MEMBERSHIP INFORMATION

Founded in 1947, ACM is the oldest and largest educational scientific society in the information technology field. Through its high-quality publications and its services, ACM is a major force in advancing the skills and knowledge of IT professionals throughout the world. From a dedicated group of 78, ACM is now 85,000 strong, with 34 special interest groups, including SIGGRAPH, and more than 60 chapters and student chapters.

For more than 25 years, SIGGRAPH and its conferences have provided the world's forum for the interchange of information on computer graphics and interactive techniques. SIGGRAPH members come from many disciplines and include researchers, hardware and software systems designers, algorithm and applications developers, visualization scientists, educators, technology developers for interactive visual communications, animators and special-effects artists, graphic designers, and fine artists.

For further information about ACM and ACM SIGGRAPH, contact:

ACM Member Services
1515 Broadway, 17th floor
New York, NY 10036-5701
Phone: 1-212-626-0500
Fax: 1-212-944-1318
E-mail: acmhelp @ acm.org

ACM European Service Center
108 Cowley Road
Oxford, OX4 1JF, United Kingdom
Phone: +44-1865-382388
Fax: +44-1865-381388
E-mail: acm_europe @ acm.org

URL: http://www.acm.org

The
Computer
Image

The Computer Image

ALAN WATT
FABIO POLICARPO

ACM Press ● SIGGRAPH Series
New York, New York

 **ADDISON-WESLEY**

Harlow, England ● Reading, Massachusetts ● Menlo Park, California
New York ● Don Mills, Ontario ● Amsterdam ● Bonn ● Sydney ● Singapore
Tokyo ● Madrid ● San Juan ● Milan ● Mexico City ● Seoul ● Taipei

Addison Wesley Longman Limited
Edinburgh Gate
Harlow
Essex CM20 2JE
England

and Associated Companies throughout the World.

Cover designed by Designers & Partners Ltd, Oxford
Typeset in 9/12pt Stone serif by 42
Printed and bound in the United States of America

First printed 1998

ISBN 0-201-42298-0

British Library Cataloguing in Publication Data
A catalogue record for this book is available from the British Library

Library of Congress Cataloging-in-Publication Data
Watt, Alan, 1942–
    The computer image / Alan Watt, Fabio Policarpo
        p.   cm.
    Includes bibliographical references and index.
    ISBN 0–201–42298–0 (alk. paper)
    1. Computer graphics. 2. Image processing––Digital techniques.
    3. Computer vision.   I. Title.
    T385.W379   1998
    006.6'6––dc21

97–40597
CIP

Contents

Preface

Computer images have come to occupy a dominant part of the computer culture and appear to be rivalling their analogue cousin – the TV image – in ubiquity; a tendency that will no doubt increase with the birth of digital TV. This book is about the computer image. Although its main emphasis is the 'how', we address from time to time the 'whys' and 'wherefores' of this new creation of the twentieth century. Where did it come from? Where is it going? What is its importance? These are questions that cannot be answered in any depth without a knowledge of the technology itself, its past and its evolutionary forces. More than most other aspects of computer technology, it is the subject of many exotic predictions, particularly in the area of virtual reality. How well will three-dimensional computer images be able to imitate reality? For example, will augmented reality in medicine and telepresence eventually lead to remote surgery? – an unthinkable proposition a few years ago.

The book is written at a time when the three main fields of computer imagery – computer graphics, image processing and computer vision – are beginning to merge in many applications. Computer vision techniques are being increasingly used in computer graphics to collect and model complex scenes; computer graphics techniques are being used to constrain the recognition of three-dimensional objects in computer vision. Image processing techniques have come out of research laboratories and are routinely used by graphic designers to manipulate photographs. The popularization of these specializations has come about mainly through the demand created by the dissemination of cheap image hardware devices on the ubiquitous PC and the resulting new applications that this has spawned.

We can say that the computer image exhibits three major guises:

- **Image synthesis** – or computer graphics – is the methodology of the creation of images using a computer. In three-dimensional computer graphics the image is generated by a program from a mathematical description or a model. Computer graphics takes a three-dimensional model (usually an abstract or mathematical model but occasionally a model constructed from real three-dimensional reality with a three-dimensional input device) and calculates a two-dimensional projection for display. It is a kind of synthetic camera.

- **Image processing** is the manipulation of an image to produce another image which is in some way different from the input image. The source image can be an image file or the program may operate directly on an image that is output by a TV-type camera. We also include **image analysis** as part of image processing. This means making calculations concerning aspects of an image as opposed to generating another version of the image.

- **Computer vision** is the extraction of information from an image. It is different from image analysis in its goal which most ambitiously attempts to emulate the human visual system. The source image in computer vision is usually a two-dimensional projection of a real scene. The goal of the process may be to recover three-dimensional information from the two-dimensional projections as in, for example, depth from stereo projections. Alternatively the output of the process may be a number, or a label as in the case, for example, of character recognition or it may be an action as in computer vision in robotics.

Thus:

- **image synthesis** or **computer graphics** is normally three-dimensional model **in**, two-dimensional image **out**;
- **image processing** is normally three-dimensional reality as two-dimensional image (or two-dimensional reality) **in**, two-dimensional image **out**;
- **computer vision** is normally three-dimensional reality as two-dimensional projection **in**, numbers, classification or action **out**. Alternatively it may be three-dimensional reality as a three-dimensional depth map **in**.

(We should note that such a classification is to some extent ephemeral and depends on current technology. It is simply the case that at the moment the most common graphics displays are two-dimensional. The most used input device in computer vision is a TV camera which gathers information from a three-dimensional scene as a two-dimensional projection. However, three-dimensional graphics display devices exist just as do devices that collect 'dense' range or three-dimensional information from a scene.)

Algorithms in computer graphics mostly function in a three-dimensional domain and the creations in this space are then mapped into a two-dimensional display or image plane at a late stage in the overall process. Traditionally computer graphics has created pictures by starting with a very detailed geometric description, subjecting this to a series of transformations that orient a viewer and objects in three-dimensional space, then imitating reality by making the objects look solid and real – a process known as rendering. In the early 1980s there was a coming together of research – carried out in the 1970s into reflection models, hidden surface removal and the like – that resulted in the emergence of a de facto approach to image synthesis of solid objects. But now this is proving insufficient for the new demands of moving computer imagery and virtual reality and much research is being carried out into how to model complex objects, where the nature and shape of the object changes dynamically, and into capturing the richness of the world without having to explicitly model every detail. Such efforts are resulting in diverse synthesis methods and modelling methods and at the moment there has been no emergence of new image generation techniques that rival the pseudo-standard way of modelling and rendering solid objects – a method that has been established since the mid-1970s.

Image processing is perhaps the oldest of the three topics with much work being done in the 1960s. It is characterized nowadays more by its migration into new application areas than the emergence of new algorithms. In particular we have seen the emergence of so-called image-based rendering techniques in virtual reality applications which have more in common with the two-dimensional world of image processing than the three-dimensional algorithms of computer graphics. Another popular application of image processing is its (now routine) use in graphic design to manipulate photographic images for presentation in advertisements and the like.

Unlike the other two areas, computer vision is a field that is characterized by difficulty and the lack of workable solutions The reason computer vision is such a demanding field is because we try to extract three-dimensional information from a series of two-dimensional projections – something that humans appear to do with consummate ease. Despite early optimism it has proved to be enduringly difficult to find solutions for most of the potential application areas. Computer vision is very much an open research problem.

Finally we should point out that with the aid of the ubiquitous PC the computer image is now firmly in the public domain. Now a significant proportion of the (middle class) population in Europe and the USA have access to a PC and are familiar with image synthesis and image processing operations that only a few years ago were the exclusive domain of computer scientists.

Reading resources

At the end of each chapter we have given a list of the most relevant literature together with a short description of each item. This is an attempt to select the most important papers and books rather than give a large unstructured reference list. Readers who wish to conduct literature research in depth will have no difficulty in doing so if they use the selected references as an entry. References are to either journals or textbooks. Of course, journals are more up to date than textbooks, but they can occasionally be difficult to understand and can be tedious to wade through. It is sometimes difficult to judge beforehand whether it is worth spending time trying to understand a paper. Always be wary of the 'Emperor's New Clothes'. In the past 30 years in scientific publishing, there has been an explosion in the amount of journals in most subject areas. The predominant reason for this is the growth in the topics and the fragmentation of mainstream subjects into many specializations. Another factor, which has led to a proliferation, is the 'publish or perish' attitude of academic researchers, who have to demonstrate, to their funding bodies, the worthwhileness of their research by the act of publication. 'If it's in a journal it's good.' This sometimes leads to papers of dubious worth, papers whose paucity of novelty or use is concealed by the apparent profundity of a difficult mathematical model, and the duplication of a work, with little or no addition in different journals.

It is often useful to browse through previous issues of a journal, rather than simply use individual issues to access a single reference given by another text. This is particularly easy to do in computer graphics. Since most of the papers are illustrated with imagery you can, in many instances, just look at the pictures until you find something that interests or stimulates you.

Structure of the book

The main topic groupings in the book are listed below. These are more or less independent of each other and the reader could start at the beginning of any one of them. The common theoretical topics have been gathered together in the final section.

- **Part 1 (Chapter 1) Introduction and overview.**

- **Part 2 (Chapters 2–8) Image synthesis and techniques** This section deals with the foundation topics in three-dimensional computer graphics required to generate two-dimensional projections from a description of a scene or an object. It excludes computer animation (dealt with in Part 5).

- **Part 3 (Chapters 9–13) Image processing techniques** Classical image processing techniques for two-dimensional imagery make up this section.

- **Part 4 (Chapters 14–16) Computer vision techniques** This section starts with pattern recognition techniques and deals with computer vision by examining both 'engineering' approaches such as CAD based vision and the 'unconstrained' shape from X approaches.

- **Part 5 (Chapters 17–19) The moving computer image** In this section we look at the way in which moving imagery has been generated (animation and morphing) and analyzed (motion analysis) and analysis/ synthesis approaches in facial animation for communication applications.

- **Part 6 (Chapters 20–23) Applications** This section looks at important current applications that utilize image synthesis and image processing techniques and includes virtual reality, image-based rendering, and the use of the computer image in medicine and art.

- **Part 7 (Chapters 24-26) Fundamentals of the computer image** Here we deal with theoretical foundations that are used throughout computer imagery and are common to all branches of it. Included in this section are the mathematics of imagery, colour considerations and image compression.

CD – contents and structure

The software on the CD enables practical experimentation with the theoretical techniques described in the text. Its purpose is to enable a deeper appreciation of the techniques. It can also provide a platform for further research and development (in this respect the source code is included for most programs).

The material consists of:

(1) A set of **executable Windows programs** as described below.

(2) Animation demonstrations.

(3) Copies of the (computer) **imagery** that appears in the book.

(4) An image study, consisting of over 400 images, called **Learning Rendering** that supports the graphics chapters.

To use the CD you should have:

- A PC running Windows 95 or Windows NT.
- Pentium Processor.
- 16-bit colour mode.
- 16 Mb RAM (32 Mb recommended).
- Internet Explorer 3 or Netscape Navigator.

(If you intend to re-compile any source code you will need Visual C++ 5.0 for all programs using MFCs and Borland C++ 5.0 or 4.5 for all 16-bit programs.)

Programs

All programs, together with sample input images and prepared demonstrations, are installed on your hard disk by running **set up**. Windows programs are executed by clicking on the program icon. Certain programs (**simpray**, **spectray** and **opticflow**) are DOS versions. Execute the **.exe** file in the program sub-directory from a DOS command line. The program returns an output file to the same directory. Operating instructions are in HTML files on the CD (**read me** button).

Animation

A selection of animations can be accessed by clicking on the thumbnail alongside the description. These are on the CD (**read me** button).

Images

Copies of all the computer generated imagery in the text are contained on the CD. These are not loaded by **set up** and can be accessed by **explore the CD** button. Viewing them on a monitor should overcome any discrepancies in the book illustration reproduction process.

Programs – brief details

Warping and morphing images

- **Warping images (WINWARP)** This program uses the feature-based warping technique to distort an image into a caricature. The image appears as an identical pair (source and destination). The program supports two kinds of feature – points and lines. The warp is created by using the left mouse button to move features around in the destination image. The corresponding feature in the source remains static. The nature of the displacement between corresponding features in the source and destination image controls the nature and extent of the warp.

- **Morphing images (WINMORPH)** This program operates in an almost identical way to the warp program, except that now the source and destination images are different. The source image and the destination image warp into each other in 'opposite directions'. The morphing is produced by cross-fading between these two sequences.

Mesh optimization and octree ray tracing

- **Mesh optimization (PROGMESH)** The purpose of this program is twofold. First it optimizes the size of the polygonal facets as a function of the local curvature of the surface in a way that minimizes the distortion of the surface. The second purpose is to clean up badly constructed models. Such models are legion in computer graphics and appear as faces collapsed into lines, two faces duplicated in the same position in space, connecting faces with their surface normal reversed, edges which are connected to more than two faces and vertices that lie on the edge of another face. These problems are commonly created by both automatic and semi-manual modelling methods and produce visual artefacts in an image created by a standard render.

- **Octree ray tracing (part of PROGMESH)** Ray tracing can be accelerated considerably by generating an octree data structure from the scene. In this case the elements used to construct the octree are polygons and this method can thus only render polygon mesh objects. Note also that the benefit of octree ray tracing is a function of scene complexity – greatest speed-ups occur for complex scenes. The ray tracer includes bump mapping, texture mapping, opacity mapping and self-illumination mapping as well as the normal ray tracing effects. These are accessible through the Material Editor. Different lighting and viewing options are available.

- **Particle simulation and spring mesh models (PARTSIM)** This is a particle animation package where the particles possess physical properties and Newtonian mechanics are employed to calculate their behaviour. It can be used to simulate classical particle animation applications – such as waterfalls and fireworks – and also to simulate the physical interaction of polygon mesh objects with gravity and other objects. In this case the object vertex points become particles and the edges become springs. (Collisions are only detected at vertices (particles) – thus in certain circumstances object edges can penetrate each other.) The shape of the object will change during interaction, but this is limited to those deformations possible by the edges moving and changing their length. The solution also depends on the relationship between the time step and the parameters used. For example, a small time step is required when using very strong springs.

Fast Fourier Transform and filtering

- **FFT for functions of a single variable (WFFT1D)**   This program generates a DFT for a function of a single variable. A selection of sample functions have already been written, alternatively you can write your own. The animate facility shows the frequency components being added to the amplitude spectrum, starting with the lowest. At the same time the inverse transform of the spectrum currently displayed is calculated and displayed. Thus, as frequencies are added to the amplitude spectrum the waveform in the space domain gets closer and closer to its original form. Thus, it is an animation of a low pass filter whose cut-off frequency increases with time.

- **FFT for functions of two variables (images) and Fourier Domain Filtering (WFFT2D)**   The program uses an FFT to transform an image into the Fourier Domain. A variety of filters are then available. The filters are built interactively after selecting one of the basic options – rectangle, circle, fan and value. Another option gives a measure of the energy in the frequency domain contained within concentric circles. After selecting a particular filter, filter shapes are controlled by click and drag operations. For example, clicking and dragging on the vertex of the rectangular filter enables you to scale the extent of the filter. The right mouse button creates a filter not centred on the origin for circles and rectangles.

Patch modelling and z-buffer rendering

- **Bezier patch modelling (BEZMODEL)**   This is a simple cross-sectional design facility that generates an object with a multi-segment spine and a variable cross-section. No continuity is 'forced' between curve segments, but end-point tangents are displayed enabling the user to obtain C1 continuity if required. Sample models stored as ready-made cross-section scripts are available for loading and experimentation.

- **Z-buffer rendering (part of BEZMODEL)**   A z-buffer renderer is included in this program. It implements flat shading, Gouraud shading and Phong shading.

General image processing and image building program (IMAGE)

This is a general purpose image manipulation and image processing program. It is best described by listing its facilities:

- **Blur**   Blurs according to the selected option using windows of a selected size. The blurring options are normal (averaging), Gaussian or median. Blurring can only be applied to a colour image and the operation can be applied to all or any colour bands.

- **Filter**   Spatial domain filtering (or convolution) using either preselected options or a custom designed filter that can be applied to all or any colour bands.

- **Stereo**
  - generates an **autostereogram** from a depth map (grey scale) image. It uses random dots or another selected image as the base image motif for the autostereogram.
  - **depth reconstruction from a stereo pair** using a correlation procedure whose options are selectable. Requires as input a pair of images exhibiting binocular disparity.

- **Projections – Build – Reconstruct**   Calculates image projections and reconstructs from them using the simple back projection method. The projection orientations are calculated by dividing 360 degrees by the number of projections selected. The projections are displayed as a single image with projection lines and associated values stacked vertically.

- **Operate**   Performs the selected arithmetic operation on two images of the same size.

- **Negate**   Negates an image.

- **Duplicate**   Duplicates an image.

- **Histogram**   Generates a histogram of the image. This may need to be scaled vertically and this is accomplished by the up and down arrows on the keyboard.

- **Equalize**   Performs a histogram equalization.

- **Tune**
  - **Brightness/contrast.**
  - **Hue/saturation** (can only be applied to a colour image).
  - **Enhance**   This operates from a piecewise linear transform function crated by the user. Initially set to input = output, the user creates and moves break points in the function by using the right mouse button and dragging with the left.

- **Threshold**   Transforms the image into binary version using a user-selected threshold.

- **Convert**
  - **To grey scale.**

- **To 8 bits** Using a median cut or popularity algorithm; also error diffusion can be used.
- **To 24 bits.**
- **To pseudo-colour.**

● **Split into RGB, into HSL** Splits an image into separate bands.

● **Combine from RGB, from HSL** Combines separate bands into a single image.

● **Transform**
  - **Resize.**
  - **Resample.**
  - **To Wavelet from Wavelet** (image size must be a power of two and the basis function used is HAAR).

● **Make IFS** Makes the IFS fern leaf image from user-selectable sizes and depth.

Thematic classification of satellite imagery (MBAND)

Operates on supplied satellite imagery using a minimum distance classifier. The user establishes 'ground truth' by selecting individual pixels and assigning a pseudo-colour to represent the nature of the landscape at that point and all matching points.

Ray tracing, implicit modelling, CSG modelling and animation

Four ray tracing programs are provided: a fast octree ray tracer (in the mesh optimization and octree ray tracing); a very simple ray tracer that works only with spheres; a more complex distributed ray tracer that also implements two-pass ray tracing; and finally the same ray tracer operating with full spectral colours. The three ray tracing programs use a command script language.

● **Simple ray tracer (DOS-SIMPRAY)** This is a simple 'whitted' ray tracer that renders only spheres. It uses a simplified version of the script language.

● **Distributed ray tracing, advanced modelling and animation (WINRAY)** This program implements distributed ray tracing and two-pass ray tracing for polygon mesh objects as well as implicitly defined objects. Distributed ray tracing enables such phenomena as soft shadows, depth of field, and blurred reflections and refractions. Two-pass ray tracing implements 'caustics' due to refraction/reflection interaction of light with glass objects and water. It also includes **implicit object modelling** facilities, using spheres as the basic implicit function. Basic **CSG modelling** is also included. Subtraction, intersection and union are implemented for any of the object types. An **animation** facility is included. This is a facility that generates a sequences of frames that captures the variation, as a function of time, of any of the parameters in the script.

- **Spectral ray tracer (DOS – SPECTRAY)** This ray tracer uses a more accurate colour model. Instead of using only RGB components (a device that results in accurate colours in the final rendered image) it uses the full colour spectrum. Colours are converted from spectral space to an RGB triple at the end of the process for display on the monitor.

Radiosity (RADI)

This is a progressive refinement radiosity rendered that uses the classical hemi-cube method to calculate the form factors. The normal progressive refinement build-up is displayed, together with a visualization of the current interaction being calculated by the program. This takes the form of a hemi-cube with the five faces projected onto the viewing plane. Colour is used as a label for each patch in the scene (thus restricting the number of patches to the maximum number of displayable colours). The hemi-cube window displays consecutively each of the five faces. The patches currently being projected onto the hemi-cube are labelled with their colour. The patch currently shooting in the scene window is highlighted in the scene window.

The radiosity phase is followed by a ray tracing phase that calculates specular reflections for shiny objects.

Video mouse (VMOUSE)

This gives an example of a set of image processing operations that implement tracking in real-time as described in the text. The user has control of certain parameters in the operations. Varying **edge threshold** alters that parameter in the edge detection filter, reducing it means an increase in the number of points classified as edge points. A point is considered to be static if its value in the previous frame and the current frame are within the **spatial coherence threshold**.

Wavelet compression package (COMPW)

The basic functions used in this program are different to those described in the text – they give better performance that Haar wavelets and are know as Daubechies Wavelets.

The program opens an image and compresses it using wavelets. A compression icon (decreasing rectangles) is on the toolbar and the compression statistics are reported. Progression can be either re-sizing the image or maintaining the image at full size and increasing the resolution. Typical compression (high quality) is from 10 to 20:1 and for lower quality 50:1.

Motion fields (DOS-OPTICFLOW)

This is a simple correlation procedure that is similar to the depth from the stereo program. It takes two images as input, and the user defines a search window size and a search area around the current pixel (the epipolar constraint used in the stereo program) is no longer valid. The motion field is superimposed on the first image as arrows.

Learning rendering

This is an image study, consisting of over 400 images, that supports the computer graphics section in the book. It is accessible on the CD through the **read me** button. The resource is a series of images/animations demonstrating the options available in mainstream rendering programs. The series is intended to support an undergraduate or postgraduate course in rendering techniques, or an instructor using the resource as appropriate to his/her course.

Most images that illustrate a rendering method are highly tuned, and are consequently of little educational value. The idea of the series provided is to demonstrate both the potential of the techniques and their deficiencies and disadvantages. Apparent in the images are the effects of the many and varied shortcomings in the methods that tend to be overlooked in standard texts. Another problem in studying images produced by renderers is that many subtle differences are lost in colour reproductions.

One of the motivations of the series is to enable a study of renderers and their behaviour without having to set them going and wait the (usually) long time for images to complete. It is hoped that the large number of images facilitates this.

The main series is structured around an old idea – to use the same scene as far as possible and inject it into a number of renderers and to use different options within a rendering method. The final results can then be compared.

The image descriptions, although reasonably comprehensive, are not meant to explain how each method works. Instead they describe the important visual ramifications of the algorithms. In other words, they are meant to be used in conjunction with the textbook and assume that the viewer already has some familiarity with the basic operation of the algorithms.

The set consists of several hundred images which are all in tiff format – these should be compatible with most popular image browsers. It is recommended that a browser with a zoom facility is used so that areas of interest can be studied more closely. The set also contains several animations. These are stored in the standard PC AVI format.

The series consists of the following general topics:

- Basic camera options.
- Basic rendering techniques for polygon mesh scenes.
- Material realism (alternative reflection models).
- Scanline rendering techniques (texture mapping, bump mapping, environment mapping).
- Sample light source options.

- Anti-aliasing.
- Global illumination.
- Ray tracing.
- Radiosity.
- Colour and rendering.
- Non-photo realistic rendering.

Acknowledgements

Brazil: we would like to thank Daniel Bezerra for his support with the programs, Eduardo Grandele (Duda) for the image of Pão de Açúcar (Fig 11.6), Gérson Lessa for the Warp, Morph and Bezmodel program icons, Leonardo Carvalho (Léo) for the images from the North East of Brazil (Figures 9.2, 9.7, 9.9, 10.2, 10.4, 10.7, 10.9, 12.2, 26.3), Fernanda and Raquel Policarpo for the warp sample images and all the people at Paralelo Computação for testing the programs.

José Antônio Borges – a man for whom all things are possible – for support and encouragement at UFRJ.

UK: we would like to thank Lee Cooper and Dan Teece for computer graphics image production. Dionéa Watt for the cover concept. The staff at Addison-Wesley Longman (Mark Ralph, Bridget Allen and Alison Martin) have been tireless in their support of a large, difficult production and the authors thank them.

The book could not have been written without the facilities and support of:
Instituto de Matemática Pura e Aplicada (IMPA), Rio de Janeiro, Brasil
Universidade Federal do Rio de Janeiro (UFRJ), Rio de Janeiro, Brasil
University of Sheffield, Sheffield, UK

The publishers wish to thank the following for permission to reproduce the following copyright material.

ACM for permission to reproduce figures from SIGGRAPH proceedings 1992, *Computer Graphics* **26** (2): 'Re-Tiling Polygonal Surfaces' by Greg Turk; 'Direct Manipulation of Free-Form Deformations' by Hse, Hughes and Kaufman.

Addison-Wesley Publishing Company for permission to reproduce figure 8.15 from Gonzalez, R C and R E Woods (1992) *Digital Image Processing*.

Morton, L and Marianne Heilig for permission to reproduce the extract plan from Mort Heilig's patent 'Virtual Reality Apparatus for Individual Use, 4 Oct. 1960.

Professor GVR Born for permission to reproduce figures from Born, G (1935) *Restless Universe* London: Blackie & Sons.

The Institute of Electrical and Electronics Engineers Inc. for permission to reproduce Figures 2c, d, e and f from Beatty and Booth (1982) *Computer Graphics*, 2nd end.

Viewpoint DataLabs International, Inc. for permission to reproduce Anatomy (3 skeletons) from Viewpoint's 3D Dataset™ catalog, 2nd edn.

While the publisher has made every attempt to trace all copyright owners and obtain permission to reproduce material, in a few cases this has proved impossible. Copyright holders of material which has not been acknowledged in the text are encourage to contact the publisher.

Dedicação

Para Dionéa – um amor verdadeiro (AW)

Para meu avô que me presenteou com seu nome e me deu meu primeiro
computador (FP)

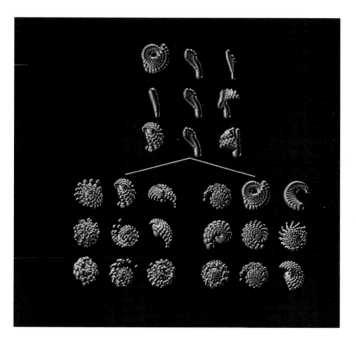

Figure 1.2
Evolutionary procedural modelling:
results obtained from the Mutator
program. (Courtesy of S. Todd and
W. Latham, IBM UK.)

SCIENTIFIC AMERICAN

VOLCANOES OF IO

January 1980

Figure 1.4
One of the most famous pictures in image
processing – an enhanced image of an
erupting volcano on the Jovian moon Io.
Source: Cover of *Scientific American*, Jan 1990
including the illustration showing 'Plume 2,
the second of eight volcanic eruption
detected on the Jovian Moon Io by The
Spacecraft Voyager I' © Hank Iken.

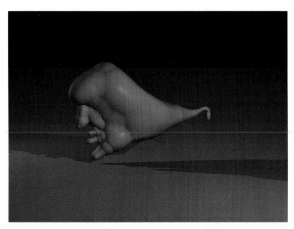
An object (based on a famous Salvador Dali painting)

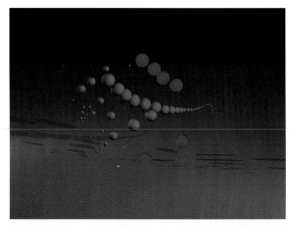
Point generators – the radius of each sphere is the influence of each generator

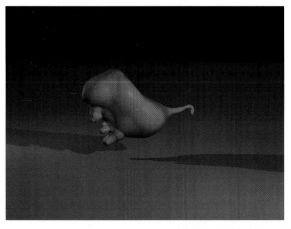

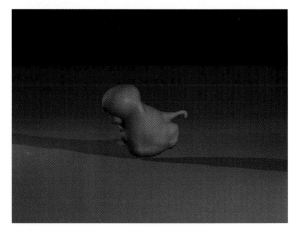
Unwanted blending as the generators are moved

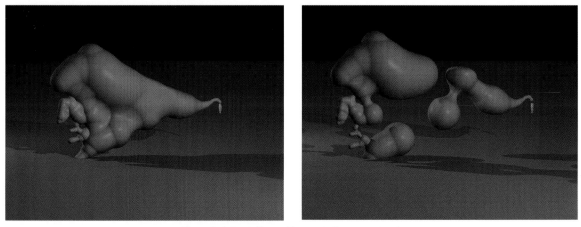
Unwanted separation as the generators are moved

Figure 2.20
An example of an implicit function modelling system. (Courtesy of Agata Opalach.)

Figure 3.15
The 'traditional' way of illustrating Phong shading. ka and kd are constant throughout. ks is increasing from left to right and the exponent is increasing from top to bottom. The model attempts to increase 'shininess' by increasing the exponent. This makes the extent of the specular highlight smaller which could also be interpreted as the reflection of a light source of varying size. (The light is a point source.)

Figure 4.6
Examples of two-part texture mapping with a solid of revolution. The intermediate surfaces are: (a) a plane (or no surface); (b) a cylinder; and (c) a sphere.

 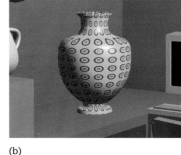 

(a)   (b)   (c)

Figure 4.7   (Left) Texture map; (right) one Bézier patch on the object; (below) recursive teapot.

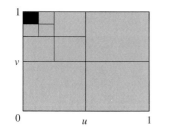

Texture map   1 Bézier patch

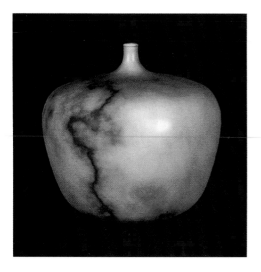

Figure 4.10
Turbulence: using the three-dimensional noise function to simulate turbulence – in this case a convincing imitation of marble.

Figure 4.11 Bump mapping. (Courtesy of J. Blinn.)

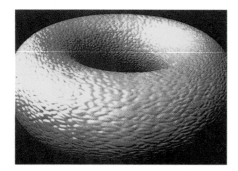 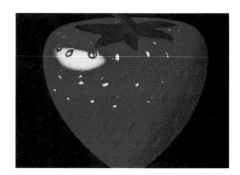

Figure 5.7 A selection of materials simulated using the model described in Section 5.3. The differences between some of the materials (for example, polished brass and gold) would be difficult to obtain by fine-tuning the parameters in Phong shading. In these images the reflection model was used as the local component in a ray tracer.

Lambertian   New model   Difference

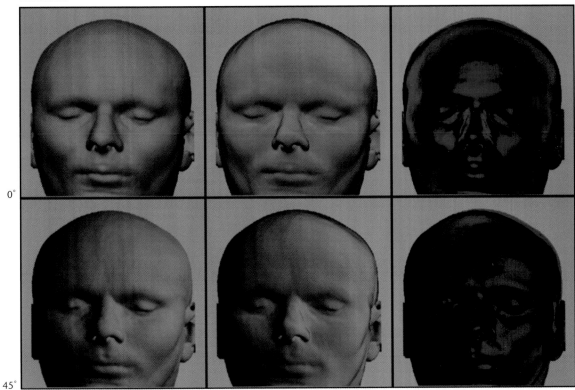

0°

45°

Figure 5.10
Hanrahan and Kreuger's model
compared with a Lambertian model for
two angles of incidence. In the difference
images, red indicates more reflection
from the new model, and blue vice
versa.

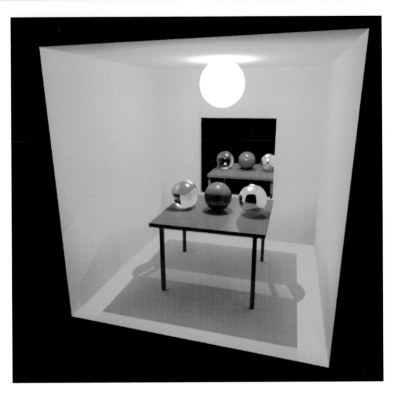

Figure 6.2
An image generated using RADIANCE. See
the black and white version of this figure
for an explanation.

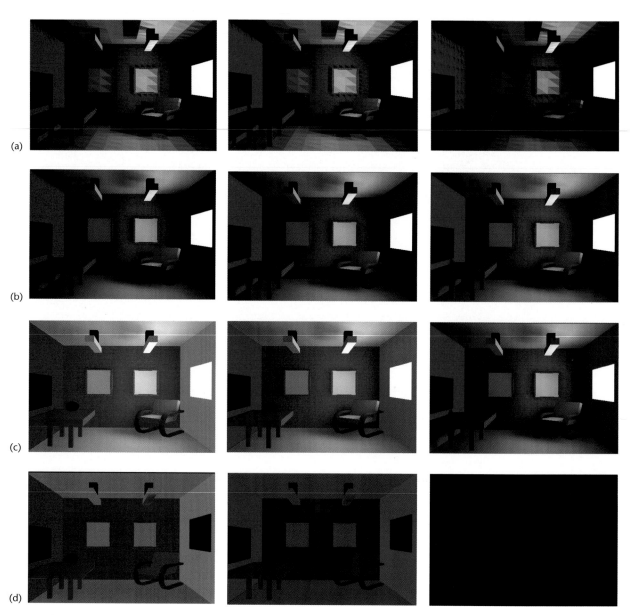

Figure 6.8
A radiosity image after 20, 250 and 5000 iterations of the progressive refinement method. From top to bottom for each column: (a) The radiosity solution as output from the iteration process. Each patch is allocated a constant radiosity. (b) The previous solution after it has been subjected to the interpolation process. (c) The same solution with the addition of the ambient term. (d) The difference between the previous two images. This gives a visual indication of the energy that had to be added to account for the unshot radiosity.

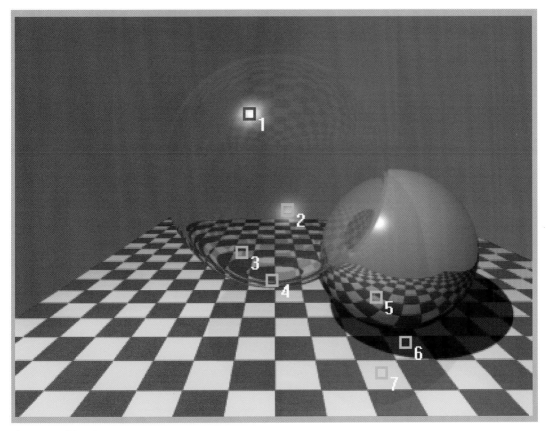

Figure 6.13(b)
The Whitted scene simple recursive ray tracing.

Figure 6.19
Two-pass ray tracing was used to generate 'pool caustics' formed by LSDE paths. These are shown as seen from the surface and with the water removed.

Figure 6.22
Radiosity illustration – Dutch interior, after Vermeer. This image was inspired by the work of the seventeenth-century Dutch painter Jan Vermeer, whose sensitivity to the interplay of light helped to give his painting a dramatic effect. The radiosity method was used to compute the global diffuse illumination during a view-independent preprocess. After the view was determined, a Z-buffer based algorithm similar to distributed ray tracing was used to compute the specular reflection on the marble floor. (Courtesy of John Wallace, Cornell University, Program of Computer Graphics.)

Figure 6.23
Radiosity illustration – simulated steel mill. The image was created using a modified version of the hemicube radiosity algorithm, computed on a VAX 8700 and displayed on a Hewlett-Packard Renaissance Display. The environment consists of approximately 55 000 elements, and is one of the most complex environments computed to date. (Courtesy of John Wallace, Cornell University, Program of Computer Graphics.)

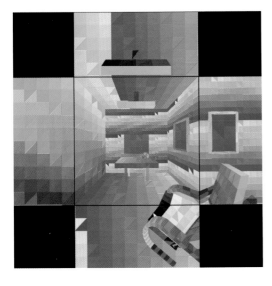

Figure 6.28
Shows the state of a hemicube placed on the window after all other patches in the scene have been projected onto it. A colour identifies each patch in the scene (and every partial patch) that can be seen by this hemicube. The algorithm then simply sums all the hemicube element form factors associated with each patch. (See also Figure 6.8)

Figure 7.20
The Utah teapot rendered by converting the patches to polygons using uniform subdivision (128, 512, 2048 and 8192 polygons respectively). (Courtesy of Steve Maddock.)

Figure 8.11
The office scene with Gouraud shading. The two defects in this image (described in detail in the text) are: Mach banding (may not be visible in the reproduction) and the interpolation artefact on the back wall.

Figure 8.13
The same scene using Phong shading. A glaring defect in Phong interpolation is demonstrated in this figure. Here the reflected light from the wall light and the image of the light have become separated due to the nature of the interpolation.

Figure 8.10
An office scene, together with a wireframe vizualization, that has been shaded using the constant ambient term only.

Figure 8.14
Zoom on one of the wall lights. The top row compares Gouraud and Phong shading. If the polygon mesh resolution is sufficiently high the difference between Gouraud and Phong shading can be quite subtle. Bottom row: Polygon resolution is reduced and the Gouraud highlight disappears.

Figure 8.15
The office scene with 'traditional'
two-dimensional texture.

Figure 8.16
The same scene with shadow
and environment mapping
(the teapot) added.

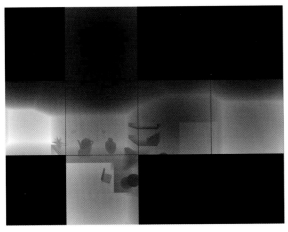

Shadow map

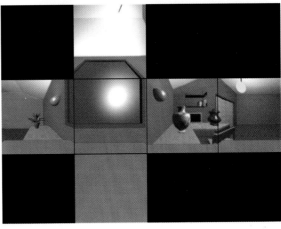

Environment map

Figure 8.17
This is a comparison between generating reflections using environment mapping (left) and ray tracing (right).

Figure 8.18
The scene ray traced using a Whitted-type ray tracer.

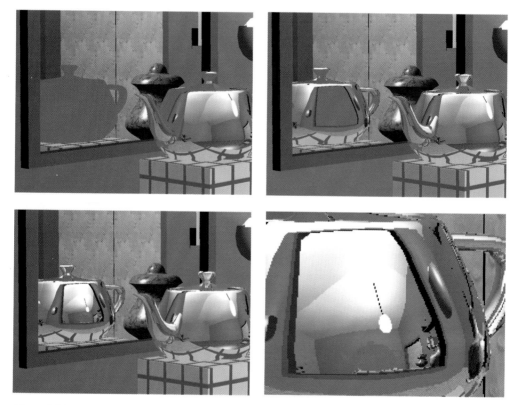

Figure 8.19
A recursive depth demonstration. The trace terminates at depth 2, 3, 4 and 5 (zoom image) respectively.
'Unassigned' pixels are coloured grey. Bad aliasing as a function of recursive depth (the light cable) is apparent.

Anti-aliasing

Supersampling (x3)

Non-uniform sampling

Figure 8.20
These illustrations demonstrate the efficiency of context-free versus context-sensitive anti-aliasing. There is little difference between the anti-aliased version despite the vast difference in the cost.

Figure 8.21
This illustration shows a radiosity version of the scene.

Figure 8.22
A photograph of the Museu de Arte Contemporânea (Museum of Contemporary Art), Niteroi, Rio de Janeiro (designed by Oscar Niemeyer), taken in the bright light of the midday sun. The colour bleeding is vividly apparent and fixed in the photograph. Do you experience it to this extent in reality?

Figure 8.23
This image, suffering from significant shadow and light leakage, was computed using a 'minimum' specification – a triangulated version of the representation shown in Figure 8.10.

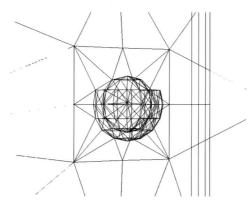

Figure 8.26
The result of meshing the area around a wall light after considering the interpenetrating geometry. Now the wall patch boundaries coincide with the light patch boundaries. The result of this mesh completely eliminates the leakage around the wall lights.

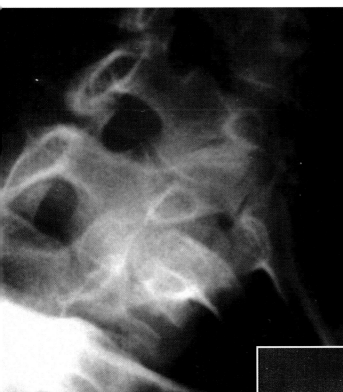

Figure 8.27
The scene rendered using the RADIANCE renderer.

Figure 9.4
The familiar pseudo-colour transform.

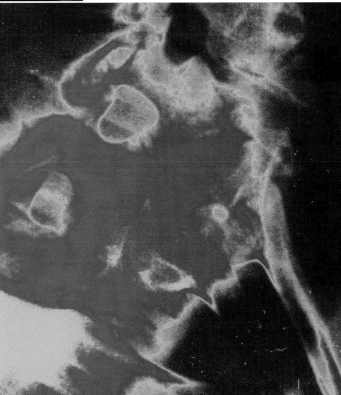

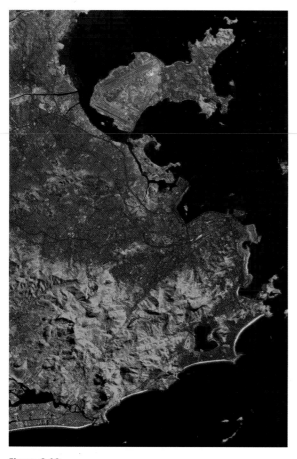

Figure 9.12
A pseudo-coloured satellite image of Rio de Janeiro.

Figure 14.6
Thematic classification of six-band satellite imagery using a minimum distance classifier.

	Class			Band 1	Band 2	Band 3	Band 4	Band 5	Band 6
	City 1	210	167	117	70	86	100	144	129
	City 2	237	288	126	94	109	113	160	147
	Lake 1	252	263	93	52	53	38	0	3
	Lake 2	290	253	81	47	45	17	0	0
	Lake 3	289	247	75	42	35	15	3	0
	Road 1	20	28	120	62	76	34	29	24
	Road 2	225	149	99	65	73	87	90	80
	Road 3	577	281	126	81	124	125	211	168
	Rock	65	69	255	161	242	147	231	255
	Sand	138	144	255	216	255	212	255	255
	Sea	351	312	75	36	33	6	3	0
	Sea Deep	696	362	72	34	28	6	2	0
	Trees 1	439	108	75	44	35	161	112	42
	Trees 2	463	76	69	42	38	125	73	24
	Trees 3	430	112	63	42	35	93	44	17

Ground truth

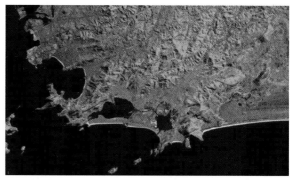

Sample band

Thematic map

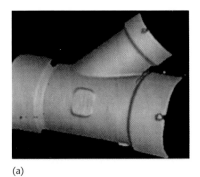

(a)

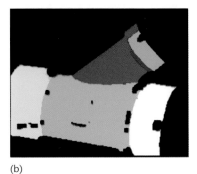

(b)

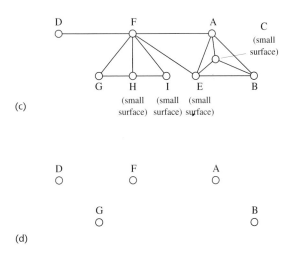

(c)

(d)

Figure 15.27
An example of Raja and Jain's method for analysing range images. The figure shows a complicated object made up of five cylindrical parts: (a) range image of the object; (b) surface segmentation showing nine surfaces; (c) surface adjacency graph (initial); (d) surface adjacency graph (final). Four small surfaces (C, E, H, I) have been removed and edges between cylindrical surfaces broken. (Courtesy of N.S. Raja and A.K. Jain.)

Left image

Left and right image superimposed

Result

Figure 16.11
A simple intensity matching algorithm for a 7×7 window.

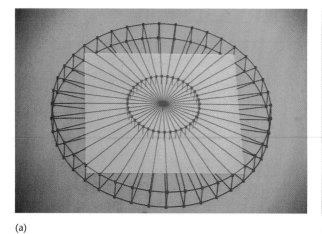

(a)

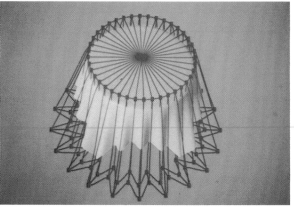

(b)

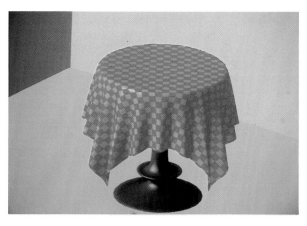

(c)

Figure 17.15
A visual simulation or geometric shape model for fabric.
(Courtesy of S. Coquillart, Inria-Rogquencourt, Le Chesnay, France).

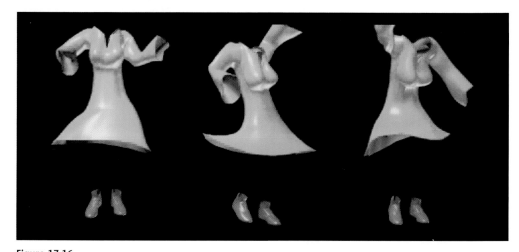

Figure 17.16
Physically-based soft object animation from Second Nature; see text for details. (Courtesy of Second Nature Industries; animation by Jim Biebl.)

(a)

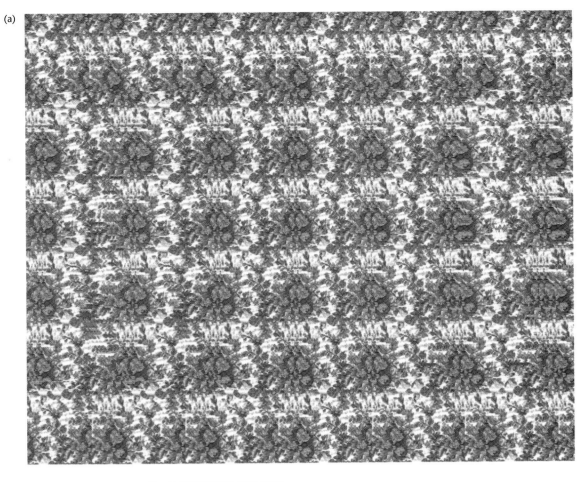

(b)

(c)

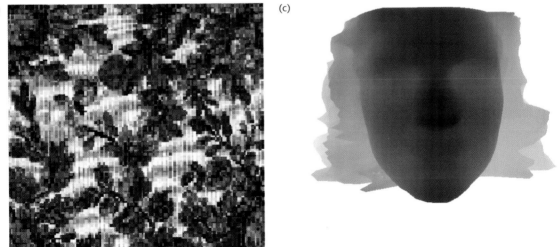

Figure 20.14
(a) A 'motif' autostereogram together with (b) the motif and (c) the depth map from which it was constructed.

1 Overlapping frames from a rotating camera

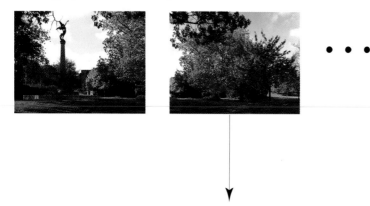

2 'Stitched' into a cylindrical panoramic image

3 A section of which is warped into a planar polygon

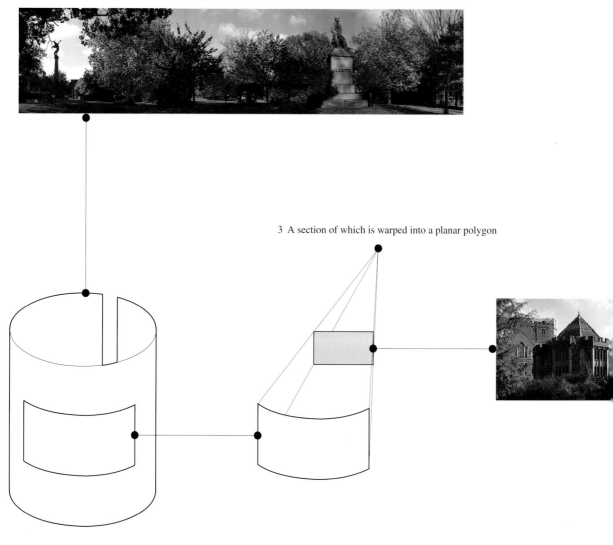

(a) One source image is used when the camera moves, holes (in blue) appear

(c) It also depends on how close the source images are, This image shows how the hole areas are reduced (see part(b)) by using more closely spaced source images

(b) The hole problem is diminished if two images are used

(d) The holes filled by interpolation

Figure 21.8
An illustration from one of the first research projects in image-based rendering. The images are produced by moving the camera to the right. (Courtesy of Eric Chen.)

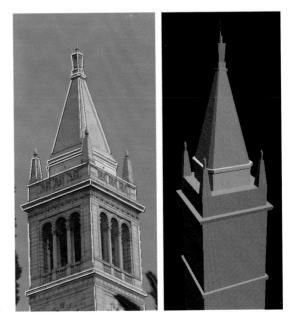

Figure 21.10
Semi-automatic fitting of a computer graphics model to a photograph. The photograph on the left is shown with a highlighted wireframe overlaid. The image on the right is a rendered version of the model extracted for the image. (Courtesy of Paul Debevec.)

Key image

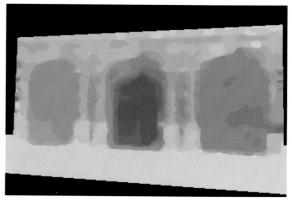

Computed warped offset image

Offset image

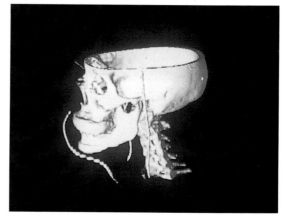

Computed depth map

Figure 21.12
Debevec et al.'s method of simplifying stereo correspondence. The computed warped offset image is produced by projecting the offset image onto the approximate model and viewing it from the position of the key camera. (Courtesy of Paul Debevec.)

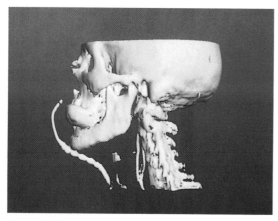

Figure 22.19
The marching cubes algorithm applied to X-ray CT data.

Figure 22.20
The same data using volume rendering with the bone voxels set to unity opacity and others set to zero.

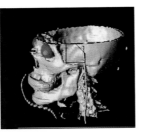

Figure 22.21
The same as previous image but with critical structures detected, stylized and rendered.

Figure 22.22
The same as previous image but now the bone is made semi-transparent. The image shows both critical structures and a (highlighted) brain tumour.

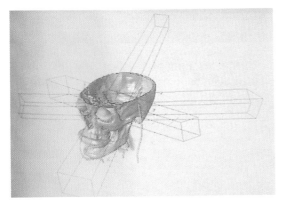

Figure 22.23
This figure shows the skull together with other superimposed information. The critical structures are detected in the data as separate objects. These objects are stylized as bounding volumes – spheres for the eyeballs and generalized cylinders for the spinal cord. They are rendered as normal using the colour orange. The idea is that the stylized bounding volumes are guaranteed to contain the actual object. A brain tumour is shown in green and three treatment beams are shown as wireframe objects. The blue on the skull shows the intersection of each beam with the skin surface. (Courtesy of Klaus de Geuss.)

Figure 22.24
This figure is rendered with the bone opacity set to a value less then unity and is viewed as though looking down a treatment beam intersecting an eyeball. (Courtesy of Klaus de Guess.)

Figure 23.1
El Pensador by Cristobal Romero. Despite the fact that this image was made by cutting and pasting, an operation easily imitated using a computer, it is difficult to imagine the utility or efficacy of a computer simulation.

a) Original photograph

b) 'Pseudo woodcut' hand-drawn by tracing the original.

c) A 'coloured woodcut' obtained by mixing a) and b). White areas in b) erase the corresponding areas in a). The colours in a) modulates the lines in b).

Figure 23.2
A typical contrivance that can be produced by image processing packages. In this case, the image was produced by a mixture of computer facilities and hand tracing.

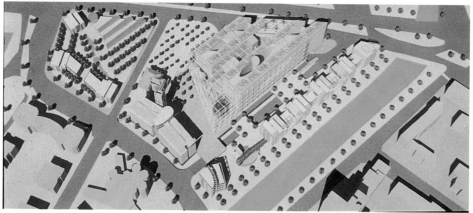

Figure 23.3
Two architectural visualizations. This is an area where many architects prefer hand produced imagery over computer graphics imagery. The computer graphics 'signature' of the bottom image somehow detracts from the illusion that the architect may want to stimulate in the viewer.

Figure 23.7
An NPR study of a machine part. All versions were produced using the information in (a) and (b). (a) Conventional rendered version; (b) depth map; (c) edge enhanced version of the depth map; (d) a simple cross-hatching algorithm; (e) a 'chalk sketch' image; (f) a brush stroke image.

(a)

(b)

(c)

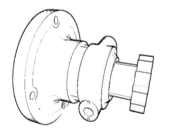

(d)

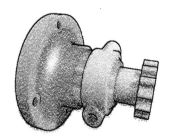

(e)

(f)

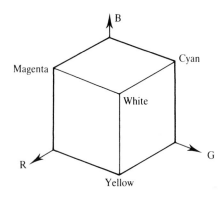

Figure 25.4
The RGB cube.

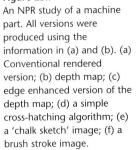

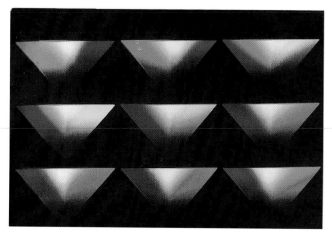

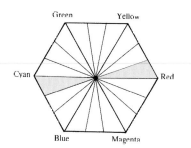

Figure 25.6
HSV colour model: slices through the value axis at 20° intervals.

Figure 25.6
HSV colour model: slices through the value
axis at 20° intervals.

Figure 25.7
(a) Marching cubes and CFD data: a Navier–Stokes CFD
simulation of a reverse flow pipe combuster. Flow occurs
from left to right and from right to left. The interface
between these flows defines a zero velocity isosurface. The
marching cubes algorithm is used to extract this surface
which is then conventionally rendered. (b) Marching cubes
and CFD data: a texture-mapped zero velocity surface. A
pseudocolour scale that represents field temperature is
combined with the colour used for shading in the previous
illustration.

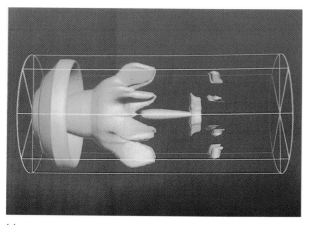

(a)

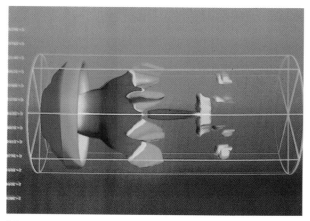

(b)

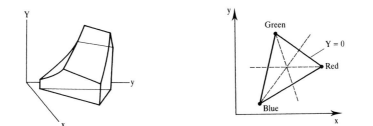

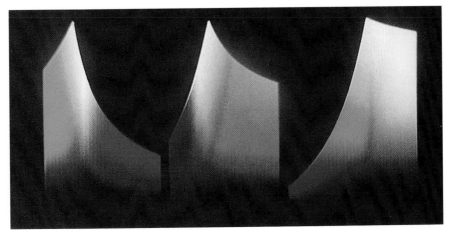

Figure 25.12
(Top left) Monitor gamut solid in CIE xyY space; (above) three cross-sections through the solid CIE xyY space; (top right) the position of the cross-sections on the plane Y=0.

Figure 25.14
Rendering in spectral space compared with RGB space for a ray traced image.

24-bit image

Figure 25.22
Colour quantization: median cut and popularity algorithm.

8-bit image
popularity algorithm

8-bit image
median cut algorithm

Figure 26.4
Comparing JPEG compression with
wavelet compression.

Original image 64 K

JPEG 13 K

Wavelet 13 K

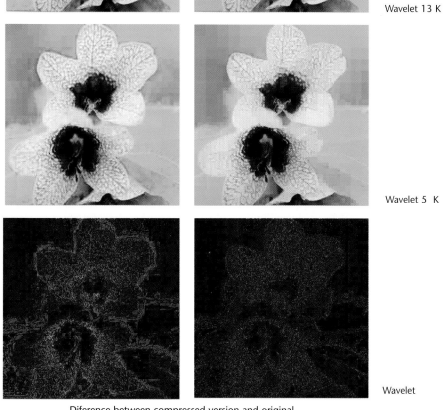

JPEG 5K

Wavelet 5 K

JPEG

Wavelet

Diference between compressed version and original

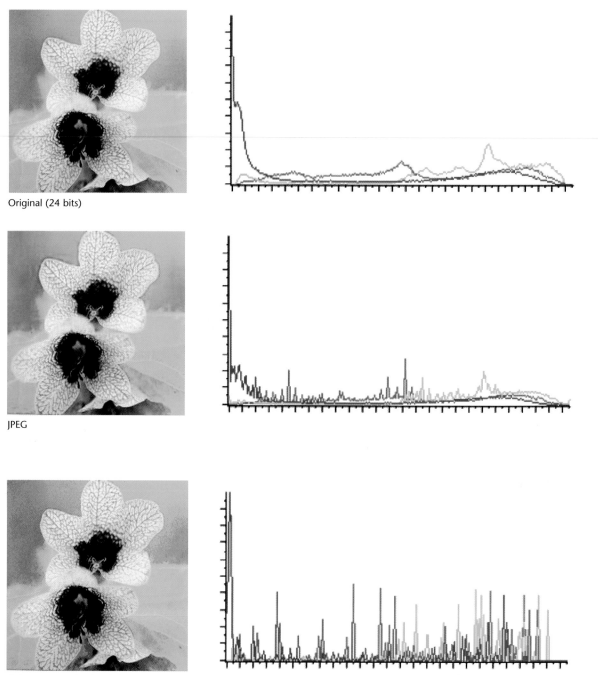

Original (24 bits)

JPEG

Colour re-quantization (8 bits)

Figure 26.7
A JPEG encoded image and an image where explicit colour reduction has been applied. In both cases the compression is reflected in similar image histograms.

Figure 26.15
Compression and animated
sequences. Inter-frame compression is
combined with wavelet compression
in this example.

No compression (192 KB/frame)

Intra frame compression (6 KB/frame)

Inter frame compression (512 bytes/frame)

1 The computer image – an overview

1.1 The nature of a computer image

1.2 Synthesizing images or computer graphics

1.3 Image processing – an overview

1.4 Computer vision

1.1 The nature of a computer image

In some respects image synthesis and computer vision are the inverse of each other. Image synthesis aims to model the way in which a light interacts with a model (which can, incidentally, be a real object scanned by a device and mapped into a data structure) and produces a two-dimensional image for display. Computer vision on the other hand attempts the inverse of this operation or mapping and is concerned with deriving information from a two-dimensional projection of a scene or an object. In other words we need to analyze an image formed as the result of light interacting with three-dimensional objects. For example, we may want to find what particular surface with what orientation produced the particular colour or intensity information in an area of the two-dimensional projection. Image processing may be used in its own right or it may be part of a computer vision process. It shares many theoretical concepts with computer graphics.

The computer graphics process has proved the most successful of these three areas and in the past two decades there has been an explosion of hardware and software that has established computer graphics as part of our visual culture. Computer vision, except for well worked out processes, is confined to research laboratories. It ranges between the extremes of established technology in narrow and highly constrained applications and ambitious research initiatives on, say, the vision capabilities of a robot operating in a human environment.

What is a computer image? Beyond what you see on the screen, it is, in reality, a two-dimensional array of numbers. Each number represents the intensity or colour of a visible picture element or pixel. Both the spatial resolution (or total number of pixels in the image) and the accuracy to which each pixel value is stored vary according to the hardware used. If we define such an image to consist of $i \times j$ pixels each of n bits, then in a high quality image, both i and j will be greater than 1000 and n will be at least 24 bits. Currently in a PC-based system the most common spatial resolution is 768×576 where each pixel is 8 bits. (Usually in such a system, although we can have only 256 or 2^8 colours on the screen, these can be any 256 from a much larger choice of colours known as a palette.)

A computer image is calculated, stored and then converted into a video or TV-type image for display on a monitor. Alternatively it may be converted from a TV image in computer vision and image processing. That quality of normal images – their permanence as ink on paper or paint on canvas – manifests as a vast array of numbers in computer imagery and it is this representation that has led to the development of the computer image as an important part of late 20th century culture. Its distinguishing features and uses are due fundamentally to the fact that it is a numerical representation of an image and can therefore be subject to manipulation by a processor.

The quality of computer images is now equal (at least in high resolution imagery) to that obtainable with film, but such has not always been the case. Prior to the advent of frame stores and a colour (TV) type display, computer images were displayed as they were generated, placing severe constraints on their quality in terms of resolution and colour and reducing them to line drawings. Using 'calligraphic' electronic displays, a moving beam would paint lines on the screen as they were generated by the program. The two fatal flaws of the early calligraphic devices were that they could only draw binary images and the drawing/refresh time was directly proportional to the complexity of the image. As soon as TV-type displays with a screen memory became available it was natural that they were replaced.

A distinguishing aspect of the computer image is its discrete nature. A pixel has a finite extent and exhibits a constant intensity. This is often visible. In computer graphics and to a lesser extent in image processing this discretization of the image both spatially and in terms of its intensity or colour leads to significant problems and much effort has to be devoted to overcoming the visual defects that arise from these. A problem connected with discretization is noise – any unwanted disturbance in an image that takes it away from an ideal form. Noise plagues many computer vision algorithms because many approaches try to make sense of small local changes in an image and when noise is present changes due to noise perturbations can be mistaken for changes in image structure. In computer graphics we generate noise-free images that are perfect to within the limitations of the synthesis algorithms but these limitations manifest themselves as visible defects in the final image and we could, using our loose definition of noise as being unwanted visible disturbance, say that computer graphics suffer from algorithmic noise. (Noise in computer graphics is called aliasing – a somewhat inappropriate term borrowed from signal processing.)

The pixel is the atomic unit of computer imagery. It is the smallest area on the view surface – almost always now a TV-type display monitor – that can be accessed by a program. The decreasing cost of memory has meant that in the 1990s the physical size of a pixel can be the same as the smallest accessible unit on the display monitor – the RGB triad that produces a tiny dot of colour on the screen. Colour resolution has also increased substantially and 24-bit frame memories mean that a pixel can be assigned any one of 16 million colours. Both these developments have meant that for synthetic imagery the pixel has become almost invisible – we do not see it on the screen except perhaps as 'staircase' patterns along silhouette edges, or when we zoom into a fixed resolution image. Only a few years ago this was not the case with mainstream computers and spatial and colour resolution had to be traded off against each other in their demands for frame memory, and we accepted images made up of large square pixels. (In fact 'pixelizing' normal images became a visual device used by graphic designers and advertisers to allude to high technology.)

The increase in resolution of the generated image towards the actual spatial resolution of the monitor has invoked a consequent increase in the time that a rendering pipeline takes to produce the image and the 1990s have seen a situation develop in which mainstream hardware is struggling to keep up with the demand of producing high resolution shaded imagery, sometimes at the requirements of interactive rates. This is particularly the case in virtual reality where the high rates required have only been possible with highly simplified environments whose lack of visual complexity obviates one of the main thrusts of virtual reality: that the user should be convinced – at least to some degree – that he or she is immersed in a real environment.

The demands of virtual reality have led recently to the development of the use of pre-rendered and/or photographic imagery to produce the image presented to the viewer. This is the first appearance of a tendency to reject the standard rendering pipeline approach, where a geometric description eventually causes an array of pixels to be output, in favour of image-based techniques. Here a new view is generated from a set of pre-rendered or pre-photographed views of an environment. New arrays of pixels are generated by warping existing ones and the scene itself is represented by pixels rather than any higher-level description.

Algorithms that analyze and process imagery generally deal initially with pixels. Algorithms that generate synthetic imagery output arrays of pixel values. The fields of image processing, computer vision and computer graphics all operate with pixel units. In the 1960s, computer graphics imagery was not made up of pixels but of units that were line segments. Although, as we shall see, some algorithms are concerned with calculations that operate with smaller units – fractions of pixels – these are concerned with increasing the accuracy of values which are eventually assigned to the pixel so that the accuracy or quality of the image is improved. In the end the pixel is of no interest to us – it is merely the means by which the computer image is visualized and any process or algorithm that deals with computer imagery is always part of a hierarchy where at the lowest level are algorithms that deal with pixel units. For example, analyzing computer imagery can be seen as a process that starts with pixels and attempts to derive structural relationships between them. Generating imagery is the reverse process. Starting with high-level structures – usually geometric descriptions of some sort – we invoke a series of processes that converts these structures into a set of pixels that forms the desired image.

The pixel representation has other ramifications that we now take for granted. One of the most important of these is that it has made possible the fast generation of shaded imagery. The fact that we can operate on individual pixels in the screen memory has spawned fast algorithms for shading and hidden surface removal for objects represented by planar polygonal facets – commonly known as polygon mesh objects. The frame memory can be divided into layers which supports the now universal GUI or windows interface that is the interface *lingua franca* of the 1990s. Another significant ramification of pixel representation is in the context of interfacing. That a subset of the image can be changed independently of the whole has been responsible for the wide acceptance of interactive (GUI) operation of machines with fairly modest processing power. The instantaneous divisibility of the computer image makes it different from other electronic imagery. We generally regard the TV image as indivisible or as something that is a copy of whatever the TV camera is currently looking at. Computer graphics images have always been divisible in this sense.

In the 1960s, although graphics terminals were a long way away from being pixel devices, interaction (with a light pen) was already established and the importance of image interaction was fully realized as exemplified by the pioneering work of Ivan Sutherland on SKETCHPAD. The output device in use then was a CRT. This operated calligraphically and an image was stored as a display list – or a list of straight line segments – which when suitably converted and fed to the display device caused a beam to plot a bright image on the screen that corresponded to the *xy* coordinates of the line segments in the display list. Interestingly the final representation of the image was structurally at a higher level (line segments) than a pixel representation. (In this connection, because the image unit was a straight line and the device calligraphic, the jagged silhouette edge that plagues pixel-based imagery was totally absent from such devices.) To cause the image to change, the display list had to be altered, and because the image was (finally) represented at a higher level than pixels, to generate the line drawings and diagrams required much less computing resources than a pixel graphics image. This significant advantage has been lost with pixel representation and even images of lines – in engineering drawings and the like – are forced into low-level pixel representation.

In the 1990s we see the common way to communicate with computers – the GUI – to be a somewhat unbalanced paradigm. Visual feedback from the computer is in the form of often quite complex imagery whereas input to the computer is via the ubiquitous mouse, a device that can only select, pick and drag. Thus we have a potentially high bandwidth output channel and an extremely low bandwidth input channel. In principle there has been little advancement in interactive techniques since Ivan Sutherland demonstrated his SKETCHPAD in 1963 – a system which involved using a light pen to interact with a line drawing on a CRT. (In fact the mouse, whose wholesale adoption was due to its simplicity and low cost, is in many ways an inferior device to other interactive input devices that were around at the same time such as the Rand Tablet and the light pen. These were never developed subsequently for the mass market, and they have found use only in certain specializations to which they are more suited than the mouse.)

Interfaces of the future are likely to exploit computer vision techniques to correct this imbalance. Already there is much research being conducted into the use of imagery as an interactive input medium. Another strong research motivator is video telephony and video conferencing where the aim is to compress moving imagery sufficiently for transmission over a low bandwidth computer link. This field has seen research approaches that use both classical compression and model-based techniques. In the latter case the transmitter sends something akin to an animation script for a model of the image, rather than the moving image itself.

It may be that in the future computer vision techniques in conjunction with speech recognition will enable 'natural' interfaces, where a user can communicate with a computer in much the same way that we communicate with each other using speech, gestures and facial expressions.

1.2 Synthesizing images or computer graphics

In 1992 Tinseltown produced another masterpiece of ephemera called *Death Becomes Her*. Starring Meryl Streep, this confection was copied onto thousands of metres of film and projected out of the darkness of thousands of cinemas throughout the planet. The absurd details of the plot are a distant memory, but Meryl was possessed of a rubber neck. She could raise her head half a metre above her shoulders and also rotate it through 180 degrees. The outstanding line of script was the resoundingly banal 'My gawd I can see my own ass'. This artful effect was produced by using complex state of the art computer graphics, using a computer graphics structure as her neck – a 'soft' object. This was fitted to a separately filmed head and body, and then choreographed along with the real movement.

This example is not atypical of the current use of computer graphics in popular culture. It has two distinguishing features: it is banal and artless and the computer graphics techniques that it employs involve elegant algorithms and advanced mathematics – a strange combination indeed. Of course, we cannot dismiss all computer graphics in this manner – as we shall see, more considered uses of the technology have made significant contributions in science and education – but the computer synthesized images that are currently seen by most inhabitants of the planet are those connected with film special effects, TV commercials and computer games.

It could be said that nowadays it is a technology with solutions – both hardware and software – aggressively hunting applications and this is tending to be reflected in the research which is moving away from image synthesis as such towards applications – particularly visualization. This is almost the opposite of the situation that persists in computer vision. There are many applications in computer vision that do not yet have a satisfactory solution.

So where did it all begin? Most of the development in computer graphics as we know it today was motivated by hardware evolution and the availability of new devices. Software rapidly developed to use the image-producing hardware. In this respect the most important development is the so-called 'raster display', a device that proliferated in the mass market shortly after the development of the PC. In this device the complete image is stored in a memory variously called a frame store, a screen buffer or a refresh memory. This information – the discretized computer image – is continually converted by a video controller into a set of horizontal scan lines (a raster) which is then fed to a TV-type monitor. The image is generated by an application program which usually accesses a model or geometric description of an object or objects. The main elements in such a system are shown in Figure 1.1. The display hardware to the right of the dotted line can be separate from the processor, but nowadays is usually integrated as in the case of an enhanced PC or a graphics workstation. The raster graphics device overshadows all other hardware developments in the sense that it made possible the display of shaded three-dimensional objects – the single most important theoretical development. The interaction of three-dimensional objects with a light source could be calculated and the effect projected into two-dimensional space and displayed by the device. Such shaded imagery is the foundation of modern computer graphics.

Figure 1.1
The main elements of a
graphics system.

The two early landmark achievements that made shaded imagery possible are the algorithms developed by Gouraud in 1971 and Phong in 1975 which enabled easy and fast calculation of the intensities of pixels when shading an

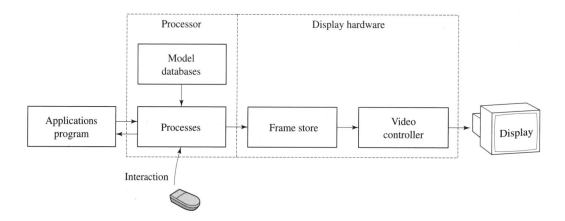

object. The Phong technique is still in mainstream use and is undoubtedly responsible for most of the shaded images in computer graphics. What image synthesis or computer graphics is depends on whether you are a consumer or a practitioner. Let us first look at the field from the common man's viewpoint.

1.2.1 ### Computer graphics and its impact on popular culture and art

You encounter, although you may not realize it, computer graphic images in many visual media, predominantly TV title sequences and film special effects. These are mostly animated sequences and seem to be motivated by two irresistible drives. First, they associate high technology with the program makers or channel owners – computer graphics as a high technology icon. Second, computer graphics images are in a sense easy to animate. Just get the computer to imitate the traditional manual technique, developed by Walt Disney – in-betweening – and before you know it you have animation (of a kind) – it can be done, so we do it. These are mostly the ubiquitous 'tumbling logo' sequences where the screen becomes filled with acrobatic characters made from chromium with rainbows reflecting in them. Decades of experience in the art of good graphic design are discarded without a further thought and a new graphics style emerges overnight. (It is not unlike the situation in typesetting, where in the 1970s computer assisted phototypesetting produced the most appalling results. This area has, however, increased in quality substantially over the past decade.) Dancing letters are a strange thing when you think that the function of a letter is to enable a word to be recognized. Despite this, it is undeniable that such productions have become part of our everyday visual culture.

A bizarre anecdote will further illustrate the 'computer graphics as a high technology icon' tendency. In 1987 in the UK a strange creation was given birth on TV. This was apparently a computer graphics-produced talking head called Max Headroom. The character had plastic-like clothes and hair, the mannerisms were jerky and the computer-like speech, together with the facial expressions, could accelerate and decelerate at will. However, this was counterfeit computer graphics. Such was the perceived demand for computer graphics that an elaborate imitation was conceived. The producers made the character by filming a real actor, then used post production techniques to make it look like a computer graphics creation. The actor was heavily made up and the post production processes simply reduced the information in the sequences by removing frames and duplicating the remainder.

The curious thing about most computer animation is that it is almost totally artless. It is at its best when the creators are presented with a specific task in film special effects. The pinnacle of achievement of this kind of animation is surely the dinosaurs and other extinct creatures in *Jurassic Park* – a Spielberg film released in 1993 (described in some detail in Chapter 17).

Computer graphics has never been seriously developed as a tool for artists, nor has it ever been accepted by the public as an art form. There are a few notable exceptions, but as far as the normal measures of works of art are concerned – books of reproductions, exhibitions, artists' names known to the public – this is true. This is strange because it is potentially a very powerful and subtle medium. Just some aspects that come to mind are the facility to precisely and subtly control the colour, the ability to experiment and manipulate images quickly and the possibility of producing creations that were not imagined by the producer but are products of a creative program. Computer graphics and art is a theme that is developed in some detail in Chapter 23.

On the other hand computer graphics is much used in creative or artistically related fields like graphic design. Here it is used as a tool of convenience rather than as an artistic medium. This means producing imagery that could be produced by hand but which is more easily and accurately produced by image manipulation in a computer. The most common manifestation of this is photomontage or cut and paste, where the computer simply replaces the scissors and the pot of glue. Such software has resulted in the 'merging' of visual images – photographic, diagrammatic or whatever – with text. These are treated uniformly – able to be displayed and manipulated on the same screen – and this has had major ramifications in, for example, the newspaper industry where before imagery and text were very much separate entities. Such facilities are a major advance in ease of use in the printing industry where the different practicalities of text and imagery were inconvenient. Another now highly developed tool facility is the routine use of classical image processing techniques in software that processes photographs.

There are a few examples of the uses of computer imagery as an art form in its own right. Perhaps the most successful of these are examples where a program is written to produce images that could not be or were not imagined by the program writer. Predominant in this genre is a technique called evolutionary procedural modelling, where objects are produced, mutated and then combined to produce child objects and so on. Notable in this field are Karl Sims and the partnership of Latham and Todd (Figure 1.2 – Colour Plate).

Another example, and probably the most well known, is a field started by Benoit Mandelbrot with his landmark book *Fractals: Form, Chance and Dimension* published in 1977. Such images are generally called fractals. They have become so ubiquitous, with so many people, intrigued by the production of such complex patterns from a few lines of code, rediscovering and producing the same thing, that their novelty and potential beauty has been destroyed. They are the visual equivalent of a popular song which on first hearing is memorable and beautiful, but which through endless repetition consumes itself and is reduced to tedium. Both of these examples reflect one of the major problems encountered when trying to use computer graphics as an artistic medium. This is that they are locked into a particular narrow type of visual imagery. We know that Figure 1.2 and anything like it has been produced by an evolutionary procedure approach and that Figure 1.3 has been produced by a Mandelbrot set formula. Whether this is the only future for image synthesis in art remains to be seen. Certainly the situation at the present time is that computer art is the production

Figure 1.3
A Mandelbrot set image – one of the most ubiquitous computer images of the 1990s.

of image synthesis programs, where there is little artistic control beyond setting up the start parameters.

1.2.2 Computer graphics and its practitioners

A brief history of shaded imagery

When we look at computer graphics from the viewpoint of its practitioners, we see that since the mid-1970s the developmental motivation has been photo-realism or the pursuit of techniques that make a graphics image of an object or scene indistinguishable from a TV image or photograph. A more recent strand of application of these techniques is to display information in, for example, medicine, science and engineering.

The foundation of photo-realism is the calculation of light/object interaction and this splits neatly into two fields: the development of local reflection models and the development of global models. Local or direct reflection models consider the interaction of an object with a light source as if the object and light were floating in dark space. That is, only the first reflection of light from the object is considered. Global reflection models consider how light reflects from one object and travels on to another. In other words the light impinging on a point on the surface can come either from a light source (direct light) or from indirect light that has first hit another object. Global interaction is for the most part an unsolved problem, although two partial solutions, ray tracing and radiosity, are now widely implemented.

Computer graphics research has gone the way of much modern scientific research – early major advances are created and consolidated. Later significant advances seem to be more difficult to achieve. We can say that most images are produced using the Phong local reflection model (first reported in 1975), fewer using ray tracing (first popularized in 1980) and fewer still using radiosity (first reported in 1984). Although there is still much research being carried out in light/scene interaction methodologies, much of the current research in computer graphics is concerned more with applications, for example with such general applications as animation, visualization and virtual reality. In the most important computer graphics publication (the annual SIGGRAPH conference proceedings), in 1985 there was a total of 22 papers concerned with the production techniques of images (rendering, modelling and hardware) compared with 13 on what could loosely be called applications. In 1995 there were 37 papers on applications and 19 on image production techniques.

Modelling surface reflection with local interaction

Two early advances which went hand in hand were the development of hidden surface removal algorithms and shaded imagery – simulating the interaction of an object with a light source. Most of the hidden surface removal research was carried out in the 1970s and nowadays, for general purpose use, the most common algorithm is the Z-buffer – an approach that is very easy to implement and combine with shading or rendering algorithms.

In shaded imagery the major prop is the Phong reflection model. Developed in 1975, this is an elegant but completely empirical model that usually ends up with an object reflecting more light than it receives. Its parameters are based on the grossest aspects of reflection of light from a surface and they are empirical or imitative. Despite this, it is the most widely used model in computer graphics, responsible for the vast majority of created images. Why is this so? Probably because users find it adequate and it is easy to implement.

Theoretically based reflection models attempt to model reflection more accurately and their parameters have physical meaning; that is, they can be measured for a real surface. For example, light reflects differently from an isotropic surface, such as plastic, compared to its behaviour with a non-isotropic surface such as brushed aluminium, and such an effect can be imitated by explicitly modelling the surface characteristics. Such models attempt to imitate the behaviour of light at a milliscale level (where the roughness or surface geometry is still much greater than the wavelength of light). Their purpose is to imitate the material signature – why different materials in reality look different. Alternatively, parameters of a model can be measured on a real surface and used in a simulation. The work on more elaborate or theoretical local reflection models does not seem to have gained any widespread acceptance as far as its implementation in rendering systems is concerned. This may be due to the fact that users do not perceive that the extra processing costs are worth the somewhat marginal improvement in the appearance of the shaded object.

All these models, while attending to the accurate modelling of light from a surface, are local models which means that they only consider the interaction of light with the object as if the object was floating in free space. No object–object interaction is considered and one of the main problems that immediately arises is that shadows – a phenomenon due to global interaction – are not incorporated into the model and have to be calculated by a separate 'add-on' algorithm.

The development of the Phong reflection model spawned research into add-on shadow algorithms and texture mapping, both of which enhanced the appearance of the shaded object and tempered the otherwise 'floating in free space' plastic look of the basic Phong model.

Modelling global interaction

The 1980s saw the development of two significant global models – light reflection models that attempt to evaluate the interaction between objects. Global interaction gives rise to such phenomena as the determination of the intensity of light within a shadow area, the reflection of objects in each other (specular interaction) and a subtle effect known as colour bleeding where the colour from a diffuse surface is transported to another nearby surface (diffuse interaction). The light intensity within a shadow area can only be determined from global interaction. An area in shadow, by definition, cannot receive light directly from a light source but only indirectly from light reflecting from another object. When you see shiny objects in a scene you expect to see in them reflections of other objects. A very shiny surface, such as chromium plate, behaves almost like a mirror, taking all its surface detail from its surroundings and distorting this geometrically according to surface curvature.

The successful global models are ray tracing and radiosity. However, in their basic implementation both models cater only for one aspect of global illumination. Ray tracing attends to perfect specular reflection – very shiny objects reflecting in each other – and radiosity models diffuse interaction, which is when light reflects off matte surfaces to illuminate other surfaces. Diffuse interaction is common in man-made interiors which tend to have carpets on the floor and matte finishes on the walls. Areas in a room that cannot see the light source are illuminated by diffuse interaction. Mutually exclusive in the phenomena they model, images created by both methods tend to have identifying 'signatures'. Ray traced images are notable for perfect recursive reflections and super-sharp refraction. Radiosity images are usually of softly lit interiors and do not contain specular or shiny objects.

Computer graphics is not an exact science. Much research in light surface interaction in computer graphics proceeds by taking existing physical models and simulating them with a computer graphics algorithm. This may involve much simplification in the original mathematical model so that it can be implemented as a computer graphics algorithm. Ray tracing and radiosity are classic examples of this tendency. Simplifications, which may appear gross to a mathematician, are made by computer graphicists for practical reasons. The reason this process 'works' is that when we look at a synthesized scene we do not generally perceive the simplifications in the mathematics unless they result in visible degeneracies known as aliases. However, most people can easily distinguish a computer graphics image from a photograph. Thus computer graphics have a 'realism' of their own that is a function of the model, and the nearness of the computer graphics image to a photograph of a real scene varies widely according to the method. Photo-realism in computer graphics means the image **looks** real, not that it approaches, on a pixel by pixel basis, a photograph. This subjective judgement of computer graphics images somewhat devalues the widely used adjective 'photo-realistic' but there you are. With one or two exceptions very little work has been done on comparing a human's perception of a computer graphics image with, say, a TV image of the equivalent real scene.

General reading in computer graphics

Journals

Computer Graphics (ACM) – the annual SIGGRAPH proceedings issue
This is the most important reference in three-dimensional computer graphics and all of the significant developments are to be found within its pages in issues of the past 15 years. It possesses the status of a journal despite being conference proceedings. It details the contributions to the annual SIGGRAPH conference which now has an attendance of around 30 000. (A curious affair with an atmosphere that is something of a cross between a religious revival meeting and a large fairground.)

IEEE Computer Graphics and Applications

The Visual Computer

Books

Foley J.D., van Dam A., Feiner S.K. and Hughes J.F. (1989). *Computer Graphics Principles and Practice*. Reading, MA: Addison-Wesley
The standard reference in computer graphics. A well-illustrated encyclopaedic work.

Glassner A.S. (1995). *Principles of Digital Image Synthesis* (Volumes 1 and 2). San Francisco, CA: Morgan Kaufmann Publishers, Inc.
This comprehensive, 1200-page text expands on explanations given by authors in the original papers. Expertly illustrated, it can be consulted whenever the reading of the original paper does not lead to a complete understanding. Although it deals with all the advanced rendering techniques in great detail, its great value is the wealth of theoretical information that is the foundation of these approaches to light object interaction.

Various editors (from) 1990. *Graphics Gems*. Academic Press
Now in its fifth volume this work, as the name implies, is a collection of programming techniques that span most of the problems that are likely to arise when implementing graphics software. Reputedly mandatory for implementors, it is of less interest to theoreticians.

Watt A.H. (1993). *The Fundamentals of Three-dimensional Computer Graphics*. Wokingham: Addison-Wesley
A comprehensive treatment of mainstream rendering techniques.

Watt M. and Watt A.H. (1992). *Advanced Animation and Rendering Techniques*. Addison-Wesley

1.3 Image processing – an overview

In January 1980 *Scientific American* published a remarkable image called *Plume 2*, the second of eight volcanic eruptions detected on the Jovian moon Io by the spacecraft Voyager 1 on 5 March 1979. The picture was a landmark image in interplanetary exploration – the first time an erupting volcano had been seen in space. It was also a triumph for image processing. An image of *Plume 2* is shown in Figure 1.4 – Colour Plate.

Satellite imagery and images from interplanetary explorers have until fairly recently been the major users of image processing techniques, where a computer image is numerically manipulated to produce some desired effect – such as making a particular aspect or feature in the image more visible. The image in Figure 1.4 is a pseudo-coloured composite, where four separate images, from different bands of the spectrum, are combined to form a single coloured image. The intensity in each of the images transmitted from the spacecraft is used as a colour component to produce a pseudo-coloured image. The image is a ratio composite of the four spacecraft images. The ultra-violet, violet and orange images have been divided by the green image and the resulting three intensity images have been used as blue, green and red components to produce the composite. The image shows a plume surrounding the core that scatters ultra-violet light. The original images – two-dimensional arrays of numbers or intensities – are subject to just one division and multiplication to produce the final RGB image.

Image processing has its roots in photo reconnaissance in the Second World War where processing operations were optical and interpretation operations were performed by humans who undertook such tasks as quantifying the effect of bombing raids. With the advent of satellite imagery in the late 1960s, much computer-based work began and the colour composite satellite images, sometimes startlingly beautiful, have become part of our visual culture and the perception of our planet.

Like computer graphics, it was until recently confined to research laboratories which could afford the expensive image processing computers that could cope with the substantial processing overheads required to process large numbers of high resolution images. With the advent of cheap powerful computers and image collection devices like digital cameras and scanners, we have seen a migration of image processing techniques into the public domain. Classical image processing techniques are routinely employed by graphic designers to manipulate photographic and generated imagery, either to correct defects, change colour and so on or creatively to transform the entire look of an image by subjecting it to some operation such as edge enhancement.

A recent mainstream application of image processing is the compression of images – either for transmission across the Internet or the compression of moving video images in video telephony and video conferencing. Video telephony is one of the current crossover areas that employs both computer graphics and classical image processing techniques to try to achieve very high compression rates. All this is part of an inexorable trend towards the digital representation of images. Indeed that most powerful image form of the twentieth century – the TV image – is also about to be taken into the digital domain.

Image processing is characterized by a large number of algorithms that are specific solutions to specific problems. Some are mathematical or context-independent operations that are applied to each and every pixel. For example, we can use Fourier transforms to perform image filtering operations. Others are 'algorithmic' – we may use a complicated recursive strategy to find those pixels that constitute the edges in an image.

Image processing operations often form part of a computer vision system. The input image may be filtered to highlight or reveal edges prior to a shape detection operation, for example. In the context of a computer vision system these processes are usually known as low-level operations. In computer graphics filtering operations are used extensively to avoid aliasing or sampling artefacts.

Recently techniques that have long been considered part of image processing have migrated into computer graphics, resulting in a new field called image-based rendering. This is considered potentially as a way of solving the scene complexity rendering time contradiction. This means that to have a quality virtual reality environment – and most applications of immersive virtual reality demand a scene rich enough in detail to emulate the real world – we need to explore alternatives to the prohibitively costly method of re-injecting the entire scene geometry into a standard rendering pipeline every time the virtual viewpoint changes slightly. Techniques such as morphing and view interpolation are being investigated as a way of supplying visually rich imagery at interactive rates. Operating in the image domain, the approaches use the current imagery under some constraint to generate new imagery when a user changes his or her viewpoint. In other words, existing images are processed in some way to supply the new imagery. Further discussion of these techniques is to be found in Chapter 21.

An example of computer graphics techniques being employed in a field that was previously the domain of image processing is the use of model-based coding in video telephony. Here the idea is to set up a photo-textured computer graphics model of a human head which might be a standard geometric model deformed to fit the characteristics of the participants. The current speaker's image is subject to an image analysis technique and those changes (lip movements, head rotations and so on) that are necessary to animate the model at the receiver are derived and transmitted. Generally we can say that we try to analyze the image so that an animation script for the model is derived. We then only need to transmit the script rather than an entire image at video rates. Although these efforts are still in the early development stage they can offer potentially far greater saving in the information rate than is available from conventional image compression techniques.

General reading in image processing

Journals

CVGIP: Graphical Models and Image Processing
This is a journal that concentrates on the synthesis methods and computation that underlies computer generated or processed imagery.

Books

Gonzalez R.C. and Woods R.E. (1992). *Digital Image Processing*. Reading, MA: Addison-Wesley
Possibly the most frequently referenced and used image processing book, this classic text is pitched at undergraduate level and contains clear and comprehensive explanations of all the mainstream image processing techniques.

Haralick R.M. and Shapiro L.G. (1992). *Computer and Robot Vision Vol 1*. Reading, MA: Addison-Wesley
This is a substantial two-volume work, the second of which is devoted mainly to computer vision. It is more detailed than most image processing texts and is written from a mathematical viewpoint. It contains many comparisons on algorithm performance.

Russ J.C. (1995). *The Image Processing Handbook 2nd Edition*. Boca Raton, FL: CRC Press
Image processing texts are notable for their variable quality images and paucity of examples. This text, biased towards the image processing user rather than the implementor, contains hundreds of high quality illuminating illustrations. It is also notable in that the author has many examples of the consecutive application of different techniques to the same image to achieve a desired result. Most illustrations in most books deal with the application of a single technique.

Sonka M., Haclav V. and Boyle R. (1993). *Image Processing, Analysis and Machine Vision*. London: Chapman and Hall
As the title implies, the book addresses computer vision and image processing. Well illustrated with ample references, sometimes the algorithm descriptions are insufficient in the detail required by an implementor.

1.4 Computer vision

And now we arrive at what is the most difficult aspect of computer imagery – the derivation of three-dimensional information from projections or computer vision. That computer vision is difficult is certain and unlike the other two areas of computer imagery that we deal with, it is still mostly a research area. Despite the fact that it is a discipline as old as image processing and, it is fair to say, older than most aspects of computer graphics, research into computer vision has not transferred in any substance into the real world of applications. There are still many computer vision applications looking for a solution. We can contrast this with the state of computer graphics, which, in a sense, is a set of solutions looking for more and more new applications.

What is computer vision? Sometimes called **image understanding**, it has come to mean the **extraction of knowledge** concerning a three-dimensional reality from one or more projections of that reality. An alternative definition is that it provides a **representation** or **description** of the scene from two-dimensional projections that can then be used in some context such as robot navigation or three-dimensional object recognition. This definition also gives us the reason why computer vision is difficult. It is because it is a 'many to one' mapping problem – many different scenes can produce the same two-dimensional projection just as a single scene is capable of producing many different projections.

What information do we need to extract from the projection of a scene? This is, of course, heavily context dependent, but most commonly we require geometric information – the position and orientation (or pose) of an object. Less commonly we may require properties associated with the object surface. We may need knowledge from time-varying information, such as extracting information about a scene from a moving camera.

What is computer vision used for? Usually it is linked with a robot function and indeed much of vision research has as its goal an imitation of human vision. But most industrial robots are non-anthropomorphic and the task required by their vision system is heavily constrained. The environment from which a practical vision system is required to extract information is usually restricted. For example, in automatic assembly, a robot arm may require information that enables it to pick up a flat part and re-orient it into a particular aspect prior to insertion in an assembly process. The vision system may only be presented with examples of this one part and may only have to recognize the orientation of the part in a flat plane. Perhaps also it may have to segment the sub-image of the part from other sub-images of overlapping parts. The parts may be illuminated from beneath (back-lit) so that their silhouette is easy to detect. Many applications do not involve a robot, for example automatic inspection of manufactured components on a conveyor belt leading to an accept/reject action. Here the goal may be to see if the shape of the component deviates sufficiently from the correct shape to be rejected. Such systems are a very long way from the unconstrained power of the human vision system.

The term computer vision as used nowadays excludes image processing – the act of operating on two-dimensional images to produce new two-dimensional images that are in some way better than the original. It also, for the purists, excludes **pattern recognition** – or **pattern classification** – the act of classifying two-dimensional images as belonging to one of a fixed set of categories. However, in this text we will take the broad view and include pattern recognition as part of computer vision. Even in pattern recognition the constrained environment approach occurs in mainstream application areas. The use of heavily constrained character sets from optical input to computers has a long history. Two everyday examples are the characters used on bank cheques to facilitate easy classification and the ubiquitous bar code. With bank cheques symbols are heavily stylized to make the classification technology simple and robust, but at the same time they are still readable by humans. In the case of bar codes, the computer readable code and its numerical human readable equivalent are printed side by side.

Although we describe computer vision as the process of providing a description of a scene and exclude image processing as belonging to another discipline, we should bear in mind that many computer vision systems will include image processing operations in their overall operation. For example, we may apply contrast enhancement or noise reduction as a pre-process in a computer vision system. We may try to describe or deduce information concerning shape after applying the process of edge detection. (Note that with processes such as edge detection there is no real agreed categorization. Some authors consider edge detection as part of computer vision, others as part of image processing. Perhaps the safest categorization comes from considering it to be part of both.)

A strong influence in computer vision research is the seemingly irresistible urge to base approaches on apparent mechanisms in human vision. The human vision system appears remarkable and seems to operate without constraints. We can, with consummate ease, derive three-dimensional information from the projections on our retinas. This is its attraction as a goal to imitate – we would like to build vision facilities that also operate without such constraints as prior knowledge of the nature of objects in the scene. An argument against going down this road stems from the obvious fact that knowledge of how the human system works is very rudimentary and fragmented, and this situation, like real knowledge of how the brain functions in general, is likely to remain so for the foreseeable future. Although much is known about how the eye itself functions, there is little knowledge available on the higher-level processes of vision and the cognitive aspects of human vision.

Also, with the human visual system it seems at the outset wrong to regard it as a perceptual sense independent of the other senses and experience. While we recognize that human beings can easily interpret and understand the projection of a three-dimensional scene, such as a photograph, we do not know how much of this ability is based on experience and knowledge. It would seem that knowledge and experience are likely to be predominant factors in the human vision system, given that we have only had (representative) two-dimensional imagery in the form of paintings and latterly photographs for a few centuries. It cannot be that our ability to interpret photographs easily is innate. We are part of the environment that we perceive and it is surely wrong to separate our visual perception as if somehow this facility exists independently of all other aspects of our consciousness. Perhaps we have no trouble with TV and photographic images because we substitute ourselves for the camera. The two-dimensional projections are simply vicarious experiences of reality.

Much of the work on computer vision as an imitator of the human visual system comes out of work done on psychophysical experiments – particularly the use of computer models to simulate their results. These simulations are strongly influential in suggesting low-level models for computer vision. Marr's work (summarized in his book *Vision*) is very influential in this respect.

For example, Marr states:

Vision is the construction of efficient symbolic descriptions from images of the world. ...To understand vision thus requires that we first have some idea of which representations to use. ...Fortunately, the human visual system offers a good example of an efficient visual processor, and therefore provides important clues to the representations that are most appropriate and likely to yield successful solutions.

Two points emerge from this (admittedly short) quotation. First, Marr seemed to see vision as an entity that we can understand and construct a theory for. He does not appear to be referring to the human visual system in the title of his book. Second, he believed that the study of the human visual system will provide strong clues for the formation of this theory. But why? Not only is there the aforementioned 'interference' from experience problem, but the human vision system can only be studied as a 'black box' – we input an image and ask an observer to describe a response. It is almost impossible to separate lower-level processes of the human vision system, that appear to be executed in the retina, from the higher-level decision-making processes. Marr's seductive theory is based on a hierarchy of processes: low-level image processing operations, such as edge detection, lead to a simpler stylization of the image which is then subject to descriptive or understanding processes. As experimental observers of the human visual system we have virtually no access to the sub-units of the 'black box'. In fact a large part of the body of knowledge from psychophysical experiments comes from studying optical illusions – a strange approach given that this is exactly where the human vision system malfunctions. Marr's elegant work is, in the main, pure theory but its influence in computer vision is significant.

The point of view that vision is a process that analyzes the two-dimensional projection of a scene without using any a priori information concerning objects that make up the scene has its most popular manifestations in the various 'shape from X' approaches. Here some aspect of a scene, such as reflected light intensity in a TV image, is analyzed and we try to regain depth information from the light intensity information. These techniques are described in detail in Chapter 16. They have met only with limited success because they are extremely sensitive to noise and also because they require constraints that are not generally experienced in practical contexts.

Unconstrained computer vision approaches exhibit a number of expectations and assumed strategies:

- The process can be seen as a hierarchy where low-level information is succeeded by higher-level processes – the whole performing an abstraction of information together with a reduction of the quantity – in the pixel sense – of information resulting in recognition or a description. A cluster of pixels in the image plane cause the systems to output something like 'the object in front of the camera is a rectangular solid with dimensions ... on top of this is a pyramid...'.

- This kind of process can be applied to two-dimensional projections of reflected light intensity. This is called passive vision to distinguish it from techniques where the computer vision system has some control over the environment – by injecting laser light into the scene as in the case of a range finder, for example.

- The system can operate without detailed prior knowledge of objects in the scene, enabling it to deal with unseen objects in terms of primitives and relationships that it does have knowledge of.

So perhaps the view of the human vision system as essentially a passive or isolated processor of low-level information through higher and more powerful levels of processing accounts only in part for our remarkable three-dimensional from two-dimensional capability. Our visual perception could owe as much to the acquisition of experience as it does to high-level passive processing by our brains.

These considerations are important in computer vision because they seem strongly to influence the nature of the research that is undertaken. Unlike the other two areas of the computer image, computer vision has two schools: crudely, the artificial intelligence/vision researcher/cognitive scientist who tries to find general solutions to vision problems and the engineer who looks for particular solutions to industrial problems. The first school tends to operate without constraints, looking for a solution that can be applied to any type of scene. The second school tries to find solutions to applications operating with constraints such as prior knowledge or by using active devices to gather information from the scene rather than relying on a reflected light intensity sensor. You can find whole textbooks devoted to one approach or the other. For this reason it is a difficult topic to write about. In this text we will keep a foot in both camps. Computer vision is an intriguing and challenging area of study and we will try to select the important developments from both schools.

Recognizing that a general vision capability may not be possible in the foreseeable future, a recent approach that has become popular is to concentrate on trying to recognize objects and scenes made up of entities of which there is prior knowledge. One of the problems then becomes: how is this knowledge to be represented and used? The approach is called CAD-based vision because it uses standard computer graphics (or CAD) models to represent stored object knowledge. The models are used in a normal computer graphics way to generate a hypothesis that is compared with the real image.

Most approaches generate an image, such as a wireframe projection, that gives the structure of the object without any shading on the faces. This reflects the fact that providing we have knowledge of the pose of the object (its position and orientation with respect to the sensor or viewer) then we are able to generate a projection from the model that should match the structure in the real image. We attempt to match structure based on the prior knowledge with structure in the image rather than attempting to match on a pixel basis. We know that the reflection models used in computer graphics are unlikely to synthesize an image that will match the input from a real scene. There is a wealth of factors (transfer characteristic of the sensor, global illumination effects due to surface irregularities and material differences, and noise) that account for the differences between a real image of a scene and its synthetic version.

Although we will examine a method that tries to match real images to synthetic ones using the shape of the specular reflections, most CAD-based vision attempts a matching process using some high-level geometric structure rather than individual pixels. This is, of course, not only because of the aforementioned difficulty with the computer graphics models, but also because the nature of the structure selected has strong ramifications for the matching process itself and the difficulty of extracting the required structure from the real image.

It needs pointing out that the obvious limitation of any CAD-based computer vision technique is the fact that computer graphics models can only represent a subset of entities that make up any real-world scene. They are particularly limiting when they are employed to represent natural objects such as trees or animals. Such limitations, which have been a feature of computer graphics for many years and have strong implications in creating convincing complex imagery for virtual reality applications, are thus reflected in the nature of the scenes that the approach can deal with in vision.

Just as computer graphics techniques are crossing over into computer vision, so are computer vision techniques now being investigated in one of the new application areas of computer graphics – virtual reality. This relates to the point that we have already discussed: the demands of high quality virtual reality systems and the inability of standard computer graphics techniques to supply quality images at low cost and at video rates. A substantial problem in virtual reality is building models of existing scenes such as cityscapes for visualization of new developments, virtual tourism or whatever. A potential solution and one the we examine in detail in Chapter 21 is to use computer vision techniques to build computer graphics models from photographs. This might involve taking photographs of a visually complex building – a twelfth-century cathedral, say – and reconstructing a model with correct geometry and surface detail from the photographs using techniques such as stereo correspondence algorithms.

General reading in computer vision

Journals

CVGIP: Image Understanding
Covers all aspects of Image Analysis from low-level processes to high-level symbolic processes of recognition and interpretation.

IEEE Transactions on Pattern Analysis and Machine Intelligence

International Journal of Computer Vision

Books

Ballard D.H. and Brown C.M. (1982). *Computer Vision.* Englewood Cliffs, NJ: Prentice-Hall
A classic early text, still eminently readable despite the absence of more up-to-date computer vision approaches such as CAD-based vision. Despite the title the book includes a good treatment of image processing.

Freeman H. (1988). *Machine Vision – Algorithms, Architectures and Systems* (Perspectives in Computing V20). Boston: Academic Press
A good text that gives an idea of current vision applications and solutions.

Gregory R.L. and Gombrich E.H. (1975). *Illusion in Nature and Art.* New York: Charles Scribner's Sons

Haralick R.M. and Shapiro L.G. (1993). *Computer and Robot Vision Vol 2.* Reading, MA: Addison-Wesley
Encyclopaedic and extremely comprehensive but somewhat inaccessible without a reasonable mathematical background.

Horn B.K.P. (1987). *Robot Vision.* Cambridge, MA: MIT Press
The classic text in the 'Shape from X' approach.

Kasturi R. and Jain R.C. (1991). *Computer Vision: Principles* and *Computer Vision: Advances and Applications.* Los Alamitos, CA: IEEE Comp. Sci. Press
A large two-volume publication in the IEEE Tutorial series containing a selection of the important papers in Computer Vision.

Marr D. (1982). *Vision – A Computational Investigation into the Human Representation and Processing of Visual Information.* San Francisco, CA: W.H. Freeman and Co.
The book that launched a thousand research projects, it espouses a low-level to high-level information extraction approach that does not rely on prior knowledge of objects.

Nalwa V.S. (1993). A *Guided Tour of Computer Vision.* Reading, MA: Addison-Wesley
Eminently readable, this is particularly good at giving an intuitive interpretation of the mathematically oriented methods.

Representation and modelling of three-dimensional objects

2.1 Introduction

In many ways modelling and representation is an unsolved problem in the computer image. The most popular way of representing an object – by approximating it with a set of planar facets – has many disadvantages when the object is complex and detailed. In mainstream computer graphics the number of polygons in an object representation can be anything from a few tens to hundreds of thousands. This has serious ramifications in rendering time and object creation cost and in the feasibility of using such objects in an animation or virtual reality environment. Other problems accrue in animation where a model has both to represent the shape of the object and be controlled by an animation system which may require collisions to be calculated or the object to change shape as a function of time.

Representational methods also have ramifications in computer vision. With the decline of the 'Marr philosophy' that computer vision should proceed from low-level processing of an image to higher and higher levels of abstraction without detailed a priori information concerning objects in the scene, came the introduction of so-called CAD-based vision. Here computer graphics models are used to store the a priori information and the scene is constrained to contain only objects that we have knowledge of. The nature of the model then has ramifications for the design of the vision system. This topic is exposed in detail in Chapter 18.

Different representational methods have their advantages and disadvantages but there is no universal solution to the many problems that still exist. Rather, particular modelling methods have evolved for particular contexts. A good example of this tendency is the development of constructive solid geometry (CSG) methods popular in interactive CAD because they facilitate an intuitive interface for the interactive design of complex industrial objects as well as a representation. CSG is a constrained representation in that we can only use it to model shapes that are made up of allowed combinations of the primitive shapes or elements that are included in the system.

In this chapter we will examine the most popular methods of representation and overview the implications they have for rendering. There are certain important modelling strategies that are dealt with in other chapters. Modelling methods that are relevant to animation – generally applications where the geometric shape model has to admit to dynamic shape control – are dealt with in Chapter 17. The important new application of photo-modelling, or extracting a scene representation from photographs, is discussed in Chapter 21. The implication of model-based video compression is discussed in Chapter 26.

A model in three-dimensional computer graphics is the word used to describe the method or way in which we represent the three-dimensional shape of an object within a program. How are models arrived at? The answer is that it depends on the nature of the object, the particular computer graphics technique that we are going to use to bring the object to life and the application. All these factors are interrelated. We can represent some three-dimensional objects exactly using a mathematical formulation – for example, a cylinder or a sphere; for others we use an approximate representation. Usually there is a trade-off between the accuracy of the representation and the bulk of information used. The standard approximate modelling method is the polygon mesh – a set of planar facets – but other more elaborate approximate models are possible. The main problem with the polygon mesh is that it is not much use for detailed objects such as, say, a human head. (See, for example, Figure 2.1 which is a rendered polygon mesh of a bust – this contains approximately 400 000 polygons.) You can only increase the veracity of the representation by increasing the polygonal resolution which then has high cost implications in rendering time.

In objects like human heads where we want to make the representation imitate the geometry of the reality as much as possible, we can use a hybrid representation. In representing a particular human head we can use a combination of a polygon mesh model and photographic texture maps. The solid form of the head is represented by a generic polygon mesh which is pulled around to match the actual dimensions of the head to be modelled. The detailed likeness is obtained by mapping a photographic texture onto this mesh. The idea here is

Figure 2.1
A rendered version of a complex polygonal object that was modelled automatically. There are approximately 400 000 polygons in the model.

that the detailed variations in the geometry are suggested by the texture map rather than by detailed geometric excursions in the geometry. Of course, it is not perfect because the detail in the photograph depends on the lighting conditions under which it was taken as well as the real geometric detail, but it is a trick that is increasingly being used (see Chapter 21 for an example of this technique in rendering architectural detail). Whether we regard the texture mapping as part of the representation or as part of the rendering process is perhaps a matter of opinion; but certainly the use of photographic texture maps in this context enables us to represent a complex object like a human head with a small number of polygons plus a photograph.

This compromise between polygonal resolution and a photographic texture map can be taken to extremes. In the computer games industry the total number of polygons rendered to the screen must be within the limiting number that can be rendered at, say, 15 frames per second on a PC. A recent football game consists of players whose heads are modelled with just a cube onto which a photographic texture is mapped.

We now list in order of approximate frequency of use the mainstream models used in computer graphics. Most of these are also used in CAD-based vision. The categories that we shall deal with are now overviewed:

(1) **Polygonal**: Objects are approximated by a net or mesh of planar polygonal facets. With this form we can represent, to an accuracy that we choose, an object of any shape. However, the accuracy is somewhat arbitrary in this sense. Consider Figure 2.1 again; are 400 000 polygons really necessary, or can we reduce the polygonal resolution without degrading the rendered image, and if so by how much? Connected with the polygonal resolution is the final projected size of the object on the screen. Waste is incurred when a complex object represented by many thousands of polygons projects onto a screen area that is made up of only a few pixels.

Fast shading algorithms use polygonal objects and are designed to visually transform the faceted representation in such a way that the piecewise planar approximation is not apparent.

Another disadvantage is that polygon objects are more or less 'fixed' – given an object it is difficult to change its shape.

This representation is technically known as a boundary representation because it explicitly represents the surface which is the boundary between the object and the surrounding space. This distinguishes it from, for example, methods that are based on volumes.

(2) **Bicubic parametric patches**: These are 'curved quadrilaterals'. Generally we can say that the representation is similar to the polygon mesh except that the individual polygons are now curved surfaces. Each patch is specified by a mathematical formula that gives the position of the patch in three-dimensional space and its shape. We can change the shape or curvature of the patch by editing the mathematical specification. This results in powerful interactive possibilities. The problems are, however, significant. It is very expensive to render or visualize the patches. When we change the shape of individual patches in a net of patches there are problems in maintaining 'smoothness' between the patch and its neighbours. Bicubic parametric patches can be either an exact or an approximate representation. They can only be an exact representation of themselves, which means that any object, say a car body panel, can only be represented exactly if its shape corresponds exactly to the shape of the patch. This somewhat torturous statement is necessary because when the representation is used for real or existing objects, the shape modelled will not necessarily correspond to the surface of the object.

(3) **CSG (Constructive Solid Geometry)**: This is an exact representation to within certain rigid shape limits. It has arisen out of the realization that very many manufactured objects can be represented by 'combinations' of elementary shapes or geometric primitives. For example, a chunk of metal with a hole in it could be specified as the result of a three-dimensional subtraction between a rectangular solid and a cylinder. Connected with this is the fact that such a representation makes for easy and intuitive shape control – we can specify that a metal plate has to have a hole in it by defining a cylinder of appropriate radius and subtracting it from the rectangular solid, representing the plate. The CSG method is a volumetric representation – shape is represented by elementary volumes or primitives. This contrasts with the previous two methods which represent shape using surfaces.

(4) **Spatial subdivision techniques**: This simply means dividing the object space into elementary cubes known as **voxels** and labelling each voxel as empty or as containing part of an object. It is the three-dimensional analogue of representing a two-dimensional object as the collection of pixels onto which the object projects. Labelling all of three-dimensional object space in this way is clearly expensive, but it has found applications in computer graphics, in particular in ray tracing where an efficient algorithm results if the objects are represented in this way.

(5) **Implicit representation**: Occasionally in texts implicit functions are mentioned as an object representation form. An implicit function is, for example:

$$x^2 + y^2 + z^2 = r^2$$

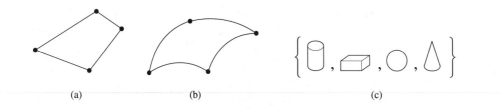

(a)　　　　　　(b)　　　　　　(c)　　　　　　(d)　　(e)

Figure 2.2
A comparison of 'atomic' elements used in computer graphics models. (a) Planar polygon: coordinates of vertices in an order that implies connectivity; (b) bicubic, parametric patch: 16 coordinates (which, when 'plugged into' a mathematical formula, generate the patch); (c) Constructive Solid Geometry: a vocabulary of primitives together with a set of combination operators; (d) spatial subdivision or labelling: a voxel and its position in space (either stated as a three-dimensional coordinate or implied as part of an octree); (e) implicit functions: a formula representing a (usually quadratic) object.

which is the implicit definition for a sphere. On their own these are of limited usefulness in computer graphics because there are a limited number of objects that can be represented in this way. Also, it is an inconvenient form as far as rendering is concerned. However, we should mention that such representations do appear quite frequently in three-dimensional computer graphics – in particular in ray tracing where spheres are used frequently – both as objects in their own right and as bounding objects for other polygon mesh representations.

Implicit representations are extended into implicit functions which can loosely be described as objects formed by mathematically defining a surface that is influenced by a collection of underlying primitives such as spheres. Implicit functions find their main use in shape-changing animation – they are of limited usefulness for representing real objects.

A simple comparison of the 'atomic' elements or primitives for each representation, together with the numerical information associated with each primitive, is shown in Figure 2.2. At this stage you can deduce a few simple facts concerning these representations which we will elaborate on later. The bicubic parametric patches, the CSG representation and the implicit functions can represent curved surfaces – the others can only approximate curved surfaces. Bicubic parametric patches represent an object by dividing it into primitive elements. With implicit functions the primitive is the object (although we will qualify this later). The CSG method is an exact representation made up of primitives; it achieves this exactness by limiting the nature of the objects. Polygons, bicubic patches and voxels can represent any objects.

2.2 Polygonal representation of three-dimensional objects

This is the classic representational form in three-dimensional graphics. An object is represented by a mesh of polygonal facets. In the general case an object possesses curved surfaces and the facets are an approximation to such a surface (Figure 2.3).

Polygonal representations are ubiquitous in computer graphics. There are two reasons for this. Creating polygonal objects is straightforward (although for complex objects the process can be time consuming and costly) and visually effective algorithms exist to produce shaded versions of objects represented in this way.

Figure 2.3
Approximating a curved surface using polygonal facets.

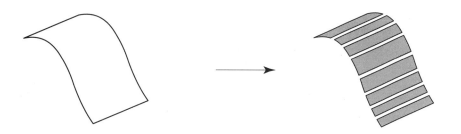

However, there are certain practical difficulties. The accuracy of the model, or the difference between the faceted representation and the curved surface of the object, is usually arbitrary. As far as final image quality is concerned, the size of individual polygons should ideally depend on local spatial curvature. Where the curvature changes rapidly, more polygons are required per unit area of the surface. These factors tend to be related to the method used for creating the polygons. If, for example, a mesh is being built from an existing object, by using a three-dimensional digitizer to determine the spatial coordinates of polygon vertices, the digitizer operator will decide on the basis of experience how large each polygon should be. Sometimes polygons are extracted algorithmically (as in, for example, the creation of an object as a solid of revolution or in a bicubic patch subdivision algorithm) and a more rigorous approach to the rate of polygons per unit area of the surface is possible.

One of the most significant developments in three-dimensional graphics was the emergence of shading algorithms that deal efficiently with polygonal objects, and at the same time, through an interpolation scheme, diminish the visual effect of the piecewise linearities in the representation. This factor, together with recent developments in fixed program rendering hardware, has secured the entrenchment of the polygon mesh structure.

In the simplest case a polygon mesh is a structure that consists of polygons represented by a list of linked (x,y,z) coordinates that are the polygon vertices (edges are represented either explicitly or implicitly as we shall see in a moment). Thus the information we store to describe an object is finally a list of points or vertices. We may also store, as part of the object representation, other geometric information that is used in subsequent processing. These are usually polygon normals and vertex normals (see Chapter 3). Calculated once only, it is convenient to store these in the object data structure and have them undergo any linear transformations that are applied to the object.

It is convenient to order polygons into a simple hierarchical structure (Figure 2.4). Polygons are grouped into surfaces and surfaces are grouped into objects. For example, a cylinder possesses three surfaces: a planar top and bottom surface together with a curved surface. The reason for this grouping is that we must distinguish between those edges that are part of the approximation – edges between adjacent rectangles in the curved surface approximation to the cylinder, for example – and edges that exist in reality. The way in which these are subsequently treated by the rendering process is different – real edges must remain

Figure 2.4
Object as a hierarchy.

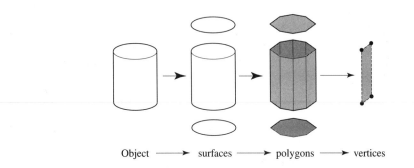

Object ——→ surfaces ——→ polygons ——→ vertices

visible whereas edges that form part of the approximation to a curved surface must be made invisible.

The way in which polygons are embedded in a data structure and the particular choice of a data structure depend to some extent on the application. Algorithms in the rendering process may exploit a hierarchical data structure for reasons of efficiency. With the demand for high scene complexity – in terms of large numbers of objects – it is becoming increasingly important to set up a scene data structure. An object may be embedded in a scene data structure such as a BSP (binary space partitioning) tree to facilitate fast hidden surface removal. (See Chapter 21 for an expansion of this point.) Scene data structures are, however, generally independent of object data structures and the leaves of a scene data structure can point to any mix of object data structures.

The important feature of this representation is that polygons can be treated as independent entities and can be dealt with as such by the renderer. This has implications in the renderer design and the most popular rendering strategy is to treat polygons independently, processing them into the frame memory using a Z-buffer hidden surface removal algorithm in conjunction with interpolative shading.

A significant problem that crops up in many guises in computer graphics is the scale problem. With polygonal representation this means that, in many applications, we cannot afford to render all the polygons in a model if the viewing distance and polygonal resolution is such that many polygons project onto a single pixel. This problem bedevils flight simulators (and similarly computer games) and virtual reality applications. The obvious solution is to have a hierarchy of models and use the one appropriate to the projected screen area. Figure 2.5 shows a simple hierarchy of three skeletons. There are two problems with this; the first is that in animation (and it is in animation applications that this problem is most critical) switching between models can cause visual disturbances in the animation sequence – the user can see the switch from one resolution level to another. The other problem is how to generate the hierarchy and how many levels it should contain. Clearly we can start with the highest resolution model and subdivide, but this is not necessarily straightforward. This topic is further explored in Chapter 20.

Figure 2.5
The art of wireframe – an illustration from Viewpoint Datalabs' catalogue. *Source*: '3D models by Viewpoint DataLabs International, Inc.' *Anatomy*, Viewpoint's 3D Dataset™ Catalog, 2e.

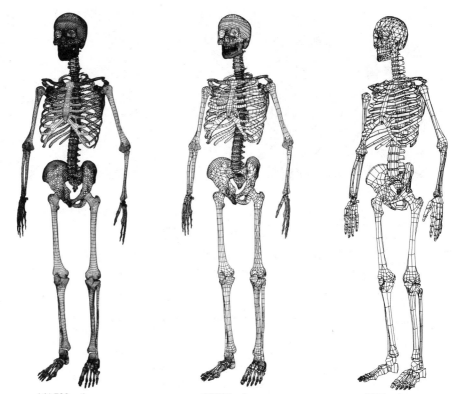

141 788 polygons   35 305 polygons   8993 polygons

2.2.1   Creating polygonal objects

Although a polygon mesh is the most common representational form in computer graphics, modelling, although straightforward, is somewhat tedious. The popularity of this representation derives from the ease of modelling, the emergence of rendering strategies (both hardware and software) to process polygonal objects and the important fact that there is no restriction whatever on the shape or complexity of the object being modelled.

Interactive development of a model is possible by 'pulling' vertices around with a three-dimensional locator device but in practice this is not a very useful method. It is difficult to make other than simple shape changes. Once an object has been created any one polygon cannot be changed without also changing its neighbours. Thus most creation methods use either a device or a program; the only method that admits user interaction is the fourth one in the following list.

Four common examples of polygon modelling methods are:

● Using a three-dimensional digitizer or adopting an equivalent manual strategy

● Using an automatic device such as a laser ranger

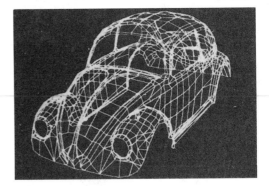

Figure 2.6

The Utah beetle – an early example of manual modelling. *Source*: Beatty & Booth (1982) *Tutorial: Computer Graphics*, 2 edn, The Institute of Electrical and Electronics Engineers, Inc: New York.

2.2.2

- Generating an object from a mathematical description
- Generating an object by sweeping.

The first two modelling methods convert real objects into polygon meshes, while the last two generate models from definitions.

Manual modelling of polygonal objects

The easiest way to model a real object is manually, using a three-dimensional digitizer. The operator uses experience and judgement to emplace points on an object which are to be polygon vertices. The three-dimensional coordinates of these vertices are then input into the system via a three-dimensional digitizer. The association of vertices with polygons is straightforward. A common strategy for ensuring an adequate representation is to draw a net over the surface of the object – like laying a real net over the object. Where curved net lines intersect defines the position of the polygon vertices. A historic photograph of this process is shown in Figure 2.6. This shows students creating a polygon mesh model of a car in 1974. It is taken from a classic paper by outstanding early pioneers in computer graphics – Sutherland, Sproull and Schumacker (1974).

2.2.3

Automatic generation of polygonal objects

A device that is capable of creating very accurate or high resolution polygon mesh objects from real objects is a laser ranger. The object is placed on a rotating table in the path of the beam. The table also moves up and down vertically. The laser ranger returns a set of contours – the intersection of the object and a set of closely spaced parallel planes – by measuring the distance to the object surface. A 'skinning' algorithm, operating on pairs of contours (Figure 2.7), converts the boundary data into a very large number of polygons. Figure 2.1 was polygonized in this way. Laser rangers are increasingly being used in computer vision to image scenes and they are readily available and accurate. For model

Figure 2.7
A skinning algorithm joins points on consecutive contours to make a three-dimensional polygonal object from the contours.

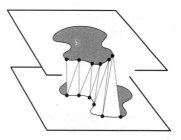

creation they suffer from the significant disadvantage that in the framework described – a fully automatic rotating table device – they can only accurately model convex objects. Objects with concavities will have surfaces which will not necessarily be hit by the incident beam.

2.2.4 Mathematical modelling of polygon objects

Generating an object from a mathematical description is most easily carried out by sweeping a cross-section. Generating a solid of revolution is a special case of this approach. The polygonal resolution is easily controlled by the generating algorithm but shape-dependent resolution problems can still occur. For example, in the case of a toroid generated by sweeping a circular cross-section around a circular path, polygons will be larger on the outer face of the toroid compared with those on the inside face. If the polygons on the outer face are deemed to be adequately small then we will have too high a polygonal resolution on the inside face.

2.2.5 Generating polygon objects by sweeping

The previous idea consists of writing a program in which the cross-section and the curve are specified by mathematical formulae. We can generalize this by allowing both the cross-section and the curve to take any form. They can, for example, be parametric curves that we generate interactively. This approach then can be encapsulated in an interactive interface, the user designing different curves for the cross-section and spine and viewing the resulting model. Another possibility is to allow the cross-section to vary in shape as it is swept. These generalizations enable the production of objects called ducted solids.

Consider a parametrically defined cubic along which the cross-section is swept. This can be defined (see Chapter 7) as:

$$\boldsymbol{Q}(u) = \boldsymbol{a}u^3 + \boldsymbol{b}u^2 + \boldsymbol{c}u + \boldsymbol{d}$$

Now if we consider the simple case of moving a constant cross-section without twisting it along the curve we need to define intervals along the curve at which the cross-section is to be placed. We also need to define points around the cross-section. Joining corresponding points in each cross-section then gives us the polygons.

Two problems present themselves. First, what should be the intervals between points placed around the cross-section, and second, what should be the orientation in three-dimensional space of the cross-section as it is swept along the curve? Clearly this should in some way be related to the spine curve, but how? For this we need a reference coordinate system, known as a frame, in which to embed the cross-section.

Consider the first problem. Dividing u into equal intervals will not necessarily give the best results. In particular, the points will not appear at equal intervals along the curve. A procedure known as arc length parametrization divides the curve into equal intervals, but this procedure is not straightforward. Arc length parametrization may also be inappropriate. What is really required is a scheme that divides the curve into intervals that depend on the curvature of the curve. When the curvature is high the rate of polygon generation needs to be increased so that more polygons occur when the curvature twists rapidly. The most direct way to do this is to use the curve subdivision algorithm (Chapter 7) and subdivide the curve until a linearity test is positive.

The second problem is somewhat easier to deal with. Having defined a set of sample points we need to define a reference frame or coordinate system at each. This is done by deriving three mutually orthogonal vectors that form the coordinate axes. There are many possibilities.

A common one is the Frenet frame. The Frenet frame is defined by the origin or sample point, P and three vectors T, N and B (Figure 2.8). T is the unit length tangent vector:

$$T = V/|V|$$

where V is the derivative of the curve:

$$V = 3au^2 + 2bu + c$$

The principal normal N is given by

$$N = K/|K|$$

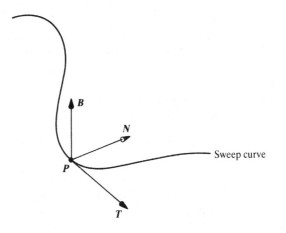

Figure 2.8
The Frenet frame at sample point P on a sweep curve.

Figure 2.9
(a) A polygonal object modelled by sweeping a varying circle along a straight line. (b) A polygonal object modelled by sweeping a varying circle along a (cubic) curve.

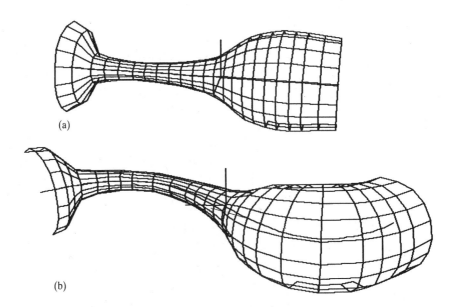

(a)

(b)

where:

$$\boldsymbol{K} = \boldsymbol{V} \times \boldsymbol{A} \times \boldsymbol{V}/|\boldsymbol{V}|^4$$

and $\boldsymbol{A}$ is the second derivative of the curve

$$\boldsymbol{A} = 6\boldsymbol{a}u + 2\boldsymbol{b}$$

Finally $\boldsymbol{B}$ is given by

$$\boldsymbol{B} = \boldsymbol{T} \times \boldsymbol{N}$$

Figure 2.9 shows examples of two objects modelled using this technique. In Figure 2.9(a) a circle of varying radius is swept along a straight line. The variation in the radius is set up by interactively defining a profile curve. Figure 2.9(b) shows the object produced by sweeping the varying radius circle along an axis that is itself a curve. This cross-sectional design philosophy is extended in Chapter 7 where we use bicubic patches as primitives instead of polygons.

2.3　Representation of objects using bicubic parametric patch nets

A (flat) quadrilateral is a polygon with four corner points joined by four straight lines. A bicubic parametric patch is a curvilinear quadrilateral. It has four corner points joined by four edges which are themselves cubic curves. The interior of the patch is a curved (cubic) surface.

Intuitively the step from polygon meshes to patch meshes is straightforward. If we consider a mesh of four-sided polygons approximating a curved surface, then a parametric patch mesh can be considered to be a set of curvilinear polygons which actually lie in the surface. Patches are treated comprehensively in Chapter 7; here we examine them in sufficient detail only to enable a comparison with other representational forms.

A bicubic parametric patch is defined as:

$$Q(u,v) = \sum_{i=0}^{3} \sum_{j=0}^{3} P_{ij} \, B_i(u) B_j(v)$$

(See Chapter 7 for further insight into this equation.) First we note that a patch is a curved surface and that every point in the patch is defined. The definition $Q(u,v)$ is in terms of two parameters u,v, where $0 < u,v < 1$, and the function Q is a cubic polynomial. The precise values of the coefficients in the cubic polynomial determine $Q(u,v)$. A special and convenient way of defining these is to use 16 three-dimensional points, P_{ij}, known as control points. Four of these points are the corner points of the patch. Such a definition is used by a predefined polynomial form known as a basis function. The 16 control points are plugged into this definition and a unique $Q(u,v)$ is obtained. The shape of the patch is determined entirely from the position of the control points. An example of a single (Bézier) patch and the relationship between the patch shape and the control points is shown in Figure 2.10.

For most applications, object modelling or building a data structure representation of a three-dimensional object is more difficult when bicubic patches are used. (This compares with creating polygonal objects where quite complex real

Figure 2.10

The relationship between the position of control points and the shape of a patch. The 16 control points are at the vertices of the polygons. One control point is moved vertically upwards.

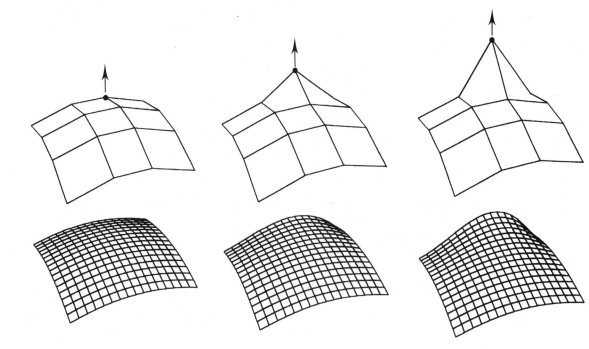

objects are easily polygonized by using a three-dimensional digitizer and operating software.) Sixteen control points have to be specified for each patch and there is another more significant practical problem. To maintain the 'integrity' of the representation, continuity constraints need to be maintained across all boundaries. A patch cannot be set up without regard to its neighbours. Because of this, patch descriptions tend to be generated semi-automatically using, for example, a sweeping strategy for modelling (Section 2.3.1).

Set against these disadvantages, there are a number of advantages that give surface patches their use in CAD. The representation is 'fluid' and by using software to adjust the position of the control points, the shape of an object can be adjusted. However, this is not as easy as it sounds, again because of the necessity to maintain the continuity conditions between patches.

Another advantage of bicubic patch representation is that because it is an exact analytical form, mass properties such as volume, surface area, moments of inertia and so on can be extracted from the description. This property is fully exploited in CAD systems.

Finally it should be mentioned that object representations at high three-dimensional resolution can demand large memory volumes. This means both high memory cost and database transfer time penalties. When rendering complex multi-object scenes, database accesses can become significant. In contrast, a bicubic parametric patch object database, an exact representation, is extremely economical.

Figure 2.11
The Utah teapot. (a) Lines of constant *u* and *v*. The teapot is made up of 32 Bézier patches. A single patch is shown shaded. (b) A wireframe of the control points. The shaded region shows the control polyhedron for the shaded patch. (c) A wireframe of the patch edges.

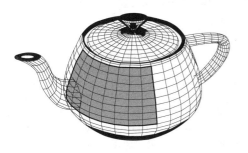

(a)

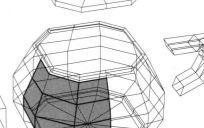

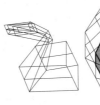

(b)

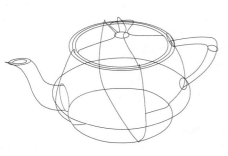

(c)

The Utah teapot will suffice as an example here. A wireframe of lines of constant u and v is shown in Figure 2.11. The object is made up of 32 Bézier patches. A single patch is shown shaded (also shown in this figure is a composite control point polyhedron). This representation consists of:

32 patches × 16 control points/patch

= 288 vertices (approximately, most patches share 12 control points)

= 288 × 3 real numbers (say)

On the other hand a 'reasonable' polygon mesh representation would be:

approximately 2048 × four-sided polygons

= 2048 × 3 real numbers

Thus the polygon mesh model, an inaccurate representation, uses more than seven times as much memory.

2.3.1 Creating objects with bicubic parametric patch nets

There are three common ways of modelling with bicubic parametric patches:

● We can work with a single patch as an object in its own right – car body panels, for example.

● We can create a net of patches from a real object by fitting parametrically defined surfaces through points sampled from the object surface – in other words, surface interpolation.

● We can use sweeping techniques as we did for the polygon mesh representation and create a ducted solid where the primitives are bicubic parametric patches instead of planar polygons.

The first method is straightforward and is not as restricted as it sounds at first sight. Many useful shapes can be modelled using a single patch. A good example of this is car body panels and in fact the first CAD program that used bicubic patches – the UNISURF system designed by P. Bézier – was set up precisely for this purpose.

The second method, called surface fitting, is basically a particular method of doing surface interpolation. A set of points is made available which lie in the surface of the object to be represented and a patch description is produced from these points. Analogous to fitting a line through a number of points in a plane, we fit a surface through a number of points in three space. Thus the method is suitable for modelling objects from some abstraction or fitting a surface to points obtained by digitizing a real object. The difference, of course, between this technique and obtaining a polygon mesh representation is that a continuous surface is obtained from the digitized points. Note, however, that in the case of a real object, the patch surface will not match exactly the surface from which the points were digitized. The exactness of the representation depends on the interpolation algorithm used and the number of points through which the surface is fitted.

The principle of the process is shown in Figure 2.12. We start with a set of points in three space. The next step fits a curve through the points in two parametric directions u and v. This curve network is partitioned into sets of curvilinear quadrilaterals. (In fact these form the edges of the individual patches – the boundary edges of a bicubic parametric patch are themselves cubic curves.) From each quadrilateral the control points for an individual patch are obtained (Chapter 7). The curve network is 'filled in' with surface patches. Figures 2.12(d) and (e) show a curve network obtained from a set of points digitized from a real object together with the rendered version of the patch description.

The third method in parametric patch modelling is cross-sectional sweeping. A schematic representation is given in Figure 2.13. A more detailed description is given in Chapter 7. Just as in polygon mesh modelling we define an axis or sweep curve, this will be a cubic curve. A cross-section is also defined, either from an single cubic curve, as shown in the figure, or as a set of cubic curve segments. The cross-section curve (or curves) is placed at appropriate intervals using the same techniques described in Section 2.2.5. If we consider a cross-section made

Figure 2.12
A schematic representation of surface fitting. (a) A set of points in three-space. (b) Fitting curves through the points in two parametric directions. (c) The grid of curves form the boundaries of the patches. (d) A curve network obtained by interpolation through digitized points. (e) A rendered version of the patch model obtained from (d).

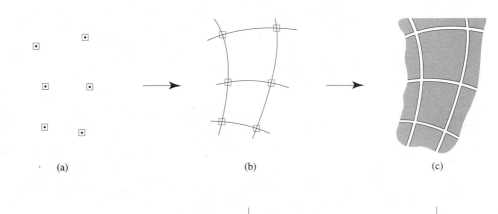

(a)   (b)   (c)

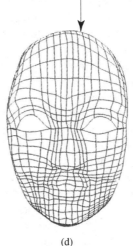

(d)

(e)

Figure 2.13
Generating bicubic parametric patches by sweeping a cross-section curve along a sweep curve.

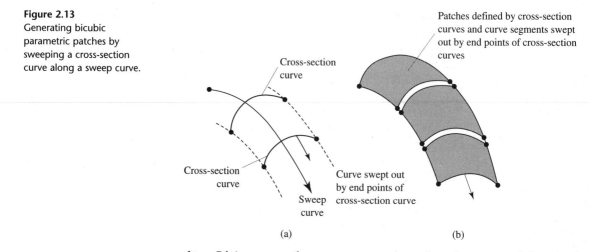

Cross-section curve

Patches defined by cross-section curves and curve segments swept out by end points of cross-section curves

Cross-section curve

Curve swept out by end points of cross-section curve

Sweep curve

(a)   (b)

up of two Bézier curves, then as we sweep along the spine we can define the four boundary curves of the patch. A single Bézier segment defines two boundary curves and the curves swept out by the end/join points define the other pair of curves. These four curves form the boundary of a patch and a patch description is then obtained. Placing another cross-section at the next sample point on the sweep curve will enable another patch to be defined and so on.

2.4 Constructive Solid Geometry (CSG) representation of objects

The motivation for this type of representation is to facilitate an interactive mode for solid modelling. The idea is that objects are usually parts that will eventually be manufactured by casting, machining or extruding and they can be built up in a CAD program by using the equivalent (abstract) operations combining simple elementary objects called geometric primitives. These primitives are, for example, spheres, cones, cylinders or rectangular solids and they are combined using Boolean set operators and linear transformations. An object representation is stored as an attribute tree. The leaves contain simple primitives and the nodes store operators or linear transformations. The representation defines not only the shape of the object but its modelling history – the creation of the object and its representation become one and the same thing. The object is built up by adding primitives and causing them to combine with existing primitives. Shapes can be added to and subtracted from the current shape. For example, increasing the diameter of a hole through a rectangular solid means a trivial alteration – the radius of the cylinder primitive defining the hole is simply increased. This contrasts with the polygon mesh representation where the same operation is distinctly non-trivial. Even although the constituent polygons of the cylindrical surface are easily accessible in a hierarchical scheme, to generate a new set of polygons means reactivating whatever modelling procedure was used to create the original polygons. Also, account has to be taken of the fact that to maintain the same accuracy more polygons will have to be used.

Boolean set operators are used both as a representational form and as a user interface technique. A user specifies primitive solids and combines these using the Boolean set operators. The representation of the object is a reflection or recording of the user interaction operations. Thus we can say that the modelling information and representation are not separate – as they are in the case of deriving a representation from low-level information from an input device. The low-level information in the case of CSG is already in the form of volumetric primitives. The modelling activity becomes the representation. An example will demonstrate the idea.

Figure 2.14 shows the Boolean operations possible between solids. Figure 2.14(a) shows the union of two solids. If we consider the objects as 'clouds' of points, the union operation encloses all points lying within the original two

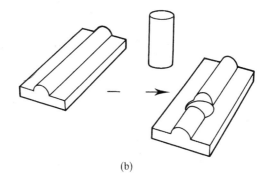

(a)

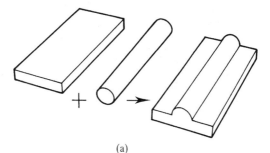

(b)

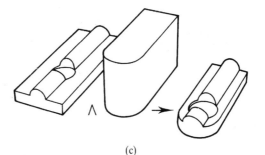

Figure 2.14
Boolean operations between solids in CSG modelling: (a) union, (b) subtraction and (c) intersection.

(c)

bodies. The second example (Figure 2.14(b)) shows the effect of a difference or subtraction operator. A subtract operator removes all those points in the second body that are contained within the first. In this case a cylinder is defined and subtracted from the object produced in Figure 2.14(a). Finally an example is shown of an intersect operation (Figure 2.14(c)). Here a solid is defined that is made from the union of a cylinder and a rectangular solid (the same operation with the same primitives as in Figure 2.14(a)). This solid then intersects with the object produced in Figure 2.14(b). An intersect operation produces a set of points that are contained by both the bodies.

Figure 2.15 shows a CSG representation that reflects the construction of a simple object. Three original solids appear at the leaves of the tree: two boxes and a cylinder. The boxes are combined using a union operation and a hole is 'drilled' in one of the boxes by defining a cylinder and subtracting it from the two-box assembly.

The power of Boolean operations is further demonstrated in the following examples. In the first example (Figure 2.16(a)) two parts developed separately are combined to make the desired configuration by using the union operator followed by a difference operator. The second example (Figure 2.16(b)) shows a complex object constructed only from the union of cylinders, which is then used to produce, by subtraction, a complex housing.

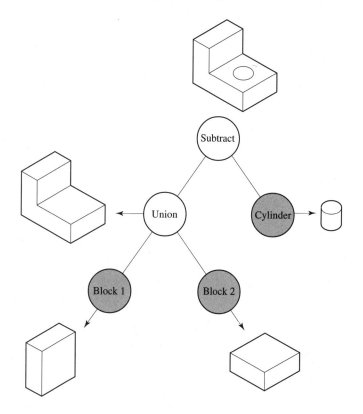

Figure 2.15
A CSG tree reflecting the construction of a simple object made from three primitives.

Figure 2.16
Examples of geometrically
complex objects produced
from simple objects and
Boolean operations.

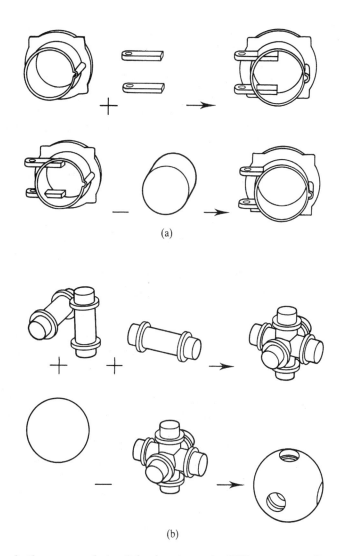

(a)

(b)

Although there are substantial advantages in CSG representations, they do
suffer from drawbacks. A practical problem is the computation time required to
produce a rendered image of the model. A more serious drawback is that the
method imposes limitations on the operations available to create and modify
a solid. Boolean operations are global – they affect the whole solid. Local operations, say a detailed modification on one face of a complex object, cannot be
easily implemented by using set operations. An important local modification
required in many objects that are to be designed is blending surfaces. For example, consider the end face of a cylinder joined onto a flat base. Normally for practical manufacturing or aesthetic reasons, instead of the join being a right angle
in cross-section a radius is desired. A radius swept around another curve cannot
be represented in a simple CSG system. This fact has led to many solid modellers

using an underlying boundary representation. Incidentally there is no reason why Boolean operations cannot be incorporated in boundary representation systems. For example, many systems incorporate Boolean operations but use a boundary representation to represent the object. The trade-off between these two representations has resulted in a debate that has lasted for 15 years. Finally, note that a CSG representation is a volumetric representation. The space occupied by the object – its volume – is represented rather than the object surface.

2.5 Space subdivision techniques for object representation

Space subdivision techniques are methods that consider the whole of object space and label each point in the space according to object occupancy. However, unlike the previous scheme, which uses a variety of volumetric elements or geometric primitives, space subdivision techniques are based on cubic elements known as voxels. A voxel is a volumetric element or primitive and is the smallest cube used in the representation. We could divide up all of world space into regular or cubic voxels and label each voxel according to whether it is in the object or in empty space. Clearly this is very costly in terms of memory consumption. Because of this, voxel representation is not usually a preferred mainstream method but is used either because the raw data is already in this form or it is easiest to convert the data into this representation – the case, for example, in medical imagery; or because of the demands of an algorithm. For example, ray tracing in voxel space has significant advantages over conventional ray tracing. This is an example of an algorithmic technique dictating the nature of the object representation. Here instead of asking the question: does this ray intersect with any objects in the scene? which implies a very expensive intersection test to be carried out on each object, we pose the question: what objects are encountered as we track a ray through voxel space? This requires no exhaustive search through the primary data structure for possible intersections and is a much faster strategy.

Another example is rendering CSG models which is not straightforward if conventional techniques are used. One strategy is to convert the CSG tree into an intermediate data structure of a spatial subdivision type and render from this. This strategy is discussed in more detail in Section 2.7.3. Voxel models can be used as an intermediate representation, most commonly in medical imaging where their use links two-dimensional raw data with the visualization of three-dimensional structures (see Chapter 22). Alternatively the raw data may itself be voxels. This is the case with many mathematical modelling schemes of three-dimensional physical phenomena such as fluid dynamics.

The main problem with voxel labelling is the trade-off between the consumption of vast storage costs and accuracy. Consider, for example, labelling square pixels to represent a circle in two-dimensional space. The pixel size/accuracy trade-off is clear here. The same notion extends to using voxels to represent a sphere except that now the cost depends on the accuracy and the cube of the radius. Thus such schemes are only used in contexts where their advantages outweigh their cost. A way to reduce cost is to impose a structural organization on the basic voxel labelling scheme.

The common way of organizing voxel data is to use an octree – a hierarchical data structure that describes how the objects in a scene are distributed throughout the three-dimensional space occupied by the scene. The basic idea is shown in Figure 2.17. In Figure 2.17(a) a cubic space is subject to a recursive subdivision which enables any cubic region of the space to be labelled with a number. This subdivision can proceed to any desired level of accuracy. Figure 2.17(b) shows an object embedded in this space and Figure 2.17(c) shows the subdivision and the related octree that labels cubic regions in the space according to whether they are occupied or empty.

There are actually two ways in which the octree decomposition of a scene can be used to represent the scene. First, an octree as described above can itself be used as a complete representation of the objects in the scene. The set of cells occupied by an object constitute the representation of the object. However, for a complex scene, high resolution work would require the decomposition of occupied space into an extremely large number of cells and this technique

Figure 2.17
Octree representation.
(a) Cubic space and labelling scheme, and the octree for the two levels of subdivision. (b) Object embedded in space.
(c) Representation of the object to two levels of subdivision.

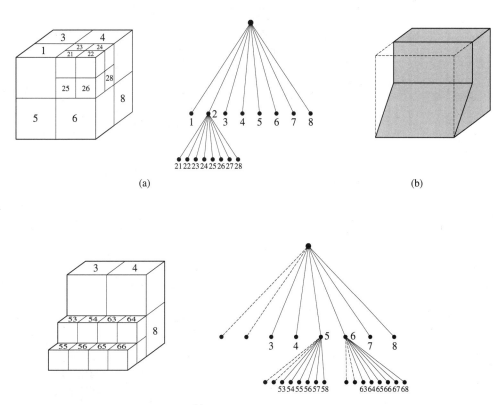

(a)

(b)

(c)

requires enormous amounts of data storage. A common alternative is to use a standard data structure representation of the objects and to use the octree as a representation of the distribution of the objects in the scene. In this case, a terminal node of a tree representing an occupied region would be represented by a pointer to the data structure for any object intersecting that region. Figure 2.18 illustrates this possibility in the two-dimensional case. Here the region subdivision has stopped as soon as a region is encountered that intersects only one object. A region represented by a terminal node is not necessarily completely occupied by the object associated with that region. The shape of the object within the region would be described by its data structure representation. In the case of a surface model representation of a scene, the 'objects' would be polygons or patches. In general, an occupied region represented by a terminal node could intersect with several polygons and would be represented by a list of pointers into the object data structures.

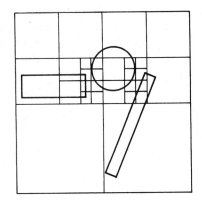

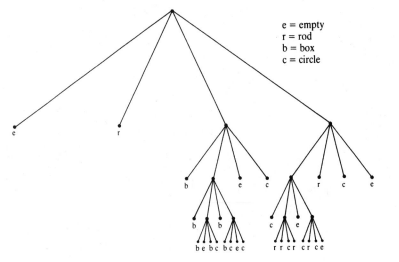

Figure 2.18
Quadtree representation of a two-dimensional scene down to the level of cells containing at most a single object. Terminal nodes for cells containing objects would be represented by a pointer to a data structure representation of the object.

Creating voxel objects

One of the mainstream uses of voxel objects is in volume rendering in medical imagery. As we detail in Chapter 22, the source data in such applications consists of a set of parallel planes of intensity information collected from consecutive cross-sections from some part of a body, where a pixel in one such plane will represent, say, the X-ray absorption of that part of the body to which the pixel physically corresponds. The problem is how to convert such a stack of planar two-dimensional information into a three-dimensional rendered object. Converting the stack of planes to a set of voxels is the most direct way to solve this problem. Corresponding pixels in two consecutive planes are deemed to form the top and bottom face of a voxel and some operation is performed to arrive at a single voxel value from the two pixel values. The voxel representation is used as an intermediary between the raw collected data, which is two-dimensional, and the required three-dimensional visualization. The overall process, from the collection of raw data through the conversion to a voxel representation and the rendering of the voxel data, is the subject of Chapter 22.

Contours collected by a laser ranger can be converted into a voxel representation instead of into a polygon mesh representation. However, this may result in a loss of accuracy compared with using a skinning algorithm.

Representing objects with implicit functions

As we have already pointed out, representing a whole object by a single implicit formula is restricted to certain objects such as spheres. Nevertheless such a representation does find mainstream use in representing 'algorithmic' objects known as bounding volumes. These are used in many different contexts in computer graphics as a complexity limiting device. In ray tracing, for example, instead of checking to see if a ray hits a complex object we can see if it intersects the sphere that contains the object (see Chapter 6 for a detailed discussion of this approach). A representation developed from an implicit formula is the representation of objects by using the concept of implicitly defined objects as components. (We use the term component rather than primitive because the object is not simply a set of touching spheres but a surface derived from such a collection.)

Implicit functions are surfaces formed by the effect of primitives that exert a field of influence over a local neighbourhood. For example, consider a pair of point heat sources shown in Figure 2.19. We could define the temperature in their vicinities as a field function where, for each in isolation, we have isothermal contours as spherical shells centred on each source. Bringing the two sources within influence of each other defines a combined global scalar field, the field of each source combining with that of the other to form a composite set of isothermal contours as shown. Such a scalar field, due to the combined effect of a number of primitives, is used to define a modelling surface in computer graphics.

Figure 2.19
An isosurface of equal temperature around two heat sources (solid line).

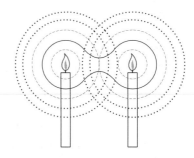

Usually we consider an isosurface in the field to be the boundary of a volume which is the object that we desire to model. Thus we have the following elements in any implicit function modelling system:

● a generator or primitive for which a distance function $d(\boldsymbol{P})$ can be defined for all points $\boldsymbol{P}$ in the locality of the generator.

● a 'potential' function $f(d(\boldsymbol{P}))$ which returns a scalar value for a point $\boldsymbol{P}$ distance $d(\boldsymbol{P})$ from the generator. Associated with the generator can be an area of influence outside of which the generator has no influence. For a point generator this is usually a sphere. An example of a potential function is

$$f(\boldsymbol{P}) = \left(1 - \frac{d^2}{R^2}\right)^2 \quad d \le R$$

where d is the distance of the point to the generator and R is its radius of influence.

● a scalar field $F(\boldsymbol{P})$ which determines the combined effect of the individual potential functions of the generators. This implies the existence of a blending method which in the simplest case is addition – we evaluate a scalar field by evaluating the individual contributions of each generator at a point $\boldsymbol{P}$ and adding their effects together.

● an isosurface of the scalar field which is used to represent the physical surface of the object that we are modelling.

An example (Figure 2.20 – Colour Plate) illustrates the point. The Salvador Dali imitation on the left is an isosurface formed by point generators disposed in space as shown on the right. The radius of each sphere indicates the radius of influence of each generator. The dark spheres represent negative generators which are used to 'carve' concavities in the model. (Although we can form concavities by using only positive generators, it is more convenient to use negative ones as we require far fewer spheres.) The example illustrates the potential of the method for modelling organic shapes. Deformable object animation can be implemented by displaying or choreographing the points that generate the object. The problem with using implicit functions in animation is that there is not a good intuitive link between moving groups of generators and the deformation that ensues because of this. Of course, this general problem is suffered by all modelling techniques where the geometry definition and the deformation method are one and the same thing. (We shall see in Chapter 17 that the most successful deformable object animation techniques separate the static shape specification from the animation framework.) In addition to this general problem, unwanted blending and unwanted separation can occur when the generators are moved with respect to each other and the same blending method retained. These are also illustrated in Figure 2.20.

A significant advantage of implicit functions in an animation context is the ease of collision detection that results from an easy inside/outside function. Irrespective of the complexity of the modelled surface, a single scalar value defines the isosurface and a point P is inside the object volume or outside it depending on whether $F(P)$ is less than or greater than this value.

2.7 Rendering strategies and representations

In this section we shall briefly overview the main or common rendering strategies that are used in conjunction with the object representation modes described above. The idea is to give the reader an overall view of the rendering process; the detailed operations that are carried out in each stage of the process are covered in later chapters. Bringing overviews of the different strategies together at this stage gives the reader a chance to consider the rendering implications of the different representational forms from a comparative point of view.

Rendering is a jargon word that has come to mean the collection of operations necessary to project a view of an object or a scene onto a view surface. The object is lit and its interaction with a light source is calculated to produce a shaded version of the scene. The common rendering strategies are determined by the object representation and algorithm options available for the internal processes. At this stage we will look at how the object representation influences things; that is, how the geometry of the representation influences how we proceed.

2.7.1 Rendering polygon objects

As we have already discussed, polygonal objects are by far the most common representational form in computer graphics and fixed program hardware is now available on many graphics workstations which renders an object or objects from a polygonal database.

The input to a polygonal renderer is a list of polygons and the output is a colour for each pixel onto which each polygon projects on the screen. The major advantage of polygonal renderers is that algorithms have evolved that treat polygons as single entities or units. Polygons become the lowest-level element that a graphics programmer has to consider. This makes for very fast and simple processing. However, we should note that these advantages are eroded as objects become more and more complex. Contexts where objects are described by hundreds of thousands of polygons are not uncommon. An example was shown in Figure 2.1. As the number of pixels onto which the polygon projects becomes smaller and smaller the renderer ends up doing a massive amount of work to allocate a value to a few pixels.

Rendering engines for polygon mesh objects perform two main tasks. The first is to process the geometry of the object as it is subject to various transformation – modelling transformations, viewing transformations and so on, followed by a process that evaluates light/object interaction – loosely called shading.

The most common polygon mesh renderers have two main components for the second process – a shading algorithm that finds the appropriate shade for each pixel within the polygons projection and a hidden surface removal algorithm that evaluates whether part of a polygon is obscured by another that is closer to the viewer.

Shading algorithms evaluate an intensity at the vertices of the polygon, then interpolate from these values to find an appropriate intensity for the polygon pixels. An equation evaluates the light intensity at the vertices, by comparing the orientation of a normal vector associated with the surface at the vertex, with the position of the light source. An interpolation scheme finds the pixel values and these two operations combine in a way that reduces the visibility of the facet edges and makes a curved surface that has been approximated by planar polygons appear to be curved.

Coincident with this operation, a similar interpolation scheme evaluates the depth of each polygon pixel from the depths at the vertices (which are evaluated from the geometry of the scene and the viewer). These depths are stored in a buffer array, known as a Z-buffer, and the stored value for a pixel is compared with the current depth value to ascertain if the current polygon pixel is neared to the viewer than the nearest previously rendered one.

This approach enables polygons to be fetched from the database in any order and rendered as independent units. It does mean that work is done evaluating the shades of polygons that may finally not be written to the screen buffer (because they are further away than previously rendered ones). It is an elegant and straightforward method of visualizing a polygon mesh object. Representational units in the database are treated as units by the renderer and the approximate geometric nature of these units is made almost invisible.

The emergence of this method was contributed to by many people, but those most often named are Gouraud and Phong who developed shading algorithms. The emergence of this approach was possibly the most significant advance in three-dimensional computer graphics and its enduring popularity, in the face of ray tracing and radiosity methods, attests to its elegant simplicity.

2.7.2   Rendering a parametric patch net

In going from a polygon mesh representation to a bicubic parametric patch one, there is an implied increase in the complexity of the rendering process. The easiest approach to rendering bicubic parametric patches is to pre-process the representation and convert the patches into planar polygons. This results in low code complexity (although there are certain problems which are discussed in Chapter 7).

On the face of it this is something of a contradiction; why, having modelled an object using the higher accuracy of patch representation, do we resort to approximating it with polygons? There are two justifications. First, it may be that the original patch representation is necessary because, for example, an interactive modelling environment is required. Second, as far as accuracy is concerned the patch representation is converted into polygons via a subdivision or splitting process and we have complete control over the extent of the sub-division and the final size of the polygons. We can even make the polygon size depend on the local curvature of the patch – an idea that we referred to when discussing polygon mesh representation. Another advantage of the method is that it acts as unification with polygon mesh rendering. As we implied earlier, rendering software and fixed program hardware for polygonal models is readily available.

Note that in general there will be far more polygons in the converted model than there were patches in the parametric model. Figure 2.21 gives an idea of the

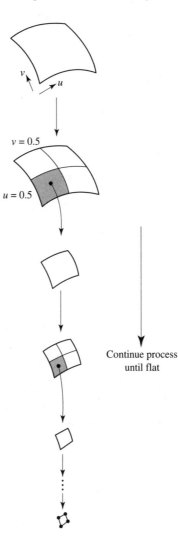

Figure 2.21
A representation of the patch splitting process.

process. A patch is simply subdivided until a flatness criterion is satisfied. Subdivision is carried out by 'drawing' isoparametric curves at each level ($u = 0.5$, $v = 0.5$) which define four patches within the original. The flatness criterion is a simple geometric test that looks at the distance between a plane through the corner points of the patch and the patch surface.

2.7.3

Rendering a CSG description

Rendering strategies for CSG models are disparate. The distinguishing feature of CSG representation is that it is not a 'direct' geometric object representation. Rather it is a formula that has to be interpreted. In CSG representation the object database is a tree that relates a set of primitive objects to each other via Boolean operations. You recall that this representation regime facilitates powerful interactivity. The price that we pay for this is an expensive and complex rendering strategy. To illustrate the point, consider, for example, an object formed by intersecting two cylinders as in Figure 2.16. The CSG description consists only of the two geometric primitives and their dimensions, their spatial relationship and the set operator that combines them. This information does not offer a 'constructed' object to a renderer; the composite object, which contains geometric features like the intersection curves which are not in the component parts, has to be derived, and it is this derivation or construction of the object that is the root of the difficulty.

The main problem involved in rendering CSG objects is to somehow derive an object representation suitable for rendering from the CSG database. Three techniques have evolved:

- CSG ray tracing
- Conversion to a voxel representation followed by volume rendering (Chapter 22)
- Using a version of the Z-buffer algorithm (Chapter 3).

Here we will briefly look at the first of these approaches. This is a fairly straightforward adaptation of standard ray tracing techniques described in Chapter 6.

The evaluation of an object from a CSG description can be achieved by reducing the problem to one dimension. To do this we cast a ray from each pixel in the view plane. In the simplest (parallel projection) case we explore the space of the object with a set of parallel rays. The process divides into two stages. First consider a single ray. Every primitive instance is compared against this ray to see if it intersects the primitive. This means solving a line quadric intersection test as described in Chapter 24. Any intersections are sorted in Z depth. We then have a ray/primitive classification for each ray (Figure 2.22(a)) and can now look at any Boolean combinations between the first two primitives encountered along the ray. From Figure 2.22(b) it is easily seen that evaluating the Boolean operations between primitives along a ray is straightforward. A shading value can then be allocated to the pixel by a simple reflection model applied at the first

Figure 2.22
(a) Deriving a ray/primitive classification. (b) Evaluating Boolean operations along a ray.

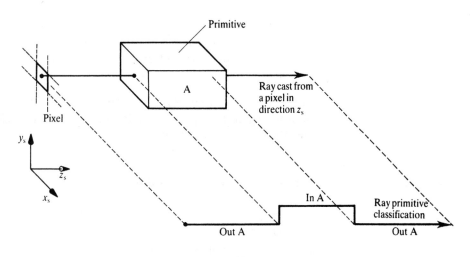

(a)

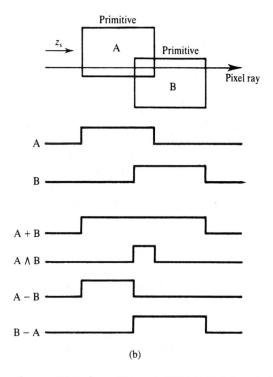

(b)

intersection along the ray. Note from Figure 2.22(b) that this point varies according to the Boolean operations between the primitives.

Ray tracing in this way is the 'classical' method of rendering the CSG model. It is, however, extremely expensive as we shall discover in Chapter 6. Finally we note that the method integrates into a single model:

- Evaluation of a boundary representation from a CSG description
- Hidden surface removal – only intersections with the two primitives nearest to the viewer are considered
- Shading.

Note that all operations take place in screen space and we would map directly from the space of the CSG description into screen space. We bypass the complexities of view space if we use a parallel projection as described above.

2.7.4 Rendering a voxel description

The choice of rendering objects ultimately represented by voxels is predetermined by the application. As we have already mentioned, a voxel representation may be chosen in a ray tracing algorithm in which case the rendering method is ray tracing. Here the voxels will represent, to an accuracy that depends on their size, solid or conventional objects.

In volume visualization a voxel usually represents a property rather than a physical object – say the X-ray absorption coefficient of a point inside a body derived from an X-ray CT scanner. Here we have to decide not only how to render but what we want to render. The implication is that the property varies throughout the data space. Each voxel no longer just represents the presence or absence of an object. Instead we have an object that is defined everywhere within the space it occupies – it is no longer just the boundary of a solid object. We are interested in looking at the variation of the information inside the object. In such an application we may want to render just the boundary information so that the voxel set looks like a solid object; or we may want to volume render which implies the use of transparency. We have the analogy of the visualization of the object – usually an internal organ of the body – as being made up of coloured glass whose colour varies according to the real property of the organ that has been imaged. Say that in a CT dataset of a head we wanted to render the skull. Then we would have to locate all those voxels that exhibited the value for bone and render these. Alternatively we may want to render the brain, but also have the skull present in the image as a transparent object.

For rendering the boundary of a voxel set, a crude approach is simply to find these voxels and shade them as if they were individual cubic objects using a standard polygon mesh renderer. Clearly this makes for a 'blocky' appearance and a more usual approach is to fit a polygonally faceted surface to the voxel set using an elegant algorithm known as the **marching cubes algorithm**.

Alternatively we can adopt a technique known as volume rendering where we try to represent all the voxels in the dataset by mapping the property of each into a transparency–colour duple and then using these properties in association with a light source to provide a transparent visualization of the data. Thus in this representation objects can be seen inside other objects. These techniques are discussed in detail in Chapter 22.

Rendering implicit functions

Like the CSG method, the implicit function representation is difficult to render. It is similar in principle to the CSG method in that the model is not a direct representation of the geometry but rather a formula from which a geometric form has to be extracted. The problem is simple to describe. We have a definition for an object whereby a point on a surface is defined by a single scalar value and selects a subset of the infinity of points within the collective sphere of influence of all the generators that are used to model the object. There are two common approaches.

The first is an approximation to evaluating the infinity of points associated with each generator. It maps the definition into a voxel set which can then be rendered using a rendering strategy for such an object. The straightforward, but costly, way to do this is: for each generator we evaluate a scalar for every voxel in its field of influence, accumulating within each voxel the sum of all the generators that encompass it. The isosurface is then extracted and rendered using, say, the marching cubes algorithm.

Another approach uses a simple extension of ray tracing spherical objects (see Chapter 6). For each ray a pair of simultaneous equations, defining the ray and the function $F(P)$, is solved giving the intersection of the ray with the isosurface. This is implemented by:

(1) finding the generators that contribute to the field of an object along the path of a ray from the intersection of the ray with the spheres of influence of each generator;

(2) calculating the ray sphere/intersection for each generator;

(3) finding the nearest and furthest intersection points which gives the intersection point with the object.

The illustration in Figure 2.20 was rendered in this way.

Summary

Object representations have evolved under a variety of influences – ease of rendering, ease of shape editing, suitability for animation, dependence on the attributes of raw data and so on. There is no general solution that is satisfactory for all practical applications and the most popular solution that has served us for so many years – the polygon mesh – has significant disadvantages as soon as we leave the domain of static objects rendered offline. We complete this chapter by listing the defining attributes of any representation. These allow a (very) general comparison between the methods.

- **Creation of object/representation**: A factor that is obviously context dependent. We have the methods which can create representations automatically from physical data (polygon mesh from range data via a skinning algorithm, bicubic parametric patches via interpolation of surface data). Other methods map input data directly into a voxel representation. Some methods are suitable for interactive creation (CSG and bicubic parametric patches) and some can be created by interacting with a 'mathematically' based interactive facility such as sweeping a cross-section along a spine (polygon mesh and bicubic parametric patches).

- **Nature of the primitive elements**: The common forms are either methods that represent surfaces – boundary representations (polygon mesh and bicubic parametric patches) – or volumes (voxels and CSG).

- **Accuracy** representations are either exact or approximate. Polygon meshes are approximate representations but their accuracy can be increased to any degree at the expense of an expansion in the data. Increasing the accuracy of a polygon mesh representation in an intelligent way is difficult. The easy brute force approach – throwing more polygons at the shape – may result in areas being 'over-represented'. Bicubic patches can be either exact or approximate depending on the application. Surface interpolation will result in an approximation but designing a car door panel using a single patch results in an exact representation. CSG representations are exact but we need to make two qualifications. They can only describe that subset of shapes that is possible by combining the set of supplied primitives. The representation is abstract in that it is just a formula for the composite object – the geometry has to be derived from the formula to enable a visualization of the object.

- **Accuracy vs. data volume**: There is always a trade-off between accuracy and data volume – at least as far as the rendering penalty is concerned. To increase the accuracy of a boundary representation or a volume representation we have to increase the number of low-level elements. Although the implicit equation of a sphere is 100% accurate and compact, it has to be converted for rendering using some kind of geometric sampling procedure that generates low-level elements.

- **Data volume vs. complexity**: There is also usually a trade-off between data volume and the complexity of the representation which has practical ramifications in the algorithms that operate with the representation. This is best exemplified by comparing polygon meshes with their counterpart using bicubic parametric patches.

- **Ease of editing/animation**: This can mean retrospective editing of an existing model or shape deformation techniques in an animation environment. The best method for editing the shape of static objects is, of course, the CSG representation – it was designed for this. Editing bicubic parametric patches is easy or difficult depending on the complexity of the shape and the desired freedom of the editing operations. In this respect editing a single patch is easy, editing a net of patches is difficult. None of the representation methods that we have described is suitable for shape changing in animated sequences, although bicubic parametric patches and implicit functions have been tried. It seems that the needs of accuracy and ease of animating shape change are opposites. Methods that allow a high degree of accuracy are difficult to animate, because they consist of a structure with maybe thousands of low-level primitives as leaves. For example, the common way to control a net of bicubic parametric patches representing, say, the face of a character is to organize it into a hierarchy, allowing local changes to be made (by descending the hierarchy and operating on a few or even a single patch) and making more global changes by operating at a high level in the structure. This has not resulted in a generally accepted animation technique simply because it does not produce good results (in the case of facial animation anyway). It seems shape change animation needs a paradigm that is independent of the object model and the most successful techniques involve embedding the object model in **another** structure which is then subject to shape change animation. Thus we control facial animation by attaching a geometric structure to a muscle control model or immerse a geometric model in the 'field' of an elastic solid and animate the elastic solid. In other words, animation of shape does not seem to be possible by operating directly on the geometry of the object.

Further reading

Sutherland I.E., Sproull R.F. and Schumacker R. (1974). A characterization of ten hidden-surface algorithms. *Computer Surveys*, **6**(1), 1–55

Basic realism – lighting polygon objects

3.1 Introduction

This chapter is about a series of techniques that can be put together to render three-dimensional graphics objects represented as polygon mesh objects. They represent a collection of algorithms that were developed mostly in the 1970s and their popularity is due to their effectiveness, ease of implementation and the development of implementations on special purpose hardware.

To visualize a polygon mesh object we need to perform a number of processes that can be placed into two groups. One group of operations can generally be entitled geometric and consists mainly of a series of transformations (these are described in Chapter 24) that finish with the object being projected into screen space. Polygon objects are made up of lists of polygons which are themselves lists of three-dimensional points of linked vertices. These vertices are passed through various transformations and end up as three-dimensional points in three-dimensional screen space (the concept of three-dimensional screen space will be explained later in the chapter). It is in this space that we perform the pixel-level processes that form the subject of this chapter.

One of the commonest strategies in polygon mesh rendering is to arrange that polygons can be fetched from the database in any order and shaded. The rendering process treats polygons as independent units and places a shaded version of each in the screen memory. To facilitate this strategy we need to adopt a particular hidden surface removal strategy – the Z-buffer algorithm. Although this rendering strategy contains some inefficiencies, its code complexity is low and it has the important advantage that there is no upper limit on the complexity (in terms of the number of polygons) in the object. As we have discussed, in offline rendering the time penalty is only reflected in cost, and very early in the development of three-dimensional computer graphics there was a fast expansion of scene complexity in terms of polygon count. Nowadays, with the demand for real-time rendering in virtual reality and computer games, the frame time places an upwards limit on polygon count for any processor.

3.2 An overview of the rendering process

Let us start by overviewing the process required to shade a polygon. We need to perform the following processes.

- **Rasterization**   In this process we have to find those pixels onto which a polygon projects, given the screen space coordinates of the polygon vertices (Figure 3.1). This is straightforward enough but we have to take care that adjacent polygons exactly jigsaw together and that no holes are left.

- **Hidden surface removal**   We have to calculate which parts of an object are visible to the viewer and which parts cannot be seen. This problem is always divided into two parts. First, we eliminate entire polygons that cannot be seen from the viewpoint – a process usually known as culling. Second, we deal with the more general hidden surface problem which occurs when only part of a polygon is hidden by another. The conceptual difference between these two problems is shown in Figure 3.2. In culling we consider the cube and the pyramid independently. By considering the orientation to the posi-

Figure 3.1
Illustrating the rasterization process. (a) A polygon as a modelling primitive (b) maps into screen space as a list of linked vertices; (c) rasterized into discrete pixels.

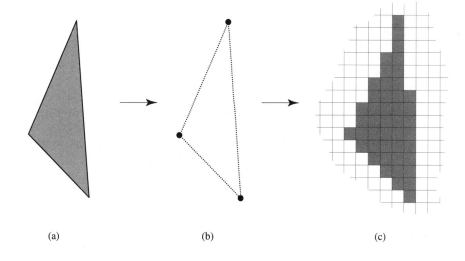

(a)   (b)   (c)

Figure 3.2
Culling and hidden space removal. (a) Culling removes complete polygons that cannot be seen; (b) hidden surface removal deals with the general problem: polygons will partially obscure others.

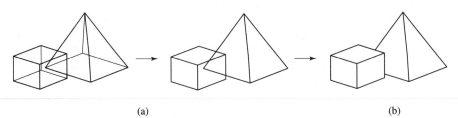

(a)   (b)

tion of the viewpoint we can remove three faces from the cube and two from the triangular pyramid. They cannot possibly be seen. However, the fact that two faces of the cube partially obscures one face of the polygon needs to be dealt with by a general hidden surface removal algorithm.

● **Shading the pixels**   Here there are three options. First, we could give all the pixels in a polygon the same shade. This is fast, but has the unfortunate effect that the underlying polygon nature of the object is glaringly obvious. Second, we can adopt one of the two classic shading techniques that were developed precisely to diminish this effect – Gouraud shading and Phong shading. In these methods each pixel onto which a polygon projects will, in general, receive a different value. The difference between these strategies is shown in the case study in Chapter 6.

The pixels onto which the polygons project need to be represented in some way. This is usually done with a structure called an edge list (Figure 3.3) where we store, for each scan line, the *x* values of the start and finish of a horizontal segment. This enables us to process a polygon by working down from the highest vertex, one scan line at a time.

The overall strategy that we will now describe makes these three processes (rasterization, hidden surface removal and shading) simultaneous rather than sequential and polygon pixels are found and given an intensity (or not depending on whether they are part of a visible polygon) as part of the same overall process that deals with one polygon at a time, starts at the top of the (projected) polygon and works downwards one scan line at a time.

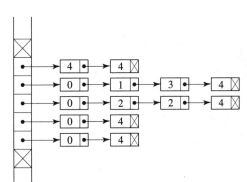
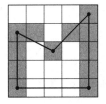

Figure 3.3
An example of a linked list maintained in polygon rasterization.

3.3   Rasterization of a polygon

We first consider that a polygon, projected into screen space by the geometric transformations, is a list of vertices connected implicitly by virtual lines known as edges. Rasterization can be approached by first rasterizing edges – obtaining pixels 'closest' to the polygon edge and then filling in between lines. This means that for each edge, we need to generate a sequence of pixels corresponding to the edge's intersections with the scan lines (Figure 3.4).

The conventional way of calculating these pixel coordinates is by use of what is referred to as a 'digital differential analyzer', or DDA for short. All this really consists of is finding how much the x coordinate increases per scan line, and then repeatedly adding this increment.

Let (xs,ys), (xe,ye) be the start and end points of the edge (we assume that $ye > ys$). The simplest algorithm for rasterizing sufficient for polygon edges is:

$x := xs$
$m := (xe–xs)/(ye–ys)$
for $y := ys$ **to** ye
    output(round(x),y)
    $x := x + m$

The main drawback of this approach is that m and x need to be represented as floating point values, with a floating point addition and real-to-integer conversion each time round the loop. (Note that although this approach is sufficient for finding those pixels that comprise a polygon edge they are an inadequate representation for a structure that is to represent an isolated line in two-dimensional graphics.)

Now that we know how to find pixels along the polygon edges, it is necessary to turn our attention to filling the polygons themselves. Finding what set of pixels constitutes a polygon projection has to be done accurately and consistently otherwise gaps can result between adjacent polygons. Since we are concerned with shading, 'filling a polygon' means finding the pixel coordinates of interior points and assigning to these a value calculated using one of the incremental shading schemes described in Section 3.6. We need to generate pairs of segment endpoints and fill in horizontally between them. This is usually achieved by

Figure 3.4
Pixel sequence required for polygon filling.

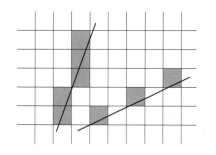

constructing an 'edge list' for each polygon. In principle this is done using an array of linked lists, with an element for each scan line. Initially all the elements are set to NIL. Then each edge of the polygon is rasterized in turn, and the x coordinate of each pixel (x,y) thus generated is inserted into the linked list corresponding to that value of y. Each of the linked lists is then sorted in order of increasing x. The result is something like that shown in Figure 3.3. Filling in of the polygon is then achieved by, for each scan line, taking successive pairs of x values and filling in between them (because a polygon has to be closed, there will always be an even number of elements in the linked list). Note that this method is powerful enough to cope with concave polygons with holes.

In practice, the sorting of the linked lists is achieved by inserting values in the appropriate position in the first place, rather than a big sort at the end. Also, as well as calculating the x value and storing it for each pixel on an edge, the appropriate shading values would be calculated and stored at the same time (for example, intensity value for Gouraud shading; x, y and z components of the interpolated normal vector for Phong shading).

A simpler and faster approach is to discard the notion of general n-sided polygons and work with triangles. Now either we have to constrain the model to consist of triangles only, or we have to pre-process the polygons in the object database and turn these into triangles. Another simplification is to split each triangle into two further triangles such that every triangle always has one horizontal edge. The complications of the previous paragraph are now overcome and the interpolation now proceeds between just two edges. Which is the right and left edge is found by a fast comparison of vertices.

One thing that has been slightly glossed over so far is the consideration of exactly where the borders of a polygon or triangle lie. For example, in Figure 3.5, the width of the polygon is 3 units, so it should have an area of 9 units, whereas it has been rendered with an area of 16 units. The traditional solution to this problem, and the one usually advocated in textbooks, is to consider the sample point of the pixel to lie in its centre, that is, at $(x+0.5,y+0.5)$. (A pixel can be considered to be a rectangle of finite area with dimensions 1.0×1.0, and its sample point is the point within the pixel area where the scene is sampled in order to determine the value of the pixel.) So, for example, the intersection of an edge with a scan line is calculated for $y+0.5$, rather than for y, as we assumed above. This is messy, and excludes the possibility of using integer-only arithmetic. A simpler solution is to assume that the sample point lies at one of the four corners of the pixel; we have chosen the top right-hand corner of the pixel. This has

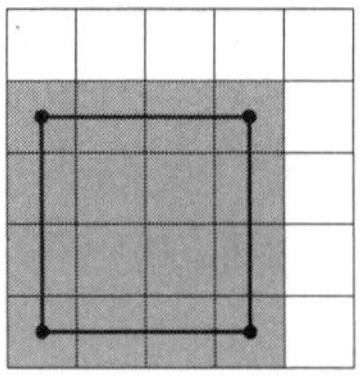

Figure 3.5
Problems with polygon boundaries – a 9-pixel polygon fills 16 pixels.

Figure 3.6
Three polygons intersecting a scan line.

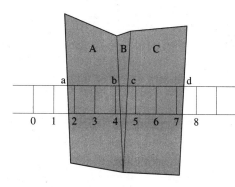

the consequence that the entire image is displaced half a pixel to the left and down, which in practice is insignificant. The upshot of this is that it provides the following simple rasterization rules:

(1) Horizontal edges are simply discarded.

(2) An edge which goes from scan line y_{bottom} to y_{top} should generate x values for scan lines y_{bottom} through to y_{top-1} (that is, missing the top scan line), or if $y_{bottom} = y_{top}$ then generate no values.

(3) Similarly, horizontal segments should be filled from x_{left} to $x_{right-1}$ (with no pixels generated if $x_{left} = x_{right}$).

Incidentally, in rules 2 and 3, whether the first or last element is ignored is arbitrary, and the choice is based around programming convenience. The four possible permutations of these two rules define the sample point as one of the four corners of the pixel. The effect of these rules can be demonstrated in Figure 3.6. Here we have three adjacent polygons A, B and C, with edges a, b, c and d. The rounded x values produced by these edges for the scan shown are 2, 4, 4, 7 respectively. Rule 3 then gives pixels 2 and 3 for polygon A, none for polygon B, and 4 to 6 for polygon C. Thus overall, there are no gaps, and no overlapping. The reason why horizontal edges are discarded is because the edges adjacent to it will have already contributed the x values to make up the segment (for example, the base of the polygon in Figure 3.3 – note also that for the sake of simplicity, the scan conversion of this polygon was not done strictly in accordance with the rasterization rules mentioned above).

3.4 Hidden surface removal

As we mentioned earlier, hidden surface removal divides into two parts – culling followed by general hidden surface removal. Although these operations, for reasons explained elsewhere, occur at different stages in the rendering process, we will treat them here together.

Figure 3.7
Culling or back-face
elimination. (a) The desired
view of the object (back
faces shown as dotted lines).
(b) A view of the geometry
of the culling operation.
(c) The culled object.

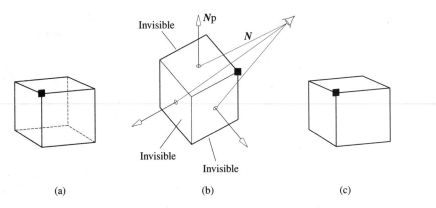

(a)   (b)   (c)

3.4.1   Culling

Refer again to Figure 3.2 which shows the difference between culling or back-face elimination and general hidden surface removal. Culling is extremely simple; we simply construct a line (the line of sight vector) to the base of the normal vector of the polygon (Figure 3.7). This can be any convenient normal vector and would in practice be associated with one of the vertices. Then we examine the magnitude of the angle between the line of sight vector and the normal vector for each face. If this is greater than 90 degrees then the face is invisible.

Thus we can write:

$$\text{visibility} := \boldsymbol{Np}.\boldsymbol{N} > 0$$

where:

$\boldsymbol{Np}$ is the polygon normal
$\boldsymbol{N}$ is the line of sight vector

On average, for a convex object, half the polygons are back-facing and it makes good sense to remove those with a simple test so that the expense of a general hidden surface removal algorithm is not invoked in these cases.

3.4.2   Z-buffer algorithm

A large amount of research into hidden surface removal algorithms was carried out in the 1970s. Many different algorithms were developed – screen subdivision algorithms, list priority algorithms, algorithms that operated in object space, and so on. The Z-buffer algorithm, developed in 1975, has survived to become the most popular approach to hidden surface removal. Interestingly, one of the main aspects of hidden surface removal that was explored and developed in the 1970s – the concept of coherence – is completely ignored by the Z-buffer algorithm. Coherence means trying to resolve the hidden surface issue with as large 'units' as possible – fragments of polygons or scan lines rather than with single pixels as is the case with the Z-buffer algorithm. Most of these algorithms are not in use today, except in special contexts (for example, in flight simulators) and the Z-buffer algorithm has become ubiquitous.

The Z-buffer hidden surface removal algorithm is extremely simple – it reduces, in effect, to a single **if** statement. The price that we pay for this simplicity is heavy memory costs and some inefficiency. The algorithm operates in three-dimensional screen space (Chapter 24) and considering a single pixel, its operation is equivalent to a search through all the polygons that project onto that pixel, to find the nearest to the viewpoint. This is achieved by using a Z-buffer – a two-dimensional array of the same dimensions as the screen buffer. At any instant in the processing this buffer contains, for each pixel, the depth of the nearest polygon so far encountered. As a polygon is rasterized and assigned an intensity, its depth in screen space is calculated. If this depth is less than the depth currently stored in the Z-buffer for that pixel, the screen buffer is overwritten with the current intensity and the current depth is placed in the Z-buffer. If the current depth is greater then the Z-buffer and screen buffer contents remain unchanged.

Herein lies the inefficiency of the process. Polygons are fetched from the database in any order. They are rasterized and assigned an intensity and placed in the screen buffer even although they may be partially or completely overwritten later by a polygon that is nearer to the viewer. In other words, as much work is performed for hidden polygons as for visible ones because the hidden surface calculation is performed last. A scene, as it builds up on the screen, may change continuously as hidden polygons are made visible and then obscured by nearer ones.

Now it may have occurred to you that when a polygon is projected into screen space we only have depth values associated with the vertices. We calculate a depth value for each pixel onto which the polygon is projected by linearly interpolating amongst the vertex depth values. (This is exactly the same solution adopted for calculating pixel intensities from vertex intensities in Gouraud shading, as we describe in the next section.) The equations required are given in Section 24.7.

In the past, Z-buffers have tended to be part of the main memory of a host processor but now graphics terminals are available with dedicated Z-buffers and this represents the best solution.

One of the major theoretical advantages of the Z-buffer is that it is independent of object representation form. Although we see it used most often in the context of polygon mesh rendering, it can be used with any representational form – all that is required is the ability to calculate a z depth for each pixel projection of the object surface. It can be used with Constructive Solid Geometry objects, and separately rendered objects can be merged into a multiple object scene using Z-buffer information associated with each object. It also finds an application in the calculation of shadows (Chapter 4). One of the easiest approaches to calculating the geometry of shadows is to use a Z-buffer approach.

As we discussed in the previous section, there was much research into the hidden surface removal problem which died out in the 1980s with the predominance of the Z-buffer algorithm. Recently there has been renewed interest in dealing with the inherent inefficiency of rendering using a Z-buffer algorithm. This is because of the demand for complex images rendered in real time in virtual reality applications. These approaches are described in detail in Chapter 21.

Shading pixels

The first quality shading in computer graphics was developed by H. Gouraud in 1971. In 1975 Phong Bui-Tuong improved on Gouraud's model and Phong shading, as it is universally known, became the de facto standard in mainstream three-dimensional graphics. Despite the subsequent development of 'global' techniques, such as ray tracing and radiosity, Phong shading has remained ubiquitous. This is because it enables reality to be mimicked to an acceptable level at reasonable cost.

There are two separate considerations to shading the pixels onto which a polygon projects. First we consider how to calculate the light reflected at any point on the surface of an object. Given a theoretical framework that enables us to do this, we can then calculate the light intensity at the pixels onto which the polygon projects. The first consideration we call 'local reflection models' and the second, 'shading algorithms'. The difference is illustrated conceptually in Figure 3.8. For example, one of the easiest approaches to shading – Gouraud shading – applies a local reflection model at each of the vertices to calculate a vertex intensity, then derives a pixel intensity using the same interpolation equations as we used in the previous section to interpolate depth values.

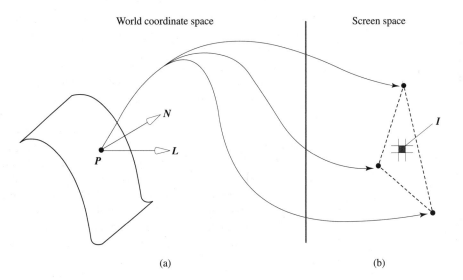

Figure 3.8
Illustrating the difference between local reflection models and shading algorithms. (a) Local reflection models calculate light intensity at any point P on the surface of an object. (b) Shading algorithms interpolate pixel values from calculated light intensities at the polygon vertices.

World coordinate space

Screen space

(a)

(b)

Basically there is a conflict here. We only want to calculate the shade for each pixel onto which the polygon projects. But the reflected light intensity at every point on the surface of a polygon is by definition a world space calculation. We are basing the calculation on the orientation of the surface with respect to a light source both of which are defined in world space. Thus we use a two-dimensional projection of the polygon as the basis of an interpolation scheme that controls the world space calculations of intensity and this is incorrect. Linear interpolation, using equal increments, in screen space does not correspond to how the reflected intensity should vary across the face of the polygon in world space. One of the reasons for this is that we have already performed a (non-affine) perspective transformation to get into screen space. Like many algorithms in three-dimensional computer graphics it produces an acceptable visual result, even using incorrect mathematics. However, this approach does lead to visible artefacts in certain contexts. The comparative study in Chapter 6 has an illustration of an artefact caused by this.

3.5.1 Local reflection models

A local reflection model enables the calculation of the reflected light intensity from a point on the surface of an object. The development of a variety of local reflection models is dealt with in Chapter 4; here we will confine ourselves to considering, from a practical viewpoint, the most common model and see how it fits into a renderer.

This model, introduced in 1975, evaluates the intensity of the reflected light as a function of the orientation of the surface at the point of interest with respect to the position of a point light source and surface properties. We refer to such a model as a local reflection model because it only considers direct illumination. It is as if the object under consideration was an isolated object floating in free space. Interaction with other objects that results in shadows and interreflection are not taken into account by local reflection models. This point is emphasized in Figure 3.9; in Chapter 6 we deal with so-called global illumination in detail.

The physical reflection phenomena that the model simulates are:

- perfect specular reflection
- imperfect specular reflection
- perfect diffuse reflection.

These are illustrated in Figure 3.10 for a point light source that is sending an infinitely thin beam of light to a point on a surface. Perfect specular reflection occurs when incident light is reflected, without diverging, in the 'mirror' direction. Imperfect specular reflection occurs when a thin beam of light strikes an imperfect mirror, that is, a surface whose reflecting properties are those of a perfect mirror but only at a microscopic level – because the surface is physically rough. Any area element of such a surface can be considered to be made up of

Figure 3.9
(a) A local reflection model calculates intensity at P_b and P_a considering direct illumination only. (b) Any indirect reflected light from A to B or from B to A is not taken into account.

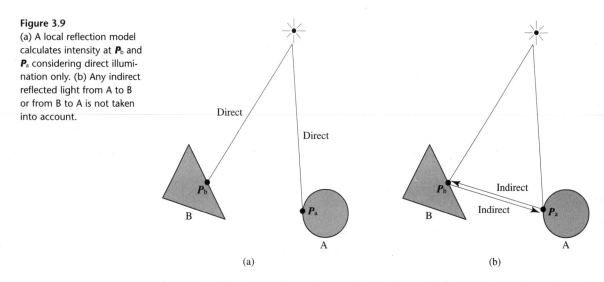

(a)   (b)

thousands of tiny perfect mirrors all at slightly different orientations. Perfect specular reflection does not occur in practice but we use it in ray tracing models – Chapter 6 – simply because calculating interaction due to imperfect specular reflection is too expensive. A perfect diffuse surface reflects the light equally in all directions and such a surface is usually called matte.

The Phong reflection model considers the reflection from a surface to consist of three components linearly combined:

reflected light = ambient light + diffuse component + specular component

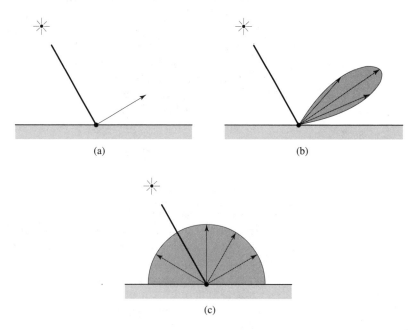

Figure 3.10
The three reflection phenomena used in computer graphics.
(a) Perfect specular reflection; (b) imperfect specular reflection;
(c) perfect diffuse reflection.

The ambient term is a constant and simulates global or indirect illumination. This term is necessary because parts of a surface that cannot 'see' the light source, but which can be seen by the viewer, need to be lit. Otherwise they would be rendered as black. In reality such lighting comes from global or indirect illumination and simply adding a constant sidesteps the complexity of indirect or global illumination calculations.

It is useful to consider what type of surfaces such a model simulates. Linear combination of a diffuse and specular component occurs in polished surfaces such as varnished wood. Specular reflection results from the transparent layer and diffuse reflection from the underlying surface (Figure 3.11). Many different physical types, although not physically the same as varnished wood, can be approximately simulated by the same model. The veracity of this can be imagined by considering looking at a sample of real varnished wood, shiny plastic and gloss paint. If all contextual clues were removed and the reflected light from each sample exhibited the same spectral distribution, an observer would find it difficult to distinguish amongst the samples.

As well as possessing the limitation of being a local model, the Phong reflection model is completely empirical or imitative. One of its major defects is that the value of reflected intensity calculated by the model is a function only of the viewing direction and the orientation of the surface with respect to the light source. In practice, reflected light intensity exhibits **bi-directional** behaviour. It depends also on the direction of the incident light. This defect has led to much research into physically based reflection models, where an attempt is made to model reflected light by simulating real surface properties. However, the subtle improvements possible by using such models – such as the ability to make surfaces look metallic – have not resulted in the demise of the Phong reflection model and the main thrust of current research into rendering methods deals with the limitation of 'localness'. Global methods, such as radiosity, result in much more significant improvements to the apparent reality of a scene.

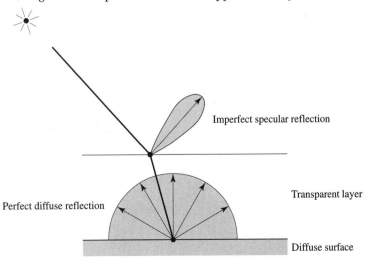

Figure 3.11
The 'computer graphics' surface.

Leaving aside, for a moment, the issue of colour, the physical nature of a surface is simulated by controlling the proportion of the diffuse to specular reflection and we have the reflected light:

$$I = k_a I_a + k_d I_d + k_s I_s$$

where the proportions of the three components, ambient, diffuse and specular, are controlled by three constants, where:

$$k_a + k_d + k_s = 1$$

Consider I_d. This is evaluated as:

$$I_d = I_i \cos \boldsymbol{\theta}$$

where:

I_i is the intensity of the incident light

$\boldsymbol{\theta}$ is the angle between the surface normal at the point of interest and the direction of the light source.

In vector notation (Chapter 24)

$$I_d = I_i \ (\boldsymbol{L \cdot N})$$

The geometry is shown in Figure 3.12. Now physically the specular reflection consists of an image of the light source 'smeared' across an area of the surface resulting in what is commonly known as a highlight. A highlight is only seen by a viewer if the viewing direction is near to the mirror direction. We therefore simulate specular reflection by:

$$I_s = I_i \cos^n \Omega$$

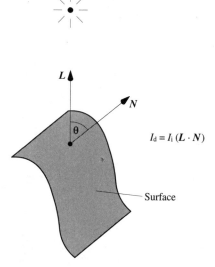

$$I_d = I_i \ (\boldsymbol{L \cdot N})$$

Surface

Figure 3.12
The Phong diffuse component.

Figure 3.13
The Phong specular
component.

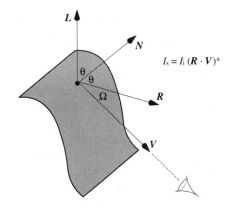

$I_s = I_i (\mathbf{R} \cdot \mathbf{V})^n$

where:

Ω is the angle between the viewing direction and the mirror direction $\mathbf{R}$,

n is an index that simulates the degree of imperfection of a surface; if $n = \infty$ the surface is a perfect mirror – all reflected light emerges along the mirror direction. For other values of n an imperfect specular reflector is simulated (Figure 3.10).

The geometry of this is shown in Figure 3.13. In vector notation we have:

$I_s = I_i (\mathbf{R} \cdot \mathbf{V})^n$

Bringing these terms together gives:

$I = k_a I_a + I_i (k_d (\mathbf{L} \cdot \mathbf{N}) + k_s (\mathbf{R} \cdot \mathbf{V})^n)$

The behaviour of this equation is illustrated in Figures 3.14 and 3.15. Figure 3.14 shows the light intensity at a single point $\mathbf{P}$ as a function of the orientation

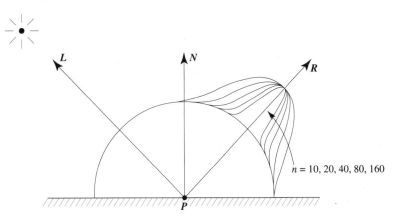

Figure 3.14
The light intensity at point
$\mathbf{P}$ as a function of the
orientation of the viewing
vector $\mathbf{V}$.

$n = 10, 20, 40, 80, 160$

of the viewing vector V. The semicircle is the sum of the constant ambient term and the diffuse term – which is constant for a particular value of N. Addition of the specular term gives the profile shown in the figure. As the value of n is increased the specular bump is narrowed. Figure 3.15 (Colour Plate) shows the equation applied to the same object using different values of k_s and n.

3.5.2 ### Practical points

A number of practical matters that deal with colour and the simplification of the geometry now need to be explained.

The expense of the above shading equation, which is applied a number of times at every pixel, can be considerably reduced by making geometric simplifications that reduce the calculation time, but which do not effect the quality of the shading. First, if the light source is considered a point source located at infinity then L is constant over the domain of the scene. Second, we can also place the viewpoint at infinity making V constant. Of course, for the view and perspective transformation, the viewpoint needs to be firmly located in world space so we end up using a finite viewpoint for the geometric transformations and an infinite one for the shading equation.

Next the vector R is expensive to calculate and it is easier to define a vector H (halfway) which is the unit normal to a hypothetical surface that is oriented in a direction halfway between the light direction vector L and the viewing vector V (Figure 3.16). It is easily seen that:

$$H = (L + V)/2$$

This is the orientation that a surface would require if it were to reflect light maximally along the V direction. Our shading equation now becomes

$$I = I_a k_a + I_i(k_d(L \cdot N) + (N \cdot H)^n)$$

because the term $(N \cdot H)$ varies in the same manner as $(R \cdot V)$. These simplifications mean that I is now a function only of N.

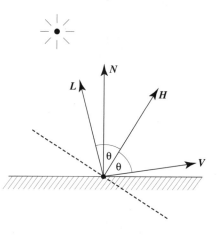

Figure 3.16
H is the normal to a surface orientation that would reflect all the light along V.

For coloured objects we generate three components of the intensity I_r, I_g and I_b controlling the colour of the objects by appropriate setting of the diffuse reflection coefficients k_{dr}, k_{dg} and k_{db}. In effect the specular highlight is just the reflection of the light source in the surface of the object and we set the proportions of the k_s to match the colour of the light. For a white light, k_s is equal in all three equations. Thus we have:

$$I_r = I_a k_{ar} + I_i((k_{dr}(\boldsymbol{L}\cdot\boldsymbol{N}) + k_s(\boldsymbol{N}\cdot\boldsymbol{H})^n)$$
$$I_g = I_a k_{ag} + I_i((k_{dg}(\boldsymbol{L}\cdot\boldsymbol{N}) + k_s(\boldsymbol{N}\cdot\boldsymbol{H})^n)$$
$$I_b = I_a k_{ab} + I_i((k_{db}(\boldsymbol{L}\cdot\boldsymbol{N}) + k_s(\boldsymbol{N}\cdot\boldsymbol{H})^n)$$

Light source considerations

One of the most limiting approximations in the above model is reducing the light source to a point at infinity. Also, we can see in Figure 3.15 that there is an unsatisfactory confusion concerning the interpretation of the parameter n, which is supposed to give the impression of 'glossiness'. In practice it looks as if we are changing the size of the light source.

A simple directional light (non-point) source is easily modelled and the following was suggested by Warn (1983). In this method a directional light source is modelled in the same way as a specularly reflecting surface, where the light emitted from the source is given by a cosine function raised to a power. Here we assume that for a directional source, the light intensity in a particular direction, given by the angle ϕ, is:

$$I_s \cos^m \phi$$

Now ϕ is the angle between $-\boldsymbol{L}$, the direction of the point on the surface that we are considering, and $-\boldsymbol{L}_s$, the orientation of the light source (Figure 3.17). The value of I_i that we use in the shading equation is then given by:

$$I_i = I_s(-\boldsymbol{L}\cdot\boldsymbol{L}_s)^m$$

Note that we can no longer consider the vector $\boldsymbol{L}$ constant over the scene.

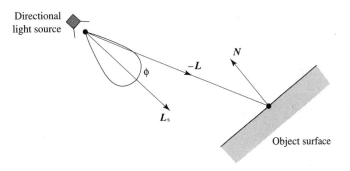

Figure 3.17
Light source represented as a specularly reflecting surface.

3.6 Interpolative shading techniques

Having dealt with the problem of calculating light intensity at a point, we now consider how to apply such a model to a polygon and calculate the light intensity over its surface. Two classic techniques have emerged – Gouraud and Phong shading. The difference in quality between these two techniques is shown and discussed in the comparative case study in Chapter 6 and we now deal with each separately. Phong interpolation gives the more accurate highlights – as we shall see – and is generally the preferred model. Gouraud shading, on the other hand, is considerably cheaper. Both techniques have been developed both to interpolate information efficiently across the face of a polygon and to diminish the visibility of the polygon edges in the final shaded image. Information is interpolated from values at the vertices of a polygon and the situation is exactly analogous to depth interpolation.

3.6.1 Gouraud shading

In Gouraud shading we calculate light intensity – using the local reflection model of the previous section – at the vertices of the polygon and then interpolate between these intensities to find values at projected pixels. To do this we use the bi-linear interpolation equations given in Chapter 24 – just as we did for depth interpolation. The particular surface normals used at a vertex are special normals called vertex normals. If we consider a polygon in isolation then, of course, the vertex normals are all parallel; however, in Gouraud shading we use special normals called vertex normals and it is this device that reduces the visibility of polygon edges. Consider Figure 3.18. Here the vertex normal N_A is calculated by averaging N_1, N_2, N_3 and N_4.

$$N_a = N_1 + N_2 + N_3 + N_4$$

N_a is then used to calculate an intensity at vertex A that is common to all the polygons that share vertex A.

Figure 3.18
The vertex normal N_A is the average of the normals N_1, N_2, N_3 and N_4, the normals of the polygon that meet at the vertex.

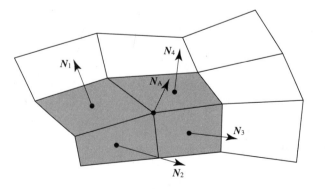

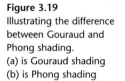

Figure 3.19
Illustrating the difference
between Gouraud and
Phong shading.
(a) is Gouraud shading
(b) is Phong shading

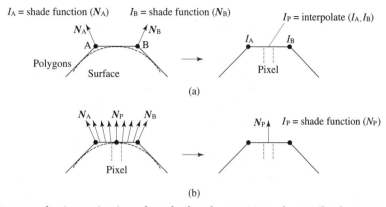

Because the intensity is only calculated at vertices the method cannot adequately deal with highlights and this is its major disadvantage. The cause of this defect can be understood by examining Figure 3.19. We have to bear in mind that the polygon mesh is an approximation to a curved surface. For a particular viewing and light source direction we can have a diffuse component at A and B and a specular highlight confined to some region between them. Clearly if we are deriving the intensity at pixel P from information at A and B we will not calculate a highlight. This situation is neatly taken care of by interpolating vertex normals rather than intensities as shown in Figure 3.19. This approach is known as Phong shading.

3.6.2 Phong shading

Here we interpolate vertex normals across the polygon interior and calculate for each polygon pixel projection an interpolated normal. This interpolated normal is then used in the shading equation which is applied for every pixel projection. This has the geometric effect (Figure 3.19) of 'restoring' some curvature to polygonally faceted surfaces.

The price that we pay for this improved model is efficiency. Not only is the vector interpolation three times the cost of intensity interpolation, but each vector has to be normalized and a shading equation calculated for each pixel projection.

3.6.3 Renderer shading options

Most renderers have a hierarchy of shading options where you trade wait time against the quality of the shaded image. This approach also, of course, applies to the addition of shadows and texture. The normal hierarchy is:

● **Wireframe** No rendering or shading at all. A wireframe display may be used to position objects in a scene by interacting with the viewing parameters. It is also commonly used in animation systems where an animator may be creating movement for objects in a scene interactively. He can adjust various aspects of the animation and generate a real-time animation sequence in wireframe display mode. In both these applications a full shaded image is obviously not necessary. One practical problem is that using the same overall renderer strategy for wireframe rendering as for shading (that is, independently drawing each polygon) will result in each edge being drawn twice – doubling the draw time for an object.

- **Flat shaded polygons**   Again a fast option. The single 'true' polygon normal is used, one shade is calculated using the Gouraud equation for each polygon and the shading interpolative process is avoided.

- **Gouraud shading**   The basic shading option which produces an intensity variation across the face of polygons. Because it cannot deal properly with specular highlights, a Gouraud shading option normally only calculates diffuse reflection.

- **Phong shading**   The 'standard' quality shading method which due to the vector interpolation and the evaluation of a shading equation at every pixel is between four and five times slower than Gouraud shading.

- **Mixing Phong and Gouraud shading**   Consider a diffuse object. Although using Gouraud shading for the object produces a slightly different effect from using Phong shading with the specular reflection coefficient set to zero, the difference is not visually important. This suggests that in a scene consisting of specular and diffuse objects we can use Gouraud shading for the diffuse objects and only use Phong shading for the specular ones. The Gouraud/Phong option then becomes part of the object property data.

These options are compared in some detail in the comparative case study in Chapter 8.

3.6.4   Bi-linear interpolation

As we have already mentioned, light intensity values are assigned to the set of pixels that form the polygon projection, not by individual calculation, but by interpolating from values calculated only at the polygon vertices. At the same time we interpolate depth values for each pixel to be used in the hidden surface determination. A general bi-linear interpolation procedure is given in detail in Section 24.7.

Further reading

Gouraud H. (1971). Continuous shading of curved surfaces. *IEEE Trans. on Computers*, (–20(6), 623–8

Phong B. (1975). Illumination for Computer Generated Pictures. *Comm. ACM*, **18**(6), 311–17

Warn D.R. (1983). Lighting controls for synthetic images. *Computer Graphics*, **17**(3), 13–21

Increasing realism – textures and shadows

Adding shadows and texture mapping became highly developed in the 1980s and was the technique used to enhance Phong shaded scenes so that they were more visually interesting, looked more realistic or looked more esoteric. Objects that are rendered using only Phong shading look plastic-like and texture mapping is the obvious way to add interest without much expense. Adding shadows increases the realism; we expect to see shadows and their absence adds to the computer signature of a rendered scene or object. (Although the addition of hard-edged shadows with arbitrary light intensity did little to reduce the computer signature, somehow the rendering was 'more complete'.)

Texture mapping and add-on shadows developed in parallel with research into global illumination algorithms – ray tracing and radiosity (Chapter 6). They were devices that could be used to enhance the visual interest of a scene rather than its photo-realism, and their main attraction was cheapness – they could be grafted onto a standard rendering method without adding too much to the processing cost. This contrasted with the global illumination methods which used completely different algorithms and were much more expensive than direct reflection models.

Another use of texture mapping that became ubiquitous in the 1980s was developed to add pseudo-realism to shiny animated objects by causing their surrounding environment to be reflected in them. Thus tumbling logos and titles became chromium and the texture reflected on them moved as the objects moved. (The over-use of this technique on TV in the 1980s is yet another example of the slow development of computer graphics as an art form because designers become locked into and constrained by variations of a technique supplied to them by the software designers. The only freedom available to designers or users of the technique is to vary the parameters made available by the software designers.) This technique – known as environment mapping – can also be used with a real photographed environment and helps to merge a computer animated object with a real environment. Environment mapping does not accomplish anything that could not be achieved by ray tracing, but it is much more efficient. A more recent use of environment mapping techniques is in image-based rendering which is discussed in Chapter 21.

As used in computer graphics 'texture' is a somewhat confusing term and generally does not mean controlling the small-scale geometry of the surface of a computer graphics object – the normal meaning of the word. It is easy to modulate the colour of a Phong shaded object by controlling the value of the three diffuse coefficients and this became the most common object parameter to be controlled by texture mapping. (Colour variations in the physical world are not, of course, generally regarded as texture.) Thus as the rendering proceeds at pixel by pixel level, we pick up values for the Phong diffuse reflection coefficients and the diffuse component (the colour) of the shading changes as a function of the texture map(s).

This simple pixel-level operation conceals many difficulties and the geometry of texture mapping is not straightforward. As usual we make simplifications that lead to a visually acceptable solution. There are three origins of the difficulties:

- We mostly want to use texture mapping with the most popular representation in computer graphics – the polygon mesh representation. This, as we know, is a geometric representation where the object surface is approximated, and this approximation is only defined at the vertices. In a sense we have no surface – only an approximation to one – so how can we physically derive a texture value at a surface point if the surface does not exist?

- We want to use, in the main, two-dimensional texture maps because we have an almost endless source of textures that we can derive from frame grabbing the real world, by using two-dimensional paint software or by generating textures procedurally. Thus the mainstream demand is to map a two-dimensional texture onto a surface that is approximated by a polygon mesh.

- Aliasing problems in texture mapping are usually highly visible. By definition, textures usually manifest some kind of coherence or periodicity. Aliasing breaks this up and the resulting mess is usually high visible. This effect occurs as the periodicity in the texture approaches the pixel resolution.

Now consider shadows. At first it may seem somewhat curious to group texture mapping and shadows into the same topic area, but shadows, like texture mapping, are commonly handled by using an empirical add-on algorithm. Shadows are pasted into the scene like texture maps. The other parallel with texture maps is that the easiest algorithm to use computes a map for each light source in the scene, known as a shadow map. The map is accessed during rendering, just as a texture map is referenced, to find out if a pixel is in shadow or not. Like the Z-buffer algorithm in hidden surface removal, this algorithm is easy to implement and has become a pseudo-standard. Also like the Z-buffer algorithm, it trades simplicity against high memory cost.

Shadows are important in scenes. A scene without shadows looks artificial. They give clues concerning the scene, consolidate spatial relationships between objects and give information on the position of the light source. To compute shadows completely we need knowledge of both their shape and the light intensity inside them. An area of the scene in shadow is not completely bereft of light. It simply cannot see direct illumination, but receives indirect illumination from another nearby object. Add-on shadow algorithms are all 'geometric'. By this we mean that they calculate the position and the shape of the shadows – they cannot compute what the light intensity should be inside the shadow area, and this is set arbitrarily. Thus we have the curious procedure of a scene, shaded using the Phong reflection model, having shadows 'pasted in', where the geometry of the shadows is accurately calculated but the light intensity is merely guessed at. (The shadow intensity can only be calculated correctly by using a global illumination model such as radiosity. In this algorithm (Chapter 6) shadow areas are treated no differently to any other area in the scene and the shadow intensity is a light intensity, reflected from a surface, like any other.)

4.1 Texture mapping – what aspects of the object to modulate

We now list the possible ways in which certain properties of a computer graphics model can be modulated with variations under control of a texture map. We have listed these in approximate order of their popularity (which also tends to relate to their ease of use or implementation). These are:

(1) **Colour** As we have already pointed out, this is by far the most common object property that is controlled by a texture map. We simply modulate the diffuse reflection coefficients in the Phong reflection model with the corresponding colour from the texture map.

(We could also change the specular coefficients across the surface of an object so that it appears shiny and matte as a function of the texture map. But this is less common, as being able to perceive this effect on the rendered object depends on producing specular highlights on the shiny parts if it is the case that we are using the basic Phong reflection model.)

(2) **Specular 'colour'**   This technique – known as environment mapping or chrome mapping – is a special case of ray tracing where we use texture map techniques to avoid the expense of ray tracing. The map is designed so that it looks as if the (specular) object is reflecting the environment or background in which it is placed.

(3) **Normal vector perturbation**   This elegant technique applies a perturbation to the surface normal according to the corresponding value in the map. The technique is known as **bump mapping** and was developed by a famous pioneer of three-dimensional computer graphic techniques – J. Blinn. The device works because the intensity that is returned by a Phong shading equation reduces, if the appropriate simplifications are made, to a function of the surface normal at the point currently being shaded. If the surface normal is perturbed then the shading changes and the surface that is rendered looks as if it was textured. We can therefore use a global or general definition for the texture of a surface which is represented in the database as a polygon mesh structure.

(4) **Displacement mapping**   Related to the previous technique, this mapping method uses a height field to perturb a surface point along the direction of its surface normal. It is not a convenient technique to implement since the map must perturb the geometry of the model rather than modulate parameters in the shading equation.

(5) **Transparency**   A map is used to control the opacity of a transparent object. A good example is etched glass where a shiny surface is roughened (to cause opacity) with some decorative pattern.

4.2 Two-dimensional textures and three-dimensional objects

The process of mapping a two-dimensional texture onto an object and rendering can be viewed (and implemented) as a forward or inverse mapping process. Consider first forward mapping (Figure 4.1). The overall mapping can be described either by two transformations as shown or as a single combined transformation. The first transformation, sometimes known as surface parametrization, takes the two-dimensional texture pattern and 'glues' it on the object. The second transformation is the standard object to screen space mapping. Two major difficulties arise in texture mapping. These are: inventing a suitable surface parametrization and anti-aliasing. The difficulty with the first transformation is due to the fact that we normally wish to stick a texture pattern on a polygon mesh object – itself a discontinuous approximation to a real object. For such objects surface parametrizations are not defined. They have to be invented. This contrasts with quadric and cubic surfaces where parametrizations are readily available. If we use the analogy of wallpaper pasting, how are we going to paste the wallpaper onto the polygon mesh object? This is a problem to which there is no good solution and a variety of ad hoc techniques have evolved. In the

Figure 4.1
Two ways of viewing the
process of two-dimensional
texture mapping.

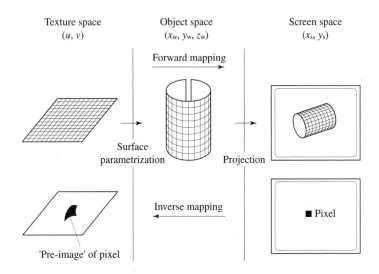

end forward mapping is only useful if we have a surface parametrization which means that we virtually treat the texture information as part of the object properties, 'collecting' the texture information when we access the geometric information associated with the object.

Now as we have seen the 'standard' object representation and 'standard' rendering regime imply algorithms driven from screen space one pixel at a time. Interpolative shading and Z-buffer hidden surface removal imply a pixel-by-pixel ordering for each polygon. This means that we have to find a single texture value for each pixel to insert into the interpolative shading scheme. The easiest way to do this is by inverse mapping – we find the 'pre-image' of the current pixel in the texture domain. Figure 4.1 shows the general idea of inverse mapping and Figure 4.2 show the process in more detail. Because the overall transform is non-linear the pixel maps into an area in texture space that in general is a curvilinear quadrilateral. To perform the inverse transformation we need to take the four pixel corner points, invert the object to screen space transformation and invert the surface parametrization. Another reason for adopting this methodology is that it facilitates anti-aliasing.

The use of an anti-aliasing method is mandatory with texture mapping. This is easily seen by considering an object retreating away from a viewer so that its projection in screen space covers fewer and fewer pixels. As the object size decreases the pre-image of a pixel in texture space will increase, covering a larger area. If we simply point sample at the centre of the pixel and take the value of $T(u,v)$ at the corresponding point in texture space, then grossly incorrect results will follow (Figures 4.2(a), (b) and (c)). Another example of this effect is shown in Figure 8.2. Here as the chequerboard pattern recedes into the distance it begins to break up in a disturbing manner. These problems are highly visible and move when animated. Consider Figures 4.2(b) and (c). Say, for example, that an object projects onto a single pixel and moves in such a way that the pre-image

Figure 4.2
Pixels and pre-images in
T(u,v) space.

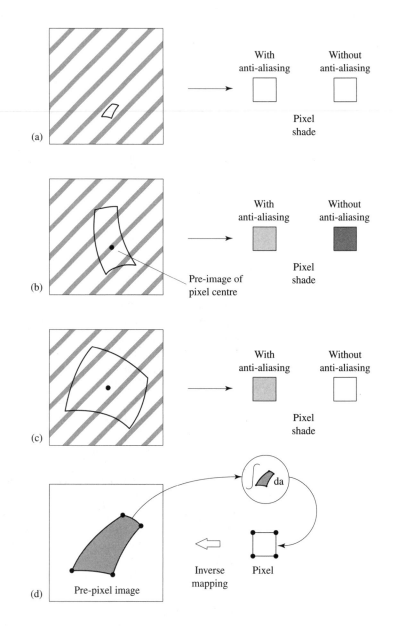

translates across the *T(u,v)*. As the object moves it would switch colour from black to white.

Anti-aliasing in this context then means integrating the information over the pixel pre-image and using this value in the shading calculation for the current pixel (Figure 4.2(d)). At best we can only approximate this integral because we have no knowledge of the shape of the quadrilateral, only its four corner points.

Polygon mesh texture mapping: two-part mapping

Two-part texture mapping is a much used technique that overcomes the surface parametrization problem in polygon mesh objects by using an 'easy' intermediate surface onto which the texture is initially projected. Introduced by Bier and Sloan, it is a method that will map two-dimensional texture onto unconstrained polygon mesh models. The method can also be used to implement environment mapping and is thus a method that unifies texture mapping and environment mapping.

The process is known as two-part mapping because the texture is mapped onto an intermediate surface before being mapped onto the object. The intermediate surface is in general non-planar but it possesses an analytic mapping function and the two-dimensional texture is mapped onto this surface without difficulty. Finding the correspondence between the object point and the texture point then becomes a three-dimensional to three-dimensional mapping.

The basis of the method is most easily described as a two-stage forward mapping process (Figure 4.3):

(1) The first stage (Figure 4.3(a)) is a mapping from two-dimensional texture space to a simple three-dimensional intermediate surface such as a cylinder.

$$T(u,v) \rightarrow T'(x_i,y_i,z_i)$$

This is known as the S mapping.

(2) A second stage (Figure 4.3(b)) maps the three-dimensional texture pattern onto the object surface.

$$T'(x_i,y_i,z_i) \rightarrow O(x_w,y_w,z_w)$$

This is referred to as the O mapping.

These combined operations can distort the texture pattern onto the object in a 'natural' way; for example, one variation of the method is a 'shrinkwrap' mapping, where the planar texture pattern shrinks onto the object in the manner suggested by the eponym.

For the S mapping Bier describes four intermediate surfaces: a plane at any orientation, the curved surface of a cylinder, the faces of a cube and the surface of a sphere. Although it makes no difference mathematically, it is useful to consider that $T(u,v)$ is mapped onto the interior surfaces of these objects. For example, consider the cylinder. Given a parametric definition of the curved surface of a cylinder as a set of points (θ,h), we transform the point (u,v) onto the cylinder as follows. We have:

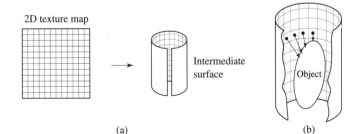

Figure 4.3
Two-stage mapping as a forward process. (a) S mapping; (b) O mapping.

$$S_{\text{cylinder}}: (\theta, h) \rightarrow (u, v)$$

$$= \left(\frac{r}{c} (\theta - \theta_0), \frac{1}{d} (h - h_0) \right)$$

where c and d are scaling factors and θ_0 and h_0 position the texture on the cylinder of radius r.

Various possibilities occur for the O mapping where the texture values for $O(x_w, y_w, z_w)$ are obtained from $T'(x_i, y_i, z_i)$, and these are best considered from a ray tracing point of view. The four O mappings are shown in Figure 4.4 and are:

(1) The intersection of the reflected view ray with the intermediate surface, T'. (This is in fact identical to environment mapping described in Section 4.5. The only difference between the general process of using this O mapping and environment mapping is that the texture pattern that is mapped onto the intermediate surface is a surrounding environment like a room interior.)

(2) The intersection of the surface normal at (x_w, y_w, z_w) with T'.

(3) The intersection of a line through (x_w, y_w, z_w) and the object centroid with T'.

(4) The intersection of the line from (x_w, y_w, z_w) to T' whose orientation is given by the surface normal at (x_i, y_i, z_i). If the intermediate surface is simply a plane then this is equivalent to considering the texture map to be a slide in a slide projector. A bundle of parallel rays of light from the slide projector impinges on the object surface. Alternatively it is also equivalent to three-dimensional texture mapping (Section 4.3) where the field is defined by 'extruding' the two-dimensional texture map along an axis normal to the plane of the pattern.

Let us now consider this procedure as an inverse mapping process for the shrinkwrap case (4). We break the process into three stages (Figure 4.5).

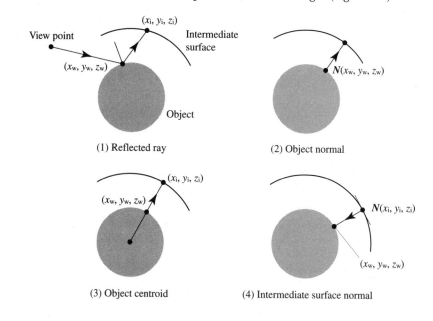

Figure 4.4
The four possible O mappings that map the intermediate surface texture T onto the object.

(1) Reflected ray

(2) Object normal

(3) Object centroid

(4) Intermediate surface normal

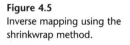

Figure 4.5
Inverse mapping using the
shrinkwrap method.

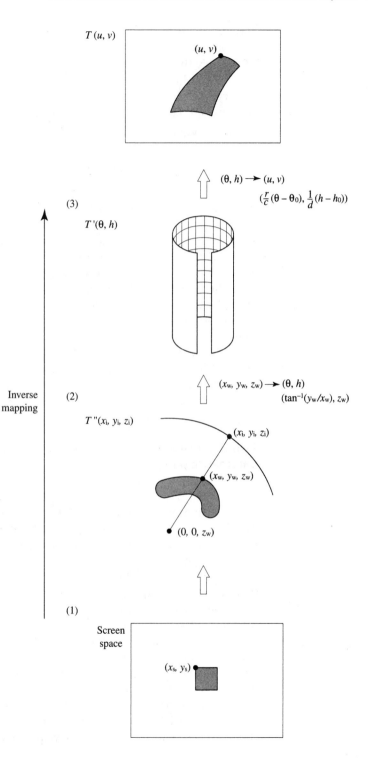

(1)   Inverse map four pixel points to four points (x_w, y_w, z_w) on the surface of the object.

(2)   Apply the O mapping to find the point (θ, h) on the surface of the cylinder. In the shrinkwrap case we simply join the object point to the centre of the cylinder and the intersection of this line with the surface of the cylinder gives us (x_i, y_i, z_i).

$$x_w, y_w, z_w \rightarrow (\theta, h)$$
$$= (\tan^{-1}(y_w/x_w), z_w)$$

(3)   Apply the S mapping to find the point (u, v) corresponding to (θ, h).

Figure 4.6 (Colour Plate) shows examples of mapping the same texture onto an object using different intermediate surfaces. The intermediate objects are a plane (equivalently no object – the texture map is a plane), a cylinder and a sphere. The simple shape of the cube was chosen to illustrate the different distortions that each intermediate object produces. There are two points that can be made from these illustrations. First, you can choose an intermediate mapping that is appropriate to the shape of the object. A solid of revolution may be best suited, for example, to a cylinder. Second, although the method does not place any constraints on the shape of the object, the final visual effect may be deemed unsatisfactory. Usually what we mean by texture does not involve the texture pattern being subject to large geometric distortions. It is for this reason that many practical methods are interactive and involve some strategy like pre-distorting the texture map in two-dimensional space until it produces a good result when it is stuck onto the object. An example of such an approach is described in Section 4.7.

4.2.2 Two-dimensional texture domain techniques: mapping onto bicubic parametric patches

If an object is a quadric or a cubic then surface parametrization is straightforward. In the previous section we used quadrics as intermediate surfaces exactly for this reason. If the object is a bicubic parametric patch, texture mapping is trivial since a a parametric patch by definition already possesses (u, v) values everywhere on its surface.

The first use of texture in computer graphics was a method developed by Catmull. This technique applied to bicubic parametric patch models; the algorithm subdivides a surface patch in object space, and at the same time executes a corresponding subdivision in texture space. The idea is that the patch subdivision proceeds until it covers a single pixel (a standard patch rendering approach described in detail in Chapter 7). When the patch subdivision process terminates, the required texture value(s) for the pixel is obtained from the area enclosed by the current level of subdivision in the texture domain. This is a straightforward technique that is easily implemented as an extension to a bicubic patch renderer. A variation of this method was used by Cook where object surfaces are subdivided into 'micro-polygons' and flat shaded with values from a corresponding subdivision in texture space.

An example of this technique is shown in Figure 4.7 (Colour Plate). Here each patch on the teapot causes subdivision of a single texture map, which is itself a rendered version of the teapot. For each patch, the u,v values from the parameter space subdivision are used to index the texture map whose u,v values also vary between 0 and 1. This scheme is easily altered to, say, map four patches into the entire texture domain by using a scale factor of two in the u,v mapping.

4.3   Three-dimensional texture domain techniques

A method that neatly circumvents the two-dimensional to three-dimensional mapping problem is to employ a three-dimensional texture domain. We can imagine that a texture value exists everywhere in the object domain or definition. Ignoring object scale problems (the texture 'size' will not vary as the size of the object changes), we can then say that given a point on the surface of an object, (x_w,y_w,z_w), its texture is given by the identity mapping $T(x_w,y_w,z_w)$. This is like the process of sculpting or carving an object out of a solid block of material. The colour of the object is determined by the intersection of its surface with the predefined three-dimensional texture field.

A fairly obvious requirement of this technique is that the three-dimensional texture field is obtained by procedural generation. Storing a complete three-dimensional field would be prohibitively expensive in memory requirements. Thus the coordinates (x_w,y_w,z_w) are used to index a procedure that defines the three-dimensional texture field for that point.

A significant advantage of the elimination of the mapping problem is that objects of arbitrary complexity can receive a texture on their surface in a 'coherent' fashion. No discontinuities occur when the texture appears on the object.

Figure 4.8 shows the overall idea of the technique. This technique is mostly used in conjunction with a three-dimensional noise function to generate the definition. This approach is now well established in three-dimensional computer graphics because it works well visually. It is particularly successful at simulating such phenomena as turbulence and has been used to model, for example, objects of marble. A three-dimensional noise function is built by assigning random integers to a three-dimensional array. This three-dimensional block of random numbers is then accessed by a three-dimensional real number and interpolation amongst the nearest integers returns a three-dimensional real noise value. This can be used to perturb the colour associated with the point on the surface of the object by using the point to access the noise function. Consider simulating a dark seam in a marble object. We could set up a block of marble as a 'sandwich' of light and dark material. We then have two fields accessed by a surface point: the light/dark definition which determines the initial colour of the point and then the noise function which perturbs this colour. The overall process is shown in Figure 4.9. Figure 4.10 (Colour Plate) is an example of an object that has been textured using this process.

Figure 4.8
Three-dimensional texture
mapping in object space.

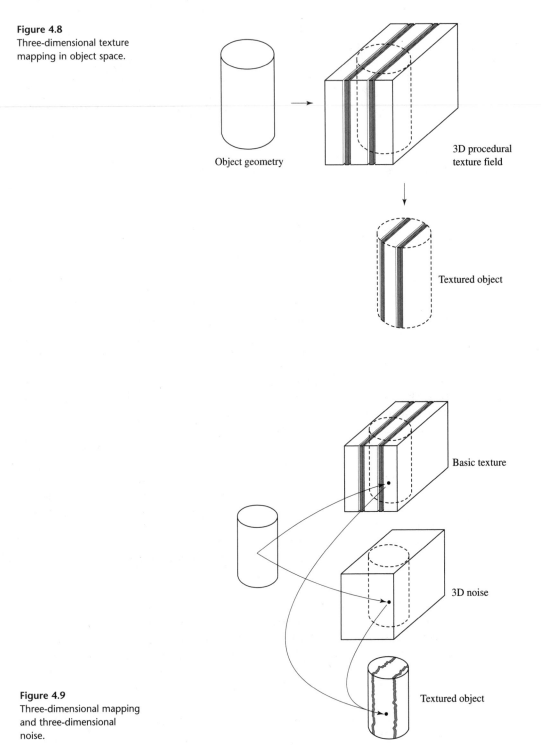

Object geometry

3D procedural
texture field

Textured object

Basic texture

3D noise

Textured object

Figure 4.9
Three-dimensional mapping
and three-dimensional
noise.

The big problem with three-dimensional texture mapping is that it is difficult to create very many procedural definitions and because of this the method lacks the flexibility and generality of two-dimensional texture mapping.

4.4 Bump mapping

Bump mapping, a technique developed by Blinn in 1978, is an elegant device that enables a surface to appear as if it was wrinkled or dimpled without the need to geometrically model these depressions. Instead, the surface normal is angularly perturbed according to information given in a two-dimensional bump map and this 'tricks' a local reflection model, wherein intensity is a function mainly of the surface normal, into producing (apparent) local geometric variations on a smooth surface. The only problem with bump mapping is that because the pits or depressions do not exist in the model, a silhouette edge that appears to pass through a depression will not produce the expected cross-section. In other words, the silhouette edge will follow the original geometry of the model.

It is an important technique because it appears to texture a surface in the normal sense of the word rather than modulating the colour of a flat surface. Figure 4.11 (Colour Plate) shows examples of this technique. The illustrations are original examples produced by J. Blinn in 1978.

Texturing the surface in the rendering phase, without perturbing the geometry, bypasses serious modelling problems that would otherwise occur. If the object is polygonal the mesh would have to be fine enough to receive the perturbations from the texture map – a serious imposition on the original modelling phase, particularly if the texture is to be an option.

In bump mapping we need to perturb the normal vector at a point on the surface in such a way that when a local reflection model is applied and the surface is shaded it looks as if the surface geometry has been perturbed by the bump map which is a two-dimensional height field. Refer to Figure 4.12 which shows an overview of the process.

If for simplicity we assume that $\boldsymbol{O}(u,v)$ is a parametrized function (Chapter 6) representing the position vectors of points $\boldsymbol{O}$ on the surface of an object, then the normal to the surface at a point is given by (Chapter 24):

$$\boldsymbol{N} = \boldsymbol{O}u \times \boldsymbol{O}v$$

where $\boldsymbol{O}u$ and $\boldsymbol{O}v$ are the partial derivatives of the surface at point $\boldsymbol{O}$ lying in the tangent plane.

We define two other vectors that lie in the tangent plane. These are:

$$\boldsymbol{P} = \boldsymbol{N} \times \boldsymbol{O}v$$

and

$$\boldsymbol{Q} = \boldsymbol{N} \times \boldsymbol{O}u$$

$\boldsymbol{D}$ is a vector that is added to $\boldsymbol{N}$ to perturb its direction to $\boldsymbol{N'}$:

$$\boldsymbol{N'} = \boldsymbol{N} + \boldsymbol{D}$$

Figure 4.12
Bump mapping geometry.

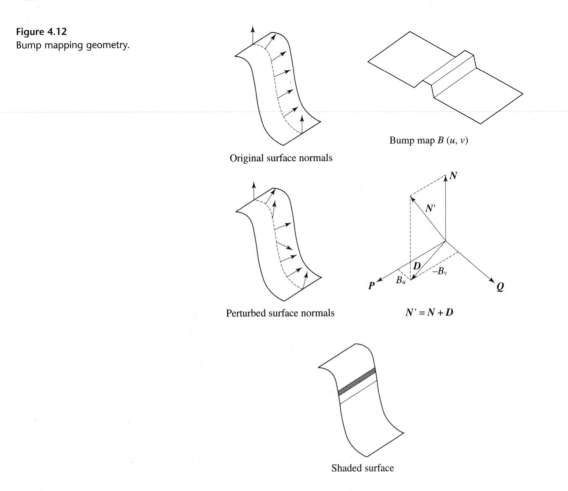

Bump map $B(u, v)$

Original surface normals

Perturbed surface normals

$N' = N + D$

Shaded surface

The vectors $\boldsymbol{P}$, $\boldsymbol{Q}$ and $\boldsymbol{N}$ form a coordinate system. $\boldsymbol{D}$ is derived from $\boldsymbol{P}$, $\boldsymbol{Q}$ and B, a bump map. The bump map is a height field and the idea is that $\boldsymbol{D}$ should transfer the variations in height in the bump map into orientation perturbations in $\boldsymbol{N}$ so that when the surface is shaded, the variation in $\boldsymbol{N}$ produces the effect specified in the bump map. In other words, the height variations in the bump map are transformed into orientation perturbations in the surface normal which makes the surface look as if it has been displaced by the height variations in the bump map. It can be shown that $\boldsymbol{D}$ is given by:

$$\boldsymbol{D} = B_u \, \boldsymbol{P} - B_v \, \boldsymbol{Q}$$

where B_u and B_v are the partial derivatives of the bump map $B(u,v)$. Thus we define a bump map as a displacement function or height field but use its derivatives at the point (u,v) to calculate $\boldsymbol{D}$.

4.5 Environment mapping

Environment mapping refers to the process of reflecting a surrounding environment in a shiny object and environment mapping was originally introduced as a cheap alternative to ray tracing. The idea is that a shiny object reflects its surroundings or environment and if this is pre-stored or rendered as a map, the texture mapping can be used when the object is rendered to give this effect. Thus the reflections are achieved by texture mapping rather than the expensive alternative of ray tracing. It is distinguished from 'normal' texture mapping in that the pattern seen on an object is a function of the view vector V. A particular detail in the environment will move across the object as V changes. The idea is shown in principle in Figure 4.13 which shows a cross-section of a spherical map surrounding an object. (Note that this is a reproduction of part of Figure 4.4 which deals with two-part texture mapping. Environment mapping is a special case of two-part texture mapping.) Reflecting a view ray V from the surface of an object produces an index into the map which is then used as a normal texture map.

Originally introduced in the 1980s, it quickly became a popular technique. The most popular manifestation of environment mapping uses a box or cube as an intermediate surface, the maps being constructed either by taking six photographs of (say) a room interior, or rendering the map using a computer graphics renderer using six mutually perpendicular viewing directions. Cubic environment maps are easier to construct than spherical maps which also suffer from distortion at the poles.

Photographic environment maps offer the potential of being used in productions in which a computer graphics object can be matted into a real environment. The object, usually animated, has the real environment reflected in its surface as it is rendered and moves about the room. The resulting effect makes the rendered object look as if it was part of the environment from which the map has been constructed. This device has been much used in TV commercials where an object – usually the advertised product – is animated in a photographed real environment.

Recently environment mapping has found a new lease of life as an image-based rendering technique (see Chapter 21). Here a person, the virtual viewer, replaces the object and that part of the map intercepted by the viewer's field of vision is presented to him as a two-dimensional projection.

Consider again Figure 4.13. In practice we have to consider four rays through the pixel point defining a reflection 'cone' with a quadrilateral cross-section. The region that subtends the environment map is then filtered to give a single shading attribute for the pixel. In other words, the technique is identical to normal inverse mapping texture mapping except that the area that a pixel intercepts may spread over one, two or three maps. Environment mapping is geometrically an approximate technique and an object that is environment mapped will not exhibit the same reflection images as a ray traced object placed in the same environment. The geometric errors are a function of the size of the object in the

Figure 4.13
Environment mapping –
principle and practice.
(a) Environment mapping
in principle. (b) Inverse
mapping produces a
reflection beam. (c) In
practice, cubic maps are
used.

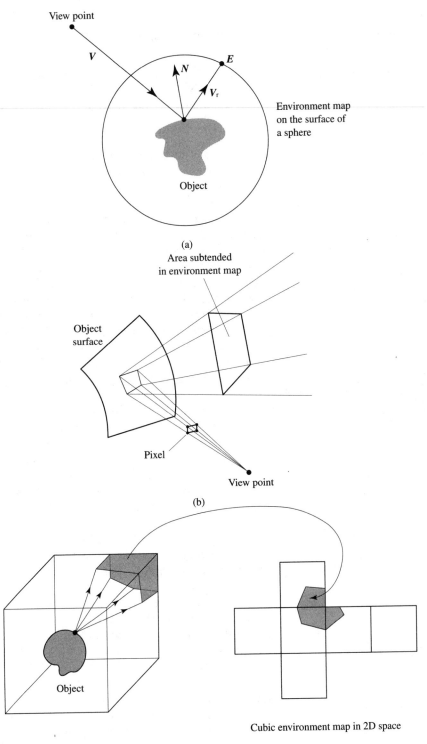

View point

V

N

E

V_r

Environment map
on the surface of
a sphere

Object

(a)

Area subtended
in environment map

Object
surface

Pixel

View point

(b)

Object

Cubic environment map in 2D space

(c)

environment. An example of environment mapping is shown in Figure 8.16 (Colour Plate). The amount of geometric distortion that is involved is shown in Figure 8.17 (Colour Plate). You should also see in the figure another drawback with environment mapping, which is that, by definition, an object cannot exhibit any self-reflections. The absence of such reflections seem to make the object look less shiny.

4.6   Anti-aliasing and texture mapping

As we have discussed in the introduction, artefacts are extremely problematic in texture mapping and most textures produce visible artefacts unless the method is integrated with an anti-aliasing procedure. Defects are highly noticeable, particularly in texture that exhibits coherence or periodicity, as soon as the predominant spatial frequency in the texture pattern approaches the dimension of a pixel. (The classic example of this effect is shown in Figure 8.2.) Artefacts generated by texture mapping are not well handled by a general anti-aliasing method – such as supersampling – and because of this standard two-dimensional texture mapping procedures usually incorporate a specific anti-aliasing technique.

Anti-aliasing is difficult because to do it properly we need to find the pre-image of a pixel and sum weighted values of $T(u,v)$ that fall within the extent of the pre-image to get a single texture intensity for the pixel. Unfortunately the shape of the pre-image changes from pixel to pixel and this filtering process consequently becomes expensive. Refer again to Figure 4.2. This shows that when we are considering a pixel its pre-image in texture space is, in general, a curvilinear quadrilateral, because the net effect of the texture mapping and perspective mapping is of a non-linear transformation. The figure also shows for the diagonal band texture that unless this operation is performed or approximated, erroneous results will occur. In particular, if the texture map is merely sampled at the inverse mapping of the pixel centre then the sampled intensity may be correct if the inverse image size of the pixel is sufficiently small, but in general it will be wrong.

In the context of Figure 4.2, anti-aliasing means approximating the integration shown in the figure. An approximate, but visually successful, method ignores the shape but not the size or extent of the pre-image and **pre-calculates** all the required filtering operations. This is **mip-mapping**, invented by Williams in 1983 and probably the most common anti-aliasing method developed specifically for texture mapping. His method is based on pre-calculation and an assumption that the inverse pixel image is reasonably close to a square. Figure 4.14(b) shows the pixel pre-image approximated by a square. It is this approximation that enables the anti-aliasing or filtering operation to be pre-calculated. In fact there are two problems. The first is more common and is known as compression or minification. This occurs when an object becomes small in screen space and consequently a pixel has a large pre-image in texture space. Figure 4.14(c) shows this situation. Many texture elements (sometimes called 'texels') need to be mapped into a single pixel. The other problem is called magnification. Here an object

Figure 4.14
Mip-mapping approximations. (a) The pre-image of a pixel is a curvilinear quadrilateral in texture space. (b) A pre-image can be approximated by a square. (c) Compression is required when a pixel maps onto many texels. (d) Magnification is required when a pixel maps onto less than one texel.

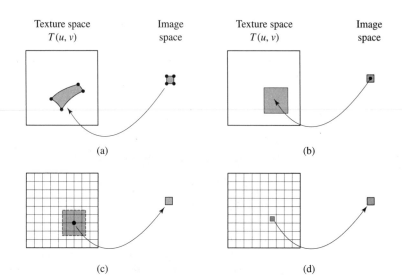

becomes very close to the viewer and only part of the object may occupy the whole of screen space, resulting in pixel pre-images that have less area than one texel (Figure 4.14(d)). Mip-mapping deals with compression and some elaboration to mip-mapping is usually required for the magnification problem.

In mip-mapping, instead of a texture domain comprising a single image, Williams uses many images, all derived by averaging down the original image to successively lower resolutions. In other words, they form a set of pre-filtered texture maps. Each image in the sequence is exactly half the resolution of the previous one. Figure 4.15 shows an approximation to the idea. An object near to the viewer, and large in screen space, selects a single texel from a high resolution map. The same object further away from the viewer and smaller in screen space selects a single texel from a low resolution map. An appropriate map is selected by a parameter D. (Note that a mip-map is an image pyramid – see Chapter 11 for a general discussion of image pyramids.)

In a low resolution version of the image each texel represents the average of a number of texels from the previous map. By a suitable choice of D, an image at appropriate resolution is selected and the filtering cost remains constant – the many texels to one pixel cost problem being avoided. The centre of the pixel is mapped into that map determined by D and this single value is used. In this way the original texture is filtered and to avoid discontinuities between the images at varying resolutions, different levels are also blended. Blending between levels occurs when D is selected. The images are discontinuous in resolution but D is a continuous parameter. Linear interpolation is carried out from the two nearest levels.

Williams selects D from:

$$D = \text{max\_of}\left(\left(\left(\frac{\partial u}{\partial x}\right)^2+\left(\frac{\partial v}{\partial x}\right)^2\right)^{1/2},\left(\left(\frac{\partial u}{\partial y}\right)^2+\left(\frac{\partial v}{\partial y}\right)^2\right)^{1/2}\right)$$

where ∂u and ∂v are the original dimensions of the pre-image in texture space and $\partial x = \partial y = 1$ for a square pixel.

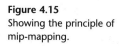

Figure 4.15
Showing the principle of
mip-mapping.

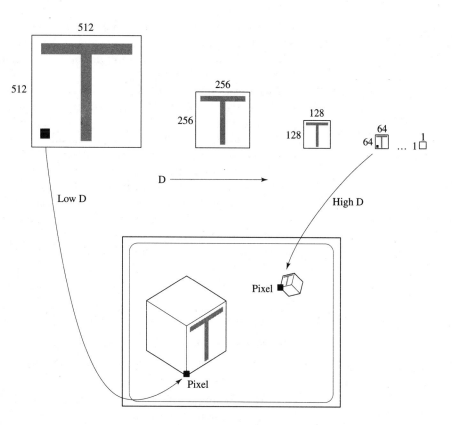

A 'correct' or accurate estimation of *D* is important. If *D* is too large then the image will look blurred; too small and aliasing artefacts will still be visible. Detailed practical methods for determining *D* depending on the mapping context are given in the book by Watt and Watt (Chapter 1).

In a theoretical sense the magnification problem does not exist. Ideally we would like mip-maps that can be used at any level of detail, but in practice, storage limitations restrict the highest resolution mask to, say, 512×512 texels. This problem does not seem to have been addressed in the literature and the following two approaches are supplied by Silicon Graphics for their workstation family. Silicon Graphics suggest two solutions: first, to simply extrapolate beyond the highest resolution mip-map, and second, a more elaborate procedure that extracts separate texture information into low and high frequency components.

Extrapolation is defined as

$$LOD(+1) = LOD(0) + (LOD(0) - LOD(-1))$$

where LOD (level of detail) represent mip-maps as follows:

LOD(+1) is the extrapolated mip-map
LOD(0) is the highest resolution stored mip-map
LOD(−1) is the next highest resolution stored mip-map

This operation derives an extrapolated mip-map of blocks of 4×4 pixels over which there is no variation. However, the magnification process preserves edges – hence the name. (Note the similarity between this idea and the wavelet transform discussed in Chapter 11.)

Extrapolation works best when high frequency information is correlated with low frequency structural information, that is, when the high frequency information represents edges in the texture. For example, consider that the texture pattern is made up of block letters. Extrapolation will blur/magnify the interior of the letters, while keeping the edges sharp.

When high frequency information is not correlated with low frequency information, extrapolation causes blurring. This occurs with texture that tends to vary uniformly throughout, for example wood grain. Silicon Graphics suggest separating the low and high frequency information and converting a high resolution (unstorable at, say, 2K×2K) into a 512×512 map that stores low frequency or structural information and a 256×256 map that stores high frequency detail. This separation can be achieved accurately using filtering techniques as described in Chapter 9. Alternatively a space domain procedure is as follows:

(1) Make a 512×512 low frequency map by simply resampling the original 2K×2K map.

(2) Make the 256×256 detail mask as follows:

    (i) Select a 256×256 window from the original map that contains representative high frequency texture.

    (ii) Resample this to 64×64 and re-scale to 256×256, resulting in a blurred version of the original 256×256 map.

    (iii) Subtract the blurred map from the original, adding a bias to make the subtrahend image unsigned. This results in a 256×256 high frequency.

Now when magnification is required a mix of the 512×512 low resolution texture with the high resolution detail is used.

4.7 Interactive techniques in texture mapping

One of the main problems in designing a conventional two-dimensional texture map is the visualization of the result on the rendered object. Say an artist or a designer is creating a texture map by painting directly in the two-dimensional uv space of the map. We know that the distortion of the map, when it is 'stuck' on the object, is a function of both the shape of the object and the mapping method that is used. To design a texture interactively the artist needs to see the final rendered object and have some intuition of the mapping mechanism so that he or she can predict the effect of changes made to the texture map.

We will now describe two interactive techniques. In the first the designer paints in uv or texture space. The second attempts to make the designer think that he or she is painting directly on the object in three-dimensional world space.

The first technique is extremely simple and was evolved to texture animals/objects that exhibit a plane of symmetry. It is simply an interactive version of two-part texture mapping with a plane as the intermediate object (Section 4.2.1). The overall idea is shown in Figure 4.16. The animal model is enclosed in a bounding box. The texture map $T(u,v)$ is then 'stuck' on the two faces of the box using the 'minimax' coordinates of the box and points in $T(u,v)$ are projected onto the object using a parallel projection, with projectors normal to the plane of symmetry.

The second technique is to allow the artist to interact directly with the rendered version on the screen. The artist applies the texture using an interactive device simulating a brush and the effect on the screen is as if the painter was

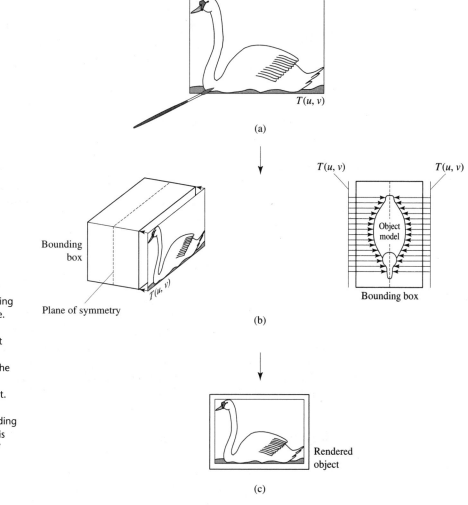

Figure 4.16
Interactive texture mapping – painting in $T(u,v)$ space. (a) Texture is painted using an interactive paint program. (b) Using the object's bounding box, the texture map points are projected onto the object. Each projector is parallel and normal to the bounding box face. (c) The object is rendered, the 'distortion' visualized and the artist repeats the cycle if necessary.

Figure 4.17
Iterative texture mapping –
painting in object space.

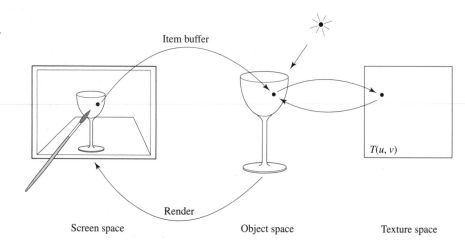

Item buffer

Render

Screen space   Object space   Texture space

$T(u, v)$

applying paint directly to the three-dimensional object. It is easy to see the advantages of such a method by looking first at how it differs from a normal two-dimensional paint program which basically enables a user to colour selected pixels on the screen.

Say we have a sphere (circle in screen space). With a normal paint program, if we selected, say, the colour green and painted the sphere, then unless we explicitly altered the colour, the sphere's projection would be filled with the selected uniform green colour. However, the idea of using a paint interaction in object space is that as you apply the green paint its colour changes according to the application of the Phong shading equation, and if the paint was shiny a specular highlight will appear. Extending the idea to texture mapping means that the artist can paint the texture on the object directly and the program, reversing the normal texture mapping procedure, can derive the texture map from the object. Once the process is complete new views of the object can be rendered and textured mapped in the normal way.

This approach requires a technique that identifies, from the screen pixel that is being pointed to, the corresponding point on the object surface. In the method described by Hanrahan and Haeberli an auxiliary frame buffer, known as an item buffer, is used. Accessing this buffer with the coordinates of the screen cursor gives a pointer to the position on the object surface and the corresponding (u,v) coordinate values for the texture map. Clearly we need an object representation where the surface is everywhere parametrized and Hanrahan and Haeberli divide the object surface into a large number of micropolygons. The overall idea is illustrated in Figure 4.17.

4.8 Adding shadows in rendering

As we mentioned in the introduction, shadows are properly part of the global illumination problem and in 'geometric' shadow algorithms we simply calculate the shape of a shadow. We have no way of knowing what the light intensity inside a shadow should be. This restriction has long been tolerated in mainstream rendering, the rationale presumably being that it is better to have a shadow pasted into the scene – as if it was a texture map – rather than having no shadow at all. Thus in the following sections we will deal with this aspect of rendering leaving the more considered discussion of shadows – as part of the global illumination problem – to Chapter 6. It is important to bear in mind that shadow algorithms of this type consider the geometry of the shadow, whereas in (most) global illumination approaches the shadow areas are **not** considered a phenomenon separate to the normal distribution of light in an environment – they are simply part of the simulation and emerge from the algorithm as an area exhibiting reflected light no different to any other area.

Shadows vary as a function of the lighting environment. They can be hard edged or soft edged and contain both an umbra and a penumbra area. The relative size of the umbra/penumbra is a function of the size and shape of the light source and its distance from the object (Figure 4.18). The umbra is that part of a shadow that is completely cut off from the light source, whereas the penumbra is an area that receives some light from the source. A penumbra surrounds an umbra and there is always a gradual change in intensity from a penumbra to an umbra. In computer graphics, if we are not modelling illumination sources, then we usually consider point light sources at large distances, and assume in the simplest case that objects produce umbrae with sharp edges. This is still only an approximation. Even although light from a large distance produces almost parallel rays, there is still light behind the object due to diffraction and the shadow

Figure 4.18
Intensity of reflected light in a shadow area: the umbra–penumbra effect due to the relative sizes of a light source and an object.

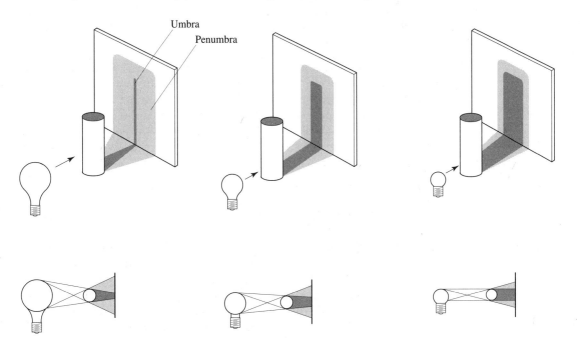

grades off. This effect also varies over the distance a shadow is thrown. These effects, which determine the quality of a shadow, enable us to infer information concerning the nature of the light source and they are clearly important to us as human beings perceiving a three-dimensional environment. For example, the shadows that we see outdoors depend on the time of day and whether the sky is overcast or not.

4.8.1 Computer graphics and shadows

A number of aspects of shadows are exploited in the computer generation of the phenomenon. These are now listed:

- A shadow from polygon A that falls on polygon B due to a point light source can be calculated by projecting polygon A onto the plane that contains polygon B. The position of the point light source is used as the centre of projection.

- No shadows are seen if the viewpoint is coincident with the (single) light source. An equivalent form of this statement is that shadows can be considered to be areas hidden from the light source, implying that modified hidden surface algorithms can be used to solve the shadow problem.

- If the light source, or sources, are point sources then there is no penumbra to calculate and the shadow has a hard edge.

- For static scenes shadows are fixed and do not change as the viewpoint changes. If the relative position of objects and light sources changes, the shadows have to be recalculated. This places a high overhead on three-dimensional animation where shadows are important for depth and movement perception.

Because of the high computational overheads, shadows have been regarded in much the same way as texture mapping – as a quality add-on. Compared with shading algorithms there has been little consideration of the quality of shadows and most shadow generation algorithms produce hard-edge point-light source shadows. Most add-on shadow algorithms deal only with polygon mesh models. We will now look at the commonest algorithm, the shadow Z-buffer algorithm, or shadow mapping.

4.8.2 Shadow mapping or the shadow Z-buffer

Possibly the simplest approach to the shadow computation, and one that is easily integrated into a Z-buffer-based renderer, is the shadow Z-buffer developed by Williams in 1978. This technique requires a separate shadow Z-buffer for each light source and in its basic form is only suitable for a scene illuminated by a single light source. Alternatively a single shadow Z-buffer can be used for many light sources and the algorithm executed for each light source.

The algorithm is a two-step process. A scene is 'rendered' and depth information is stored into the shadow Z-buffer using the light source as a viewpoint. No intensities are calculated. This computes a 'depth image' from the light source, of those polygons that are visible to the light source.

The second step is to render the scene using a normal Z-buffer algorithm. This process is enhanced as follows: if a point is visible, a coordinate transformation is used to map (x,y,z), the coordinates of the point in three-dimensional screen space (from the viewpoint), to (x_l,y_l,z_l), the coordinates of the point in screen space from the light point as a coordinate origin. The coordinates (x_l,y_l) are used to index the shadow Z-buffer and the corresponding depth value is compared with z_l. If z_l is greater than the value stored in the shadow Z-buffer for that point, then a surface is nearer to the light source than the point under consideration and the point is in shadow, thus a shadow 'intensity' is used, otherwise the point is rendered as normal. Examples of the algorithm are shown in Figure 8.16 (Colour Plate).

Apart from extending the high memory requirements of the Z-buffer hidden surface removal algorithm, the algorithm also extends its inefficiency. Shadow calculations are performed for surfaces that may be subsequently 'overwritten' – just as shading calculations are.

Anti-aliasing and the shadow Z-buffer

In common with the Z-buffer algorithm, the shadow Z-buffer is susceptible to aliasing artefacts due to point sampling. Two aliasing opportunities occur. First, straightforward point sampling in the creation phase of the shadow Z-buffer produces artefacts. These will be visible along shadow edges – we are considering a hard-edged shadow cast by a point light source. The second aliasing problem is created when accessing the shadow Z-buffer. It is somewhat analogous to the problem created in texture mapping (described in Section 4.6). This problem arises because we are effectively projecting a pixel extent onto the shadow Z-buffer map. This is shown schematically in Figure 4.19. If we consider the so-called pre-image of a square pixel in the shadow Z-buffer map, this will in general be a quadrilateral that encloses a number of shadow Z-buffer pixels. It is this 'many map pixels to one screen pixel' problem that we have to deal with. It means that a pixel may be partly in shadow and partly not and if we make a binary decision then aliasing will occur. We thus consider the fraction of the pixel that is in shadow by computing this from the shadow Z-buffer. This fraction can be evaluated by the z_l comparisons over the set of shadow Z-buffer pixels that the screen pixel projects onto. The fraction is then used to give an appropriate shadow intensity. The process in summary is:

(1) For each pixel calculate four values of (x_l,y_l) corresponding to the four corner points. This defines a quadrilateral in shadow Z-buffer space.

(2) Integrate the information over this quadrilateral by comparing the z value for the screen pixel with each value in the shadow Z-buffer quadrilateral. This gives a fraction that reflects the area of the pixel in shadow.

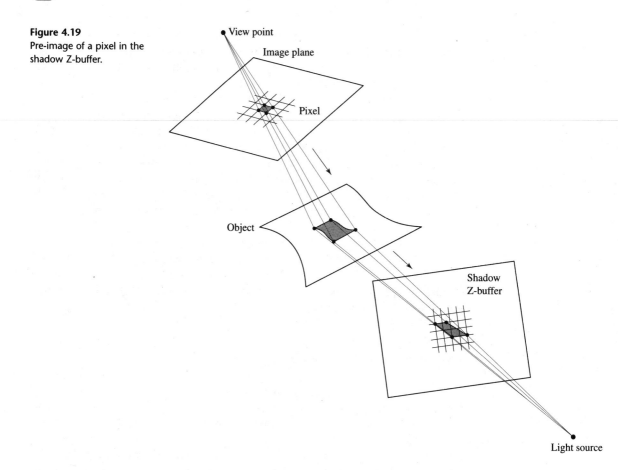

Figure 4.19
Pre-image of a pixel in the shadow Z-buffer.

(3)   We use this fraction to give an appropriate attenuated intensity. The visual effect of this is that the hard edge of the shadow will be softened for those pixels that straddle a shadow boundary.

Further reading

Texture mapping is not covered too well outside research publications. An exception to this is the book by Ebert et al. The two-part mapping idea, together with examples of different combinations of S and O mappings, is described in the paper by Bier and Sloan. The first use of texture mapping in computer graphics seems to be the article by Catmull which mapped two-dimensional texture onto parametrically defined objects.

The three-dimensional texture idea was reported simultaneously by Peachey and Perlin. The work contains impressive illustrations that demonstrate the visual efficacy of this technique. The paper by Blinn on bump mapping contains a full mathematical treatment of his elegant technique together with a discussion of some of its difficulties. (The ubiquitous scale problem appears here.)

The classic mip-map technique is described in the paper by Williams. This does not contain much elaboration on the calculation of the parameter D. More details on the determination of D are to be found in Watt and Watt.

The strategies for dealing with texture magnification do not appear to be dealt with in the literature, and those we have described were abstracted from *Graphics Library* (user manual) 1992 by Silicon Graphics.

Hanrahan and Haeberli developed the three-dimensional paint approach that we have described. Their paper also contains many possible extensions to this technique that we have not mentioned – such as geometry painting which is using the brush to make small scale changes to the geometry of the surface.

Full details of anti-aliasing with the shadow Z-buffer approach are given in the paper by Reeves.

Papers

Bier E.A. and Sloan K.R. (1986). Two-part texture mapping. *IEEE Computer Graphics and Applications*, **6**(9), 40–53

Blinn J.F. (1978). Simulation of wrinkled surfaces. *Proc SIGGRAPH 1978*, 286–92

Catmull E. (1974). Subdivision algorithm for the display of curved surfaces. PhD Thesis, University of Utah

Hanrahan P. and Haeberli P. (1990). Direct WYSIWYG painting and texturing on 3D shapes. *Proc. SIGGRAPH 1990*, 215–23

Peachey D.R. (1985). Solid texturing of complex surfaces. *Proc SIGGRAPH 1985*, 279–86

Perlin K. (1985). An image synthesizer. *Proc SIGGRAPH 1985*, 287–96

Reeves W., Salesin D. and Cook R. (1987). Rendering antialiased shadows with depth maps. *Proc SIGGRAPH 1987*, 283–91

Silicon Graphics User Manual – Graphics Library Vol 2, 1992

Williams L. (1978). Casting curved shadows on curved surfaces. *Proc. SIGGRAPH 1978*, 270–4

Williams L. (1983). Pyramidal parametrics. *Proc SIGGRAPH 1983*, 1–11

Books

Ebert D.S., Musgrave F.K., Peachey D., Perlin K. and Worley S. (1994). *Texturing and Modeling, A Procedural Approach.* New York: Academic Press (Professional)

5 Increasing realism – the evolution of local reflection models

5.1 Perfect reflection models

5.2 Perfect diffuse – empirically spread specular (Phong)

5.3 Physically based specular reflection (Blinn, Cook and Torrance)

5.4 Pre-computing BRDFs

5.5 Physically based diffuse component

Local reflection models, and in particular the Phong model, have been part of mainstream rendering since the mid-1970s. Combined with interpolative shading of polygons, local reflection models are incorporated in almost every conventional renderer. The obvious constraint of locality is the strongest disadvantage of such models but despite the availability of ray tracers and radiosity renderers the mainstream rendering approach is still some variation of the strategy described earlier – in other words, a local reflection model is at the heart of the process. However, nowadays it would be difficult to find a renderer that did not have ad hoc additions such as texture mapping and shadow calculation. Texture mapping adds interest and variety and geometrical shadow calculations overcome the most significant drawback of local models.

Despite the understandable emphasis on the development of global models, there has been some considerable research effort into improving local reflection models. However, not too much attention has been paid to these, and most renderers still use the Phong model – in one sense a tribute to the efficacy and simplicity of this technique, in another an unfortunate ignoring of the real advances that have been made in this area.

An important point concerning local models is that they are used in certain global solutions. As will be discovered in Chapter 6, most simple ray tracers are hybrid models that combine a local reflection model with a global ray traced model. A local model is used at every point to evaluate a contribution that is due to any direct illumination that can be seen from that point. To this is added a (ray traced) component that accounts for indirect illumination. (In fact this is inconsistent because different parameters are used for the local and global contribution, but it is a practice that is widely adopted.)

In this chapter we will look at a representative selection of local models, delving into such questions as: how do we simulate the different light reflection behaviour between, say, shiny plastic and metal that is the same colour? We can mostly perceive such subtle differences in real objects and it is appropriate that we should be able to simulate them in computer graphics.

In general, light reflected from a point on the surface of an object is categorized by a bi-directional reflection distribution function, or BRDF. This term emphasizes that the light reflected in any particular direction (in computer graphics we are mostly interested in light reflected along the viewing direction V) is a function, not only of this direction, but also of the direction of the incoming light. A BRDF can be written as:

$$\mathrm{BRDF} = f(\theta_{in}, \phi_{in}, \theta_{ref}, \phi_{ref}) = f(L, V)$$

and many models used in computer graphics differ amongst themselves according to which of these dependencies are simulated. Figure 5.1(a) shows these angles together with a a BRDF computed for a particular set of angles. The r endered surface shows the magnitude of the reflected light (in any outgoing direction) for an infinitely thin beam of light incident in the direction shown. In practice light would be incident on a surface point from more than one direction and the total reflected light would be obtained by considering a separate BRDF for each incoming light beam.

For many years computer graphics has worked with simple, highly constrained BRDFs. Figure 5.2 gives an idea of the difference between such computer graphics models and what actually happens in practice. The illustrations are cross-sections of the BRDF in the plane containing L and R, the mirror direction, for different angles of θ, the angle of incidence (and reflection). In particular, note the great variation in the shape of the reflection lobes as a function of the wavelength of the incident light, the angle of incidence and the material. In the case of aluminium we see that it can behave like either a mirror surface or a directional diffuse surface depending on the wavelength of the incident light. When we also

Figure 5.1
Bi-directional reflectivity function. (a) A BRDF relates light incident in direction L to light reflected along direction V as a function of the angles θ_{in}, ϕ_{in}, θ_{ref}, ϕ_{ref}. (b) An example of a BRDF.

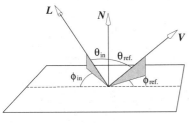

(a)

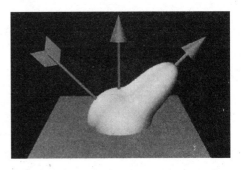

Figure 5.2
BRDF cross-section for different materials and wavelengths (after an illustration by He *et al.* (1991)).

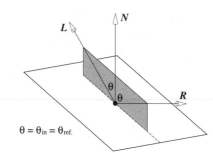

$\theta = \theta_{in} = \theta_{ref.}$

Plane containing *L* and *R* the mirror direction

(a)

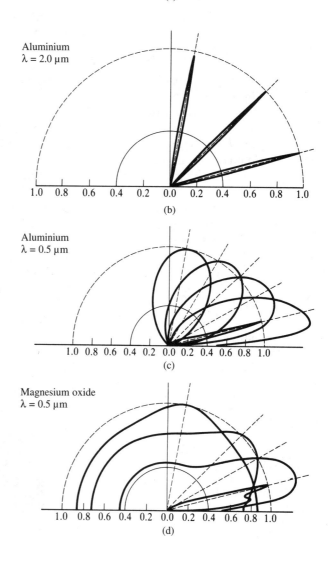

take into account that in practice incident light is never monochromatic (and we thus need a separate BRDF for each wavelength of light that we are considering) we see that the behaviour of reflected light is a far more complex phenomenon than we can model with simple approximations like the Phong model.

Another complication that occurs in reality is the nature of the atmosphere. Most BRDFs used in local reflection models are constrained to apply to light reflected from opaque materials in a vacuum. We mostly do not consider any scattering of reflected light in an atmosphere (in the same way that we do not consider light scattered by an atmosphere before it reaches the object). The reason for this is, of course, simplicity and the subsequent reduction of light intensity calculations to simple comparisons between vectors categorizing surface shapes, light directions and viewing direction.

What follows is a review of the early local reflection models and a short selection of more recent advances. In particular we start by looking at the defects inherent in the Phong model and how these can be overcome. The material is by no means a comprehensive review, but is intended as a representation of these departures from the Phong model that have been simulated to provide ever more subtle variations on the way in which light 'paints' an object.

5.1 Perfect reflection models

As we have discussed, local reflection models used in computer graphics are normally a combination of a diffuse and a specular component. Perfect specular reflection occurs when light strikes a perfect mirror surface and a thin beam of light incident on such a surface reflects according to the well-known law – the outgoing angle is equal to the angle of incidence. Perfect diffuse reflection occurs when incident light is scattered equally in all directions from a perfect matte surface, which could in practice be a very fine layer of powder. Combining separately calculated specular and diffuse components imitates the behaviour of real surfaces and is an enabling assumption in many computer graphics models. Imitating the subtle visual differences between real surfaces has mostly been achieved by incorporating various effects into the specular component as we shall now examine, by looking at a selection of such models. These are:

- The Phong model – perfect diffuse reflection combined with empirically spread specular reflection (1975).
- A physically based specular reflection model developed by Blinn and by Cook and Torrance (1977 and 1982).
- Precalculating BRDFs to be indexed during a rendering process (1987).
- A physically based diffuse model (1993).

This selection is both an historical sample and an illustration of the diverse approaches of researchers to local reflection models.

5.2 Perfect diffuse – empirically spread specular (Phong)

This is in fact the Phong reflection model. We have already discussed the practicalities of this, in particular how it is integrated into a rendering system or strategy. Here we will look at it from a more theoretical point of view that enables a comparison with other direct reflection models.

The Phong reflection model accounts for diffuse refection by Lambert's Cosine Law, where the intensity of the reflected light is a function of the cosine between the surface normal and the incoming light direction.

Phong used an empirically spread specular term. Here the idea is that a practical surface, say, shiny metal, reflects light in a lobe around the perfect mirror direction because it can be considered to be made up of tiny mirrors all oriented in slightly different directions, instead of being made up of a perfectly smooth mirror that takes the shape of the object. Thus the coarseness or roughness of the (shiny) surface can be simulated by the index n – the higher n is the tighter the lobe and the smoother the surface. All surfaces simulated by this model have a plastic-like appearance.

A more subtle aspect of real behaviour, and one that accounts for the difference in the look of plastic and shiny metal, is missing entirely from this model. This is that the amount of light that is specularly reflected depends on the angle of the incoming light. Drive a car into the setting sun and you experience a blinding glare from the road surface – a dull surface at midday has little or no specular component. It was to account for this behaviour, which for any object accounts for subtle changes in the shape of a highlight as a function of the incoming light direction, that an early local reflection model, based on a physical microfacet simulation of the surface, emerged.

We can say that, although the direction of the specular bump in the Phong model depends on the incident direction – the specular bump is symmetrically disposed about the mirror direction – its magnitude does not vary and the Phong model implements a BRDF 'reduced' to:

$$\text{BRDF} = f(\theta_{ref}, \phi_{ref})$$

The BRDF shown in Figure 5.1(b) was calculated using the Phong reflection model.

5.3 Physically based specular reflection (Blinn, Cook and Torrance)

Two years after the appearance of Phong's work in 1975, J. Blinn published a paper describing how a physically based specular component could be used in computer graphics. In 1982 Cook and Torrance extended this model to account for the spectral composition of highlights – their dependency on material type and the angle of incidence of the light. These advances have a subtle effect on the size and colour of a highlight compared to that obtained from the Phong model. The model still retains the separation of the reflected light into a diffuse and a specular component and the new work concentrates entirely on the specular component, the diffuse component being calculated in the same way as before. The model is most successful in rendering shiny metallic-like surfaces, and through the colour variation in the specular highlight being able, for example, to render similar coloured metals differently.

The problem of highlight shape is quite subtle. A highlight is just the image of a light source or sources reflected in the object. Unless the object surface is planar, this image is distorted by the object, and as the direction of the incoming light changes, it falls on a different part of the object, and its shape changes. Therefore we have a highlight image whose overall shape depends on the curvature of the object surface over the area struck by the incident light and the viewing direction, which determines how much of the highlight is visible from the viewing direction. These are the primary factors that determine the shape of the patches of bright light that we see on the surface of an object and are easily calculated by using the Phong model. (In fact highlight shape has recently been proposed as a methodology for three-dimensional object recognition; where we are saying that under certain conditions, the highlight shape is a unique reflection of the shape of the object. This is further discussed in Chapter 15.)

The secondary factor which determines the highlight image is the dependence of its intensity and colour on the angle of incoming light with respect to a tangent plane at the point on the surface under consideration. This identifies the nature of the material to us and enables us to distinguish between metallic and non-metallic objects.

Curiously, despite producing more accurate highlights, these models were not taken up by the graphics community and the cheaper and simpler Phong model remained the more popular, as indeed it does to this day. The possible reason for this is that the differences produced by the more elaborate models are subtle. Objects rendered by the Phong model, although inaccurate and incorrect in highlight rendering, produce objects that look real. In most graphics applications, then and now, this is all that is required. Photo-realism, the much stated goal of three-dimensional computer graphics, depends on very many factors other than local reflection models. To make objects look more real only in this manifestly narrow sense was perhaps not deemed to be worth the cost.

What is meant by a physical simulation in the context of light reflection is that we attempt to model the micro-geometry of the surface that causes the light to reflect, rather than simply imitating the behaviour, as we do in the Phong model, with an empirical term.

This early simulation of specular highlights has four components, and is based on a physical microfacet model consisting of symmetric V-shaped grooves occurring around an average surface (Figure 5.3). We now describe each of these components in turn.

Figure 5.3
Simulating a rough surface
with a collection of
microfacets each considered
as a perfect mirror.
(a) Modelling a surface as
a collection of V-shaped
grooves. (b) Reflection lobes
for different values of *m* in a
Gaussian distribution.

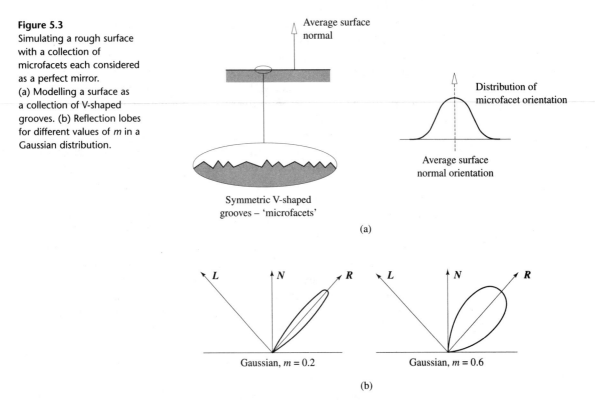

Symmetric V-shaped
grooves – 'microfacets'

(a)

Gaussian, *m* = 0.2   Gaussian, *m* = 0.6

(b)

5.3.1   Modelling the micro-geometry of the surface

A statistical distribution is set up for the orientation of the microfacets (Figure 5.3(a)) and this gives a term D for the light emerging in a particular (viewing) direction. A simple Gaussian can be used:

$$D = k \exp[-(\alpha/m)^2]$$

where α is the angle of the microfacet with respect to the normal of the (mean) surface, that is, the angle between **N** and **H**, and m is the standard deviation of the distribution. Evaluating the distribution at this angle simply returns the number of microfacets with this orientation, that is, the number of microfacets that can contribute to light emerging in the viewing direction. Two reflection lobes for $m = 0.2$ and 0.6 are shown in Figure 5.3(b).

Using microfacets to simulate the dependence of light reflection on surface roughness makes two enabling assumptions:

● it is assumed that the microfacets, although physically small, are large with respect to the wavelength of light;

● the diameter of the incident beam is large enough to intersect a number of microfacets that is sufficient to result in representative behaviour of the reflected light.

In BRDF terms this factor controls the extent to which the specular role bulges.

5.3.2 Shadowing and masking effects

Where the viewing vector or the light orientation vector begins to approach the mean surface, interference effects occur. These are called shadowing and masking. Masking occurs when some reflected light is trapped and shadowing when incident light is intercepted as can be seen from Figure 5.4(a).

The degree of masking and shadowing is dependent on the ratio l_1/l_2 (Figure 5.4(b)) which describes the proportionate amount of the facets contributing to reflected light that is given by:

$$G = 1 - l_1/l_2$$

In the case where l_1 reduces to zero then all the reflected light escapes and

$$G = 1$$

A detailed derivation of the dependence of l_1/l_2 on L, V and H was given by Blinn in 1977. For masking:

$$G_m = 2(N.H)(N.V)/V.H$$

For shadowing the situation is geometrically identical with the role of the vectors L and V interchanged. For masking we have:

$$G_s = 2(N.H)(N.L)/V.H$$

The value of G that must be used is the minimum of G_s and G_m. Thus:

$$G = \text{min\_of } \{1, G_s, G_m\}$$

5.3.3 Viewing geometry

Another pure geometric term is implemented to account for the glare effect mentioned in the previous section. As the angle between the view vector and the mean surface normal is increased towards 90 degrees, an observer sees more and more microfacets and this is accounted for by a term:

$$1/N.V$$

that is, the increase in area of the microfacets seen by a viewer is inversely proportional to the angle between the viewing direction and the surface normal. If there is incident light at a low angle then more of this light is reflected towards the viewer than if the viewer was intercepting light from an angle of incidence close to normal. This effect is countered by the shadowing effect which also comes into play as the viewing orientation approaches the mean surface orientation.

Figure 5.4
The interaction of light with a microfacet reflecting surface. (a) Shadowing and masking. (b) Amount of light which escapes depends on $1 - l_1/l_2$.

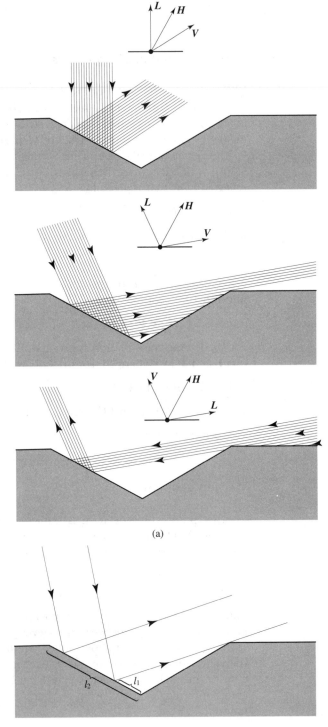

(5.3.4)

Electromagnetic effects

The next term to consider is the Fresnel term F. This term concerns the amount of light that is reflected as opposed to being absorbed – a factor that depends on the material type considered as a perfect mirror surface – which our individual micro-facets are. In other words, we now consider the behaviour for a perfect planar surface, having previously modelled the entire surface as a set of such micro-facets which individually behave as perfect mirrors. This factor determines the strength of the reflected lobe as a function of incidence angle and wavelength. The wavelength dependence accounts for subtle colour effects in the specular high-light.

The Fresnel equation expresses the reflectance of a perfectly smooth mirror surface in terms of the refractive index of the material, μ, and the angle of inci-dence of the light source.

$$F = \frac{1}{2} \frac{\sin^2 (\phi - \theta)}{\sin^2 (\phi + \theta)} + \frac{\tan^2 (\phi - \theta)}{\tan^2 (\phi + \theta)}$$

where:

ϕ is the angle of incidence, that is, $\cos^{-1}(\boldsymbol{L}.\boldsymbol{H}) = \cos^{-1}(\boldsymbol{V}.\boldsymbol{H})$

θ is the angle of refraction

$\sin\theta = \sin\phi/\mu$ where μ is the refractive index of the material

These angles are shown in Figure 5.5(a). F is minimum, that is, most light is absorbed when $\phi = 0$ or normal incidence. No light is absorbed by the surface and F is equal to unity for $\phi = \pi/2$. The wavelength-dependent property of F comes from the fact that μ is a function of wavelength. F is not usually known and Cook and Torrance suggest a practical compromise which is to use the known (measured) value of F_0 to calculate μ and then to use the above equation to evaluate F for any angle of incidence. At normal incidence the above equation reduces to:

$$F_0 = \frac{(\mu - 1)^2}{(\mu + 1)^2}$$

The practical effect of this term is to account for subtle changes in colour of the specular highlight as a function of the angle of incidence. For any material, when the light is incident at an angle nearly parallel to the surface then the colour of the highlight approaches that of the light source. For other angles the colour depends on both the angle of incidence and the material. An example of this dependency is shown for polished copper in Figure 5.5(b).

The effect of this term is to cause the reflected intensity to increase as the angle of incidence increases (just as did the previous term $1/\boldsymbol{N}.\boldsymbol{V}$) – less light is absorbed by the material and more is reflected. (A more subtle effect is that the peak of the specular lobe shifts away from the perfect mirror direction as the angle of incidence increases.)

Figure 5.5
Fresnel equation and polished copper. (a) Angles in the Fresnel equation. (b) Reflectance F as a function of wavelength (λ) and angle of incidence (polished copper). (c) The dependence of F on ϕ for red, green and blue wavelengths.

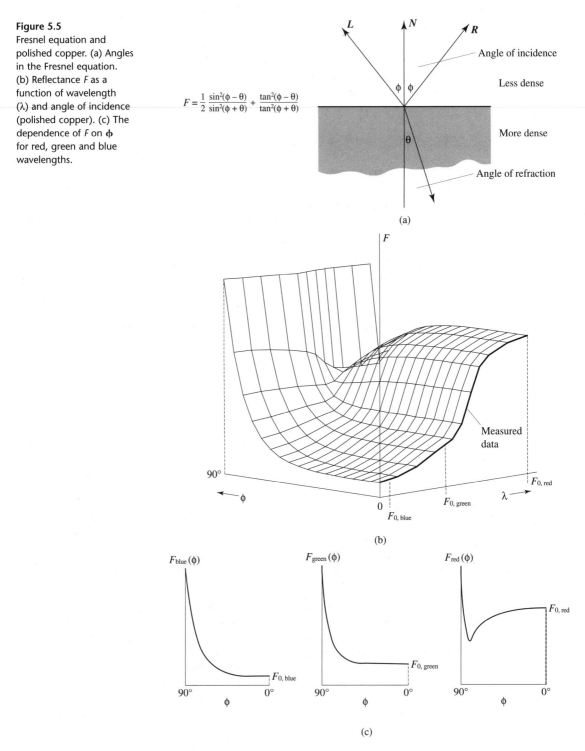

$$F = \frac{1}{2} \frac{\sin^2(\phi - \theta)}{\sin^2(\phi + \theta)} + \frac{\tan^2(\phi - \theta)}{\tan^2(\phi + \theta)}$$

Thus putting these together the specular term now becomes:

specular component = $DGF/(\mathbf{N}.\mathbf{V})$

where D is the micro-geometry term

      G is the shadowing/masking term

      F is the Fresnel term

      $(\mathbf{N}.\mathbf{V})$ is the glare effect term

Summarizing we have:

- a factor that models reflected light intensity as a function of the physical nature of the surface to within the approximations of the geometric simulation;

- two interacting factors that simulate the behaviour of the 'glare' effect which occurs when light is incoming at a high angle (with respect to $\mathbf{N}$, the surface normal) of incidence;

- a factor that relates the reflected light intensity at each (perfect mirror) microfacet to the electro-optical properties of the material. This is a function of the direction of the incoming light and controls subtle second order effects concerning the shape and the colour of the highlight. This effect is important when trying to simulate the difference between, say, shiny plastic and metals. Gold, for example, exhibits yellow highlights when illuminated with white light and the highlight only tends to white when the light grazes the surface.

The specular term is separately calculated and combined with a uniform diffuse term:

$\text{BRDF} = sR_s + dR_d$ where $s+d = 1$

For example, metals are usually simulated with $d = 0$ and $s = 1$ and shiny plastics with $d = 0.9$ and $s = 0.1$. Note that if d is set to zero for metals the specular term controls the colour of the object over its entire surface. Compare this with the Phong reflection model where the colour of the object is always controlled by the diffuse component. The Phong model, because of this, is incapable of producing metallic-looking surfaces and all surfaces objects rendered using Phong have a distinct plastic look.

In this model the reflected light intensity depends on the elevation angle of the incoming light but the model is independent of the azimuth angle of the incident light. Whatever the azimuthal direction of the incoming light, it encounters the same statistical distribution of long, parallel symmetric V-shaped grooves (a somewhat impossible situation in practice). Thus:

$\text{BRDF} = f(\boldsymbol{\theta}_{in}, \boldsymbol{\theta}_{ref}, \boldsymbol{\phi}_{ref})$

A pair of BRDFs for a low and high angle of incidence are shown in Figure 5.6. This shows a specular lobe increasing in value (and also moving away from the mirror reflection direction) as the angle of incidence is increased towards the

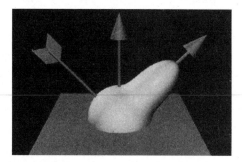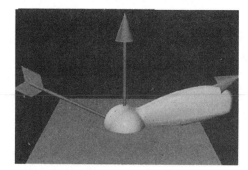

Figure 5.6
BRDFs for different angles of incidence in the Blinn reflection model.

grazing angle. Figure 5.7 (Colour Plate) gives an idea of the variety of object appearances that can be achieved using this model.

5.4 Pre-computing BRDFs

One of the main inadequacies of the previous approach is that it cannot be used to model anisotropic surfaces. Many surfaces exhibit anisotropy reflection characteristics. Cloth and 'brushed' metal used in 'decorative' engineering applications – like car wheels – are two examples. Consider cloth, for example: this exhibits anisotropic reflection because it is made up of weaves of parallel threads with circular cross-sections. Each thread scatters light narrowly when the incident light is in a plane parallel to the direction of the thread, and more widely when the incident plane is parallel to the circular cross-section of the thread. The two popular approaches to including anisotropic behaviour in BRDFs have been to set up special surface models, usually based on cylinders and pre-calculation.

In 1987 a model was reported that could deal with the dependence of the azimuth angle of the incoming light. The model pre-calculates a BRDF for each L represented by a hemisphere divided into bins indexed by V. The BRDF is calculated by ray tracing for each incoming direction a bundle of parallel, randomly positioned rays as they strike the surface and reflect to hit the surrounding hemisphere. The dependency of the BRDF on angles is then:

$$\text{BRDF} = f(\theta_{\text{in}}, \phi_{\text{in}}, \theta_{\text{ref}}, \phi_{\text{ref}})$$

The BRDF is generated by firing rays or beams onto a surface element that encompasses a sufficiently large area of the microsurface. The surface element is modelled by an array or grid of triangular microfacets. The rays that hit the element without being shadowed and emerge without being masked make a contribution to the BRDF, and the complete function is the sum of all such contributions. This information is built up by dividing a hemisphere into a number of cells or bins. A representation of this process is shown in Figure 5.8. The surface microfacets are perturbed out of the mean plane by a bump map as the

Figure 5.8
Modelling a surface with
height-field perturbed
triangular microfacets.

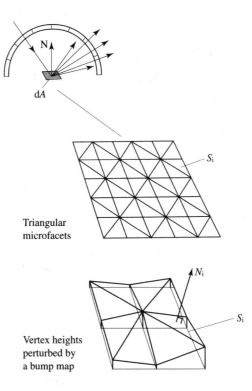

Hemisphere surrounding microsurface element
is divided into 24 × 24 cells

N

dA

S_i

Triangular
microfacets

N_i

S_i

Vertex heights
perturbed by
a bump map

figure suggests. Note that an advantage of this approach is that there is no restriction on the small-scale geometry – the microfacets do not need to form a Gaussian distribution, for example.

The BRDF is then a coarsely sampled version of a continuous BRDF. The pre-calculation is built up by considering each cell to be a source of incoming light and calculating the resulting reflection into the hemisphere. When a surface is being rendered the hemisphere closest to the angle of incident light is selected. The north pole of this distribution then has to be aligned with the surface normal at the point and the pre-calculated BRDF then gives the reflected intensity in the viewing direction.

5.5 Physically based diffuse component

Until fairly recently local reflection models in computer graphics have concentrated almost exclusively on the specular component of reflected light and, as we have seen, these have been based on physical micro-surface modelling.

Diffuse light is usually modelled on Lambert's Cosine Law which assumes that reflected light is isotropic and proportional in intensity to the cosine of the angle of incidence. Surface simulations of diffuse light are not possible because diffuse reflection originates from light that actually enters the material. This component is absorbed and scattered within the reflecting material. The wavelength-dependent absorption accounts for the colour of the material – incident white light is in effect filtered by the material. It is the multiple scattering within the material that causes the emerging light to be (approximately) isotropic. Thus a physical simulation of diffuse reflection would have to be based on subsurface scattering.

We could ask the question: what is wrong with sticking with Lambert's Law? The answer to this would be the same as the motivation for the development of physically based specular models – there are subtle effects produced by diffusely reflecting light that are responsible for the distinctive look of certain materials. Recent work by Hanrahan and Krueger develops a physically based model for diffuse reflection that the authors claim is particularly appropriate for layered materials appearing in nature, such as biological tissues (skin, leaves and so on) and inorganic substances like snow and sand. The outcome of the model is, of course, anisotropy – reflecting the fact that very few real materials exhibit isotropic diffuse behaviour.

Hanrahan and Kreuger specify the reflected light form a point on the surface as

$$L_r = L_{rs} + L_{rv}$$

where L_{rs} is the reflected light due to surface scattering – imperfect specular reflection – and L_{rv} is the reflected light that is due to subsurface scattering. The algorithm that determines the subsurface scattering is based on a one-dimensional transport model solved using a Monte Carlo approach. The details are outside the scope of this text; more important for our purposes is a conceptual understanding of the advances made by these researchers and the visual ramifications of them.

The combination of those two components produces anisotropic behaviour because of a number of factors that we will now describe. First, consider the angle of incidence of the light. For a plane surface the amount of light entering the surface depends on Fresnel's law – the more light that enters the surface, the higher will be the contribution or influence from subsurface events to the total reflected light L_r. So the influence of L_{rv} depends on the angle of incidence. Subsurface scattering depends on the physical properties of the material. A material is modelled by a suspension of scattering sites or particles and parametrized by absorption and scattering cross-sections. These express the probability of occurrence per unit path length of a scattering or absorption. The relative size of these parameters determines whether the scattering is forward, backward or isotropic.

The effect of these two factors is shown, for a simple case, in Figure 5.9. The first row shows high/low specular reflection as a function of angle of incidence. The behaviour of reflected light is dominated by surface scattering or specular reflection when the angle of incidence is high and by subsurface scattering when

Figure 5.9
Reflection behaviour due to Hanrahan and Kreuger's model (courtesy of Pat Hanrahan).

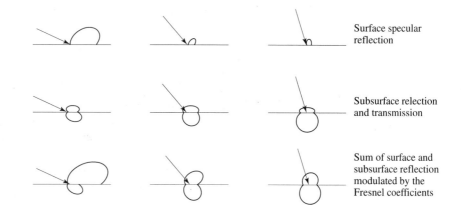

Surface specular reflection

Subsurface relection and transmission

Sum of surface and subsurface reflection modulated by the Fresnel coefficients

the angle of incidence is low. As we have seen this behaviour is modelled, to a certain extent, by the Cook and Torrance model mentioned in Section 5.3. The second row shows reflection lobes due to subsurface scattering and it can be seen that materials can exhibit backward, isotropic or forward scattering behaviour. (The bottom lobes do not, of course, contribute to L_r but are nevertheless important when considering materials that are made up of multiple layers and thin translucent materials that are back lit.) The third row shows that the combination of L_{rs} and L_{rv} will generally result in non-isotropic behaviour which exhibits the following general attributes:

- reflection increases as material layer thickness increases due to increased subsurface scattering,

- subsurface scattering can be backward, isotropic or forward, and

- reflection from subsurface scattering tends to produce functions that are flattened on top of the lobe compared with the (idealized) hemisphere of Lambert's law.

Such factors result in the subtle differences between the model and Lambert's law. Hanrahan and Kreuger provide demonstrations of a human face (albeit dead) and leaves. Figure 5.10 (Colour Plate) shows the model as tested on human skin. Hanrahan and Kreuger considered skin to consist of two layers with both layers having the same refractive index and a different density of randomly distributed absorbers and scatterers. The image demonstrates that a more 'silk-like' appearance is obtained with the multi-layer model.

Further reading

The most comprehensive general reference to this material is Vol. 2 of the textbook by Glassner (see Chapter 1).

Blinn J.F. (1977). Models of light reflection for computer synthesized pictures. *Proc SIGGRAPH 1977*, 192–98

Cook R.L. and Torrance K.E. (1982). A reflectance model for computer graphics. *Proc. SIGGRAPH 1982*, 307–16

Hanrahan P. and Krueger W. (1993). Reflection from layered surfaces due to sub-surface scattering. *Proc. SIGGRAPH 1993*, 165–74

He X.D., Torrance K.E., Sillion F.X. and Greenberg D. P. (1991). A comprehensive physical model for light reflection. *Computer Graphics*, **25**(4), 175–86

6 Increasing realism – global illumination or following the light

6.1 The evolution of global illumination algorithms

6.2 Towards L(D|S)*E

6.3 Whitted ray tracing – the details

6.4 Further developments in ray tracing illumination model

6.5 Classical radiosity

This chapter begins with a definition of global illumination in terms of light interaction mechanisms at object surfaces and categorization of global paths from a light source. It then overviews the main algorithms that offer a (partial) solution to the global illumination problem. The chapter is completed with a more detailed study of ray tracing and radiosity – the two most common global illumination algorithms. These studies are concerned with the algorithmic detail whereas the overview describes the algorithms in terms of that part of the global illumination problem that they attend to. The material in this chapter should be read in conjunction with the comparative image study in Chapter 8. This compares all image synthesis methods, including global illumination methods. The idea of this study is to examine side by side the visual advantages and defects of all the rendering methods dealt with in the text.

It is probably the case that in the general pursuit of photo-realism, most research effort has gone into solving the global illumination problem. Although, as we have seen in Chapter 5, considerable parallel work has been carried out in light/surface interaction, workers have been attracted to the difficult problem of simulating the interaction of light with an entire environment. Light has to be tracked through the environment from emitter(s) to sensor(s), rather than just from an emitter to a surface and then directly to the sensor or eye. Such an approach does not then require add-on algorithms for shadows which are simply areas in which the global illumination level is reduced due to the proximity of a nearby object. Other global illumination effects such as reflection of objects in each other and transparency effects can also be correctly modelled.

It is not clear how important global illumination is to photo-realism. Certainly it is the case that we are accustomed to 'closed' man-made environments where there is much global interaction but the extent to which this interaction has to be simulated to achieve a degree of realism acceptable for most computer graphics applications is still an open problem. Rather the problem has been vigorously pursued as a pure research problem in its own right on the assumption that improvements in the accuracy of global interaction will be valuable.

As we discussed in the introductory chapter, two accepted methods have now emerged. These are ray tracing and radiosity and, for reasons that will soon become clear, they both, in their most commonly implemented forms, simulate only a subset of global interaction, ray tracing attending to (perfect) specular interaction and radiosity to (perfect) diffuse interaction. In other words, current practical solutions to the problem deal with its inherent intractability by attending to particular global interactions, ignoring the remainder and by considering interactions to be perfect. In the case of specular interaction 'perfect' means that an infinitesimally thin beam hitting a surface reflects without spreading – the surface is assumed perfect. In the case of perfect diffuse interaction we assume that an incoming beam of light reflects equally in all directions into the hemisphere centred at the point of reflection.

Ignoring finite computing resources, a solution to the global interaction problem is simply stated. We start at the light source(s) and follow every light path (or ray of light) as it travels through the environment, stopping when the light hits the eye point, has its energy reduced below some minimum due to absorption in the objects that it has encountered, or travels out of the environment into space. To see the relevance of global illumination algorithms we need ways of describing the problem – models that capture the essence of the behaviour of light in an environment.

The first model that we will look at was introduced into the computer graphics literature in 1986 by Kajiya and is known as the rendering equation. It encapsulates global illumination by describing what happens at a point x on a surface in terms of the light travelling from that point in a particular direction. It is a completely general mathematical statement of the problem and global illumination algorithms can be categorized in terms of this equation. In fact Kajiya states that its purpose:

is to provide a unified context for viewing them (rendering algorithms) as more or less accurate approximations to the solution for a single equation

The integral in Kajiya's original notation is given by:

$$I(x,x') = g(x,x')[\varepsilon(x,x') + \int_s \rho(x,x',x'')I(x',x'')dx'']$$

where

$I(x,x')$ is the transport intensity or the intensity of light passing from point x' to point x

$g(x,x')$ is the visibility function between x and x'. If x and x' cannot see each other then this is zero. If they are visible then g varies as the inverse square of the distance between them.

$\varepsilon(x,x')$ is the transfer emittance from x to x'

$\rho(x,x',x'')$ is the scattering term or bi-directional reflectivity function with respect to direction x' and x''. It is the intensity of the energy scattered towards x by a surface point located at x' arriving from point or direction x''

The integral is over s, all points on all surfaces in the scene, or equivalently over all points on the hemisphere situated at point x'. The equation states that the transport intensity from point x' to point x is equal to (any) light emitted from x' towards x plus the light scattered from x' towards x from all other surfaces in the scene – that is, that originate from direction x''.

Another way of categorizing the behaviour of global illumination algorithms is to detail which surface to surface interactions they implement or simulate. This is a much simpler non-mathematical categorization and it enables an easy comparison and classification of the common algorithms. We consider which interactions between pairs of interacting surfaces are implemented as light travels from source to sensor. Thus at a point, incoming light may be scattered or reflected diffusely or specularly and may itself have originated from a specular or diffuse reflection at the previous surface in the path. We can then say that for pairs of consecutive surfaces along a light path we have (Figure 6.1):

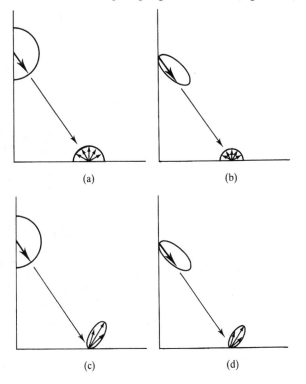

(a)

(b)

(c)

(d)

Figure 6.1

The four 'mechanisms' of light transport: (a) diffuse to diffuse; (b) specular to diffuse; (c) diffuse to specular; (d) specular to specular (after Wallace et al. (1987)).

- diffuse to diffuse transfer
- specular to diffuse transfer
- diffuse to specular transfer
- specular to specular transfer

In an environment where only diffuse surfaces exist, only diffuse–diffuse interaction is possible and such scenes are solved using the radiosity method. Similarly an environment containing only specular surfaces can only exhibit specular interaction and (Whitted) ray tracing deals with these. Basic radiosity does not admit any other transfer mechanism except diffuse–diffuse and it excludes the important specular–specular transfer. Ray tracing, on the other hand, can only deal with specular–specular interaction. More recent algorithms, such as 'backwards' ray tracing and enhancements of radiosity for specular interaction, require a categorization of all the interactions in a light journey from source to sensor, and this led to Heckbert's string notation for listing all the interactions that occur along a path of a light ray as it travels from source (L) to the eye (E). Here a light path from the light source to the first hit is termed L, subsequent paths involving transfer mechanisms at a surface point are catego-

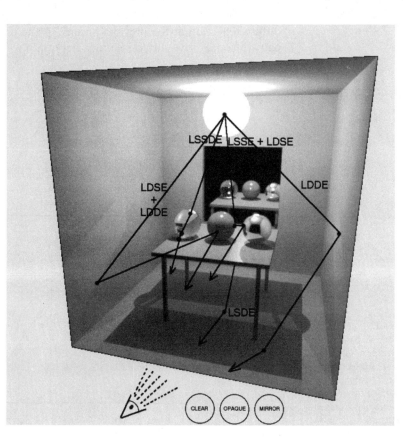

Figure 6.2
A selection of global illuminations paths in a simple environment. See also the colour plate version of this figure.

rized as DD, SD, DS or SS. Figure 6.2 (also a Colour Plate) shows an example of a simple scene and various paths. The path that finally terminates in the eye is called E. The paths in the example are:

- LDDE For this path the viewer sees the shadow cast by the table. The light reflects diffusely from the right-hand wall on to the floor. Note that any light reflected from a shadow area must have a minimum of two interactions between L and E.

- LDSE + LDDE Here the user sees the dark side of the sphere which is not receiving any direct light. The light is modelled as a point source, so any area below the 'equator' of the sphere will be in shadow. The diffuse illumination reflected diffusely from the wall is directed towards the eye and because the sphere is shiny the reflection to the eye is both specular and diffuse.

- LSSE + LDSE Light is reflected from the perfect mirror surface to the eye and the viewer sees a reflection of the opaque or coloured ball in the mirror surface.

- LSDE Here the viewer sees a shadow area that is lighter than the main table shadow. This is due to the extra light reflected from the mirror and directed underneath the table.

- LSSDE This path has three interactions between L and E and the user sees a caustic on the table top which is a diffuse surface. The first specular inter-action takes place at the top surface of the sphere and light from the point source is refracted through the sphere. There is a second specular interaction when the light emerges from the sphere and hits the diffuse table surface. The effect of the reflection is to concentrate light rays travelling through the sphere into a smaller area on the table top than they would occupy if the transparent sphere was not present. Thus the user sees a bright area on the diffuse surface.

A complete global illumination algorithm would have to include any light path which can be written as L(D|S)*E, where | means 'or' and * indicates repetition. The application of a local reflection model implies paths of type LD|S (the intensity of each being calculated separately then combined as in the Phong reflection model) and the addition of a hidden surface removal algorithm implies simulation of types LD|SE. Thus local reflection models only simulate strings of length unity (between L and E) and viewing a point in shadow implies a string which is at least of length 2.

6.1 The evolution of global illumination algorithms

We will now look at the development of popular or established global illumination algorithms using as a basis for our discussion the preceding concepts. We will deal with the algorithms in order of their historical appearance. The idea of this section is to give a view of the algorithms in terms of global interaction.

Details more concerned with the implementation of the algorithms will come later. (The terminology for some ray tracing algorithms is confusing; we will use the most popular or original form of the terminology together – in brackets – with the alternatives.)

Return to consideration of the brute force solution to the problem. There we considered the notion of starting at a light source and following every ray of light that was emitted through the scene and stated that this was a computationally intractable problem. Approximations to a solution come from constraining the light/object interaction in some way and/or only considering a small subset of the rays that start at the light and bounce around the scene. The main approximations which led to ray tracing and radiosity constrained the scene to contain only specular reflectors or only (perfect) diffuse reflectors, respectively.

We will now describe global algorithms starting with ray tracing (and its popular variations) and classical radiosity. This will be followed by a brief discussion on how – in principle – ray tracing and radiosity can be extended to a full global solution. The selection of the global algorithms is necessarily incomplete. This topic is one of the most vigorously researched subjects in rendering and a substantial number of approaches have been reported in the past decade. Finally we give a comprehensive description of the original or classical ray tracing and radiosity algorithms – the foundation algorithms that started it all, and the algorithms that are now commonly found in practical or commercial systems.

6.1.1 Whitted ray tracing

Whitted ray tracing (visibility tracing, eye tracing) traces light rays in the reverse direction of propagation from the eye back into the scene towards the light source. To generate a two-dimensional projection of a scene using ray tracing we are only interested in those light rays that end at the sensor or eye point and therefore it makes sense to start at the eye and trace rays out into the scene. A simple representation of the algorithm is shown in Figure 6.3. The process is often visualized as a tree where each node is a surface hit point. At each node we spawn a light ray and a reflected ray or a transmitted (refracted) ray or both.

Whitted ray tracing is a hybrid of a global illumination model onto which is added a local model. Consider the global interaction. The classic algorithm only includes perfect specular interaction. Rays are shot into the scene and when they hit a surface a reflected (and transmitted) ray is spawned at the point of intersection and themselves are then followed recursively. The process stops when the energy of a ray drops below a predetermined minimum or if it leaves the scene and travels out into empty space or if a ray hits a surface that is perfectly diffuse. Thus the global part of ray tracing only accounts for pure specular–specular interaction. Theoretically there is nothing to stop us calculating diffuse global interaction, but at every hit point an incoming ray would spawn reflected rays in every direction into a hemispherical surface centred on the point.

Figure 6.3

Whitted ray tracing: when a ray strikes a partially transmitting sphere, a transmitted and a reflected ray are 'spawned' at the first hit point.

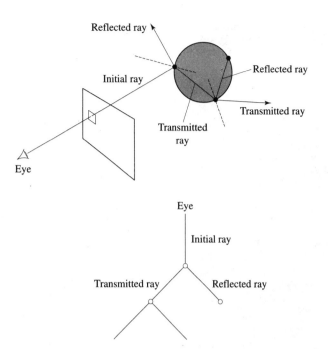

To the global specular component is added a direct contribution calculated by shooting a ray from the point to the light source. The visibility of the point from the light source and its direction can be used to calculate a local or direct diffuse component and thus (direct) diffuse reflection (but not diffuse–diffuse) interaction is considered. This is sometimes called the shadow ray or shadow feeler because if it hits any object between the point under consideration and the light source then we know that the point is in shadow. However, a better term is light ray to emphasize that it is used to calculate a direct contribution (using a local reflection model) which is then passed up the tree. The main problem with Whitted ray tracing is its restriction to specular interaction – most practical scenes consist of predominantly diffuse surfaces.

If we restrict ourselves to considering global specular interaction then we can only consider objects that have perfect mirror surfaces – we could not have objects that possessed their own colour. To add coloured objects into a Whitted ray tracer we consider a direct diffuse component by considering objects to exhibit (separate) diffuse and specular reflection as in local reflection models. Consider the LSSE + LDSE path in Figure 6.2 reproduced in Figure 6.4 together with the ray tree. The initial ray from the eye hits the perfect mirror sphere. For this sphere there is no contribution from a local diffuse model. At the next intersection we hit the opaque sphere and trace a global specular component which hits the ceiling (ignoring the light source), a perfect diffuse surface, and the recursion is terminated. Also at that point we have a contribution from the local diffuse model for the sphere and the viewer sees in the pixel associated with that ray the colour of the reflected image of the opaque sphere in the mirror sphere.

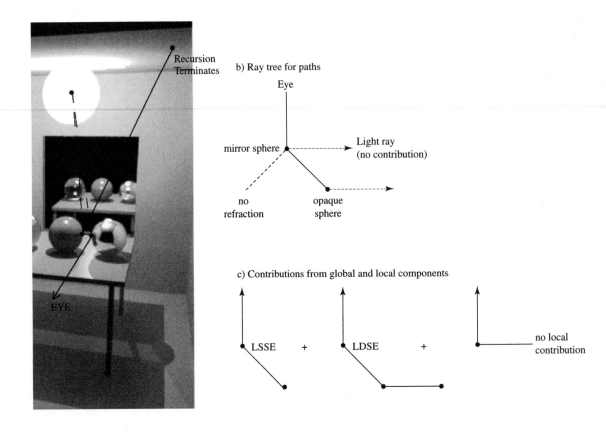

Figure 6.4

Whitted ray tracing: the relationship between light paths and local and global contributions for one of the cases shown in Figure 6.2.

A little thought will reveal that the paths which can be simulated by Whitted ray tracing are constrained to be LS*E and LDS*E. Ray traced images therefore exhibit reflections in the surfaces of shiny objects of nearby objects. If the objects are transparent any objects that the viewer can see behind the transparent object are refracted. Also, as will be seen shortly, shadows are calculated as part of the model – but only 'perfect' or hard-edged shadows.

6.1.2 Distributed ray tracing

Distributed ray tracing (distribution ray tracing, stochastic ray tracing), developed by Cook in 1986, was presumably motivated by the need to deal with the fact that Whitted ray tracing could only account for perfect specular interaction which would only occur in scenes made up of objects that consisted of perfect mirror surfaces or perfect transmitters. The effect that a Whitted ray tracer produces for (perfect) solid glass is particularly disconcerting or unrealistic. For example, consider a sphere of perfect glass. The viewer sees a circle inside which perfectly sharp refraction has occurred (Figure 6.5). There is no sense of the

Figure 6.5
Perfect refraction through
a solid glass sphere is
indistinguishable from
texture mapping.

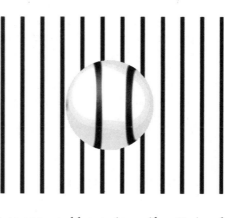

sphere as an object as one would experience if scattering due to imperfections had occurred.

Distributed ray tracing again only considers specular interaction but this time imperfect specular interaction is simulated by using the ray tracing approach and constructing at every hit point a reflection lobe. The shape of the lobe can depend on the surface properties of the material. Instead of spawning a single transmitted or reflected ray at an intersection, a group of rays is spawned which samples the reflection lobe. It is a Monte Carlo technique which replaces the integral over the reflection lobe in the outgoing direction with a set of samples. This produces more realistic ray traced scenes. The images of objects reflected in the surfaces of nearby objects appear blurred, transparency effects are more realistic because scattering imperfections can be simulated and shadows can be soft edged. Consider again the previous example redrawn in Figure 6.6. If, as would

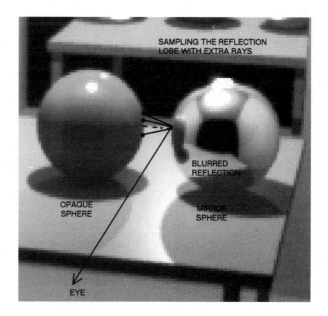

Figure 6.6
Distributed ray tracing for
reflection (see Figure 6.2 for
the complete geometry of
this case).

be the case in practice, the mirror surface of the sphere was not physically perfect, then we would expect to see a blurred reflection of the opaque sphere in the mirror sphere.

Thus the path classification scheme is again LDS*E or LS*E but this time all the paths are calculated (or more precisely an estimation of the effects of all the paths is calculated by judicious sampling). In Figure 6.6 three LDSE paths are discovered by a single eye ray. The points on the sphere hit by these rays are combined into a single ray (and eventually a single pixel).

6.1.3 Two-pass ray tracing

Two-pass ray tracing (or bi-directional ray tracing) was originally developed to incorporate the specular to diffuse transfer mechanism into the general ray tracing model. This accounts for caustics which is the pattern formed on a diffuse surface by light rays being refracted through a medium like glass or water (see Figure 6.19 – Colour Plate). Thus one can usually see on the bottom and sides of a swimming pool beautiful elliptical patterns of bright light which are due to sunlight refracting at the wind-disturbed water surface, causing the light energy to vary across the diffuse surface of the pool sides. Figure 6.7 shows a ray from the scene in Figure 6.2 emanating from the light source refracting through the sphere and contributing to a caustic that forms on the (diffuse) table top. This is an LSSD path.

In general, two-pass ray tracing simulates paths of type LS*DS*E. The algorithm 'relies' on there being a single D interaction i encountered from both the light source and the eye. The first pass consists of shooting rays from the light source and following them through the specular interactions until they hit a

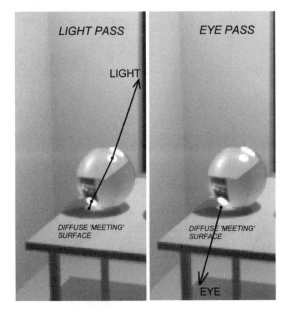

Figure 6.7
Two-pass ray tracing for the LSDDE path in Figure 6.2.

diffuse surface (Figure 6.7(a)). The light energy from each ray is then deposited or cached on the diffuse surface, which has been subdivided in some manner, into elements or bins. In effect the first pass imposes a texture map or illumination map – the varying brightness of the caustic – on the diffuse surface. The resolution of the illumination map is critical. For a fixed number of shot light rays, too fine a map may result in map elements receiving no rays and too coarse a map results in blurring.

The second pass is the eye trace – conventional Whitted ray tracing – which terminates on the diffuse surface and uses the stored energy in the illumination map as an approximation to the light energy that would be obtained if diffuse reflection was followed in every possible direction from the hit point. In the example shown the second pass simulates a DE path (or ED path with respect to the trace direction). The 'spreading' of the illumination from rays traced in the first pass over the diffuse surface relies on the fact that the rate of change of diffuse illumination over a surface is slow. It is important to note that there can only be one diffuse surface included in any path. Both the eye trace and the light trace terminate on the diffuse surface – it is the 'meeting point' of both traces.

6.1.4

Radiosity

Classic radiosity implements diffuse–diffuse interaction. Instead of following individual rays, 'interaction' between patches (or polygons) in the scene are considered. Radiosity differs from other global illumination algorithms in two respects. The solution is view independent and consists of a constant radiosity for every patch in the scene. This is known as the constant radiosity assumption. View independence means that a solution is calculated for every point in the scene rather than just those points that can be seen from the eye (view dependent). This implies that a radiosity solution has to be followed by another process or pass that computes a projection, but most work is carried out in the radiosity pass. A problem or contradiction with classical radiosity is that the initial discretization of the scene has to be carried out before the process is started but the best way of performing this depends on the solution. In other words, we do not know the best way to divide up the scene until after we have a solution or a partial solution. This is an outstanding problem with the radiosity method and accounts for its difficulty of use.

A way of visualizing the radiosity process is to start by considering the light source as an (array of) emitting patches. We shoot light into the scene from the source(s) and consider the diffuse–diffuse interaction between a light patch and all the receiving patches that are visible from the light patch – the first hit patch. An amount of light is deposited or cached on these patches which are then ordered according to the amount of energy that has fallen onto the patch and has yet to be shot back into the scene. The one with the highest unshot energy is selected and this is considered as the next shooting patch. The process continues iteratively until a (high) percentage of the initial light energy is distributed around the scene. This convergence test derives from the fact that the reflectivity coefficient associated with each patch is, by definition, less than unity and at each phase in the iteration more and more of the initial light is absorbed. A series of illustrations now illustrates the idea. Figure 6.8 (Colour Plate) shows a solution in progress using this algorithm. The stage shown is the state of the solution after 20, 250 and 5000 iterations. The four illustrations in each case are:

- The radiosity solution as output from the iteration process. Each patch is allocated a constant radiosity.

- The previous solution after it has been subject to interpolation process.

- The same solution with the addition of an ambient term. The ambient 'lift' is distributed evenly amongst all patches in the scene, to give an early well-lit solution (this enhancement is described in detail in Section 6.5.4).

- The difference between the previous two images. This gives a visual indication of the energy that had to be added to account for the unshot radiosity.

The transfer of light between any two patches – the diffuse–diffuse interaction – is calculated by considering the geometric relationship between the patches (expressed as the form factor). Compared to ray tracing we follow light from the light source through the scene as patch to patch diffuse interaction, but instead of following individual rays of light, the form factor between two patches averages the effect of the paths that join the patches together. This way of considering the radiosity method is in fact implemented as an algorithm structure. It is called the progressive refinement method. The iteration shown visually in Figure 6.8 is in fact a stage in the solution of a very large set of linear equations.

This simple concept has to be modified by a visibility process (not to be confused by the subsequent calculation of a projection which includes, in the normal way, hidden surface removal) that takes into account the fact that in general a patch may be only partially visible to another because of some intervening patch. The end result is the assignment of a constant radiosity to each patch in the scene – a view-independent solution which is then injected into a Gouraud-style renderer to produce a projection. In terms of path classification, conventional radiosity is LD*E.

The obvious problem with radiosity is that although man-made scenes usually consist mostly of diffuse surfaces, specular objects are not unusual and these cannot be handled by a radiosity renderer. A more subtle problem is that the scene has to be discretized into patches or polygons before the radiosities are computed and difficulties occur if this polygonization is too coarse. We discuss these problems in Section 6.5.3 and also in Chapter 8.

6.2 Towards L(D|S)*E

The main approaches to global illumination have been to extend radiosity to include specular–specular transfer and to develop a form of ray tracing that is not restricted to specular–specular interaction. We will now briefly describe three such approaches.

6.2.1 Extending radiosity

By combining radiosity with two-pass ray tracing the path classification LS*DS*E can be extended to LS*(D*)S*E, the inclusion of radiosity extending the D component to D*. This implies the following ordering for an extended radiosity algorithm. Light ray tracing is employed first and light rays are traced from the source(s) through all specular–specular transports until a diffuse surface is reached and the light energy is deposited. This accounts for the LS* paths. A radiosity solution is then invoked using these values as emitting patches and the deposited energy is distributed through the D* chain. Finally an eye pass is initiated and this provides the final projection and the ES* or ES*D paths.

Comparing the string LS*(D*)S*E with the complete global solution, we see that the central D* paths should be extended to (D*S*D*)* to make LS*(D*S*D*)*S*E which is equivalent to the complete global solution L(S|D)*E. Conventional or classical radiosity does not include diffuse to diffuse transfer that takes place via an intermediate specular surface. In other words, once we invoke the radiosity phase we need to include the possibility of transfer via an intermediate specular path DSD.

The first and perhaps the simplest approach to including a specular transfer into the radiosity solution was based on modifying the classical radiosity algorithm for flat specular surfaces such as mirrors and is called the virtual window approach. This idea is shown in Figure 6.9. Conventional radiosity calculates the geometric relationship between the light source and the floor and the LDE path is accounted for by the diffuse–diffuse interaction between these two surfaces. (Note that since the light source is itself an emitting diffuse patch we can term the path LDE or DDE.) What is missing from this is the contribution of light energy from the LSD or DSD path that would deposit a bright area of light on the floor. The DSD path from the light source via the mirror to the floor can be accounted for by constructing a virtual environment 'seen' through the mirror

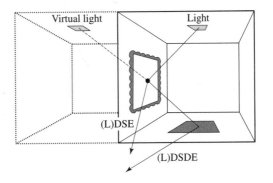

Figure 6.9
The virtual environment method for incorporating DSD paths in the radiosity method.

as a window. The virtual light source then acts as if it was the real light source reflected from the mirror. However, we still need to account for the LSE path which is the detailed reflected image formed in the mirror. This is view dependent and is determined during a second pass ray tracing phase. The fact that this algorithm only deals with what is in effect a special case illustrates the inherent difficulty of extending radiosity to include other transfer mechanisms.

Path tracing

Path tracing is a generalization of Whitted ray tracing where rays are traced from the eye into the scene in reverse direction of light propagation. Previously we have said that there is no theoretical bar to extending ray tracing to handle all light surface interactions including diffuse reflection and transmission for a hit point, just the impossibility of the computation. Suggested by Kajiya in 1986, path tracing is another Monte Carlo approach which initiates a large number of initial rays at each pixel (instead of (usually) one with Whitted ray tracing) and follows a single path for each ray through the scene rather than allowing a ray to spawn multiple reflected children at each hit point. The method is best understood by comparing it with the other two ray tracing algorithms (Whitted ray tracing and distributed ray tracing). Figure 6.10 encapsulates this comparison in the form of three ray trees which express the generation of rays that are produced by an initial ray as it passes through the scene. Whitted ray tracing exhibits a binary tree with a light ray emanating from each node (a single light ray for every light source). Distributed ray tracing is a 'bushy' version of this tree, and path tracing reduces the ray tree to a single path. Kajiya uses such a diagram to point out that Whitted ray tracing is wasteful in the sense that as the algorithm goes deeper into the tree it does more and more work. At the same time the contribution to the pixel intensity from events deep in the tree becomes less and less. In Kajiya's approach the tree has a branching ratio of one, and at each hit point a random variable, from a distribution based on the specular and

Figure 6.10
Ray trees for each ray tracing method compared.
(a) Whitted ray tracing.
(b) Distributed ray tracing.
(c) Path tracing.

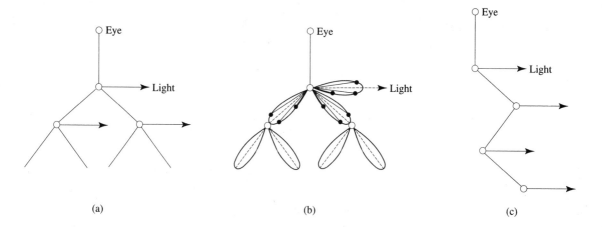

(a)   (b)   (c)

diffuse BRDFs, is used to shoot a single ray. Kajiya points out that this process has to maintain the correct proportion of reflection, refraction and shadow rays for each pixel. The process is truncated by accumulating the probabilities associated with each hit along the path and stopping when this falls below a threshold. As with conventional ray tracing a light or shadow ray is cast from each hit and light energy at each node is passed back up the path, however, the paths followed are no longer restricted to specular interaction and the method simulates full L(D|S)*E interaction.

The quality of the final image depends on the number of rays shot per pixel (Kajiya used 40 rays per pixel) and the way in which the pixel is subdivided is controlled by an importance sampling technique.

6.2.3 The RADIANCE renderer

The RADIANCE renderer is probably the most well-known global illumination renderer. Developed by Ward over a period of nine years, it is a strategy, based on light-backwards or eye ray tracing, that solves a version of the rendering equation under most conditions. The emphasis of this work is firmly on the accuracy required for architectural simulations under a variety of lighting conditions varying from sunlight to complex artificial lighting set-ups. The algorithm is effectively a combination of deterministic and stochastic approaches and Ward describes the underlying motivations as follows:

The key to fast convergence is in deciding *what* to sample by removing those parts of the integral we can compute deterministically and gauging the importance of the rest so as to maximise the payback from our ray calculations.

This aim is accomplished by removing the specular reflections, transmissions and direct illumination contribution from the integral. As in conventional ray tracing from the eye, a full evaluation of the rendering equation is performed for the direct and specular components on a per pixel basis. For a single light source scene (such as the sun) a light ray is spawned from the evaluation point and if it is unobstructed, the direct contribution can be calculated. Indirect diffuse illumination is calculated by spawning rays over the hemisphere centred on the point of interest. These are then traced recursively. The strategy that controls the potential combinatorial explosion consists of performing this evaluation once for every few pixels rather than for every pixel. Diffuse illumination changes gradually over a surface and the rationale is that the effect of a single evaluation can be spread over a number of pixels. In addition, values are cached as they are generated and when a hemisphere is sampled the algorithms looks around to see if there are any previously calculated values available. If there are, the required sample is interpolated from them. This basic approach is elaborated by determining the 'irradiance gradient' in the region currently being examined, which leads to the use of a higher order (cubic) interpolation procedure for the interpolation. This information is retrieved from the hemisphere samples themselves.

An important consequence of Ward's strategy is that it effectively decouples the shading from the geometry of the scene representation – the main problem with the radiosity method. The sampled values are cached in an octree data structure that is indexed by the world coordinates of the sample point that requires a shading value.

Finally Ward expresses some strong opinions about the practical efficacy of the radiosity method. It is unusual for such criticisms to appear in a computer graphics paper and Ward is generally concerned that the radiosity method has not migrated from the research laboratories. He says:

For example, most radiosity systems are not well automated, and do not permit general reflectance models or curved surfaces … Acceptance of physically based rendering is bound to improve, but researchers must first demonstrate the real-life applicability of their techniques. There have been few notable successes in applying radiosity to the needs of practising designers. While much research has been done on improving efficiency of the basic radiosity method, problems associated with more realistic complicated geometries, have only recently gotten the attention they deserve. For whatever reason it appears that radiosity has yet to fulfil its promise, and it is time to re-examine this technique in the light of real-world applications and other alternatives for solving the rendering equation.

An example of the use of the RADIANCE renderer is given in the comparative image study in Figures 6.2 and 8.27.

Having looked at the general problem of global illumination and overviewed approaches we will now look at the details of basic ray tracing and radiosity. There is a wealth of algorithmic variations possible, particularly in ray tracing, and the reader interested in a more in-depth approach should consult the reference list. The algorithms that we will describe are the mainstream approaches which tend to be found in most current commercial implementations.

6.3 Whitted ray tracing – the details

Whitted ray tracing, despite the flaws that we have discussed, is an elegant algorithm, and combines in a single model:

- hidden surface removal
- shading due to direct illumination
- global specular interaction effects such as the reflection of objects in each other and refraction of light through transparent objects
- shadow computation (but only the geometry of hard-edged shadows is calculated).

It usually 'contains' a local reflection model such as the Phong reflection model, and the question arises: why not use ray tracing as the standard approach to rendering, rather than using a Phong approach with extra algorithms for hidden surface removal, shadows and transparency? The immediate answer to this is cost. Ray tracing is expensive, particularly for polygon objects because effectively each polygon is an object to be ray traced. Much research in the 1980s concentrated on efficiency schemes for Whitted ray tracing. This is the dilemma of ray tracing. It can only function in reasonable time if the scene is made up of 'easy' objects. Quadric objects such as spheres are easy, and if the object is polygonal the number of facets needs to be low for the ray tracer to function in reasonable time. If the scene is complex (many objects each with many polygons) then the basic algorithm needs to be burdened with efficiency schemes whose own complexity tends to be a function of the complexity of the scene. However, we are just about at a point in hardware development where ray tracing is a viable alternative for a practical renderer and the clear advantages of the algorithm are beginning to overtake the cost penalties. In this chapter we will develop a program to ray trace spheres. We will then extend the program to enable polygonal objects to be dealt with. The topic is completed with an extension to the model that allows rays to be traced from both the eye and the light source.

Although the ray tracing algorithm is easy to implement and understand there are some subtleties and hacks that are best got out of the way before we look at ray tracing in detail.

6.3.1 Tracing rays – initial considerations

We trace infinitesimally thin light rays through the scene, following each ray to discover perfect specular interactions. Tracing implies testing the current ray against objects in the scene – intersection testing – to find if the ray hits any of them. At each boundary, between air and an object (or between an object and air) a ray will 'spawn' two more rays. For example, a ray initially striking a partially transparent sphere will generate at least four rays for the object – two emerging rays and two internal rays (Figure 6.3). The fact that we appropriately bend the transmitted ray means that geometric distortion due to refraction is taken into account. That is, when we form a projected image, objects that are behind transparent objects are appropriately distorted. If the sphere is hollow the situation is more complicated.

To perform this tracing we follow light beams in the reverse direction of light propagation. That is, we trace light rays from the eye. We do this eye tracing because tracing rays by starting at the light source(s) would be hopelessly expensive. This is because we are only interested in that small subset of light rays which pass through the image plane window.

6.3.2 Inclusion of a local reflection model

At each point P where a ray hits an object, we spawn, in general, a reflected and a transmitted ray. Also we evaluate a local reflection model by calculating L at that point and shooting a ray to the light source which we consider as a point. Thus at each point the intensity of the light consists of up to three components:

- a local component
- a contribution from a global reflected ray that we follow
- a contribution from a global transmitted ray that we follow

We linearly combine or add these components together to produce an intensity for point P. It is necessary to include a local model because there may be direct illumination at a hit point. However, it does lead to this confusion. The use of a local reflection model does imply empirically blurred reflection (spread highlights); however, the global reflected ray at that point is not blurred but continues to discover any object interaction along an infinitesimally thin path. This is because we cannot afford to blur global reflected rays – we can only follow the 'central' ray. This results in the classic visual contradiction in ray traced images, which is that the reflection of the light source in an object – the specular highlight – is blurred, but the images of other objects are perfect.

It is also necessary to account for local diffuse reflection as we explained in Section 6.1.1. We cannot in ray tracing handle diffuse interaction (such as that, for example, that illuminates the wall of a room that cannot see the sun through a window). This would mean spawning, for every hit, a set of diffuse rays that sampled the hemispherical set of diffuse rays that occurs at the hit point on the surface of the object, if it happens to be diffuse. Each one of these rays would have to be followed and may end up on a diffuse surface, and a combinatorial explosion would develop that no machine could cope with.

6.3.3 Shadows are easy

Shadows are easily included in the basic ray tracing algorithm. We simply calculate L and insert it into the intersection test part of the algorithm. That is, L is considered a ray like any other. If L intersects any objects, then the point from which L emanates is in shadow and the intensity of direct illumination at that point is consequently reduced (Figure 6.11). This generates hard-edged shadows with arbitrary intensity. The approach can also lead to great expense. If there are

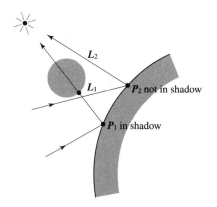

Figure 6.11
Shadow shape is computed by calculating L and inserting it into the intersection tester.

Figure 6.12
A reflected 'hidden' surface.

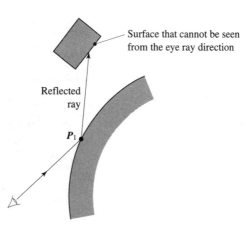

Figure 6.12
A reflected 'hidden' surface.

Surface that cannot be seen
from the eye ray direction

Reflected
ray

P_1

n light sources, then we have to generate n intersections tests. We are already spawning two rays per hit point plus a shadow ray, and for n light sources this becomes $(n+2)$ rays. We can see that as the number of light sources increases, shadow computations are quickly going to predominate since the major cost at each hit point is the cost of the intersection testing.

6.3.4 Hidden surface removal is easy

Hidden surface removal is 'automatically' included in the basic ray tracing algorithm. We test each ray against all objects in the scene for intersection. In general this will give us a list of objects that the ray intersects. Usually the intersection test will reveal the distance from the hit point to the intersection and it is simply a matter of looking for the closest hit to find, from all the intersections, the surface that is visible from the ray-initiating viewpoint. A certain subtlety occurs with this model, which is that surfaces hidden from the point of view of a standard rendering or hidden surface approach may be visible in ray tracing. This point is illustrated in Figure 6.12 which shows that a surface, hidden when viewed from the eye ray direction, can be reflected in the object hit by the incident ray.

6.3.5 Using recursion to implement ray tracing

We will now examine the working of a ray tracing algorithm using a particular example. The example is based on a famous image, produced by Turner Whitted in 1980, and it is generally acknowledged as the first ray traced image in computer graphics. An imitation is shown in Figure 6.13 (Colour Plate). It is an image that has spawned many imitations.

First some symbolics. At every point P that we hit with a ray we consider two major components, a local and a global component:

Figure 6.13
The Whitted scene.

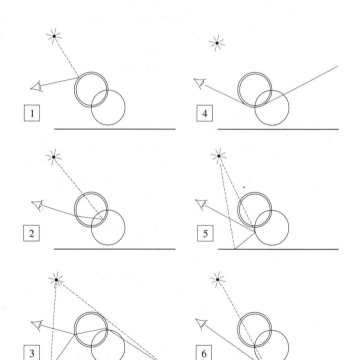

$$I(\boldsymbol{P}) = I_{\text{local}}(\boldsymbol{P}) + I_{\text{global}}(\boldsymbol{P})$$
$$= I_{\text{local}}(\boldsymbol{P}) + k_{\text{rg}}\, I(\boldsymbol{P_r}) + k_{\text{tg}}I(\boldsymbol{P_t})$$

where

$\boldsymbol{P}$ is the hit point

$\boldsymbol{P_r}$ is the hit point discovered by tracing the reflected ray from $\boldsymbol{P}$

$\boldsymbol{P_t}$ is the hit point discovered by tracing the transmitted ray from $\boldsymbol{P}$

k_{rg} is the global reflection coefficient

k_{tg} is the global transmission coefficient

This recursive equation emphasizes that the illumination at a point is made up of three components, a local component, which is usually calculated using a Phong local reflection model, and a global component, which is evaluated by finding $\boldsymbol{P_r}$ and $\boldsymbol{P_t}$ and recursively applying the equation at these points. The overall process is sometimes represented as a tree (Figure 6.3).

A procedure to implement ray tracing is easily written and has low code complexity. The top-level procedure is recursive and calls itself to calculate the reflected and transmitted rays. The geometric calculation for the reflected and transmitted ray directions are give in Chapter 24, and details of intersection testing a ray with a sphere will also be found there.

The basic control procedure for a ray tracer consists of a simple recursive procedure that reflects the action at a node where, in general, two rays are spawned. Thus the procedure will contain two calls to itself, one for the transmitted and one for the reflected ray. We can summarize the action as:

ShootRay (ray structure)
    intersection test
    if ray intersects an object
        get normal at intersection point
        calculate local intensity (I_{local})
        decrement current depth of trace
        if depth of trace > 0
            calculate and shoot the reflected ray
            calculate and shoot the refracted ray

where the last two lines imply a recursive call of ShootRay(). This is the basic control procedure. Around the recursive calls there has to be some more detail which is:

Calculate and shoot reflected ray elaborates as

    if object is a reflecting object
        calculate reflection vector and include in the ray structure
        Ray Origin := intersection point
        Attenuate the ray (multiply the current k_{rg} by its value at the previous invocation)
        ShootRay(reflected ray structure)
        if reflected ray intersects an object
            combine colours ($k_{\text{rg}}I$) with I_{local}

Calculate and shoot refracted ray elaborates as

 if object is a refracting object
  if ray is entering object
   accumulate refractive index of space
   increment number of objects that the ray is currently inside
   calculate refraction vector and include in refracted ray structure
  else
   de-accumulate refractive index
   decrement number of objects that the ray is currently inside
   calculate refraction vector and include in refracted ray structure
  Ray origin := intersection point
  Attenuate ray (k_{tg})
  if refracted ray intersects an object
   combine colours ($k_{tg}I$) with I_{local}

The ray structure needs to contain at least the following information:

- origin of the ray
- its direction
- its intersection point
- its current colour at the intersection point
- its current attenuation
- the distance of the intersection point from the ray origin
- the refractive index the ray is currently experiencing
- current depth of the trace
- number of objects we are currently inside

Thus the general structure is of a procedure calling itself twice for a reflected and refracted ray. This is necessarily enhanced with some detail. The first part of the procedure finds the object closest to the ray start. Then we find the normal and apply the local shading model, attenuating the light source intensity if there are any objects between the intersection point P and the object. We then call the procedure recursively for the reflected and transmitted ray.

 The number of recursive invocations of ShootRay() is controlled by the depth of trace parameter. If this is unity the scene is rendered just with a local reflection model. To discover any reflections of another object at a point P we need a depth of at least 2. To deal with transparent objects we need a depth of at least 3. (The initial ray, the ray that travels through the object and the emergent ray have to be followed. The emergent ray returns an intensity from any object that it hits.)

(6.3.6)   **The adventures of seven rays – a ray tracing study**

Return to Figure 6.13 which is shown as both a black and white and a colour illustration. We consider the way in which the ray tracing model works in the

Table 6.1

Very transparent hollow sphere

k_d (local)	0.1	0.1	0.1	(low)
k_s (local)	0.8	0.8	0.8	(high)
k_{rg}	0.1	0.1	0.1	(low)
k_{tg}	0.9	0.9	0.9	(high)

Opaque (white) sphere

k_d (local)	0.2	0.2	0.2	(white)
k_s (local)	0.8	0.8	0.8	(white)
k_{rg}	0.4	0.4	0.4	(white)
k_{tg}	0.0	0.0	0.0	

Chequerboard

k_d (local)	1.0	0.0	0.0/1.0	1.0	0.0	(high red or yellow)
k_s (local)	0.2	0.2	0.2			
k_{rg}	0					
k_{tg}	0					

Blue background

k_d (local)		0.1	0.1	1.0	(high blue)

Ambient light	0.3	0.3	0.3
Light	0.7	0.7	0.7

context of the seven pixels shown highlighted. The scene itself consists of a thin walled or hollow sphere, that is almost perfectly transparent, together with a partially transparent white sphere, both of which are floating above the ubiquitous red and yellow chequerboard. Everywhere else in object space is a blue background. The object properties are summarized in Table 6.1. Note that this model allows us to set k_s to a different value from k_{rg} – the source of the contradiction mentioned in Section 6.2.2; reflected rays are treated differently depending on which component (local or global) is being considered.

Consider the rays associated with the pixels shown in Figure 6.13.

Ray 1

This ray is along a direction where a specular highlight is seen on the highly transparent sphere. Because the ray is near the mirror direction of **L**, the contribution from the specular component in $I_{local}(\mathbf{P})$ is high and the contributions from $k_{rg}I(\mathbf{P_r})$ is low. For this object k_d, the local diffuse coefficient, is low (it is multiplied by 1 – transparency value) and k_s is high with respect to k_{rg}. However, note that the local contribution only dominates over a very small area of the surface of the object. Also note that, as we have already mentioned, the highlight should not be spread. But if we left it as occupying a single pixel it would not be visible.

Ray 2

Almost the same as Ray 1 except that the specular highlight appears on the inside wall of the hollow sphere. This particular ray demonstrates another accepted error in ray tracing. Effectively the ray from the light travels through the sphere without refracting (that is, we simply compare L with the local value of N and ignore the fact that we are now inside a sphere). This means that the specular highlight is in the **wrong** position but we simply accept this because we have no intuitive expectation of the correct position anyway. We simply accept it to be correct.

Ray 3

Ray 3 also hits the thin walled sphere. The local diffuse contribution at all hits with the hollow sphere is low and the predominant contribution is the chequerboard. This is subject to slight distortion due to the refractive effect of the sphere walls. The red (or yellow) colour comes from the high k_d in $I_{local}(P)$ where P is a point on the chequerboard. k_{rg} and k_{tg} are zero for this surface. Note, however, that we have a mix of two chequerboards. One is as described and the other is the superimposed reflection on the outside surface of the sphere.

Ray 4

Again this hits the thin walled sphere, but this time in a direction where the distance travelled through the glass is significant (that is, it only travels through the glass, it does not hit the air inside) causing a high refractive effect and making the ray terminate in the blue background.

Ray 5

This ray hits the opaque sphere and returns a significant contribution from the local component due to a white k_d (local). At the first hit the global reflected ray hits the chequerboard. Thus there is a mixture of:

  white (from the sphere's diffuse component)
  red/yellow (reflected from the chequerboard)

Ray 6

This ray hits the chequerboard initially and the colour comes completely from the local component for that surface. However, the point is in shadow and this is discovered by the intersection of the ray L and the opaque sphere.

Ray 7

The situation with this ray is exactly the same as for ray 6 except that it is the thin walled sphere that intersects L. Thus the shadow area intensity is not reduced by as much as the previous case. Again we do not consider the recursive effect that L would in fact experience and so the shadow is in effect in the wrong place.

Ray tracing polygon objects – interpolation of a normal at an intersection point in a polygon

Constraining a modelling primitive to be a sphere or at best a quadric solid is hopelessly restrictive in practice and in this section we will look at ray tracing polygonal objects. Extending the above program to cope with general polygon objects requires the development of an intersection test for polygons and a method of calculating or interpolating a normal at the hit point P. We remind ourselves that the polygonal facets are only approximations to a curved surface and, just as in Phong shading, we need to interpolate, from the vertex normals, an approximation to the surface normal of the 'true' surface that the facet approximates. This entity is required for the local illumination component and to calculate reflection and refraction. Recall that in Phong interpolation we used the two-dimensional component of screen space to interpolate, pixel by pixel, scan line by scan line, the normal at each pixel projection on the polygon. We interpolated three of the vertex normals using two-dimensional screen space as the interpolation basis. How do we interpolate from the vertex normals in a ray tracing algorithm, bearing in mind that we are operating in world space? One easy approach is to store the polygon normal for each polygon as well as its vertex normals. We find the largest of its three components x_w, y_w and z_w. The largest component identifies which of the three world coordinate planes the polygon is closest to in orientation, and we can use this plane in which to interpolate, using the same interpolation scheme as we employed for Phong interpolation (Chapter 24). This plane is equivalent to the use of the screen plane in Phong interpolation. The idea is shown in Figure 6.14. This plane is used for the interpolation as follows. We consider the polygon to be represented in a coordinate system where the hit point P is the origin. We then have to search the polygon vertices to find the edges that cross the 'medium' axis. This enables us to interpolate the appropriate vertex normals to find N_a and N_b from which we find the required normal N_p (Figure 6.15). Having found the interpolated

Figure 6.14

A polygon that lies almost in the $x_w y_w$ plane will have a high z_w component. We choose this plane in which to perform the interpolation of vertex normals.

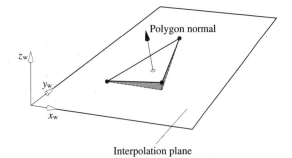

Figure 6.15
Finding an interpolated
normal at a hit point **P**.

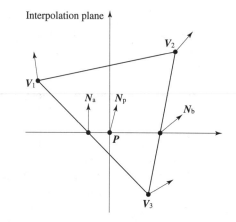

normal we can calculate the local illumination component and the reflected and the refracted ray. Note that because we are 'randomly' interpolating we lose the efficiency advantages of the Phong interpolation, which was incremental on a pixel-by-pixel, scan line by scan line basis.

We conclude that in ray tracing polygonal objects we incur two significant costs. First, the more overwhelming cost is that of intersection testing each polygon in an object. Second, we have the cost of finding an interpolated normal on which to base our calculations.

6.3.8 Bounding objects with simple shapes

Given that the high cost of ray tracing is embedded in intersection testing, we can greatly increase the efficiency of a recursive ray tracer by making this part of the algorithm as efficient as possible. An obvious and much used approach is to enclose the object in a 'simple' volume known as a bounding volume. Initially we test the ray for intersection with a bounding volume and only if the ray enters this volume do we test for intersection with the object.

Two properties are required of a bounding volume. First, it should have a simple intersection test – thus a sphere is an obvious candidate. Second, it should efficiently enclose the object. In this aspect a sphere is deficient. If the object is long and thin the sphere will contain a large void volume and many rays will pass the bounding volume test but will not intersect the object. A rectangular solid, where the relative dimensions are adjustable, is possibly the best simple bounding volume. Details of intersection testing both spheres and boxes is given in Chapter 24.

The dilemma of bounding volumes is that you cannot allow the complexity of the bounding volume scheme to grow too much, or it obviates its own purpose. Usually for any scene, the cost of bounding volume calculations will be related to their enclosing efficiency. This is easily shown conceptually. Figure 6.16 shows a two-dimensional scene containing two rods and a circle represent-

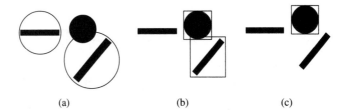

        (a)   (b)   (c)

Figure 6.16
Three different bounding volumes, going from (a) to (c). The complexity cost of the bounding volume increases together with its enclosing efficiency.
(a) Circles (spheres) as bounding volumes;
(b) rectangles (boxes) as bounding volumes;
(c) rectangles (boxes) at any orientation.

ing complex polygonal objects. Figure 6.16(a) shows circles (spheres) as bounding volumes with their low enclosing efficiency for the rods. Not only are the spheres inefficient, but they intersect each other, and the space occupied by other objects. Using boxes aligned with the scene axes is better (Figure 6.16(b)) but now the volume enclosing the sloping rod is inefficient. For this scene the best bounding volumes are boxes with any orientation (Figure 6.16(c)); the cost of testing the bounding volumes increases from spheres to boxes with any orientation.

6.3.9   Secondary data structures

Another common approach to efficiency in intersection testing is to set up a secondary data structure to control the intersection testing. The secondary data structure is used as a guide and the primary data structure – the object database – is entered at the most appropriate point.

Bounding volume hierarchies

Bounding volumes can be organized into hierarchies if the spatial juxtapositioning of objects in the scene is appropriate. Consider Figure 6.17, a two-object scene consisting of a table supporting a pyramid (again we assume that the objects are made up of a large number of polygons). A hierarchy of box bounding volumes is shown. Note that the bounding volume hierarchy can enter into and segment the object, as it does in the case of the table. Also note that for a table a box is a very inefficient bounding volume, but a two-level hierarchy of five boxes is perfect.

    The problem with bounding volume hierarchies is that they may not be appropriate for a scene. Objects must cluster into groups and if they themselves are to be segmented by bounding volumes, they must split up in a way that complements the bounding volume scheme (as in the example of the table). Automatically pre-processing the database is a difficult problem and we are left with the tedium of finding a suitable hierarchy manually.

Tracking labelled space

A brute force reorganization of the intersection problem is to label all of the object space with an object occupancy label. We then, instead of asking the question:

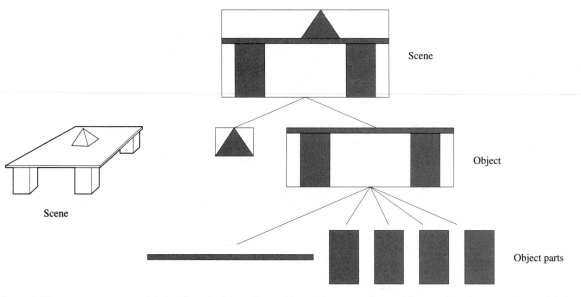

Figure 6.17
A bounding volume
hierarchy for a simple scene.

which (if any) object does this ray intersect? are able to pose the question: which
objects are encountered by this ray in its passage through labelled space?

An octree is a representation of the objects in a scene that allows us to exploit
spatial coherence – objects that are close to each other in space are represented
by nodes that are close to each other in the octree (Chapter 2).

When tracing a ray, instead of doing intersection calculations between the ray
and every object in the scene, we can now trace the ray from subregion to subregion in the subdivision of occupied space. For each subregion that the ray
passes through, there will be only a small number of objects (typically one or
two) with which it could intersect. Provided that we can rapidly find the node
in the octree that corresponds to a subregion that a ray is passing through, we
have immediate access to the objects that are on, or close to, the path of the ray.
Intersection calculations need only be done for these objects. If space has been
subdivided to a level where each subregion contains only one or two objects,
then the number of intersection tests required for a region is small and does not
tend to increase with the complexity of the scene.

In order to use the space subdivision to determine which objects are close to
a ray, we must determine which subregion of space the ray passes through. This
involves tracking the ray into and out of each subregion in its path. The main
operation required during this process is that of finding the node in the octree,
and hence the region in space, that corresponds to a point (x,y,z).

The overall tracking process starts by detecting the region that corresponds to
the start point of the ray. The ray is tested for intersection with any objects that
lie in this region and if there are any intersections, then the first one encountered is the one required for the ray. If there are no intersections in the initial
region, the ray must be tracked into the next region through which it passes.
This is done by calculating the intersection of the ray with the boundaries of the

region and thus calculating the point at which the ray leaves the region. A point on the ray a short distance into the next region is then used to find the node in the octree that corresponds to the next region. Any objects in this region are then tested for intersections with the ray. The process is repeated as the ray tracks from region to region until an intersection with an object is found or until the ray leaves occupied space.

The simplest approach to finding the node in the octree that corresponds to a point (x,y,z) is to use a data structure representation of the octree to guide the search for the node. Starting at the top of the tree, a simple comparison of coordinates will determine which child node represents the subregion that contains the point (x,y,z). The subregion, corresponding to the child node, may itself have been subdivided and another coordinate comparison will determine which of its children represents the smaller subregion that contains (x,y,z). The search proceeds down the tree until a terminal node is reached. The maximum number of nodes traversed during this search will be equal to the maximum depth of the tree. Even for a fairly fine subdivision of occupied space, the search length will be short. For example, if the space is subdivided at a resolution of $1024 \times 1024 \times 1024$, then the octree will have depth 10 ($=\log_8(1024 \times 1024 \times 1024)$).

6.4 Further developments in ray tracing illumination model

The main deficiencies in ray tracing are consequences of two aspects of the standard model:

● the use of infinitesimally thin rays reflecting from and refracting through perfect surfaces;

● the need to use a local **and** a global model at the point P.

The effect of the first two problems was illustrated in Figure 6.5. This visual problem was more or less eliminated in an elegant development of ray tracing, known as distributed ray tracing, implemented by Cook et al. in 1984.

6.4.1 Distributed ray tracing

This method overcomes the visual problem of 'perfection' in ray traced imagery. Because traced rays are not spread but continue from intersection to intersection as infinitely thin beams, a super real 'signature' results. This means that we have 'sharp' shadows, sharp reflection and sharp refraction, as well as aliasing artefacts.

Some of these problems can be overcome by both increasing the number of initial rays and spawning extra rays at intersections but this approach very soon becomes completely impractical because of the overheads. Distributed ray tracing is an elegant method that circumvents the straightforward solution of adding a large number of extra rays. Both the anti-aliasing problem and the modelling of what Cook calls fuzzy phenomena are solved by distributed ray tracing.

Reflecting surfaces produce, in general, blurred reflections due to surface imperfections; similarly, transmitting surfaces blur transmitted rays due to scattering in the material. As we discussed above, the hybrid nature of a naive ray tracer allows reflections from a direct light source to cause a blurred reflection (or specular highlight) but global reflection/transmission is deemed to be perfect. In distributed ray tracing these problems are overcome by causing the rays to follow paths other than that predicted by the exact reflection and transmission direction. This produces blurred reflection and transmission. The same model incorporates new effects – blurred shadows, depth of field, motion blur and anti-aliasing. The method uses 16 rays per pixel and its main attributes are:

● The process of distributing rays means that stochastic anti-aliasing becomes an integral part of the method.

● Distributing reflected rays produces blurry reflections.

● Distributing transmitted rays produces convincing translucency.

● Distributing shadow rays results in penumbrae.

● Distributing ray origins over the camera lens area produces depth of field.

● Distributing rays in time produces motion blur (temporal anti-aliasing).

The algorithm works by approximating or sampling the reflection and transmission lobes. Figure 6.18 shows a single ray from a pixel hitting two objects. At the first hit the direction of the reflected ray is not necessarily the 'true' reflected direction, *R* (and this deviation, of course, gives blurred reflections as we pointed out in Figure 6.6). Instead jitter is used to implement 'importance' sampling. Here an emerging reflected direction is chosen on the basis of a precalculated importance sampled reflection function. Given the angle between the reflected ray and the surface normal, a lookup table stores a range of reflection angles and a jitter magnitude.

The fact that rays emerge at some direction other than the previous reflected direction means that the second hit will occur at a different position to that given by the hit of the precise reflected direction (dotted lines in Figure 6.18). Each object may exhibit a different specular reflection function and so the second object may index into a different table.

So far we have said nothing about how each lookup table index is chosen. Each ray derives an index as a function of its position in the pixel. The primary ray and all its descendants have the same index. This means that a ray emerging from a first hit along a direction relative to *R* will emerge from all other hits in the same relative *R* direction for each object. This ensures that each pixel intensity, which is finally determined from 16 samples, is based on samples that are distributed, according to the importance sampling criterion, across the complete range of the specular reflection functions associated with each object. Note that

Figure 6.18
Distributed ray tracing and
reflected rays.

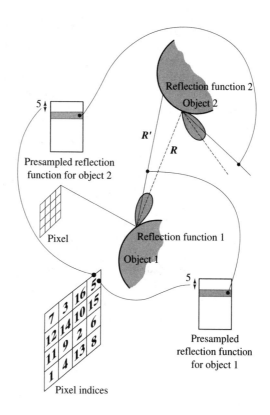

there is nothing to prevent a lookup table being two-dimensional and indexed also by the incoming angle. This enables specular reflection functions that depend on angle of incidence to be implemented. Finally note that transmission is implemented in exactly the same way using specular transmission functions about the refraction direction.

6.4.2

Generalizing the trace direction – two-pass ray tracing

We recall from Section 6.1.1 that Whitted ray tracing simulates paths LDS*E or LS*E and that this could be extended to LS*DS*E which incorporates the important SD path. The SD path is covered by tracing rays both from the eye and from the light. An important and beautiful visual phenomenon associated with the specular to diffuse mechanism is caustics. A caustic is a local increase in illumination on a diffuse surface and is caused by light passing through an object, such as a glass, that acts as a lens. A caustic is like a 'bright shadow'. If the geometry of the transparent object is such that it concentrates light rays on the receiving or next surface in the ray path, then a patch of concentrated light, a caustic, will appear on the receiving surface.

This phenomenon is also associated with water, whose surface disturbances, due to wind or vortices, cause the sun to form beautiful moving caustics on the receiving surface. Such patterns on the base of a swimming pool were stylized by the painter, David Hockney, in his Californian pools paintings. They represent specular (the transmission of rays through water) to diffuse (the pool bottom) transfer. Figure 6.19 (Colour Plate) shows an image generated using two-pass ray tracing.

It is easy to see that we cannot simulate this phenomenon by eye tracing alone. Eye rays do not necessarily hit the light and we have no way of finding out if a surface has received extra illumination due to specular to diffuse transfer. This is illustrated for an easy case of an LSDE path in Figure 6.20. (Return to Figures 6.2 and 6.7 for other examples of SDE paths.)

Two-pass ray tracing was first proposed by Arvo in 1986. In Arvo's scheme rays from the light were traced through transparent objects and from specular objects. When these rays hit the (diffuse) surface (the result of the first specular to diffuse transfer) we can 'remember' this effect and take this into account during the eye trace. Thus two-pass ray tracing means showering the scene with rays from the light, the first pass, then doing conventional eye tracing, taking any information from the first pass into account.

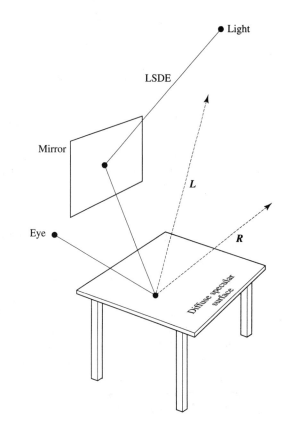

Figure 6.20
An example of an LSDE path (see also Figures 6.2 and 6.7 for examples of SDE paths). An eye ray can 'discover' light ray **L** and reflected ray **R** but cannot find the LSDE path.

Central to the working of such a strategy is how information derived during the first pass is communicated to the second. Arvo suggests achieving this with a light or illumination map, consisting of a grid of data points, which is pasted onto each object in the scene in much the same way that a conventional texture map would be. A given illumination ray, originating from the light, strikes an object at a point and deposits a certain amount of energy in the light map associated with that object. The first pass consists of 'showering' the scene with these rays. During the second pass a ray striking the object will pick up a value for this indirect illumination. When we have completed the first pass we have a light map for all the objects that require such a map. Some objects do, others do not. For example, consider Figure 6.7. The table top gets a light map, the sphere does not. After the light maps are completed we need to blur them. Bear in mind that a light map is simply a 'sprinkling' of contributions from the light rays. There is no guarantee that all pixels in the light map receive a contribution.

The process is illustrated in Figure 6.21. A light ray strikes a surface at **P** after being refracted. It is indexed into the light map associated with the object using a standard texture mapping function **T** (Chapter 4). During the second pass an eye ray hits **P**. The same mapping function is used to pick up any illumination for the point **P** and this contribution weights the local intensity calculated for that point.

An important point here is that the first pass is view independent: we construct a light map for each object which is analogous in this sense to a texture map – it becomes part of the surface properties of the object. We can use the light maps from any viewpoint after they are completed and they need only be computed once for each scene.

A Whitted ray tracer is easily extended into a two-pass ray tracer as follows:

Figure 6.21
Two-pass ray tracing and light maps. (a) First pass: light is deposited in a light map using a standard texture mapping *T*. (b) Second pass: when object 2 is conventionally eye traced extra illumination at *P* is obtained by indexing the light map with *T*.

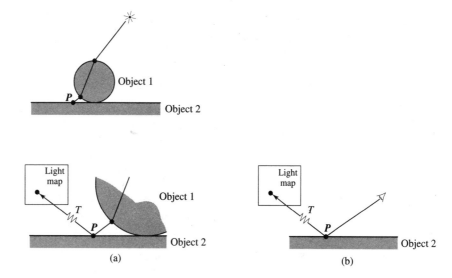

(a) (b)

First pass

```
ShootLightRay(ray structure)
    find the closest intersection (a light ray always hits something)
    if the ray intersects an object
        get the normal
        decrement depth of trace
        if it is an object for which a light map is to be built
            inverse map from intersection point to find (u,v) – the light
            map co-ordinates
            accumulate the intensity in the light map
            decrement depth of trace
            calculate and shoot reflected ray
            calculate and shoot refracted ray
```

Second pass

The second pass is the same as ShootRay() for normal ray tracing except that at the end of the procedure that calculates the local intensity we 'add' any contribution from the light map to the diffuse component. In practice, we multiply or weight the diffuse component by the light map contribution. Thus:

$$CalculateLocalIntensity(I_{local})$$

$$.$$
$$.$$

if object has an associated light map
    inverse map to find (u,v)
    get light map value at (u,v)
    $I_{local}(\boldsymbol{P}) := I_{local}(\boldsymbol{P}) + \text{LightMap}\ (u,v) * I_d(\boldsymbol{P})$

Further reading

Ray tracing appeared to be one of the most exhaustively researched areas in computer graphics in the 1980s and any of the computer graphics textbooks mentioned in Chapter 1 have coverage of this topic. A good cross-section of the research can be found in SIGGRAPH proceedings of the 1980s. Research into ray tracing divides into a number of categories, including:

● efficiency or speed-up schemes using either bounding volumes or a labelled space.

● elaborations of the model to diminish its shortcomings – distributed ray tracing, for example.

● use of ray tracing in conjunction with radiosity to solve the 'mutual exclusion' problem.

● work on special hardware designs for ray tracing implementation

● work on ray tracing 'special' objects such as CSG or bicubic patch representation.

A useful book devoted exclusively to ray tracing and with chapters written by different authors is edited by Glassner. This goes into many of the topics just described. As far as the original papers are concerned, Whitted's is only useful for historical reasons – it contains no details that are not more easily accessible in a textbook. Cook's pioneering paper on distributed ray tracing is somewhat short on implementation details but he gives more detail in the Glassner reference, to which he contributed. Arvo's work on two-pass ray tracing only appears to have been reported in SIGGRAPH course notes for 1986. These are generally not available and we have not included them as references.

Cook R.L., Porter T. and Carpenter L. (1984). Distributed ray tracing. *Computer Graphics*, **18**(3), 137–44 (Proc. SIGGRAPH '84)

Glassner A., ed. (1989). *An Introduction to Ray Tracing*. New York: Academic Press

Kajiya J. (1986). The rendering equation. *Computer Graphics*, **20**(4), 143–50

Wallace J. R., Cohen M. F. and Greenberg D. P. (1987). A two-pass solution to the rendering equation: a synthesis of ray tracing and radiosity methods. *Computer Graphics*, **21**(4), 311–20

Whitted T. (1980). An improved illumination model for shaded display. *Comm. ACM*, **26**(6), 342–9

6.5 Classical radiosity

Ray tracing, the first computer graphics model to embrace global interaction – or at least one aspect of it – suffers from an identifying visual signature: you can usually tell if an image has been synthesized using ray tracing. It only models one aspect of the light interaction – that due to perfect specular reflection and transmission. The interaction between diffusely reflecting surfaces, which tends to be the predominant light transport mechanism in interiors, is still modelled using an ambient constant (in the local reflection component of the model). Consider, for example, a room with walls and ceiling painted with a matte material and carpeted. If there are no specularly reflecting objects in the room, then those parts of the room that cannot see a light source are lit by diffuse interaction. Such a room tends to exhibit slow and subtle changes of intensity across its surfaces.

In 1984, using a method whose theory was based on the principles of radiative heat transfer, researchers at Cornell University developed the radiosity method. This is now known as classical radiosity and it simulates LD*E paths; that is, it can only be used, in its unextended form, to render scenes that are made up in their entirety of (perfect) diffuse surfaces.

To accomplish this, every surface in a scene is divided up into elements called patches and a set of equations is set up based on the conservation of light energy. A single patch in such an environment reflects light received from every other patch in the environment. It may also emit light if it is a light source – light sources are treated like any other patch except that they have non-zero self-emission. The interaction between patches depends on their geometric relationship, that is, distance and relative orientation. Two parallel patches a short distance apart will have a high interaction. An equilibrium solution is possible if, for each patch in the environment, we calculate its interaction between it and every other patch in the environment.

One of the major contributions of the Cornell group was to invent an efficient way – the hemicube algorithm – for evaluating the geometric relationship between pairs of patches; in fact in the 1980s most of the innovations in radiosity methods have come out of this group.

To keep processing costs down the patches are made large and the light intensity is assumed to be constant across a patch. This immediately introduces a quality problem – if illumination discontinuities do not coincide with patch edges artefacts occur. The cost of the algorithm is N^2 where N is the number of patches into which the environment is divided. This size restriction is the practical reason why the algorithm can only calculate diffuse interaction, which by its nature changes slowly across a surface. Adding specular interaction to the radiosity method is expensive and is still the subject of much research. Thus we have the strange situation that the two global interaction methods – ray tracing and radiosity – are mutually exclusive as far as the phenomena that they calculate is concerned. Ray tracing cannot calculate diffuse interaction and radiosity cannot incorporate specular interaction.

Despite this, the radiosity method has produced some of the most realistic images to date in computer graphics. Two images, Figures 6.22 and 6.23 (Colour Plates), produced at Cornell demonstrate the quality of the method. The first is based on the work of the seventeenth-century Dutch painter Vermeer and attempts to simulate the subtle variation of the slow changes across the walls of a room lit by a window. Although much is lost in the printing process, the soft feel of the light interplay is apparent. This image also contains an enhancement that calculates specular reflection (of the floor). The second image, of a steel mill, shows that, ignoring computing time restrictions, complex environments can be modelled with the method. In this case the factory is synthesized using 55 000 patches.

The radiosity method deals with shadows without further enhancement. As we have already discussed, the geometry of shadows is more or less straightforward to calculate and can be part of a ray tracing algorithm or an algorithm added on to a local reflection model renderer. However, the intensity within a shadow is properly part of diffuse interaction and can only be arbitrarily approximated by other algorithms. The radiosity method takes shadows in its stride. They drop out of the solution as intensities like any other. The only problem is that the patch size may have to be reduced to delineate the shadow boundary to some desired level of accuracy. Shadow boundaries are areas where the rate of change of diffuse light intensity is high and the normal patch size may cause visible aliasing at the shadow edge.

The radiosity method is an object space algorithm, solving for the intensity at discrete points or surface patches within an environment and not for pixels in an image plane projection. The solution is thus independent of viewer position. This complete solution is then injected into a renderer that computes a particular view by removing hidden surfaces and forming a projection. This phase of the method does not require much computation (intensities are already calculated) and different views are easily obtained from the general solution.

Radiosity theory

Elsewhere in the text we have tried to maintain a separation between the algorithm that implements a method and the underlying mathematics. It is the case, however, that with the radiosity method, the algorithm is so intertwined with the mathematics that it would be difficult to try to deal with this in a separate way. The theory itself consists of nothing more than definitions – there is no manipulation. Readers requiring further theoretical insight are referred to the book by Siegel and Howell.

The radiosity method is a conservation of energy or energy equilibrium approach, providing a solution for the radiosity of all surfaces within an enclosure. The energy input to the system is from those surfaces that act as emitters. In fact a light source is treated like any other surface in the algorithm except that it possesses an initial (non-zero) radiosity. The method is based on the assumption that all surfaces are perfect diffusers or ideal Lambertian surfaces.

Radiosity, B, is defined as the energy per unit area leaving a surface patch per unit time and is the sum of the emitted and the reflected energy:

$$B_i dA_i = E_i dA_i + R_i \int_j B_j F_{ji} dA_j$$

Expressing this equation in words we have for a single patch i:

Radiosity $\times$ area = emitted energy + reflected energy

E_i is the energy emitted from a patch. The reflected energy is given by multiplying the incident energy by R_i, the reflectivity of the patch. The incident energy is that energy that arrives at patch i from all other patches in the environment; that is, we integrate over the environment, for all j ($j \neq i$), the term $B_j F_{ji} dA_j$. This is the energy leaving each patch j that arrives at patch i. F_{ji} is a constant, called a form factor, that parametrizes the relationship between patch j and i.

We can use a reciprocity relationship to give:

$$F_{ij} A_i = F_{ji} A_j$$

and dividing through by dA_i gives:

$$B_i = E_i + R_i \int_j B_j F_{ij}$$

For a discrete environment the integral is replaced by a summation and constant radiosity is assumed over small discrete patches, giving:

$$B_i = E_i + R_i \sum_{j=1}^{n} B_j F_{ij}$$

Such an equation exists for each surface patch in the enclosure and the complete environment produces a set of n simultaneous equations of the form:

$$\begin{bmatrix} 1-R_1F_{11} & -R_1F_{12} & \ldots & -R_1F_{1n} \\ -R_2F_{21} & 1-R_2F_{22} & \ldots & -R_2F_{2n} \\ \cdot & \cdot & & \cdot \\ \cdot & \cdot & \ldots & \cdot \\ \cdot & \cdot & & \cdot \\ -R_nF_{n1} & -R_n\,F_{n2} & \ldots & 1-R_nF_{nn} \end{bmatrix} \begin{bmatrix} B_1 \\ B_2 \\ \cdot \\ \cdot \\ \cdot \\ B_n \end{bmatrix} = \begin{bmatrix} E_1 \\ E_2 \\ \cdot \\ \cdot \\ \cdot \\ E_n \end{bmatrix}$$

Solving this equation is the radiosity method. Out of this solution comes B_i the radiosity for each patch. However, there are two problems left. We need a way of computing the form factors. And we need to compute a view and display the patches. To do this we need a linear interpolation method – just like Gouraud shading – otherwise the subdivision pattern – the patches themselves – might be visible.

The E_i's are non-zero only at those surfaces that provide illumination and these terms represent the input illumination to the system. The R_i's are known and the F_{ij}'s are a function of the geometry of the environment. The reflectivities are wavelength-dependent terms and the above equation should be regarded as a monochromatic solution; a complete solution being obtained by solving for however many colour bands are being considered. We can note at this stage that $F_{ii} = 0$ for a plane or convex surface – none of the radiation leaving the surface will strike itself. Also from the definition of the form factor the sum of any row of form factors is unity.

Since the form factors are a function only of the geometry of the system they are computed once only. The method is bound by the time taken to calculate the form factors expressing the radiative exchange between two surface patches A_i and A_j. This depends on their relative orientation and the distance between them and is given by:

$$F_{ij} = \frac{\text{Radiative energy leaving surface } A_i \text{ that strikes } A_j \text{ directly}}{\text{Radiative energy leaving surface } A_i \text{ in all directions in the hemispherical space surrounding } A_i}$$

It can be shown that this is given by:

$$F_{ij} = \frac{1}{A_i} \iint_{A_iA_j} \frac{\cos\phi_i\cos\phi_j}{\pi r^2} \, dA_j dA_i$$

where the geometric conventions are illustrated in Figure 6.24. In any practical environment A_j may be wholly or partially invisible from A_i and the integral needs to be multiplied by an occluding factor which is a binary function that depends on whether the differential area dA_i can see dA_j or not. This double integral is difficult to solve except for specific shapes.

Figure 6.24
Form factor geometry for
two patches *i* and *j*. (After
Goral et al. (1984).)

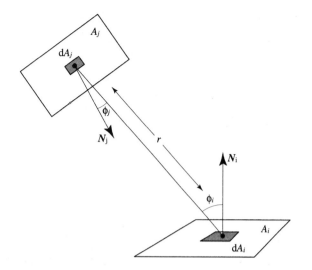

6.5.2

Form factor determination

An elegant numerical method of evaluating form factors was developed in 1985 and this is known as the hemicube method. This offered an efficient method of determining form factors and at the same time a solution to the intervening patch problem.

The patch to patch form factor can be approximated by the differential area to finite area equation

$$F_{dA_iA_j} = \int_{A_j} \frac{\cos\phi_i\cos\phi_j}{\pi r^2} \, dA_j$$

where we are now considering the form factor between the elemental area dA_i and the finite area A_j. dA_i is positioned at the centre point of patch i. The veracity of this approximation depends on the area of the two patches compared with the distance, r, between them. If r is large the inner integral does not change much over the range of the outer integral and the effect of the outer integral is simply multiplication by unity. A theorem called the Nusselt analogue tells us that we can consider the projection of a patch j onto the surface of a hemisphere surrounding the elemental patch dA_i and that this is equivalent in effect to considering the patch itself. Also patches that produce the same projection on the hemisphere have the same form factor. This is the justification for the hemicube method as illustrated in Figure 6.25. Patches A, B and C all have the same form factor and we can evaluate the form factor of any patch j by considering not the patch itself, but its projection onto the faces of a hemicube.

A hemicube is used to approximate the hemisphere because flat projection planes are computationally less expensive. The hemicube is constructed around the centre of each patch with the hemicube Z axis and the patch normal coin-

Figure 6.25
The justification for using a hemicube. Patches *A*, *B* and *C* have the same form factor.

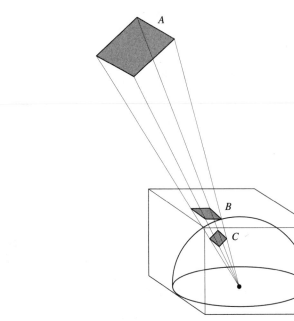

cident (Figure 6.26). The faces of the hemicube are divided into pixels – a somewhat confusing use of the term since we are operating in object space. Every other patch in the environment is projected onto this hemicube. Two patches that project onto the same pixel can have their depth compared and the further patch rejected, since it cannot be seen from the receiving patch. This approach is analogous to a Z-buffer algorithm except that there is no interest in intensities at this stage. The hemicube algorithm only facilitates the calculation of the form factors that are subsequently used in calculating diffuse intensities and a 'label buffer' is maintained indicating which patch is currently nearest to the hemicube pixel.

Each pixel on the hemicube can be considered as a small patch and a differential to finite area form factor, known as a delta form factor, defined for each pixel. The form factor of a pixel is a fraction of the differential to finite area form factor for the patch and can be defined as:

$$\Delta F_{dA_iA_j} = \frac{\cos\phi_i\cos\phi_j}{\pi r^2} \Delta A$$

$$= \Delta F_q$$

where ΔA is the area of the pixel.

These form factors are pre-calculated and stored in a lookup table. This is the foundation of the efficiency of the hemicube method. Again using the fact that areas of equal projection onto the receiving surface surrounding the centre of patch A_i have equal form factors, we can conclude that F_{ij}, for any patch, is obtained by summing the pixel form factors onto which patch A_j projects (Figure 6.27).

Figure 6.26

Evaluating the form factor F_{ij} by projecting patch j onto the faces of a hemicube centred on patch i.

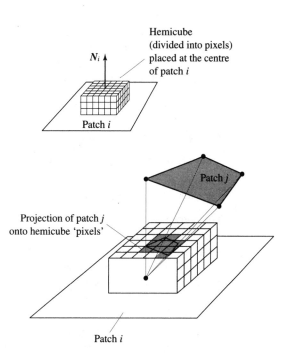

Thus form factor evaluation now reduces to projection onto mutually orthogonal planes and a summation operation.

Figure 6.28 (Colour Plate) is an interesting image that shows the state of a hemicube placed on the window (Figure 6.8) after all other patches in the scene have been projected onto it. A colour identifies each patch in the scene (and every partial patch) that can be seen by this hemicube. The algorithm then simply summates all the hemicube element form factors associated with each patch. The original scene representation is shown as a wireframe. This scene has been carefully constructed to avoid problems that arise out of 'interpenetrating' geometry

Figure 6.27

F_{ij} is obtained by summing the form factors of the pixels onto which patch i projects.

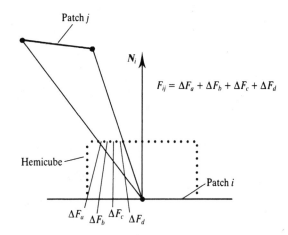

which gives rise to the common defects of light and shadow leakage (see the comparative image study in Chapter 8 for a full discussion of this defect). In particular note that the table edge coincides with a subdivision line on the wall.

The method can be summarized in the following stages:

(1) Computation of the form factors, F_{ij}. Each hemicube emplacement calculates $(n-1)$ form factors or one row in the equation.

(2) Solving the radiosity matrix equation.

(3) Rendering by injecting the results of stage 2 into a bi-linear interpolation scheme.

(4) Repeating stages 2 and 3 for the colour bands of interest.

This process is shown in Figure 6.29. Form factors are a function only of the environment and are calculated once only and can be reused in stage 2 for different reflectivities and light source values. Thus a solution can be obtained for the same environment with, for example, some light sources turned off. The solution produced by stage 2 is a view-independent solution and if a different view is required then only stage 3 is repeated. This approach can be used, for example, when generating an animated walk-through of a building interior. Each frame in the animation is computed by changing the viewpoint and calculating a new view from an unchanging radiosity solution. It is only if we change the geometry of the scene that a recalculation of the form factors is necessary. If the lighting is changed and the geometry is unaltered, then only the equation needs resolving – we do not have to recalculate the form factors.

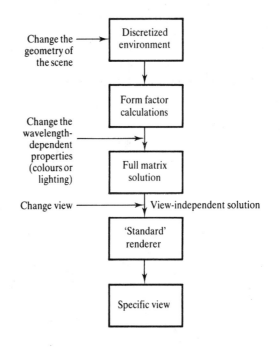

Figure 6.29
Stages in a complete radiosity solution. Also shown are the points in the process where various modifications can be made to the image.

Stage 2 implies the computation of a view-independent rendered version of the solution to the radiosity equation which supplies a single value, a radiosity, for each patch in the environment. From these values vertex radiosities are calculated and these vertex radiosities are used in the bi-linear interpolation scheme to provide a final image. A depth buffer algorithm is used at this stage to evaluate the visibility of each patch at each pixel on the screen. (This stage should not be confused with the hemicube operation that has to evaluate inter-patch visibility during the computation of form factors.)

The time taken to complete the form factor calculation depends on the square of the number of patches. A hemicube calculation is performed for every patch (onto which all other patches are projected). The overall calculation time thus depends on the complexity of the environment and the accuracy of the solution. as determined by the hemicube resolution. Although diffuse illumination changes only slowly across a surface, aliasing can be caused by too low a hemicube resolution and accuracy is required at shadow boundaries (see next section). Storage requirements are also a function of the number of patches required. All these factors mean that there is an upward limit on the complexity of the scenes that can be handled by the radiosity method.

6.5.3 Increasing the accuracy

Above we pointed out that environments are divided into large patches because diffuse reflection changes slowly and because the radiosity method is an $O(N^2)$ algorithm. However, in any environment there are usually areas, such as shadow boundaries, which need smaller patches. There is a contradiction here which is that we need to subdivide the scene on the basis of the solution; but we need this subdivision as input to the algorithm that produces the solution. The resolution of this contradiction has resulted in one of the main research areas in radiosity and we describe some approaches in Chapter 8.

6.5.4 Seeing a partial solution – progressive refinement

Using the radiosity method in a practical context, such as in the design of building interiors, means that the designer has to wait a long time to see a completed image. This is disadvantageous since one of the *raisons d'être* of computer-based design is to allow the user free and fast experimentation with the design parameters. A long feedback time discourages experimentation and stultifies the design process.

In 1988 the Cornell team developed an approach called 'progressive refinement' that enabled a designer to see an early (but approximate) solution. At this stage major errors can be seen and corrected, and another solution executed. As the solution becomes more and more accurate, the designer may see more subtle changes that have to be made.

The general goal of progressive or adaptive refinement can be taken up by any slow image synthesis technique and it attempts to find a compromise between the competing demands of interactivity and image quality. A synthesis method that provides adaptive refinement would present an initial quickly rendered image to the user. This image is then progressively refined in a 'graceful' way. This is defined as a progression towards higher quality, greater realism and so on, in a way that is automatic, continuous and not distracting to the user. Early availability of an approximation can greatly assist in the development of techniques and images, and reducing the feedback loop by approximation is a necessary adjunct to the radiosity method.

The two major practical problems in the radiosity method are the storage costs and the calculation of the form factors. For an environment of 50×10^3 patches, even although the resulting square matrix of form factors may be 90% sparse (many patches cannot see each other), this still requires 10^9 bytes of storage (at four bytes per form factor).

Both the requirements of progressive refinement and the elimination of pre-calculation and storage of the form factors are met by an ingenious restructuring of the basic radiosity algorithm. The stages in the progressive refinement are obtained by displaying the results as the iterative solution progresses. The solution is restructured and the form factor evaluation order is optimized so that the convergence is 'visually graceful'. This restructuring enables the radiosity of all patches to be updated at each step in the solution, rather than a step providing the solution for a single patch. Maximum visual difference between steps in the solution can be achieved by processing patches according to their energy contribution to the environment. The radiosity method is particularly suited to a progressive refinement approach because it computes a view-independent solution. Viewing this solution (by rendering from a particular viewpoint) can proceed independently as the radiosity solution progresses.

In the conventional evaluation of the radiosity matrix (using for example a Gauss–Seidel method) a solution for one row provides the radiosity for a single patch i:

$$B_i = E_i + R_i \sum_{j=1}^{n} B_j F_{ij}$$

This is an estimate of the radiosity of patch i based on the current estimate of all other patches. This is called 'gathering'. The equation means that (algorithmically) for patch i we visit every other patch in the scene and transfer the appropriate amount of light from each patch j to patch i according to the form factor. The algorithm proceeds on a row by row basis and the entire solution is updated for one step through the matrix (although the Gauss–Seidel method uses the new values as soon as they are computed). If the process is viewed dynamically, as the solution proceeds, each patch intensity is updated according to its row position in the radiosity matrix. Light is gathered from every other patch in the scene and used to update the single patch currently being considered.

The idea of the progressive refinement method is that the entire image of all patches is updated at every iteration. This is termed 'shooting', where the contribution from each patch i is distributed to all other patches. The difference between these two processes is illustrated diagramatically in Figures 6.30(a) and (b). This reordering of the algorithm is accomplished in the following way.

A single term determines the contribution to the radiosity of patch j due to that from patch i:

$$B_j \text{ due to } B_i = R_j B_i F_{ji}$$

This relationship can be reversed by using the reciprocity relationship:

$$B_j \text{ due to } B_i = R_j B_i F_{ij} \, A_i/A_j$$

and this is true for all patches j. This relationship can be used to determine the contribution to each patch j in the environment from the single patch i. A single radiosity (patch i) shoots light into the environment and the radiosities of all patches j are updated simultaneously. The first complete update (of all the radiosities in the environment) is obtained from 'on the fly' form factor computations. Thus an initial approximation to the complete scene can appear when only the first row of form factors has been calculated. This eliminates high start-up or pre-calculation costs.

This process is repeated until convergence is achieved. All radiosities are initially set either to zero or to their emission values. As this process is repeated

Figure 6.30
(a) Gathering and (b) shooting in radiosity solution strategies (based on an illustration in Cohen et al. (1988a)).

Gathering: a single iteration (k) updates a single patch i by gathering contributions from all other patches.

$$B_i^{(k+1)} = E_i + R_i \sum_{j=1}^{N} F_{ij} B_j^{(k)}$$

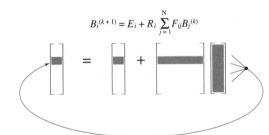

Equivalent to gathering light energy from all the patches in the scene.

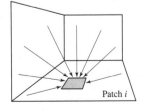

(a) Gathering

Shooting: a single step computes form factors from the shooting patch to all receiving patches and distributes (unshot) energy ΔB_i

for all j:
$$B_j^{(k+1)} = B_j^{(k)} + R_j F_{ji} \Delta B_i$$

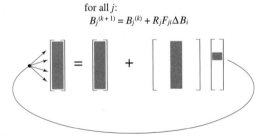

Equivalent to shooting light energy from a patch to all other patches in the scene.

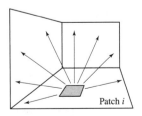

(b) Shooting

for each patch *i* the solution is displayed and at each step the radiosities for each patch *j* are updated. As the solution progresses the estimate of the radiosity at a patch *i* becomes more and more accurate. For an iteration the environment already contains the contribution of the previous estimate of B_j and the so-called 'unshot' radiosity – the difference between the current and previous estimates – is all that is injected into the environment.

If the output from the algorithm is displayed without further elaboration, then a scene, initially dark, gradually gets lighter as the incremental radiosities are added to each patch. The 'visual convergence' of this process can be optimized by sorting the order in which the patches are processed according to the amount of energy that they are likely to radiate. This means, for example, that emitting patches, or light sources, should be treated first. This gives an early well-lit solution. The next patches to be processed are those that received most light from the light sources and so on. By using this ordering scheme, the solution proceeds in a way that approximates the propagation of light through an environment. Although this produces a better visual sequence than an unsorted process, the solution still progresses from a dark scene to a fully illuminated scene. To overcome this effect an arbitrary ambient light term is added to the intermediate radiosities. This term is used only to enhance the display and is not part of the solution. The value of the ambient term is based on the current estimate of the radiosities of all patches in the environment, and as the solution proceeds and becomes 'better lit' the ambient contribution is decreased.

Four main stages are completed for each iteration in the algorithm. These are:

(1) Find the patch with the greatest (unshot) radiosity or emitted energy.

(2) Evaluate a column of form factors, that is, the form factors from this patch to every other patch in the environment.

(3) Update the radiosity of each of the receiving patches.

(4) Reduce the temporary ambient term as a function of the sum of the differences between the current values calculated in step 3 and the previous values.

An example of the state of the image at various stages of the process is shown in Figure 6.8 (Colour Plate).

Further reading

The radiosity method is based on the theory of thermal radiation heat transfer described in the classic text by Siegel and Howell.

Although there is much research into the radiosity method, most of the significant early developments emerged from the Cornell University team in the 1980s in a series of classic papers listed below. Inevitably, work into radiosity has gone the way of all research. An early idea is presented and consolidated and methods or algorithms are worked out. Later more and more workers enter the field and look at narrower and narrower aspects of the problem. This is just what happened with the ray tracing method five years earlier.

Now a similar tendency can be observed in radiosity research. The seminal paper was by Goral in 1984. This was followed in 1985 (Cohen and Greenberg) by a paper describing the classic hemicube method. In 1986 the substructuring method of Cohen *et al.* was reported. This paper also contains details on merging texture mapping with the radiosity solution. The progressive refinement method is described in a report by Cohen et al. in 1988.

The Cornell team have also conducted significant research into including specular reflection into the method. The significant problem with this is the extremely large overheads. A description of this work together with an overview of more recent approaches is given in the book by radiosity pioneers Cohen and Wallace.

Papers

Cohen M.F., Chen S.E., Wallace J.R. and Greenberg D.P. (1988a). A progressive refinement approach to fast radiosity image generation. *Proc SIGGRAPH '88*, 75–84

Cohen M.F. and Greenberg D.P. (1985). A radiosity solution for complex environments. *Proc SIGGRAPH '85*, 31–40

Cohen M.F., Greenberg D.P. and Immel D.S. (1988b). An efficient radiosity approach for realistic image synthesis. *IEEE Computer Graphics and Applications*, **6**(2), 26–35

Goral C., Torrance K.E., Greenberg D.P. and Battaile B. (1984). Modelling the interaction of light between diffuse surfaces. *Proc SIGGRAPH '84*, 212–22

Ward G.J. (1994). The RADIANCE lighting simulation and rendering system. *Proc. SIGGRAPH '94*, 459–71

Books

Cohen M.F. and Wallace J.R. (1993). *Radiosity and Realistic Image Synthesis*. Boston: Academic Press Professional, Harcourt Brace and Co.

Siegel R. and Howell J.R. (1984). *Thermal Radiation and Heat Transfer*. Washington DC: Hemisphere Publishing

Bicubics and image synthesis

7.1 Introduction

In Chapter 2 we overviewed the representation of objects using bicubic parametric patches. We introduced the concept of a patch as a curvilinear quadrilateral whose shape is determined by a mathematical equation which is a cubic polynomial in two parametric variables.

Representing surfaces of objects using bicubic parametric patches finds two applications in computer graphics:

● As an alternative representational form to polygon mesh – the representation which services the normal computer graphics requirement of transforming a real object into a representational form. In this application we usually wish to exploit the accuracy of the parametric representation. Here we may obtain a parametric representation from a real object by some (surface) interpolation technique.

● As a basis for interactive design in CAD. Here we may obtain the model by an interactive process – a designer building up a model by interacting with a program. In many CAD applications the representational form is transformed **directly** into a real object (or a scaled-down model of the real object). The computer graphics representation is used to control a device such as a numerical milling machine which sculpts the object in some material. This is exactly the opposite of the 'normal' computer graphics methodology – instead of transforming a real object into a representation we are using the computer graphics model to make the real object.

The apparent advantages of this representation over the polygon mesh representation are:

● it is an exact analytical representation;
● it has the potential of three-dimensional shape editing;
● it is a more economical representation.

Given these advantages it is somewhat surprising that this form is not the mainstream representation in computer graphics. It is certainly no more difficult to render an object represented by a net of patches and so we must conclude that its lack of popularity in mainstream computer graphics (it is, of course, used in industrial CAD), is due to the mathematical formalistics associated with it.

These factors need careful qualification. A real object (or a physical model of a real object) can be represented by a net or mesh of patches (Figure 2.12 showed an example) but the representation may not be completely 'exact'. We can obtain a suitable set of points that lie in the surface of the object from a three-dimensional digitizer and we could, say, use the same set of points that we would use to build a polygon mesh model. We then use an interpolation technique known as surface fitting, to determine a set of patches that represent the surface. However, the patch surface and the object surface will not necessarily be identical. The exactness of the fit depends both on the nature of the interpolation process and on how closely the physical surface conforms to the shape constraints of the bicubic patch representation. But we do end up with an object representation that is a smooth surface which has certain advantages over the polygon mesh representation – the silhouette edge problem is cured, for example. It is possible to model subtly shaped objects such as a human face with a net of patches. An adequate representation of such an object using a polygon mesh would need an extremely high polygonal resolution (see Figure 2.12, for example). Despite this there is a perceived complexity associated with bicubic parametric patches and in many applications we can avoid this – the polygon mesh representation suffices. When we digitize real objects we are normally working with an application that does not demand exact representation. We may be building a model of a product for an animated TV commercial, for example, in which case a good polygon mesh model will do.

In fact the most common applications of the bicubic parametric patch representation are not to build very complex models but as a representation for fairly simple objects in industrial CAD or CAGD applications. The real value of the representation here is that it can be used to transform an abstract design, built up within an interactive program, directly into a physical reality. The description can be made to drive a sculpting device such as a numerically controlled milling machine to produce a prototype object without any human intervention. It is this single factor more than any other that make bicubic parametric patches important.

Part of their value in CAD comes from the ability to change the shape of an object represented by patches in a way that maintains a smooth surface. Sometimes the allusion to sculpting is made. We can view the representation as a kind of 'abstract clay' model that can be pulled around and deformed into any desirable shape – giving the same freedom to create as a sculptor would have with a real clay model (see Figure 20.11). Here we should beware of the some-times audacious claims that are made in the computer graphics literature con-cerning the efficacy of free-form sculpting using bicubic parametric patches. We can distinguish between methods that attempt the free-form sculpting model which places no constraints on the shape complexity of the object formed, and the much more well-established techniques in CAD where the object tends to be fairly simple. A common, early example of this category is the design of car body panels. Bicubic parametric patches are manifestly successful in such applica-tions; their success as a metaphor for clay sculpting is more debatable.

We distinguish between objects that are represented by a single patch and objects whose form demands that they are represented by a net of patches. Shape editing a single patch is straightforward but the objects that we can design with a single patch are restricted. Shape editing an object that is represented by a net of patches is much more difficult. One problem is that if we have to alter the shape of one patch in a net, we have to maintain its smoothness relationship with the neighbouring patches in which it is embedded. Another difficulty is yet another manifestation of the scale problem. Say we want to effect a shape change that involves many patches. We have to move these patches together and maintain their continuity with all their neighbouring patches.

Despite these difficulties we should recognize that this representation has a strong potential for shape editing compared with the polygon mesh representa-tion. This is already an approximation and pulling vertices around to change the shape of the represented object results in many difficulties. The accuracy of the polygon mesh representation changes as soon as vertices are moved, resulting perhaps in visual defects. It is almost certain that we would always have to move groups of points rather than moving a single polygon vertex around in three space. Pulling a single vertex would just result in a local peak.

In this chapter we will mainly confine ourselves to the study of single patches and simple shapes formed from nets of a few patches using rudimentary but powerful CAD devices such as generating a solid object by sweeping a profile through 360 degrees.

The analytical representation of patches differs according to the formulation and some have been named after their instigators. One of the most popular for-mulations is the Bézier patch developed in the 1960s by Pierre Bézier for use in the design of Renault cars. His CAD system, called UNISURF, was one of the first to be used. In what follows we will concentrate mainly on the Bézier formulation. The usual approach in considering parametric representation is to begin with a description of three-dimensional space curves and then to generalize to surfaces or patches. A three-dimensional space curve is a smooth curve that is a function of the three spatial variables. An example would be the path that a particle traced as it moved through space. Incidentally curves by themselves also find applications in computer graphics. For example, we can script the path of an object in three-dimensional computer animation by using a space curve. We can model a 'ducted' solid by sweeping a cross-section along a space curve.

7.2 Bézier and the secret curves

In this section we will look at the pioneering developments of Bézier, who was amongst the first to develop computer tools in industrial design. We will draw on Bézier's own descriptions of the evolution of his method, not just because of their historical interest but because they give a real insight into the relationship between the representation, the physical reality and the requirements of the designers who were to use his methods.

Bézier's development work was carried out in the Renault car factory in the 1960s and he called his system UNISURF. Car designers are concerned with styling free-form surfaces which are then used to produce master dies which produce the tools that stamp out the manufactured parts. Many other industries use free-form surfaces. Some parts such as ships' hulls, airframes and turbine blades are constrained by aerodynamic and hydrodynamic considerations and shapes evolve through experience and testing in wind tunnels and test tanks – but a designer still needs freedom to produce new shapes albeit within these constraints. Before the advent of this representational form such free-form surfaces could not be represented analytically and once developed could only be stored for future reproduction and evolution by sampling and storing as coordinates.

The process of going from the abstract design to the prototype was lengthy and involved many people and processes. The following description, abstracted from Bézier's account in Piegl's book, is of the process of car design at the time:

(1) Stylists defined a general shape using small-scale sketches and clay mock-ups.

(2) Using offsets (world coordinates in computer graphics terminology) measured on the mock-up, designers traced a full-scale shape of the skin of the car body.

(3) Plasterers built a full-scale model, weighing about 8 tons, starting from plywood cross-sections duplicating the curves of the drawing. The clay model was then examined by stylists and sales managers, and modified according to taste.

(4) When at last the model was accepted, offsets were again measured and the final drawings were made. During this period, which could be a year or

more, tooling and production specialists often suggested minor changes to avoid difficult and costly operations during production.

(5) The drawings were finalized, and one three-dimensional master was built as the standard for checking the press tools and stamped parts.

(6) The plaster copies of the master were used for milling punches and dies on copy-machine tools...

Bézier's pioneer development completely changed most aspects of these processes by enabling a representation of free-form surfaces. Before, a designer would produce curves using, say, a device such as a French curve. The designer used his skill and experience to produce a complete curve that was built up a step at a time using segments along some portion of the French curve. A curve so generated could not be stored in any convenient way except as a set of samples. Bézier's development was a definition that enabled such curves to be represented as four points, known as control points, and an implicit set of basis or blending functions. When the four points are injected into the definition the curve is generated or reproduced. This has two immediate consequences. The definition could be used to directly drive a numerically controlled milling machine and the part is produced exactly without the intervention of complications and delays. (Numerically controlled milling machines had been in existence since 1955 and were another motivation for the development of CAGD.) The definition could be used as a basis of a CAD program in which modifications to the curve could be made to a computer visualization.

Bézier describes an intriguing difficulty that he experienced at the time:

When it was suggested that these curves replace sweeps and French curves, most stylists objected that they had invented their own templates and would not change their methods. It was therefore solemnly promised that their secret curves would be translated into secret listings and buried in the most secret part of the computer's memory, and that nobody but them would keep the key of the vaulted cellar. In fact, the standard curves were flexible enough and secret curves were soon forgotten; designers and draughtsmen easily understood the polygons and their relationship with the shape of the corresponding curves.

Many simultaneous developments were occurring in other industries – notably aircraft and ship manufacture, and much of the research was carried out under the auspices of particular manufacturers, who, like Bézier at Renault, developed their own CAD systems and surface representations suited to their own requirements. This has led to a number of parametric definitions of surfaces and the interested reader is best referred to Piegl's book in which each chapter is written by a pioneer in this field.

Bézier states that one of the most important requirements of his representation was that it should be founded on geometry and that the underlying mathematics be easily understood. He introduced the concept of a space curve being contained in a cube which when distorted into a parallelepiped distorts the curve (Figure 7.1). The curve is 'fixed' within the parallelepiped as follows:

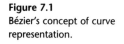

Figure 7.1
Bézier's concept of curve
representation.

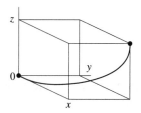

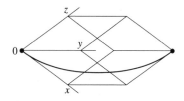

Curve 'contained' by a cube

Drawing the cube into a
parallelepiped changes the curve

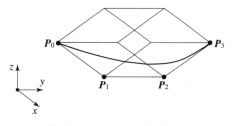

Vertices used as control points

- The start and end points of the curve are located at opposite vertices of the parallelepiped.
- At its start point the curve is tangential to OX.
- At its end point the curve is tangential to OZ.

This geometric concept uniquely defines any space curve (if it is understood that the curve is a polynomial of a certain degree) and also gives an intuitive feel for how the curve changes shape as the parallelepiped changes. Now the parallelepiped, and thus the curve, can be completely defined by four points – known as **control points** – P_0, P_1, P_2 and P_3 which are just vertices of the parallelepiped as shown in the figure. Given that the position of the end points of the curve is fixed and its behaviour at the end points is determined, the shape that the curve traces out in space between its extremities needs to be defined. A parametric definition was chosen which means that the space curve $Q(u)$ is defined in terms of a parameter u ($0 \leq u \leq 1$). As u varies from 0 to 1 we arrive at values for the position of a point on $Q(u)$ by scaling or blending the control points. That is, each point on the curve is determined by scaling each control point by a cubic polynomial known as a basis or blending function. The curve is then given by:

$$Q(u) = \sum_{i=0}^{3} P_i B_i(u)$$

and in the case of a Bézier curve the basis or blending functions are the Bernstein cubic polynomials:

$$B_0(u) = (1-u)^3$$
$$B_1(u) = 3u(1-u)^2$$
$$B_2(u) = 3u^2(1-u)$$
$$B_3(u) = u^3$$

Figure 7.2 shows these polynomials and a Bézier curve (projected into the two-dimensional space of the diagram).

A useful intuitive notion is the following. As we move physically along the curve from $u=0$ to $u=1$ we simultaneously move a vertical line in the basis function space that defines four values for the basis functions. Weighting each basis function by the control points and summing, we obtain the corresponding point in the space of the curve (Figure 7.2). We note that for any value of u (except $u=0$ and $u=1$) all the functions are non-zero. This means that the positions of all the control points contribute to every point on the curve (except at the end points). At $u=0$ only B_0 is non-zero. Therefore:

$$\boldsymbol{Q}(0) = \boldsymbol{P}_0$$

similarly

$$\boldsymbol{Q}(1) = \boldsymbol{P}_3$$

We also note that:

$$B_0(u) + B_1(u) + B_2(u) + B_3(u) = 1$$

Figure 7.2

Moving along the curve by increasing u is equivalent to moving a vertical line through the basis functions. The intercepts of this line with the basis functions give the values of B for the equivalent point.

Joining the four control points together gives the so-called control polygon and moving the control points around produces new curves. Moving a single control point of the curve distorts its shape in an intuitive manner. This is demonstrated in Figure 7.3. The effect of moving the end points is obvious. When we move the inner control points $\boldsymbol{P}_1$ and $\boldsymbol{P}_2$ we change the orientation of the tangent vectors to the curves at the end points – again obvious. Less obvious is that the position of $\boldsymbol{P}_1$ and $\boldsymbol{P}_2$ also control the magnitude of the tangent vectors and it can be shown that:

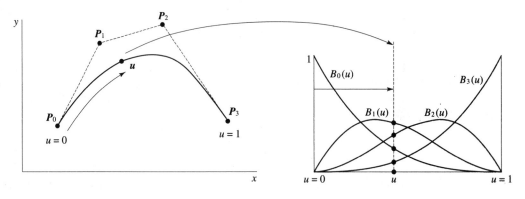

Space of curve   Space of basis functions

Figure 7.3
Effects of moving control
point P_1.

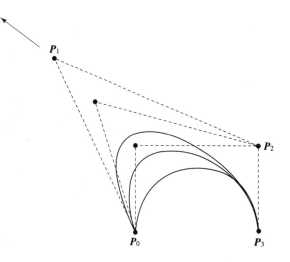

$$Q_u(0) = 3(P_1 - P_0)$$
$$Q_u(1) = 3(P_2 - P_3)$$

where Q_u is the tangent vector to the curve (first derivative) at the end point. It can be seen that the curve is pulled towards the tangent vector with greater magnitude which is controlled by the position of the control points.

Bézier's original cube concept, encapsulating a curve of three spatial variables, seems to have been lost and most texts simply deal with the curves of two spatial variables enclosed in a control polygon. Applications where three-dimensional space curves have to be designed, three-dimensional computer animation for example, can have interfaces where two-dimensional projections of the curve are used. (Note that for a three-dimensional curve the parallelepiped determines the plane in which the tangents to the curve – the edges of the control polygon – are oriented.)

At this point it is useful to consider all the ramifications of representing a curve with control points. The most important property, as far as interaction is concerned, is that moving the control points gives an intuitive change in curve shape. Another way of putting it is to say that the curve mimics the shape of the control polygon. An important property from the point of view of the algorithms that deal with curves (and surfaces) is that a curve is always enclosed in the convex hull formed by the control polygon.

The convex hull of a two space curve is illustrated in Figure 7.4 and can be considered to be the polygon formed by placing an elastic band around the control points. This follows from the fact that the basis functions sum to unity for all u.

Now consider transforming curves. Since the curves are defined as linear combinations of the control points, the curve is transformed by any affine transformation (rotation, scaling, translation and so on) in three-dimensional space by applying the appropriate transformations to the set of control points. Thus to transform a curve we transform the control points and then compute the points

Figure 7.4
Convex hull property for
cubic spline. The curve is
contained in the shaded
area formed from the
control points.

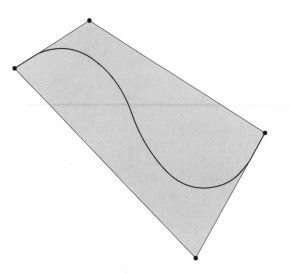

on the curve. In this context note that it is not easy to transform a curve by computing the points and then transforming (as we might do with an implicit description). For example, it is not clear in scaling how many points are needed to ensure smoothness when the curve has been magnified. Note here that perspective transformations are non-affine, so we cannot map control points to screen space and compute the curve there.

7.3 From curves to surfaces

The treatment of parametric cubic curve segments given in the foregoing sections is easily generalised to bi-parametric cubic surface patches. A point on the surface patch is given by a bi-parametric function and a set of blending or basis functions are used for each parameter. A cubic Bézier patch is defined as:

$$Q(u) = \sum_{i=0}^{3} \sum_{j=0}^{3} P_{ij} B_i(u) B_j(v)$$

Mathematically the three-dimensional surfaces are said to be generated from the Cartesian product of two curves. A Bézier patch and its control points are shown in Figure 7.5 where the patches are displayed using iso-parametric lines. The 16 control points form a characteristic polyhedron and this bears a relationship to the shape of the surface, in the same way that the characteristic polygon relates to a curve segment. From Figure 7.5(a) it can be seen intuitively that 12 of the control points are associated with the boundary edges of the patch (four of them specifying the end points). Only the corner vertices lie in the surface. In fact if we consider the control points to form a matrix of 4×4 points then the four groups of four points forming the edges of the matrix are the control points for the boundary curves of the patch. Thus the edges of the patch are made up of

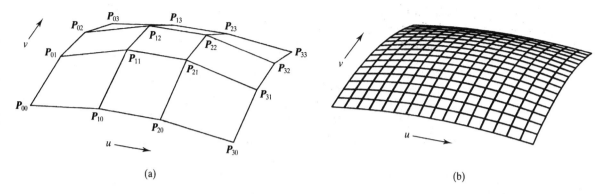

(a)

(b)

Figure 7.5
(a) A control polyhedron and (b) the resulting bicubic Bézier patch.

Figure 7.6
The effect of 'lifting' one of the control points of a Bézier patch.

four Bézier curves. We can now see that the remaining four control points must specify the shape of the surface contained between the boundary edges.

The properties of the Bézier curve formulation are extended into the surface domain. Figure 7.6 (which is Figure 2.10 reproduced here for convenience) shows a patch being deformed by 'pulling out' a single control point. The intuitive feel for the surface through its control points and the ability to ensure first order continuity are maintained. The surface patch is transformed by applying transformations to each of the control points.

The way in which the control points 'work' can be seen by analogy with the cubic curve. The geometric interpretation is naturally more difficult than that for the curve and, of course, the purpose of the Bézier formulation is to protect the

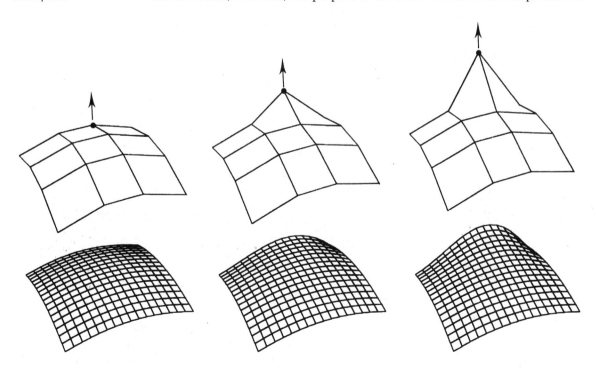

designer against having to manipulate tangent vectors and so on, but it is included for completeness.

The matrix of control points is:

$$P = \begin{bmatrix} P_{00} & P_{01} & P_{02} & P_{03} \\ P_{10} & P_{11} & P_{12} & P_{13} \\ P_{20} & P_{21} & P_{22} & P_{23} \\ P_{30} & P_{31} & P_{32} & P_{33} \end{bmatrix}$$

It is instructive to examine the relationship between control points and derivative vectors at the corner of a patch. For example, consider the corner $u = v = 0$. The relationship between the control points and the vectors associated with the vertex P_{00} is as follows:

$$Q_u(0,0) = 3\,(P_{10} - P_{00})$$
$$Q_v(0,0) = 3\,(P_{01} - P_{00})$$
$$Q_{uv}(0,0) = 9\,(P_{00} - P_{01} - P_{10} + P_{11})$$

Figure 7.7 shows these vectors at a patch corner. $Q_u(0,0)$ is a constant times the tangent vector at $Q(0,0)$ in the u parameter direction. Similarly $Q_v(0,0)$ relates to the tangent vector in the v parameter direction. The cross derivatives at each endpoint, sometimes called twist vectors, specify the rate of change of the tangent vectors with respect to u and v. It is a vector normal to the plane containing the tangent vectors.

Figure 7.7
Vectors at P_{00}. (a) Tangent vectors at P_{00}. (b) Elements of control point matrix involved in vectors at P_{00}.

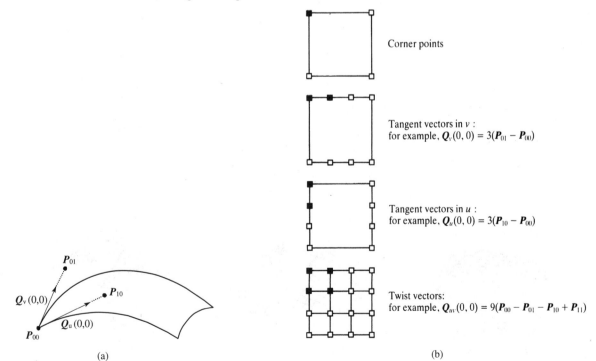

Corner points

Tangent vectors in v :
for example, $Q_v(0,0) = 3(P_{01} - P_{00})$

Tangent vectors in u :
for example, $Q_u(0,0) = 3(P_{10} - P_{00})$

Twist vectors:
for example, $Q_{uv}(0,0) = 9(P_{00} - P_{01} - P_{10} + P_{11})$

(a)

(b)

Analogous to the control points in Bézier curves, patches are specified in terms of four end points, eight tangent vectors (two at each corner) and four twist vectors. Consider Figure 7.7(b) which shows the elements of the control point polyhedron that are involved in the derivatives. Four pairs of points specify the tangent vectors in u at each corner (two rows in the matrix), four pairs specify tangent vectors in v (two columns in the matrix) and all 16 elements specify the twist vectors.

If we set $\mathbf{Q}_{uv}(i,j) = 0$ then we have a so-called zero twist surface or a surface with four zero twist vectors. For such a surface the inner control points can be derived from the three adjacent edge points. For example, at the (0,0) corner we have:

$$0 = 9\,(\mathbf{P}_{00} - \mathbf{P}_{01} - \mathbf{P}_{10} + \mathbf{P}_{11})$$

This is important when we wish to derive the 16 control points of a patch when we only have knowledge of the boundary curves. This situation occurs in surface fitting or interpolation when we wish to fit a patch through a set of points in three space. We do this by first using curve interpolation to define the boundary curves of the patches – giving 12 of the control points for a patch – and estimating in some way the four internal control points. The zero twist solution is a particularly easy way to estimate what the four internal control points should be.

For shading calculations we need to calculate certain surface normals. One of the easiest ways to shade a patch is to subdivide it until the products of the subdivision are approximately planar (this technique is discussed fully later in the chapter). The patches can then be treated as planar polygons and Gouraud or Phong shading applied. Vertex normals are calculated from the cross-product of the two tangent vectors at the vertex. For example:

$$\mathbf{a} = (\mathbf{P}_{01} - \mathbf{P}_{00})$$
$$\mathbf{b} = (\mathbf{P}_{10} - \mathbf{P}_{00})$$
$$\mathbf{N} = \mathbf{a} \times \mathbf{b}$$

A normal can be computed at any point on the surface from the cross-product of the two partial derivatives $\partial \mathbf{Q}/\partial u$ and $\partial \mathbf{Q}/\partial v$ but shading a patch by exhaustive calculation of internal points from the parametric description is computationally expensive and is subject to other problems. The advantages of using a parametric patch description of a surface are not contained in the fact that a precise world coordinate is available for every point in the surface – the cost of retrieving this information is generally too high – but in advantages that patch representation has to offer in object modelling.

7.4 Modelling with Bézier patches

The Bézier representation is excellent for single segment curves and single patch surfaces. When we want to make a curve (or surface) that is more complex, we have to join Bézier curves together using a continuity constraint. At the beginning of this chapter and in Chapter 2 we discussed the general issues in modelling with bicubic parametric patches. We will now develop these in detail. First we have to look at the way in which we have to join patches together to maintain continuity over a surface and we will do this by developing the argument from the joining of Bézier curve segments.

7.4.1 Joining Bézier curve segments

Curve segments, defined by a set of four control points, can be joined to make up 'more complex' curves than that obtainable from a single segment. This results in a so-called piecewise polynomial curve. An alternative method of representing more complex curves is to increase the degree of the polynomial, but this has computational and mathematical disadvantages and it is generally considered easier to split the curve into cubic segments. Connecting curve segments implies that constraints must apply at the joins. The default constraint is positional continuity, the next best is first order (or tangential continuity). The difference between positional and first order continuity for a Bézier curve is shown in Figure 7.8. Positional continuity means that the end point of the first segment is coincident with the start point of the second. First order continuity means that

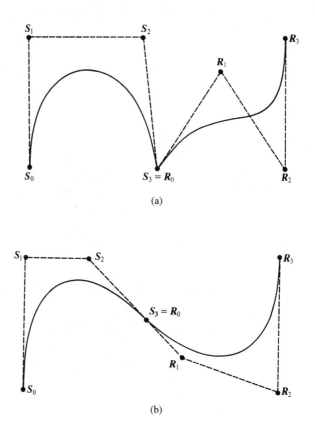

(a)

(b)

Figure 7.8
Continuity between Bézier curve segments.
(a) Positional continuity between Bézier points.
(b) Tangential continuity between Bézier points.

the edges of the characteristic polygon are collinear as shown in the figure. This means that the tangent vectors, at the end of one curve and the start of the other, match to within a constant. In shaded surfaces, maintaining only positional continuity would possibly result in the joins being visible in the final rendered object.

If the control points of the two segments are S_i and R_i then first order continuity is maintained if:

$$(S_3 - S_2) = k(R_1 - R_0)$$

Using this condition a composite Bézier curve is easily built up by adding a single segment at a time. However, the advantage of being able to build up a composite form from segments is somewhat negated by the constraints on local control that now apply because of the joining conditions.

7.4.2

Joining Bézier surface patches

Maintaining first order continuity across two patches is a simple extension of the curve joining constraints and is best considered geometrically. Figure 7.9 shows two patches, S and R, sharing a common edge. For positional or zero order continuity:

$$S(1,v) = R(0,v) \text{ for } 0 < v < 1$$

This condition implies that the two characteristic polygons share a common boundary edge (Figure 7.10) and:

$$S_{33} = R_{03}$$
$$S_{32} = R_{02}$$
$$S_{31} = R_{01}$$
$$S_{30} = R_{00}$$

or

$$S_{3i} = R_{0i} \quad i = 0 \ldots 3$$

To satisfy first order continuity the tangent vectors at $u = 1$ for the first patch must match those at $u = 0$ for the second patch for all v. This implies that each of the four pairs of polyhedron edges that straddle the boundary must be collinear (Figure 7.10). That is:

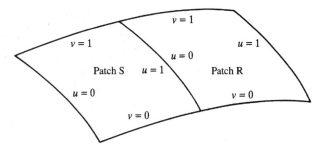

Figure 7.9
Joining two patches.

Figure 7.10
(a) Positional continuity
between bicubic Bézier
patches and (b) tangential
continuity between bicubic
Bézier patches.

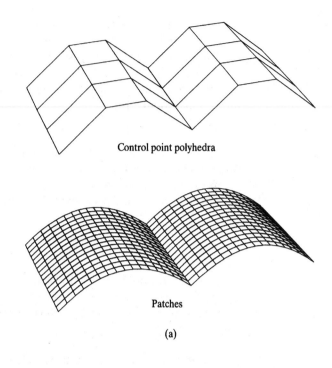

Control point polyhedra

Patches

(a)

Four sets of three control points must be collinear

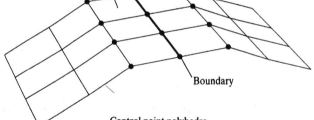

Boundary

Control point polyhedra

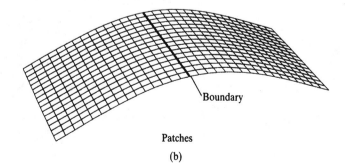

Boundary

Patches

(b)

$$(\boldsymbol{S}_{3i} - \boldsymbol{S}_{2i}) = k(\boldsymbol{R}_{1i} - \boldsymbol{R}_{0i}) \quad i = 0 \dots 3$$

Faux in 1979 pointed out that in CAD contexts, this constraint is severe, if a composite surface is constructed from a set of Bézier patches. For example, a composite surface might be designed by constructing a single patch and working outwards from it. Joining two patches along a common boundary implies that eight of the control points for the second patch are already fixed and joining a patch to two existing patches implies that 12 of the control points are fixed.

A slightly less restrictive joining condition was developed by Bézier in 1972. In this patch corners have positional but not gradient continuity. However, tangent vectors of edges meeting at a corner must be co-planar. Even with this marginally greater flexibility, there are still problems with the design of composite surfaces.

It should be mentioned that although the foregoing treatment has dealt with rectangular patches, such patches cannot represent all shapes. Consider, for example, a spherically shaped object. Rectangular patches must degenerate to triangles at the poles. Farin points out that perhaps the main reason for the predominance of rectangular patches in most CAD systems is that the first applications of patches in car design were to the design of the outer body panels. Those parts have a rectangular geometry and it is natural to break them down into smaller rectangles and use rectangularly shaped patches.

7.4.3 Modelling and interaction with Bézier patches

From the preceding section it is clear that we have to maintain continuity between patches when we perform any kind of shape interaction. In practice, because in many industrial design applications we are dealing with fairly simple objects, we can control the shape of patches by editing and maintaining continuity with curves. The curve editing controls 'global' stylistic alterations according to the constraints of the application. Contextual constraints such as symmetry enable us to control the shape of surfaces by controlling the shape of curves.

Therefore let us start at how we can move the control points of curves around in a two-segment Bézier curve. Consider Figure 7.11. This shows three cases of simple editing protocols that will maintain continuity between the two curve segments. We can:

Figure 7.11
Examples of possible shape editing protocols for a 2 segment Bézier curve.
(a) Maintain the orientation of $\boldsymbol{R}_1\boldsymbol{S}_2$ and move any of the three control points $\boldsymbol{R}_1$, $\boldsymbol{S}_3/\boldsymbol{R}_0$, $\boldsymbol{S}_2$ along this line.
(b) Rotate the line $\boldsymbol{R}_1\boldsymbol{S}_2$ about $\boldsymbol{S}_3/\boldsymbol{R}_0$. (c) Move the three control points $\boldsymbol{R}_1$, $\boldsymbol{S}_3/\boldsymbol{R}_0$, $\boldsymbol{S}_2$ as a 'locked' unit.

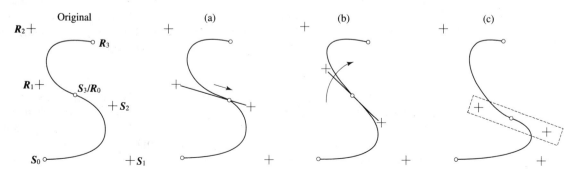

Figure 7.12
Four adjoining Bézier
patches and their
control points. Continuity
constraints imply that the
central control point
cannot be moved without
considering its eight
neighbours. All nine points
can be moved together and
continuity maintained.

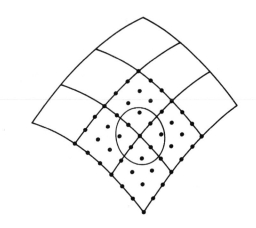

- maintain the orientation of the line R_1S_2 and move any of the three control points along this line (Figure 7.11(a));
- rotate the same line about the common point R_0S_3 (Figure 7.11(b));
- move all three points as a locked unit (Figure 7.11(c)).

Trying to extend these interactive procedures to patches is difficult. Consider Figure 7.12. This shows that if we apply the third curve editing procedure to a the corner point where four patches meet then we would have to move the encircled nine points as a unit. The shape editing becomes difficult and the interface would be cumbersome. In addition, moving groups of nine control points simultaneously may not give us the desired alteration to the shape of the surface that we required.

We will now look at an example where the design constraints enable us to work and interface with curves and then use these curves to derive an object made up of a net of patches.

7.5 Patch CAGD example

Consider using an eight-patch surface to design containers or bowls that in cross-section have four-fold symmetry. That is, the final object can be considered to be made by sweeping some kind of cross-section along a linear axis or spine. Many industrial objects fall into this category. We will develop a hierarchy of three manifestations of this design each increasing in complexity in the nature of the variation of the cross-section.

It may be that a patch model (rather than a polygon mesh representation) is important in this context because we want the ability to make global stylistic changes and also because we want a high quality visualization of the object. Objects such as bottles have most of their shape defined in projection by their silhouette edge and we may not want to encounter the silhouette edge degradation that would come from using a polygon mesh model for the visualization.

We decide that to give us a reasonable degree of shape control the minimum number of patches that we can tolerate is eight.

The possibilities and the interactive protocol required are now dealt with. The illustrations show models constructed with 8 patches, the formulae given relate to a single patch.

Linear axis design – scaled circular cross-sections

Here we can only have circular cross-sections and the objects that we can design are of the form shown in Figure 7.13. (Actually Bézier curves can only approximate a perfect circle, but this complication we shall ignore.) To derive the eight patches in this case we need only interact with a two-segment Bézier curve. This is known as a profile curve. This gives the control points for two patches and the other control points for the other six patches are obtained by symmetry. Such objects are also well known as solids of revolution.

If we take the z axis as the spine of the object the control points of a bottom patch are given by:

$$
\begin{bmatrix} P_{00} & P_{01} & P_{02} & P_{03} \\ P_{10} & P_{11} & P_{12} & P_{13} \\ P_{20} & P_{21} & P_{22} & P_{23} \\ P_{30} & P_{31} & P_{32} & P_{33} \end{bmatrix} = \begin{bmatrix} T_{00} \\ T_{10} \\ T_{20} \\ T_{30} \end{bmatrix} \begin{matrix} r_0 & r_1 & r_2 & r_3 \end{matrix} + \begin{bmatrix} k \\ k \\ k \\ k \end{bmatrix} \begin{matrix} z_0 & z_1 & z_2 & z_3 \end{matrix}
$$

where T_{00}, T_{10}, T_{20} and T_{30} are the control points for the quarter circle forming a cross-section segment circle:

$T_{00} = (0, 1, 0)$

$T_{10} = (c, 1, 0)$

$T_{20} = (1, c, 0)$

$T_{30} = (1, 0, 0)$

$c = 0.552$ (approx.)

Figure 7.13

Linear axis design – circular cross-section, object is designed by a single profile curve.

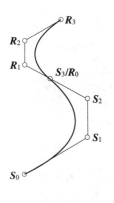

Profile design

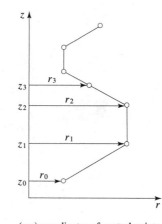

(r, v) coordinates of control points

Object

and the control points for the surface patch lie on circles of radius r_0, r_1, r_2 and r_3 at distances z_0, z_1, z_2 and z_3 along the z axis. The segments S_0S_1, S_2R_1 and R_2R_3 sweep out to form truncated cones. The designed surface is tangential to these conical sections at the top, bottom and join cross-section. We can derive the top patch similarly.

Linear axis design – non-circular scaled cross-sections

This time we allow the quarter cross-section to be any shape and we design now with a profile curve as before and also a curve for the quarter cross-section (Figure 7.14). The cross-section maintains its shape and only varies in scale.

The control points for a bottom patch are again given by the equation given in the previous section, except that T_{00}, T_{10}, T_{20} and T_{30} are obtained from the cross-section design rather than being predefined.

Linear axis design – non-circular varying cross-sections

There are many options for blending different cross-section curves. An easy approach is to confine the blend to a single segment of the profile curve – the upper say. Thus in this example the upper four patches will exhibit a varying cross-section, while the lower four will have a constant cross-section as before.

Here we allow the cross-section to vary in shape and we design two cross-sections which form the top and bottom edge of a single patch (Figure 7.15). Now we need to define intermediate curves from the top and bottom curves of a patch. This can be done simply by defining:

$$Q(u,v) = Q(u,0)\,(1 - r(v)) + Q(u,1)r(v)$$

Figure 7.14
Linear axis design – scaled (non-circular) cross-section. Object is designed by one profile curve and one (1/4) cross-section curve.

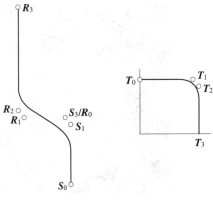

Profile design   Cross-section design   Object

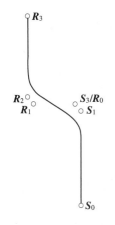

Profile design

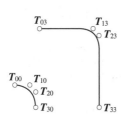

Cross-section design

Object

Figure 7.15
Linear axis design –
non-circular varying cross-
section. Object is designed
by one profile curve and
three cross-sections.

where

$$r(0) = 0 \text{ and } r(1) = 1$$

Figure 7.16 is a representation of this procedure from which it can be seen that the curve $Q(u,v)$ has a characteristic polygon whose control points lie on lines joining the control points of the two cross-sections.

The control points of a patch are now given by

$$\begin{bmatrix} P_{00} & P_{01} & P_{02} & P_{03} \\ P_{10} & P_{11} & P_{12} & P_{13} \\ P_{20} & P_{21} & P_{22} & P_{23} \\ P_{30} & P_{31} & P_{32} & P_{33} \end{bmatrix} = \begin{bmatrix} T_{00} & T_{03} \\ T_{10} & T_{13} \\ T_{20} & T_{23} \\ T_{30} & T_{33} \end{bmatrix} \begin{bmatrix} 1 & 1-r_1 & 1-r_2 & 0 \\ 0 & r_1 & r_2 & 1 \end{bmatrix} + \begin{bmatrix} k \\ k \\ k \\ k \end{bmatrix} [z_0 \ z_1 \ z_2 \ z_3]$$

where T_{00}, T_{10}, T_{20} and T_{30} are the control points for the first cross-section (bottom edge) and T_{03}, T_{13}, T_{23} and T_{33} are the control points for the second cross-section.

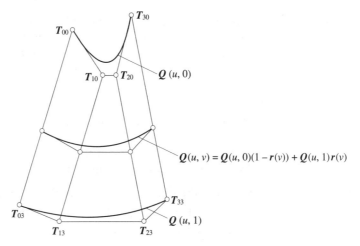

Figure 7.16
Blending two different cross-
sections using the profile
curve.

7.6 Deriving a net of patches from an object – surface fitting

This process was reviewed in Chapter 2 where a particular example was given. We will now supply a little more detail of this somewhat difficult technique. The basic idea is that we perform three-dimensional interpolation and fit a surface to a set of points that have been sampled, in some way, over the surface of an object. The algorithm is as follows.

(1) Fit iso-parametric curves through the points to give a net of cubic curves in u and v (Figure 2.12). Obviously this requires context-dependent knowledge of the organization of the data points. That is, which set of points form into sequences in u and which into sequences in v? Standard interpolation techniques can be used (see, for example, Farin's book) and the easiest method is B-spline interpolation. This gives a net of cubic parametric curves where each element in the net is a curvilinear quadrilateral made up of four curves that form the boundary segments of a patch.

(2) Convert the curves into patches. We now have, for each patch, 12 out of the 16 control points for each patch because we have found the boundary curves for each patch. We have to derive the inner four control points and then we have a complete patch description for the entire net.

(3) The easiest solution, given the boundary curve control points, is to assume the surface is everywhere a zero twist surface and derive the inner control points from the existing 12 (boundary curve) control points. (Obviously this will give a zero twist surface. A zero twist surface is a so-called translational surface (Section 7.3) where the surface can be generated by sweeping an isoparametric curve in u with one of its end points embedded in an iso-parametric curve in v. In other words, the surface can be generated from two curves. The uv net to which we want to fit patches will not, in general, be made up of translational curves and this solution, although it 'fits' the boundary curve, makes the surface patch behave internally as if it was a translational surface.)

The B-spline Bézier complication in the approach arises from the fact that it is easiest to perform B-spline interpolation to provide the uv curve network, but fitting patches to this net is best done in the Bézier basis domain. Full details of the algorithm are given in the Watt and Watt book.

7.7 Rendering parametric surfaces

Algorithms that scan convert surfaces represented by bicubic parametric patches divide naturally into two categories:

● those that render directly from the parametric description, and

● those that approximate the surface by a polygon mesh and use a planar polygon scan converter to render this approximation.

Currently the second approach appears to be the more popular. It is certainly the easier to implement and is computationally less expensive.

Approximation to a surface patch using a polygon mesh

In Chapter 2 we overviewed the process of patch splitting as a rendering strategy for objects modelled from bicubic parametric patches. We now investigate this process in more detail.

A planar polygon mesh is easily generated from a surface patch. The patch can be divided using iso-parametric curves. (Splitting up a patch into iso-parametric curves is a common method of display in CAD systems, permitting a wireframe visualization of the surface sufficient for the requirements of such systems.) This yields a net or mesh of points at the intersection of these curves with each other and the boundary edges. This net of points can be used to define the vertices for a mesh of planar polygons which can then be rendered using a planar polygon renderer. There are two basic flaws in this rudimentary approach. Visible boundary edges and silhouette edges may exhibit discontinuities. In general, a finer polygon resolution will be necessary to diminish the visibility of piecewise linear discontinuities on edges than is necessary to maintain smooth shading within the patch. There is also the subtlety that an internal silhouette edge in the patch will generally be of higher degree than cubic.

Connected with this is the question: how fine should the iso-parametric division be? Too fine a subdivision is computationally expensive, too coarse implies visible discontinuities. A possible approach is to relate the number of divisions to the area projected by the patch on the screen.

A subtler approach is a varying 'resolution'. Areas of the patch that are 'flattish' are subject to few subdivisions. Areas where the local curvature is high are subject to more subdivisions. Effectively the patch is subdivided to a degree that depends on local curvature.

Patches are subdivided until the products of the subdivision submit to a flatness criterion. Such patches are now considered to be approximately planar polygons and are scan converted by a normal polygon renderer using the corner points of the patches as vertices for rectangles in the polygon mesh. The set of patches representing the surface can be pre-processed, yielding a set of polygons which are then scan converted as normal.

There are two significant advantages to patch splitting:

- it is fast, and
- the speed can be varied by altering the depth of the subdivision. This is important for interactive systems.

Subdivision algorithms are best considered for a curve. These are then easily extended or generalized to deal with a patch. The crux of the method is that rather than evaluate points along a curve, the curve is approximated by a piecewise linear version obtained by subdividing the control points recursively. This gives a finer and finer approximation to the curve. The level of subdivision/ recursion terminates when a linearity criterion is satisfied. It can be shown that the piecewise linear approximation to the curve will eventually 'collapse' onto the curve, providing enough subdivisions are undertaken.

A Bézier curve is subdivided into two curves by subdividing the control points, forming two new sets of control points R_i and S_i. The point R_3/S_0 is the end point of the first curve and the start of the second. The formula is:

$$R_0 = Q_0 \qquad\qquad S_0 = R_3$$
$$R_1 = (Q_0 + Q_1)/2 \qquad\qquad S_1 = (Q_1 + Q_2)/4 + S_2/2$$
$$R_2 = R_1/2 + (Q_1 + Q_2)/4 \qquad S_2 = (Q_2 + Q_3)/2$$
$$R_3 = (R_2 + S_1)/2 \qquad\qquad S_3 = Q_3$$

Figure 7.17(a) shows how, after a single subdivision, the piecewise linear curve joining the two new sets of control points is a better approximation to the curve

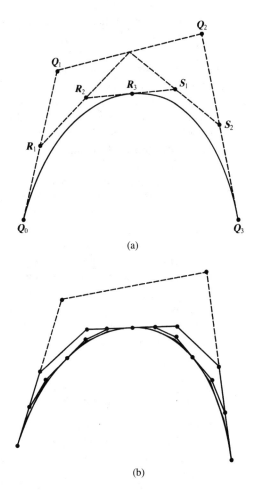

(a)

(b)

Figure 7.17
Recursively splitting a
Bézier curve. (a) First split.
(b) Drawing the control
points at each level of
subdivision.

than the original. The approximation after three levels of subdivision is shown in Figure 7.17(b).

The curve splitting process is easily extended to patches as is demonstrated in Figure 7.18. We can either split in the u parametric direction and then v or vice versa – it does not matter. Interpret, say, rows of the control point matrix as the control polygons of Bézier curves and apply the curve splitting formula to the four rows. This results in 2×4×4 control points splitting the patch along a v iso-parametric curve. We then apply the same procedure to split the patch along a u curve by applying the same formula to columns of each of the new control nets resulting in 4×16 control points for the four sub-patches into which the original is now split.

This efficient formula (which uses only additions and divide by twos) makes the subdivision rapid. The depth of the subdivision is easily controlled using a linearity criterion. The Bézier basis functions sum identically to 1. This means that the curve lies in the convex hull formed by the control points P_i. The piece-wise linear subdivision product will coincide with the curve when it 'merges' with the line joining the two end points. The degree to which this is achieved, that is, the linearity of the line joining the four control points, can be tested by

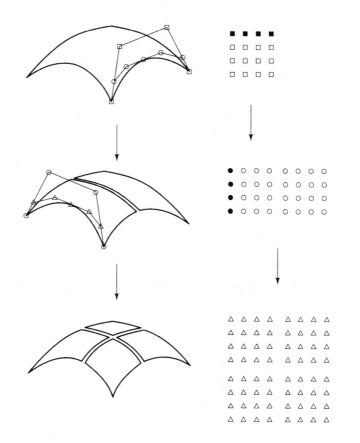

Figure 7.18
A conceptual illustration of patch subdivision.

Figure 7.19
A cubic Bézier curve with control points P_0, P_1, P_2, P_3.

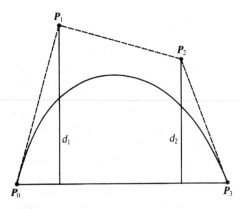

measuring the distance from the middle two control points to the end point joining line (Figure 7.19).

The philosophy of this test is easily extended to surface patches. A plane is fitted through three non-collinear control points. The distance of each of the other 13 control points from this plane is then calculated. If one of these distances lies outside a pre-specified tolerance, then the patch is further subdivided.

A practical problem that occurs when considering non-uniform subdivision (until a flatness criterion is satisfied) compared with uniform subdivision to some predetermined level, is the cost of the flatness test. It is debatable if it is a simpler and better, but less elegant approach, simply to adopt uniform subdivision and ignore the fact that some areas are going to be unnecessarily subdivided (because they are already flat). Figure 7.20 (Colour Plate) shows a uniform subdivision approach for the Utah teapot at subdivisions of one, two and three. This shows predictably that the difference in quality between the rendered images is mainly visible along silhouette edges.

If uniform subdivision is adopted then rendering bicubic patches can reduce to a pre-processing phase of a normal Z-buffer renderer. A polygon mesh model is generated from the parametric representation. This method requires a large database for the subdivision products. If sufficient memory is not available, and the extra complexity of a scan line algorithm needs to be introduced, then it is not a big step to use non-uniform subdivision.

7.8 From patches to objects

We have stressed that one of the main *raisons d'être* of this representation is that it can be used to program a numerically controlled cutting device enabling the abstract design to be converted directly into an object or a model of the object.

In most applications this involves programming a cutting tool to remove material from a stock shape, such as a rectangular prism, to produce the desired object (Figure 7.21 shows an example of this process). The practical techniques depend on many factors such as the nature of the model, the material and the

Figure 7.21
Converting a computer
graphics model into a
real object. Courtesy of
H. Chiyokura.
Source: Chiyokura, H (1988)
Solid Modelling with
DESIGNBASE, Singapore:
Addison-Wesley Longman
Singapore Pte Ltd.

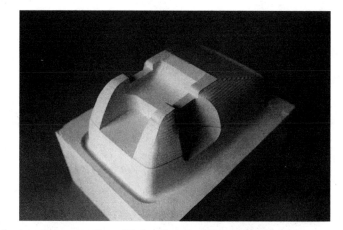

cutting device. For example, with hard material such as metal it may not be possible to remove all the material in one go. The cutter must be programmed to produce intermediate shapes to eventually arrive at the desired object. There is a minimum radius of curvature that the cutter can cope with due to its physical extent. This is easily imagined in the case of a tool with a hemispherical tip. The actual paths that the cutter must take need to be determined. So we will simply outline the principle here.

In the simplest possible case we can consider a tool tip positioned in a cutting device at a distance d from the reference point of the cutter. That is the three-dimensional point in the machine that the cutter needs to control. This point, leaving aside the issue of actual paths, generally has to move on a 'parallel' surface to the defined surface. This is known as an **offset surface**. A simple offset surface for a patch $Q(u,v)$ is given by

$$O(u,v) = Q(u,v) + dN(u,v)$$

This defines a normal surface $O(u,v)$ at a distance d along the normal $N(u,v)$. Having derived this surface cutter paths could be derived from suitably spaced iso-parametric curves that lie in the offset surface.

Further reading

One of the best examples of the free-form sculpting metaphor is a hierarchical method developed by Forsey and Bartels in which they use a B-spline patch representation. This method facilitates a continuum of editing possibilities between fine and coarse shape changes.

In this chapter we have emphasized mainly one historical thread – the developments of Bézier. An excellent historical reference that is contributed to by most of the important pioneers of CAGD (including Pierre Bézier) is the book edited by Piegl. Anyone interested in CAGD should treat this volume as mandatory reading.

For serious study of bicubic parametric patch representation the best general texts are by Faux and Pratt and by Farin. The former is oriented towards practical CAD methods and although it was first published in 1979, as an introduction to practical methods in CAD it has not been superseded. Farin's book is more theoretical, but is still eminently accessible to a non-specialist. It is more recent.

Many implementation details on patch algorithms, which have not been included in this text, are to be found in the Watt and Watt book.

Farin G. (1990). *Curves and Surfaces for Computer Aided Design*. Boston: Academic Press

Faux I.D. (1979). *Computational Geometry for Design and Manufacture*. Chichester, UK: Ellis Horwood

Forsey D.R. and Bartels R.H. (1988). Hierarchical B-spline refinement. *Computer Graphics*, **20**(4), 205–12 (Proc. SIGGRAPH 1988)

Piegl L. (1993). *Fundamental Developments of Computer-Aided Geometric Modelling*. New York: Academic Press

Watt A. and Watt M. (1992). *Advanced Animation and Rendering Techniques*. Wokingham, UK: Addison-Wesley

8 Defects in computer graphics images

8.1 Introduction – the difficulty of categorization

Defects in image synthesis could be said to fall into two categories. First there are algorithm signatures – defects or not depending on your point of view – that enable a knowledgeable viewer to discern the type of algorithm that produced the image. We know that a ray traced image is exactly that – because of the perfection of the specular interaction and other give-aways. We can perceive that it is not a photograph of reality. Another example that we discussed in Chapter 3 was the 'glossy' specular coefficient in Phong shading. Here we decided that the coefficient could equally be interpreted as a parameter that made it appear that a larger light source was illuminating the object. As we discussed in the introductory chapter the pursuit of photo-realism has long been accepted as a goal in image synthesis and from this point of view algorithm signatures are image defects because they do not imitate reality as accurately as we would like. This type of shortcoming we have dealt with in the course of describing the synthesis methods. We might term these defects as 'shortcomings'.

The other kind of defect is usually known as an alias – a somewhat confusing term, as we shall see, that derives from signal processing. We could define an alias as a noticeable or intolerable defect in an image that we need to eliminate.

Usually such defects are said to be caused by 'undersampling' and there is much theoretically based work that depends on the concept of undersampling. However, this is not the whole story. Because of the diverse nature of image synthesis algorithms, the way in which an algorithm samples the geometry of a scene determines the cause and the nature of the defects, and thus their cure. In simple ray tracing, a scene is sampled initially by dividing up the image plane and shooting a bundle of rays into the scene. As the rays 'recurse' they proceed to sample the scene geometry in a way that depends on their reflection and refraction directions at the previous level. In classical radiosity defects arise because of the finite size of patches and also because of the finite size of hemicube pixels. The way in which these defects arise and their visual manifestation are due more to the particular mechanisms of the radiosity algorithm. Certain defects in image synthesis do not admit an undersampling model. A good example of this is the interpolation defect in Phong shading which is due to the fact that the interpolation is performed after a perspective transformation.

Another difficulty with intolerable defects is that depending on their noticeability they take on different status – meaning that we decide, on the basis of their severity, that it is mandatory (or not) to try to eliminate them. For example, conventional texture mapping almost always produces unacceptable results and we normally incorporate an anti-aliasing procedure with the mapping algorithm (as we discussed in Chapter 4). Similarly in radiosity we need some kind of integral subdivision scheme if we are going to avoid patch boundaries becoming visible as shadow edges.

In this chapter we will first discuss the theoretical foundation for sampling and then look at the way in which defects arise out of the main image synthesis techniques.

8.2 Sampling and image synthesis

Fourier theory is not used to any great extent in image synthesis but it is nevertheless fundamental to the understanding and modelling of many (but not all) aliasing artefacts. In particular it gives a theoretical framework which facilitates quantification and comparison of various anti-aliasing algorithms.

Classically the term 'aliasing' means the distortion of information due to undersampling. It is easily demonstrated using a sine wave to represent an information signal (although a sine wave does not contain any information anyway, this does not matter for our purposes). Figure 8.1 shows a sine wave being sampled at different rates (with respect to the frequency of the sine wave). Undersampling the sine wave, and reconstructing a continuous signal from the samples (dotted line in the figure), produces an 'alias' of the original signal – another sine wave at a lower frequency than the one being sampled. We can say that this happens because the coherence or regularity of the sampling pattern is interfering with the regularity of the information. This effect is shown for an

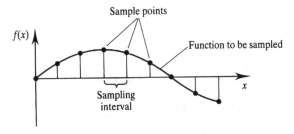

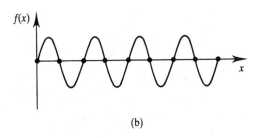

(a)

(b)

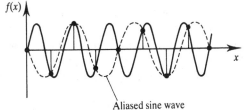

Aliased sine wave

(c)

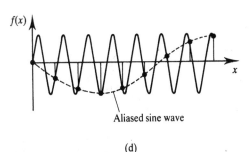

Aliased sine wave

(d)

Figure 8.1
Space domain representation of the sampling of a sine wave: (a) sampling interval is less than one-half the period of the sine wave; (b) sampling interval is equal to one-half the period of the sine wave; (c) sampling interval is greater than one-half the period of the sine wave; (d) sampling interval is much greater than one-half the period of the sine wave.

image in Figure 8.2. We can see that the aliased spatial frequencies are manifested as disturbances that break up the chequerboard pattern.

To avoid aliasing artefacts we have to sample at an appropriately high frequency with respect to the signal or image information and we normally consider the process of calculating an image function at discrete points in the image plane to be equivalent to sampling.

In computer graphics the term aliasing is used extremely loosely to describe any unwanted image artefact. In fact there is much confusion surrounding the terms sampling and aliasing. This arises because sampling in image synthesis is different in many ways to sampling in image processing. In particular, what we mean by sampling is strongly dependent on the rendering algorithm that we are using.

The defects that arise in computer graphics that are due to insufficient calculations or samples and which are easily modelled by an image plane sampling model are coherent patterns breaking up – the case that we have already discussed – and small fragments that are missed because they fall between two sample points.

Now we will look at the chequerboard example in more detail. Consider a chequerboard pattern that extends a long way from a view point (Figure 8.2(a)) – a commonly used texture in computer graphics. Very quickly the pattern units approach the size of a pixel and the pattern 'breaks up'. High spatial frequencies are aliasing as lower ones and forming new visually disturbing coherent patterns. Now consider Figure 8.2(b) where we render the same image onto a view plane with double the resolution of the previous one. Aliasing artefacts still appear but at a higher spatial frequency. In Fourier terms we have increased the sampling

(a)   (b)

Figure 8.2
The pattern in (b) is a super-sampled version of that in (a). Aliases still occur but appear at a higher spatial frequency.

frequency, but the pattern remains the same, causing aliasing at a higher spatial frequency. This demonstrates two important facts. Spatial frequencies in a computer graphics image are unlimited because they originate from a mathematical definition. You cannot get rid of aliases by simply increasing the pixel resolution. The artefacts simply occur at a higher spatial frequency (although they are, of course, less noticeable).

The most familiar defects in computer graphics are called jaggies. These are produced by the finite size of a (usually) square pixel when a high contrast edge appears in the image. These are particularly troublesome in animated images where their movement gives them the appearance of small animated objects and makes them glaringly visible. These defects are easier to get rid of because they do not arise out of the algorithm *per se* – they are simply a consequence of the resolution of the image plane.

Jagged edges are recognized by everyone and described in all computer graphics textbooks; but they are not aliasing defects in the classical sense of an aliased spatial frequency, where a high spatial frequency appears as a disruptive lower one. They are defects produced by the final limiting effect of the display device. We can certainly ameliorate their effect by, for example, calculating an image at a resolution higher than the pixel resolution, but the problem is due to the display device and not to undersampling with respect to information in the image. In the case of jaggies, edge information is 'forced' into the horizontal and vertical edges of the pixels. Consider Figure 8.3 which shows a perfect rectangle and a pixelized version. The Fourier transform for the perfect rectangle maps the edge information into high energy components along directions corresponding to the orientation of the edges in the image. The Fourier version of the pixel version also contains this information together with high energy components along the axes corresponding to the false or pixel edges. Jaggies do not arise because of high spatial frequencies aliasing as lower ones, but because more energy is concentrated along the horizontal and vertical axes in the Fourier domain. The terminological confusion is further compounded by the fact that the same anti-aliasing filter will reduce the visibility of both types of artefacts.

Let us now look in more detail at the notion of sampling in the image plane. In image synthesis what we are doing is performing, for each pixel, a number of

(a) Simulation of a perfect line

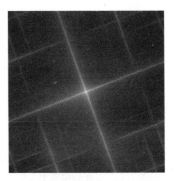

(b) Fourier transform of (a)

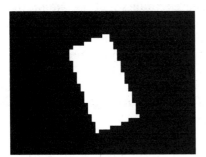

(c) Simulation of a jagged line

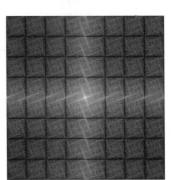

(d) Fourier transform of (b)

Figure 8.3
The effect of jaggies is to rotate high energy components onto the horizontal and vertical axes in the Fourier domain.

(sometimes very complicated) operations that eventually calculate, for that pixel, a constant value. Usually we calculate a value at the centre of the pixel and 'spread' that value over the pixel extent.

We assume that in principle this is no different from having a continuous projection image in the view plane and sampling this with a discrete two-dimensional array of sample points (one for each pixel). We say that this assumption is valid because we can approach such an image by continually increasing the sample resolution and calculating a value for the image at more and more points in the image plane. However, it is important to bear in mind that we do not have access to such an image in computer graphics and this limits and conditions our approaches to anti-aliasing measures. And furthermore the nature of the generated image – the defects that it contains – as we go on increasing the sampling resolution depends on the rendering method that we are using.

In fact both the terms 'sampling' and 'reconstruction' – another term borrowed from digital signal processing – are used indiscriminately and, we feel, somewhat confusingly in computer graphics and we will now emphasize the difference between an image processing system, where their usage is wholly appropriate, and their somewhat artificial use in computer graphics.

Consider Figure 8.4 which shows a schematic diagram for an image processor and a computer graphics system. In the image processor a sampler converts a two-dimensional continuous image into an array of samples. Some operations are then performed on the digital image and a reconstruction filter converts the processed samples back into an analogue signal.

Not so in image synthesis. Sampling does not exist in the same sense – the operations involved in assigning a value to a pixel depend on the rendering algorithm used and we can only ever calculate the value of an image function at these points.

Reconstruction in image synthesis does not mean generating a continuous image from a digital one but may mean, for example, generating a low (pixel) resolution image from an image stored at a higher (undisplayable) resolution. We are not reconstructing an image since a continuous image never existed in the first place. An appreciation of these differences will avoid confusion. (In reality we do reconstruct a continuous image for display on a computer graphics monitor, but this is done by fixed electronics that operate on the image produced in the framestore by a graphics program. A comprehensive approach to anti-aliasing would need to take the transfer characteristics of the conversion electronics into account but we will not do so in this text.)

To return to the problem of aliasing artefacts. Fourier theory tells us that aliasing occurs because we sample a continuous image (or the equivalent operation in computer graphics) and we do not do this at a high enough resolution to cap-

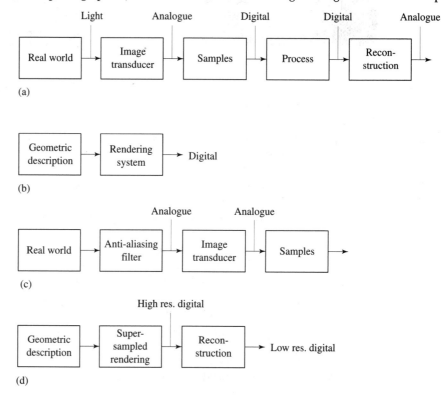

Figure 8.4
Sampling, reconstruction and anti-aliasing in image processing and image synthesis. (a) Image capture and processing; (b) image synthesis; (c) anti-aliasing in image capture; (d) anti-aliasing in image synthesis.

•

ture the high spatial frequencies or detail in the image. The sampling theorem states that if we wish to sample an image function without loss of information then our (two-dimensional) sampling frequency must be at least twice as high as the highest frequency component in the image. The minimum sampling frequency is known as the Nyquist limit.

So what does this mean in terms of practical computer graphics? Just this: if we consider we are sampling a continuous image in the view plane with a grid of square pixels, then the highest frequency that can appear along a scan line is:

$$f = 1/2d$$

where d is the distance between pixel centres.

Having fixed these concepts it is easy to see why anti-aliasing is so difficult in computer graphics. The problem stems from two surprising facts. There is no limit to the value of the high frequencies in computer graphics – they extend to infinity – and there is no direct way to limit (the technical term is band-limit) these spatial frequencies.

This is easily seen by comparing image synthesis with image capture through a device like a TV camera (Figure 8.4(c)). Prior to sampling a continuous image we can pass it through a band-limiting filter (or an anti-aliasing filter). Higher frequencies than can be handled by the process are simply eliminated from the image before it is sampled. We say that the image is pre-filtered. In such systems aliasing problems are simply not allowed to occur.

In image synthesis our scene database exists as a mathematical description or as a set of points connected by edges. Our notion of sampling is inextricably entwined with rendering. We sample by evaluating the projection of the scene at discrete points. We cannot band-limit the image because no image exists – we can only define its existence at the chosen points.

We will now look at practical anti-aliasing measures in the context of these facts. Such approaches fall into two categories. The first and easiest is where the anti-aliasing method is separate from or not dependent on the nature of the rendering algorithm. In other words, it can be used as an option. An example of this is the so-called super sampling approach (Figure 8.4(d)). Second, methods exist which are considered part of the rendering algorithm or strategy. Indeed many algorithms (distributed ray tracing is an example) have been specifically developed in their entirety to give a good anti-aliased image. The first approach is usually context independent – a big disadvantage as far as rendering expense is concerned. This means that the anti-aliasing method devotes the same effort to all parts of the image irrespective of the image content. Whether we are rendering the interior of a flat shaded polygon or rendering pixels that straddle an edge, the anti-aliasing proceeds regardless. Anti-aliasing measures that are integrated into the rendering strategy are usually context sensitive – they devote most energy to those parts of the image that require most attention.

Context-independent anti-aliasing measures in computer graphics are some approximation to the ideal of generating a continuous image, band-limiting it to the pixel resolution and then sampling. We will now discuss two such approaches.

8.3   The ultimate – filtering a continuous image

We start with a scheme that is too costly to be implemented except with highly constrained images. It compares with using a band-limiting filter in image capture and its near impossibility highlights some of the practical problems in anti-aliasing, in particular the unsuitability of common rendering techniques for the incorporation of anti-aliasing.

The technique is easily explained by referring to Figure 8.5. A continuous image has superimposed on it a filter of finite extent which has a circular cross-section. We centre the filter on a pixel and evaluate the sum of the product of the filter weights and the corresponding image value. We assume that the filter is defined by a large enough set of weights and that this discrete operation closely approximates the continuous integral. This value – the integral – would then be assigned to the pixel under consideration. The same operation would be performed on the next pixel and so on and the complete operation is convolution. We convolve the filter with the image to gain a filtered image.

What is it that we are doing with this filter? The end result is to produce a set of samples from a continuous image. We are combining the operations of sampling, band-limiting and reconstruction in the single operation of convolution. We are sampling by moving the filter in steps of one pixel. Since we are integrating over an area larger than a pixel, to calculate a pixel intensity, we are blurring the image or low pass filtering it – removing those high spatial frequencies that we cannot display.

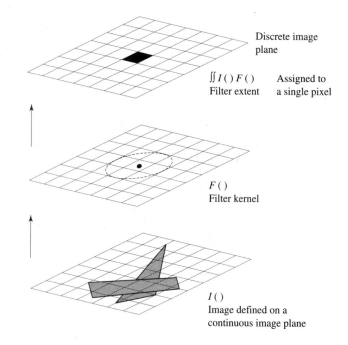

Discrete image plane

$\iint I(\,)\,F(\,)$ Assigned to
Filter extent   a single pixel

$F(\,)$
Filter kernel

$I(\,)$
Image defined on a continuous image plane

Figure 8.5
The concept of a 'perfect' filtering operation. A continuous image is filtered and the result assigned to a single pixel.

We now consider why this would be so difficult to perform in practice. First, how can we define the shape of the image elements in a continuous view plane? In most computer graphics applications we do not have a continuous representation of the objects in the scene. We normally have a sparse representation of the boundary of the objects in terms of a list of vertices. And even if we had a complete representation that could be transformed into a continuous representation in the view plane, how would we handle hidden surface removal? The visibility of objects would also have to be continuously defined. How can we represent that variation in shading over the projection of the objects in the view plane? In practice, with most rendering algorithms we calculate illumination values at discrete points. Consider ray tracing, for example; we can certainly generate more than one ray per pixel, but the algorithm cannot be implemented in a way that provides us with an analytic illumination for an object projection. And even if we could generate the continuous representation that we required, this would be an expensive strategy in that we are generating undisplayable detail that we then proceed to remove.

So the best that we can do is to approximate this approach by increasing the sampling interval – the rendering interval in the view plane – to sub-pixel resolution and filter this to the final pixel resolution. This is the basis (and justification) for the most common approach which is known as supersampling.

8.4 Supersampling – the best filtering we can do

Supersampling is the most common from of anti-aliasing and it usually used with polygon mesh rendering. It involves calculating a virtual image at a spatial resolution higher than the pixel resolution and 'averaging down' the high resolution image to a lower (pixel) resolution. In broad terms, subject to the previous reservations about the use of the term sampling, we are increasing the sampling frequency. The advantage of the method is trivial implementation which needs to be set against the high disadvantage of cost and increased Z-buffer memory. In terms of Fourier theory we can:

(1) generate a set of samples of $I(x,y)$ at some resolution (higher than the pixel resolution);

(2) low pass filter this image which we regard as an approximation to a continuous image;

(3) resample the image at the pixel resolution.

Steps 2 and 3 (often confusingly referred to as reconstruction) are carried out simultaneously by convolving a filter with the virtual image and using as steps in the convolution intervals of pixel width. That is, for a $3 \times$ virtual image, the filter would be positioned on (super) pixels in the virtual image, using a step length of three superpixels. Figure 8.6 is a representation of the method working and two examples of filters tabulated as weights (note that these are unnormalized – the filter weights must sum to unity). For an (odd) scaling factor S and a filter h of dimension k

Figure 8.6
'Reducing' a virtual image
by convolution.

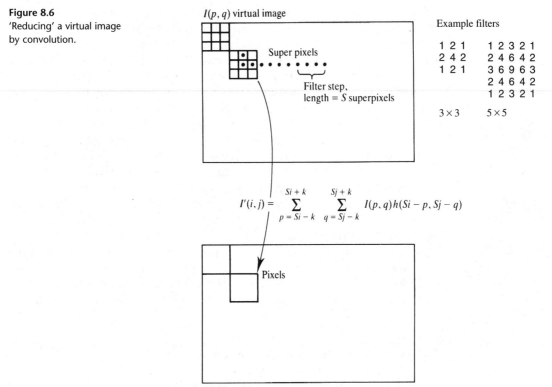

$$I'(i, j) = \sum_{p = Si - k}^{Si + k} \sum_{q = Sj - k}^{Sj + k} I(p, q)h(Si - p, Sj - q)$$

Although it is simple to implement, supersampling is somewhat difficult when it comes to the underlying theory. Intuitively it is obvious what is going on. We are generating a higher resolution image, averaging it, and so diminishing by blurring, aliasing artefacts. Bear in mind the ideal – we would like to be able to band-limit a continuous image then sample it at pixel resolution. This means that it should not contain any frequencies greater than $1/2d$. We approach the continuous image ideal by generating our supersampled image and we can look upon this image as a better approximation to a continuous image than the pixel resolution version. This is then band-limited by the filter which reduces the high resolution image to pixel resolution.

8.5 Sampling and algorithms

It is useful to consider what is meant by sampling with respect to the main rendering techniques and to ask the question: does increasing the resolution of the rendered image in the view plane have the same effect as increasing the frequency at which a continuous image is sampled (if one was available)? We should try to answer this question with respect to the three main rendering approaches – polygon mesh rendering, ray tracing and radiosity. The short answer is no; but we need to look at how far away these methods are from the theoretical ideal.

Polygon mesh rendering is the most straightforward of the three to consider and the easiest to construct a classical theory around. An image in such a renderer is generated by changing the representation of a polygon from a list of vertices to a set of pixels and applying an intensity to every pixel in the projected set. Calculating an image at a higher and higher resolution will lead to a higher number of pixels that represent each polygon and each polygon, as far as its outline is concerned, will be projected more and more accurately. It departs from the sampling ideal in one very important respect. The scene is already geometrically sampled – each object being represented by a certain number of polygons. This results in what is usually called 'geometric aliasing', which in this method manifests itself visually by piecewise linear silhouette. This is just as much of a problem as 'jaggies' and it not cured by calculating a higher resolution image. In polygon mesh rendering our ideal of increasing the pixel resolution to sample more and more accurately is thwarted in this way by the geometric representation.

Now consider simple recursive ray tracing. In this method a bundle of initial rays emerging from the image plane will usually diverge/converge at the first hits and will travel on to sample the environment more and more sparsely. The nature of the divergences depends entirely on the geometry of the scene that is being traced. The severity of aliasing artefacts that appear in a ray traced image depend on what depth a ray was at when it sampled that part of the scene that produced the artefact. If we consider the images of a once, twice and thrice reflected object in a first hit object, then any aliasing will be worse in the thrice reflected object than in the first reflected one. (However, the images of the once, twice and thrice reflected objects do get smaller and smaller as a function of their hit depth.) Thus the effect of increasing the sampling in the image plane by firing more rays for each pixel has an effect that depends primarily on the geometry of the scene and on the depth that the ray is at when it hits the object.

A simple strategy in ray tracing is to adopt a non-uniform approach. Here a solution is calculated at one ray per pixel, the solution examined for possible aliasing artefacts, and then those areas of the image plane that need more work have more rays per pixel initiated. The process can be recursive with areas continually subdividing until a 'goodness' criterion is passed. These context-dependent approaches in ray tracing have emerged because of the expense of the method – simply supersampling by firing more rays for every pixel would result in wasteful traces in areas of the images that were stationary. It is also the case that the nature of the algorithm is such as to easily facilitate a non-uniform approach.

In radiosity things are even more complicated. The accuracy of the final rendered image depends on the extent to which the scene representation is subdivided. Aliasing artefacts, in classical radiosity, appear as visible patch boundaries, turning such image components as curved shadow boundaries into steps that have a shape which is the geometric projection of the patch boundaries on the image plane. This is because in classical radiosity we assume that the radiosity is constant over a patch and because patches are generally large enough to project onto a number of pixels. In this sense the main aliasing artefacts depend on scene subdivision and these are thus in the same category as geometric aliasing in polygon mesh rendering (although there are other sampling problems in classical radiosity such as errors that result from the hemicube method of form factor calculation).

Classical radiosity is more or less unusable without attending to this problem and an anti-aliasing method is a vital part of any practical system. In fact because of this point such problems are not usually described as aliasing artefacts, *per se*. The only way to increase the accuracy of a radiosity image is to subdivide the scene more accurately. Like ray tracing, context-dependent approaches are taken and we subdivide those parts of the scene that require more accuracy. However, whereas subdivision in a ray tracing algorithm means initiating more rays per pixel, subdivision in radiosity means increasing the modelling accuracy of the objects in a way that eliminates the undesired effect – a much more difficult problem.

The conclusion from this is that in image synthesis the notion of sampling has to be used very carefully, and its exact meaning varies from algorithm to algorithm. The traditional approach of trying to fit these methods into a theory that is only correct for the sampling of a continuous image is of limited utility. When we increase the resolution in the image plane we are simply calculating a picture more accurately with respect to the algorithm that we are using. The way in which this improves the image quality depends as much on the nature of the algorithm signature as it does on classical theory.

8.6 Non-uniform sampling – some theoretical concepts

Non-uniform sampling has become of great interest in computer graphics because it addresses the high cost problem of conventional anti-aliasing techniques. It does this by getting away from the idea of uniform sampling and allows us to address the issue of context-sensitive anti-aliasing measures, or devoting computing resources to those parts of the image that need attention. The way in which this is done invariably means that we study algorithms where there is no separation between the rendering part and the anti-aliasing part. We cannot, as we did above with supersampling, render without using the anti-aliasing strategy.

Another benefit of considering non-uniform sampling is that it enables algorithms where we can convert aliases into noise. That is, we can design algorithms in such a way that, for a given pixel resolution, the algorithm produces noise where a conventional algorithm would produce aliases. Approaches that do this are called stochastic sampling methods and they function by making uniform intervals between samples irregular.

Here note the similarity with the image compression problem (Chapter 26). In image compression we wish to represent a uniformly sampled image as economically as possible. Space domain strategies work by devoting more samples to those parts of the image where it changes most. Fewer samples are devoted to regions where the image function changes slowly.

In computer graphics the equivalent process is to generate an image using most effort in busy regions and least in regions where the illumination is changing slowly. The crux of the matter in image synthesis is: how do we know which regions to devote most attention to before we have generated the image? This consideration leads us naturally to the most common strategy which is to generate a low resolution image, examine it, and use this to generate a higher resolution image in those areas of the low resolution image that appear to need further attention. We can go on repeating this process recursively until we come up against some pre-specified limit. This is called adaptive refinement.

A simple, but by no means complete, taxonomy of non-uniform sampling would be the two main categories of non-uniform subdivision and stochastic sampling. There are many subdivisions – different ways of effecting the stochastic sampling and ways of combining the two approaches into a single sampling strategy. For example, a stochastic sampling pattern may be generated at different scales (number of samples per unit area) so that it can be incorporated in an adaptive refinement scheme.

The approaches are represented schematically in Figure 8.7. Both these methods are applied after an initial sampling of the image plane has taken place. Most commonly in computer graphics this is uniform sampling, usually but not necessarily at pixel level. The techniques then become non-uniform supersampling in that the non-uniform strategy operates at sub-pixel level.

Non-uniform subdivision is a general strategy that appears in many algorithms in computer science. It naturally fits into an adaptive refinement scheme in image synthesis which consists of dividing the image plane into a grid of initial (say square) sampling boxes, then recursively subdividing these into squares until a resolution limit is reached. There is another subtle problem with such methods. This is that the output from an algorithm that uses this kind of strategy is going to be a set of non-uniform samples. These have to be converted into a uniform set of (pixel) samples prior to display. Alternatively we can say that we have to reconstruct the image from non-uniform samples and then resample at a uniform rate. There is no worked out theory that encompasses reconstruction

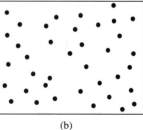

Figure 8.7
The two main non-uniform sampling techniques.
(a) Non-uniform subdivision;
(b) stochastic sampling.

Sampling domain

(a)   (b)

from non-uniform samples and a variety of ad hoc techniques exist. A simple scheme is shown in Figure 8.8.

Stochastic sampling seems at first sight a strange idea but an intuitive explanation of its efficacy is straightforward. Aliases appear in an image as a direct consequence of the regularity of the sampling pattern 'beating' with regularities or coherences in the image. If we make the samples irregular then the higher frequency coherences in the image will appear as noise rather than aliases. This perturbation of regular sampling, and consequent trade-off of aliasing against noise, is stochastic sampling.

An easy demonstration of the functioning of this trade-off is to return to our sine wave example of Figure 8.9. This shows a sine wave, again being sampled by a regular sampling pattern. Now we can invoke a stochastic sampling technique by 'jittering' each sample by some random amount about the regular sampling instant. Consider the effect of doing this on a sine wave whose frequency is below the Nyquist limit (Figure 8.9(a)). Here our procedure will sample the sine wave inaccurately, introducing amplitude perturbations, or noise, that depends on the extent of the sample instant jitter. For a sine wave whose frequency is well above the Nyquist limit (Figure 8.9(b)), the sample jitter extent encompasses many cycles and the effect of sampling successive such packets of waves will simply be to produce a set of random numbers. Thus the aliased sine wave that would be produced by a regular sampling interval is exchanged for noise.

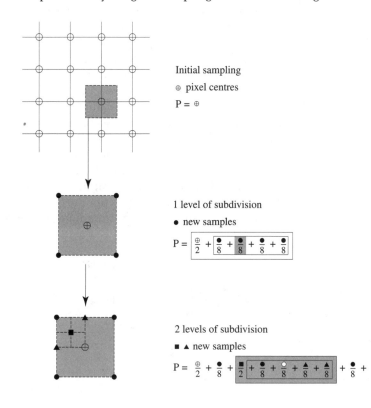

Initial sampling

⊕ pixel centres

$P = \oplus$

1 level of subdivision

● new samples

$$P = \frac{\oplus}{2} + \frac{\bullet}{8} + \frac{\bullet}{8} + \frac{\bullet}{8} + \frac{\bullet}{8}$$

2 levels of subdivision

■ ▲ new samples

$$P = \frac{\oplus}{2} + \frac{\bullet}{8} + \frac{\blacksquare}{2} + \frac{\bullet}{8} + \frac{\circ}{8} + \frac{\blacktriangle}{8} + \frac{\blacktriangle}{8} + \frac{\bullet}{8} + \frac{\bullet}{8}$$

Figure 8.8
Simple reconstruction for non-uniform subdivision.

Figure 8.9
Sampling a sine wave whose frequency is (a) below and (b) above the Nyquist limit. (After Cook.)

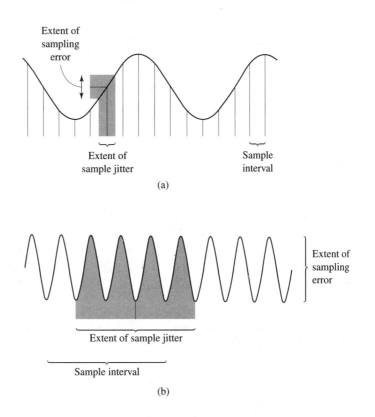

(a)

(b)

Jittering is easily carried out within a two-dimensional area, such as a pixel, by starting with a uniform grid and applying two component jitters in the x and y direction. This is cheap and easy to do and for this reason it is probably the most common strategy in computer graphics.

Stochastic sampling has an interesting background. In 1982 Yellot pointed out that the human eye contains an array of non-uniformly distributed photoreceptors and he suggested that this is the reason that the human eye does not produce its own aliasing artefacts. Photoreceptor cells in the fovea are tightly packed and the lens acts as an anti-aliasing filter. However, in the region outside the fovea, the spatial density of photoreceptors is much lower and for this reason the cells are non-uniformly distributed.

We will now look at the nature of image defects and their causes for the main rendering techniques. We will find that the way in which they are cured in most cases involves more calculations. In this very general sense we are increasing the number of samples that we calculate. We will find that the concept of more samples applies to structures deep in the algorithm itself (like increasing the resolution of the hemicube in radiosity) or it consists of making more calculations in the image plane (ray tracing) or it consists of making the geometry that the renderer deals with more accurate. All images, however synthesized, suffer from the general defect of jagged edges which we will henceforth ignore.

8.7 Comparative image study

A series of images will now be used to illustrate and support the discussion of image defects. The treatment is based on an old idea of using the same scene (as far as possible) as input to different renderers. This enables a good comparison of the wide differences between the methods, visual differences that are not apparent when one views individual scenes 'tuned' for a particular renderer. The imagery is used to illustrate both the advantages and defects of the different methods. The main scene used contains around 10 000 polygons. This is too many for a naive intersection test ray tracer and far too many for a radiosity renderer where one polygon equals one patch. The ray tracing problem can be solved by using spatial partitioning. In the radiosity case the relationship between the representation and the rendering method is far more difficult and we will demonstrate some possibilities with an example.

The material deals with the following topics:

- local reflection models and interpolative shading
- texture and shadow mapping
- light backwards or eye ray tracing
- radiosity using scene subdivision
- RADIANCE renderer

8.7.1 Local reflection models

The first series of illustrations (Figures 8.10 and 8.11 – Colour Plate) represent the standard cost/image quality used in computer graphics. Low quality images are used to preview and tune work. Figure 8.10 shows an office scene, together with a wireframe visualisation, that has been shaded using the constant ambient term only. Figure 8.11 is the office scene with Gouraud shading.

There are three highly visible defects in shaded imagery that uses interpolative techniques. The first always occurs in Gouraud shaded imagery and is called Mach banding. This is almost impossible to reproduce in a text and we will restrict ourselves to a description. If we consider the light intensity profile across the surface of a polygon mesh object then this will be piecewise linear as shown in Figure 8.12. When the surface is viewed on the screen the human visual system sees bands or lines on the surface that correspond to the polygon edges. These do not physically exist but are the response of low-level processing in the retina to the piecewise linear changes in the light intensity. They appear as faint but still discernible bands that appear to exhibit a lighter intensity than the surrounding surface. (They also appear in radiosity images that use Gouraud-style interpolation to calculate the final projected image.)

Interpolation defects in Gouraud shading manifest as unwanted changes in light intensity across a surface. This problem is clearly visible in Figure 8.11 on

Figure 8.12
Mach bands in Gouraud shading.

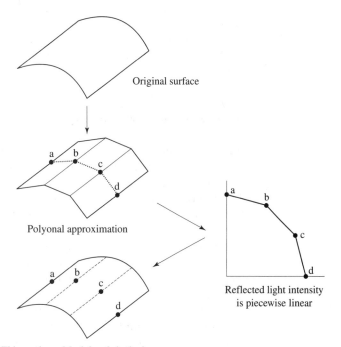

Original surface

Polyonal approximation

a b c d

Reflected light intensity
is piecewise linear

This produces Mach bands in the image

the wall adjacent to the door. Here the discontinuities occur on scan lines as the edges that are being used in the interpolation switch. This can be solved by sub-dividing the large polygon into triangles – in other words, we have to sample the geometry more accurately; we cannot simply map large flat areas into single polygons without considering the consequences in the renderer.

Figure 8.13 (Colour Plate) shows the same scene using Phong shading. A glaring defect in Phong interpolation is demonstrated in this figure. Here the reflected light from the wall light and the image of the light have become separated due to the nature of the interpolation. In this case to calculate the reflection we have interpolated using equal steps along a scan line in screen space. However, the image of the light appears in a different position because this has been mapped from world space using a perspective projection. In other words, the screen space projection treats as equal pixel units along the wall but these do not correspond to equal length units in world space. This problem, and others that occur when we try to include a light source as part of the scene, is the reason for excluding lights from rendered scenes. Consider the spherical light. Treating it as a shaded object doesn't quite work. In this case the point light source is inside the surrounding sphere and cannot by definition illuminate it. The light object can only get illumination from the wall light and we have to turn up the ambient component for the point light to make it look more like a source.

Figure 8.14 (Colour Plate) shows a zoom on one of the wall lights. The top row compares Gouraud and Phong shading. If the polygon mesh resolution is sufficiently high, the difference between Gouraud and Phong shading can be quite subtle. As the size of the polygons approaches single pixels in screen space, Gouraud shading approaches Phong shading. In the bottom row the polygonal resolution has been reduced. Here the Gouraud highlight disappears because none of the mesh vertices are close to it.

8.7.2 Texture and shadow mapping

We continue down the cost/image quality hierarchy with the standard 'add-on' effects of texture mapping and shadow mapping.

Figure 8.15 (Colour Plate) shows the office scene with 'traditional' two-dimensional texture maps. The addition of apparently complexity/ 'reality' /visual interest of simple textures to a Phong shaded scene is the reason for its enduring popularity. If anything, the addition of textures makes a scene look less real in the sense that its obvious computer signature is increased.

Figure 8.16 (Colour Plate) shows the same scene with shadow and environment mapping (the teapot) added. The resolution on the shadow maps are 256×256 and this causes geometric aliasing – as is apparent in the leaf shadow on the wall which has actually broken up. Note that there is 'interaction' between shadow mapping and environment mapping; the order of operations is important. In this image the environment map was computed before the shadow map and hence the shadow of the teapot does not appear in the reflections of the teapot.

Figure 18.17 (Colour Plate) gives a comparison between generating reflections using environment mapping and ray tracing. The demonstration illustrates the extent of geometric distortion introduced by environment mapping.

8.7.3 Ray tracing

The next three illustrations are demonstrations of certain aspects of the mainstream ray tracing technique – Whitted or recursive ray tracing using infinitesimally thin beams traced through a subdivided object space.

In Figure 8.18 (Colour Plate) the scene ray has been traced using a Whitted type ray tracer. In this scene there are around 10,000 polygons and a naive or brute force intersection text, where each spawned ray is tested against every polygon in the scene, would result in impossibly long execution times. The scene was thus traced using an octree representation as described in Section 6.3.9.2. Although the differences between Figure 8.18 and the Phong shaded scene are obvious, a few points are worth observing. The shadows are hard edged which is the normal option in ray tracing. (At each intersection point a light ray is shot to the point source.) These look wrong and it is far more difficult to implement or approximate soft shadows in a ray tracer compared with building such a facility into a shadow mapper (see Figure 8.17).

We generate a set of initial rays that sample the scene geometry. In the simple case of an orthographic projection, this bundle would emerge from the image plane parallel. After the first hit all this parallel bundle will diverge and converge depending on the nature of the surfaces that the initial rays hit. In general this will mean that all the second hit surfaces will be sampled with a lower density of rays and so on down through the recursion. This means that reflected images become poorer as a function of the recursive depth (see Figure 8.19). At the same time the defects become less noticeable as the reflections within reflections become smaller and smaller.

Figure 8.19 (Colour Plate) is a recursive depth demonstration. Shown is the teapot/mirror interaction for a depth of 2, 3, 4 and 5 respectively. Both objects are perfect reflectors and have no local component. All colour has to come from the global specular component. Terminating the recursion results in an unknown component which is rendered grey. A grey 'shadow' of the teapot recurses into the mirror. The interesting point here is shown in zoom images. These show the light cord breaking up as a function of recursive depth.

Alternatively ray tracing is particularly appropriate for the incorporation of a non-uniform sampling approach (Figure 8.7) because it allows us to generate initial rays anywhere in the image plane. (This contrasts with polygon mesh rendering, where the most commonly used rendering strategy dictates that calculation intervals are equally spaced in the image plane.)

Non-uniform sampling appears in Whitted's original paper where he uses a classic adaptive refinement scheme. Initial rays are generated at the rate of one per pixel – the standard first approximation. The calculated intensity values at four pixel corners are then compared and if they differ by more than a pre-specified threshold then the pixel is recursively subdivided until the threshold limit is achieved or the resolution limit is reached. To reconstruct a final value for a pixel the contribution of each sub-pixel area is weighted by its area. The process is represented in Figure 8.8 which details the numerical weighting of the samples when a pixel is subdivided. Embedded in this algorithm is a refinement test and a method of combining (or reconstructing and filtering) the intensities returned from the new rays into a single value. The refinement test uses intensity values on a weighted area basis. These are particular solutions and since Whitted published his classic paper many other approaches to the refinement strategy and reconstruction problem have been published.

The illustrations in Figure 8.20 (Colour Plate) demonstrate the efficacy of context-free versus context sensitive anti-aliasing. The images are respectively: no aliasing, super-sampling at 3x the screen resolution, and the context sensitive scheme just described. Note that there is no apparent difference between the two anti-aliased versions. The normal scheme involves 9x the work of the anti-aliased version, whereas the context sensitive scheme is just over 1.5x

8.7.4 Radiosity

The radiosity illustrations in this section were produced using a progressive refinement hemicube-based method.

Figure 8.21 (Colour Plate) shows a radiosity version of the scene. One of the noticeable differences between this image and previous ones is the effect of so-called colour bleeding – the image colours are different. As a result of diffuse-diffuse interaction the colour from a diffuse surface is transmitted to adjacent patches. This is particuarly noticeable on the ceiling. The 'apparentness' of colour bleeding in real life is debatable. In other words, we may not perceive much colour bleeding – which can be measured instrumentally – because of the perceptual predominance of colour constancy. This means that we as human beings tend to see the colour of an object as a constant attribute of the object irrespective of the colour of the light illuminating it. Thus the question arises: should we include this effect in image synthesis or not? Certainly colour bleeding is 'fixed' in photographs and seems to be more apparent in a photograph of a scene than is experienced by actually viewing the scene from the camera point. Figure 8.22 is a photograph taken at midday in the bright light of Rio de Janeiro. The colour bleeding is vividly apparent even at a distance.

Most serious defects in the radiosity method are due to inadequate meshing. Although there are other visual defects produced by the radiosity method – notably problems due to the finite size of the hemicube cells and Mach banding due to the interpolation – those that result from inadequate meshing or subdivision are usually the most visible. The most common results of inadequate meshing are blocky shadows, shadow leakage and light leakage. Unless the scene is extremely simple or constructed to take these artefacts into account (as in Figure 6.8), they will always occur.

As we know, the radiosity method calculates a view-independent solution from a scene database that has been subdivided into elements called patches. The solution assigns a constant radiosity to each patch and Gouraud-type interpolation is then used to provide a linearly varying light intensity across the patches. The radiosity method can only be made to work in a reasonable time by making these patches fairly large and this implies that a basic radiosity algorithm that uses arbitrary subdivision will always produce image defects.

To calculate a more accurate image we have to subdivide the scene further and because of this the notion of increased resolution sampling in the image plane seems inappropriate. However, the effect of subdivision of the three-dimensional scene into smaller and smaller patches, whose projection onto the image plane is consequently smaller, is in effect no different to subdivision of the image plane itself. The final result in the image plane is a form of non-uniform sampling. The subdivision has to be done 'intelligently'; the processing demands of the method are such that to initially subdivide the scene uniformly into smaller and smaller patches would result in too expensive a solution. Further subdivision needs to occur only where it is required – context-dependent measures are vital in radiosity.

Defects in radiosity are difficult to correct and since the introduction of radiosity in 1984, one of the main research areas has been to develop methods that automatically subdivide the scene so as to guarantee a final image free of defects to within some limit.

High radiosity gradients appear, as we have already discussed, at shadow edges. They also appear on surfaces such as ceilings adjacent to light sources which 'paint' beams of light on them. We should also remember that it is not only shadow boundaries that have to be delineated but the graduation across the boundary (soft shadows). This implies adequate subdivision of both the receiving area and the light source. The attention given to shadows in the radiosity method is extremely important. One of the motivations for the radiosity method is that it is a global illumination method that correctly calculates the intensity of the reflected light in a shadow area. This feature contributes to the quality of the realism in the final image and to use the benefit of the illumination calculations in the radiosity method using inadequate geometry would be a foolish strategy.

The question is: how do we know in advance where to apply finer subdivision? We can either predict the position of the radiosity discontinuities and subdivide before the calculation (a priori methods) or we can effect subdivision during a solution.

We will now look at the interaction between subdivision and light and shadow leakage.

The image in Figure 8.23 (Colour Plate) was computed using a 'minimum' representation. The wireframe is a triangulated version of the representation shown in Figure 8.10, and is the most basic subdivision that we could try a radiosity solution with. Despite the fact that there are many more polygons than in the original scene, the quality is unacceptably low due to shadow and light leakage.

Shadow or light leakage is not due to inadequate sub-division *per se* – although the effect can be reduced by finer subdivision. It occurs when the sub-division boundaries do not coincide with intersecting surfaces. The simple scene shown in Figure 8.24 demonstrates the idea. This is a room divided by a floor to ceiling partition, which does not coincide with patch boundaries. One half of the room contains an emitter, the other is completely dark. Depending on the precise position of the partition with respect to the patch boundaries, the interpolation will either produce light leakage into the dark region or shadow leakage into the lit region.

Further subdivision of a scene is vital in areas such as shadow boundaries in a radiosity image and the first approach to this problem is analogous to adaptive refinement sampling in ray tracing. The solution itself is used to determine where further subdivision is necessary by comparing the radiosity of adjacent patches for areas of high change. We cannot use the image plane in the radiosity method to effect adaptive refinement because we are interested in the difference in radiosity between adjacent patches in the three-dimensional solution and not between adjacent areas in the image plane which contains, in general, overlapping patches. This method cannot, by definition, deal with the light and shadow leakage problem. Finer subdivision of the scene can reduce leakage but cannot eliminate it entirely. Complete elimination of leakage can only be achieved by creating patch boundaries that coincide with the intersection of object surfaces.

Figure 8.24
Shadow and light leakage.

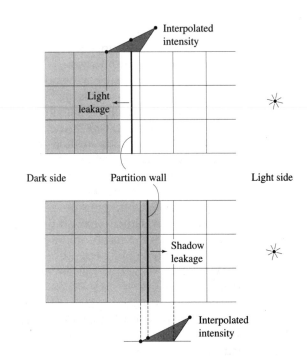

Subdivision strategy is a difficult problem and accounts for a major research effort in the radiosity method. Using a fairly naive approach the sequence in Figure 8.25 shows the difficulties encountered as subdivision, performed after every iteration, proceeds around one of the wall lights. Originally two large patches situated away from the wall provide general illumination of the object. This immediately causes subdivision around the light/wall boundary because the program detects a high difference between vertices belonging to the same patches. These patches have vertices both under the light and on the wall. However, this subdivision is not fine enough and as we start to shoot energy from the light source itself light leakage begins to occur. Light source patches continue to shoot energy in the order in which the model is stored in the database and we spiral up the sphere, shooting energy onto its inside and causing more and more light leakage. Eventually the light emerges onto the wall and brightens up the appropriate patches. As the fan of light rotates above the light more and more inappropriate subdivision occurs. This is because the subdivision is based on the current intensity gradients which move on as further patches are shot. Note in the final frame this results in a large degree of subdivision in an area of high light saturation. These redundant patches slow the solution down more and more and we are inadvertently making things worse as far as execution time is concerned.

Possible alternative strategies are:

● Limit the initiation of subdivision by only initiating it after every *n* patches instead of after every patch that is shot.

Figure 8.25
This sequence shows the difficulties encountered as subdivision, performed after every iteration, proceeds around one of the wall lights. As the fan of light rotates above the light more and more inappropriate subdivision occurs. This is because the subdivision is based on the current intensity gradients which move on as further patches are shot. Note in the final frame this results in a large degree of subdivision in an area of high light saturation. These redundant patches slow the solution down more and more and we are inadvertently making things worse as far as execution time is concerned.

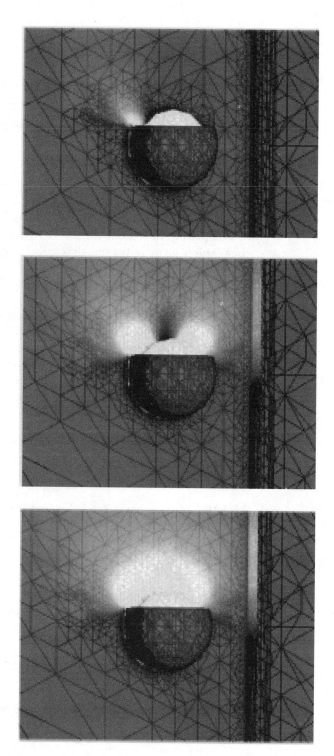

- Limit the initiation of subdivision by waiting until the illumination is representative of the expected final distribution.

- Aid the initial mesh generation by taking account of interpenetrating geometry. This means adding edges to objects that coincide with boundaries of other objects. This solution is applied before the radiosity solution begins.

Figure 8.26 is the result of meshing the area around a wall light after considering the interpenetrating geometry. Now the wall patch boundaries coincide with the light patch boundaries. The result of this mesh eliminates the leakage.

Figure 8.27 is the scene rendered using The RADIANCE renderer. This has a slight grainy appearance compared to the other images which is due to the way in which the diffuse interreflection is sampled (see Section 6.2.3).

Comparing the various images in Figures 8.26 and 8.27, it is apparent that they exhibit many noticeable differences, especially concerning light levels and colour shifts.

Only a cursory attempt was made to match object properties and light levels through each interface – apart from the obvious algorithmic attributes (hard-edged vs. soft-edged shadows, for eaxmple) it is difficult to deduce what differences are due to the different models and methodology of the algorithms and which are due to inadequate tuning through the renderers' interfaces. This is an enduring practical problem with using renderers.

Further reading

The benchmark papers on ray tracing and radiosity are given in the appropriate chapters. The references listed here concern only the enhancements described in this chapter. Volume 2 of Glassner's mighty tome (see Chapter 1) and Cohen and Wallace's book on radiosity (see Chapter 6) are particularly good on recent radiosity developments.

Baum D.R., Mann S., Smith K.P. and Winget J.M. (1991). Making radiosity useable: automatic pre-processing and meshing techniques for the generation of accurate radiosity solutions. *Proc. SIGGRAPH 1991*, 51–60

Campbell A.T. and Fussell D. (1990). Adaptive mesh generation for global diffuse illumination. *Proc. SIGGRAPH 1990*, 155–64

Cohen M., Greenberg D., Immel D.S. and Brock P.J. (1986). An efficient radiosity approach for realistic image synthesis. *IEEE Computer Graphics and Apps.*, **6**(3), March, 26–35

Cook R. L., Porter T. and Carpenter L. (1984). Distributed ray tracing, *Computer Graphics*, **18**(3), 137–44 (Proc. SIGGRAPH '84)

Hanrahan P., Salzman D. and Aupperle L. (1991). A rapid hierarchical radiosity algorithm. *Proc. SIGGRAPH 1991*, 197–206

Lischinski D., Tampieri F. and Greenberg D.P. (1992). Discontinuity meshing for accurate radiosity. *IEEE Computer Graphics and Applications*, **12**(6), November, 25–39

Image processing for enhancement or basic processing in image space

9.1   Pixel processing

9.2   Transforming the position of pixels – image warping

As soon as imaging technology made it possible for computers to treat images as collections of pixels each with a numerical value and separately manipulatable, the science of image processing began.

The classic operation in image processing is to enhance an input image in some way so that the output image is more easily interpretable. The goal of the operation may be just that – a human interpreter wants to view an image that has the relevant information made more visible. We may want to make detail in the image more easily visible or alternatively we may want to reduce noise. We gave a classic example of this in Chapter 1 where an enhanced image from the interplanetary explorer, Voyager 2, revealed an erupting volcano on a moon of Jupiter (Figure 1.4 – Colour Plate). Alternatively an enhancement operation may form the pre-processing part of a system that automatically analyzes an image. Here the goal may be simple, as in cloud cover analysis where the number of bright pixels are counted to provide an area measure. A more complex system, such as a computer vision facility, where objects are to be recognized, may contain an enhancement phase as part of a whole series of image operations. A more recent application of basic image processing techniques dealt with in Chapter 23 is in graphic design where operations are applied and tuned to impart some kind or 'artistic effect' to the image. The popularity of packages like Adobe's Photoshop has meant that image processing operations, once confined to research institutions, are now routinely used by designers.

Generally image enhancement transformations use some prior knowledge concerning the nature of the degradation. This knowledge may vary from the rudimentary: 'the image is dark', to detailed knowledge of the degradation: 'the image is blurred due to linear relative velocity between the camera and the scene, with the camera moving horizontally with respect to the scene'.

Although some image enhancement operations have always been used in photography, the advent of digital images and the ability to manipulate elements of the image numerically inside a program has made many impressive enhancement techniques possible and made image processing an exact science.

Figure 9.1 is an example of 'manual' image processing. It is an early postcard of Florence Cathedral and it is typical of the way in which photographs were retouched prior to being reproduced as postcards. In this case the retouching is so substantial that the photograph almost has the appearance of a drawing. Lines have been inked in (equivalent to detail enhancement) and dark areas (shadow area on the left of the picture) have been repainted (equivalent to contrast enhancement). It is a good example of a black art that was first superseded by darkroom techniques and eventually by computer image processing.

This chapter is concerned with point or pixel processing in the **spatial domain**. This means that we operate on the pixel intensity or colour. We make this distinction because a major area of image processing is concerned with operating on images that have been transformed into, for example, the **Fourier domain** – a representation of an image that enables many processing operations to be carried out more easily and conveniently than their spatial domain equivalents. Fourier processing is dealt with at length in Chapter 11.

Figure 9.1
Manual image processing – edge enhancement in an early picture postcard.

Although processing the intensity of pixels still accounts for the most common usage in image processing, operating on the position of pixels is becoming extremely important in many applications. Image warping is a term that means that we operate on the position of pixels, rather than their intensity. In image processing it is used to correct geometric distortions due to the image collection system. In morphing (Chapter 17) in film special effects it is used to distort a source image towards a target image. In three-dimensional graphics the mapping of a texture (Chapter 4) onto a three-dimensional object and then projecting into screen space is a warping operation from two-dimensional texture space to two-dimensional screen space. Another application of warping is view interpolation an application explored in Chapter 21. Finally warping transformation can be used in volume rendering to efficiently rotate a three-dimensional data volume into a desired orientation for viewing.

In any application where a sampled image is transformed from one coordinate system to another, sampling, aliasing and filtering issues arise. These issues are dealt with in the chapters that describe the applications of image warping. Although there are general theoretical considerations involved, anti-aliasing algorithms tend to be specific to an application. The theory of anti-aliasing is dealt with in Chapter 8.

The most common class of planar or spatial transformations are affine and perspective mappings. The most common applications of image warping in popular culture are real-time video effects and morphing in the film industry. Real-time video effects are, for example, the ubiquitous 'flying paper' device in which an image, say the image already on the screen, is mapped onto a quadrilateral. The mapping changes as the quadrilateral translates, giving the illusion of a flat image on a piece of paper flying around in three space. Morphing has been used as a special effect in the film industry for many years and is described in detail in Chapter 17. Both of these applications depend, for efficiency, on structuring the warp as a two-pass transform and this will be one of the main topics of this chapter.

The way in which warps are specified or derived depends on the application. In the processing of satellite imagery the warp can be due to the curvature of the Earth and the correcting warp characteristics can be derived from known geometry. Alternatively if the distortion is due to non-linearities in the image collection system this information is sometimes obtained by imaging a phantom (such as a regular grid). In this case the warp may be modelled by low order polynomials and the coefficients of these specify the nature of the compensating warp. In special effects in film morphing the warp is specified by an animator setting up some kind of correspondence between a source and target frame. Note that in image processing we are generally trying to correct a distortion whereas in special effects we deliberately introduce a distortion. In computer graphics (texture mapping) the specification of the warp derives from the rendering process and varies with many factors such as the shape of the object and the viewpoint. The renderer calculates a mapping from such parameters that warps the texture into screen space.

9.1 Pixel processing

Pixel or point processing is one of the oldest and easiest operations that can be used to effect some kind of image transformation. It means that we operate, using a linear or non-linear transform, on pixel values one at a time. The transform may be derived by considering some global property of the image – most commonly a histogram of pixel values – or by considering the values of pixels in the immediate neighbourhood of the one under consideration. In this way such operations as noise removal and contrast enhancement are effected.

The intuitive basis of the power of point processing is easily considered. Say, for example, we have an image that was acquired under poor conditions and consequently exhibited a very small dynamic range. It may be that we are interested in an object that is more or less invisible to the eye because the pixels representing the object may only differ from the background pixels by a very small amount (in the limit we may have in an 8-bit image a difference of just 1 in 256). Thus although the naked eye is unable to detect the object a numerical technique can sense and enhance this difference.

The fact that we can write programs to manipulate images as sets of numbers means that we can effect image enhancement/manipulation in a much more flexible way than would be possible using traditional or optical techniques. This simple fact is the underlying basis for the impressive results of pixel or point processing.

9.1.1 Intensity transformations

Intensity or grey scale transformations are so called because we apply the same transformation to every pixel in the image. The transform in the value of the pixel does not vary from pixel to pixel as it may do in methods where we consider pixels in a small neighbourhood. The classic grey scale transformation is **contrast stretching**. Low contrast images are those whose pixels do not occupy their full dynamic range. This could be due to inadequacies in the image recording process. We can apply a correction function:

$$z' = T(z)$$

where: z is the input grey level
z' is the output grey level

Such a function can be piecewise linear and derived interactively as shown in the illustration of Figure 9.2. Here we decide that we wish to stretch the contrast of the original image in the middle range at the expense of compressing the contrast for high and low grey levels. (If $T < 1$ then contrast is compressed; if $T > 1$ contrast is expanded.) The function can be derived by setting the two

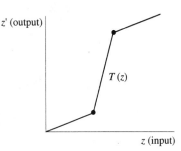

Original (N.E. Brazil)

Contrast stretched

Figure 9.2
Contrast stretching.

breakpoints while viewing the processed image, or better still both images side by side.

9.1.2 Intensity level slicing

This simple technique selects a particular contiguous range of grey levels to display. It is used in contexts where intensity variations of interest in an image are too slight to be seen well by the viewer. Providing these variations occupy contiguous intensity levels and the information occupying other intensity levels is of no interest, we can highlight those areas that occupy the levels of interest. Figure 9.3 gives an illustration. In the first case the application of T results in a binary image that displays in white the selected range of pixels. Here we would be interested in the shape of the area occupied by such intensity levels. A special case of this transformation is thresholding where T is a step function. Thresholding, as an image segmentation technique, is taken up in more detail in Chapter 12. In the final example in Figure 9.3, grey levels of interest are enhanced while the others remain at their original values.

Figure 9.3
Intensity level 'slicing'.

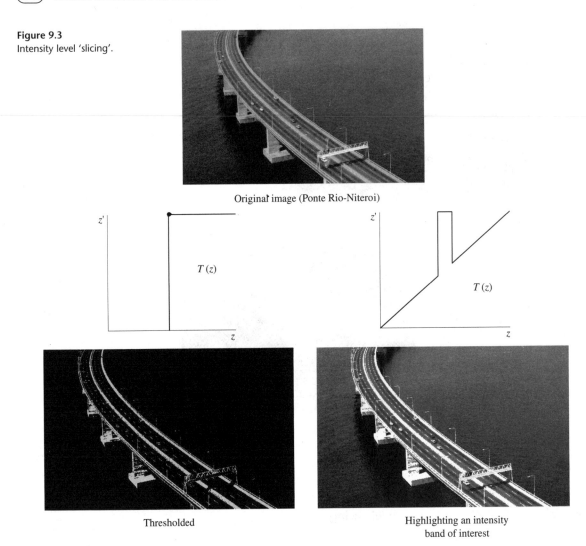

Original image (Ponte Rio-Niteroi)

Thresholded

Highlighting an intensity
band of interest

9.1.3 Intensity level to colour – pseudo-colour enhancement

A commonly used transformation, which is basically the same as those in the previous section except that colour is exploited, is called pseudo-colour enhancement and maps a grey scale image into a colour image. This operation is not really an enhancement operation at all (in the sense of enhancement operations where pixel intensities are actually changed) but a re-encoding of the image. Its purpose is to present images that consist of some kind of data, rather than photographic images of reality, in a way that is more easily interpretable. In use since the advent of image processing, it is an early example of something that is now called scientific visualization. It is called **pseudo-colour** because the colours used generally have no real relationship to the context from which the image was produced. Indeed in most contexts the image consists of data for which there is no real association with colour. We may, for example, have data from the cross-section through a structural element where the image or data consists of stress or temperature.

Pseudo-colour utilizes the human visual system's sensitivity to colour contrast. Small differences in grey scale that may not be visible can be mapped into highly contrasting colour. Herein lies the significant disadvantage of pseudo-colour enhancement – false contours. Imagine the following example. Say we have a rectangle or strip that exhibits a slow linear grey scale increase as a function only of x, from the left to the right. We may not perceive the change if the difference between the left and right values is small. Mapping into pseudo-colour would give a series of vertical strips whose boundaries are false contours. As well as visualizing the change in greyness in the image we have introduced discontinuities that do not exist in the original image. This may be particularly troublesome in, for example, medical images such as X-rays. Here clinicians have to examine images that represent structures that cannot be seen in reality. They may be searching for the outline of a tumour, for example. In this context the 'interference' from the structures of a false contour may be highly undesirable.

Pseudo-colour images have now become part of our everyday visual culture. They are used in TV weather presentations and recently they have been used in TV commercials for ice cream where actors are 'photographed' with a thermal imaging camera. In other words, almost everyone now routinely makes the association between an entity such as pressure or temperature using red for high values through the spectrum to blue for low values.

We can define pseudo-colour mapping generally as follows:

$$I_R(x,y) = T_1(I(x,y))$$

$$I_G(x,y) = T_2(I(x,y))$$

$$I_B(x,y) = T_3(I(x,y))$$

and a useful practical implementation is to define the three T functions as piecewise linear transfer functions that can be altered interactively.

The most commonly used fixed pseudo-colour transformation is to map grey scale values into hue in, say, HSV space leaving saturation and value at unity.

$$H(x,y) = T(I(x,y))$$

$$S = 1$$

$$V = 1$$

This gives the familiar mapping where Red (hot) is used for high values of I and Blue (cold) is used for low values. This ubiquitous mapping is perhaps not optimal for many applications. For example, the harshness of false contours can be reduced by reducing S. Figure 9.4 (Colour Plate) shows a typical use of this technique.

9.1.4

Image histograms and their uses

Operations based on image histograms are carried out in two stages. The accumulation of the histogram and its analysis is followed by an enhancement oper-

Figure 9.5
Images with 'unsatisfactory' histograms.

ation based on the **shape** of the histogram. The first stage gives us global knowledge about the nature of the image as far as its intensity levels are concerned and enables a suitable transformation to be derived.

One way of characterizing an image in terms of its overall visual impression is to look at the shape of its histogram of grey values. Figure 9.5 illustrates the point, showing respectively the histogram of a dark image that only occupies low levels. The second case shows the histogram of an image that is predominantly grey. In the general case, even if we did not see the original image, we would expect that images exhibiting such histograms were visually unsatisfactory. In particular we would expect that the narrow band of grey levels occupied would mean that detail in the image would be difficult to see. For most images we would expect a histogram that is reasonably distributed with pixels tending to occupy the complete range. Ideally we would like a uniform distribution although, of course, the histogram depends not only on the distribution of intensities over the complete range of values but also on the image structures that exhibit these intensities. We cannot observe intensity histograms independently of image content. A picture of a chess board, for example, would exhibit an ideal histogram that only had two non-zero values.

Histogram equalization

Histogram equalization can be seen as an extension of the interactive contrast stretching technique described in Section 9.1.1. Here we effected a grey scale transformation by interactively specifying one or more breakpoints of a piece-wise linear function $T(z)$. In histogram equalization the process is automatic. The histogram of the input image is analyzed and a $T(z)$ is derived from this so that when the transformation is applied to the input image, it is transformed into an image that will tend towards an equiprobable histogram – hence the name of the technique.

In histogram equalization $T(z)$ can be derived as follows. First we assume that z is continuous and the input image has a continuous probability density function $P(z)$ and the output image an equiprobable distribution $Q(z)$ (which as we have already remarked may be inappropriate). If we consider a single grey level z_i corresponding to the output image grey level z_i' then we have (Figure 9.6)

$$\int_0^{z_i} P(z)\mathrm{d}z = \int_0^{z_i'} Q(z)\mathrm{d}z$$

$$= \frac{MN}{z_{max}} z_i'$$

where $M{\times}N$ is the pixel dimension of the image.

Thus the transformation $T(z)$ is given by

$$z_i' = T(z_i) = \frac{z_{max}}{MN} \int_0^{z_i} P(z)\mathrm{d}z$$

and the discrete approximation to this is

$$z_i' = \frac{z_{max}}{MN} \sum_{i=0}^{z_i} H(z)$$

where $H(z)$ is the (discrete) histogram of the input image.

Figure 9.7 shows an example of this technique. The original image and histogram is shown together with a histogram equalized image. Although histogram equalization is automatic this does imply that only one result is possible. It may be that this is not an optimal result. A better $T(z)$ may be possible.

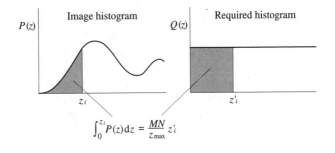

Figure 9.6
Histogram equalization.

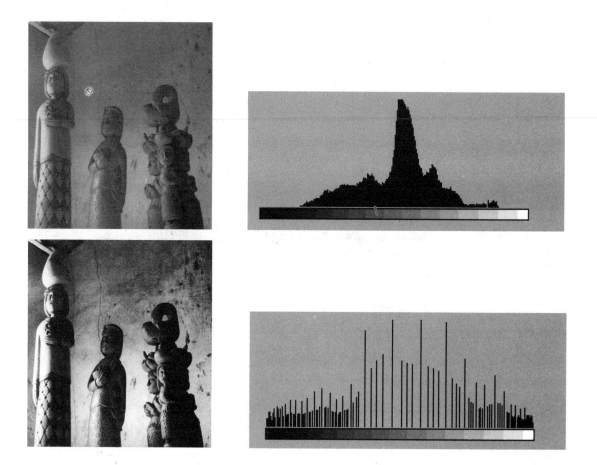

Figure 9.7
Histogram equalization.

Variations on histogram equalization are possible. For example, we could apply the technique to local regions. A related technique is **histogram specification** where, as the name implies, the user specifies the histogram that the output image is required to have. These variations are fully described in Gonzalez and Woods see page 15.

9.1.6 Image subtraction

This is one of the simplest techniques in point processing. It is used when we need to isolate the motion that occurred between two frame captures in a sequence and it has applications in the contexts of both enhancement and segmentation. One of the most common and recent applications of image subtraction is the compression of video images where the idea is to transmit or store only the information that changes from frame to frame (see Chapter 26 for a full discussion of image subtraction in the context of image compression techniques). Figure 9.8 is a simple example of image subtraction. The idea is that given a 'start'

Figure 9.8
Two images of moving
traffic and their difference.

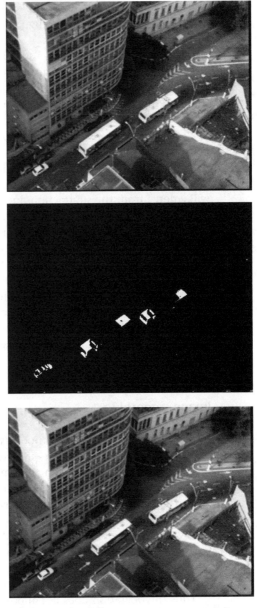

image and a series of images of the same scene containing motion, the subtrahends contain only that information that moves – static information is reduced to zero (or near zero) grey levels by the operation.

A classic (non-computer) example is **mask mode radiography**. Here X-ray images are obtained from an image intensifier which is viewing an area of blood vessels after an X-ray opaque substance has been injected into the bloodstream. Successive frames are subtracted from an image obtained from the same region before injection of the dye. The resulting subtrahends form a moving sequence of the passage of the dye through the blood vessels. All other (static) information is diminished or zeroized.

Another classic use of image subtraction is in quality control, particularly in the context of detecting missing parts in a flat assembly such as an electronic circuit board. An image of a perfect part is produced and the image of the part that is being inspected is subtracted from this.

If the subtracted images are not for human consumption, but are also to be analyzed by computer, then some obvious problems present themselves. If we consider, for example, the quality control example, how are the subtrahends going to be analyzed? In most practical cases the information that should be identical between the two frames will not in reality be so. Non-zero pixel values will emerge from the subtraction due to misalignment, changes in illumination and noise. It may be sufficient to remove differences between similar, but not identical, pixels and then count. Alternatively it may be necessary to search for spatially coherent groups of pixels in the subtrahend.

To measure relative velocity accurately it is necessary to identify in each subtrahend the same point on the object whose speed is to be measured. This may be non-trivial. Thus image subtraction is a deceptively simple technique whose practical application may involve certain problems of a complexity much greater than the subtractive process itself. Even the apparently simple case of a single object moving against a background exhibits difficulties when subtrahends are formed.

9.1.7 Image smoothing

Image smoothing or neighbourhood averaging is used to remove noise. We may, for example, employ it as a pre-processing step in edge detection as we describe in Chapter 10. Gaps in broken edges may be less troublesome in an edge detector if the image is first passed through a smoothing operation.

It is a simple filtering operation where we move a small array of weights over the image and for each pixel over which the filter is placed we compute the average of the pixels over, say, a 3×3 neighbourhood (Figure 9.9) by taking the sum of the products of the surrounding pixels with the filter weights. This has the effect of removing noise. At the same time the operation produces a blurring effect and the degree of blurring is proportional to the size of the filter.

Thus the operation does not alter slow changes but blurs fast changes in the image. If the noise consists of isolated spots of white in areas of black and vice versa then the blurring effect also removes the noise. This blurring effect may be desirable, in the case of an edge detection pre-processor, or it may be undesirable if it removes detail which is not noise, but information that we want to retain.

If we want to smooth without blurring we can employ **median filtering** which, using the same algorithmic framework, replaces the centre pixel value with the median of all the values in the neighbourhood. Figure 9.10 shows an

Figure 9.9
Smoothing an image by local averaging.

Original

Original + noise

$^1/_9$	$^1/_9$	$^1/_9$
$^1/_9$	$^1/_9$	$^1/_9$
$^1/_9$	$^1/_9$	$^1/_9$

Filter

Smoothed image

example of median filtering. Other more elaborate non-blurring techniques are described in Sonka et al (Chapter 1).

The operation is, in effect, a crude approximation to a low pass filtering operation in the Fourier domain – described in Chapter 11. The larger the area of the filter the smaller is the cut-off frequency in the corresponding Fourier domain filter. We should, however, note the two significant differences between this operation and low pass filtering in the Fourier domain. The first is a disadvan-

Figure 9.10
Median smoothing produces a better result in this case than local averaging (see Figure 9.9).

tage: the filter is empirical – it is in no sense an accurate space domain equivalent of a low pass filter, which (within the limitations of the discrete Fourier transform) blurs on the precise basis of spatial frequency. The second difference is a comparative advantage: we can perform smoothing as a spatial filter operation with none of the computational complexity of transforming into the Fourier domain, filtering and performing the reverse transform.

Sharpening or detail enhancement

Just as smoothing is equivalent to low pass filtering, sharpening or detail enhancement is equivalent to high pass filtering in the Fourier domain. Again it is implemented as a spatial filter operation and possesses the same advantage and disadvantage compared with Fourier domain filtering as we discussed for smoothing in the previous section. A 3×3 example is shown in Figure 9.11 and it is clear that if such a spatial filter is contained by a region homogeneous in grey scale, the pixel on which the spatial filter is centred will be zeroized – equivalent to removing low spatial frequencies. On the other hand, spatial changes that occur within the compass of the spatial filter will be retained. Thus fine detail – specifically changes that occur within the spatial dimensions of the filter – in the image will appear emphasized against a dark background.

An alternative way of looking at the operation is that it is equivalent to forming a new pixel value z' by taking the average of the eight surrounding neighbours and subtracting this from z. This is like taking a blurred copy of the image and subtracting this blurred copy from the original – a technique known photographically as **unsharp masking**.

Figure 9.11
Detail/edge enhancement in the image domain (compare with Figure 11.10).

−1	−1	−1
−1	8	−1
−1	−1	−1

It is instructive to consider the similarity and difference between this spatial filter and those used in edge detection (Chapter 10). Both are essentially concerned with detail enhancement but in edge detection we use spatial filters from which we can derive some information concerning edge orientation. That is, we may use the filters to extract information from an image like 'this variation is part of a vertical edge' rather than to simply transform the image from one form to another. Note also that the filter used in this section is a form of the Laplacian also described in Chapter 10.

9.1.9

Colour and image processing

Up to now we have dealt with grey scale images and the field of image processing, now around 35 years old, grew up with such images. Now that we have the ability to deal with colour images on modestly priced machines it is important that we briefly examine the enhancement techniques of the preceding sections in the context of colour images. The following material should be read in conjunction with Chapter 25 which describes colour representations in general.

Consider colour images in the context of spatial filtering. Here there is no problem: we can simply use any of the described techniques separately on each of the RGB components, combining them after processing in the normal way for display. However, we should note that although there is a correlation between the image structures that appear in the RGB components, processing structure in the components will in general also affect colour. In the case of contrast enhancement techniques, for example, we may want to operate on the luminance component of the image only, leaving the colour information undisturbed, by using an RGB to YIQ transformation (see Chapter 25).

At this stage we should make an important point concerning images and colour representations. With most images the colour representation (such as RGB) is just that; it is the three components that we have to specify for the colour image. As the word component implies, we do not generally consider one component separately from the others. However, in the important case of multiband satellite imagery, the components, four or eight wavelength bands, are image entities in their own right that reveal different properties concerning the imaged surface according to wavelength. They cannot be regarded as colour components which when sent to a conventional display device will produce a colour image of the ground area that produced them (although, of course, they are combined in this way to produce the beautiful colour composites that have become part of our perception of planet Earth). Figure 9.12 (Colour Plate) is a pseudo-colour image of a single wavelength band image of Rio de Janeiro.

In multi-band satellite images the commonly used techniques are pseudo-colour, subtraction between bands and division of one band by another. Subtraction of neighbouring bands to form a difference image is a technique that will accentuate reflectivity variations between the two bands.

The satellite bands can be combined in different ways to produce different effects. Ratio images of pairs of bands provide a normalization for the illumination

Figure 9.13
Using a ratio image to remove shadows. The third image is the dividend of the first two.

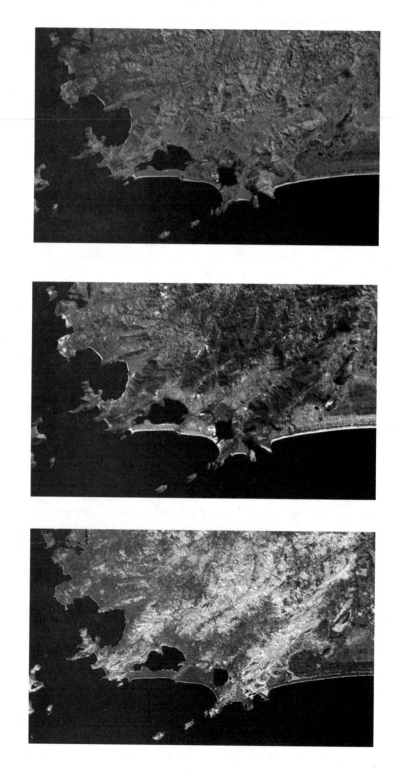

Figure 9.14
Using a ratio image to enhance road detail in Figure 9.13. The third image is the dividend of the first two.

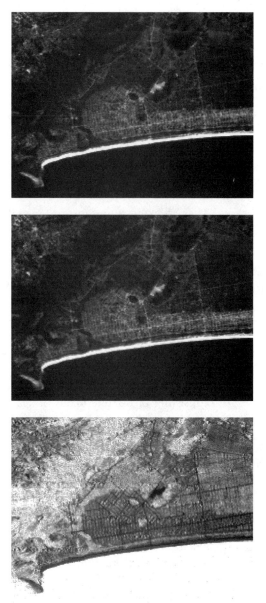

of a scene which is of course a function of the relative positions of the sun and the satellite and changes with time. This assumes that we consider that each image has been produced as a product of a reflectivity function and an illumination function. We assume that although the reflectivity function changes from band to band, the illumination function remains constant. Dividing images will thus remove such differences as shadows as shown in Figure 9.13. Ratio images can also be used to emphasize the difference in the slopes of the reflectivity curves between two bands. Figure 9.14 shows road detail emphasized by taking a ratio image.

9.2

Transforming the position of pixels – image warping

An important feature of image warping is whether we use forward or inverse mapping to effect the warp. Consider an input and an output image (in morphing we refer to a source and a target image). If the (unwarped) input image has pixel coordinates (u,v) that correspond to pixels with coordinates (x,y) in the (warped) output image, then we can define the mapping as:

$$(x,y) = (X(u,v), Y(u,v))$$

or

$$(u,v) = (U(x,y), V(x,y))$$

The first expression is forward mapping and the second inverse mapping. In forward mapping we scan the input image and copy the pixel intensity at (u,v) to the corresponding output pixel using the mapping X,Y. In inverse mapping we scan the pixels of the output image and use U,V to find the corresponding pixels in the input image. Each mapping direction has its own problems and advantages as we will now discuss.

9.2.1

Forward mapping

In practice, in forward mapping the 'bare' mathematical definition needs to be enhanced with a number of algorithmic details. With an input and output image consisting of discrete pixels of spatial extent, we cannot simply map a single point from the input image with integer coordinates (u,v) into (x,y) coordinates that will be real valued in general. If we simplistically round the (x,y) coordinates to nearest integer values and assign the intensity associated with (u,v) into the resulting output pixel, there is no guarantee that we will not end up with holes and overlaps in the output image. Many pixels in the input image may map into a single pixel in the output image, causing overlaps; alternatively a single pixel in the input image may need to be spread over many pixels in the output image – a situation that may result in holes. Holes and overlaps are particularly problematic in view interpolation (Chapter 21) where we are dealing with three-dimensional information using manipulations confined to image-plane space.

If we must consider the input pixel as a square whose four corners map into a quadrilateral in the (x,y) or output plane (Figure 9.15(a)), this means that each input pixel has to be mapped, its shape in the output plane found and an appropriate weighted value accumulated in those output pixels that the quadrilateral overlaps. For this we need an accumulator array and a calculation to determine what fraction of the input intensity should be apportioned to each of the accumulator cells that the input pixel overlaps. The input intensity must be scaled, for a cell, according to the area overlap for that cell.

There are two problems with forward mapping. First, the weight determining intensity calculation is costly. Second, there is a problem with magnification. If

Figure 9.15
(a) Forward and (b) inverse
mapping.

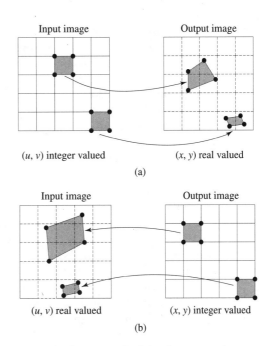

(a)

(b)

the transformation is such that one pixel in the source image maps into many in the target – magnification, or zooming – then distributing the single source pixel intensity across the corresponding quadrilateral in the target image will lead to a characteristic 'blocky' appearance. The cure to this problem is to subdivide the pixel into sub-pixels until the area of the subdivision product, transformed into the target domain, reduces to approximately one pixel extent, to gain more information within or under a pixel (Figure 9.16(a)). This implies that

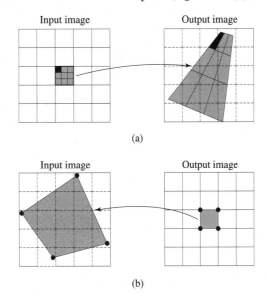

Figure 9.16
Magnification and
minification in forward and
inverse mapping. (a) The
magnification problem in
forward mapping can be
solved by subdividing input
pixels. (b) The minification
problem in inverse
mapping.

we have an application where we can sample the input image at a higher rate. The diagram reveals yet another problem which is that unless the transformation is affine, uniform sampling of the input image does not correspond to uniform sampling of the output image. The example shows the non-linear transformation that would be, for example, the image plane result of a perspective transformation in three-dimensional computer graphics.

9.2.2 Inverse mapping

Simply the reverse of forward mapping (Figure 9.15(b)), inverse mapping has the property that the hole problem is avoided and guarantees that all output pixels are computed. Now, however, there is a problem with minification. If one pixel in the output image maps into many in the input image we have to somehow integrate over the projected area of the pixel in the source – the 'pre-image' of the output pixel – to calculate a correct intensity. This is a problem that has stimulated much research in computer graphics where the minification problem routinely occurs in texture mapping. Consider an easy example that demonstrates the nature of the problem. Say an object becomes very small and approaches one pixel when projected into screen space. Again an anti-aliasing filter is needed and the extreme case is minification. Thus we see that magnification in forward mapping and minification in inverse mapping are the extreme cases where anti-aliasing is most required and most efficacious. Consider a chequerboard texture map has to be pasted onto the object. The precise inverse mapping may correspond to a black or white area in the texture domain and if this single value is used the object would end up being completely black or completely white. When the object was animated it would alternatively switch between black and white. The correct approach is to integrate or filter over the pre-image and allocate, in this case, a grey intensity.

9.2.3 Two-pass transforms

A two-pass transform is a method of implementing an image transformation that makes for efficiency, ease of hardware implementation and ease of anti-aliasing. It can be defined as

$$(x,y) = (X(u,v),Y(u,v))$$
$$= T(u,v)$$
$$= P_1(u)P_2(v)$$

where (x,y) and (u,v) are the coordinates of pixels in the output and input image as before and it is understood that T decomposes into the sequential application of P_1 and P_2.

Consider the simple example of rotation demonstrated in Figure 9.17. P_1 is a shear and scale operation produced by scanning the input image in rows or scan-

Figure 9.17
An example of a two-pass
transform.

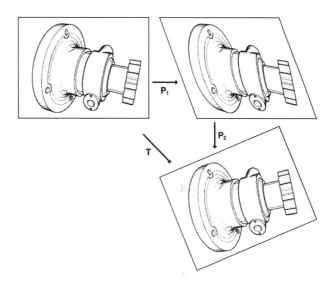

line order. This generates an intermediate image. The intermediate image is then scanned in column order and P_2 is applied, generating the output image. Operating on consecutive rows then columns of an image has major practical advantages. Incremental calculations are possible and the row/column coherence makes for efficient hardware design.

Consider the first pass. This generates the intermediate image where all the pixels have a y coordinate that is the same as their y coordinate in the final image. That is, when the second pass of the transfer is applied the y coordinate of the intermediate image pixels does not change. Now the first pass must be row preserving. Rows in the input image map into corresponding rows in the intermediate image. Thus we can write the first pass as

$$(x,v) = (P_1(u),v)$$

where P_1 varies from row to row, that is, it is a function of the row coordinate v.

In the second pass each column in the intermediate image is scanned and P_2 is applied to generate the output image. The problem is to find P_2.

Let us return to the rotation example (Figure 9.17). We can define the overall transfer as

$$\begin{bmatrix} \cos\theta & \sin\theta \\ -\sin\theta & \cos\theta \end{bmatrix}$$

The first pass is given by

$$(x,v) = (u\cos\theta - v\sin\theta, v)$$

or

$$P_1(u) = u\cos\theta - v\sin\theta$$

This results in a horizontal shear together with a scale. For the second pass we hold x (in the intermediate image) constant and apply P_2, a function of x, to consecutive columns in the intermediate image. We cannot simply use

$$y = u\sin\theta + v\cos\theta$$

since the intermediate pixels have coordinates (x,v), that is, x is referenced, not u. Therefore we need to express u in terms of x. Now

$$x = u\cos\theta - v\sin\theta$$

so

$$u = \frac{x + v\sin\theta}{\cos\theta}$$

giving

$$y = \frac{x\sin\theta + v}{\cos\theta}$$

$$= P_2(v)$$

where P_2 is also a function of the column coordinate x varying from column to column. We can summarize the general process as:

(1) Execute the first pass using $P_1(u)$ which is directly derived from the transform matrix.

(2) Find an auxiliary function which removes u from the mapping $X(u,v)$.

(3) Use this expression to find $P_2(u,v)$. This is a function of v but varies from column to column as x.

Returning to conventional notation we can easily show the operations as a two-pass decomposition of a rotation as follows:

$$\begin{bmatrix} \cos\theta & \sin\theta \\ -\sin\theta & \cos\theta \end{bmatrix} = \begin{bmatrix} \cos\theta & 0 \\ -\sin\theta & 1 \end{bmatrix} \begin{bmatrix} 1 & \tan\theta \\ 0 & \dfrac{1}{\cos\theta} \end{bmatrix}$$

(9.2.4) The bottleneck problem

The major problem with the two-pass transform is the bottleneck problem. This is when significant information is lost by 'compression' of the input image during the first pass. Consider, for example, 90 degree rotation. The intermediate image collapses into a diagonal line of pixels. The first row in the input image is mapped into a single pixel at the top right of the intermediate image. All the other rows also map into a single point. When the second pass is performed there is little or no information available. The information cannot be recovered. Continuing with the second pass would be geometrically correct but the colour information in the input image is lost. Now, of course, a 90 degree rotation is not a problem. We do not need any special technique to rotate through 90 degrees

– we simply transpose rows and columns. But the bottleneck problem occurs in rotation as we approach 90 degrees. We can solve this for, say, an 85 degree rotation by first rotating 90 degrees (by transposition) and then using the two-pass transform to rotate back through –5 degrees. Another way of solving the bottleneck problem is simply to reverse the order of the horizontal and the vertical pass. These two solutions taken together provide a general strategy. We select the particular strategy that maximizes the area of the intermediate image. In other words we select one of the following:

(1) Horizontal pass followed by a vertical pass

(2) Vertical pass followed by a horizontal pass

(3) Transpose rows and columns (90 degree rotation) followed by (1)

(4) Transpose rows and columns followed by (2)

Another way in which the bottleneck problem is avoided is to decompose the rotation into three passes as follows:

$$\begin{bmatrix} \cos\theta & \sin\theta \\ -\sin\theta & \cos\theta \end{bmatrix} = \begin{bmatrix} 1 & 0 \\ -\tan\dfrac{\theta}{2} & 1 \end{bmatrix} \begin{bmatrix} 1 & \sin\theta \\ 0 & 1 \end{bmatrix} \begin{bmatrix} 1 & 0 \\ -\tan\dfrac{\theta}{2} & 1 \end{bmatrix}$$

This is because each component in the overall transformation only involves a shear, whereas in the two-pass decomposition a shear and a scale are involved.

Further reading

For basic pixel processing any of the texts in Chapter 1 are recommended. The book by Wolberg contains an expert treatment of warping transforms (Chapter 17).

10 Edges and their detection

10.1 The origin and nature of edges

10.2 Edge detection

10.3 Global processing and the Hough transform

10.4 Edges and segmentation – explicit edge detection or boundary following

Edge detection, as we remarked in the introduction, is an area that embraces both image processing and computer vision. It is used as a pre-process in many computer vision tasks, principally in shape recognition or description. It is perhaps the most assiduously researched and most successful aspect of computer vision and this is due to the assumption of its importance as a 'low-level' vision operation. By this is meant that it almost seems mandatory to detect edges in an image if we are going to be able to extract geometric or shape information from the image – shapes are delineated by edges. If we are trying to extract structural information from an image without using any a priori information on the nature or shape of the structure, then detecting edges seems an obvious approach.

The classic problem that edge detection is plagued with is noise. This manifests itself as small perturbations in the input edge which cause large perturbations in the output image. Consider an edge which has been broken into two segments by a single noisy pixel. If we do nothing about this then our output image would consist of two line segments instead of one. This may have serious implications in higher-level processes. Doing something about this problem we have treated separately. This is called edge linking or aggregation.

The sources of the noise problem are fairly clear. First, we have perturbation noise which means that the value of a pixel is not what it should be due to the addition of random noise. This kind of noise is independent of the image structure and is scattered throughout the image. If we rely on changes in (say) pairs of pixels which are horizontal to detect a vertical edge, then noise perturbation in one of the pixels may reduce their difference and we may miss labelling a pixel as belonging to an edge. Such noise does not occur in a computer graphics image. Another problem which interferes with edge detection is the extent of the edge. An ideal edge is a step edge (Figure 10.1(a)) but this rarely occurs in a sampled image because it is unlikely that the end to end effect of the sampling process is such that it will cause a pixel boundary to line up with an edge. In practice a real scene will include deficiencies introduced by the transfer characteristic of the sampling system (distortion due to lenses, inadequacies in the image sensor array, and so on). This manifests in ramp edges (Figure 10.1(b)) where the edge is spread over a number of pixels at a slower rate of change than the step edge. Again this does not occur in computer graphics images.

We assume that edges are visually important to human beings. Certainly prior to the 20th century, we existed in an environment that consisted mostly of static objects. If relative motion existed between us and the scene, then it was of low magnitude. We are interested in recognizing or perceiving the shape of objects in our environment and undoubtedly edges of an object play an important role in such recognition, although the extent of this importance is not clear.

The most general way in which the use of edges can be described is to say that they are normally used in some type of segmentation process. They are a straightforward way of (possibly) highlighting features of interest in an image – features that we want to jump out of the background.

The main role that edges play in computer vision is to get an image containing an object or objects to 'reveal' its structure. We can then use the edges in a matching scheme that relates them to stored or prior knowledge. Usually we try to group edges into higher-level structures.

Images need not necessarily be segmented on the basis of edges. Satellite images are usually segmented according to wavelength or even texture to divide the image into parts that reflect the different types of ground area. However, segmentation based on edges is the most common form and is routinely used in many computer vision systems.

We conclude this section by demonstrating that the 'success' of an edge detection procedure depends as much, if not more, on the nature of the image (and thus on the application) than on the method used. Figure 10. 2 is an example of a simple edge detection procedure operating on three very different images. The first is a computer graphics image which is characterized by total lack of noise. The second is a photograph where the edges are fairly well differentiated. The final image is one where there is much edge detail. If an image of this type

Figure 10.1
(a) Step and (b) ramp edges.

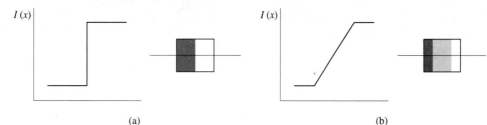

(a)   (b)

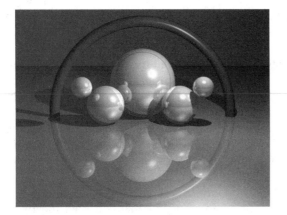
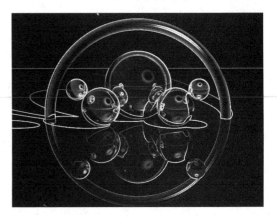

(a)

(b)

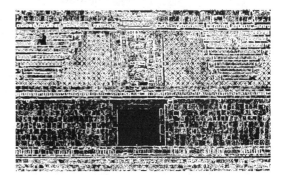

(c)

Figure 10.2

A simple edge detection process applied to an easy, moderate and hard image. (a) A computer graphics image. (b) An image with long explicit edge structure. (c) An image where practically every pixel belongs to some kind of edge structure.

occurred in an application then it would be difficult to distinguish edges of interest from 'textual' variations.

10.1 The origin and nature of edges

In a projection of a scene an edge manifests itself as a spatially coherent discontinuity in image intensity. We can usually identify edge information that originates from four different types of sources in the scene. Let us now look at these and the nature of the information that they contain.

The silhouette edge of an object

This may be the edge of a continuous surface – the projection formed by a sphere, for example – or it may be an edge from a surface normal discontinuity as in the case of the projection of a cube. Silhouette edges may not contain sufficient information to facilitate shape recognition and the value of the information tends to depend on viewing direction. An obvious example, where the utility of the information depends on the viewpoint, is the silhouette of a human face. In profile the outline of the nose, lips and jaw may be sufficient to identify the person. On the other hand, the silhouette of a frontal view may only contain sufficient information to identify it as a person (and perhaps the gender). Another problem with silhouette edges is that objects may overlap in projection to produce a composite silhouette edge. Sometimes, particularly in image processing applications, the shape of edges is not important. It is only necessary to reliably segment an object from its background by thresholding and then perform, say, some image analysis operation. An easy example is cloud cover analysis. Here we may have a satellite image of clouds against a dark background. We threshold the scene and produce a binary image with clouds represented as 1 and ground or sea as zero. Counting the 1s gives the area of cloud cover. Although the operation highlights the edges of the clouds they themselves are of no significance.

Surface normal discontinuities

When we use the word edge it is usually a surface normal discontinuity to which we refer – the edge of a table, for example. The discontinuity in a surface normal produces a discontinuity in the reflected light intensity from the object and ideally this appears as a detectable edge in the projection. Note that a surface normal discontinuity can also be a silhouette edge, but in general it will be an edge contained within the boundary projection of an object. You will recall from our simple local reflection models in computer graphics that a diffuse component of reflected intensity was calculated as a function of the surface normal and the position of a point light source and any discontinuity in the surface normal will produce a discontinuity in the shading on the surface. We saw that such simple models produced an acceptable illusion of reality and in the real situation, except in obscure cases, we would always expect a surface normal discontinuity to produce a detectable edge in the image. Detecting both silhouette edges and edges that result from surface normal discontinuities may enable us to recover information concerning the three-dimensional shape of the object. While silhouette edges are usually fairly easy to detect, we cannot normally always detect edges within the outline of an object projection by using the same means because the contrast across the edge may be much less. In simple cases the visibility of the shading discontinuity is a function of the magnitude of the difference in surface normal between the two faces that form the edge.

Illumination discontinuities

Such discontinuities can occur from shadows cast by another object on the object of interest or from the edge of a specular highlight. Usually such edges are of no interest to us. By 'us' we mean implementors of computer vision. Shadows to us as human beings are important and contain much information concerning the nature of the illumination and the spatial relationships of objects to each other. Although there has been some recent work on object recognition from the geometry of the specular highlights (described in Chapter 15), they have normally been ignored, that is, simply considered as a nuisance. As we know from computer graphics, specular highlights depend on the nature of the surface and the viewpoint as well as the shape of the surface. Shadow boundaries depend on the nature, position and number of light sources. The question is, if we apply an edge detection operator over an image, how do we distinguish between edges that are of interest to us and edges in which we have no interest? As far as an edge detection algorithm is concerned, there will normally be no difference between an edge that resulted from a surface normal discontinuity and one that appeared because of an illumination discontinuity.

Object reflectivity discontinuities

Yet another discontinuity in reflected intensity can occur if the imaged object exhibits changes in reflectivity over its surface. For example, we may be imaging an object that is coloured differently in different areas or contains a brand name. Whether this object property produces unwanted or wanted edges is clearly context dependent.

10.2 Edge detection

Edges are usually detected by a two-stage process. First, a small spatial filter – a mask or edge detector – is cross-correlated with the image to detect pixels in the image which according to the nature of the mask may form part of an edge. This process is an approximation to some kind of spatial differentiation of the image intensity and such masks are sometimes called difference operators as they produce a digital estimate of derivatives at a point on the image surface $I(x,y)$. Such operations are essentially local and, depending on the size of the mask, are sensitive to noise so a second operation is often performed to aggregate the points into connected edges.

A rigid mathematical approach to local edge detection would require a model of the edges that we are going to detect (the nature of the illumination changes across an edge) and because we do not want the operation to be sensitive to noise, we also require knowledge of the nature of the noise.

10.2.1 Edge detection using difference operators

The principle of edge detection using derivatives can be summarized easily in a figure (Figure 10.3). We can see from the figure that:

- The first derivative is positive or negative depending on the direction of the intensity change with respect to the order in which we are examining or scanning the image.

- The first derivative is zero in areas of constant intensity and low in areas of slow changing intensity.

- The second derivative has the property of crossing zero at either a positive or negative edge. The sign change of the zero crossing depends on the sign of the first derivative.

In Chapter 24 we describe a digital approximation to the gradient of an image $I(x,y)$ and introduced the 3×3 Prewitt operator. This is reproduced for convenience in Figure 10.4. A mask implies the operation cross-correlation, which means that the centre of the mask is placed 'over' the current pixel and a sum of products (the result of the cross-correlation) is evaluated by weighting and summing the image pixels that lie 'under' the mask. It is easily seen from the figure that Δ_1 detects vertical edges and Δ_2 detects horizontal edges. The sum of each of the mask weights is zero – as should be the case for a derivative operator. If the

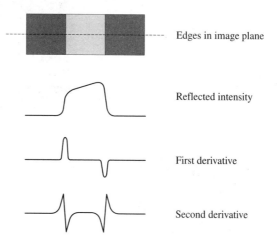

Edges in image plane

Reflected intensity

First derivative

Second derivative

Figure 10.3
Two ideal edges exhibiting linearly varying reflected intensities.

Figure 10.4
3×3 Prewitt operator for
edge detection; the result of
cross-correlating the image
in Figure 10.2 with each
mask together with the
sum.

1	1	1
0	0	0
−1	−1	−1

Horizontal

−1	0	1
−1	0	1
−1	0	1

Vertical

Sum

mask is placed over a region of constant or slow varying intensity then the response should be zero or very low. The result of applying this operator to an image is shown in Figure 10.4. Note that we have omitted a multiplicative factor which is required to scale the result. This does not affect the edge detection ability of the mask.

Detecting edges of predefined orientation

Now we know that the gradient is a vector whose direction is normal to the iso-brightness contour at the point (x,y) (see Chapter 24). The direction of this vector is given by:

$$\boldsymbol{\theta} = \tan^{-1}(\Delta_2/\Delta_1)$$

where

Δ_1 and Δ_2 represent the x and y components of the gradient

We can use this fact to perform an operation that selects lines of a particular orientation.

The complete edge detection process operation breaks down into two or three separate processes:

(1) Apply the gradient approximation (see Chapter 24) to give

$$\nabla I(x,y) = \Delta_1 + \Delta_2$$

Calculate also if required $\boldsymbol{\theta}(x,y)$

$$\boldsymbol{\theta} = \tan^{-1}(\Delta_2/\Delta_1)$$

(2) Threshold $\nabla I(x,y)$ to give a binary edge image.

(3) If required transform $\nabla I(x,y)$ into a binary edge image that only contains edges of a particular orientation by using those parts of $\boldsymbol{\theta}(x,y)$ that have the required value to effect the selection.

Figure 10.5
(a) Sobel edge detection and the image from Figure 10.2. (b) The same image using the Prewitt operator.

A number of differencing masks have been suggested. Figure 10.5(a) shows a pair of Sobel edge detecting masks. Figure 10.5(b) shows the result of applying this operator to the 'difficult' image of Figure 10.2 together, for comparison, with an extract from that figure. Rotating the basic differencing configuration into a num-

(a)

−1	0	1
−2	0	2
−1	0	1

−1	−2	−1
0	0	0
1	2	1

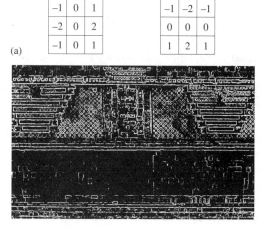

(b) Sobel

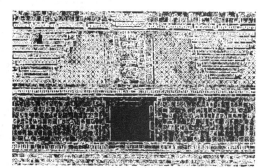

(c) Prewitt

Figure 10.6
Compass masks or edge detectors.

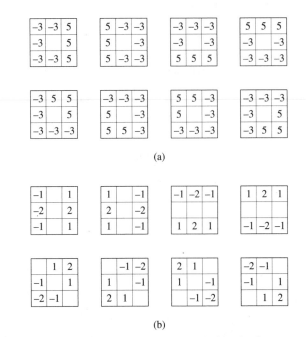

(a)

(b)

ber of orientations gives us so-called compass masks which act as an alternative to evaluating edge direction by comparing Δ_1 and Δ_2 responses. Figure 10.6 shows Kirsch and Robinson compass masks.

(10.2.3) Edge masks with 'combined' properties

In this section we look at masks that combine properties, in effect from separate component masks, into a single operation or mask. It may seem from the previous sections that one can choose any arbitrary differencing configuration but each of the above mask sets perform differently. We can measure their performance with respect to such properties as: edge contrast, edge direction, gradient magnitude and gradient direction. Their behaviour is a function of their configuration and the geometry of the edge. Another problem that we have already touched on is noise and in this section we will deal with more complex, second generation masks which attempt to detect edges in the presence of noise. They also address another problem which is scale – we need different operators to function at different scales.

The two approaches that we will now examine attempt to deal with these problems; they are methods developed by Marr and Hildreth and Canny. First we consider the Marr–Hildreth approach.

The developers of this edge detection technique claim that it is based on evidence that biological low-level vision systems exhibit a function that is similar. A Marr–Hildreth mask is a combination of a Gaussian smoothing function and a Laplacian difference operator. The Laplacian, or second spatial derivative, is described in Chapter 24 and returning to Figure 10.3 we see that the second derivative crosses zero at exactly that point where the first derivative is maximal. In the Marr–Hildreth technique the Laplacian is used to detect edges by finding zero crossings, the key idea being that edges as zero crossings are easier to detect than edges as extrema, the case with derivative images. The function $I'(x,y)$ obtained after cross-correlating $I(x,y)$ with the Marr–Hildreth operator has positive and negative values. Edges are marked in this function by some operation such as:

for all x,y:
    if $(I'(x,y) < -t$ **and** any_neighbour_of$(I'(x,y)) > t)$
      or $(I'(x,y) > t$ **and** any_neighbour_of$(I'(x,y)) < t)$
        then $I'(x,y)$ is an edge pixel

where

any_neighbour_of() means any of the eight neighbours of (x,y)

t is a threshold

The Gaussian part of the operation is a more considered smoothing operation than the smoothing component of the Sobel operator and overall the method works better than simple gradient edge detection, particularly when edges are more blurred and the noise level is high. Figure 10.7 shows a result of using the Marr–Hildreth operation.

Let us now look at how the Marr–Hildreth operator is constructed. This has to be done analytically rather than intuitively as we did before. Also, any meaningful implementation has to be reasonably exact and this means that we end up with a much larger mask than we had with the simple gradient operators. (Our final filter is expressed practically as weights spaced one pixel apart. The more accurately we require a filter function to be represented in this way, the more pixels we require. In other words, we need many more pixels to sample and accurately reflect the shape of the filter function. In the case of step function type edge filters we can represent these accurately with 3×3 pixels. With the Marr–Hildreth operator we require more.) This means that much more computation is involved. Because of the nature of convolution, smoothing $I(x,y)$ by convolving it with a Gaussian smoothing filter and then convolving the result with a Laplacian is exactly equivalent to taking the Laplacian of the Gaussian filter and convolving $I(x,y)$ with the result. Thus we have:

$$M_H(x,y) = \nabla^2 G$$

$$= \frac{\partial^2 G}{\partial x^2} + \frac{\partial^2 G}{\partial y^2}$$

where $G = \exp\left(\frac{x^2 + y^2}{2\sigma^2}\right)$

writing $r^2 = x^2 + y^2$

we have $M_H = \left(\frac{r^2 - \sigma^2}{\sigma^4}\right) \exp\left(\frac{-r^2}{2\sigma^2}\right)$

Figure 10.7
Marr–Hildreth edge
detection.

```
0    0    0   -1   -1   -2   -1   -1    0    0    0
0    0   -2   -4   -8   -9   -8   -4   -2    0    0
0   -2   -7  -15  -22  -23  -22  -15   -7   -2    0
-1   -4  -15  -24  -14   -1  -14  -24  -15   -4   -1
-1   -8  -22  -14   52  103   52  -14  -22   -8   -1
-2   -9  -23   -1  103  178  103   -1  -23   -9   -2
-1   -8  -22  -14   52  103   52  -14  -22   -8   -1
-1   -4  -15  -24  -14   -1  -14  -24  -15   -4   -1
0   -2   -7  -15  -22  -23  -22  -15   -7   -2    0
0    0   -2   -4   -8   -9   -8   -4   -2    0    0
0    0    0   -1   -1   -2   -1   -1    0    0    0
```

Digital implementation of the Man-Hildreth filter

After convolulution of image
with filter of 6 = 1.5

After convolulution of image
with filter of 6 = 5

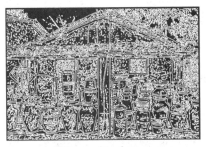

Zero crossings from
above image

Zero crossings from
above image

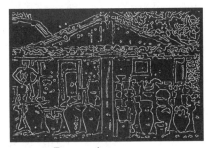

Zero crossing common
to both

Result from the
'difficult' image

σ is the standard deviation of the Gaussian and controls its width. The higher the value of σ the greater the smoothing and at the same time the more the image is blurred. Figure 10.7 shows a digital implementation of the mask and a slice through the continuous function that the digital implementation is a sampled version of. We note that the mask is circularly symmetric. After applying this filtering operation zero crossings are detected as described earlier.

The value of σ can be used to extract edge detail in the image at different scales. A common example of an image that may exhibit different scales is of an object that possesses surface texture. A small-scale edge detector may produce edges of the texture, whereas a large-scale detector may produce the physical edges that characterize the shape of the object. That such scale differences are important is perhaps obvious. But having recognized this, what is less obvious is how to combine and use the output of multiple scale edge detectors. One way in which to do this is to filter the images separately with different values of σ and consider only those zero crossings that are present in the output from all filters. The two values used in Figure 10.7 were 1.5 and 5.

The Canny edge detector, reported in 1986, also uses Gaussian smoothing. This operator detects edges at zero crossings of the second directional derivative of the Gaussian smoothed image in the direction of the gradient (where the magnitude of the gradient must be above a threshold). That is:

$$C(x,y) = \frac{\partial^2 G}{\partial n^2}$$

where

> n is the direction of the gradient of the smoothed image

The implementation of this operator is most easily carried out by a series of steps:

(1) We start with a one-dimensional Gaussian filter that we will call G, together with one-dimensional derivative filters G_x and G_y.

(2) Cross-correlate $I(x,y)$ with G along rows to give I_x and down columns to give I_y.

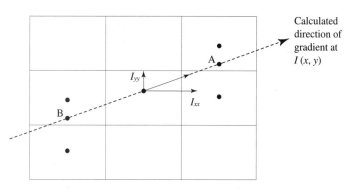

Figure 10.8
Interpolating gradient values.

(a)

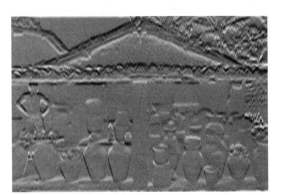

(b)

Figure 10.9
Canny edge detection
6 = 4. (a) x and y
components of the one-
dimensional Gaussian
convolution; (b) x and
y components of the
derivative Gaussian
convolution; (c) the final
image after non-maximum
suppression.

(c)

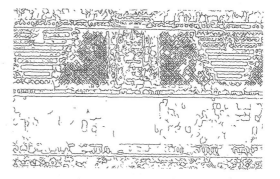

Figure 10.10
Canny edge detection for
6 = 1.5 and 5.

(3) Cross-correlate along I_x with G_x and I_y with G_y along rows and columns to give I_{xx} and I_{yy}.

(4) I_{xx} and I_{yy} are now the smoothed x and y components of the gradient $\nabla I(x,y)$ from which we can find the direction of the gradient to complete the process. We will now describe this operation in some detail.

The reason why the final step requires an algorithm in its own right is that the direction estimation given by I_{xx} and I_{yy} is not necessarily accurate, and unless the calculated direction is exactly horizontal or vertical it will follow a path that lies between pixel centres. Canny calls this process non-maximum suppression.

Refer to Figure 10.8 which shows the pixel (x,y) under consideration. The gradient direction calculated from I_{xx} and I_{yy} is shown as a dotted line. We require the value of the gradient on either side of pixel (x,y), say at positions A and B. For example, the value of the gradient at A can be linearly interpolated from the values along the line joining pixel $(x,y+1)$ to pixel $(x+1,y)$. Similarly for the value at B. We can now find the magnitude of the difference between the magnitude of the gradient at (x,y) and A and between (x,y) and B and mark (x,y) as an edge pixel accordingly. This process can be further enhanced by a further thresholding operation called hysteresis thresholding. This uses two thresholds, a high value and a low value. Any pixel in the image that has a gradient magnitude greater than the high value is marked as an edge pixel, and pixels that are connected to marked ones and have a value greater than the lower threshold are also marked as belonging to an edge. The process can be applied recursively. This is an example of an edge linking process which we will now describe in general terms. An example of the stages in taking an image through a Canny edge detecting process is shown in Figures 10.9 and 10.10.

10.2.4 **Edge linking or aggregation**

Although the operations described in the previous section are known universally as edge detection, possibly a better term is edge emphasis. As is apparent from the examples, an image is transformed into a binary domain that contains a set of pixels which belong to an edge. (Such pixels are sometimes called **edgels**.) However, such pixels also contain pixels that manifestly do not belong to an edge (false positives) and edges in the images may exhibit breaks (false negatives). Difference operators are particularly prone to producing false positives because of their sensitivity to noise. Even if they deal with noise satisfactorily by smoothing, they can respond to non-edge regions where the intensity gradient is sufficiently steep.

In general such problems will always occur with the inherently parallel operation of edge detection by using masks. We only consider a single pixel and some neighbourhood of that pixel independently of all other pixels. A more intelligent strategy may be a serial operation where an edge is **followed** and we can make decisions and ask questions at a current pixel such as where to look next; is the gap manifested by the next pixel likely to be noise, for example?

Another approach is to follow 'parallel' edge detection by some process called linking or aggregation. In its simplest manifestation this attempts to diminish the effect of spurious pixels that are not part of an edge and to form continuous edges from likely fragments. We will examine two of the simplest operations – one which is local in that it deals with neighbourhoods of points in an image to which edge detection has been applied and one which is global.

10.2.5 Local edge linking

For a local approach to succeed it is intuitively obvious that the neighbourhood over which we detected the edge must now be expanded. The aggregation process must be able to span gaps between segments of a line or edge produced by the edge detection process. This of course is the tricky part. The neighbourhood must be sufficiently large to close unwanted gaps but not so large as to join line segments that should not be joined.

A direct local approach is easily implemented by considering similarity in magnitude and direction between pixels in some neighbourhood in, say, a gradient image. We can say that two pixels (x,y) and (x',y') are linked or lie on the same edge if:

$$| \nabla I(x,y) - \nabla I(x',y') | < t_1$$

and

$$| \theta(I(x,y)) - \theta(I(x',y')) | < t_2$$

where

x',y' lies in a predefined neighbourhood of x,y

θ is the orientation of the gradient

t_1, t_2 are thresholds

This operation tends to eliminate false positives in the gradient image. Depending on the context it can be followed by further processing that eliminates short line segments and short breaks.

10.3 Global processing and the Hough transform

The Hough transform is a global technique that finds the occurrence of curves of a predefined shape. We will look at two examples – detection of straight lines and circle detection. The literature on the Hough transform is sometimes confusing because an implementation, rather than the transform, is often described. We will try to avoid this confusion and we will describe two implementations – a brute force algorithm and an algorithm due to O'Gorman and Clowes. A comparison and understanding of these two approaches should make everything clear.

The Hough transform is the image mapped into the parameter domain of a predefined curve, the occurrences of which we want to detect in the image. This domain allows us to make a quantitatively considered decision on the existence of the sought curves because it reveals both the position and the 'strength' of the curve. For example, consider finding all occurrences of straight lines of any orientation:

$$y = ax + b$$

in $I(x,y)$. We have a two-dimensional domain $A(a,b)$ to represent every possible straight line. This is the parameter domain or space. A single point (a,b) in this space represents a straight line.

A slight problem with straight lines is that as the line approaches the vertical both a and b approach infinity and a better parametrization is (d,θ):

$$d = x \cos\theta + y \sin\theta$$

where

d is the perpendicular distance from the line to the origin

θ is the angle this perpendicular makes with the x axis

The transform works as follows. Consider Figure 10.11. We have a single point in the image $I(x,y)$ and we wish to find the evidence for the occurrence of any straight line passing through that point. Clearly there are an infinity of straight lines passing through this point so we consider lines at, say, every 10 degrees. We evaluate the evidence for a particular straight line, having parameters d and θ, by searching $I(x,y)$ from (x,y) along the direction θ. If the pixels we encounter are, say, greater than some predefined threshold then we increment the cell $A(d,\theta)$ which corresponds to the line we are currently searching for. The strength of the evidence for any line is then given by examining the value of the accumulators $A(d,\theta)$.

Figure 10.11
Hough transform: an
image point is tested for
membership of a straight
line segment. (a) A single
image point $I(x,y)$ is tested
to see if it lies on any of a
set of straight lines.
(b) Parameter space:
the accumulator cells
corresponding to the lines
in (a).

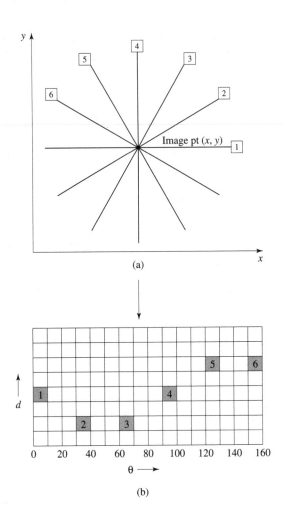

(a)

(b)

10.3.1 Hough transform – brute force implementation

A brute force algorithm of the Hough transform would be first a pass through the image:

```
for each point I(x,y) in the image
    for each point I(x',y') along line (d,θ)
        if I(x',y') > t then
            A(d,θ) := A(d,θ) + 1
```

This is then followed by a search of parameter space, $A(d,\boldsymbol{\theta})$, for peaks which identify the occurrences, by position and orientation, of all the straight lines in the image.

Hough transform – O'Gorman and Clowes

If a and b are quantized into Q values and n is the number of pixels in $I(x,y)$ then the brute force implementation of the Hough transform requires nQ invocations. This is somewhat expensive and an algorithm that requires just n invocations was developed by O'Gorman and Clowes. This tests for a straight line in a small neighbourhood of (x,y) using a measure of local edge strength and direction based on the gradient, and accumulates the appropriate $A(d,\theta)$ if an edge is found. The idea is illustrated in Figure 10.12. The algorithm can be summarized as:

> **for** each point $I(x,y)$ in the image
>   **if** strength_of_gradient $> t$ **then**
>   evaluate the direction of the line and increment appropriate $A(d,\theta)$

The Hough transform can be used as an edge linking scheme because it can locate the set of disjoint pixels that may be part of a fragmented line. Consider a structure in the image that exhibits gaps. This will map into a high value in the Hough transform. From such values and information on the structure that we are searching for, we can use cells in the Hough transform to direct us to potential gap pixels in the image. In other words, the Hough transform highlights the gaps in fragmented lines. The idea is shown in Figure 10.13 for a circular structure. A further examina-

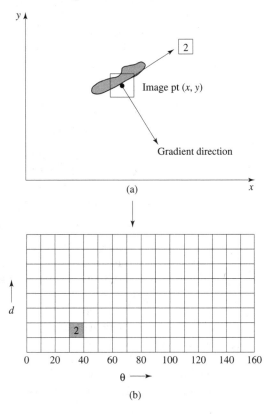

Figure 10.12
O'Gorman and Clowes implementation of the Hough transform. (a) The gradient strength and direction are measured at point $I(x,y)$. (b) If the gradient is greater than a threshold the line direction is calculated and the appropriate accumulators all incremented.

Figure 10.13
Hough transform technique
for circles: any structures
lying on the circumference
of a circle with given radius
have gradients at that
point in the direction of
the centre.

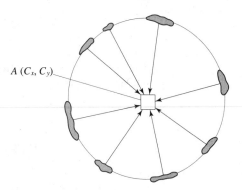

$A\,(C_x, C_y)$

tion of the gaps can then be made in the image domain. Alternatively we can say that the value A gives us a direct numerical indication of the likelihood of a circular structure being present even if it appears in the image as a broken form.

Hough transform – circles

To extend the Hough transform to find circles or any other parametrized curve is straightforward. Consider finding the evidence for all circular structures in $I(x,y)$ of a fixed radius r. Look again at Figure 10.13. If the structures form themselves into a circle then the components will have gradient directions that point to the centre of the circle. Points (x,y) on the circumference of a circle centred at (Cx,Cy) satisfy

$$x = Cx + r\cos\theta$$
$$y = Cy + r\sin\theta$$

The algorithm can be summarized as:

> **for** each point (x,y) in the image
>   **if** strength_of_gradient $> t$ **then**
>   evaluate direction of gradient and
>   **increment** $A(Cx,Cy)$ where
> $Cx = x - r\cos\theta$
> $Cy = x - r\sin\theta$

This approach is easily extended to detect circles of any radius by extending the dimension of A to 3 and adding an extra loop to the algorithm.

Edges and segmentation – explicit edge detection or boundary following

It would seem self-evident that a good way to segment an image is to use boundaries or edges. However, as we have seen, even an edge emphasis image that has been subject to linking or aggregation does not produce a closed boundary which we would require for segmentation.

We can say that one way of solving the segmentation problem is boundary detection where we try to find an explicit boundary as opposed to using an edge-emphasized version of the original image. In general this will only work for simple 'loop' boundaries such as silhouette edges rather than internal edges in a two-dimensional projection of a three-dimensional object. This leads to a class of boundary finding algorithms which, instead of operating independently on individual pixels (edge emphasis), use some kind of strategy like 'we are currently positioned on a boundary point, which is the best direction to look for the next boundary point and if we find a candidate what is its strength as a boundary candidate?'. Most algorithms thus attempt to track, follow or grow a boundary sequentially from point to point, starting with a seed point.

This can be a difficult or an easy problem. When we have simple objects silhouetted against a high contrast background we can use thresholding to segment the image, and if the parts for which we want to find boundaries do not overlap the process is trivial. However, note that in the special case when we have a priori knowledge of the shape of the object that we are trying to segment from a background then we can use the (generalized) Hough transform to find a boundary but such contexts are limited. Another, relatively new, approach that can be used is the active contour model or 'snakes' described in Chapter 14 but again some a priori knowledge of shape is required.

One of the most powerful strategies for explicit edge detection is graph searching. This can incorporate a variety of weak and strong a priori knowledge and the technique finds a minimum cost path from a known start position to a known stop position. Also it can be made highly resistant to noise.

The first step in the process is to map the image into a directed graph. A directed graph is a structure consisting of nodes n_i and arcs that connect the nodes $[n_i, n_j]$. Each node on the graph represents either a pixel intensity or the magnitude of the gradient. The basic requirements to represent the problem as a graph search are:

- We need a method of generating the graph. To generate a graph we expand the nodes. Expanding a node means that if we consider being positioned at node n_i, what pixels do we select as being candidates for the next in the boundary sequence? This determines the node connected to node n_i in the graph.

- We need to be able to evaluate a cost function for any path through the graph. Specifically if we are currently positioned at node n_i we need to be able to evaluate the costs incurred in getting to n_i from n_s (the start node) and from n_i to n_f (the goal node).

Consider the first requirement – moving from node n_i representing pixel X_i to node n_j representing pixel X_j. If we have a gradient image with magnitude

$$G(X) = |\nabla I(x,y)| = \Delta_1 + \Delta_2$$

and direction $\theta(X) = \tan^{-1}(\Delta_2/\Delta_1)$

we can use, for example:

- X_j must be one of the three neighbours (eight connected) that lie 'in front' of X_i, that is, in the direction

$$d \in \left[\boldsymbol{\theta}(X_i) - \frac{\pi}{4}, \boldsymbol{\theta}(X_j) + \frac{\pi}{4} \right]$$

- $G(X_i)$ and $G(X_j)$ must both be greater than some threshold indicating edge significance.

- The change in angle of the gradients should be, say, less than 90 degrees. That is

$$\left| [\boldsymbol{\theta}(X_i) - \boldsymbol{\theta}(X_j)] \bmod 2\pi \right| < \frac{\pi}{2}$$

An example of a thresholded gradient image and a graph constructed according to the above criteria is shown in Figure 10.14.

The second requirement involves evaluating a cost function:

$$g(n_i) + h(n_i)$$

where $g(n_i)$ is the cost associated with the path from the start node to n_i and $h(n_i)$ is the cost of the path from n_i to the end node. $g(n_i)$ is evaluated by working back from the current node and summing the cost associated with each arc in the path. This means that we have to assign costs to the outcomes of the test that produce the successful candidate nodes during the expansion of a node. $h(n_i)$ requires an estimate which can be as crude and as simple as the Euclidean distance from the current node to the end node. We can also just set $h(n_i)$ equal to zero and this will, for the search algorithm given below, result in a 'breadth first search' and a path that is optimal with respect to the cost criteria used. In general $h(n_i)$ controls the behaviour of the search algorithm in terms of the time it takes and a breadth first search will take much longer than one which is based on an estimate of $h(n_i)$; however, note that in this particular case we have already introduced, in the node expansion part of the problem, criteria that narrow the search.

Figure 10.14
Mapping (a) a gradient
image in (b) a graph.

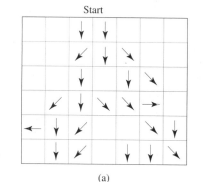

(a)

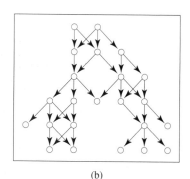

(b)

The search algorithm is as follows:

(1) Expand the start node and put the successors – the candidates that pass the test criteria – on a list of open nodes and set up pointers back to the start node. Evaluate the cost function at the same time.

(2) Find the open node of minimum cost and remove it from the open list. If the current node, n_i, is the end node then follow back through the pointers to find the optimum path and stop.

(3) Else expand n_i and go to step 2.

Further reading

An exhaustive treatment of techniques for evaluating edge detector performance is given in *Computer Vision* (Volume 1) by Haralick and Shapiro (see Chapter 1).

Canny J. (1986). A computational approach to edge detection. *IEEE Trans. on Pattern Analysis and Machine Intelligence*, **8**(6), 679–98

Hough J. (1962). A Method and Means for Recognizing Complex Patterns. U.S. Patent No. 3,069,654

Kirsch R. (1971). Computer determination of the consistent structure of biological images. *Comput. Biomed. Res.*, **4**, 315–28

Marr D. and Hildreth E. (1980). Theory of edge detection. *Proc. of Royal Soc. of London*, Series B, **207**, 187–217

O'Gorman F. and Clowes M.B. (1976). Finding picture edges through collinearity of feature points. *IEEE Trans. Comput.*, **C25**(4), 449–54

Prewitt J. (1970). Object enhancement and extraction. In *Picture Processing and Psychopictorics* (Lipkin, B. and Riosenfeld, A. eds) pp. 75–149. New York: Academic Press

Robinson G.S. (1977). Edge detection by compass gradient masks. *Computer Graphics and Image Processing*, **6**, 492–591

Image transforms

Image transforms are alternative ways of representing the information in an image. The motivation is to exploit some property possessed by the image transform that is not available in the image domain. Most commonly we do this to facilitate image processing, image compression, or image editing. The operations that we wish to carry out on the image are easier to perform when the image information is reordered according to the nature of the transform. The commonest image transform, the Fourier transform, decomposes an image into its (spatial) frequency components (analogous to the way in which a musical note can be expressed as the sum of its harmonic components). This has the effect of 'bringing together' certain forms of information that exists in the image. For example, if an image exhibits much of a certain texture, this will be reflected in the Fourier domain as a high energy component whose attributes specify the nature of the texture – how busy it is and whether it possesses a coherent direction. This information concentrates into a small area in the Fourier domain even although it may be dispersed throughout the image.

The transforms that we will discuss are reversible or invertible. This means that the image can be reconstructed from the transform without any loss of information. The common implementation model of an operation that involves an image transform is:

(1)   Transform the image from the image or space domain into the transform domain.

Figure 11.1
Image processing and
transforms. (a) Processing
in a transform domain;
(b) image compression
in a transform domain.

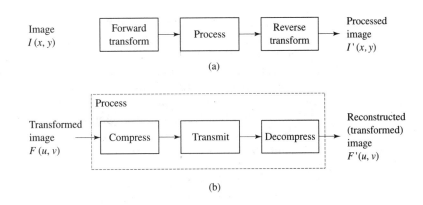

(2) Operate on, or process, the image in the transform domain (when we are dealing with the Fourier domain we use the term 'filtering'). If we are dealing with image compression the operation would be transmission of a compressed version of the transform over a communications link.

(3) Transform the results of the transform domain operations back into the image domain for display.

These general processes are shown in Figure 11.1. If the motivation of the process is image compression then the process stage expands as shown: an encoding stage followed by a decoding after the image has been transmitted over a communications link (or stored on, say, a CD-ROM). The point of this operation is that we can make a more measured decision in a transform domain concerning the information that we should discard to achieve the compression than we could in the spatial or image domain.

In this chapter we will look at three common image transforms – the Fourier transform, the (related) cosine transform and the wavelet transform. The Fourier transform has many applications in image processing. The cosine transform is mainly used as a basis for lossy compression (as in Figure 11.1(b)) and the wavelet transform has applications in compression and other areas such as multi-resolution representation. Compression issues using wavelets and cosine transforms are dealt with in Chapter 26 and the use of the wavelet transform in multi-resolution representation is dealt with in Chapter 23.

11.1 The Fourier transform of images

The Fourier transform is one of the fundamental tools of modern science and engineering and it finds applications particularly in both analogue and digital electronics, where information is represented (usually) as a continuous function of time and in work associated with computer imagery where the image $I(x,y)$ is represented as an intensity function of two spatial variables.

Calculating the Fourier transform of an image, $I(x,y)$, means that the image is represented as a weighted set of spatial frequencies (or weighted sinusoidally undulating surfaces) and this confers, as far as certain operations are concerned, particular advantages. The individual spatial frequencies are known as basis functions.

Any process that uses the Fourier domain will usually be made up of three main phases. The image is transformed into the Fourier domain. Some operation is performed on this representation of the image and it is then transformed back into its normal representation – known as the space domain. The transformations are called forward and reverse transforms. Fourier transforms are important, and this is reflected in the fact that the algorithms which perform the transformations are implemented in hardware in image processing computers.

There is no information lost in transforming an image into the Fourier domain – the visual information in the image is just represented in a different way. For the non-mathematically minded it is, at first sight, a strange beast. One point in the Fourier domain representation of an image contains information about the entire image. The value of the point tells us how much of a spatial frequency is in the image.

Operating with this representation makes certain image processing operations that involve a degree of complexity if carried out in the image domain much simpler when implemented in the Fourier domain. It enables lossy image compression to be implemented with precise user control over the resulting degradation in the quality of the image. Finally it enables objective discussions on the important problem of aliasing in computer graphics.

We define the Fourier transform of an image $I(x,y)$:

$$F(u,v) = \iint I(x,y) \exp\left[-j2\pi\,(ux + vy)\right]\,dxdy$$

and the reverse transform as:

$$I(x,y) = \iint F(u,v) \exp\left[\,j2\pi\,(ux + vy)\right]\,dudv$$

The Fourier transform is a complex quantity and can be expressed as a real and an imaginary part:

$$F(u,v) = \text{Real}(u,v) + j\,\text{Imag}(u,v)$$

and we can represent $F(u,v)$ as two functions known as the amplitude and phase spectrum respectively:

$$|F(u,v)| = (\text{Real}^2(u,v) + \text{Imag}^2\,(u,v))^{1/2}$$
$$\varphi(u,v) = \tan^{-1}(\text{Imag}(u,v)/\text{Real}(u,v))$$

Now it is important to have an intuitive idea of the nature of the transform and in particular the physical meaning of a spatial frequency. We first consider the easier case of a function of a single variable $I(x)$. If we transform this into the Fourier domain then we have the transform $F(u)$. The amplitude spectrum, $|F(u)|$, specifies a set of sinusoids that when added together produce the original function $I(x)$ and the phase spectrum specifies the phase relationship of each sinusoid (the value of the sinusoid at $x = 0$). That is, each point in $|F(u)|$ specifies the amplitude and frequency of a single sine wave component. Another way of putting it is to say that any function $I(x)$ decomposes into a set of sine wave co-efficients. This situation is shown in Figure 11.2. The first part of the figure shows the amplitude spectrum of a single sinusoid which is just a single point (actually a pair of points symetrically disposed about the origin) in the Fourier domain. The second example shows a function that contains information – it could be a speech signal. This exhibits a spectrum that has extent in the Fourier domain. The spread from the minimum to the maximum frequency is called the bandwidth.

A two-dimensional function $I(x,y)$ – an image function – decomposes into a set of **spatial** frequencies $|F(u,v)|$. A spatial frequency is a surface – a sinusoidal 'corrugation' whose frequency or rate of undulation is given by the distance of the point (u,v) from the origin:

$$\sqrt{u^2 + v^2}$$

and whose orientation – the angle the peaks and troughs of the corrugation make with the x axis – is given by

$$\tan^{-1}(u/v)$$

A single point $F(u,v)$ tells us how much of that spatial frequency is contained by the image. Figure 11.3 is a two-dimensional analogue of Figure 11.2. Here a sinusoid has spatial extent and maps into a single point (again actually a pair of points) in the Fourier domain. If we now consider an image $I(x,y)$, this maps into a two-dimensional frequency spectrum that is a function of the two variables u and v. Different categories of images exhibit different categories of Fourier transforms as we shall demonstrate shortly by example. However, most images have Fourier representations with the amplitude characteristic peaking at (0,0) and decreasing with increasing spatial frequency. Images of natural scenes tend to exhibit Fourier representations that contain no coherent structures. Images of man-made scenes generally exhibit coherences in the Fourier domain reflecting the occurrence of coherent structures (roads, buildings and so on) in

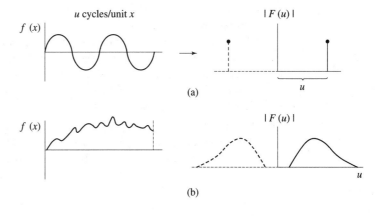

Figure 11.2
One-dimensional Fourier transform. (a) A sine wave maps into a single point. (b) A 'window' of an 'information wave' maps into a frequency spectrum.

Figure 11.3
An image made up of a
single spatial frequency
and its Fourier transform.

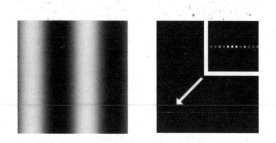

the original scene. Computer graphics images often have high energy in high spatial frequency components, reflecting the occurrence of detailed texture in the image.

A property of the Fourier representation that is of importance in image processing is that the circumference of a circle, centred on the origin, specifies a set of spatial frequencies of identical rate of undulation

$$r = \sqrt{u^2 + v^2}$$

having every possible orientation.

We will now look at the nature of the transform qualitatively by examining three different examples of amplitude spectra.

- Figure 11.4(a) is an image from nature. It produces a Fourier transform that exhibits virtually no coherences. Despite the fact that there is much line structure manifested in the edges of the leaves, the lines are at every possible orientation and no coherence is visible in the Fourier domain.

- Figure 11.4(b) is an image of a man-made scene. It is a photograph of the Arches of Lapa in Rio de Janeiro – a small toast-rack tramcar trundles over the top to go to the old district of Santa Tereza. There is obvious structure in the Fourier domain that relates to the scene. First, there is the line structure that originates from the tramline discontinuity (top of the arches). Second, there is the discontinuity between the upper and lower arches that manifests as another line in the Fourier domain. There are 'fan-like' coherences around the u axis that are due to the vertical structure or edges of the arches. Because the orientation of these lines varies about the vertical, due to the camera perspective, they map into the u axis fan in the Fourier domain. There is a vertical coherence in the Fourier domain that relates to scan lines in the data collection device and is also due to horizontal discontinuities manifested by the long shadows. The remainder of the contributions in the Fourier domain originate from the natural components in the image such as the texture on the arch walls.

- Figures 11.5(a) and 11.5(b) are two man-made textures. The relationships between the coherences of the texture and the structures in the Fourier domain should be clear. In both cases the textures have been overlaid with a leaf, which manifests as a blurry 'off-vertical' line in the Fourier domain.

Figure 11.4
Fourier transforms of natural and man-made scenes.

(a) Bush

Fourier transform | $F(u, v)$ |

(b) Arcos da Lapa
(Rio de Janeiro)

Fourier transform | $F(u, v)$ |

What can we conclude from these examples? A very important observation is that information that is 'spread' throughout the space domain separates out in the Fourier domain. In particular we see that in the second example the coherences in the image structure are reflected in the Fourier domain as lines or spokes that pass through the origin. In the third example, the texture produces components that are strictly localized in the Fourier domain at their predominant spatial frequencies. This property of the Fourier domain is probably the most commonly used and accounts for spatial filtering, where we may want to enhance some spatial frequencies and diminish others to effect particular changes to the image. It is also used in image compression where we encode or quantize the transform of the image, rather than the image itself. This gives us the opportunity to use less information to encode those components of the transform that we know have less 'importance'. This is a powerful approach and it happens that much less information can be used to encode certain parts of the transform without any significant fall in image quality. The original information in the image is reordered in the transform in a way that enables us to make easy judgements about its relative importance in the image domain.

An extremely important property of the Fourier domain is demonstrated in Figure 11.6. This shows that most of the **image power** is concentrated in the low frequency components. The figure shows circles superimposed at different

Figure 11.5
Fourier transforms of
textures.

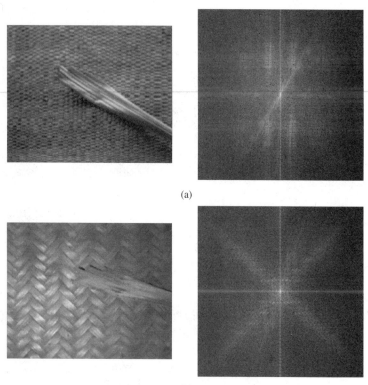

(a)

(b)

radii on the Fourier transform of the image shown in the figure. If we calculate
the proportion of the total sum of $|F(u,v)|^2$ over the entire domain contained
within each circle, then we find the relationship shown in Figure 11.6(b).

A property of the Fourier transform pair that is fundamental in image processing is known as the **convolution theorem**. This can be written as:

$$I(x,y) * h(x,y) = \Im^{-1}(F(u,v)H(u,v))$$

where * means convolution.

In words: the convolution of the image function $I(x,y)$ with $h(x,y)$ in the space
domain is equivalent to (or the inverse transform of) the multiplication of $F(u,v)$
and $H(u,v)$ in the Fourier domain, where:

$$I(x,y) = \Im^{-1}(F(u,v))$$

and

$$h(x,y) = \Im^{-1}(H(u,v))$$

Analogously we have

$$I(x,y)h(x,y) = \Im^{-1}(F(u,v) * H(u,v))$$

Both of these results are known as the convolution theorem. Convolution, and
its special case, cross-correlation, is an extremely common operation as we

| Pão de Açúcar | (a) | Fourier transform |
| (Rio de Janeiro) | | $\lvert F(u,v) \rvert$ |

Radius (pixels)	% image power
8	95
16	97
32	98
64	99.4
128	99.8

(b)

Figure 11.6
The percentage of image power enclosed in concentric circles of increasing radius.

describe in Chapter 24. For the purposes of this chapter we need only note that it can be performed by multiplication in the Fourier domain. It is this theorem that underlies the convenience property of filtering in the Fourier domain.

In practice the images that we have just studied were sampled versions of a continuous $I(x,y)$ and we use a discrete version of the continuous integral, known as a Discrete Fourier Transform (DFT), to compute the Fourier transform of a digital image. The transform pair is:

$$F(u,v) = \frac{1}{MN} \sum_{x=0}^{M-1} \sum_{y=0}^{N-1} I(x,y)\exp\left(-j2\pi\left(\frac{ux}{M}+\frac{vy}{N}\right)\right)$$

$$I(x,y) = \sum_{u=0}^{M-1} \sum_{v=0}^{N-1} F(u,v)\exp\left(j2\pi\left(\frac{ux}{M}+\frac{vy}{N}\right)\right)$$

where M and N are the dimensions of the image.

DFTs are always computed using an algorithm called a Fast Fourier Transform or FFT. For a one-dimensional array of N values this reduces the number of arithmetic operations from a factor of N^2 to $N\log N$. The operation and properties of an FFT are described fully in many textbooks (in particular the classic text by Bracewell (1965)) and we will not repeat the treatment here.

Image processing and the Fourier domain

The general idea of filtering in the Fourier domain is shown in Figure 11.7. Here we have an image $I(x,y)$ transformed into the Fourier domain where it is represented as $F(u,v)$. The figure shows that we can operate on the image transform $F(u,v)$ by multiplying by a **filter** $H(u,v)$. The product, $F(u,v)H(u,v)$, is then transformed back into the space domain where it is now $I'(x,y)$ – a processed version of $I(x,y)$.

We can write:

$$I'(x,y) = \Im^{-1}(H(u,v)F(u,v))$$

where

$$F(u,v) = \Im(I(x,y))$$

At this point an obvious question arises: what is the point of enhancement operations in the Fourier domain, with the implied extra complexity of transforming the image into the Fourier domain, performing the operation and then transforming back into the space domain? There are a number of answers to this question. One is that it is easier and more intuitive to specify a multiplicative operation with respect to spatial frequencies in the image than it is to think up the appropriate function $h(x,y)$ with which to convolve the image in the space domain. A simple example illustrates the point. We know that the image is in a form where low spatial frequencies are near the origin. As we move away from the

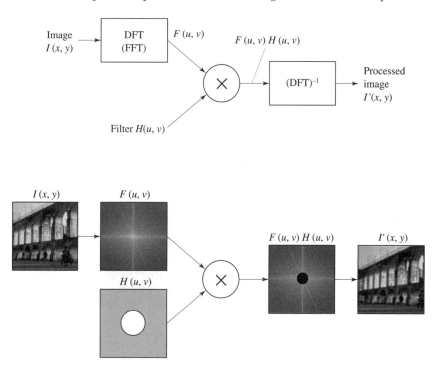

Figure 11.7

Schematic illustration of the computational steps in the process of filtering in the Fourier domain.

origin in the Fourier domain we encounter higher and higher spatial frequencies. If we want to deblur an image and emphasize detail we can simply delete low frequencies and retain higher ones by using a circularly symmetric $H(u,v)$:

$$H(u,v) = 0 \quad \textbf{if } u^2 + v^2 < r^2$$
$$H(u,v) = 1 \quad \textbf{if } u^2 + v^2 \geq r^2$$

This is known as a high pass filter. Thus we have an exact (at least to within the limitations of the discrete process) specification of an operation based on the concept of spatial filtering. This filtering operation which weights frequency components is well established in electronics where we deal with information that is a function of a single variable – time. For example, everyone is familiar with the tone or frequency controls on an audio amplifier. These controls enhance or diminish certain frequency components in a signal (usually) representing music. The conceptual convenience of this process is universally understood and everyone has a certain expectation of how the sound of the music is going to be changed by turning this or that control.

Consider, now, the nature of the filtering process in the space domain, by using the example of a low pass filter (Section 11.1.2). Such a circular symmetric filter is shown in Figure 11.8(a) and is the 'opposite' of a high pass filter – it passes low frequencies. The convolution theorem tells us that the equivalent operation in the space domain would be convolution with the Fourier transform of the cylindrical filter function $H(u,v)$. The convolution filter in the space domain is the solid of revolution formed by rotating a sinc function $(\sin(x)/x)$ through 2π. This is shown in Figure 11.8(b). A digital implementation of a two-dimensional sinc function is far more difficult than that of the cylindrical function. We have not only the problem of approximating the shape digitally, but there is also the problem that it is of infinite extent (and therefore has to be truncated) and the fact that it has negative weights (a pixel cannot have a negative intensity). Note, however, that this filter is used as a component of a composite filter for edge detection in Chapter 10.

Note that not all spatial domain filtering techniques have their equivalent Fourier domain operations. The equivalence of spatial domain convolution to Fourier domain multiplication only applies to linear filters. Non-linear filters, such as median filters, fall outside this rule and cannot be implemented as a

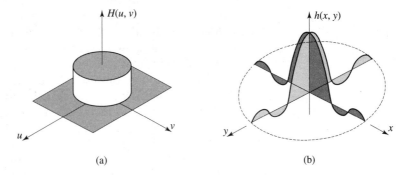

Figure 11.8
Ideal filters in the Fourier and space domains. (a) An ideal low pass (multiplicative) filter $H(u,v)$. (b) The equivalent (convolving) filter $h(x,y)$.

(a)　　　　　　　(b)

Fourier domain operation. Thus in practice the choice of the space domain or the Fourier domain depends on many factors.

In the operations described in this chapter we are only going to consider filters, $H(u,v)$, that effect the amplitude and phase spectrum identically. Such filters are called **zero phase shift** filters. We will now look at filters in detail.

Low pass filters

As we saw in Figure 11.6 most of the power in an image is concentrated in the low frequency components. Very little energy appears in the high frequency components. However, the **detail** in an image maps into high spatial frequencies. This is intuitively obvious. Detail in an image means structures such as edges where there is a sharp or fast spatial rate of change of image intensity. Such intensity transitions occur, by definition, over one or two pixels and will produce high frequency components in the Fourier domain.

High frequency information in an image can consist of wanted or unwanted information. Two examples of unwanted high frequency information are shown in Figure 11.9. In the first case there are unwanted edges due to inadequate sampling (we have seen in other parts of this book that these are more commonly dealt with by 'dithering' where the unwanted edges, or false contours, are spatially disrupted to reduce their visibility). In the second case we have corrupted the image with 'salt and pepper' or high frequency noise. This kind of noise is often generated within electronic equipment and manifests in an image as black specks in white regions or white specks in dark areas.

The effects of both kinds of noise can be diminished, as can be seen from the figure, by simply deleting high frequency components that occur in $F(u,v)$ at a radius greater than r:

if $\sqrt{u^2 + v^2}$ > r **then** $F(u,v) := 0$

or equivalently we can specify a filter $H(u,v)$

$H(u,v) = 1$ **if** $u^2 + v^2 < r^2$

$H(u,v) = 0$ **if** $u^2 + v^2 \geq r^2$

This is called **low pass** filtering because the low frequency components are retained while the high frequency components are deleted.

We also note from the illustration the important point that the price we pay for getting rid of unwanted high frequencies is that we also diminish those high frequencies that we want to retain. In other words, the image is blurred and we trade off unwanted information against blurring. However, our visual system would rather tolerate blurring than unwanted high frequency information. Our eyes are extremely sensitive to high frequencies in an image and a 'defocused' image to us seems preferable to high frequency noise.

We recall that the locus of points of equal spatial frequency lie on the circumference of a circle centred on the point (0,0) and simple low pass filters of the type we have described have the shape of circles centred on $H(0,0)$. Such filters are also

'Pixelized' image

Image with added noise

Figure 11.9
Examples of low-pass filtering
to diminish the effects of two
types of high-frequency noise.

called **ideal** filters because every spatial frequency up to those at radius *r* is passed unattenuated while those at radius greater than *r* are completely deleted.

11.1.3

High pass filters

High pass filtering is the converse of low pass filtering – here low frequencies are deleted and high frequencies are retained:

if $\sqrt{u^2 + v^2}$ $< r$ **then** $F(u,v) := 0$

or equivalently we can specify a filter $H(u,v)$

$$H(u,v) = 1 \text{ \bf if } u^2 + v^2 \geq r^2$$
$$H(u,v) = 0 \text{ \bf if } u^2 + v^2 < r^2$$

An example of high pass filtering is shown in Figure 11.10 together with the same image low pass filtered for comparison. The effect of high pass filtering is to emphasize edges or detail at the expense of slow varying changes in a scene.

Figure 11.10
High pass vs. low pass
filtering.

This realization – that high frequency components originate from the object edges and low frequency components from shading – can be used to make filters that operate differently on the high and low frequency components. The idea is to retain the advantages of a high or low pass filtering operation and at the same time diminish the disadvantages. For example, the purpose of high pass filtering is usually to make detail more visible – we may still want to retain the low frequency shading variations. In such a case we can use high frequency **emphasis** by simply adding a constant to the high frequency filter. In this way the low frequency components are still retained. An even better result can be obtained by following the high pass emphasis filter with histogram equalization which reduces the 'unbalancing' effect of the predominance of the higher brightness values of the high frequency components.

Finally we note that the effect of high frequency emphasis has been traditionally employed in the printing industry. Before the advent of modern digital computers, the effect could be achieved by subtracting a blurred copy of an image from the original. This technique is called **unsharp masking**.

11.2 Other Fourier domain filtering techniques

So far we have considered two cylindrical filters centred on the origin. These are shown schematically in Figure 11.11 which also shows simple extensions of

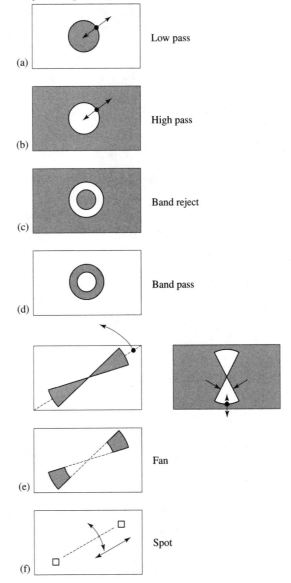

(a) Low pass

(b) High pass

(c) Band reject

(d) Band pass

(e) Fan

(f) Spot

Figure 11.11
A selection of Fourier domain filtering possibilities: (a) removes noise that manifests as high frequency components; (b) emphasizes detail such as edges which are high frequency transitions; (c) removes spatial frequencies of a particular value; (d) removes all spatial frequencies except those of a certain value; (e) emphasizes or de-emphasizes coherent structure at certain orientations; (f) removes texture that appears localized in one or more positions.

Figure 11.12
The effects of using various settings of a fan-shaped filter.

$H(u,v)$. (Note that we still are considering filters where $H = 0$ or $H = 1$ – binary valued filters.) The two extra configurations manipulate structure in imagery that is either oriented along a line in the Fourier domain or is localized into a small area. For example, coherent structure which comes from regular or repeat-

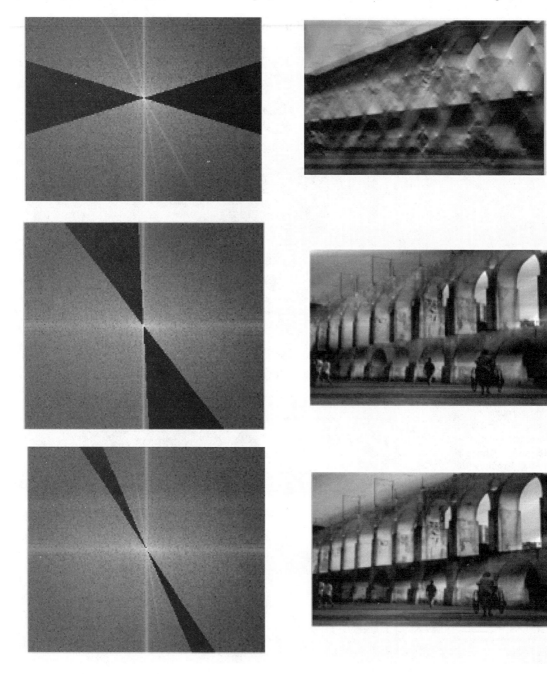

ing patterns in a man-made scene 'clusters' in the Fourier domain into certain frequency components. An image of a skyscraper produces high values along the u and v axes in the Fourier domain because all the high frequency edges and also the lower frequency changes (that manifest in the image as repetition of horizontal and vertical blocks) occur in the horizontal and vertical directions. Uniform texture concentrates into a few spikes in the Fourier domain which are oriented according to the principal directions of the texture pattern. These observations can be used in many ways in image processing and analysis and we will now consider, using simple examples, some of these applications. Figure 11.12 shows the effect of applying a fan-shaped filter to the man-made scene. This removes/enhances coherent structure at the orientation set by the filter.

As well as image processing, filters can be used in image matching applications. A rotating fan filter could be used to detect the occurrence of texture or structure at a certain frequency but of unknown orientation.

Inverse filtering or deconvolution

Inverse filtering is an elegant technique in theory that can present significant practical problems. The operation relies on knowledge of the nature of a degradation in an image. Division (multiplication by an **inverse filter**) in the Fourier domain can then restore the image. The classic example is the restoration of an image that has been blurred due to relative motion between the camera and the scene. It seems that in the space domain all information of interest has been destroyed, but it so happens that a simple division in the Fourier domain will make everything right. We will use this impressive example to explain the technique and to highlight its problems.

Suppose the relative motion is linear and takes place along the x axis due to the camera moving with velocity V for its exposure time T. In this case the image is blurred horizontally and can be modelled in the space domain as the convolution of a perfect image with a square wave of width VT.

Let us consider the general case first and return to this particular example later. If the perfect image is $I(x,y)$ and the degraded image is $g(x,y)$, then we have in general

$g(x,y) = I(x,y)*h(x,y)$

where $h(x,y)$ is the degrading function

In the Fourier domain we have

$G(u,v) = F(u,v)H(u,v)$

where $H(u,v)$ is the Fourier transform of $h(x,y)$

Inverse filtering simply means dividing $G(u,v)$ by $H(u,v)$ giving the Fourier transform of the undegraded image $F(u,v)$:

$$\frac{G(u,v)}{H(u,v)} = F(u,v) \frac{H(u,v)}{H(u,v)}$$

(Note that dividing in the Fourier domain means dividing the magnitude components and subtracting the phase components.)

Let us now consider the motion blur example. In this case $H(u,v)$ is given by

$$H(u,v) = \frac{\sin(\pi VTu)}{\pi VTu}$$

which is a function of u only because $H(x,y)$ is a function of x only.

Other degradations that can be modelled by analytic functions are atmospheric turbulence and blurring due to a lens system not being focused properly.

Let us now examine the problems associated with this technique. There are three basic problems. First – the obvious one – degradations are not always known a priori and even if they are it may not be possible to model them analytically. Sometimes $H(u,v)$ can be estimated from a posteriori examination of $G(u,v)$ if the general nature of $H(u,v)$ is known. For example, in the case of image blur due to simple relative motion, examination of the coherences in the pattern $G(u,v)$ will give both the direction of the relative motion and the interval VT. The second problem is the occurrence of zeros or very small values in $H(u,v)$. The dividend becomes very high causing overflow. This has to be handled.

A related problem is noise. In practice an image will not be perfect but will usually contain noise. Let us assume for simplicity that the noise is simple additive. This means that the degraded image in the Fourier domain can be modelled as:

$$G(u,v) = F(u,v)H(u,v) + N(u,v)$$

where $N(u,v)$ is the Fourier transform of the noise pattern

The restored image is now given by:

$$F(u,v) = \frac{G(u,v)}{H(u,v)} - \frac{N(u,v)}{H(u,v)}$$

and the last term will produce high values where $H(u,v)$ is small, amplifying the noise to such an extent, when the reverse transform is performed, that artefacts are produced which 'drown' the first or restoration term.

One way in which to minimize the problems caused by small values of H is to use a multiplicative weighting W:

$$F(u,v) = \frac{G(u,v)}{H(u,v)} \quad W = \frac{G(u,v)}{H(u,v)} \frac{|H(u,v)^2|}{|H(u,v)^2|+k}$$

k can be estimated interactively, where the deblurring of the image is appropriately balanced against the interference due to high noise terms. Alternatively a form of this filter, known as a **Weiner filter**, can be used. In this case both H and N need to be known. This technique is described in detail in Gonzalez and Woods.

The Discrete Cosine Transform (DCT)

In this section we introduce the Discrete Cosine Transform or DCT, used predominantly in data compression as we describe in Chapter 26. Also we deal (informally) with the properties of the DCT that make it attractive for lossy data compression (compared with the Discrete Fourier Transform), namely its superior energy packing facility and its relative immunity to blocking artefacts. This is the visibility of boundaries which occur when a picture is divided up into, say, 16×16 elements and a DCT is performed independently on each of these blocks – the method used in practical compression schemes.

It is useful to define the DCT by comparing it with the DFT definition. For simplicity we will consider a one-dimensional definition of each. First the one-dimensional DFT:

$$F(u) = \frac{1}{N} \sum_{x=0}^{N-1} I(x)\exp\left(-j2\pi\frac{ux}{N}\right)$$

This should be compared with the one-dimensional DCT which is

$$C(u) = c(u) \sum_{x=0}^{N-1} I(x)\cos\left[\frac{(2x+1)u\pi}{2N}\right]$$

where

$$c(u) = \sqrt{\frac{1}{N}} \quad u = 0$$

$$= \sqrt{\frac{2}{N}} \quad u \neq 0$$

We note that for $u = 0, 1, 2, 3, \ldots, N-1$, instead of using the frequencies $0, 1, 2, 3, \ldots, N-1$, we use frequencies $0, 0.5, 1, 1.5 \ldots (N-1)/2$. In the DFT we produce $2N$ real and imaginary numbers (actually only N independent coefficients whereas in the DCT we produce $2N$ real numbers or N independent numbers). In fact we can consider that we invoke a Fourier transform but in such a way that only real components are concerned.

The easiest way of understanding the DCT is to consider how it can be developed from the DFT. This is done in the following way. First we generate a symmetrical version of $I(x)$ by reflecting it about the point of symmetry. We then take a DFT about the point of symmetry (from $-N$ to $N-1$). Because we are now dealing with a symmetrical $I(x)$ the DFT **only** generates real (or cosine) components. This property means that the DCT deals better with the artefacts that arise from the arbitrary subdivision of the picture into small (say 16×16) blocks. Thus we see informally that a DCT is equivalent to making $I(x)$ symmetric and taking a DFT over $2N$ points.

It is easily demonstrated (see, for example, Rosenfield and Kak (1982)) that although a fast DCT can be written, a DCT can be achieved from an FFT by zero padding. This means that we generate an $I'(x)$ from $I(x)$ as follows:

$$I'(x) = I(x) \quad x = 0, 1, 2, \ldots, N-1$$
$$ = 0 \quad\quad x = N, N+1, \ldots, 2N-1$$

and use a conventional FFT with $2N$ points.

The two-dimensional DCT pair is given by:

$$C(u,v) = c(u)c(v) \sum_{x=0}^{M-1} \sum_{y=0}^{N-1} I(x,y) \cos \left[\frac{(2x+1)u\pi)}{2M} \right] \cos \left[\frac{(2y+1)v\pi}{2N} \right]$$

and

$$I(x,y) = \sum_{x=0}^{M-1} \sum_{y=0}^{N-1} c(u)c(v)C(u,v) \cos \left[\frac{(2x+1)u\pi)}{2M} \right] \cos \left[\frac{(2y+1)v\pi}{2N} \right]$$

11.4 Image pyramids

Image pyramids are image transforms where multiple copies of an image at different resolutions are formed. Two of the main applications of this transform are in image communication where the resolution transmitted is appropriate to the needs of the receiver and multi-resolution painting systems in interactive image editing where a user can edit or alter an image at any desired resolution level. An image pyramid consists of an image at the bottom of the pyramid which is the highest or limiting resolution together with copies at lower and lower resolution.

We will describe three types of image pyramid, a low pass pyramid, a bandpass pyramid and a wavelet pyramid. Examples of the first two are shown in Figure 11.13. A low pass image consists of the finest resolution image, followed by a half resolution version, followed by a quarter resolution version, and so on. Each version is formed from the previous one by an averaging process. The top of the image is a single pixel which is the average of the entire image. In a low pass pyramid each image is 'independent' and we simply select an image appropriate to current use by indexing into the required resolution level. An early example of this type of image transform was developed in computer graphics in 1983. Here a texture map is stored in this way and when the texture is to be mapped onto the object a metric that relates to the screen size or projection of the object is used to select a map at the appropriate resolution level. Objects far away from the user would select a small or coarse resolution map. This is called mip-mapping and we use it to prevent artefacts forming in the mapped texture. We say that the texture maps are 'pre-filtered'. Mip-mapping is described in detail in Chapter 4.

In a bandpass pyramid the top of the pyramid is again a single pixel – the average of the entire image. Every other level contains detail imagery required to generate an image at a desired resolution level n from the previous resolution level $n-1$. Thus to generate a 4×4 image from the top of the pyramid we assign the final average value to all four pixels and add the detail stored at the second

Low-pass pyramid

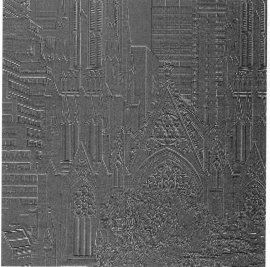

Band-pass pyramid

Figure 11.13
Image domain pyramids
(compare with Figure
11.15).

level of the pyramid. Now we cannot index into any level for the required image; we have to generate an image at the required level by starting at the top and working down in this way. The pyramid only stores at each level the information required to go from a coarse level n to a finer level $n{-}1$. A bandpass image is generated by averaging down to the next (coarser level). For example, if we have $m \times m$ pixels in the highest resolution image we generate an averaged version at $(m/2) \times (m/2)$. This averaged image is then 'expanded' back to $m \times m$ and subtracted from the original to form the detail image.

The third type of image pyramid is the most frequently used one. This is the wavelet transform and it can be thought of as a type of bandpass pyramid, but one which stores separate detail images for horizontal, vertical and diagonal information. It is somewhat more complicated to discuss and we shall devote an entire section to it. We shall begin by comparing a wavelet approach with Fourier techniques.

Wavelet transform

The Fourier transform finds its main application in classical image processing and in image compression in the guise of the DCT. With the inexorable growth of image traffic on the Internet and the use of imagery in CD-ROM-based multimedia its use as a standard tool in JPEG is surely its most common application. Outside of providing a theoretical base for anti-aliasing, it does not find many applications in computer graphics. The wavelet transform is being increasingly used in computer graphics and it may well become as standard a tool in computer graphics as the Fourier transform is in image processing. We will begin by looking at an inherent disadvantage of the Fourier transform as an image transform. It is this disadvantage that is addressed by the wavelet transform and the removal of this drawback may open up many applications in computer graphics.

In a Fourier transform a single point in the Fourier domain contains information from everywhere in the image. It specifies the amount or strength of that particular spatial frequency that exists in the image. Considered in the image domain, a single spatial frequency is a sinusoidal 'corrugation' that exists over the entire image space. The existence of a strong high frequency component, for example, means that there are edges in the image – we know their orientation relates to the orientation of the spatial frequency but the frequency domain information does not tell us where they exist in the image. In fact we do not even know if the edge information is constrained to one particular area of the image or if it is dispersed over the entire image as a texture pattern. Technically we say that the Fourier basis functions have infinite support. Practically this fact has important ramifications. In image compression, for example, we can invoke a lossy compression by only retaining part of the Fourier domain. The loss in information is manifested across the entire image as blurring. In other words, image compression using the Fourier transform is independent of image context. This is in many cases a disadvantage. Often what is needed in image compression is a scheme that retains detail where required and compresses non-significant areas of the image.

Wavelets, on the other hand, have compact or finite support and they enable different parts of the image to be represented at different resolutions. They can be used in image compression where parts of the image are represented by a quantity of information – the wavelet coefficients – that is appropriate for the nature of the image. Busy parts of the image are represented using more information than that used for smooth parts. (An example of image compression using wavelets is discussed in Chapter 26.) Wavelets enable approaches in computer graphics that are the same in effect as the adaptive sampling methods that we describe in Chapter 8.

In computer graphics they can be used for efficient representation of the radiosity function in global illumination, where the nature of the variation in the radiosity function is such that it exhibits slow changes over relatively large parts of the image interrupted by fast variations. Radiosity algorithms using wavelets can deal with one of the major inaccuracies inherent in classical radiosity techniques, namely the Constant Radiosity Assumption (Chapter 6). Finally the representation can be used in image interaction at any level of resolution. This new area has potentially major applications in image editing and painting. (We discuss this application in Chapter 23.)

Wavelet transforms are more difficult to understand than Fourier transforms and we will approach them informally by describing how a transform is performed then working backwards to intuitively deduce the attributes of the process. The particular transform of interest to us is called the standard decomposition and the basis functions used are called Haar bases which are rectangular waves.

First we show a wavelet transform of a stylized image Figure 11.14 (a square against a background) and of a real image (Figure 11.15). In the stylized image the absolute amplitude of the wavelet transform coefficients is indicated and from this simple example we can make the following observations:

- The number of pixels in the transform is equal to the number of pixels in the image.

- The transform has a recursive structure (shown to three resolution levels in the figure) based on quadrants where each bottom left quadrant contains a copy of itself at half the resolution of the copy one level up. The final bottom left quadrant contains a copy of the image at 1/8 resolution of the original.

- At each level the three quadrants which are not subdivided contain edge information and if we consider the wavelet bases as edge detectors then these respond maximally to horizontal, vertical and diagonal edges. They are, however, not just simple edge detectors but functions that respond to differential information concentrated in different parts of the image and existing at different scales.

The same transform is shown in Figure 11.15 for a real image.

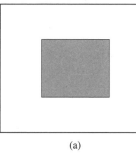

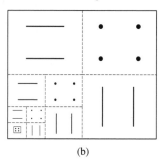

Figure 11.14
A wavelet transform of an image (see next figure for a real image). (a) Original image; (b) wavelet transform.

(a)

(b)

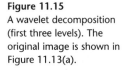

Figure 11.15
A wavelet decomposition
(first three levels). The
original image is shown in
Figure 11.13(a).

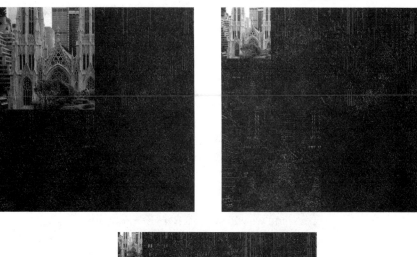

We could consider the generation of a transform as a recursive process where we generate lower and lower resolution copies of itself. This is called decomposition and is illustrated conceptually in Figure 11.16(a). The reverse of the process is called reconstruction (Figure 11.16(b)). In decomposition at each step in the recursion we generate an image averaged to 1/2 its previous resolution together with three copies of 'detail' lost in the averaging operation (Figure 11.16(c)).

Now to generate the transform in this way we can use an algorithm that alternates between operations on rows and operations on columns. The algorithm is extremely simple:

(1) Perform an averaging and differencing operation on each row of the image (we will explain exactly what is meant by 'averaging and differencing' in a moment).

(2) Perform an averaging and differencing operation on each column of the result of (1).

(3) Repeat this process recursively on the bottom left-hand quadrant of the result of (2).

Figure 11.16
Decomposition and
reconstruction in a wavelet
transform.

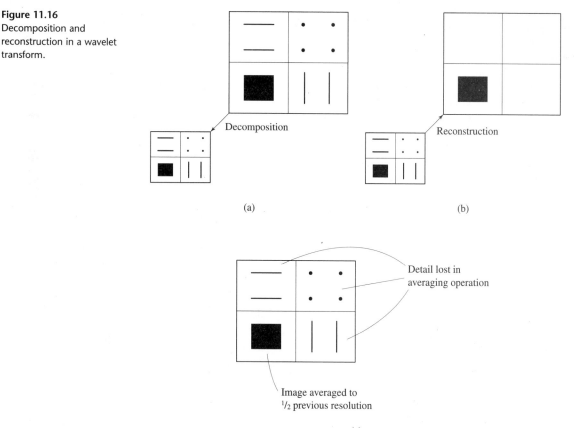

(a)

(b)

Detail lost in
averaging operation

Image averaged to
$^1/_2$ previous resolution

(c)

You can see from the illustration that this produces a series of intermediate images where the original image appears at lower and lower resolution in the bottom left-hand quadrant. Eventually it shrinks to a single pixel that contains the average of the entire image. This is called a non-standard decomposition. An alternative method is the standard decomposition and this corresponds to the transform that would be obtained using the basis functions shown in Figure 11.17. The algorithm that generates this decomposition is:

(1) Perform an averaging and difference operation on each row of the image.

(2) Apply the same operation to each column of the results obtained in (1).

We now need to explain what is meant by averaging and differencing and we will consider this process using simple examples in one-dimensional space. Consider the sequence:

6 8 4 2

which may be the intensity values of four pixels along a scan line. Averaging this one-dimensional image means forming, at each resolution level (or each level of the recursion), the average of consecutive pairs. That is:

Figure 11.17
Decomposition of $I(x)$ into a scaling function ϕ and four wavelets.

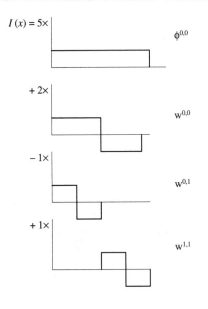

6 8 4 2
7   3
5

Averaging, by definition, involves a loss of detail information – in image terms it is a blurring operation – and at each level in the process we retain the lost detail in the form of detail coefficients. We now have:

Resolution level	Average	Detail coefficients	
4	6 8 4 2		
2	7 3	–1	1
1	5	2	

In this case our wavelet transform is the final average together with the detail coefficients – the wavelet transform for the sequence 6 8 4 2 is:

5 2 –1 1

and, for example, to reconstruct from this information the average image at resolution level 2, we have:

$7(= 5+(2))\ 3\ (=5+(-2))$

That is, to reconstruct from level n the average image at level $n-1$ we construct two intensity values at level $n-1$ by adding and subtracting the detail coefficients to/from the value at level n. Thus the wavelet transform for an entire image consists of a single pixel representing the average of the entire image together with the complete hierarchy of detail coefficients. This form immediately emphasizes its potential in image compression because the detail coefficients are usually very small in magnitude and can be stored in a lossy form with little reduction in image quality.

Let us now use this same example and introduce some formalistics which will give us some insight into the nature of the basis functions. We write the wavelet transform

5 2 –1 1

as

$$I(x) = 5\phi^{0,0}(x) + 2w^{0,0}(x) - w^{1,0}(x) + w^{1,1}(x)$$
$$= b^{0,0}\phi^{0,0}(x) + c^{0,0}w^{0,0}(x) + c^{1,0}w^{1,0}(x) + c^{1,1}w^{1,1}(x)$$

a graphical interpretation of which is given in Figure 11.18. We can see that the function $I(x)$ is built from a scaling function $\phi^{0,0}(x)$, wavelet coefficients $c^{a,b}$ and

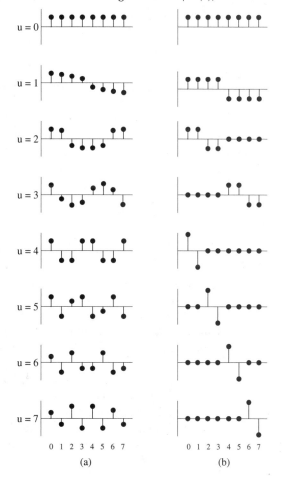

Figure 11.18
Compares basic vectors for DCT and wavelets (a) Basis vectors for the DCT; (b) basis vectors for the Haar transform.

wavelets $w^{a,b}$. The indices (a,b) on the wavelets refer to the level of the wavelet and its position. As the index a increases the wavelet base of support halves and the number of wavelets at this level doubles. These are the Haar basis wavelets which are step functions taking the values +1 and –1, specifically:

$$W(x) = \begin{cases} 1 & 0 \leq x < 1/2 \\ -1 & 1/2 \leq x < 1 \\ 0 & \text{otherwise} \end{cases}$$

The translated and scaled wavelet basis functions are then defined as:

$$w^{a,b}(x) = w(2^b x - a) \qquad a = 0,\ldots,2^b - 1$$

From Figure 11.18 can be seen the origin of the term 'wavelet'. The basis functions only have local extent. They are in every case a single rectangular waveform, which for a given 'frequency' differ in that they are all translates of each other. They are wavelets rather than waves. A wavelet can be any basis function that satisfies certain requirements which are that it must be oscillatory and that it must decay quickly to zero in both the positive and negative direction. The rectangular wave is the simplest possible manifestation of these requirements.

11.5 Image transforms and basis matrices

In this chapter we have looked fairly informally at three image transforms – the Fourier transform, the cosine transform and the wavelet transform (using the Haar basis). In all these transforms we can consider that we are performing the same general process only differing by the basis functions that we use. We could write a transform in general terms as:

$$T(u,v) = \sum_{x=0}^{M-1} \sum_{y=0}^{N-1} I(x,y)b(x,y,u,v)$$

where

$b(x,y,u,v)$ is the kernel of the transformation that contains the basis functions

The value of each component in the transform is the 'strength' or amount of each basis function in $I(x,y)$. For a particular value of (u,v) in the transform domain we calculate this by multiplying each sample of $I(x,y)$ by the equivalent sample in the basis function and summing and averaging. In the one-dimensional case we can therefore define a set of basis vectors the components of which form the product with the image samples. This is shown in Figure 11.18 for the cosine transform and the Haar transform (the basis functions for the Fourier transform are complex). The number of basis vectors is equal to the number of components in each vector – in the illustration, eight. The important concept of an image transform as a general process that can select any one of a number of basis functions or vectors then becomes clear. In the case of the two-dimensional transform the basis vectors become basis matrices or basis images.

Figure 11.19
Basis functions or basis 'images' for the two-dimensional Haar wavelet.

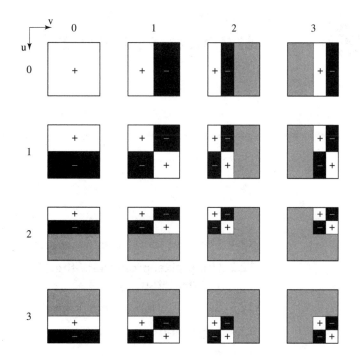

Shown in Figure 11.19 are the 8×8 basis images for the Haar wavelet transform. Note that the Haar/wavelet image only contains three values: 1, 0 and –1.

Further reading

All general image processing texts (see Chapter 1) contain treatments of the transform coding of images. An excellent text, devoted entirely to image transforms, is the book by Clarke. In particular, this contains a detailed treatment of the properties of the transforms from the point of view of image compression. Recently there has been an explosion of texts on wavelets; the one listed here is eminently readable.

Papers

Stollnitz E.J., DeRose T.D. and Salesin D.H. (1995). Wavelets for computer graphics – Parts 1 and 2. *IEEE Computer Graphics and Applications*, May, 76–84 and July, 75–84

Books

Bracewell R. (1965). *The Fourier Transform and its Applications*. New York: McGraw-Hill

Clarke R.J. (1985). *Transform Coding of Images*. New York: Academic Press

Rosenfield A. and Kak A. C. (1982). *Digital Picture Processing*. New York: Academic Press

12 Image segmentation

12.1 Segmentation – grey scale thresholding

12.2 Using pixel properties other than intensity – texture-based segmentation

12.3 Segmentation by region growing

12.4 Edges and segmentation

12.5 Case study

Image segmentation means breaking up an image into regions that have some meaning with respect to the image content and application. There may be objects of interest in the image and we wish to isolate those pixels that make up the objects. A simple example is cloud cover analysis where we may want to measure the area of the clouds in a satellite photograph. The clouds make up the areas of interest or objects and we need to 'label' those pixels in the image which we decide belong to clouds. Traditionally image segmentation has been seen as a processing stage prior to recognition or analysis. We segment the image and then process the results of the segmentation.

The general approach of most segmentation methods is to somehow cluster pixels with similar properties in the belief that objects are going to exhibit pixels with similar intensities and such a clustering will isolate objects, for example, from their backgrounds. We want to divide the image up into non-overlapping regions or parts, in a way that is desired by a particular application.

Segmentation tends more towards image analysis than image processing. Although there is no clear borderline between the two we can loosely say that image processing is image in, image out, whereas image analysis involves some reduction in the information content of the image, some extraction of knowledge. Like many methods in image analysis it is a deceptively simple idea whose easy application is limited to certain special cases. In the case of cloud cover analysis this may involve a simple strategy like thresholding the image to binarize it. In more demanding applications segmentation is difficult.

Segmentation appears to be an operation that we as humans perform with ease but of course we possess a visual system that involves considerable parallel processing and it seems that our recognition of objects in an image is instantaneous. We recognize or segment objects in their entirety by considering the image in its entirety. (Although it is the case that we may also use depth information to aid segmentation we appear to be remarkably adept at segmenting two-dimensional images. Objects often seem to jump out of their background. We even infer object boundaries where none exist as the Kanizsa illusion (Figure 12.1) demonstrates, where a triangular illusory contour is generated by three black 'pac-man' figures positioned at the virtual vertices of the non-existent triangle.)

With simple computer approaches to segmentation we generally consider one pixel at a time and mostly do not use information already obtained from previous operations on pixels in the same neighbourhood. To us as human beings it seems that the recognition task in such a simple case is trivial because we do not perform any segmentation task independent of our knowledge that the scene is a projection of a familiar object or objects. We use knowledge or experience to decode the image and it is difficult or impossible to comment on the possible lower-level processes that may or may not be part of this overall process.

Using a segmentation operation phase as part of image analysis is a perfect example of the way in which much computational research into difficult problems proceeds. We try to force the problem into steps for which we know we can write programs, produce special hardware, or utilize an existing body of knowledge. It is the evolutionary or bootstrapping approach of much computer science research. In this case we are saying that a sensible way to proceed in any image analysis problem is to first subject the image to low-level pixel by pixel operations as the first step in a hierarchy of operations that gradually reduce the volume of information in an image and enable us to make decisions about structures of interest in the image.

The simplest approach to segmentation is thresholding. Consider an image that consists of a sphere and a background, where the sphere is illuminated by a single light source. We know from our shading simulation (Chapter 3) that the pixels forming the projection of the sphere can exhibit (in grey scale), say, the complete dynamic range of eight bits. Thus attempting to isolate the sphere by assuming that it will exhibit intensities clustered around one value and the background a different small set of intensities clearly will not work even for such a simple example of a single object scene.

Figure 12.1
The illusory contours of the Kanizsa illusion.

There is nothing to stop us using prior knowledge of object properties to assist segmentation but first we will concern ourselves with classic segmentation techniques that do not use object-based knowledge. These divide neatly into two or three categories (depending on your opinion). These are:

- Segmentation based on simple **global** knowledge concerning pixel intensities. In this case we try to decide how an image should be segmented by basing a strategy on an examination of (usually) the image histogram. Note that in the simple sphere example this would not generally work because the background may exhibit the same range of pixel values as the sphere. Also note that an image histogram, although we can say that it exhibits global information, is confined to telling us about variations in pixel intensity that are not related to structural variations. There is no form information in an image histogram. A pixel-sized chequerboard would exhibit the same histogram as an image which was a large white rectangle adjacent to a large black rectangle. This is why image histograms are of limited utility in segmentation – although they are perfect for classic intensity processing operations like contrast enhancement.

- **Region-based** segmentation is where we proceed by dividing the image into regions that exhibit similar properties. Here we look at the properties in the neighbourhood of a pixel and 'grow' a region while neighbouring pixels exhibit similar values. This seems to be a more powerful strategy than the previous one but again this would not work in our sphere example. The specular highlight would be considered a separate region (if we were using intensity or colour) and the edge of the sphere may merge into the background in a dark area.

- **Edge-based** segmentation is a technique that in its simplest application means utilizing edge detection processes (Chapter 10) to find a **closed** boundary such that an inside and an outside can be defined. Again this will not work for the case of the sphere. There will be an edge around the specular highlight and the geometric or silhouette edge may be broken. In general, detected edges contain breaks. Edges are detected from areas in images that are not wanted object edges. Objects may exhibit edges that do not generally relate to the geometric edge of the object. This is not only true for such pseudo 'objects' as specular highlights but it is also true that objects may not exhibit, in any easily measurable sense, an edge that we want to isolate. Consider the canopy of a tree. We can easily see the outline but an edge detection operation may not produce a simple figure with an inside and an outside.

Thus we have three possible approaches and a very common example that will not work with any of them and this brings us back to a point made earlier, which is that like most image analysis tasks we are limited with each method to certain special classes of images.

12.1 Segmentation – grey scale thresholding

This is the oldest segmentation technique but it is only appropriate in a limited number of applications. These are images where the object(s) of interest exhibits reasonably homogeneous brightness values against an (unwanted) background which also exhibits homogeneous but different brightness values. Examples of images in this class might be text in an OCR (Optical Character Recognition) machine or flat machine parts in a quality control inspection system.

We decide on a **threshold** and any pixel with a value above (or below) the threshold is deemed to belong to the object; and a value below (or above) the threshold is deemed to be part of the background. The result of the operation is a binary image. We can then perform operations on this image such as counting the number of parts in the image, measuring their area or some other geometric property of the parts, comparing a part with a standard part, and so on.

If we have no idea what the threshold should be, then we can examine the image histogram to select a suitable value. If the image is suitable for this type of segmentation then the histogram should exhibit peaks corresponding to the clusters of object/background pixels into a narrow range of grey levels. By suitable we mean that the objects produce a clustering in grey scale space. In the simple cases suggested above, the image histogram should be distinctly bi-modal and we set the threshold by finding the valley between the two peaks and setting the threshold to the corresponding grey scale value. An extreme example of an image that exhibits peaks at each end of its histogram is shown in Figure 12.2. Note that an image with a clear bi-modal distribution does not imply that the image consists of objects against a background. A structureless image that consisted entirely of random noise – dark spots and light spots – would exhibit a clear-cut bi-modal histogram. Also note that such an approach will be completely useless for images, common, for example, in nature, where regions are distinguished by different texture. Grey scale thresholding may segment a textured region into many different parts.

Finding a threshold from a histogram can be done either interactively or by using a simple heuristic that will find the valleys automatically. We might, for example, examine the histogram curve itself, searching for a significant minimum. Alternatively we can iterate towards a threshold without using the image histogram using the following strategy:

(1) Assume that the four corner pixels belong to the background set and define an initial mean for the background intensity and for the object intensity assuming that all of the remaining pixels belong to the object.

(2) Iterate using a threshold definition until there is a sufficiently small difference between T^{i+1} and T^i:

$$T^{i+1} = \frac{\mu^i_{\text{background}} + \mu^i_{\text{object}}}{2}$$

where $\mu^i_{\text{background}}$ and μ^i_{object} are calculated after applying T^i

Figure 12.2
An example of an image that exhibits peaks at each end of the histogram.
(a) Original image;
(b) thresholded image;
(c) histogram.

(a)

(b)

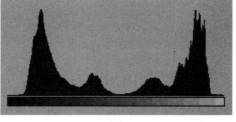

(c)

It is obvious that thresholding approaches will produce a number of misclassification errors, the extent of which depends on the individual histograms exhibited by the objects in the image as Figure 12.3 demonstrates. This shows that an image histogram is the sum of two individual object histograms which will exhibit pixel intensities on the 'wrong' side of the threshold, demonstrating that the selection of a single threshold can never be correct in such a case.

The obvious extension to a single threshold strategy is to assume that we can still use the approach but now the threshold has to be applied to sub-regions of

Figure 12.3
Misclassification in
histogram-based
thresholding.

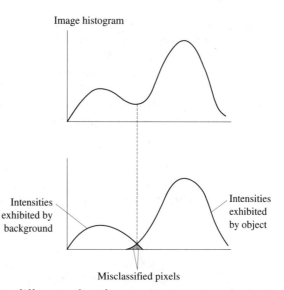

Image histogram

Intensities
exhibited by
background

Intensities
exhibited
by object

Misclassified pixels

the image, taking different values from region to region. Assuming, say, that we
have an object(s) background scene, we divide the image into small regions and
look for a bi-modal histogram in each region. We need also to identify regions
that do not exhibit bi-modality and assume that these are either all object or all
background. (Otherwise we would 'force' a segmentation where there should be
none, based on insignificant variations such as noise.) A method developed by
Chow and Kaneko in 1972 is based on this approach. They divide images into
(64×64 pixel) overlapping regions and test for bi-modality in each region histogram by trying to fit a pair of Gaussian curves to the histograms. If a region
does not exhibit bi-modality it is assumed to be all object or background and
assigned a threshold from a neighbouring region. The final stage involves allo-
cating a threshold to each pixel within a region by performing bi-linear interpolation (Chapter 24) between the threshold defined by the previous process at
each region corner.

(**12.1.1**)

Thresholding multi-band or colour images

The extremely simple technique of the previous section involves certain complications when extended to colour images or multi-band satellite images. With
black and white images we used the image histogram to find clusters in a one-
dimensional measurement space – the value of the pixel. Now we have three or
more values associated with each pixel and we have two choices in extending
the technique of threshold detection.

Consider colour images (the problems are the same for multi-band satellite
images except that we have to extend the arguments into *n*-dimensional space).
For colour images we can either treat the problem as three separate
one-dimensional problems and try to apply the same techniques used in the

previous section, or we can try to extend the techniques into three space and use three-dimensional colour space as the domain in which we attempt to find clusters so as to effect segmentation.

At first sight this should not be a difficult problem because we suppose that it may be the case that pixels which cannot be separated into different categories in one component band may be distinguishable in another. Thus simplistically we could apply histogram-based thresholding separately to each colour component, and then combine the three results into a single image by an AND operation.

That this approach will generally not work is easily demonstrated. If we select a region in each colour component using two thresholds and combine the resulting three images by ANDing them together, we are defining in RGB space a region that is a rectangular solid bounded by planes through the thresholds and parallel to the axes. This sub-region of RGB space cannot have any other shape. Thus we are making the assumption that objects of interest to us are going to possess pixels which will form clusters in RGB space and that these clusters are separable by using planes parallel to the axis planes. This is not generally true of RGB space which is the space of the detector and the display system. It is not a space that relates to our perception of colour (as we discuss in Chapter 25). It may be that better separability is achievable in HSV space or some other colour space and this hypothesis leads us to a technique which is a recursive application of the technique where we use a histogram to automatically guide us to an appropriate threshold.

The first step in this method is to construct, say, nine histograms by mapping into two extra colour spaces. As well as RGB space we construct histograms based on, say, a space such as HSV and YIQ space (Chapter 25). Of course no new information is added by such a process but it is simply an application of the hypothesis that better clustering may occur in another space. Segmentation then proceeds by searching all the histograms for significant peaks or applying some kind of priority (we may want to segment primarily on the basis of image intensity). The component with the most significant peak determines two thresholds – one either side – and the image is segmented on this basis. When the initial segmentation is achieved the same process is applied to each of the segmented parts and the process continues until either the histograms become unimodal or until it is judged manually that a suitable level of segmentation is achieved. Note the similarity between this problem and the colour quantization problem examined in Chapter 25. There we are attempting to divide up a high resolution colour space in such a way that the low resolution colour space is used optimally to display the majority of the colours in the image. Figure 12.4 shows an image that has been segmented using this technique.

Instead of working with many one-dimensional histograms we could construct an n-dimensional histogram for an image with n-valued pixels. However, a simple extension of the one-dimensional technique of the previous section into three or more dimensions is difficult and quickly becomes impossible as the number of dimensions increases.

Original colour image shown in black and white

Sky

Land

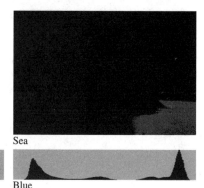

Sea

Red	Green	Blue

Figure 12.4
Segmenting a colour image by setting thresholds derived from the colour component histograms. In this case the original image is segmented into land, sea and sky. (Pão de Açúcar, Rio de Janeiro.)

There are a number of related problems. First, consider the size problem. Haralick and Shapiro point out that in a six-band image, where each pixel takes a value between 0 and 99, the histogram array would require 100^6 or 10^{12}, a very large number which is also many orders of magnitude larger than the number of pixels in the image. (However, they also point out that it is likely that because of the correlation between bands and within bands, such data may only exhibit 10^4–10^5 distinct 6-tuples.)

Second, in the case of the univariate histogram simple programs or an interactive technique could be used to find suitable thresholds. With even three-dimensional data interactively placing thresholds is difficult. (Unless we resort to the rectangular prism constraint of the previous section. However, a common approach with three-dimensional data is to project the histogram data onto each of the three axis planes and define three two-dimensional thresholds, then project these limits back into the colour space to define the selected sub-space.)

Third, automatically finding clusters in n-dimensional space is difficult and is similar to finding clusters in classic pattern recognition.

12.1.2 Thresholding and approximate boundary information

Reliable segmentation based on intensity histogram(s) depends on being able to identify peaks and valleys and whether this is possible or not depends on the nature of the image. One obvious problem is that the size of the peaks in a histogram depends on the size of the objects that produce the intensity levels that contribute to a peak. A large object will produce a large peak and vice versa for a small one. A strategy suggested by Gonzalez and Woods is to apply the histogram technique to an image that has been edge emphasized using, say, a gradient operator. They point out that this has the immediate advantage of removing the object size dependency of the histogram peaks. Consider a small object silhouetted against a large background. The background pixels will dominate the histogram. If, however, the histogram contains only those pixels that are located on or around the boundary then we should tend to see two peaks of equal size reflecting pixel intensities from both sides of the boundary.

Thus for an image consisting of a single object or object type against a single background, the histogram of gradient values should produce a good bi-modal distribution with two dominant modes. The procedure can be further elaborated, Gonzalez and Woods suggest, by using the Laplacian. The complete procedure is as follows:

(1) Evaluate a gradient image, ∇I, and gradient histogram from which a threshold T can be deduced.

(2) Evaluate the Laplacian $\nabla^2 I$.

(3) Evaluate a three-level image as follows:

$$I'(x,y) = \begin{cases} 0 \text{ if } \nabla I < T \\ + \text{ if } \nabla I \text{ and } \nabla^2 I \geq 0 \\ - \text{ if } \nabla I \text{ and } \nabla^2 I \leq 0 \end{cases}$$

This produces a thresholded image where pixels not deemed to be on an edge are labelled 0, pixels on the dark side of an edge are labelled + and those on the light side –. Scanning this image and noting the transitions produces a conventional object/background segmentation. Thus we are using the gradient image to isolate those pixels that are likely to belong to an edge and the Laplacian to indicate whether a pixel lies on the dark (or background) or on the light (or object) side of an edge.

12.2 Using pixel properties other than intensity – texture-based segmentation

It is easy to think of images that cannot be segmented by clustering in grey-level histogram space. Many images of man-made and natural scenes contain areas that are differentiated clearly by texture and in this section we will examine methods of measuring or labelling texture as a means of achieving segmentation. There are many ways of measuring texture in an image. Consider possibly the two most popular: give a texture label to a pixel by examining the intensity variations over a small neighbourhood and map the complete image into the Fourier domain where particular textures that exist over areas of the image map into distinct points or lines in the frequency domain (see the examples in Chapter 11).

What is texture? This is somewhat difficult to answer linguistically and this difficulty is reflected when we try to invent methods that quantify texture in an image. Generally we mean a region that exhibits some kind of recognizable variation over an area. Repetition is involved when we say that an area has a texture. In coherent texture, such as we would see in a close-up image of woven fabric, the repetition is clear. In amorphous texture, such as an aerial picture of a natural landscape, repetition means sameness of granularity and we use this concept to distinguish between, say, grassland and dense forest. We have many words for texture – fineness, coarseness, directionality, regularity, granularity and so on – and what we need to do is to devise a measure that will quantify these concepts.

We begin with measurements made directly in the image domain – sometimes called statistical texture measures. In such measurements we not only have to capture or measure texture variations in the neighbourhood of a pixel by examining grey scale variations, but we also have to consider the spatial organization of the texture. Thus if we are looking at the difference in grey scale between the reference pixel and a pixel in the neighbourhood we have to consider **both** the difference between the pixels and their spatial relationship. Coherent textures, by definition, have one or more directions associated with them. A fabric weave, for example, may exhibit horizontal and vertical structures.

Ideally we would like to consider an area centred on a particular pixel and return a single number or texture label that measures these descriptive factors. We would then have a single texture label for each pixel and hopefully simple thresholding would reduce the image into a number of meaningful regions. To have a single label for a neighbourhood implies some compromise between brightness difference and distance/orientation information in one number. Thus in general a texture label will be an N-tuple. However, we start by looking at a simple technique that attempts to classify texture with a single number and does not take direction into account.

12.2.1 Texture segmentation – Hurst coefficient

The **Hurst coefficient** is a single number that is derived from an octagonal neighbourhood. It is most easily explained by first ignoring pixel geometry and considering a continuous image. The coefficient is evaluated as follows:

(1) Place a circle on the point (pixel that is to be categorized) increasing the radius of the circle until we have covered the desired neighbourhood extent.

(2) For each radius we examine all the image points on the circumference of the circle and find the highest and lowest values whose difference defines a **range**.

(3) A graph is plotted of the log of brightness vs. the log of radius and the slope fitted to this data gives the Hurst coefficient.

A little thought will confirm that a smooth area with little texture variation will exhibit a lower Hurst coefficient than a highly textured area.

The digital application uses an octagonal configuration of pixels. An octagonal neighbourhood of dimension 7 would be:

```
        h   g   h
    f   e   d   e   f
h   e   c   b   c   e   h
g   d   b   a   b   d   g
h   e   c   b   c   e   h
    f   e   d   e   f
        h   g   h
```

where the distances of each pixel from the reference pixel **a** are:

b	1
c	√2
d	2
e	√5
f	√8
g	3
h	√10

This is a particular implementation of the relationship:

$$D = \frac{\log N}{\log \dfrac{1}{s}}$$

for a set of pixels where the set has been partitioned into N (non-overlapping) copies of a basic shape, each one scaled by a factor s from the original.

12.2.2 Texture segmentation – co-occurrence matrices

Originally introduced by Haralick more than 20 years ago, this comprehensive scheme of statistical categorization of texture enables a number of measurements to be made concerning the texture of a region. The single number measurements are made on one or a number of **co-occurrency matrices** which reflect grey-level variations over a region. Haralick reported that such measurements or features were used to segment satellite images into eight terrain classes (old residential, new residential, lake, swamp, marsh, urban railroad yard, scrub or woodland) with 82% identification accuracy. In this usage the method is applied to blocks of the image measuring 64×64 pixels. The method can also be applied to the neighbourhood of each pixel, using, say, the octagonal neighbourhood of the previous section. Whatever the size or shape of the window or region chosen, the method produces, for each pixel, a set of property labels quantifying the nature of the texture within a window or region centred on the pixel. The method, as we shall see, is extremely expensive.

A co-occurrence matrix, $P_{\phi,d}(i,j)$, is a matrix where the (i,j)th element describes the frequency of occurrence of two pixels, separated by distance d in the direction ϕ. For an $N{\times}N$ region that can exhibit four grey levels $(0,\ldots,3)$ the grey-level differences that single pairs of pixels can exhibit are:

(0,0)　(0,1)　(0,2)　(0,3)
(1,0)　(1,1)　(1,2)　(1,3)
(2,0)　(2,1)　(2,2)　(2,3)
(3,0)　(3,1)　(3,2)　(3,3)

For example, if we consider constructing the matrix $P_{0,1}(i,j)$ which looks at pairs of pixels in a horizontal direction ($\phi = 0$) separated by distance 1 ($d = 1$) for the following sub-image:

0 0 1 1
0 0 1 1
2 0 2 2
2 0 3 3

then we have

$$P_{0,1}(i,j) = \begin{vmatrix} 4 & 2 & 0 & 1 \\ 0 & 4 & 0 & 0 \\ 2 & 0 & 2 & 0 \\ 0 & 0 & 0 & 2 \end{vmatrix}$$

and we could construct any co-occurrence matrix that would capture the textural variations in a region by varying ϕ and d. Rather than use the co-occurrence matrices directly we characterize the nature of them by making measurements. Thus the co-occurrence matrices are obtained directly from the image and we base textural categorization on measurements made on them.

For each co-occurrence matrix we can make a number of global measurements. For example:

$$M1 = \sum_{i=1}^{L} \sum_{j=1}^{L} \frac{P(i,j)^2}{R}$$

where: L is the number of grey levels
　　　　R is the total number of pixels in the region

This measures the homogeneity of the region. Each term in P is squared and large values in the matrix – which will result from a homogeneous region – will have a greater effect than a few small values. Another common measure is:

$$M2 = \sum_{i=1}^{L} \sum_{j=1}^{L} (i - j)^2 \frac{P(i,j)}{R}$$

which is the element difference moment. This weights elements in P as a function of their distance from the main diagonal, or elements that exhibit high differences in grey scale values. Other possible measures and their semantics are described in detail in Haralick et al.

If we have no prior knowledge of the nature of the texture that is being categorized then a minimum set of co-occurrence matrices is four ($\phi = 0$, 45, 90 and 135 degrees respectively; $d = 1$). The size of the matrix is a function of the number of grey levels in the image and calculating a matrix for each pixel in an 8-bit image would be prohibitively expensive and in practice the grey levels can be set to, say, 32 or 64 – although this of course results in a loss of accuracy.

Haralick states that the power of the co-occurrence approach is that it characterizes the spatial interrelationships of the grey levels in a textural pattern, and can do so in a way that is invariant under monotonic grey-level transformations. He also points out that its weakness is that it does not work well for coherent texture whose primitive is large. Consider, for example, the matrices that would be produced by a black and white checkerboard pattern, where each square occupied four pixels, compared with randomly distributed black squares. The measures would simply reflect the existence of regular areas of black, regular areas of white and the horizontal and vertical boundary edges regardless of the spatial juxtaposition of the squares.

It is clear from the foregoing that calculating a co-occurrence matrix for each pixel window is extremely expensive. A fast method due to Unser uses sum and difference histograms to calculate approximations to the measurements. The histograms are a sum and difference histogram S and D. For a 256-level image a bin in the sum histogram between 0 and 511 is indexed by the sum of the two pixels d apart. Similarly the distance histogram (–255 to 255) is incremented by the difference of the two pixels. This leads to the following approximations for the co-occurrence matrix measures:

$$\text{mean} = \frac{1}{2} \sum_i iS(i)$$

$$\text{contrast} = \sum_j j^2 D(j)$$

$$\text{homogeneity} = \sum_j \frac{1}{1 + j^2} D(j)$$

$$\text{entropy} = -\sum_i S(i)\log(S(i)) -\sum_j D(j) \log (D(j))$$

$$\text{energy} = \sum_i S(i)^2 \sum_j D(j)^2$$

Figure 12.5 shows a simple example of these measures for a simple chequerboard example. The examples demonstrate the way in which the measures change as a function of the value of the distance parameter. Note that the vertical coher-

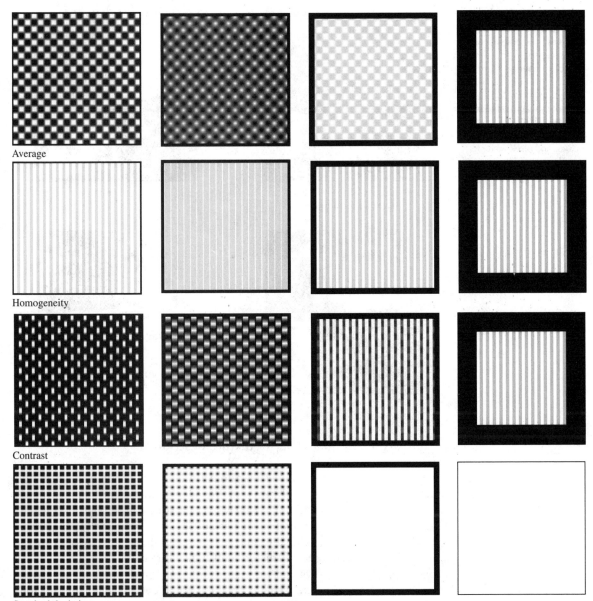

Average

Homogeneity

Contrast

Standard deviation

Figure 12.5
Approximate co-occurrency matrix measures due to Unser (Section 12.2.2). The test image is a chequerboard and the measurements are horizontal. Along a row $d = 0.5$, 1, 2 and 4 squares.

ences are because the measures were made in a horizontal direction. An example using such measures to segment images is shown in Figure 12.6. Here a composite image is made up of four textures. The texture measures are used to distinguish between each pair of images in each row. Note that the segmentation in the bottom row is always worse than that in the top row regardless of the measures used to effect the segmentation. This is because the patterns on the bottom row exhibit two distinct texture components.

Figure 12.6
Using co-occurrency matrix measures for segmentation. The images are mapped into co-occurrency matrix measures then thresholded to effect segmentation. The result of the segmentation is coloured white/black for the top left and bottom right images, and black/white for the other two.

Original image made up
of 4 natural textures

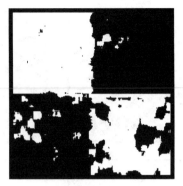

Contrast

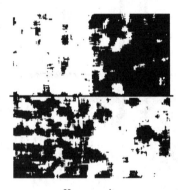

Homogeneity

Standard deviation

12.2.3 Texture segmentation – Fourier texture descriptors

Figure 8.3 shows the well-known relationship between coherent texture and peaks in the amplitude spectrum of the Fourier transform of the image. Coherent texture is characterized by a few spatial frequencies of high energy. The further away from the origin a texture peak is (the higher the spatial frequency) then the more 'busy' it is in the image. The angle of the texture peak in the amplitude spectra relates to the direction of the texture coherence (if any) in the image. The question is: how do we use this information to characterize texture in an image? This raises the same problem as we encountered in the previous section. We cannot simply classify texture with a single label.

One way in which the energy in the amplitude spectrum has been characterized is to reduce $|F(u,v)|$ to two functions of a single variable. To do this we consider $|F(u,v)|$ expressed in polar coordinates (r,θ). We can then calculate the functions:

$$S(r) = \int_0^{2\pi} |F(r,\theta)| \mathrm{d}\theta$$

Figure 12.7
Fourier domain texture signatures.

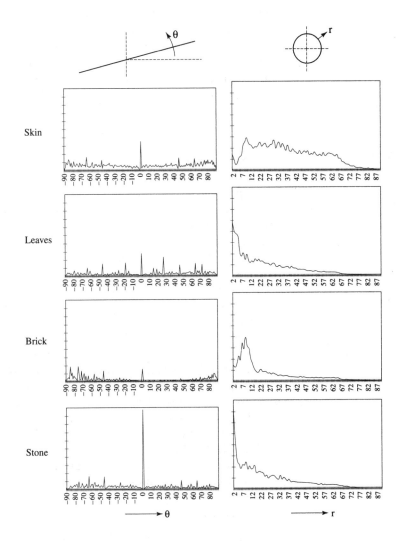

and

$$S(\boldsymbol{\theta}) = \int_{0}^{R} |F(r, \boldsymbol{\theta})| \mathrm{d}r$$

The first function is obtained by summing around circles of radius r centred on the origin of the amplitude spectrum and the second sums values along a line of orientation $\boldsymbol{\theta}$ passing through the origin. These functions will display peaks characteristic of the texture in the image. Calculating each function for a particular image gives a 'texture signature'. Single labels for segmentation could be obtained from an LUT that stored specimen signatures. Figure 12.7 shows the signatures for the texture patterns in Figure 12.6.

Note the structural similarity between the Hurst coefficient (Section 12.2.1) and the function $S(r)$. Both operate by examining values around the circumference of circles of increasing radius.

The method can also be used to answer the question: 'is texture with Fourier descriptor X present anywhere in the image and if so to what strength?'. The information in the Fourier domain that identifies the occurrence of a particular texture is independent of the spatial position of the texture in image space.

12.2.4 Texture segmentation – applying texture measures

In the previous two sections we derived multi-valued categorizations of texture. In the case of the co-occurrence matrices, we can make up to, say, seven measurements on four matrices resulting in an N-tuple of 28 values. In the Fourier transform technique the derived texture measure is a pair of functions of a single variable. Both techniques are expensive and do not produce a single value that can be directly applied to a simple thresholding algorithm to produce segmentation. Rather a classification algorithm is required.

Another consideration is whether we apply the technique by centring a neighbourhood on each pixel and evaluating the metric for each and every pixel, or evaluate measures for contiguous blocks of pixels and assign the same result to each pixel in the block. In an area where the texture does not change over an area that is larger than the block or pixel neighbourhood, there is no advantage in doing a pixel by pixel evaluation – we simply end up doing much more work. The only advantage of the every pixel approach is that the boundaries between regions of different texture will tend to be better defined. For example, if we consider a boundary running through a block in such a way that the block is split into two equal parts, then there will be incorrect or uncertain texture measures assigned to every pixel in the block. With pixel neighbourhoods correct metrics will be assigned in general closer to the actual boundary (although there will still be uncertainty as a function of the dimension of the neighbourhood).

Segmentation by region growing

In Section 12.1 we attempted to find clusters in pixel intensity space. The rationale was that objects of interest to us would tend to exhibit similar pixel values. These sets of values could be found and thresholding produced the desired segmentation. **Region growing** generally does the same thing in a different way. We find regions that exhibit homogeneous pixel values by operating directly in image space instead of in intensity space and we should see that region growing is a technique that is potentially more powerful than histogram-based approaches. This is because the implicit assumption that clustering in intensity space reflects clustering in image space is not necessarily true.

First, it is useful to try to define what is meant by a region. Gonzalez and Woods suggest that a region should possess the following properties:

- Every pixel in an image must be labelled as belonging to a region. We should have no unclassified pixels left after region growing has been applied to an image.

- All points in a region must be connected. This means that we must be able to reach a neighbouring pixel, from a current pixel, according to some connectivity definition. The two isomorphic connectivity definitions are four-connectivity, which means that the neighbours of $I(x,y)$ indicated by * are:

$$
\begin{array}{ccc}
  & 1 & \\
1 & * & 1 \\
  & 1 &
\end{array}
$$

and eight-connectivity, which means:

$$
\begin{array}{ccc}
1 & 1 & 1 \\
1 & * & 1 \\
1 & 1 & 1
\end{array}
$$

A moment's thought will confirm that a four-connected region will generally have a different shape to an eight-connected region.

- The regions must not overlap – each pixel should only have one label.

- Each pixel in a region R_i must conform to a predicate $P(R_i)$. For example, we might say that $P(R_i)$=TRUE if all pixels in R_i have the same intensity (to within some small interval).

- Two regions R_i and R_j are different regions if they are different in the sense of the predicate P.

Region growing

The easiest way to grow a region is by pixel aggregation. For this we need to start the growth of each region with a 'seed' point. The algorithm then proceeds by growing from that point using a connectivity rule and a predicate or property rule P. Thus all pixels that are connected to the seed pixel, and which satisfy the property rule P between the seed pixel and the pixel currently being examined are labelled as belonging to the same region as the seed pixel.

The algorithm is identical to a flood fill algorithm in two-dimensional computer graphics. Here a four- or eight-connected region is filled with a particular colour. In region growing we fill a region with a particular label. Naive implementation of such an algorithm merely involves, for a four-connected region, four recursive procedure calls from each of the neighbours of the pixel currently being examined. Code would be written for this in the following style:

procedure label_region_of(I,x,y,label,intensity);
:
:

if I(x,y) = intensity **then**
    I(x,y) := label;
    label_region_of(I,x,y-1,label,intensity)
    label_region_of(I,x,y+1,label,intensity)
    label_region_of(I,x-1,y,label,intensity)
    label_region_of(I,x+1,y,label,intensity)

This is a good example of the elegance of recursion as a high-level programming tool. Unfortunately this implementation conceals a tendency to run out of memory space quickly as the housekeeping associated with the recursive calls builds up.

Of course, the main problem with this simplistic approach is obtaining the original seed points. We could fall back on the image histogram, using as seed points, for each region, any pixel that had a value corresponding to the histogram peak value. We then end up with a segmentation that should give us similar results to histogram mode techniques except that now we have the potential of varying the predicate to satisfy the goal of the segmentation.

A strategy suggested by Haralick and Shapiro is to grow regions simultaneously in image and intensity space. Initially a segment is seeded from a pixel whose value is a peak on the histogram. The region is grown in the normal way but with an extra criterion. This is that a neighbouring pixel is considered if its intensity is close enough to the current pixel's intensity and if its probability is not larger than the probability of the pixel that we are growing from.

12.3.2   Region splitting and merging

This is a classic divide and conquer strategy that can be implemented as a recursive procedure. We simply divide the image space into smaller and smaller regions until we are left with a region that is homogeneous. An advantage over the previous technique is that no seed points are required. A significant disadvantage is that the segmentation boundaries are, to a greater or lesser extent, blocky. A naive recursive implementation of the algorithm is:

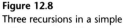

Figure 12.8
Three recursions in a simple split merge algorithm (based on an illustration by Gonzalez and Woods).

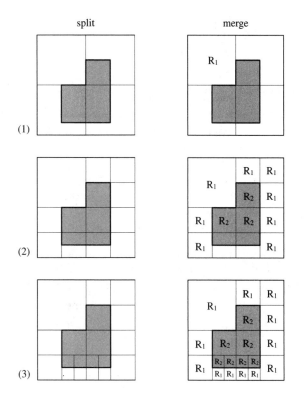

split   merge

(1)

(2)

(3)

if current region homogeneity test is FALSE

then split into four quadrants
    attempt to merge these quadrants
    recursively call the procedure for each subdivision

find any remaining merges

A simple demonstration of the progress of the recursion in this example is shown in Figure 12.8. We could use the same uniformity test for splitting and merging. Since we are generally concerned with many values in a region we can use statistical tests involving, say, the mean and variance of the values in the region. For example, we could say that a region was homogeneous if there was no difference, to within some tolerance, between the means of each of its quadrants. Similarly we could merge two regions on the same basis.

12.4 Edges and segmentation

It would seem that the most direct way to segment an image is to find boundaries of entities. Points inside the boundary are part of the entity and those outside are not (or vice versa). We see, however, that finding a boundary is a difficult process involving edge linking and using this as a strategy for segmentation implies that the boundary be closed. This means a class of boundary finding algorithms where we track or follow a boundary from a start point back to the same point.

Case study

We finish this chapter with an example of the application of some of the techniques discussed above. This is an example that operates in real time on a PC and is a simple example of the use of a vision technique in interfaces. Here the idea is to replace a mouse with a finger pointing gesture. The processing operations are to locate the position of the finger (Figure 12.9) in screen space and also find an approximation to the distance of the finger from the camera. The operations performed were as follows:

(1) The stationary information in the frames was eliminated by forming a subtrahend between frame n and frame $n-1$. (See also Chapters 17 and 26 for a discussion of image subtraction.)

(2) Threshold the interframes, using the technique discussed in Section 12.1.

(3) Apply a Laplacian filter (Chapter 9) to the nth frame and threshold it.

(4) Combine the images from steps 2 and 3 using an AND operation.

(5) Find the middle topmost point of the output from step 4.

Figure 12.9
'Videomouse'. An example of real-time processing involving thresholding and segmentation. The + in the top illustration is the final detected point. The size of the + indicates depth. The bottom illustrations are the output from Step 4.

(6)   Find the mean radius of the output from step 4. This is indicated in Figure 12.9 as the size of the cursor and it gives an approximate measure of depth.

Further reading

Papers

Chow C.K. and Kaneko T. (1972). Automatic boundary detection of the left ventricle from cineangiograms. *Computers in Biomedical Research*, **5**, 388–410

Unser M. (1986). Sum and difference histograms for texture classification. *IEEE Trans. on Pattern Analysis and Machine Intelligence*, **PAMI-8**(1), 118–25

Books

All of the books by Gonzalez and Woods, Haralick and Shapiro and Russ contain substantial treatment of segmentation techniques (see Chapter 1, p.15). Many of the techniques used to analyze texture are based on exactly the same models as those used to synthesize or generate texture (procedurally) for two-dimensional texture mapping (such methods as fractals and Fourier synthesis, for example). In this respect the book *Texturing and Modeling* by Ebert et al. (see Chapter 4) contains much information of potential use in textural analysis.

Images and mathematical morphology

13.1 Binary image morphology

13.2 Grey scale morphology

Mathematical morphology is a set of techniques that is biased towards image analysis – the quantitative description of shape, for example – rather than shape-independent image processing operations such as those described in Chapter 9. Although some operations are equivalent to low-level pixel by pixel techniques, and in this sense no different to 'standard' low-level image processing techniques, the methods do have a reliance on shapes. Its principle applications are:

- noise filtering using shape 'simplification' as a goal
- structural decomposition of objects into constituent parts
- quantitative descriptions of objects (areas, perimeters and so on)
- generally operations which consider the underlying structure of an image (in some way) and ignore irrelevant information such as noise.

Mathematical morphology operates on images as point sets and is most easily applied to binary images. A binary image can be treated as a two-dimensional point set by listing all the coordinates of the black pixels (conventionally) using row notation. For example:

x 1 0 0 0   can be written as
0 1 0 0 0
0 1 0 0 0 $I = \{(0,1), (1,1), (2,1), (3,1), (3,2), (3,3)\}$
0 1 1 1 0
0 0 0 0 0   where x denotes the origin

In this way a binary object is represented as a set in two-dimensional integer space. A grey scale object could be represented as a set in three-dimensional integer space and a colour object would be a set in five-dimensional space.

The basic morphological operations are **dilation** and **erosion** and from these the operations of **opening** and **closing** are constructed. The latter two operations implicitly include shape information and can be used to decompose the object into parts.

It is useful to compare morphological operations on images with spatial filtering (Chapter 9). Many operations can be considered as a kind of 'shape filtering'. With morphological operations the position of certain shapes can be located in an image, an object can be decomposed into its constituent parts, and so on. Consider the fundamental difference between this and filters that operate on spatial frequencies. Spatial frequencies reflect properties of the entire image and the use of, for example, a bandpass/bandreject filter affects information over the complete extent of the image. This comparison brings out the difference between the two classes of operations. Spatial filtering is general to all of the image whereas morphological techniques operate only on parts of the image, leaving the remainder unaltered. Because shape is a specific property, a priori knowledge is required for morphological operations – we need to know the nature of the shape that we want to operate on. This contrasts with spatial filtering where we can invoke a general operation, such as enhancement of high frequency content, without possessing any a priori knowledge concerning the image.

In this chapter we will take a non-mathematical or algorithmic approach to mathematical morphology. A comprehensive treatment of mathematical morphology that combines the formalism of this topic with an algorithmic approach is to be found in Haralick and Shapiro. The point of the formal approach is that it enables quite complex image processing operations to be expressed as an algebraic expression that specifies a series of morphological operations. The expressions themselves can be manipulated using the algebraic relations between the operations. We will introduce simple examples of this but the generality of the technique is outside the scope of this text. We have also not attempted to be comprehensive in the sense of trying to include all the morphological operations that have been proposed or used. The idea is to give insight into the approach and for an excellent comprehensive treatment of both binary and grey scale images the reader is referred to Haralick and Shapiro.

13.1 Binary image morphology

13.1.1 Binary dilation

Binary dilation is an operation that expands a binary image in some way. It is accomplished by combining two sets. One set is the binary object or image of interest, I, and the other set, X, usually smaller, is known as the structuring element, for reasons that will shortly be clear. At this stage X can be regarded as a shape that operates on the image I. The operation is written as $I \oplus X$. An example of dilation of a simple image is shown in Figure 13.1(a). The * in both the

Figure 13.1
Simple examples of dilation.
(a) *I* is dilated by *X*. (b) The
structuring element does
not contain the origin.

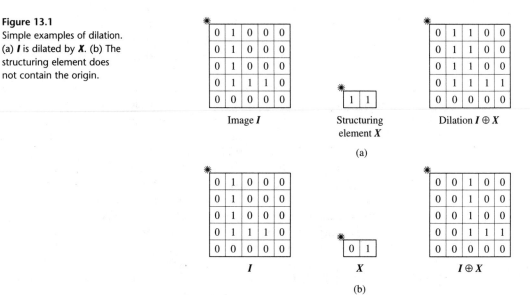

Image *I*

Structuring
element *X*

Dilation *I* ⊕ *X*

(a)

I

X

I ⊕ *X*

(b)

image and the structuring element is the origin or reference point. We will now define the operation of dilation mathematically and algorithmically. First let us consider the mathematical definition. The dilation of the set *I* by the set *X* is defined as:

$$I \oplus X = \{j | j = i + x, i \in I, x \in X\}$$

which defines the translation of the set *I* by members of the set *X*. For our example this can be written as:

$$I \oplus X = (I + \{(0,0)\}) \cup (I + \{(0,1)\})$$

In this case:

$$I = \{(0,1),(1,1),(2,1),(3,1),(3,2),(3,3)\}$$

so

$$I + \{(0,0)\} = \{(0,1),(1,1),(2,1),(3,1),(3,2),(3,3)\}$$

and

$$I + \{(0,1)\} = \{(0,2),(1,2),(2,2),(3,2),(3,3),(3,4)\}$$

Taking the union of these two sets gives us:

$$I \oplus X = \{(0,1)\ (0,2),(1,1),(1,2),(2,1),(2,2),(3,1),(3,2),(3,3),(3,4)\}$$

Dilation is also known as Minkowski addition.

Algorithmically we could define this operation as: we consider the structuring element as a mask. The reference point of the structuring element is placed on all those pixels in the image that have value 1. All of the image pixels that corre-spond to black pixels in the structuring element are given the value 1 in *I* ⊕ *X*.

Now consider Figure 13.1(b). This shows the same image dilated by a structuring element that does not contain the origin I. You deduce from these examples that dilation by disk structuring elements will produce isotropic expansion. Another observation is that dilation can be used to fill in small holes in an image – noise removal.

Note the similarity to convolving or cross-correlating I with a mask. Here for every position of the mask, instead of forming a weighted sum of products, we place the elements of X of into the output image.

13.1.2   Binary erosion

Erosion, also known as Minkowski subtraction, is the dual operation of dilation and erosion shrinks an object in some way. (In fact the operations are dual in the sense that dilation of an object is equivalent to erosion of the background and erosion of an object is equivalent to dilation of the background.) Whereas dilation can be expressed as a union of translation of the structuring element using an OR operation, erosion uses AND, or containment, as its basis set. The operation is written as $I \ominus X$ defined as:

$$I \ominus X = \{j | (X)_j \subseteq I\}$$

In other words the set of all pixels j that correspond to the structuring element translated by j.

Algorithmically we can define erosion as: the output image $I \ominus X$ is set to zero. X is placed at every black point in I. If I contains X (that is, if I AND X is not equal to zero) then X is placed in the output image. The output image is the set of all elements for which X translated to every point in I is contained in I. Figure 13.2 shows two simple examples of erosions Note how in the first example the vertical limb is deleted – it does not contain X. In the second example,

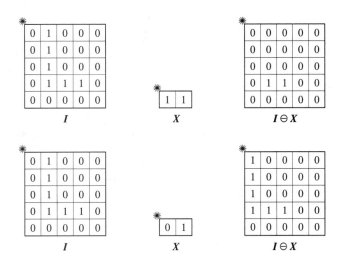

Figure 13.2
Simple examples of erosion.

Figure 13.3
Erosion by different
structuring elements
on the same image.

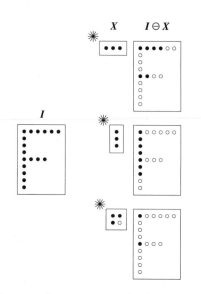

X, the structuring element does not contain the origin. In Figure 13.3 a more elaborate example shows that erosion is 'marking' occurrences of patterns in the image. It is as if the structuring element was a probe which is moved over the image, recording a 'hit' whenever it corresponds to the same structure.

13.1.3 Combining dilation and erosion – boundaries and contours

Because isotropic shrinking is accomplished by erosion, we can use the composite operation:

$$I - (I \ominus X)$$

to perform boundary extraction. Here we are shrinking the image and subtracting the result from the original. The subtrahend is thus the set of pixels 'lost' by the erosion process. For isotropic shrinking we can use a 3×3 or a 5×5 structuring element of 1's. The dimension of the structuring element will determine the width of the boundary detected. For example, using a 5×5 structuring element will result in a boundary set that is between 2 and 3 pixels thick.

13.1.4 Combining dilation and erosion – hit and miss transforms

Although Figure 13.3 suggests that we can use erosion to detect structure in an image this is not true in general – in that case we chose the somewhat artificial example of a pattern that was one pixel wide. A more powerful operation for detecting structure is the hit and miss transform, which is an operation that is used to select sub-images that exhibit certain properties. As the name implies it is a combination of two transforms (erosions) and is somewhat similar to

Figure 13.4
The hit and miss transform used to detect features forming an upper right-hand corner.

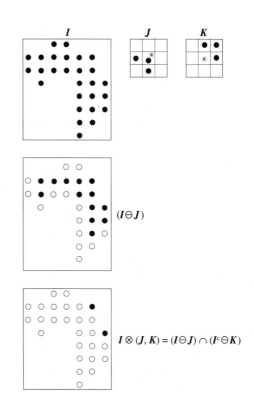

template matching, where an input is cross-correlated with a template or mask that contains a sub-image of interest. The hit and miss transform is expressed as:

$$I \otimes (J,K) = (I \ominus J) \cap (I^c \ominus K)$$

where I is the object as before

$\quad\quad I^c$ is the complement (or background) of I

$\quad\quad J,K$ are structuring elements

Thus the operation is performed by ANDing together two output images, one formed by eroding the input image with J and the other by eroding the complement of the input image by K. The name derives from the fact that the output image consists of the set of points where J found a match in I (the hit) and (simultaneously) K found a match in I^c (the miss). An example will make things clear. Figure 13.4 shows the structuring elements J and K required to detect upper right-hand corners.

13.1.5 Combining dilation and erosion – opening and closing

Two of the most important operations in mathematical morphology are **opening** and **closing**. Opening is just erosion followed by dilation, or:

$$I \bigcirc X = (I \ominus X) \oplus X$$

and closing is simply dilation followed by erosion:

$$I \bullet X = (I \oplus X) \ominus X$$

Opening an image with a disk structuring element tends to smooth the boundary of an image. It breaks narrow connections, or 'isthmuses', and eliminates small protrusions. Closing an image with a disk element tends to smooth the boundary but will also fuse components connected by a narrow gap and will fill narrow gulfs formed by protrusions. In other words, 'opening' tends to open up small gaps or spaces between just touching image structures and 'closing' tends to close up small gaps.

A useful algorithmic definition of opening is obtained by following Haralick and Shapiro, which is:

> The structuring element X swept across the image I, but no part of the structuring element is allowed to appear outside I. The set of all points where X can be contained by I is the output image.

This gives an interpretation of opening in terms of shape matching – the ability to select from a set or object all those subsets that match the structuring element. Figure 13.5 shows an example of this property. Note that the radius of the disk structuring element must be larger that the widths of the image subsets that are to be eliminated.

An important property of opening and closing is that they are idempotent which means that repeated application of either has no further effect on the result. (Note that this is also the case with spatial filtering – the comparison of which we made in the introduction. Once an image has been filtered using, say, a perfect bandpass filter, any further application of the filter has no effect on the image.) This property is exploited when the operations are used repeatedly for decomposition of an object into its constituent parts. A simple example of a series of openings and image subtractions is shown in Figure 13.6. Of course, as was pointed out in the introduction, to use this device implies precise a priori knowledge of the component shapes into which the object is going to be decomposed. We are not, by any stretch of the imagination, imitating our (human) immediate ability to analyze shapes and decompose or recognize immediately those components that are 'round', those that are 'vertical' and those that are 'horizontal'.

Figure 13.5
Opening a binary image with a disk structuring element.

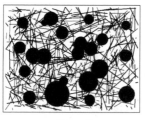
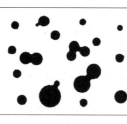
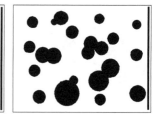

Image   After erosion   After dilation

Figure 13.6
A series of opening/
subtracting operations
(based on an illustration
by Haralick and Shapiro
(1992)).

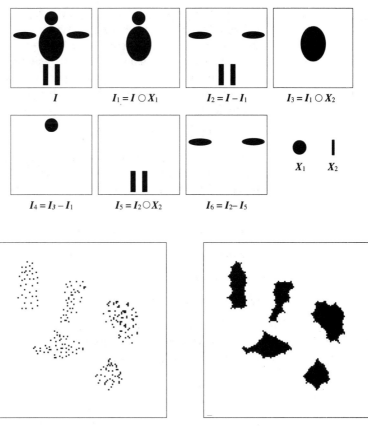

I

$I_1 = I \bigcirc X_1$

$I_2 = I - I_1$

$I_3 = I_1 \bigcirc X_2$

$X_1 \quad X_2$

$I_4 = I_3 - I_1$

$I_5 = I_2 \bigcirc X_2$

$I_6 = I_2 - I_5$

Figure 13.7
Using the closing operation
to cluster points.

Original image

After closing with a disk

An example of an application of closing is shown in Figure 13.7. Here clusters of points are changed into connected sets. Thus each point can now be labelled as belonging to a certain cluster.

13.1.6 Thickening and thinning

Thickening and thinning transformations are generally used sequentially. Sequential transformations can be used to derive a 'digital skeleton' easily.

The skeleton of an object is most easily defined informally with respect to two-dimensional Euclidean space and is:

> Let $C(x)$ be the largest circle centred at x that is contained in the object. Then x is a part of the skeleton of the object if there is no larger disk C1 which is both contained by the object and contains C. C_1 need not be centred at x.

> Alternatively it is the union of the points x, the centres of all circles $C(x)$, which just touch the boundary of the object in at least two distinct points.

A simple example (Figure 13.8) illustrates this definition. In a sense it is an information-reducing shape-preserving transformation or decomposition in terms of maximal disks contained in the object. Each point on the skeleton is the centre of a maximal disk. Another way of looking at a skeleton is as the dual of a boundary. Just as a boundary specifies shape, so does a skeleton.

Sequential thinning is defined with respect to a sequence of structuring elements X as:

$$((...((I \oslash X_1) \oslash X_2)...) \oslash X_n)$$

That is, the image is thinned by X_1. The result of this process is thinned by X_2, and so on until all the n structuring elements have been applied. Then the entire process is repeated until there is no change between two successive images. That is:

$$I_{n+1} = ((...((I_n \oslash X_1) \oslash X_2)...) \oslash X_n)$$

The operation $\oslash$ is defined in terms of the hit and miss transform:

$$I \oslash X = I - (I \otimes X)$$

where X is conveniently defined as a composite structuring element where:

1 means an element belonging to J (object)
0 means an element belonging to K (background)
R means – can be either

A set of eight structuring elements that can be used for thinning is:

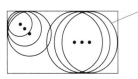

Largest circles that can be constructed within the object and which cannot be contained by another (larger) circle

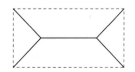

Skeleton of a rectangle formed by the centres of such circles

Skeleton of an H object

Figure 13.8
Illustrating the definition of the skeleton of an object.

Figure 13.9
A one-dimensional demonstration of grey-scale dilation (adapted from an illustration by Gonzalez and Woods (1992)).

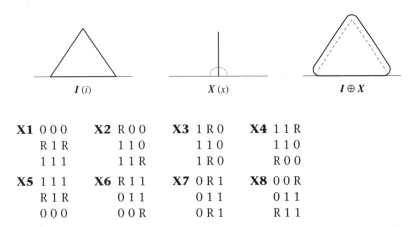

$I\,(i)$ $\qquad$ $X\,(x)$ $\qquad$ $I \oplus X$

X1	0 0 0	**X2**	R 0 0	**X3**	1 R 0	**X4**	1 1 R
	R 1 R		1 1 0		1 1 0		1 1 0
	1 1 1		1 1 R		1 R 0		R 0 0
X5	1 1 1	**X6**	R 1 1	**X7**	0 R 1	**X8**	0 0 R
	R 1 R		0 1 1		0 1 1		0 1 1
	0 0 0		0 0 R		0 R 1		R 1 1

where the origin in each case is the centre element.

Each pass through the image erodes it by any structure successfully detected. Alternate application of structuring elements that detect straight line boundaries (at least three pixels long) and ones that detect corners (at least containing 2×2 pixels) ensure that the objects shrinks to its digital skeleton. (Notice the difference between sequential thinning and what would happen if we shrank an object by its entire boundary at each pass. Such a procedure would shrink the object to zero.)

13.2　Grey scale morphology

13.2.1　Dilation and erosion

Extending the concepts of binary image morphology to grey scale imagery is non-trivial. The images can no longer be regarded as point sets and the question that immediately arises is: what do such operations as dilation mean with respect to a grey scale image? A definition of grey scale dilation can be formed by extending the binary definition by use of a maximum operator:

$$(I \oplus X)(i,j) = \max\{I(i - x, j - y) + X(x,y) \mid (i - x),(j - y) \in D_I; (x,y) \in D_X\}$$

where D_I and D_X are the domains of I and X and both I and X are now functions of two spatial variables.

The algorithmic definition of this operation is perhaps more accessible and is defined as:

for each pixel:

  position the structuring element over the pixel and calculate the sum of each pair of corresponding pixels

  find the maximum of the sums and output this value

Note the similarity of this operation to cross-correlation. Here, instead of calculating the sum of products over the corresponding mask and image elements we

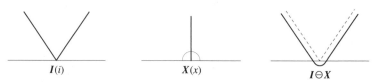

Figure 13.10
A one-dimensional demonstration of grey-scale erosion (adapted from an illustration by Gonzalez and Woods (1992)).

select the maximum of the sums of corresponding pixels in the image and structuring element. We can describe the effect of the operation qualitatively in the following terms. First, because of the addition operation and the selection of the maximum sum, the image being dilated will tend to be brighter (assuming positive values in the structuring element). Second, dark details will tend to be reduced and relatively large dark structure will be undisturbed. This effect depends on the nature and extent of the structuring element with respect to image structure or detail. A simple one-dimensional illustration is shown in Figure 13.9. In this case there is no shape information in the structuring element, but the effect of the grey scale variation in the structuring element on the image is clear.

Grey scale erosion can be similarly defined. In this case we extend the binary definition by using a minimum operator and subtraction:

$$(I \ominus X)(i,j) = \min\{I(i + x, j + y) - X(x,y) \mid (i + x),(j + y) \in D_I; (x,y) \in D_X\}$$

where D_I and D_X are the domains of I and X and both I and X are now functions of two spatial variables. Figure 13.10 is a simple one-dimensional effect of this operation. The effect on an image is first, to tend to make it darker because of the subtraction, and bright details in the input image that are contained within the structuring element are diminished.

13.2.2 Combined operations

Opening and closing can now be defined as for the binary case except now the grey scale dilation and erosion operators are used. Consider opening, here the effect is to remove small bright detail – depending on the nature and extent of the structuring element – and also to darken the image. The following dilation operation increases the brightness (diminished during erosion) without reintroducing the deleted detail. Closing, on the other hand, first removes dark detail at the same time brightening the image. The subsequent erosion operation tends to restore the image to its original brightness levels without reintroducing the deleted dark detail.

An excellent and insightful visualization of the operations of opening and closing, which appears to be due to Gonzalez and Woods, is shown in Figure 13.11. This is a demonstration of a single scan line of an image being opened and closed by a hemispherical structuring element. In the opening operation the effect is equivalent to pushing the sphere against the underside of the image function and then 'rolling' along, at the same time maintaining the upwards pushing force. The output of the opening operation, at any point along the scan

Figure 13.11
Gonzalez and Woods' rolling
sphere analogy of grey-scale
opening and closing.

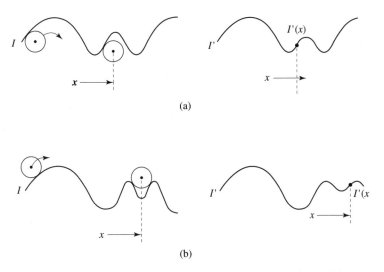

(a)

(b)

line, is then given by the curve of highest points reached by the sphere. Closing has the opposite sense in that the ball is rolled along the top of the image function. Here it is easily seen that small light peaks are bridged by the sphere in opening and small dark valleys are similarly bridged by the closing operation.

A common practical application of grey scale opening and closing is morphological smoothing where it is necessary to attenuate both light and dark detail which is regarded as noise. Another example is the morphological gradient defined by:

$$G(x,y) = (I \oplus X) - (I \quad X)$$

The advantage of this operation over gradient methods discussed in Chapter 9 is that the morphological gradient for a symmetrical element depends less on the direction of the edges in the image.

Further reading

For a comprehensive treatment of this subject see the book by Haralick and Shapiro (Vol 1) described in Chapter 1.

Classical pattern recognition and image matching

14.1 Rigid image matching – template matching

14.2 Statistical classifiers

14.3 Adaptive image matching or feature extraction strategies

14.4 Trainable pattern recognizers – neural nets or multi-layer perceptrons

14.5 Image measurements

14.6 Decomposition of regions

14.7 Real-time strategies – the recognition of handwriting

In this chapter we look at techniques that deal with analyzing images that are in reality two-dimensional, rather than two-dimensional projections of three-dimensional scenes. The common examples are optical character recognition, where the scene is a two-dimensional pattern of black ink on white paper; analysis of photomicrographs, where the scene is a very thin slice of tissue; a satellite image where the reflectivity information is independent of the height of the reflecting feature; or a TV image of a flat or flattish machine part on a conveyor belt where the camera is positioned vertically above the belt surface. Thus we could refer to the techniques in this chapter as two-dimensional computer vision methods. The problems that arise when we consider two-dimensional projections of three-dimensional reality, generally a far more difficult area, are dealt with in Chapter 15.

Pattern recognition is the name that is usually given to a particular image analysis problem where the aim is to recognize or categorize an image or part of an image as being the same as a sample or prototype image. We distinguish the field from scene recognition or scene understanding or computer vision where we are attempting to extract information from a two-dimensional projection of a three-dimensional scene. In pattern recognition we are generally trying to answer the question: which one of n categories does the input image belong to? Because of this, pattern recognition includes theory that has evolved techniques that are related to how the decision is made. The two main branches of decision theory are statistically based techniques and learning or training techniques. In pattern recognition we usually have much prior knowledge about the pattern categories. A good example is character recognition where we know the general shapes of the characters. Pattern recognition may not be concerned with making a one out of n decision but may itself be part of some higher-level image understanding process. A good example is the use of pattern recognition (that is, decision-based techniques) to effect the segmentation of multi-band satellite images. It may also take the form of image matching where we are usually trying to answer the question: is sub-image or feature X present in the input image?

Classical pattern recognition has been around for a long time – since the late 1950s. Much research was carried out in the 1960s and at the time optimism was in the air and many future extrapolations were made that predicted an early and complete solution to most applications of interest. It turned out that such optimism was ill-founded and 35 years on we are no nearer to solving most of the classic pattern recognition problems. First let us define what we mean by classical pattern recognition by discussing it in terms of its most intensively studied application – optical character recognition or OCR. (The apparently redundant use of the word 'optical' is due to the fact that pattern recognition systems for character recognition function with non-optical information such as the magnetic field from magnetized ink or real-time information from a stylus tracking device.)

As we have stated, most classical pattern recognition problems are two-dimensional – the images that we analyze originate from a two-dimensional entity such as ink on paper. Here we present a device with an image of a single printed character and require the machine to place it in one out of 26 categories. (There are of course associated problems of segmenting from a printed page an image of a single isolated character, but we shall ignore these.) This seems at first sight like a simple problem. The images are of two-dimensional objects. Usually characters are easily distinguished from their backgrounds – they are black images on white paper. There only 26 (or 52) of them. Human beings find the task remarkably easy. Never the less, the problem has proved extremely difficult unless the characters are fairly constrained in size and type variations. In particular, unconstrained block printed character recognition is still the subject of much research and recognizing cursive script – handwriting – still seems as far away as it was in the 1960s.

Classical pattern recognition is usually presented as having the general structure shown in Figure 14.1. The first process will involve some image processing operation or a procedure that segments an area of interest. In the case of OCR this may involve segmenting a line of characters into individual letters and thresholding. The second process makes measurements on the image. In most applications the recognition phase is not carried out on the original pattern –

Figure 14.1
The structure of a classical
pattern recognizer.

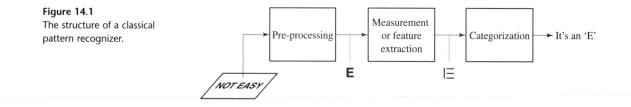

image processed or not. Instead we try to map the pattern into some form that is more amenable to categorization. This is usually called feature extraction. Generally, we can state that we should attempt to extract measurements that in some way reflect the uniqueness of the pattern amongst the set of all categories. For example, in OCR we generally want to be able to deal with a number of different typefaces. Thus we want to extract features from a letter 'a' that empha- size its 'a-ness'. We need measurements that diminish or are tolerant to the **intra-category** variations between 'a's; but which at the same time maintain or emphasize the **inter-category** variations. By this we mean that shape varia- tions between 'a's are to be ignored while at the same time shape variations between 'a's and the other 25 character classes are to be maintained. It is this that has proved difficult – shape variations between characters of the same class are difficult and sometimes impossible to distinguish from shape variations that exist between classes. Perhaps this is not surprising. Intra-category variations in typefaces are in fact substantial despite the fact that we as human beings seem to ignore them easily. (At least we ignore them as far as the identity of the letter is concerned, while at the same time appreciating the aesthetics of the typeface that the character is cloaked in. And despite the fact that typographical design- ers make their reputations by creating forms that are different to existing fonts, we are always immediately aware of the identity of the letters.) The third process is making a decision based on the measurements, which in the case of OCR is a one out of 26 categorization.

Another way of interpreting Figure 14.1 is to see the three stages as different spaces. The data is transformed from space to space (Figure 14.2). The first space is conventional image space and the character may be represented as a normal image intensity function or as a binary image. This data is transformed into mea- surement or feature space by making measurements on the original data. These may be simple geometric measurements or 'feature measurements' like detecting whether or not a T junction or some other feature exists in the image. In these terms the goal of this part of the process is to ensure that patterns from the same categories form clusters in the measurement space, the clusters reflecting the intra-category variations. The measurement space can then be divided up into mutually exclusive labelled regions and a pattern is categorized according to which part of labelled measurement space it falls into. If the application is such that pattern clusters overlap then we cannot make a decision using this tech- nique. To ensure that this does not happen we either have to design patterns

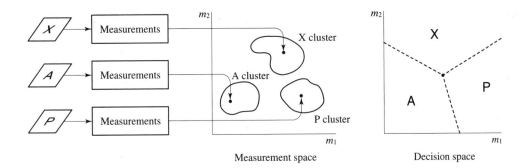

Measurement space   Decision space

Figure 14.2

Image, measurement and decision space in pattern recognition.

with respect to the measurement space to produce separable clusters, or we have to design adequate measurements with respect to the patterns. Many practical machines use the former approach; in particular, most early OCR machines used stylized characters.

Thus the inherent difficulty of character recognition led to the early emergence of special OCR fonts which are heavily stylized to avoid these problems and simplify the recognition technology. Simplistically we can say that these are designed to be read by both humans and machines – stylized for easy and reliable OCR technology without losing their identity to humans. The oldest of these is the internationally used E13B font for bank cheques. Each letter is designed so that a single 'slit' reading head (the characters are printed with magnetic ink) produces a unique one-dimensional signal for each character. This function is proportional to the rate of change of black area 'seen' by the slit as it moves horizontally over the letter. Crude sampling of this signal results in a unique N-dimensional measurement vector for each character which is compared with 14 prototype vectors for assignment to 1 out of 14 classes. Examples of E13B charters and the corresponding waveforms are shown in Figure 14.3. The advantage of the system is that the reading technology is cheap, fast and reliable. (However, even in this highly constrained application we should note that the system does not result in complete automation of the cheque clearance system. Only the bank code, accountee code and cheque number can be preprinted on the cheque. When the cheque is processed manual intervention is necessary to handle payee information and the amount, which is either handwritten or typed. It is interesting to note that this problem is of diminishing importance as electronic methods of cash transfer replace cheques.)

A more extreme example of stylization for machine reading, and one that is now so ubiquitous that it is a familiar part of our visual culture, is the bar code. Here the information is totally invisible to human beings but is easily interpreted by simple reading devices These two examples demonstrate our recent failure to build machines that can deal with our graphical culture and how we have instead evolved a new symbology suited more to machines than human beings. Although the E13B font is readable, it is less than ideal and anyway only includes numerals.

OCR technology, that is, methods that recognize normal, rather than specially designed typefaces, at first adopted a brute force approach and utilized an

Figure 14.3
American Bankers
Association E-13B
font characters and
corresponding waveforms.

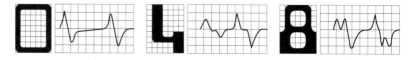

approach known as template matching where sample measurements of all characters of every typeface (that the machine is to recognize) are stored internally in the machine. The measurements made on incoming characters are compared with these templates for a match. The plain disadvantage of such an approach is that the machine can only recognize characters that it has prior knowledge of – a somewhat limiting situation.

The difference between using a feature extractor to somehow measure the essence of a pattern belonging to a certain class, independent of intra-category variations, and storing **all** likely variations within a category is profound as far as the machine structure and computational cost are concerned. In the first case we expect a powerful feature extractor to produce a set of 26 different feature lists, one for each character category. We store 26 feature lists – one for each character class. In the second case we have to store 26 feature lists multiplied by the number of typefaces that we want to recognize.

A useful conceptualization of this kind of pattern recognition problem comes from considering the N-dimensional measurement that is made on the image as a single point in N-dimensional feature or measurement space – an N-dimensional vector or N-tuple. Consider again Figure 14.2 which shows a two-dimensional analogue of this space together with measurements made on images that originate from three categories. Each pattern is a single point in this space. We hope that patterns which belong to the same category produce clusters in the measurement space. We can then divide the space up into regions, one for each category.

The extent of the clusters is due to intra-category variations within each category, that is, shape variations between characters in a class and noise. We hope that we can make measurements that produce category clusters that are tight enough to facilitate the division of the measurement space into mutually exclusive regions. The simple case exemplified in Figure 14.2 possesses two important attributes:

- the clusters are separable
- we can use straight lines to separate the categories and define decision space.

The first attribute is an obvious requirement and if it is not met we have to use statistically based techniques; the second relates to the practical problem of implementation. If the categories are linearly separable then there are available techniques that we can use. If they are not, the practicalities are much more difficult for reasons that we will shortly explore. It is the case that in most unsolved problems of interest to us, we cannot make measurements that result in category problems that are linearly separable – most problem are non-linear.

What do we mean by making measurements on a pattern? In general we could define a measurement as any extracted information that is a higher-level structure than simply the collection of pixels and associated intensities that make up the low-level detailed image. In a sense, if we knew what measurements to make, what structures to try to extract from the image, we would have solved the problem. Consider again the OCR problem. The simplest measurements that we could make for each character would be just the value of each pixel after, say, thresholding. This identifies the structure of interest or extracts it from the background – a process called segmentation. Our N-tuple would then be an N-bit binary word (where N is the number of pixels in the image). That this is a useless approach for most applications is immediately apparent. It would be sensitive to noise, position and size changes as well as shape differences. Intra-category clusters in measurement space would merge into these clusters exhibited by other categories. To proceed down the path of utilizing low-level pixel information, we would have to implement at least position and size 'normalization' by, say, enclosing each character in a minimum area rectangle and dividing this up into the same number of squares each time, sampling a value from these subdivisions. Alternatively, as we have discussed, we have to employ a strategy of extreme stylizations of the patterns so as to ensure that low-level measurements result in non-overlapping and linearly separable category clusters.

For characters we may try to achieve a **structural description**. We might, for example, manage to describe an '**E**' as a single vertical line plus three horizontal lines in a particular spatial juxtaposition. This seems like the obvious way to proceed; but finding particular features to extract that result in linearly separable clusters in measurement space has proved extremely elusive, and recently the attention given to neural nets has returned the problem to low-level measurement space because these machines have the ability to deal with clusters that are not linearly separable – they are trainable machines that adjust their structure automatically during a training phase and remove from the designer the problem of finding appropriate measurements.

Thus we see that if we conceptualize the problem in this way we end up with two sub-problems: selecting a feature set or measurement space and dividing this up to into categories. The first of these problems, as we have discussed, is difficult and heavily context dependent. The second is more straightforward and a number of so-called decision-theoretic techniques have been developed to deal with this. We will look at two common approaches – template matching and statistical classifiers.

14.1 Rigid image matching – template matching

The most familiar and possibly the earliest technique employed in pattern recognition, template matching, means storing a prototype or template of each class, comparing the unknown pattern with each template in turn and recognizing the pattern as belonging to the class of the template that it is most similar to, that is, the template that it matches best. Matching is most commonly carried out by cross-correlating the template with the pattern. In other words, it is a spatial filtering operation like those in Chapter 9. Cross-correlation is also used as a method of feature detection. We could look for corners of a particular orientation in an image by using a corner template. The process in that case returns a corner present/absent as a result rather than a categorization.

Basic cross-correlation is defined as:

$$C(i,j) = \sum_x \sum_y I(x,y)T(x-i,y-j)$$

where $C(i,j)$ is the cross-correlation function, $I(x,y)$ is the image and $T(x,y)$ is the template. Usually the template is a sub-image smaller than $I(x,y)$ and the summation is over that area of I overlapped by T. The maximum value of C is where the image and the template best match and the maximum over all categories gives us our classification. Because this measure is sensitive to amplitude or intensity variations in $I(x,y)$ it is usually normalized as:

$$C(i,j) = \frac{\sum_x \sum_y (I(x,y) - \bar{I}(x,y))(T(x-i,y-j) - \bar{T})}{\sqrt{\sum_x \sum_y (I(x,y) - \bar{I}(x,y))^2 \sum_x \sum_y (T(x-i,y-j) - \bar{T})^2}}$$

where the mean of T is constant and calculated once, and the mean of I is calculated over the current area of overlap. The technique can only be used successfully in contexts where the image will potentially match the template exactly, or at least very closely. For example, it could be used in single font OCR. It is often used in applications to detect the presence/absence of an object rather than to categorize an object as belonging to a certain class. In this kind of application it may be important to report the position of the object searched for, which is given by the maximum value of $C(i,j)$. Again the implication is that the template is an exact match. The main disadvantage of this technique is that it is sensitive to orientation and scale changes in $I(x,y)$. This, of course, is why it is ruled out as a technique for multi-font OCR where the intra-category variations are just that.

(14.1.1)

Rigid vs. flexible image matching

Although we are approaching the comparison of one image with another from the (mostly historical) point of view of pattern recognition, this term is now tending to fall into disuse and the more general term of image matching predominates. This generalizes the applications of techniques like template matching. We may be interested not in seeing if an image matches a stored prototype but if a small part of an image contains a stored prototype. This may form part of a pattern recognition application where we attempt to recognize a global pattern by first recognizing the presence (and spatial juxtaposition, say) of components usually known as features. Alternatively we may be looking for the existence of a special feature in an image such as a tumour in a medical image.

In the previous section the image matching method that we used is called rigid matching. (Note that although we have described it elsewhere (Chapter 10) the Hough transform is another rigid matching technique.) Rigid matching can only be used when we have reasonably precise prior knowledge of the pattern, feature or sub-image that we are looking for. In many applications we may not have precise enough prior knowledge of the feature and in such contexts flexible or adaptive matching strategies are required. We describe an important branch of such approaches in Section 14.3.

14.2 Statistical classifiers

The idea behind making statistically based decisions is that we can specify the shape of the intra-category clusters as a multivariate probability distribution function (PDF). If we can do this for each category on the basis of a representative set in each category, then we can implement optimum decision making for an unknown pattern. We can also take into account, in the same scheme, such factors as the cost of making an error and the frequency of occurrence of each category.

The approach relies upon being able to represent an intra-category cluster analytically as a particular PDF. If the approach is to be valid the variations within the cluster have to be such that they can be accurately described by a particular distribution. This may be fine in contexts where a pattern is represented by a large number of low-level measurements that are subject to variations due to noise. But in contexts like OCR, where the intra-category variations are likely to be less 'well behaved', statistical techniques may be totally inappropriate. Because of these factors the success of this approach in classical pattern recognition and similar applications has been somewhat low. However, most books on pattern recognition will have a good few chapters on this topic, reflecting the never-ending desire for elegant mathematical solutions to practical problems that stubbornly refuse fit into the models. We will deal very briefly with the topic here, but a practical example will be given where the approach works quite well.

Consider Figure 14.4 which shows the simplest possible analogue of this approach. This shows two pattern classes or categories, where each pattern is represented by a single measurement. The PDFs derived from the set of samples of each category have a different mean, as we would expect, and also have a different variance. The decision boundary in one-dimensional measurement space (for equal probability of occurrence of each category) is given by x_b, where:

$$p(x_b|\omega_1) = p(x_b|\omega_2)$$

An unknown pattern x is classified as:

if $x < x_b$ then the category is ω_1 **else** ω_2

There are two important points to note from this simple example. First, the shaded area on the graph indicates that misclassifications can occur. A measure-

Figure 14.4
A simple two-category (one measurement) statistical classifier.

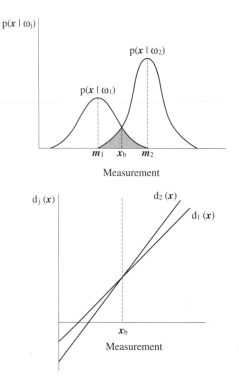

ment less than x_b can originate from a pattern belonging to category ω_2 and vice versa. This is inevitable because we are now considering a situation where our pattern clusters overlap in measurement space. That is, statistical methods can deal with applications where patterns do not form separable clusters. Second, note that any such machine or program must operate in two phases. The first phase, sometimes called the training or learning phase, presents the machine with a sufficient number of samples from each category so that the parameters of p can be determined. In the second phase, or operating phase, the machine classifies unknown patterns that are presented to it on the basis of the information gathered in the training phase. Note that this implies that we have prior knowledge of, or can assume a particular form of, distribution.

In general we have to consider a multidimensional pattern and also include the possibility that the categories are not equiprobable. In the simple example in Figure 14.4, if the two categories were not equiprobable then the boundary x_b would move away from the PDF crossover point towards the more frequently occurring category.

For a multidimensional pattern x and M categories we use a so-called **Bayes** classifier which includes the probability of occurrence of each category and assigns a pattern x to category i, if

$$p(x|\omega_i)\, f(\omega_i) > p(x|\omega_j)\, f(\omega_j) \qquad j = 1,2,\ldots,M;\, j \neq i$$

where $f(\omega_j)$ is the probability of occurrence of category ω_j

A complete derivation of this expression is given in Gonzalez and Woods whose notation we follow here. As we have already pointed out, the estimation of $p()$ is difficult, if not impossible, and in most cases where this technique is used it is 'traditional' to assume that $p()$ will be a Gaussian distribution in which case:

$$p(\mathbf{x}|\omega_j) = \frac{1}{(2\pi)^{N/2}|\mathbf{C}_j|^{1/2}} \exp\left(-\frac{1}{2}(\mathbf{x}-\mathbf{m}_j)^T \mathbf{C}_j^{-1}(\mathbf{x}-\mathbf{m}_j)\right) \tag{14.1}$$

where $\mathbf{m}_j$ is the mean measurement vector for patterns in category j

$\mathbf{C}_j$ is the covariance matrix for patterns in category j

N is the number of components in the pattern vector $\mathbf{x}$

These can be approximated from the samples in the training phase as follows:

$$\mathbf{m}_j = \frac{1}{N_j} \sum_{x \in \omega_j} \mathbf{x}$$

and

$$\mathbf{C}_j = \frac{1}{N_j} \sum_{x \in \omega_j} \mathbf{x}\mathbf{x}^T - \mathbf{m}_j\mathbf{m}_j^T$$

We define a **decision function** as:

a pattern $\mathbf{x}$ is assigned to category ω_i **if** $d_i(\mathbf{x}) > d_j(\mathbf{x})$ $\qquad j = 1,2,\dots,M$

where $d_i(x) = p(\mathbf{x}|\omega_i)f(\omega_i)$ and taking logs $d_i(\mathbf{x})$ can be written as:

$$d_i(\mathbf{x}) = \ln p(\mathbf{x}|\omega_i) + \ln f(\omega_i) \tag{14.2}$$

and we can write a decision function for j as:

$$d_j(\mathbf{x}) = \ln f(\omega_j) - \frac{1}{2} \ln|\mathbf{C}_j| - \frac{1}{2} ((\mathbf{x}-\mathbf{m}_j)^T \mathbf{C}_j^{-1}(\mathbf{x}-\mathbf{m}_j)) \tag{14.3}$$

This is arrived at by substituting Equation (14.1) into Equation (14.2) and ignoring the term $(N/2) \ln 2\pi$ which is the same for all the M decision functions. From this we can see that components in $\mathbf{x}$ exist in no higher degree than 2 and in fact the classifier implements hyperquadrics in N-dimensional space. The PDFs themselves are hyperellipsoids in N-dimensional space.

In the event that all distributions have the same shape, all covariance matrices are equal and Equation (14.3) reduces to:

$$d_j(\mathbf{x}) = \ln f(\omega_j) + \mathbf{x}^T\mathbf{C}^{-1}\mathbf{m}_j - \frac{1}{2} \mathbf{m}_j^T\mathbf{C}^{-1}\mathbf{m}_j$$

and these are now linear decision or discriminant functions or hyperplanes in N-dimensional space.

If $\mathbf{C}$ is the identity matrix $\mathbf{I}$ and $f(\omega_j) = 1/M$ for all j, then the equation further reduces to:

$$d_j(\mathbf{x}) = \mathbf{x}^T\mathbf{m}_j - \frac{1}{2} \mathbf{m}_j^T\mathbf{m}_j$$

In this case all the PDFs are hyperspheres in N-dimensional space. This expression is known as a **minimum distance classifier**. If we consider for simplicity a two-category problem in two-dimensional measurement space, it implements a decision boundary which is the perpendicular bisector of the line joining the two means $\boldsymbol{m_i}$ and $\boldsymbol{m_j}$. It is called a minimum distance classifier because any unknown pattern has its distance to the mean of every category calculated and it is assigned to that category for which this distance is a minimum. The one-dimensional example of this case is shown in Figure 14.4 which shows the two linear decision functions $d_1(\boldsymbol{x})$ and $d_2(\boldsymbol{x})$.

Finally note that any machine or procedure that implemented template matching or statistically based classification that resulted in linear decision functions would conform to the structure shown in Figure 14.5. A pattern is presented to a set of category filters or detectors. Inside each category box there exists a structure that in general performs a component-by-component weighting followed by a summation. An example of a minimum distance classifier applied to satellite imagery is shown in Figure 14.6 (Colour Plate). This shows a thematic map made from six wavelength bands. Each 'ground truth' point shown in the illustration was set manually, and formed the mean of the category

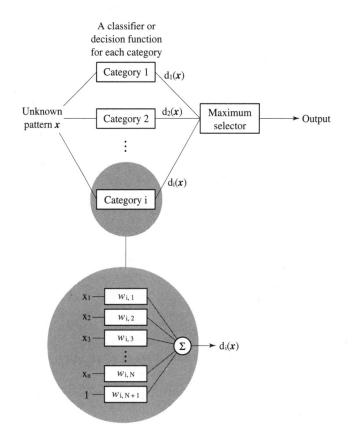

Figure 14.5
The structure of a linear machine.

(note that the analysis was applied to unprocessed imagery; the issue of shadows and satellite imagery is dealt with in Chapter 9).

It is obvious that basic template matching is only effective within certain limits. If the shape of a feature is too distorted compared with the 'stored' feature in the template, or if imaging conditions (say, for example, lighting) change, then the result of the convolution will signal a mismatch. The same shortcomings, although less severe, are inherent in statistical classifiers. Statistical classifiers only work in contexts where the variations can be modelled by a PDF which by definition implies that patterns cluster in measurement space in a way that enables separation by decision surfaces as we have described. Although they have the advantage that noise and misclassification costs can be taken into account they cannot cope with wide intra-category variations. An approach which tries to overcome the limitations inherent in these two techniques is called elastic matching or deformable templates – a matching process that deals with both geometric and intensity 'distortion'.

14.3 Adaptive image matching or feature extraction strategies

14.3.1 Deformable templates

Deformable templates come in many different guises and have been proposed by many different authors. The idea of a deformable template is easy to describe; however, the way in which the template is set up, and the exact matching strategies used, vary widely according to the image context in which it is to be used. The power of the method lies not just in the ability, as the name implies, of the template to adapt in some way to the pattern, but also in the fact that it implements both image matching (in the sense of cross-correlation type matching of image intensities with prototype image intensities – the template approach) and relational matching. Relational matching is where we specify that a subfeature X_1 in the image must have a certain relationship to subfeature X_2 (say, for example, X_1 must be 'to the left of' X_2). (Relational matching is further described in Chapter 15 in the context of three-dimensional object recognition.)

The simple physical analogue is elastic matching – the prototype is considered to be a rubber sheet which is stretched to match the image that is being analyzed. The goodness of fit is metricized in some way that relates to the minimal amount of stretching that the prototype undergoes when it is matched. This is just the stored energy of the (virtual) elastic material. The power of elastic matching is its potential ability to cope with complex distortions.

An early version of this approach, implemented as a dynamic programming algorithm, was described in 1973 by Fischler et al. This involved a series of templates connected together by virtual springs. Figure 14.7 shows the idea for a set of facial features. Individual iconic or image-based features are connected by springs and the scheme enables a cost function, which consists of the sum of the intensity matching template costs plus the spring costs, to be calculated. These

Figure 14.7
Fischler and Elschlager's templates and springs model of a face.

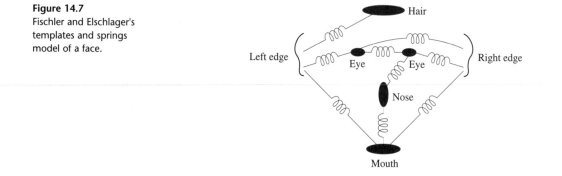

are just the tensions in the springs or the amount of energy that is required to stretch the iconic templates with respect to each other to match the image. Thus the templates measure dissimilarity between image components and the stored sub-images and the springs measure the relational dissimilarity between the features. Costs can also be assigned if features are missing in the image.

This kind of approach is usually described in terms of internal and external energy. The internal or constraint energy is the energy stored in the springs and relates the degree of distortion of the template. The external energy is the dissimilarity between the image intensities and the template. A total energy function is set up which depends on the template parameters and the problem becomes the minimization of this function by iteratively altering the template parameters. In other words we have:

$$E_{total} = W_{internal}E_{internal} + W_{external}E_{external}$$

where $E_{internal}$ is a function of the (internal) constraint parameters of the template and $E_{external}$ is a function of the interaction between template parameters and image information. Many implementations are hierarchical, enabling a coarse match followed by a finer match. This is important in the design of iterative strategies that minimize the total energy. Finer matches are guided by the result of previous coarser matches which should improve convergence.

As an example of this technique, we will describe an approach by Yuille et al. (1989) which was applied to facial feature extraction, in this case the eyes and lips. (Facial feature extraction is becoming an increasingly important application area that uses elastic matching. As we describe in Chapter 26, one of the approaches to achieving high compression for video telephony is to transmit changes – in effect an animation script – that relate to a common model that both the transmitter and the receiver can access. This requires that facial features be extracted and tracked.) We have chosen to describe this particular technique because it seems typical, relevant and comprehensive. Yuille et al. categorize their method as consisting of three elements:

(1) A parametrized geometric or shape model for the feature. In this case a circle for the eye and a pair of parabolae that define the upper and lower eyelids. This model is shown in Figure 14.8 and when incorporated into the

Figure 14.8
The eye template. The geometry, see text, is specified by the parameters x_e, x_c, p_1, r, a, b, c with an additional parameter θ specifying the orientation. The iris, R_c, is represented by the circle centred on x_c and the whites, R_w, by the region outside the circle but inside the two parabolae.

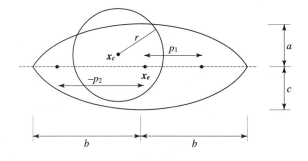

Figure 14.8
The eye template. The geometry, see text, is specified by the parameters x_e, x_c, p_1, r, a, b, c with an additional parameter θ specifying the orientation. The iris, R_c, is represented by the circle centred on x_c and the whites, R_w, by the region outside the circle but inside the two parabolae.

algorithm it encapsulates the structural relationship between subfeatures that make up the eye feature. This model is correlated with processed versions of the image – specifically an edge-detected version, an image containing peaks only and an image containing valleys only.

(2) An imaging model which, operating on image intensities, enumerates how closely the actual image values match the prototype or model.

(3) An algorithm that controls the parameters of the model iteratively to minimize an overall energy.

The structural template parameters are as follows:

x_c, r	the centre and radius of the iris
x_e	the centre of the template
θ	the orientation of the template
e_1, e_2	$(\cos\theta, \sin\theta)$, $(-\sin\theta, \cos\theta)$
a, b, c	the parameters of the parabolae defining the upper and lower eyelid boundaries
p_1, p_2	the position of the centres of the expected image peaks

Energy terms are defined as follows:

$$E_{\text{prior}} = \frac{k_1}{2} (|x_e - x_c|)^2 + \frac{k_2}{2} (p_1 - p_2 - (r + b))^2 + \frac{k_3}{2} (b - 2r)^2$$

This constrains the centre of the eye to be close to the centre of the iris. The remaining energy terms are integrations of image information, or derived image information, over regions defined by template areas. In terms of conventional template matching, we are correlating each manifestation of the deformable template with the image.

$$E_{\text{valley}} = -\frac{c_1}{|R_c|} \int_{R_c} \varphi_{\text{valley}}(x) \, dA$$

Here the region R_c is the set of pixels in the image $I(x)$ that are enclosed by the iris of the template and $\varphi_{\text{valley}}(x)$ is the valley processed version of $I(x)$. c_1 is a parameter used in the iteration. Minimization of this term causes the valley image to drag the template towards the eye part of the image.

$$E_{\text{edge}} = -\frac{c_2}{|\partial R_c|} \int_{\partial R_c} \varphi_{\text{edge}}(\boldsymbol{x})\, \mathrm{d}s - \frac{c_3}{|\partial R_w|} \int_{\partial R_w} \varphi_{edge}(\boldsymbol{x})\, \mathrm{d}s$$

∂R_c and ∂R_w are the boundary of the iris and the white regions respectively and $\varphi_{\text{edge}}(\boldsymbol{x})$ is the edge processed version of $I(\boldsymbol{x})$.

$$E_{\text{peak}} = -c_4(\varphi_{\text{peak}}(\boldsymbol{x}_e + p_1\boldsymbol{e}_1) + \varphi_{\text{peak}}(\boldsymbol{x}_e + p_2\boldsymbol{e}_2)$$

$\varphi_{\text{peak}}(\boldsymbol{I})$ is the peak processed version of $I(\boldsymbol{x})$.

$$E_{\text{image}} = \frac{c_5}{|R_c|} \int_{R_c} I(\boldsymbol{x})\mathrm{d}A - \frac{c_6}{|R_w|} \int_{R_w} I(\boldsymbol{x})\mathrm{d}A$$

This last energy term is positive and operates directly on the image, fine-tuning the template parameters to maximize the difference in intensity between the iris and the white.

The algorithm implements a strategy based on steepest descent in the total energy:

$$E_{\text{total}} = E_{\text{prior}} + E_{\text{valley}} + E_{\text{edge}} + E_{\text{peak}} + E_{\text{image}}$$

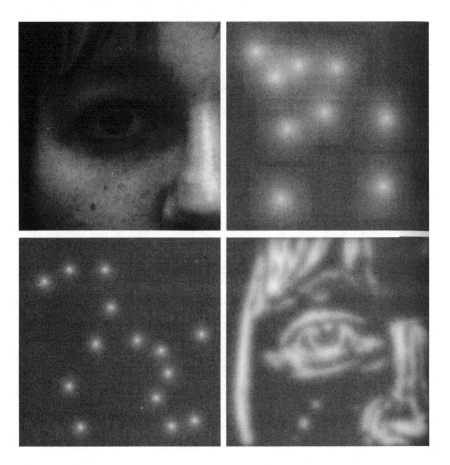

Figure 14.9

The potential fields for a typical eye (top left). The valley (top right), peak (bottom left) and edge (bottom right) fields. (Courtesy of A.L. Yuille and J.J. Clarke.)

That is, for each iteration the parameters are adjusted in a way that selects the highest negative change in E_{total} with respect to the parameter. Yuille et al. divide the search into 'epochs' by controlling the parameters c_i and k_i. For example, in the first epoch c_1 is the only non-zero parameter, x_e is set equal to x_c and the valley image drags the template towards the eye. This is followed by the next epoch which switches on parameters c_2 and c_5 which fine-tune the position and the size of the iris. In this way the template is gradually switched on and a solution emerges which considers the most salient parts of the eye in order. Figure 14.9 shows an image and valley, peak and edge fields extracted using this method.

14.3.2 Active contour models or snakes

Active contour models, or snakes, were first proposed by Kass et al. in 1987. They are a specialized form of deformable template but differ from them in that they detect image contours (as opposed to features) and are modelled using B splines or some other basis function (see Chapter 7). They are energy-minimizing curves, rather than templates representing specific patterns, with extent in two spatial variables.

In Chapter 7 we dealt with the use of cubic parametric functions in image synthesis or computer graphics. Most of these applications involved the use of bicubic parametric surfaces. Here we are interested in curves that are functions of two spatial variables or a single parameter:

$$\mathbf{Q}(u) = (x(u), y(u))$$

An illustration that shows various uses of such functions in two-dimensional imagery is shown in Figure 14.10. Figure 14.10(a) shows the use of Bézier functions in the interactive design of fonts. Here the silhouette of the character being designed is controlled interactively by the designer who moves the associated control points. In the second example, a variety of different handwritten 'a's are synthesized using the same basic 'a' template. This might be the basis of an analysis by synthesis approach for the recognition of such characters (further discussed in Section 14.7) where characters generated from splines are made to fit (skeletonized) and drawn characters. The third shows the flexibility of contours specified in this way – an E is morphed into a Z by interpolating between the sets of control points that represent each character. Finally the application of active contours is shown applied to an image where a contour of interest is detected by the snake method. This illustration points out an important difference between using deformable templates, in which is usually embedded prior shape knowledge, and the idea of detecting contours of interest in an image without prior knowledge of the final shape of the contour. In such a context the algorithm is supplied only with prior knowledge concerning the desired image properties that the contour is to exhibit and the snake moves and changes shape dynamically, matching itself to image contours that have the desired property.

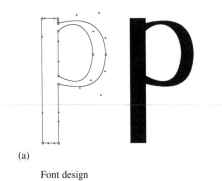

(a)

Font design

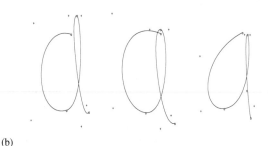

(b)

Synthesis of handwritten characters (see Chapter 14)

(c)

Shape morphing in
two-dimensional space

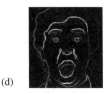

(d)

Using 'snakes' to track facial
expressions (see Chapter 19)

Figure 14.10
Four applications of cubic
parametric functions in
computer imagery.

Snakes need to be initialized in some way That is, an approximate starting shape and position near to the desired contour has to be supplied to the algorithm. This may originate interactively from a user, be supplied by some higher-level process or from a previous snake process – for example, in tracking facial features in video sequences.

When using active contour models with an image, again the energy to be minimized is a weighted sum of a term that originates from the current state of the deformation of the snake. We have:

$$E_{\text{total}} = \int_0^1 E_{\text{internal}}\, \boldsymbol{Q}(u)\mathrm{d}u + E_{\text{external}}\, \boldsymbol{Q}(u)\mathrm{d}u$$

The overall energy term E_{total} thus depends on both the shape of the snake and the value of the image function along its path. The internal spline energy consists of an elasticity and rigidity term:

$$E_{\text{internal}} = w_1 \left|\frac{\mathrm{d}\boldsymbol{Q}}{\mathrm{d}u}\right|^2 + w_2 \left|\frac{\mathrm{d}^2\boldsymbol{Q}}{\mathrm{d}u^2}\right|^2$$

where w_1 and w_2 are respectively elasticity and stiffness constants. The implication of this term is that when the snake fits a contour then by definition this will be some kind of coherent structure such as an edge. A snake modelled to fit such an image structure will exhibit a lower internal energy than one that exhibits many random excursions along its path.

The external term is derived from interaction between image information and $Q(u)$. For example, if we define:

$$E_{external} = -|\nabla I(\mathbf{x})|$$

then the curve is attracted to the local maximum of the gradient, that is, edges. Note that the term is negative and the curve moves towards areas of high gradient to minimize the sum of the two energy terms. Other image constraints can be applied. For example, lines can be used as attractors; the area enclosed by the curve can be constrained, forcing the curve to enclose homogeneous regions only. Constraints may exist between multiple snakes – Kass et al. describe a stereo snake where a pair of snakes operate in a stereo image pair.

14.4 Trainable pattern recognizers – neural nets or multi-layer perceptrons

Neural nets is the term given to the practical implementation of devices that in their simplest form implement linear discriminant functions 'automatically' from a training phase. It is a device, almost always simulated by a program running on a normal processor, that adjusts its structure as it is presented with patterns in a training or supervised phase. Neural nets have applications in many areas of computer science and we will only consider their use in pattern recognition where they were originally known as multi-layer perceptrons.

The term **neural nets** is perhaps as inappropriate as one that emerged in the 1950s describing early computers as 'giant brains'. It is not just the scale of a human neural network that is unachievable artificially – around 100 billion neurons – where each individual element may be connected to thousands of others; but the complexity of the tasks it performs are inimitable and our knowledge of how human neural nets function is sadly extremely limited. Artificial neurons are extremely simple devices that can be interconnected to form large networks. The size of the network and the number of interconnections make its behaviour difficult to model or predict. However, this fact does not imply that the network is somehow more than the sum of its parts as the term 'neural net' tends to imply. The point is that we should decouple the computer science structures from any allusion to the human brain and should not invent jargon that does the opposite.

In the context of this section a neural net is a system formed by interconnecting a number of simple devices. The interconnections are fixed but the weight or influence of each connection is variable. Nodes in a network have N inputs and produce a single output. The N inputs can be the components of an N-dimensional pattern vector. An interconnection joins the output of a node to one of the inputs of a node in the next layer. This simple structure is shown in Figure 14.11. It consists of a set of nodes forming an input layer, a set of nodes

Figure 14.11
Neural net: convention for
interconnections.

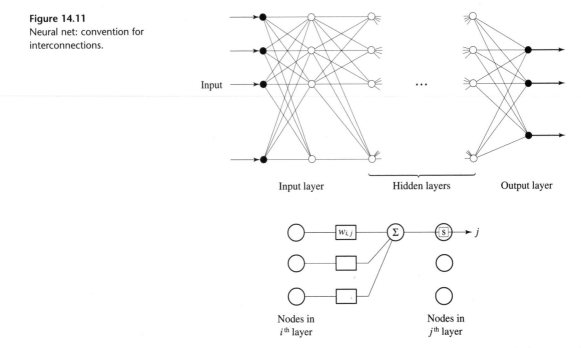

forming an output layer and a set of intermediate nodes curiously known as hidden layers. The insert shows the set-up in more detail. At each node j we have a single input I_j which is the sum of the weighted outputs from all the nodes i in the previous layer. This is then operated on by the sigmoid function S to provide the output O_j. The output from the sigmoid unit varies continuously, but not linearly, as the input changes, in a manner that will be explained. We can observe that each node in a layer is presented with the same pattern – the output from the previous layer. However, the input to each node is weighted differently according to how the weights contained in its input line are adjusted.

Such a network is **trainable**. This means that we can present the device with a number of patterns in a training set and adjust the weights in the network until all the patterns in the training set are correctly categorized. We then suppose that if pattern classes are well represented by the training set, the machine will function well in the operating phase. This is no different in effect from decision functions derived from a training set by using statistical methods. However, instead of deriving a decision function from statistical properties of the training set we 'evolve' a decision function by a kind of trial and error method. The machine adjusts its internal structure to effect the correct classification during the training phase.

The important attribute of neural nets is that they can be trained to deal with pattern classes that are not linearly separable. Many if not most practical pattern recognition classes are not linearly separable and it appears that it is extremely difficult to invent a set of features that makes them so. Thus the importance of one of the early tenets of classical pattern recognition – that we should extract features that make the classes linearly separable – is diminished and replaced by research into neural nets that do not make the difficult demand of linear separability.

Research into such machines has an interesting history. There was much excitement in the late 1950s and early 1960s centred around a device called a **perceptron** that could be trained on linearly separable training sets. In fact a mathematical proof was developed which demonstrated that a solution would converge after a finite number of iterations in the training phase. It was also known that to deal with training sets that were not linearly separable the perceptron had to be extended into a multi-layer device – a so-called multi-layer perceptron or MLP. The stumbling block then was the lack of effective training algorithms for such devices. Renewed interest in MLPs emerged in 1986 with the popularization of a training algorithm, known as the **delta rule for learning by back propagation**, which was originally developed in 1974. This, together with hardware developments and a plethora of potential applications, has caused a resurgence of interest in the field.

The individual element in an MLP is a perceptron for two linearly separable pattern classes and it is with this device that we begin.

(14.4.1)

Perceptron for two linearly separable pattern classes

This is a simple device that uses a (fixed increment) training algorithm to evolve a linear discriminant function between two linearly separable pattern classes. The device takes as input the pattern vector x. Each input is weighted by a weight coefficient w_i and is fed into a summing device (Figure 14.12). Note that it is just a two-category version of the structure shown in Figure 14.5 where we now have just a single discriminant function and the maximum selector has been replaced with a threshold element. Thus the device implements the linear decision function

$$d(x) = \sum_{i=1}^{N} w_i x_i + w_{N+1}$$

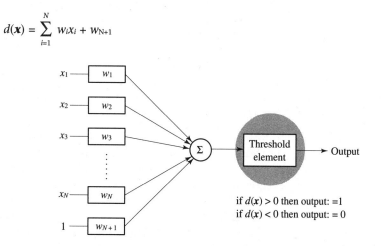

Figure 14.12
Perceptron model for two linearly separable pattern classes.

if $d(x) > 0$ then output: $= 1$
if $d(x) < 0$ then output: $= 0$

and this is a hyperplane in feature or measurement space whose orientation is determined by the first N coefficients of the weight vector $\mathbf{w}$ and whose distance from the origin is set by w_{N+1}. This sum is then tested by an element, called an activation element, to determine its sign and assign the pattern class to which $\mathbf{x}$ belongs depending on whether it is greater than or less than zero.

The training algorithm is, for linearly separable categories, guaranteed to find a separating hyperplane and it is known as the **fixed increment correction rule**. The algorithm is more easily stated if we redefine the pattern vector $\mathbf{x}$. We do this by augmenting $\mathbf{x}$ with an $(N+1)$th component of unity.

Augmented pattern vector $= \mathbf{y} = x_1, x_2, \ldots, x_N, 1$

The weighting of the pattern vector can then be written as a dot product:

$d(\mathbf{y}) = \mathbf{w}^T \mathbf{y}$

where:

$\mathbf{w} = (w_1, w_2, \ldots, w_N, w_{N+1})^T$

is called the weight vector.

The algorithm proceeds by presenting the training set (a sample from one class followed by a sample from the other) adjusting $\mathbf{w}$ if the current iteration results in an erroneous classification and stopping when a loop through the algorithm results in 100% correct classification.

Consider a training set consisting of augmented pattern vectors that are known to belong to either category ω_1 or ω_2. The algorithm is:

Assign arbitrary values to $\mathbf{w}$ (say small random numbers)

(k is the iteration number)

repeat

    for each pattern $\mathbf{y}$ in the training set

        evaluate $d^k(\mathbf{y})$

        if $d^k(\mathbf{y}) <= 0$ **and** $\mathbf{y} \in \omega_1$

        then $\mathbf{w}^{k+1} := \mathbf{w}^k + \delta\mathbf{y}$

          an_error := TRUE

          if $d^k(\mathbf{y}) >= 0$ **and** $\mathbf{y} \in \omega_2$

          then $\mathbf{w}^{k+1} := \mathbf{w}^k - \delta\mathbf{y}$

            an_error := TRUE

    until NOT(an_error)

In this algorithm δ is a fixed number in the range $0, \ldots, 1$. Thus when an complete iteration through the training sets has occurred without any adjustment to $\mathbf{w}$ the process halts and a decision function has been found. Geometrically this process is equivalent to placing a hyperplane in N-dimensional hyperspace. The hyperplane forms the boundary between the two categories and dichotomizes the measurement space. Pattern vectors lying on one side of the plane belong to one category and those on the other side belong to the other category.

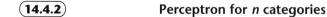

Perceptron for *n* categories

The two-category approach can be extended to a multi-category problem in which we try to find weight vectors $\boldsymbol{w}_i$, one per category, such that for all categories except $i = j$:

$$\boldsymbol{w}_i{}^T\boldsymbol{y} > \boldsymbol{w}_j{}^T\boldsymbol{y}$$

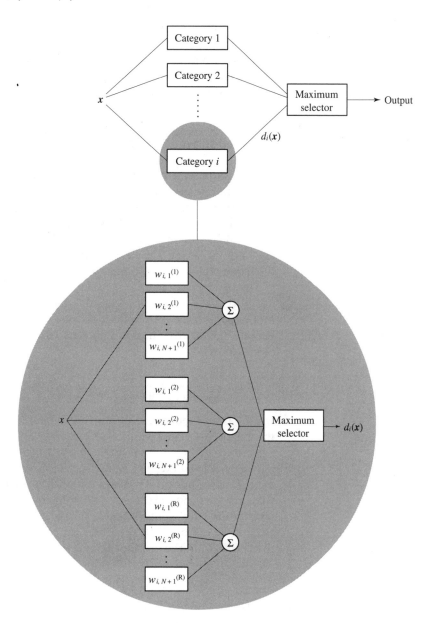

Figure 14.13
The structure of a worst case piecewise linear machine. Each category box contains R weight vectors rather than one.

for all ys belonging to the jth training set. Now we no longer have the geometric concept of a separating hyperplane, but we still have only one weight vector per class. We now have the general structure shown in Figure 14.13 where we have a maximum selector instead of a threshold element. In practical recognition problems the disposition of category clusters in measurement space may be such that we require many weight vectors per category as shown in the expanded part of the figure. Here each set of category weight vectors is implementing a collection of R hyperplanes or a single piecewise linear hyperplane per category. In the worst case we need for category i a set of weight vectors that discriminates patterns in the ith class from each of the other categories. However, with this extension many problems arise. For example, to design a training algorithm we need to know how many weight vectors to use for each category – too few may be chosen for some classes and too many for others.

14.4.3　MLP feed-forward neural nets

For our purposes a neural net or an MLP is just a device that implements the multi-category structure of Figure 14.13 by extending the two-category perceptron in such a way that the one weight vector per class constraint is avoided and where the potential difficulties associated with a training algorithm for the Figure 14.13 structure are also avoided. It does this by having a number of layers made up of nodes each of which contain a two-category perceptron, hence the name multi-layer perceptron.

The basic device used as a node in the MLP is the two-category perceptron except that the activation element, which in the case of the simple perceptron for two pattern classes outputs a –1 or a +1, is changed so that it produces a value between 0 and 1 that depends on $d(x)$. This is called a **sigmoid** function and is modelled by:

$$S(I_j) = \frac{1}{1+\exp(-(I_j + \theta_j)/\theta_0)}$$

where I_j is the input to the sigmoid unit after it has been weighted and summed by the weights associated with the jth layer. The form of the function $S(I)$ is shown in Figure 14.14. θ_j is an offset threshold and $S(I)$ gives a high response (but not 1) for any value of $I > \theta_j$ and a low value (but not 0) for a value of $I < \theta_j$. θ_0 is a shape parameter for the function. The reasons for the use of a continuous function are somewhat involved and they emerge out of the mathematical model on which the back propagation training rule is based. Full details are given in Gonzalez and Woods.

Now we can define I_j, the input pattern to every node in layer j, in terms of the output from the previous layer i:

$$I_j = \sum_i w_{ij}O_i$$

giving

Figure 14.14
The sigmoid function $S(I)$.

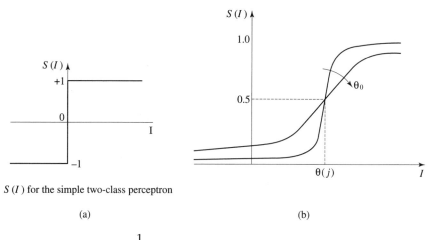

$S(I)$ for the simple two-class perceptron

(a)   (b)

$$O_j = S(I_j) = \frac{1}{1+\exp(-(\sum_i w_{ij}O_i + \theta_j)/\theta_0)}$$

We now develop an intuitive justification for MLPs and look at the shape of the hyperplane decision surfaces that can be implemented by them. Consider again the single layer perceptron. We have seen that this implements a single hyperplane and can thus only be used to discriminate between linearly separable pattern classes. In most practical pattern recognition tasks we cannot seem to invent a feature or measurement space in which pattern classes map into clusters that are linearly separable. Figure 14.15 shows two examples of pattern classes in two-dimensional space that cannot be separated by a single line. In one case the pattern clusters 'break' in feature space and in the other case the clusters 'mesh' into one another.

Consider now extending the single layer perceptron to two layers as shown in Figure 14.16. With the two perceptrons in the first layer we can implement two lines and position these anywhere in measurement space. Say for the example in Figure 14.16(a) we position these as shown. If the first layer perceptrons output

Figure 14.15
Two examples of category clusters that cannot be separated by a single decision function of a single layer perceptron.

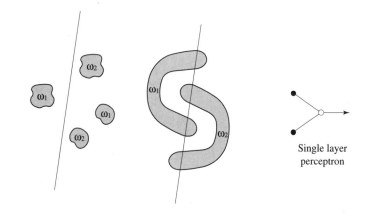

Single layer
perceptron

Figure 14.16
Two-layer perceptron can distinguish between classes in (a) but not in (b).

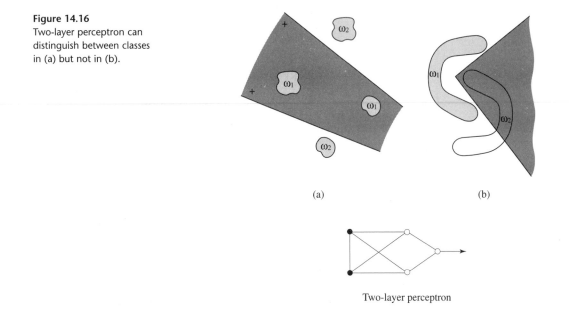

(a)   (b)

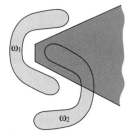

Two-layer perceptron

a 1 or 0 depending on whether the pattern falls on the positive or negative side of the decision function or line, then the inputs feeding the single perceptron in the second layer are 01, 10 and 11. Thus the perceptron in the second layer simply has to distinguish between an input of two 1's and an input of a single 1. Note that we still cannot fit a decision function for the case in Figure 14.16(b).

If we extend the number of nodes in the first layer we can implement a decision function that consists of a piecewise linear line but this is still not sufficient for the case of the meshing categories. For example, Figure 14.17 shows a possible outcome of extending the number of nodes in the input layer to three. Separation is still not possible. In fact what we need for this case is a piecewise linear line that is not restricted to being convex.

We can do this by extending the number of layers to three. Again if we consider our simple two-dimensional meshed category example, Figure 14.18 shows that discrimination can be achieved in this case by using two sets of convex piecewise linear lines, one of three segments and one of two segments. Thus by increasing the number of nodes in the first layer to five we can implement these.

Two-layer perceptron

Figure 14.17
Increasing the number of nodes cannot deal with this case.

Figure 14.18
A three-layer perceptron can implement a non-convex piecewise linear decision function.

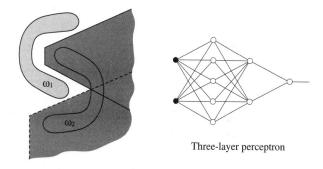

Three-layer perceptron

We are now dividing the space into three regions and the second layer makes a decision that the pattern belongs to ω_2 if it falls in either of the shaded regions bounded by the component convex piecewise linear functions. Thus we can use a three-layer perceptron to simulate or approximate non-linear, non-convex decision functions.

⟨14.4.4⟩

Back propagation algorithm

The back propagation algorithm is used for the training phase of an MLP feed-forward neural net. It is best described initially in words. In general terms it is controlled in much the same way as the fixed increment correction rule. That is, we have to adjust the weights associated with each node in such a way that the error between the actual output and the desired output is minimized. The back propagation algorithm, however, does this by calculating the error derivatives of the weights. In other words, it calculates how the error is affected for incremental changes in each weight. It can be considered as two phases:

Phase 1:
Set all weights to small arbitrary (say random) values.

Input a pattern vector y which will produce an output vector O at the output nodes.

The output vector O is compared with the desired output and a vector of error terms (the deltas of the algorithm's name) is generated.

Phase 2:
We work back through the network passing error signals backwards from layer to layer (hence the name of the algorithm) by using an error term derived for each node to influence the weight changes that are made to all weights that are connected to the node. That is, for each node in the layer or level currently being considered, we adjust all the weights that feed into that node.

We now flesh out this basic idea with some detail. Consider the penultimate layer and the output layer to be i and j respectively. The input to the output layer is then:

$$I_j = \sum_i w_{ij} O_i$$

and using a simplified sigmoid function we have:

$$O_j = \frac{1}{1 + \exp(-I_j)}$$

This enables us to define a performance or error measure as the total squared difference between the required output R_j and the actual output O_j as:

$$E_o = \frac{1}{2} \sum_j (R_j - O_j)^2$$

the sum of the squares of the node differences summed over the number of nodes. The general idea is to adjust the weights w_{ij} in such a way that the error function E_o is minimized. This is done by making the adjustment proportional to the derivative of E_o with respect to the weights. That is, the change in w_{ij} is given by:

$$w_{ij}^{k+1} - w_{ij}^{k} = -\alpha \frac{\partial E_o}{\partial w_{ij}}$$

It can be shown (see Gonzalez and Woods for a detailed derivation) that:

$$w_{ij}^{k+1} = w_{ij}^{k} + \alpha \delta_j O_i + \beta (w_{ij}^{k} - w_{ij}^{k+1})$$

where α and β are learning constants and:

$$\delta_j = \begin{cases} O_j(1 - O_j)(R_j - O_j) & \text{if } j \text{ is the output node} \\ O_i (1 - O_i) \sum_j \delta_j w_{ij} & \text{if } i \text{ is an internal layer and } j \text{ is the next to the right} \end{cases}$$

The main problem with simulating or implementing this algorithm as a program is the many hours of computing resources it can swallow. Tens of thousands of iterations may be necessary. Convergence may be very slow and it may be necessary to weaken the stopping criteria. As we stated in the summary of the algorithm at the beginning of the section, the weights w_{ij} need to be initialized throughout the network. In practice many researchers choose random values between 0.1 and 0.3 and initial values of 0.5 and 0.9 for α and β. After initialization a training pattern is presented to the network, the output is compared with the desired response and the error is propagated back through the network, adjusting the weights in each layer. A common practical implementation of this involves accumulating the δs for an entire training set, adding them and propagating back an error based on the total vector. This is called batch or epoch training. A pattern is deemed to be classified correctly if the output node associated with that pattern is high and all the other output nodes are low. In the operating phase the weights are fixed and patterns are assigned a category according to which output node is high.

14.5 Image measurements

Up to now we have looked at strategies for matching or recognizing patterns. The implication is that a pattern is an image that has been processed and segmented to produce a sub-image that comprises the pattern. We have stated that the matching or recognition may not necessarily be made on a segmented sub-image but we may adopt a strategy of extracting features or making measurements on the image. It is then this set of features or measurements that are subject to the decision-making process rather than intensity data from the original image. Any pattern recognition or image analysis context involves making measurements on image segments and in this section we will look at some of the many and varied ways of making measurements on sub-images.

We remind ourselves that the motivation for such an approach in classic pattern recognition applications is to achieve a set of measurements that represent the pattern and which are insensitive to intra-category variations; in other words, the choice or design of the measurements is to enable categorization. Image measurement applications outside the pattern recognition domain are extremely varied, as are their goals. We may want to simply count the number of cells on a photomicrograph. Alternatively we may want to make geometric measurements on each cell to determine if any abnormalities exist in the population. The type of measurements that we make depend, of course, on the application and the ones that we deal with here are those that are useful in many contexts.

Although there is no standard definition of the term 'measurement' in the context of imagery, we are usually representing shape in some way. Simple and familiar measurements such as area and elongatedness are two examples of single global measurements that may be applied to the complete pattern. Alternatively we may try to extract those features in the image that describe the nature of the image in terms of entities that are of interest to the context. Thus in the recognition of handprinted characters a goal may be to map the input patterns into a description such as: 'a semicircular curve joined to the right-hand side of a vertical stroke'. The difficulty in obtaining such descriptions is the root of the relative lack of success of many pattern recognition tasks. In the case of handprinted characters, intra-category variations are as many and varied as the human beings who write them. The problem appears to be due to the fact that although we appear to have an immediate intuitive notion of shape, categorizing or quantifying shape seems to be very difficult. Making measurements on an image can be seen as an information reduction process. We generally want to reduce the quantity of low-level information in the original intensity image by grouping pixels together into structures that have significance to the task in hand. Thus we can say that any categorization of the shape of an image segment will form part of a continuum at one end of which is a representation of the segment (for example, a list of boundary elements) and which at the other end is a simple global measurement such as area.

Probably the most common measurement categories are:

- Methods that are representations of the input image – for example, we may segment an object, subject it to boundary following, then represent the coordinates of the boundary pixels in some way. Alternatively we may represent the segment by a transformation of itself – the medial axis transformation, or skeleton, is an example of this. These methods carry the implication that they are to some extent reversible. The original image can, to some extent, be recovered from the representation.

- Methods that make geometrical measurements – for example, we may assume that all segmented objects in the image conform to an elliptical shape and find the lengths of the major and minor axes of each object. Alternatively we may enclose the object in a bounding box and categorize the shape of the box. These methods are irreversible; there is no possibility of recovering the image on which the measurement was made.

The measurements themselves will posses attributes such as: they may be invariant to translation, rotation and scale transformations in the segmented objects – the ideal requirement in optical character recognition.

Simple measurements of shape depend on the entire object being visible. They are global measurements of the object. This will be the case in character recognition, but in many industrial processes involving flat parts occlusion occurs and non-global measurements must be made on that part of the object that is visible.

Most simple shape descriptors are sensitive to scale. Scale changes occur either because the size of the object of interest varies or because its projected size on the image plane varies. The first category should cause pure magnification but the second causes shape changes which simple geometric descriptors will capture. As the sampling resolution decreases the pixel shape starts to interfere with the shape of the object resulting in a loss of information. Here we are doing no more than rewording the undersampling problem – it is obvious that problems will occur as the number of pixels representing an image segment is reduced. At the other end of the sampling continuum noise problems can occur and the shape description can capture or reflect excursions in shape which are simply due to noise.

(14.5.1)

Boundary-based measurements and descriptions

Using boundary information to categorize or describe shapes seems natural, providing that we are dealing with a problem that is essentially two-dimensional, such as the recognition of characters, the recognition of the orientation of flat machine parts in an industrial process, and so on. Although we could just as well choose to represent the segmented object by categorizing, in some way, the internal region of the object, much more work has been carried out on boundary representations. In most contexts the properties that we are interested in depend directly on shape rather than 'internal' attributes that may depend on the object surface reflectivity or texture and this is why there is a concentration of effort on boundary information. If there is no interest in such internal variations, then working with a boundary gives a substantial reduction in information while retaining all the information of interest. We are saying essentially that in many, if not most, two-dimensional problems we can consider only the boundary information. Note that in the case of three-dimensional object recognition the boundary of the object's projection – its silhouette edge – is not generally a reliable or sufficient representation of the object.

Boundary representations are ubiquitous, being commonly used in two-dimensional computer graphics applications, and prior to the advent of raster graphics devices, the machines that produced the images – calligraphic CRTs and incremental plotters – worked directly from the boundary representations by drawing small vectors from a list representing a boundary or contour of the object to be visualized.

Most ways of representing boundaries simply map the list of pixel coordinates into a form that exhibits some advantage such as economy, invariance to scale and rotation of the object, and resistance to noise excursions, all of which assist the efficacy of the shape measurements which may be then made on the boundary list.

⟨14.5.2⟩ **Chain codes**

Chain encoding of a boundary is one of the earliest forms of boundary representation and involves encoding the boundary pixels as directions using four or eight connectivity relationships between consecutive elements in the list as shown in the example in Figure 14.19. To reduce the effects of noise, the main problem with chain codes, the boundary information can be resampled at a coarser resolution but this, of course, reduces the accuracy of the resolution. This is just a restatement of the fact that the main problem with boundary detection is noise: when is a small excursion in a boundary noise and when is it a genuine part of the outline of the object? In its basic form, the chain code depends on

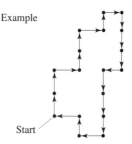

Example

Direction convention

Chain code: 110110103332333212
Derivative: 303103133003100331

Start

Figure 14.19
Chain code convention for boundary elements.

the starting point and to ensure that the same code is always obtained for the same shape, we can consider the chain elements as a circular sequence, and move the start point so that the sequence forms an integer of minimum magnitude (considering the chain as a base four integer). Rotational invariance can be achieved by constructing a 'derivative' code from the initial code. In a derivative code the difference between pairs of consecutive elements is calculated and the subtrahends replace the absolute direction elements.

The success of these normalizations depends on the noise in the original boundary list, and its sensitivity to noise is the main disadvantage of the chain code scheme.

Univariate functions of boundaries

A common technique for categorizing boundary information is to transform it into a function of a single variable. Again the motivation is the ease of normalizing unwanted variations such as scale, rotation and translation together with the reduction in dimensionality which should simplify any recognition procedure.

Such descriptions are sometime called signatures and the simplest is obtained by mapping boundary points into an $r(\theta)$ representation where r is the distance from the centroid of a shape and θ the angle between r and a reference direction. Figure 14.20 shows a simple example. Invariant to translation an $r(\theta)$ representation can be normalized for rotation by shifting the function until the maximum value is positioned at $\theta = 0$, assuming that such a unique point exists. Scale normalization can be achieved by, for example, scaling the function so that the amplitude values are mapped into the range [0,1]. An alternative signature can be computed by plotting the angle that the tangent to the boundary curve makes, with respect to a reference direction, as a function of position around the boundary.

Fourier descriptors of boundary information have been used in such contexts as handprinted character recognition. The method used retains the usual Fourier domain attribute of mapping image detail into high frequency components

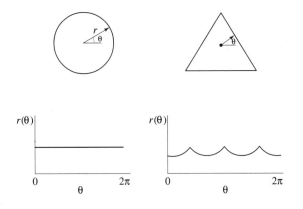

Figure 14.20
$r(\theta)$ for two boundary shapes.

while the basic shape information is transformed into low frequency components. In the context of handprinted characters we presume that the intra-category variations are contained in detailed variations of a standard basic shape. The hope is that the underlying shape uniqueness of the character is mapped into low frequency components and the unwanted intra-category variations into high frequency components. It is important to bear in mind that we are not considering a two-dimensional transformation of the image where consideration of low frequency components only just gives us a blurred version of the original. With the one-dimensional transform of the ordered boundary elements we are using as input information the boundary shape of the character. Consideration of the low frequency components in this case results in a kind of 'shape blurring' rather than a global blurring of the entire pattern.

A one-dimensional Fourier transform is calculated by considering the boundary information to form a complex sequence. That is, the image x and y axes are considered as the real and imaginary axes for the purpose of the Fourier transform. The (x,y) coordinates of the boundary points become the function:

$$b(n) = x(n) + j\, y(n)$$

The input to the transform then consists of a one-dimensional sequence of complex numbers. The Fourier descriptors possess the following properties:

- Translation – translation of all the boundary points by the same amount. The Fourier descriptors remain the same except for the value at the origin.

- Scaling – shrinking or expanding the boundary. The Fourier descriptors are scaled in the same way. That is, a scaling factor S applied to $b(n)$ results in the descriptors being multiplied by the same factor.

- Rotation – rotation of the boundary points by an angle results in a constant phase shift in the phase spectrum of the Fourier descriptors and no change in the amplitude spectrum.

Figure 14.21 shows an example of this technique that demonstrates the way in which shape details map into the Fourier domain.

Another obvious approach to boundary representation is to emulate the polygonal approximation strategy in computer graphics and represent an image segment with a polygon – sometimes called a polyline. The problem is to represent an image segment by allotting a polygon with a number of edges sufficient to represent the shape, without being influenced by small excursions that are due to noise. Thus the problem is to find the vertices of the polygon. (Note that a chain code is already a polygon or polyline at limiting resolution.)

A simple way to do this is to invoke a straightness criterion between a segment formed between the current point and several points ahead and the segment formed between the current point and the last vertex found. When the straightness falls below a threshold then the current point becomes a vertex.

A variation on this idea is a tolerance-based approach. In this scheme, a maximum tolerable error is decided on and used to construct a pair of parallel lines

Figure 14.21
In this illustration descriptors are formed by considering the (x,y) coordinates of the boundary points to be the real and imaginary parts of a complex number. The sequence of boundary points forms a sequence of complex numbers which are then used as the input of a one-dimensional Fourier transform. The figures are reconstructed from the Fourier descriptor/transform by including more and more frequency components (m), and show the way in which shape detail is mapped into higher components. (Courtesy of R.C. Gonzalez and R.E. Woods.) *Source*: Gonzalez, R.C. and R.E. Woods (1992) *Digital Image Processing*, Menlo Park, Calif.: Addison Wesley Longman

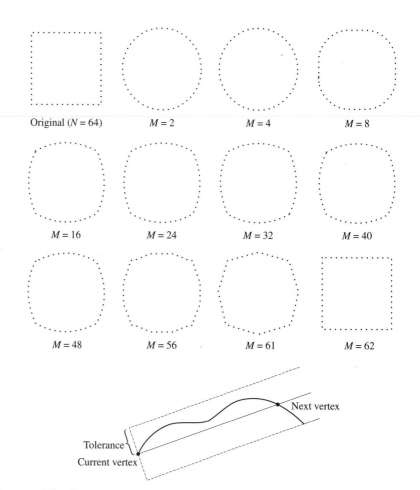

Figure 14.22
Finding a piecewise linear approximation to a curve. A pair of parallel lines, appropriately oriented and equidistant from the current vertex, are defined.

that straddle the curve (Figure 14.22). The longest possible line is then found that lies between the parallel lines, and this defines the next polygon segment. These approaches make one pass thorough the boundary list and allocate vertices which may not be in the best position. Gonzalez and Woods report a more robust technique that segments the boundary. This involves first finding the convex hull of the segment which we deal with in the next section.

 14.5.4

Enclosing image segments

The three most common enclosures are the bounding rectangle, the minimum bounding rectangle and the convex hull (Figure 14.23). The standard analogy of a convex hull is that it is the figure formed when we stretch an elastic band around the boundary – it is the 'minimum' convex figure that encloses the object. A less common one is the convex deficiency, whose definition should be apparent from the figure. The bounding rectangle can be found quickly from the

Figure 14.23
Enclosing an image
segment and segmenting
a boundary.
(a) Bounding box
(b) Minimum bounding box
(c) Convey hull
(d) Convex deficiency
(e) Segmenting the
boundary

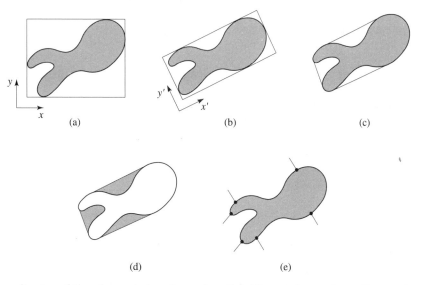

coordinates of the elements in a boundary list. The minimum bounding rectangle is the smallest rectangle enclosing the object that is also aligned with the orientation θ which is a moment-based feature (Section 14.5.5). When it is known we can apply the following transformation to the boundary elements:

$$x' = x \cos \theta + y \sin\theta$$
$$y' = -x \sin\theta + y \cos\theta$$

Searching for the maximum and minimum in x' and y' now gives the intersections of the sides of the minimum enclosing rectangle with the x' and y' axes.

A convex hull can be evaluated using mathematical morphology (Chapter 13) or by using a classic algorithm due to Aki and Toussaint (1978). An example of this algorithm working is shown in Figure 14.24. A brief description follows:

(1) Given a set of points characterizing a region or a set of boundary points, the extreme points, E_1, E_2, E_3 and E_4 in the x and y directions are determined.

(2) This defines a quadrilateral. All points inside this region are deleted from further consideration.

(3) The extreme points F_1, F_2, F_3 and F_4 in the two diagonal directions are determined and all points inside the triangular regions formed by E_i, F_i, E_{i+1} are deleted.

(4) The remaining points are sorted by their x coordinates in ascending order (if they are in R_1 or R_2) and in descending order (if they are in R_3 or R_4).

(5) This gives an ordering for the vertices of a polygon that includes these remaining points from which the convex hull polygon can be obtained.

The convex deficiency – the difference between the convex hull and the image segment – can then be calculated and compared with the boundary list. The excursion of a boundary point into or out of a convex deficiency area defines points at

Figure 14.24
The Aki-Toussaint algorithm
for finding a convex hull.

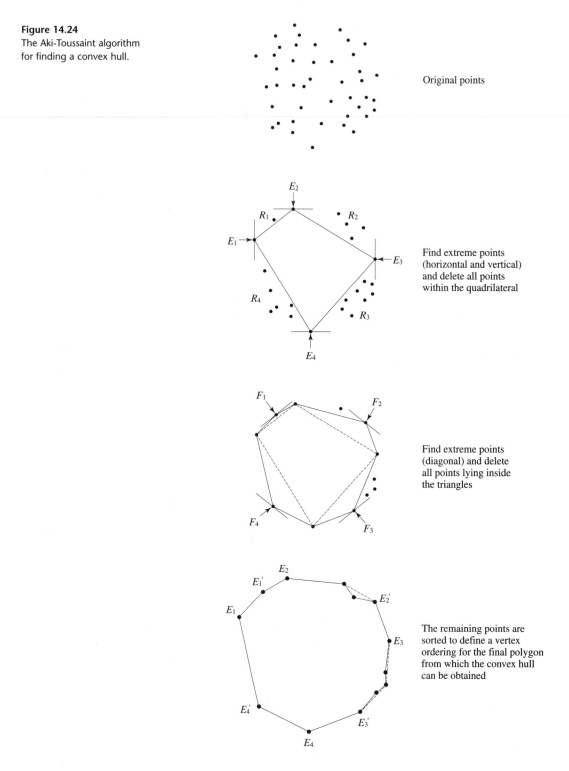

Original points

Find extreme points
(horizontal and vertical)
and delete all points
within the quadrilateral

Find extreme points
(diagonal) and delete
all points lying inside
the triangles

The remaining points are
sorted to define a vertex
ordering for the final polygon
from which the convex hull
can be obtained

which the boundary should be segmented (Figure 14.23). Global properties of the convex hull and its deficiency can be used as region descriptors (the topic of the next section). For example, the area of the convex hull compared to the area of the convex deficiency, the number of parts in the convex deficiency, and so on.

14.5.5 Region-based measurements and descriptions

At the lowest level a region is described by a list of pixels that it comprises. In this form, as we have discussed, it is not particularly useful for the purposes of recognition. Most common region-based descriptors are global. Simple obvious examples are area and perimeter length and combinations of such parameters. Such measurements cannot effectively describe the nature of complex shapes and do not carry any possibility of reconstruction of image segments. It is in this sense that they differ from representations from which some reconstruction of the image segments can be achieved. In other words, they tend to be measurements rather than representations. We start by considering the most common global shape measurements:

Global shape measurements

(1) **Area of a segment**   This most familiar measure is obtained by:

    (a)   counting the number of pixels in the segment

    (b)   from a polygonal representation:

$$\text{area} = \frac{1}{2} \left| \sum_{k=0}^{n-1} (i_k j_{k+1} - i_{k+1} j_k) \right|$$

    where (i_k, j_k) is the kth vertex in the list of n polygon vertices

    (c)   from a chain code (four-connectivity) representation by the following algorithm:

        area := 0; vert_postn := x-coordinate_of(start postn);

        for each element in the code

            if code = 0 **then** area := area − vert_postn

            if code = 1 **then** vert_postn := vert_postn + 1

            if code = 2 **then** area := area + vert_postn

            if code = 3 **then** vert_postn := vert_postn − 1

(2) **Eccentricity of a segment**   The eccentricity (Figure 14.25) is simply the ratio of the length of the longest chord (A) to the length of the longest chord perpendicular to A.

(3) **Elongatedness of a segment**   The intuitive notion of elongatedness is quantified by the aspect ratio of the minimum bounding rectangle. Note that this measurement is useless if the segment curves in the sense of a

Figure 14.25
Simple shape
measurements.

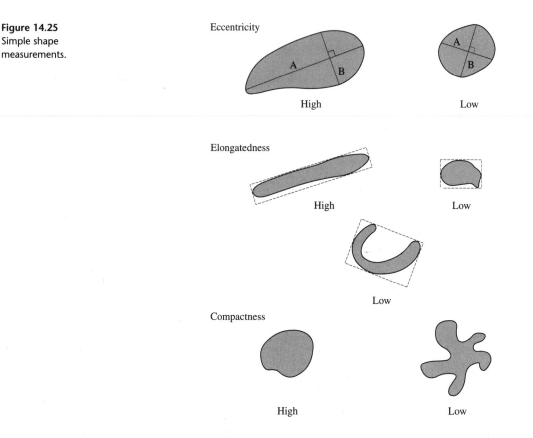

letter C. A related measure is **rectangularity** which is the ratio of the area of the image segment to the area of the minimum bounding rectangle.

(4) Compactness Compactness is the ratio of the square of the boundary length to the area of the segment, giving for a circular shape – the most compact region – a value of 4π.

Moments

Moments can be used to describe image segments by considering pixels in the region to be point bodies of unity mass. We can then define the centre of mass as:

$$\bar{x} = \frac{1}{N} \sum_{(x,y)} \sum_{\in R} x \qquad \bar{y} = \frac{1}{N} \sum_{(x,y)} \sum_{\in R} y$$

for a region R of N pixels. The (p,q) order central moment is defined by:

$$\mu_{pq} = \frac{1}{N} \sum_{(x,y)} \sum_{\in R} (x - \bar{x})^p (y - \bar{y})^q$$

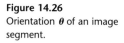

Figure 14.26
Orientation θ of an image
segment.

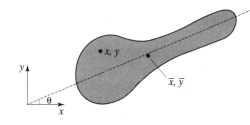

Rotation, scale and translation invariant measurements can be derived from normalized combinations of central moments.

Orientation of an image segment, which can be used to find the minimum bounding rectangle, is obtained by finding the least moment of inertia, that is, by minimizing with respect to θ (Figure 14.26):

$$\sum_{(x,y)\,\in R}\sum ((x - \overline{x})\cos\theta \,(y - \overline{y})\sin\theta)^2$$

which gives

$$\theta = \frac{1}{2}\,\tan^{-1}\left[\frac{2\mu_{1,1}}{\mu_{2,0} - \mu_{0,2}}\right]$$

Moments can also be defined by considering the region grey scale values, but the corresponding measures no longer have a geometric interpretation with respect to the shape of the region.

14.5.6 ### Skeleton or medial axis transform

The skeleton of a region can be considered as an alternative representation to the boundary. Like the boundary it is non-trivial to compute and it is also sensitive to noise excursions in the boundary. Also known as the medial axis transform, it is defined as follows. For each point in the region, we find the closest boundary point. If, for any point, it has more than one closest in the boundary set, then this point lies on the skeleton of the region. Therein lies the major disadvantage of this representation – its high computational cost.

An alternative geometric interpretation and an algorithm for deriving the skeleton of an image region is given in Chapter 13. A skeleton (which will not necessarily be the same as the medial axis transform) can be obtained by using a thinning algorithm as described in Chapter 13. Although skeletons are to be found in most textbooks, they do not seem to have met with much practical success. The problem is not just that they are sensitive to noise, but that they produce a description that is 'structurally' more complicated than the original region – albeit that the representation uses much less information. An example is given in Figure 13.8 which shows that the skeleton of an H object consists of 15 line segments – whereas we would conceive of the object as being made of a structure with three components.

14.6 Decomposition of regions

We can deduce that the above simple shape descriptors are inadequate when a complex shape is to be described. Returning to our representation versus measurement argument, we need to represent complicated shapes in some way, rather than make global measurements on them. An obvious approach is to subject a region to further decomposition. We could call this internal segmentation and it means that we need to further segment the region in a way that will fully represent the complexity of the shape. We may then categorize the segmented parts with global measurements. This segmentation is distinct from the general segmentation techniques that we considered in Chapter 12, where the segmentation was performed according to, for example, low-level image criteria like similarity of intensity. A simple example illustrates the idea in Figure 14.27. Here the original image is a segmented handprinted character. We might decide that a good feature extraction strategy for recognizing such characters is to further segment the character into three regions representing the horizontal and two vertical strokes. The essence of the shape of the character can then be represented by some structure that specifies this information together with the spatial relationship between the components. The crux of the matter here is to perform the region decomposition. Relatively straightforward for machine printed characters, the wild variations that occur in handprinted characters pose a challenge.

Decomposition of a skeleton representation can be achieved by categorizing its points. In particular it can be mapped directly into a graph representation. If the medial axis definition is used then a minimum radius circle whose centre is on the skeleton point and which just touches a boundary point can be drawn. (See Figure 13.8 for a simple illustration.) If a such a circle is drawn for each skeleton point, then skeleton points can be categorized according to whether they touch one boundary point (an end point), two boundary points (a normal point) or three boundary points (a node point). Graph node points can then be the end points and node points and two graph nodes are connected if the equivalent skeleton points are connected by a set of normal points in the skeleton.

Figure 14.27
(a) The image of a handpainted F after segmentation.
(b) Decomposition of the segmented region.

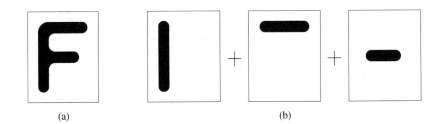

(a)   (b)

Real-time strategies – the recognition of handwriting

In the 1990s we have seen the consolidation of the graphical user interface or GUI. The inertia of this methodology has meant that outside the research laboratory there is little attention paid to alternative interface techniques. Despite its limitation – as a device which can do little more than function as a pick and drag – the use of the mouse is now as ubiquitous as the keyboard and an earlier, potentially more powerful device – the graphic tablet – has been almost totally ignored. A strange situation, given that the GUI was developed as a desktop metaphor and a writing stylus is a common part of any desktop. In Chapter 20 we further discuss the potential role of computer imagery in alternative interfaces; in this section we will look at how pattern recognition techniques can benefit from the real-time information available from a virtual pen – a stylus moving across some kind of sensitive surface that outputs a continuous stream of coordinates as the stylus is moved across it. The use of stylus devices, outside of special applications, and the development of recognition techniques for such applications as the input of cursive script fell into abeyance in the 1970s but has recently enjoyed a resurgence of interest. Offline recognition of handwriting has long been felt to be an extremely difficult task but the use of real-time information brings it into the realm of possibility. Another potential application of this kind of recognition technology is the input of sketches and diagrams. A recent hardware development, related to the graphics tablet, and which may encourage the popularity of handwriting and drawing input, is a combination of an input and an output device in the same facility. Sometimes known as 'electronic ink', the user writes on a flat panel and a visible trace of the stylus motion immediately appears under the tip.

The real-time information available from such devices adds the dimension of time to the pattern and this can be exploited simply as a sequence of points in two-dimensional space – a position time model. Alternatively it has been suggested that for cursive script recognition, measuring the velocity and acceleration of the strikes as they are generated can result in measurements that diminish the variations that an individual will make when writing the same section of script at different times.

Let us look first at an early (1968) example by Bernstein that uses position time information, embellished with some velocity information, that uses the occurrence of a corner feature to recognize hand block-printed characters. Figure 14.28 demonstrates the idea. Maximum/minimum coordinates are determined from the list of coordinates output by the stylus/tablet device and the sample points are enclosed by a minimum area rectangle divided into five labelled regions. This enables a simple code, such as the code shown for the example **G**, to be produced quickly and easily. The code also contains corner occurrences where a corner is detected by the change in direction of the path formed by consecutive points sweeping through some angle approaching 90 degrees. (A corner detection is also reinforced by a decrease in the local velocity of the path.) These descriptions are mapped into 'strokes' and then applied to a dictionary in the

Figure 14.28
Real-time information and character recognition (after Bernstein (1968)).

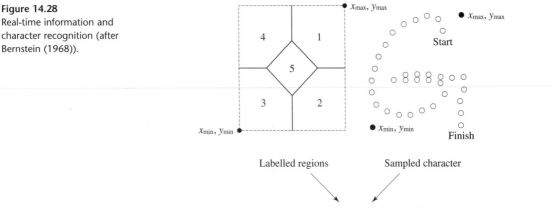

Code produced 1 4 3 2 5 3 (corner) 5 2 (corner)

form of a tree in which only the legitimate successor strokes are linked to a given stroke at each level. A vertical down-stroke followed by a curve nearby and north-east of the first stroke is classified as a **P**.

Such a simple system performs extremely well and should be compared with the processing that would have to be done offline to skeletonize or stylize the printed character. (Although it is apparent that unwanted information is also provided by a real-time system. Consider the many ways of printing an **E** in terms of the number of strokes used and their order of writing. This information is, of course, lost in the static image.)

The real-time recognition of cursive script or handwriting has proved to be as difficult as continuous speech recognition and predictably it is the segmentation problem in both applications that has proved to be the main difficulty. In cursive script, groups of letters or even whole words are formed by a single continuous stroke; segmenting the pattern prior to the recognition of individual characters is extremely difficult, if not impossible, and this observation has led to strategies that look at the whole word rather than individual characters. (This is not surprising – much handwriting is indecipherable to human beings if contextual clues are removed. It seems obvious that we do not recognize individual characters but the word as a whole.)

Practical systems require a user to perform segmentation and adopt a style of one stroke per letter. This situation also currently exists in practical speech recognition systems where the speaker uses a clipped single word utterance mode of speech.

An approach that has similarities to CAD-based vision (Chapter 15) is called analysis by synthesis. In CAD-based vision we use an explicit model of an object to synthesize a projection – a hypothesis. In analysis by synthesis in pattern recognition we use a parametrized or mathematical model that can generate a pattern that is similar to the one to be recognized. The values of the parameters produce a likeness to the pattern that then enables us to classify it. The hope is that when a human writes a word, the parameters that describe the physical process of performing this act are simpler than any description that we could obtain by looking (offline) at an image of the word. This implies a process that generates test patterns and homes in on a pattern that is similar if not identical to the input pattern. That this approach seems feasible at all is due to the fact that we have from the input sensor a coarse two-dimensional space curve parametrized in time. We have a pattern that is represented in a way that depends on the underlying neuro-muscular process used by the human writer. This is what we are dealing with, rather than the image of ink on paper.

An early, and oft quoted, analysis by synthesis approach was reported by Eden in 1962. In this work and other similar approaches, a handwritten word is segmented into a set of strokes. This might be done, for example, by obtaining the horizontal and vertical components of the pen's velocity over the paper and defining a stroke as a segment of the curve between the instants that the vertical velocity is equal to zero. Having performed this segmentation, each stroke is then matched against two quarter wave sinusoidal generators by adjusting the phase and frequency of each component. The model equations are:

$$\dot{x}(t) = \alpha_1 \sin[\omega_1(t - t_0) + \phi_1] + \gamma$$

$$\dot{x}(t) = \alpha_2 \sin[\omega_2(t_2 - t) + \phi_2] + \gamma$$

$$\dot{y}(t) = \beta \sin[\omega_1(t - t_0)]$$

$$\dot{y}(t) = \beta \sin[\omega_2(t_2 - t)]$$

In this way, because the generated strokes now match the actual strokes, the actual strokes are parametrized by the values required to match the stroke and

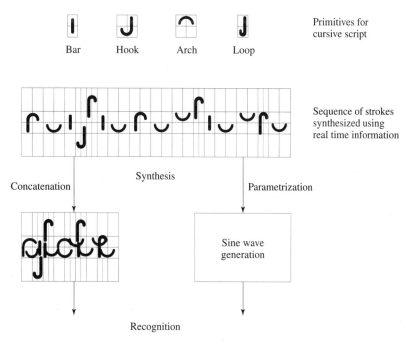

Primitives for cursive script

Bar   Hook   Arch   Loop

Sequence of strokes synthesized using real time information

Concatenation   Synthesis   Parametrization

Sine wave generation

Recognition

Figure 14.29
Eden's analysis by synthesis approach for real-time recognition of cursive script. A description is generated/synthesized by a combination of concatenating the segmented strokes and matching their parameters according to a sine wave generation (based on an illustration by Eden (1962)).

these parameter values enable word recognition. Figure 14.29, an example from Eden's work, shows a sequence of strokes for the word 'globe'. In this way handwritten words are transformed into a sequence of idealized, classified strokes. The precise way in which the word is 'expanded' into a sequence of strokes as shown in the illustration is governed by a set of stroke concatenation rules that depend of local conditions.

A modern variation of this technique due to Williams et al. uses elastic matching. Here a set of prototype characters are stored using spline-based models or prototypes. (An example of the synthesis of handprinted characters using splines was given in Figure 14.9.) The amount of effort that is required to 'pull' the unknown character into the shape of each prototype is then measured and the character is characterized according to that prototype category for which the least 'energy' was expended in deforming the unknown character. It is a version of the deformable template approach (Section 14.3.1) particularized for character recognition.

Further reading

There have been many texts written on pattern recognition techniques in the past three decades, the ones listed here are a small selection. The classic early text on perceptron-like structures is the book by Nilsson. There has been a recent explosion in the literature published on neural nets; the book by Rummelhart and McClelland is the reference for the back propagation algorithm.

Papers

Aki S.G. and Toussaint G.T. (1978). Efficient convex hull agorithms for pattern recognition algorithms. In *Proc. 4th Int. Pattern Recognition Conf.*, Kyoto, Japan, 1978

Bernstein M.I. (1968). A method for recognizing handprinted characters in real time. In *Pattern Recognition* (ed. L.N. Kanal), Washington DC: Thompson Book Co.

Eden M. (1962). Handwriting and pattern recognition. *IRE Trans. Inform. Theory*, **IT-8**

Fischler M.A. and Elschlager R.A. (1973). The representation and matching of pictorial structures. *IEEE. Trans. Computers*, **22**, January, 69–77

Kass M., Witkin A. and Terzopoulos D. (1987). Snakes: active contour models. *Int. J. Comput. Vision*, **1**, 321–31

Tappert C.T., Suen C.Y. and Wakahara T. (1990). The state of the art in on-line handwriting recognition. *IEEE Transactions on Pattern Analysis and Machine Intelligence*, **12**(8), August

Williams C.K.I., Revow M.D. and Hinton G.E. (1993). Hand-printed digit recognition using deformable models. In *Spatial Vision in Humans and Robots* (ed. Harris, L. and Jenkin, M.), pp. 127–47. Cambridge: Cambridge University Press

Yuille A.L., Cohen D.S. and Halliman P.W. (1989). Feature extraction from faces using deformable templates. *IEEE Proc. of CVPR*, San Diego, 1989, pp. 104–9

Books

Bow S.T. (1992). *Pattern Recognition and Image Processing*. New York: Marcel Dekker

Duda R.O. and Hart P.E. (1973). *Pattern Classification and Scene Analysis*. New York: Wiley

Fu K.S. (1974). *Syntactic Methods in Pattern Recognition*. New York: Academic Press

Nilsson N.J. (1965). *Learning Machines: Foundations of Trainable Pattern-Classifying Systems*. New York: McGraw-Hill

Rummelhart D.E. and McClelland J.L. (1986). *Parallel Distributed Processing: Explorations of the Microstructure of Cognition*. Cambridge, MA: MIT Press

Tou J.T. and Gonzalez R.C. (1974). *Pattern Recognition Principles*. Reading, MA: Addison-Wesley

15 Towards recognition, understanding and description of three-dimensional scenes

15.1 Using knowledge – hypothesizing and testing

15.2 Special representational models used in computer vision

15.3 Example approaches – systems dealing with two-dimensional data

15.4 Example approaches – systems dealing with range data

We will see in the Shape from X chapter (Chapter 16) that deriving or recovering information from projections of general scenes is difficult and many methods are experimental. Many constraints on the nature of the illumination and the reflective behaviour of the surfaces are necessary.

We can view these approaches as bottom-up techniques involving no top-down or goal-driven strategies. Raw image data is processed and we expect to reduce the data in such a way that we can extract useful information concerning, for example, shape from the projection. We attempt to 'integrate' pixel information into structural information. There are no constraints on the nature or type of object that we deal with.

Alternatively we can view Shape from X strategies as image processing techniques that convert a two-dimensional projection into a three-dimensional form like a dense range image where every pixel has a depth assigned to it. We then suppose that extracting the information that we require, such as: is object A present and if so what is its position and orientation?, is possible with some further (rudimentary) procedure. Shape from X strategies, as we discuss in Chapter 16, have met with only limited success, and the other mainstream approach that has been pursued in computer vision is the use of a priori information in the form of geometric models or descriptions to assist in the interpretation of information in two-dimensional projections of a scene.

We can describe the idea in the most general terms as: given knowledge of the objects that we are likely to encounter in some form of structured way – a geometric model – can we use this information to deal with a three-dimensional scene made up of such objects? Can we use such models to determine the orientation of the object with respect to the viewpoint – what is its pose? Explicit knowledge of pose may be required, not only to recognize any projection of an object, but, for example, in robot vision where the machine and/or the vision facility needs to interact with the scene.

Compare this idea with the template matching approach of classic pattern recognition (Chapter 14). There we store a priori knowledge of patterns that we expect to encounter as a set of measurements that are representative of a category and are reasonably immune to intra-category variations. The recognition problem in two-dimensional contexts is generally seen as segmentation of a sub-image of interest from the main image followed by application – in two-dimensional space – of some heuristic that enables us to compare a priori knowledge with the sub-image. Because our operations are constrained to two-dimensional space, such simple strategies as template matching and its multifarious extensions are easy and obvious approaches.

The (potentially) infinite number of intra-category variations that result from the different projections of a three-dimensional object and the addition of other problems such as occlusion by other objects means that we cannot economically store a representative measurement set of projections. We need to store a description that is capable of generating the version of the object that we can observe in the image under examination. In this way we hope to bring the problem within the domain of a two-dimensional matching problem.

Most of the material in this chapter is an examination of important past and promising current methods. These form only a small selection of the vast amount of work that has been carried out in this area in the past two decades. Studying these examples will give a good feel for the nature of the problem, the underlying general principles that are employed and the complexity of the problem. A good reflection of its complexity is the fact that many books exist which are devoted in their entirety to describing a single system. Although some theoretical principles are specific to particular methodologies, general principles should emerge from the examples. This treatment of the subject is, we feel, a reflection of the state of the art of three-dimensional object recognition.

15.1 Using knowledge – hypothesizing and testing

The most common strategy for using stored knowledge in computer vision is called hypothesizing and testing. Here we try to match an input image from a real scene with an image generated from our stored knowledge. Usually this matching process will not take place at a pixel level and we generally try to match structures extracted from the image with structures generated from our object database.

As you would expect, knowledge about objects is stored in the form of geometric information and models or descriptions similar or identical to those used in computer graphics are employed (although there are important representations that are unique to computer vision, which are described in Section 15.2). The problem then becomes, for example, describing or classifying a scene when it is reduced (edge enhanced, say) to something like a scene produced by a wire-frame renderer in computer graphics. The description of the object is capable of producing an infinity of wireframe projections of the object as a computer graphics image; so given an extracted wireframe image of a real scene, we should be able to describe it in terms of our stored geometric models. Of course, the idea immediately restricts us to considering scenes that are capable of being described by the models. This may not be too much of a restriction in an industrial environment but would be a long way from being able to analyze everyday scenes that human beings deal with easily.

It is thus both a bottom-up and a top-down approach. We apply low-level processing to produce some structural version of the image, such as, for example, an edge image or a dense range image. With such an image we then use a knowledge base or structured or geometric model of information to try to make sense of the scene. In this way we attempt to bridge the chasm between the raw two-dimensional image data and our three-dimensional geometric knowledge of objects in the scene. Of course, the two approaches are not independent of each other. We have to use the model information in a way which both encapsulates our geometric knowledge and makes demands on the required bottom-up processing which are achievable. In other words, we use high-level information to try to make sense of the low-level information flowing from the image, a situation depicted in Figure 15.1. This shows low-level scene information subject to primitive extraction producing a description in terms of some extracted structure where the structure is more apparent or accessible than the input image. At the same time a description is generated in terms of the same primitives from the object database. The hypothesis and the real image are then compared. Figure 15.2 shows two important elaborations of this structure. First, we note that part of the hypothesis generation may be done offline. We may have available a 'standard' computer graphics description such as a polygon mesh structure from which we require another description that is used to generate a hypothesis for matching. An example, described shortly, is where we generate an aspect graph of the object. We will usually have an indexing strategy (unless we are only looking for a single object) where extracted primitives index the database to find those objects that contain a particular primitive. We may use the model descriptions themselves to guide or assist the primitive extraction process.

Figure 15.1
A mainstream CV approach.

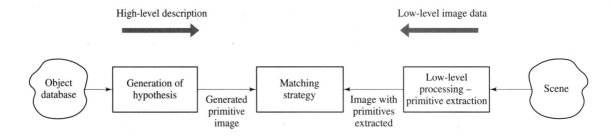

High-level description

Low-level image data

| Object database | → | Generation of hypothesis | → Generated primitive image → | Matching strategy | ← Image with primitives extracted ← | Low-level processing – primitive extraction | ← | Scene |

Figure 15.2
Elaborations to basic
structure of Figure 15.1.

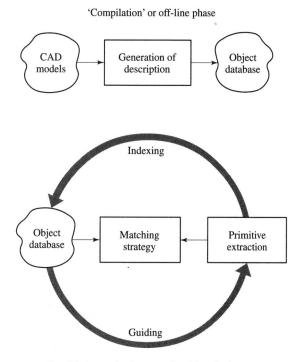

Possible interaction between the object database
and the primitive extraction

We note that there are three basic attributes that such systems will posses:

- **knowledge representation**: what primitives are going to be used to represent the object and how this representation is structured;

- **primitive extraction**: whatever primitives are used have to be extracted from the image;

- **matching domain**: usually matching is carried out at a higher level than the basic primitives. Thus, for example, lines may be grouped into faces or vertices. Faces can be grouped into volume primitives.

Because this approach may use computer graphics-type models that are readily available in industrial applications it is called CAD-based vision. The physical constraints used in such environments can also be used to simplify the vision problem. For example, a common vision application is to determine the pose and identity of objects travelling on flat conveyor belts. Here the degrees of freedom of the pose is reduced from 6 to 3 and it may be, depending on the shape of the object, that it can only take up certain poses – stable poses – when lying on a flat surface.

Thus we can see computer vision as a methodology that in part employs the same image generation strategies as computer graphics. We may synthesize some two-dimensional projection of the image from a geometric model and compare this stylization with the real image. This is sometimes called hypothesizing and testing. We hypothesize that an object exists in the image and estimate its view parameters using some heuristic. We can then use these to generate a projection from the stored object model and look for correspondence, again using some heuristic, between the projection of the model and the real projection.

The type of models that are used are in the main identical or similar to those used in computer graphics as we describe in Chapter 2. The factors that are involved in the choice of a particular representational scheme are also similar to those involved in computer graphics. We may require a model that reflects a (hierarchical) structure of the object. We may require a model that is capable of generating a projection efficiently at any scale, and so on.

With such an approach we expect to be able to output information like: object A is present. It is upside down and three metres from the camera. Alternatively we would expect to be able to output descriptions in terms of geometric primitives such as: an object is present. It is made up of a pyramid placed on top of a rectangular solid.

Two important factors are implied here. The type of scenes that we can approach with such a strategy are more or less the same as those that we can generate in computer graphics. We do not have models that efficiently describe, and therefore efficiently generate, projections of many objects that exist in reality. This is particularly true of complex natural objects like trees. The strategy is a long way from a general vision system, like that possessed by humans, for example. We can only output descriptions of fairly simple structures that we have stored as a geometric model.

Dickenson et al. in a typical application of the CAD-based vision approach identify six interacting design factors that are involved in such systems. They discuss these from the point of view of the complexity of the indexing primitive – the unit that is used to access the object database to identify objects that contain the primitive.

The first factor is **primitive complexity** – this may range from three-dimensional volume primitives, down through two-dimensional structures formed from collections of lines down to individual points. Primitive complexity is probably the most important attribute of a computer vision system. The complexity of the primitive extraction process is directly related to the complexity of the primitive and edge features have perhaps been the most commonly used. The difficulty of grouping edge features into higher-level structures has meant that many recognition approaches have operated with fairly low-level features such as lines. Primitive complexity determines **search complexity** which can be loosely defined as the number of matching tests that have to be made between the image and the hypothesis. Primitive complexity also determines the **model complexity** or the complexity of the object representation – a few high-level primitives give a simpler object description compared with a description made from low-level features such as individual lines. The next factor, **reliance on verification**, encapsulates the fact that when we describe a complex object with simple features it is more difficult to verify than the same object described by higher-level features. Objects described in terms of volume features will be easier to match than those described by two-dimensional line segments. **Model flexibility** describes the powerfulness of the model in coping with minor changes that may be unimportant in the context of the recognition system. A rectangular solid can be described as just that by a single volume primitive. This will be less sensitive to minor changes than a lower-level description in terms, say, of line segments. If complex high-level features are used then we have the more difficult problem of extracting them from the image data (**ease of recovery**) but we would expect that the matching problem is easier and less effort would have to be expended here. Figure 15.3 summarizes the interdependence of these factors.

Dickenson et al. point out that most existing systems use fairly simple primitives such as two-dimensional line segments. Considering the interaction of the above factors, they conclude that it is best to work with complex three-dimensional primitives which then places the major burden on the extraction problem They conclude with the following insightful statement:

The inefficiency of most three-dimensional object recognition systems is reflected in the relatively small number of objects in their database (on the order of 10); in many cases, algorithms are demonstrated on a single model. The major problem is that these systems terminate the bottom-up primitive extraction phase very early, resulting in simple primitives such as lines, corners and inflections. These primitives do not provide very discriminating indices into a large database, so that normally there are a large number of hypothesized matches. Consequently the burden of recognition falls on the top-down verification, which for simple geometric image features requires both accurate estimates of the object's pose and prior knowledge of the object's geometry.

We will now relate these factors to a simple example. Consider Figure 15.4. If we are to attempt to match a wireframe image of three stored objects then pixel by pixel matching of the hypothesis with the image implies the following. First, we require knowledge of the objects' pose or the sensor viewpoint to generate the appropriate wireframe view from the database. Without this we are faced with generating a (theoretically) infinite number of hypotheses. Second, even if we have a way of dealing with the pose problem, the matching is not necessarily straightforward. The edge-enhanced image is noisy and we are not in a sense matching lines (in the hypothesis) with lines (in the image) but pixels in the hypothesis with pixels in the edge image. However, in trying to match at this level we do not encounter the difficulty of extracting a higher-level description from the image. The potential advantage of the approach is that it allows us to

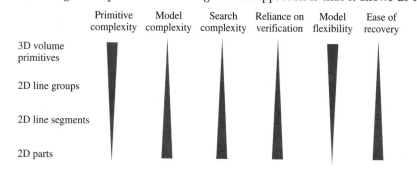

Figure 15.3
The interaction of design factors in a computer vision system (after Dickenson et al. (1992)).

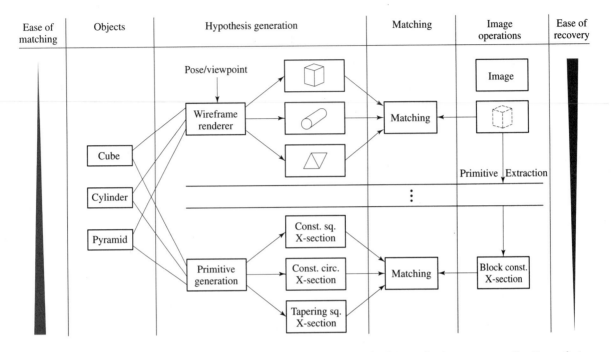

Figure 15.4
Hypothesize and test computer vision. Ease of matching vs. ease of recovery.

set a matching domain somewhere in the hierarchy between a collection of pixels and a high-level description at a level which is consistent with our ability to process the input images to that level. We may, for example, attempt to match the cross-section 'signature'. Note also that in this particular case the hypothesis generator in the case of the wireframe projections would have to operate online using information from the image while the hypothesis generators for the high-level primitives could compile knowledge offline.

A recent application of a similar (in principle) approach in the extraction of a computer graphics geometric model from photographic images is described in Chapter 21. Here there is a degree of user interaction – the process is not entirely automatic. In effect the user replaces the need for pose/viewpoint determination by invoking a particular model and aligning edges in the model with edges in the image. The matching process involves altering the parameters of the wireframe until its projection fits the image. A user invokes a (solid) geometric model and then gives the program some guidance on how this is to match structures in the photographic image. The act of matching a simple geometric model to the image enables the program to derive a detailed computer graphics image that exhibits a photographic level of complexity when used in rendering.

15.1.1 Using knowledge – geometric matching

Geometric matching techniques are designed to match features extracted from the image with features extracted from the object model(s). The principal distinction in most systems is the nature (level) of the features extracted and the dimensionality or nature of the matching space. A more recent dichotomy is the dimensionality of the image with an increasing amount of research operating with three-dimensional range images rather than a two-dimensional intensity image. Active sensing techniques, which provide dense range data directly, are potentially able to operate in a 3D/3D matching space, while passive techniques which usually provide an intensity image operate in a 2D/2D matching space (although as we shall see in Section15.3 approaches exist that try to extract three-dimensional features from intensity images). The potential of range data for simplifying object recognition is great and in recent years, with the increasing accuracy and decreasing cost of sensors, more and more methods are concentrating on this type of data.

Three-dimensional scene data has the potential of being compared directly with model data. We simply need to extend two-dimensional image matching techniques into three-dimensional space. Ignoring scale problems and assuming a 3D/3D matching the pose transformation of a rigid object is specified by a general rotation and translations:

$$Tp = \begin{bmatrix} r_{11} & r_{12} & r_{13} & T_x \\ r_{12} & r_{22} & r_{23} & T_y \\ r_{31} & r_{32} & r_{33} & T_z \\ 0 & 0 & 0 & 1 \end{bmatrix}$$

In other words, when an object changes pose the movement is specified by a rotation and translation.

The basic goal is to put the model and the image data into correspondence and by doing this determine at the same time T_p. The rigid object constraint implies that certain pairwise relationships between features must hold. For example, the distance between a pair of features in the model must be the same as the distance between the same features extracted from the data. Angular relationships and connectivity between features must also be preserved. This means that a higher-level matching strategy is to identify extracted features in the image data and put these into correspondence with the model data. Each such correspondence produces a possible pose.

A number of problems occur. Usually there will be fewer detected features than model features. In both active and passive sensing about half of the object is not seen by the sensor. Features occlude other features unless the object is completely convex. Features may not be extracted from the image data because of noise and the inadequacy of the extraction process. A pose candidate obtained from a matching pair of image and model features will match these features locally but it may not be the correct pose. Thus many poses have to be evaluated and some strategy invoked to find the correct one. Using a conventional hypothesize and test approach we could, for each feature extracted from the image data, attempt to find a potential match in the model in the model data by checking that the constraints in the extracted data match those in the model data. When sufficient information is built up, the pose transformation can be estimated and this estimation used to map the model data into the image or processed image space and verify the hypothesis.

This basic process can be embedded in a conventional back-tracking algorithm and it is easy to see that the difficulty of the overall process and the processing time relate to the number of features. This in turn relates to the feature complexity, a point we discussed in the previous section. In 2D/2D matching we may use lines and/or structures formed from groups of related lines. In 3D/3D matching surface segments and three-dimensional geometric primitives are used.

15.1.2 Using knowledge – relational matching

Another way of using stored knowledge is relational matching. It is similar to the previous strategy except that we concentrate exclusively on the structural relationships between geometric entities in the objects of interest, rather than a pure geometric description.

In relation matching schemes an object is specified by a set of component parts and a set of relationships between these parts. Thus we might describe a rectangular solid as consisting of six faces and specify that each face is connected to four others together with the parallel relationship between the three pairs of faces. A relational description is then just a set of relations that encapsulate the spatial juxtaposition of parts of an object. Such a scheme can be used to compare two objects described in this way. We measure the relational similarity between objects, calling this metric relational distance. If we are applying this kind of approach to compare a stored description with that of a description extracted from a real image then we presuppose that:

(1) it is possible to extract such a description from the image. For example, with a single view of a rectangular solid we can only see one, two or three faces and none of the hidden faces that are parallel to the visible ones;

(2) we can match or map parts from the object description with those extracted from the image.

It is clear that a useful way in which we might measure the 'goodness' of a match between a stored model and an object description from an image is to devise a similarity metric that measures the similarity between the relation set of each. Two rectangular solids, for example, that are described by face connectivity and parallel relationships will result in an exact match independent of scale and the aspect ratio of the rectangles. It may be useful to quantify inexact matches – a truncated wedge object is similar to a rectangular solid. The only difference is that the parallel relationship between a pair of faces falls down.

The following example and associated conventions illustrate the basic idea. It is based on a more formal treatment of this topic in the book by Haralick and Shapiro.

Let

$$D_A = \{R_1,\dots,R_i\}$$

be a set of relations among the parts of object A and

$$D_B = \{S_1,\dots,S_i\}$$

be a set of relations among the parts of object B.

f is a one-to-one mapping corresponding parts in set A with parts in set B. If the number of parts in one set is less than those in the other the discrepancy is made up by adding dummy parts to the smaller set. We define the best mapping f as the mapping which minimizes the total error of f with respect to D_A and D_B. We define the structural error as the number of tuples in R_i that are not mapped by f to tuples in S_i and the number of tuples in S_i that are not mapped by f^{-1} to tuples in R_i. The total error is the sum of structural errors for each pair of corresponding relations and is a quantification of the difference between the two relational descriptions D_A and D_B with respect to the mapping f. The relational distance is the minimal total error obtained for all possible mappings.

Now refer to the example shown in Figure 15.5 and consider the following possible matches. The objects have two relationships – a connectivity relationship specifying pairs of faces that are connected and a relationship that gives pairs of faces that are parallel.

M₁ to M₂

The best mapping f is 1 Ø 1'
2 Ø 2'
3 Ø 3'

Connection relationship (R_1, S_1) is isomorphic

Parallel relationship (R_2, S_2) – (2,3) exists in **M₁** but (2',3') does not hold in **M₂**.

Relational distance = 1

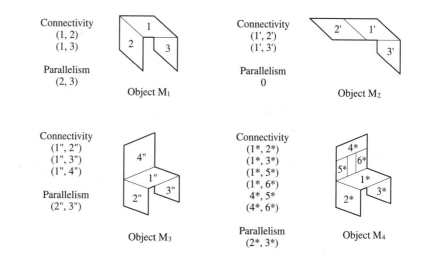

Figure 15.5
Connectivity and parallelism relationships in four simple objects. Relational matching gives M₁ is similar to M₂ and M₃. M₃ is dissimilar to M₄. (After Haralick and Shapiro (1993) for reference details see Chapter 1; p. 15.)

M_1 to M_3

The best mapping f is 1 $\emptyset$ 1"

2 $\emptyset$ 2"

3 $\emptyset$ 3"

4d $\emptyset$ 4" (d is the dummy part in M_1)

Parallel relationship (R_2, S_2) is isomorphic

Connection relationship (R_1, S_1) – (1",4") exists·in M_3 but (1,4d) does not hold in M_1 by definition.

Relational distance = 1

M_3 to M_4

The best mapping f is 1" $\emptyset$ 1*

2" $\emptyset$ 2*

3" $\emptyset$ 3*

4" $\emptyset$ 4*

5d $\emptyset$ 5*

6d $\emptyset$ 6*

Connection relationship (R_1, S_1) – (1*,4*) does not hold in M_4

(4",5d), (4",6d), (1",5d) and (1",6d) do not hold in M_3

Parallel relationship (R_2, S_2) – (5d,6d) does not hold in M_2

Relational distance = 6

An observation that we might make from this example is that as human beings we would almost certainly say that M_3 was more similar to M_4 than it was to M_1. We can note that the relative unimportance of the difference between the two 'chairs' – the different structure of the backs – is not taken into account. All faces regardless of their physical function are given equal consideration in this scheme. In this case the supports (faces 5* and 6*) are considered equal to face 4* as far as the matching scheme is concerned.

15.2 Special representational models used in computer vision

The geometric models that are used in computer vision are similar or identical to those used in computer graphics – refer to Chapter 2 for a comprehensive description of these. Their advantages and disadvantages have equivalent ramifications in computer vision. The most general disadvantage common to both fields is their specificity – we favour different models for different object classes and we have no good models for complex natural objects. The polygon mesh in particular can only deal with scenes made up of polygonal or polyhedral objects. When we use polygons to represent complex objects in the context of computer vision the processing problem of matching internal descriptions that contain tens of thousands of polygons would quickly become intractable – far more quickly than it becomes a problem in computer graphics. Thus we can synthesize objects from detailed polygonal descriptions but we cannot invoke a matching strategy beyond a polygonal resolution that would be considered primitive in many computer graphics contexts. There is also the problem that matching generates more problems as the description becomes more detailed and thus more subject to noise problems. Volume representations are used in both fields for the same reason that a small number of primitives can generate a very large number of objects that can be made from these parts. In computer graphics we call the modelling technique CSG and here we exploit the primitive representation mainly in interactive CAD where the representation enables a designer to build up a model by adding and subtracting parts. In computer vision such primitives are called 'geons' (for geometric ions). Here the problem is to extract the primitives from a two-dimensional projection of the object. The problems are obvious. Not only do we have to deal with occlusion but in using such a representation both the primitives and their relationship to each other in an object have to be found.

Two representation techniques that are exclusive to computer vision are now described. They are view representations and the Gaussian sphere. View representations try to deal with the problem that there is no restriction on the number of views that a three-dimensional object can produce on a two-dimensional image surface.

15.2.1 View or aspect representation

This representational method is used in hypothesize and test strategies and is a technique for categorizing and storing all the views that can be generated by an object description. In its simple form the method is restricted to objects that are made up of a collection of planar faces. The representation is generated from a geometric description such as a polygon mesh structure. The idea is that if we can generate and represent all possible views of an object from our stored object description, then we can potentially use these to match real images of an object of unknown pose and hence effect three-dimensional object recognition.

For an unconstrained viewing system there is theoretically an infinite number of two-dimensional projections. In practice it is common to deal with this problem with a two-level hierarchy consisting of a view class or view aspect and a particular view within a class. A view aspect is defined as follows. All possible views of an object are grouped into a small number of view classes which is the set of all projections that are topologically equivalent. Topologically equivalent means that the same faces, edges and vertices appear in a view aspect.

This definition leads to a method for generating the aspects of polygonal objects. They can be rendered together with an identity label using a standard graphics pipeline. An examination of the identity labels in the projections leads to a merging of views into classes from which some representation of the aspects can be derived. To generate the projections we consider a unit sphere surrounding the object and quantize or tessellate its surface. (An easy way to tessellate a sphere is to consider it as an icosahedron and then subdivide the 20 (triangular) faces as required to generate a multi-faceted polyhedron with approximately equal faces.) Views are computed by positioning the viewpoint on every (view) patch on the sphere and computing a projection with the view directed along the radius connecting the viewpoint to the centre of the sphere. The complete set of views can then be partitioned into topologically equivalent sets.

The number of view classes that an object possesses depends on its complexity; a simple object defined by a few polygons has a low number of classes. Actual views within a class are then related by an affine transformation. The method encapsulates the fact that small changes in the viewpoint do not effect the view class until a traversal suddenly takes the viewer into a new class.

The idea is shown in Figure 15.6(a) for three view classes of a cube. In each of the seven aspects the same faces of the object are visible in an image taken from that set of viewpoints that forms the view class. Different views within a class can be related by the coefficients of an affine transformation.

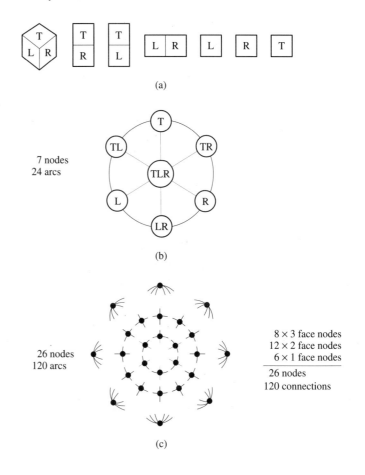

Figure 15.6
Aspects and aspect graphs for a cube. (a) Characteristic views or visual aspects of three faces of a cube; (b) aspect graph for three faces of a cube; (c) increase in complexity for all six faces of a cube.

A method for characterizing the relationship between view classes is called an aspect graph (also called the visual potential of the object). The nodes in such a graph are the aspects and the arcs represent the relationship between the aspects. A path through the graph is equivalent to a viewer orbiting around the object. Figure 15.6(b) shows an aspect graph for the three faces of a cube, containing seven nodes and 24 arcs. An idea of the increase in the complexity of the graph when the six faces of a cube are considered is given in Figure 15.6(c). We now have 26 nodes and 120 arcs. If we return to the concept of a camera orbiting over the surface of a sphere, then the view aspects are equivalent to regions on the surface of the sphere that are separated by curves. A traversal between two nodes on the graph is equivalent to crossing a curve on the sphere. Such a traversal is called a visual event.

One of the main problems with this representation is the scale problem. The scale problem in computer vision causes many problems just as it does in computer graphics. In this context the problem it manifests is: at what scale do we compute view aspects? Some visual events may happen at a small scale only. Also, in its simplest form any recognition strategy that employs this technique needs to know the camera distance.

Another problem occurs with object complexity, particularly if we are using polygon mesh models. As we know from computer graphics, a complex object represented by small polygonal facets will probably contain tens of thousands of polygons leading to an aspect graph that is unmanageably large because there are graph size ramifications in the matching and indexing operations of any recognition strategy. The simple method of generating a graph for a polyhedral object suggested above very quickly falls down as the number of polygons increases for a given view sphere tessellation. On the positive side, however, we can generate the graphs offline.

Also associated with object complexity is the problems that arise when we consider non-convex objects. So far we have implicitly assumed that the objects being dealt with are convex. Occlusion of parts of an object by other parts disrupts the simple notions described above. Consider a simple non-convex object – an L-shaped solid shown in Figure 15.7. Here the criteria for determining whether a view is part of a view class become more complicated. In the example shown two views are given where face visibility is the same but vertex visibility is not.

It may be possible in certain situations to effect object recognition by matching stored aspect graphs with ones extracted from the image. Because aspect graphs of polyhedra are not unique, if they are to be used for matching then it

Figure 15.7
A non-convex object. Two views where face visibility is the same but vertex visibility is not.

will be necessary to append attributes to the nodes. That is, the nodes should contain information concerning the properties of the faces to which they relate. If spatial relationships between faces are also used in the representation, then matching becomes another form of relational matching as we described in Section 15.1.2. The representation in its simplest form is just an icon of a view – nothing more. To effect a match with an image implies that we can classify information in the image in the same way.

Gaussian sphere

A representation that has the potentially useful property that it is invariant under both translation and scaling of the surface that it represents is the Gaussian image. This is simply the collection of all surface normals that the object exhibits. The representation takes the form of considering each surface normal as a point on a unit sphere as shown for the two simple examples of a cube and a cylinder in Figure 15.8. The tail of each surface normal is placed at the centre of the sphere and the point of intersection of the vector with the surface of the sphere gives the point in the Gaussian image that corresponds to the corresponding surface element. Thus every planar element on the surface of an object is represented by a single point in the representation. Because of this the Gaussian image is not invertable (for planar objects) and the so-called extended Gaussian image is sometimes used where each point is a pair – the spherical coordinates of the surface normal and a weighting proportional to the area of the patch to which the normal corresponds. Thus an extended Gaussian image of a polyhedron can be thought of as a collection of point masses on the surface of the sphere.

The main problem with using such a representation in matching is the difficulty of obtaining the extended Gaussian object from the image. Here we have to resort to the techniques outlined in Chapter 16.

Object   Gaussian sphere

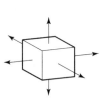

Figure 15.8
Gaussian image of a cube and a cylinder.

15.3 Example approaches – systems dealing with two-dimensional data

The following sections describe three example approaches and systems for the interpretation of three-dimensional scenes from two-dimensional detail which are manifestations of the general approach of matching geometric knowledge with information from the scene in some way. All of them restrict, to a greater or lesser extent, the nature of the objects to be recognized. Two out of the three fall into the hypothesize and test category, differing only in the way in which the information from which the hypothesis is obtained and how the objects are represented. In the first case the information is in the form of a constraint system common to all objects in a 'block world'. This early classic example uses no matching or stored knowledge as such but outputs a description of any scene made up of 'allowable' elements. The second example is the system derived from the hypothesize and test conclusion given at the end of Section 15.1. This uses knowledge in the form of volume primitives and extracts volume primitives from the input image. In the third example, the information is in the form of standard computer graphics models of known objects. In this example the matching takes place at the image level and the hypotheses are generated from standard computer graphics representations using a standard graphics pipeline. The selection is not comprehensive nor is it reasonably representative of the large body of research that exists in three-dimensional object recognition. The variety exhibited amongst the approaches and their varying practical applicability are a good reflection of the current state of computer vision.

15.3.1 Example 1: Interpretation of polygonal objects from wireframe projections – vertex labelling

We will first look at a method that was proposed many years ago – in 1971 – for the interpretation of scenes that are constrained to consist of polygonal objects. At first glance this is perhaps a not unreasonable restriction considering that many contexts of computer vision are in engineering applications and many objects in such a context are going to be polygonal. However, the method that we are about to describe, although it raised expectations at the time, does not seem to have been extended into any practical application. One of the reasons for this is the difficulty of obtaining a line drawing from a practical scene. Edge detection, which gives us explicit knowledge of the projected image of edges, and 'shape from x', which gives us a dense range image, are potentially capable of supplying a line drawing or wireframe projection but taking them together, both techniques are not capable of supplying a perfect line drawing or wireframe projection.

The method assumes that the scene projections can be reduced to perfect wireframe projections. These projections are exactly equivalent to wireframe projections in computer graphics with the hidden lines removed. Although edge detection is one of the most extensively used and worked out techniques in computer vision it tends to perform badly at corners or edges where lines meet to form a vertex – precisely the regions where we need accurate information to build a wireframe projection. However, let us ignore this problem and proceed on the basis that we are going to have perfect wireframe projections to interpret. In addition we assume that we have none of the other problems that would occur in practice, such as interference from shadows.

Despite a few well-known counter-examples – such as the Necker cube (the famous orthographic projection of a wireframe cube that produces two equally plausible interpretations – the vertical faces interchange their depth priority), human beings are extremely adept at inferring shape from line drawings. Many people have argued that this is the most important aspect of our high-level visual abilities and that we see edges as the significant structure of the scene, then make an understanding of the three-dimensional nature of the scene from the relationship between edges.

The classic work on the interpretation of wireframe projections was developed simultaneously by Huffman and Clowes in 1971 (although some earlier work is not without significance, they are the names most often referred to in this field). In this work it was assumed that vertices in the objects consisted of a conjunction of exactly three faces or three edges and the recognition problem was solved by reducing it to a **consistent labelling** problem. What is meant by this is that we have a set of objects, in this case constrained to be the type of objects that we have described, and a constrained set of labels for parts of these objects. In this problem the labels are vertex and edge types. We can then fit a set of vertex types to the object – a consistent labelling. This is possible because of 'constraint propagation' – once a corner has been labelled it constrains those corners to which it is connected by an edge.

First let us look at the labels and then we can develop an approach for applying these labels to the object.

The taxonomy of Hoffman is as follows:

Edges – three types

(1) An occluding edge, symbolized by an $\rightarrow$. An occluding edge is an edge that we have referred to elsewhere as a silhouette edge. An edge is a line between two planar faces and with an occluding edge only one face is visible. The arrow is oriented with respect to the edge such that the visible face is to the right of the arrow.

(2) A non-occluding convex edge (+) . Here both faces are visible and the angle between the surface normals for each face is greater than 180 degrees.

(3) A non-occluding edge (–). Both faces are visible and the angle between the surface normals is less than 180 degrees.

An example of an object with such labels is shown in Figure 15.9. Huffman made the observation that for an edge between two planar surfaces, the edge possesses a constant label along its entire length. The opposite of this is easily demonstrated. Figure 15.10 shows a curved edge and how its label must change.

Figure 15.9
Line labelling of the
projection of a wireframe
object.

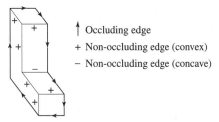

Having labelled edges in this way, a dictionary can be set up containing all possible vertices where three lines meet – more commonly known as corners. The power of this dictionary comes from the realization that only 18 ways of labelling corners exist in practice. These are shown in Figure 15.11. They divide into four types: **Y**, **W**, **V** and **T**. For example, the corners of a cube can only appear as a **Y** or a **W** or a **V** (Figure 15.12).

To find a labelling scheme automatically from a line drawing, we use the obvious fact that an edge joining two vertices, or corners, can only have one label. For a particular scene we have to find a set of labels that are consistent (given that there may be more than one way of labelling a scene). A brute force approach would be simply to test all possible ways of labelling the edges against the dictionary. A more reasoned approach is to start with a corner, give it a valid label, then move to the corners connected to the first corner and try to give them valid labels, given that they are now constrained by the edges that con–nect to the first corner. If this cannot be done we back up and relabel the first corner.

What do we do when we find a consistent labelling scheme? The answer is that the act of applying such a scheme should reveal a description of the object. For example, if we were to set about labelling a cube we might discover the description shown in Figure 15.13 given that, in general, a cube will appear as three faces. This gives us the following description for a cube:

> The object is made up of one **Y** junction. Each leg of the **Y** junction is con–nected to a **W** junction. Each arm of each of the **W** junctions is connected to a **V** junction.

The English description is, however, inadequate in describing the complete con–nectivity relationship between the vertices and a complete description is the con–nectivity diagram shown in Figure 15.13. The important point about such a description is that it is a description of a three-dimensional cube, recovered from the projection, and it is independent of scale, orientation and so on. Given the constraints that we have outlined, only an object that is a cube could produce such a description. We could continue this process and describe a scene made up of rectangular solids with such descriptions as: 'A cube on top of another cube' or

Figure 15.10
A curved edge has a label
that changes.

Figure 15.11
The complete dictionary of
18 trihedral vertices.

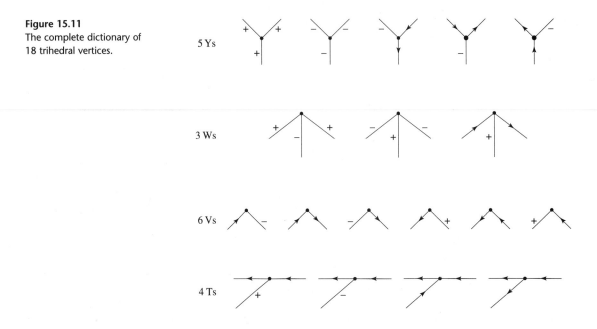

'a cube to the right of another', and so on. The apparent power and soundness of this approach led to a large amount of research into so-called 'block worlds' that now appears to have evaporated. Despite initial optimism this approach has not been extended to account for practical scenes. One reason we have already mentioned is the difficulty of attaining perfect line drawings from practical scenes. Another is that most real scenes of interest do not decompose into blocks.

Another important restriction of such schemes is that they invoke a **general viewpoint assumption**. This rules out 'accidental' alignment of certain scene features, such as edges, so that in the case of the cube we ignore the cases where the cube projects as a single square or as two squares. We are insisting with this assumption that the properties of interest to us in the object persist as the viewpoint is altered. The goal of this scheme is to produce a description of the scene and the description should be independent of viewpoint perturbations.

The above approach is considered of interest because it is an early example of a model-based approach to computer vision. Although it is a not matching

Figure 15.12
The only three possible
labellings for a vertex of a
cube.

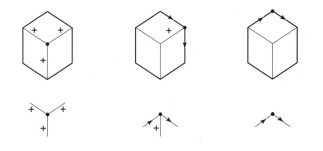

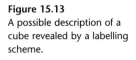

Figure 15.13
A possible description of a cube revealed by a labelling scheme.

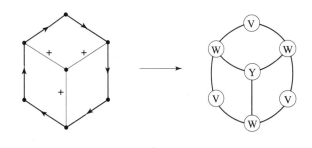

scheme where we attempt to find correspondence between a stored entity or model and the real image, it does not work with specific geometric models but rather invokes a general model for an entire class of objects.

15.3.2

Example 2: Object recognition using Probabilistic Three-dimensional Interpretation of Component Aspects (OPTICA)

We will now describe a system that, although it was designed two decades after the previous one, still depends on a constrained world where objects are composed of a set of 10 volume primitives and which, at its lowest level, considers extraction of these volume primitives from edges. It is an elegant, classic example of a hypothesize and test approach, and is the work of the authors (Dickenson et al.) that we quoted in Section 15.1 where their arguments concerning the interacting factors in a three-dimensional recognition system working with prior knowledge suggested that despite the difficulty of extracting or recovering high-level complex primitives from an image, it is best to work with primitives such as volumes.

Both OPTICA (Object recognition using Probabilistic Three-dimensional Interpretation of Component Aspects) and the system of Raja and Jain that we describe in Section 15.4 use as primitive components 'geon'-like objects that are based on Biderman's theory of 'Recognition By Components', which in simple terms states that given a small number of fundamental part primitives (called geometric ions or geons), recognition of an object made up of such components can be achieved by recognizing the identity and spatial relationships of an object's component geons. Identification of component geons can proceed by analysis of the properties of edges in the image – curvature, collinearity, parallelism and so on. Geons are generalized cones whose shape is controlled by four attribute parameters. Three attributes describe characteristics of the cross-section – its shape, symmetry and its size as it is swept along the primitive axis or spine (constant, increasing, or increasing and decreasing). The remaining attribute describes the shape of the axis (straight or curved). Dickenson et al. use a set of 10 primitives (Figure 15.14) and Raja and Jain use 12 (Figure 15.23).

An important and powerful attribute of OPTICA is that it utilizes multi-view representations or aspects as stored knowledge. However, it only stores the

Figure 15.14
Geons used in OPTICA (compare with Figure 15.23).

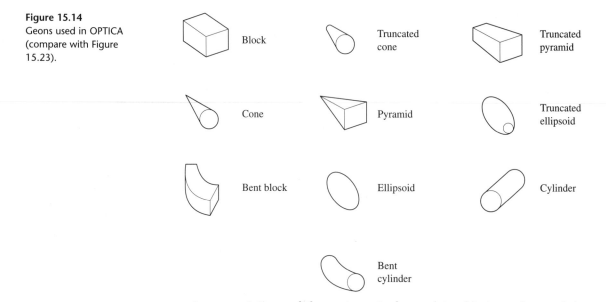

Block

Truncated cone

Truncated pyramid

Cone

Pyramid

Truncated ellipsoid

Bent block

Ellipsoid

Cylinder

Bent cylinder

aspect representations of the parts, not of complete objects made up of these parts. This makes it feasible to use an aspect-based scheme for recognition without incurring the penalty associated with generating the large number of aspects for complete objects. Also, the number of stored aspects is independent of the number of objects in the database. As Figure 15.6 demonstrates, aspect representations grow very quickly as a function of object complexity. Another innovation in this work is the use of probabilistic information gathered from the phase that generates the aspect representations to guide primitive recovery. Thus it conforms in general terms to the structure shown in Figures 15.1 and 15.2, with the aspect representations generated offline.

The core of the stored knowledge in OPTICA is an aspect hierarchy. The organization of this enables conditional probabilities – evaluated when the knowledge is compiled – to be included. The hierarchy enables the system to deal with occlusion by guiding the primitive recovery operation to the appropriate level. Aspects comprise the topmost level of the hierarchy and these consist as usual of the topologically distinct views of each primitive. Figure 15.15(a) is a small part of the hierarchy showing four aspects (from a total of 37). An aspect may be common to a number of primitives, and associated with each link from an aspect to a primitive is a conditional probability expressing the probability that the aspect belongs to the primitive with which it is linked. Thus where only one link exists between an aspect and a primitive the associated probability is 1.0. When more than one link exists a fractional probability is associated with each link – all probabilities emanating from an aspect node summing to unity. The next level down comprises faces or face types that make up the aspect and the bottom level is boundary groups which are subsets of the faces bounding contours.

Reliable identification of an aspect can lead to identification of a primitive but because of occlusion part of the aspect may be missing from the image. If this

Figure 15.15
Representations in OPTICA:
(a) part of the aspect
hierarchy; (b) example of
a face graph; (c) example
of a boundary group graph.

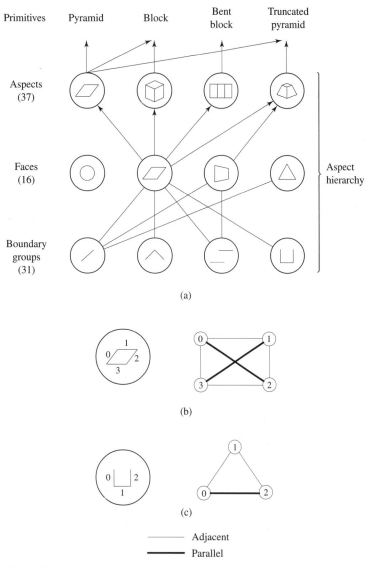

occurs then the remaining faces can be analyzed from the face level. Similarly if contours are missing in the faces because of occlusion the arrangement of the visible contours can be analyzed at the contour level.

Conditional probabilities relating levels in the hierarchy are generated when the knowledge is compiled by (orthographically) projecting each primitive onto an image plane using a viewing direction given by quantizing a viewing sphere (Section 15.2.1). For each primitive the number of occurrences of each boundary group, face and aspect divided by the total number of occurrences of the feature give the required conditional probabilities. By examining all these probabilities, Dickenson et al. were able to show that the mapping from faces to aspects is much less ambiguous than the mapping from boundary groups to aspects and they concluded from this that for geon-like primitives the most appropriate feature for recognition is the face. Only when a face is occluded do they descend to analysis at the boundary group level. This means that the primitive recovery attempts to extract faces from the image before attempting a match with the aspect hierarchy or the hierarchy is entered at the face level, unless a face is occluded. Thus a contour algorithm determines boundaries and these are, if possible, identified as a face from the graphs representing a face in the face-level nodes. For example, Figure 15.15(b) shows the graph corresponding to a parallelogram face. The thin lines between each node represent edge intersection and the thick lines the parallel relationship. In the event of occlusion the counters are applied to the boundary group level. For example, Figure 15.15(c) shows a boundary group for the same face with one edge occluded.

Face extraction implies not only identification or labelling of individual faces but the construction of a face graph in which nodes represent faces and arcs represent face adjacencies. A face graph for a simple object is shown in Figure 15.16(a). It may be that there is more than one face hypothesis at each face. In the case of a perfect match with a face in the aspect hierarchy, the list contains a single hypothesis with a probability of 1.0. If there are a number of hypotheses, because of occlusion, then associated with each is a probability determined from the probabilities of mapping boundary groups to faces.

The next step is to match the extracted face graph with the aspects. This problem can be stated as: find a covering of the face graph using aspects in the aspect hierarchy, such that no face is left uncovered and each face is covered by only one aspect. This graph matching problem is constrained by the conditional probabilities in the aspect hierarchy. Aspect hypotheses are generated for each face hypothesis and their probabilities evaluated (from the product of the face to aspect mapping probability and the face hypothesis probability).

Figure 15.16
Object face and aspect graphs. (a) Face graph for an object; (b) aspect graph of the object in (a).

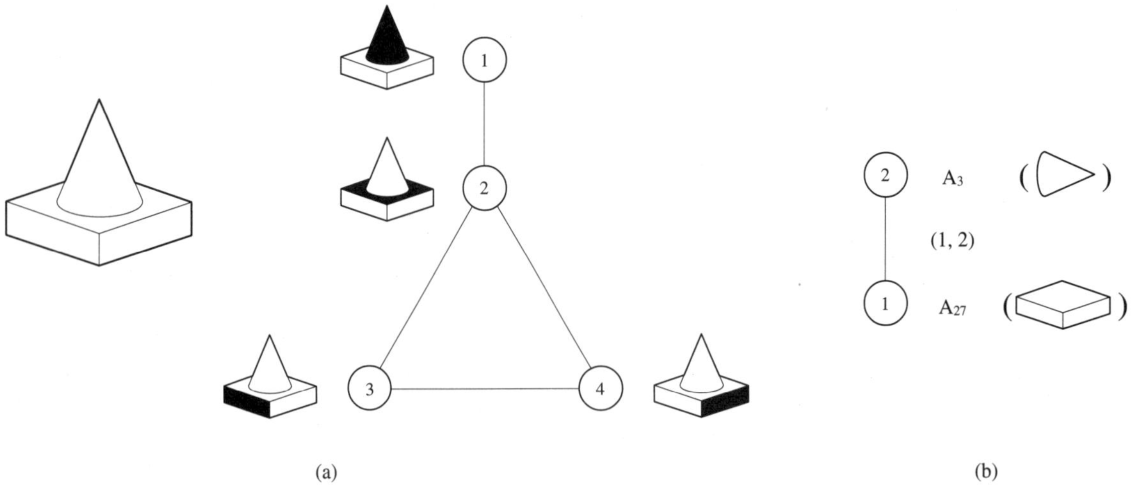

(a)

(b)

Once an aspect covering has been made the next step is to extract the primitives that the imaged object is made up of prior to object recognition. An aspect covering can be represented by a graph where the nodes represent aspects and the arcs face adjacencies that specify the connectivity between the primitives. Figure 15.16(b) shows an aspect graph for the object in Figure 15.16(a). The arc (1,2) in the graph indicates that face number 1 is adjacent to face number 2. This process is similar to the face aspect matching step and a primitive covering of the aspect graph is evaluated. Again hypotheses are generated and all possible primitive coverings (one primitive per aspect) are evaluated until the objects in the scene are recognized.

Dickenson et al. conclude:

> The cost of extracting more complex primitives from the image is the difficulty of grouping less complex features into more complex features; the number of possible groupings is enormous. Our recovery algorithm uses a statistical analysis of the aspects (explicitly generated in the aspect hierarchy) to rank-order the possible groupings. The result is a heuristic that has been demonstrated to quickly arrive at the correct interpretation. Note, however, that our approach will, if need be, enumerate *all* possible interpretations (or groupings); the correct interpretation of any scene, no matter how ambiguous or unlikely, will eventually be generated.

15.3.3   Example 3: Specular highlights as primitives

A proposal that utilizes standard three-dimensional computer graphics techniques to generate the hypothesis uses specular reflections as the extracted primitives. This means that the stored models no longer use solely geometric information to generate, for example, a wireframe projection as a hypothesis, but employ an entire computer graphics pipeline (geometric model plus a local refection model) on the generative side.

The approach described here is based on work reported by Sato et al. in 1992 who point out that in the overall context of computer vision some categories of images are made up entirely of specular reflections (radar imagery and ultrasonic imagery are two examples). They also point out that a strong potential advantage of using specular reflections as a matching primitive is their ease of detection – simple thresholding will suffice. On first consideration this may not seem like a good idea: specular highlights depend on both the shape of the object and the viewpoint and thus violate the constraint invoked in the previous section – the general viewpoint assumption. As we know from Chapter 3, we can only see specular highlights when the viewing direction is aligned with the direction of the reflected light to within the limits of the reflection lobe. However, if we invoke the constraint that the sensor and the light source are located at the same point then we can remove the variation due to the relative position of the light source and the viewpoint. We are still left with the problem that specular reflections change their shape abruptly and may suddenly disappear under viewpoint perturbations.

In this work the suitability of specular reflections as features is ranked according to two descriptive parameters: detectability (generally the size of the feature) and stability – the sensitivity of the appearance or non-appearance of the feature to perturbations of the viewing direction or equivalently the pose of the object. An example of the interaction of these factors for four different surface types is shown in Figure 15.17 which exhibits an inverse relationship between detectability and stability. The right-hand column is a Gaussian sphere representation of the viewing directions (assuming the sensor and light source are located at the same point) along which a specular highlight will be seen. In the case of a planar surface the stability is low – the light source/sensor has to be oriented near to the surface normal. When in this position, all of the surface reflects specularly and the detectability is therefore high. For an elliptical surface the light/source sensor can take any orientation – stability is high – but only a small part of the surface reflects specularly and the detectability is consequently low.

The shape of a specular highlight depends on the shape of the object, its pose, the shape of the light source illuminating it and to a lesser extent the nature of the surface. We can assume that in many practical applications we will have a single fixed source (optical, radar or ultrasonic) and that objects of the same shape will have the same surface reflectivity properties which leaves the shape and pose of the object determining the shape of the specular highlight.

The overall structure falls into the general hypothesize and test category described in Section 15.1 with an offline compilation phase for the generation of an object database for matching from standard computer graphics representations of known objects. The compilation phase consists of the following steps:

(1) Visual aspects are extracted from the object models by using a sensor simulator to generate images. In computer graphics terminology a sensor simulator is just a ray tracer – tracing rays from each pixel backwards along the direction of light propagation. This is done by generating all possible views of objects (by tessellating a view sphere as we describe in Section 15.2.1).

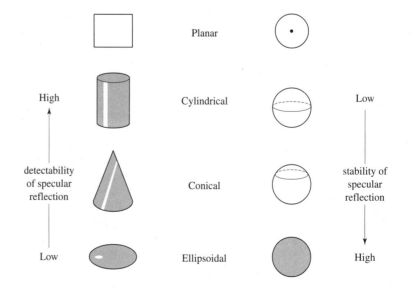

Figure 15.17
Detectability and stability of specular reflections for different surface types (after Sato et al. (1992)).

(2)   These views are analyzed for the existence of specular features which are detectable and stable by using a metric based on the idea exemplified in Figure 15.17. These views are grouped into aspects where in this case the definition of an aspect is a grouping of similar specular features. Figure 15.18 shows some specular aspects of an example (compound) object made up of a cone cylinder and a sphere. The aspects are positioned according to the region they occupy on the surface of the unit (hemi)sphere.

The overall specular reflection of an object is divided into components produced by each object part. In the example shown in Figure 15.17 the

Figure 15.18
Specular aspects for a group of objects.

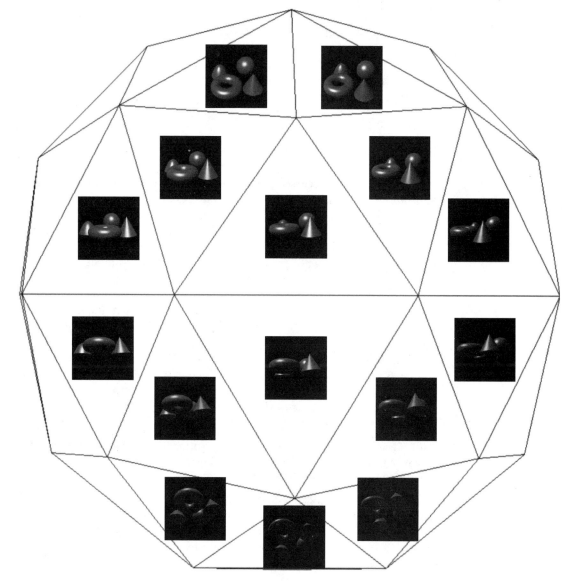

components originate from either the cone, cylinder or sphere part. This is to facilitate a particular matching methodology.

(3) Deformable templates (see Chapter 14) are prepared for verification. This particular problem seems a perfect application for deformable templates – a specular feature changes its shape as well as its apparent position.

The run time phase is as follows:

(1) The input image is classified into candidate aspects. This is done by a two-level process – coarse matching and ordering possible matches in order of significance followed by fine matching using deformable templates.

The report of Sato et al. is based on the verification of the existence of a single object of some complexity – a toy airplane – and the work determines that the object in the image matches the 'compiled' model and determines its pose from the matched aspect. It is not clear how easily this work can be extended to deal with the general recognition problem.

15.4 Example approaches – systems dealing with range data

Up to now we have discussed schemes that operate with two-dimensional image data, and we have seen that all of the strategies operate with constraints of one form or another, regardless of whether we are using a bottom-up approach where we try to recover three-dimensional data from the projection (the shape from X paradigm) or a model-based approach where we try to match image projections with projections generated from prior knowledge stored as models. We will now look at analyzing dense range or depth data.

Depth data supplied by a device such as a laser ranger is known as active sensing. (Perfect depth data for a scene generated in a computer graphics program is shown in Figure 8.16.) Active sensing means introducing radiation into the scene and controlling it. Passive sensing means measuring radiation – usually reflected light – that already exists in the scene. Despite its potential and the fact that it is extremely difficult to recover dense three-dimensional information from a two-dimensional projection, there appears to be two schools of thought concerning active sensing in the vision community. For example, Nalwa comments in the introduction to his book:

Further, we shall restrict ourselves to passive sensing ... Although active sensing ... can greatly simplify the computation of scene structure, it interferes with the state of the world, and is therefore not always tolerable.

Certainly there are cases where this will be true. (If a robot is coming into your office to empty your wastebasket, you do not want it firing laser light in your direction.) But it seems not unlikely that if ranging devices continue to develop, they will be adopted in many applications. Recently there has been much emphasis on the use of dense range data in object recognition. The two main factors that have led to this may be the extreme difficulty of considering object recognition in a two-dimensional domain and the concomitant scene constraints that are usually employed, and the increasing accuracy (and decreasing cost) of laser rangers.

It seems intuitively obvious that the recognition of three-dimensional objects from three-dimensional data ought to be easier than working with two-dimensional data. What advantages accrue in an active sensing system where three-dimensional information, in the form of a two-dimensional array of depth values, is the low-level input to the system and what is the difference in the strategies that we have to invoke to deal with this data?

At first sight it would seem that the advantages ought to be substantial. However, we have to bear in mind that although we have three-dimensional scene information, it is in an unstructured or raw form. We may have an array of pixels that correspond to the depth of the three visible faces of a cube but they are in a completely unstructured form. There is nothing in the data that tells us that there are three quadrilaterals connected together in a certain way. Other problems that exist in two-dimensional projections persist – the data is still view dependent and occlusion still occurs.

When an image – a single projection – is analyzed, most strategies, as we have seen, are based on some kind of structural information derived from edges. As we have seen in Chapters 3 and 5, the light reflected from an object depends on many variables other than the surface geometry (light source position and intensity, surface material, and so on) and using this information is difficult. Thus strategies in many systems concentrate on scenes made up of entities that have (piecewise) constant surface geometry – polyhedral objects. They do not generally attempt to extract information that reflects surface curvature. Consider, for example, the curved surface of a cylinder. If no curvature information is available from the strategy then this will always appear as a quadrilateral with two straight edges and two curved edges. The curved edges give a clue to the nature of the surface but it could still be just a planar patch with the silhouette of a cylinder unless we extract curvature information from the intensity variation across the surface of the cylinder. Range data of sufficiently high resolution, on the other hand, gives us curvature information directly. Matching strategies that utilize range maps have the potential of matching a three-dimensional model representation with the three-dimensional range data. The extension of the matching space dimensionality from 2D/2D to 3D/3D naturally deals with curved surfaces.

A system based on dense range data will have the same basic features as a 2D/2D hypothesize and test system – knowledge representation, primitive extraction and a matching domain for comparing the knowledge representation with the structures extracted from the image. The most obvious primitive that can (theoretically) be obtained directly from range data is surfaces and their categorization based on curvature. A discontinuity in surface curvature implies a boundary between faces and the nature of the curvature (positive/negative and so on) categorizes the shape of the face. In other words, we should be able to perform three-dimensional segmentation directly from the image data. The image data depends only on surface geometry and not on factors such as surface reflectance and the nature and position of the light sources.

It is difficult to make any firm conclusions about the future of range data vs. intensity data, but what appears to be clear is that low-level processing is greatly simplified and that a rich surface description of the object is potentially available from low-level data.

15.4.1 The nature of range data and possible strategies

From the point of view of low-level processing we can view range data in a number of ways. We could consider the data as a set of unconnected points through which we fit a surface–surface interpolation. An example of such a strategy that fits bicubic parametric patches to the data was given in Chapter 7. Here the goal of the process was to gain a computer model of a range-scanned object so that the object could be rendered. We could adopt the same process in computer vision and indeed the example given could be considered an application of the use of computer vision techniques in deriving models for computer graphics. However, there are potential problems in using such an interpolation technique in computer vision. The interpolation depends on first fitting a *uv* net through the data points and this net defines the patch boundaries. The net is defined in the image plane and would vary depending on the viewpoint, which would imply a viewpoint-dependent description. Also, the problem is considerably easier in computer graphic derivation of an object model because there is no object/background or object/object segmentation necessary and usually the whole of the object is scanned (the normal device is a rotating table in the path of a laser beam).

Another surface interpolation approach taken by Faugeras is described in Section 15.4.4. In both of these approaches we are attempting to gain knowledge of the nature of the structure and at the same time describe it in a way that is suitable for matching to a model.

A direct approach is to describe the surface by considering a pixel neighbourhood and locally, for each pixel, label it with a surface curvature identity – locally flat, cylindrical and so on. In this scheme a particular view of a cylinder would map into a region labelled cylindrical connected to a region labelled flat. A region growing scheme would then produce a description of the object in the image plane as a set of (homogeneously) labelled regions. The method is different in principle to surface interpolation. With the interpolation procedure we are fitting a separate entity to the data using some type of best fit criterion. Such a scheme is comprehensively described in Besl (1990). Its predictable problem is that the labelling, derived from small pixel windows centred on the point of interest, is sensitive to noise and this results in a physically homogeneous region being inhomogeneously labelled which then requires further processing (exactly the problem that bedevils local processing of intensity images). One of the goals of the approach is to achieve surface characterization and surface segmentation without using a priori knowledge. Matching can then be achieved in a 3D/3D domain by directly comparing the object description with the surface characterization. Another important motivation for not using a priori knowledge in the initial image processing operations is the potential ability to deal with scenes that contain objects for which there is no a priori knowledge – unseen objects.

(15.4.2)

Example 1: Use of surface curvature to categorize and segment surfaces

We begin with some definitions relating to the curvature of a surface. Surface shape can be effectively characterized by two scalar functions – Gaussian curvature (K) and mean curvature (H). Reasons for using such measures are:

● they are invariant to translations and rotations of the object surface;

● since they are local measures they are unaffected by partial occlusion;

● they can be obtained directly from input data providing it is sufficiently dense;

● they can be used to segment the input data directly. All the image information (potentially) contributes to the process, none is discarded. This results in a 'rich' description where each projected point of a surface contributes to its description.

Gaussian curvature (Figure 15.19(a))is defined as the signed ratio of the area of the Gaussian image (Section 15.2.2) of a surface patch to the area of the surface patch:

$$K = \frac{dA}{dS}$$

Thus the Gaussian curvature of a planar patch is zero, because its Gaussian image is a single point, as is that of a cylindrical surface (its Gaussian image being a line). Also, the Gaussian curvature of a sphere is everywhere on the surface unity. Figures 15.19(b) and (c) show that the Gaussian curvature of a peak and a valley are respectively positive and negative.

We now consider measures of surface curvatures that are based on curves that lie in the surface. For a point on the surface we define a direction of maximum normal curvature and minimal normal curvature from all curves that lie in the surface (Figure 15.20), that pass through the point and have (curve) normals that align with the surface normal at the point. At the point of interest there is therefore a direction the maximum and minimum curvatures and associated with each curve, curvature values h_1 and h_2. We define the mean curvature as:

$$H = \frac{h_1 + h_2}{2}$$

Figure 15.19
(a) Gaussian curvature.
(b) Gaussian curvature of a peak is positive. (c) Gaussian curvature of a valley is negative.

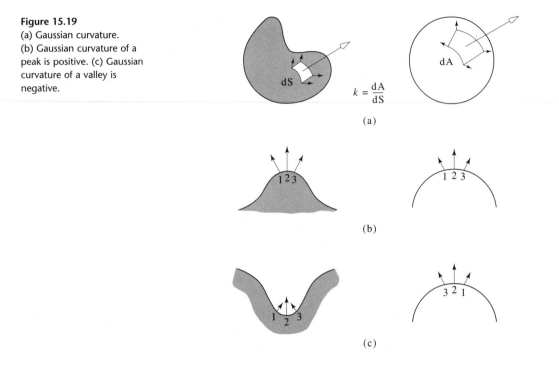

We are now able to categorize eight surface types based on the signs of H and K. For every pixel in the range image, the pixel is part of a surface that is locally:

(1)	Planar	$H=0$	$K=0$
(2)	Ridge	$H<0$	$K=0$
(3)	Valley	$H>0$	$K=0$
(4)	Peak	$H<0$	$K>0$
(5)	Pit	$H>0$	$K>0$
(6)	Saddle ridge	$H<0$	$K<0$
(7)	Saddle valley	$H>0$	$K<0$
(8)	Minimal surface	$H=0$	$K<0$

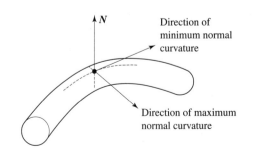

Figure 15.20
Maximum and minimum normal curvature.

Besl calls this categorization of a range image an *HK* sign map. *K* and *H* can be computed from the range image derivatives as follows:

$$H = \frac{1}{2} \frac{(1 + I_y^2)I_{xx} + (1 + I_x^2)I_{yy} - 2I_xI_yI_{xy}}{(1 + I_x^2 + I_y^2)^{\frac{3}{2}}}$$

$$K = \frac{I_{xx}I_{yy} - I_{xy}^2}{(1 + I_x^2 + I_y^2)^2}$$

The practical disadvantage of this theoretically promising approach is its reliance on direct numerical differentiation of the range data. Image differentiation is sensitive to noise and the second partial derivatives are particularly troublesome. In this case the result of the operation is a mapping of each pixel into one out of eight surface curvature labels and the classic problem of information extraction occurs – small perturbations in input levels, due to noise and so on, lead to large perturbations in output. Besl approaches this problem by smoothing the image and fitting a quadratic surface to the neighbourhood of each point, but he points out that this involves making a priori assumptions, which is contrary to the goal of using as few a priori assumptions as possible.

The *HK* sign map is noisy and it is not in a form suitable for matching with a model description. The information in the *HK* sign map needs integrating into complete surface segments. Besl approaches this with a fairly complex variable order surface fitting and region growing procedure. In other words, the region grows as a surface is fitted and grows. The *HK* sign map exhibits groups of identically labelled pixels and small subsets of these are used as seed regions to initiate the process.

The underlying principle of variable order surface fitting is a simple to complex hypothesis testing. Starting with the simplest hypothesis – the surface is planar – this is tested to see if it is true. If it is, the region is grown. If it is false, the algorithm tests the next hypothesis in order of complexity – the surface is biquadratic. Four types of surfaces are fitted: planar, biquadratic, bicubic and biquartic polynomials. If the image surface bends faster than the highest order approximating surface, it is broken into two or more regions that will join smoothly. A number of terminating criteria are applied, such as: the current surface fit error, the maximum allowable error threshold, the current and previous region sizes and the current and previous fit orders. The main output is an array of explicitly labelled regions with surface equations.

Besl also implements a 'stimulus bound philosophy' which is that the output from all lower-level vision modules should be made available to higher-level modules. This means that without checking higher-level structures against the original data the complete information extraction structure is only as strong as its weakest link. Such checking is possible with surface-based algorithms by simple image differencing. For example, the final interpretation can be used to reconstruct an image which can then form a difference image which can then be interpreted to evaluate the quality of the information. The overall idea of this

Figure 15.21
Stimulus bound approach
to bottom-up analysis;
higher-level processes are
continually checked against
image information.

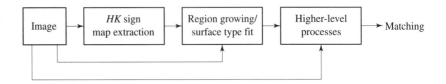

process is shown in Figure 15.21 where at each separate process the original image can be used in some comparison.

An important summary point concerning this model is that it is entirely data driven. There is no intermediate matching domain where a representation obtained from the model description is matched with a representation extracted from the image. It can thus be viewed as a three-dimensional analogue of the classic pattern recognition paradigm where an image is transformed into a structural description and matched with one out of n stored descriptions.

(15.4.3) Example 2: A generic parts-based description of range data

This more recent work was reported in 1994 by Raja and Jain. It differs in a number of fundamental ways from the previous work. It is, however, similar in its approach for the low-level image processing stages. The description extracted from the data is a three-dimensional 'parts'-based object representation in terms of a specific set of 12 three-dimensional parts or primitives. The stored or a priori knowledge uses a representation known as a SAG or surface adjacency graph. This is a multi-view representation of the parts description. The stored knowledge – the parts catalogue – is in this case not used for matching but to facilitate segmentation of an object into parts, which enables the object description in terms of the primitives. The output from the process is thus a parts-based description. The method also combines information from both intensity and range imagery.

An overall view of the approach is shown in Figure 15.22. This also shows that the original data is employed at each step in the process – another manifestation of the 'stimulus bound' approach expounded in the previous section. Surface segmentation means the same as it did in the previous method – an initial sur-

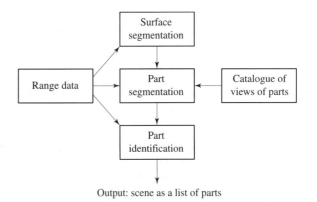

Figure 15.22
Raja and Jain's system for
categorizing range data as
a collection of three-
dimensional primitives
or parts.

Output: scene as a list of parts

face segmentation based on surface curvature measurements made directly from the range data. This is followed by a parts segmentation which simultaneously relates surfaces to parts and segments a part. At this stage a priori knowledge is used to guide the process. Finally the individual parts are identified.

The primitives used – the parts-based representation – are another variation of the computer graphics modelling method known as CSG or constructive solid geometry. (In fact in their work Raja and Jain obtain their a priori knowledge descriptions from a CSG modelling system.) As we saw in Chapter 2, a small number of three-dimensional geometric primitives can represent a very large number of the kind of objects that are encountered in a manufacturing environment, and the major rationale of CSG representations in computer graphics was to facilitate a powerful user modelling interface where a designer could build up a complex part by specifying primitives related to each other by three-dimensional Boolean operators. In computer vision this description is used for exactly the same reason – a small number of primitives can represent a very large number of objects and they can provide a powerful index into stored knowledge.

Similar to the representation used in Section 15.3.2, Raja and Jain selected 12 parts for their three-dimensional primitives. These are a class of objects that can be generated by sweeping a cross-section along a spine curve (see Chapter 2), allowing the cross-section to vary as it is swept. The parts are shown in Figure 15.23 and are categorized according to the shape of the spine curve (straight or bent), the cross-section edges (straight or curved) and the cross-section area

Axis shape	Cross-section edges	Cross-section size	Example
s	s	co	
b	s	co	
s	s	id	
b	s	id	
s	s	t	
b	s	t	
s	c	co	
b	c	co	
s	c	t	
b	c	t	
s	c	id	
b	c	id	

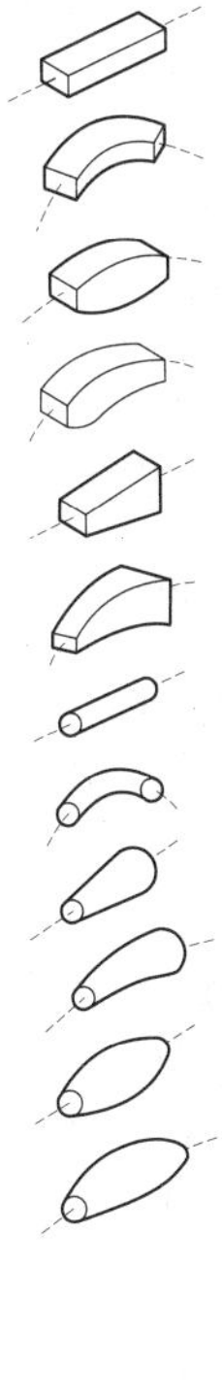

s straight
b bent
c curved
co constant
id increasing/decreasing
t tapered

Figure 15.23
Geons used by Raja and Jain (compare with Figure 15.14).

(constant, increasing/decreasing, tapered). The final description simply identifies each part in the scene as one of these 12. In this way each segmented part is defined by qualitative shape properties.

In Section 15.2.1 a method of representing characteristic views or aspects was explained. A modified version of such a scheme, which exploits information available (in principle) directly from range data, is employed in this method. A qualitative surface classification, based on principal curvatures (Section 15.4.2), is used to set up SAGs or surface adjacency graphs which specify the surface type (nodes) and the angular relationship between surfaces. Two examples of such graphs are shown for the parts s-s-id and b-s-co in Figure 15.24. It can be seen from this that both the nodes and the connecting edges possess attributes. The node attribute is the duple maximum curvature, minimum curvature which distinguishes five surface types as:

maximum curvature	minimum curvature
+	+
+	0
+	−
0	0
−	0

The edge attributes, using the constraint that the parts are convex, can be one of four types that specify the angle between the two surfaces:

———————————	right angle
- - - - - - - - - - - - - - -	obtuse angle
....	acute angle
ıııııııııııııııııııııııııııııı	zero angle

SAGs contains as sub-graphs, aspects in which the number, types, adjacencies and angles of the surfaces are the same and can be used to generate the aspects. Removing impossible views and duplicates results in a total of only 74 aspects for the 12 parts.

As we have already stated, the stored representations are used, not to effect recognition, but to assist in the segmentation of a scene into parts. The scene data is represented originally as a large SAG using surface curvature information

Figure 15.24
Example surface adjacency graphs for two parts.

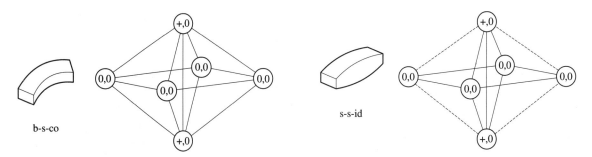

derived from the range data. Segmentation is effected by fragmenting the SAG into individual SAGs that represent parts. This is achieved by removing edges in the graph that connect parts rather than connecting adjacent surfaces of the same part. If we assume that every surface in the scene SAG belongs to exactly one part then every edge potentially represents a connection between two surfaces that belong to different parts. Thus each edge can be examined against the multi-view representation to see if a part can contain two surfaces of the attributed type connected together via an edge of the attributed type. For example, the object shown in Figure 15.25 would be segmented into two parts because the two adjacent surfaces do not match any specification in the stored representation.

Raja and Jain point out that this process can also account for the common problem of over-segmentation where insignificantly small surfaces emerge from the surface segmentation stage. If such a surface connects two larger surfaces which are also connected to each other, the small surface can be safely removed.

The output of the parts segmentation process is a set of sub-graphs of the original scene sub-graph. The parts that are represented by the sub-graphs now need to be identified. This cannot be done simply from the sub-graphs themselves because the surface curvature information is restricted to the sign. For example, in Figure 15.25 the single node surface which has curvature attribute (+,0) could be a tapered cylinder or a normal cylinder.

Raja and Jain have developed a number of tests that operate directly (see Figure 15.26) on the original data. One of these computes the variation of cross-section size for a segmented part by constructing a histogram of surface normals. As Figure 15.26 shows, surface normal direction histograms should exhibit a peak around 90 degrees with respect to the principal axis direction, a peak some distance from 90 degrees or a spread about 90 degrees, depending on whether the cross-section is constant, tapering or increasing/decreasing. This test also requires the principal axis, the reference direction for the surface normals, to be computed.

Figure 15.27 (Colour Plate) shows a result from Raja and Jain's approach. It shows a complicated object made up of five cylindrical parts. Figure 15.27(b) shows the surface segmentation obtained; parts (c) and (d) show the initial and final surface adjacency graphs. The initial SAG has four small surfaces which arise due to imperfect surface segmentation. These are removed. Five remaining large surfaces are all classified as having positive maximum curvature and zero negative curvature. The catalogue of part views shows no example of two adjacent surfaces of this type and the corresponding SAG links are removed to give a correct segmentation.

Figure 15.25
Parts segmentation by removing edges from the scene SAG.

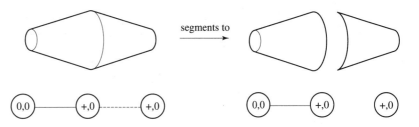

Figure 15.26
Range data enables direct measurement of cross-section variation from surface normals.

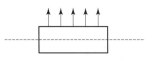

Constant cross-section

Exhibits surface normals with constant orientation of 90° with respect to the principal axis

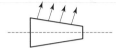

Tapering cross-section

Constant orientation of ≠ 90°

Increasing/decreasing cross-section

Spread of orientations

15.4.4

Surface interpolation and representation

Both the preceding methods extract surface curvature from the image data and use this as a basis for higher-level processing. In both methods the most fragile part of the process is the segmentation of the object or scene data on the basis of surface curvature and this is, as we discussed, because the direct measurement of surface curvature involves both first and second derivatives which are sensitive to noise perturbations.

A more direct approach which avoids this problem and which could be used for single object scenes would be to fit a surface to the range data and directly match this against a stored model by moving it into correspondence with each of the models – a kind of three-dimensional cross-correlation process. This is broadly the approach taken by Faugeras (1993) and described in his book *Three-dimensional Computer Vision – A Geometric Viewpoint.*

Faugeras obtains a computer graphics-type representation of the object – in this case a mesh of planar triangular facets – from the range data. As we have already mentioned, such surface interpolation is used routinely in computer graphics applications to obtain models of real objects. However, the computer graphics situation differs in a number of ways from computer vision applications. First, the input device is usually some kind of arrangement, such as a platform rotating in the path of a laser beam, that measures depth all the way round an object. Second, consider the issue of the accuracy of representation – the amount of information used to specify the surface. In the computer graphics case the interest is in achieving an accurate rendered version of the model and the number of facets in the model only incurs a rendering time penalty which in most offline applications is tolerable. In real-time applications such as virtual reality, high rendering times are unacceptable and the required compromise between photo-realism and frame generation time has led to a number of diverse techniques to reduce the rendering time (as we discuss in Chapter 21). One of the approaches that has been given consideration is the reduction of the number of polygons in a model to, say, an extent that does not degrade too much the quality of the rendered version. Thus in computer graphics the motivation is processing time and the trade-off is between model complexity and image quality. In computer vision a similar trade-off exists, this time between model accuracy – the number of facets in the original representation – and the time it takes to use such a representation in a scheme that matches the extracted object to the model. Clearly using tens of thousands of facets – the norm in offline rendering – would be completely out of the question in computer vision and one of the problems that Faugeras addresses is the generation of a faceted model and its subsequent approximation.

Further reading

There are textbooks and journals on general approaches to computer vision described and listed in the introductory chapter. As we mentioned in that chapter, there are whole books devoted to particular approaches to three-dimensional object recognition. A selection of these is now listed. An instructive debate on representation in computer vision, to which many leading researchers in computer vision contribute, is to be found in *CVGIP: Image Understanding* (Special Issue on Directions in CAD based Vision), **60**(1), July 1994.

Journals

Clowes M.B. (1971). On seeing things. *Artificial Intelligence*, **2**, 79–116

Dickenson S.J., Pentland A.P. and Rosenfeld A. (1992). From volumes to views: an approach to 3-D object recognition. *CVGIP: Image Understanding*, **55**(2), March, 130–54

Huffman D.A. (1971). Impossible objects as nonsense sentences. In *Machine Intelligence 6*, B. Meltzer and D.Michie (eds), New York: American Elsevier

Raja N.S. and Jain A.K. (1994). Obtaining generic parts from range images using a multi-view representation, *CVGIP: Image Understanding*, **60**(1), July, 44–64

Sato K., Ikeuchi K. and Kanade T. (1992). Model based recognition of specular objects using sensor models. *CVGIP: Image Understanding*, **55**(2), March, 155–69

Books

Besl P.J. (1990). *Surfaces in Range Image Understanding*, Springer Series in Perception Engineering. New York: Springer-Verlag

Faugeras O. (1993). *Three-dimensional Computer Vision: A Geometric Viewpoint*. Cambridge, MA: MIT Press

Jain R.C. and Jain A.K., eds (1990). *Analysis and Interpretation of Range Images*, Springer Series in Perception Engineering. New York: Spriner-Verlag

Sugihara K. (1986). *Machine Interpretation of Line Drawings*. Cambridge, MA: MIT Press

16 Shape from X

In this chapter we look at techniques that attempt to extract shape information from a single projection – shape from shading, or from two projections – shape from stereo. We distinguish between the case of stereo, which normally involves a pair of images, and shape or structure from motion which involves determining structure from a series of images, although the latter is a generalization of the former. Structure from motion is dealt with in Chapter 18. This area of computer vision is still firmly a research area and the practical work in the chapter is as much a demonstration of the underlying problems as a set of solutions. Deriving shape information from intensity variations in a single image seems to be an extremely difficult problem and there is only one well-known algorithm which requires the scene to conform heavily to constraints. In shape from stereo (at least) two different views are available and it is by comparing these images that we attempt to extract information. The differences in the image tell us about depth. This is also an extremely difficult problem and does not have a robust solution despite having had around three decades of research devoted to it.

The main distinguishing factor between the material in this chapter and that in Chapter 15 where we look at the recognition of three-dimensional objects is that here we look at the recovery of three-dimensional information from a scene using two-dimensional passive sensors and without prior knowledge of the scene. They are both, however, computer vision approaches.

We can thus define the problem in the broadest possible terms by saying that we wish to recover three-dimensional information from two-dimensional projections. Additionally we wish to do this without any assistance from prior knowledge of the shapes or type of shapes that form the scene that we are viewing.

In most approaches to shape recovery we are firmly up against the major computer vision problem – the many to one mapping. This means that given any particular two-dimensional projection of a scene there are many three-dimensional configurations of that scene that could have produced the projection.

How are we to tackle this problem? That it is possible is evident from the human vision system. We can immediately perceive shape from a black and white photograph. (Although experience may be significant in this respect. Most of the photographs that we see contain objects whose shape we are already aware of. Also, we presumably make much use of edge information.) At first sight it seems impossible. The task is concerned with the recovery of depth information where most of such information has been destroyed by the projection process. In an orthographic projection only the depth order of objects – or which object is in front of another – is retained in the projection.

It is reasonable to assume that it is the relative lack of success of the 'shape from' techniques that have led to the parallel development of techniques that utilize existing knowledge. Why then, you may ask, do we persist with this approach to computer vision problems? The simplest answer is that in any completely general computer vision system we must be able to describe scenes that we have never seen before. The systems or approaches described in Chapter 15 can only output information like 'object A is present in such and such a pose'.

To describe scenes we have first to extract low-level information such as depth information before proceeding to a higher level of shape description. Another oft-quoted but arguable motivation is that human beings appear to be able to interpret two-dimensional pictures of reality with remarkable ease. In this respect Julesz's experiments (see Chapter 20) were especially influential in supporting this view, notably in shape from stereo approaches. Before this experiment it was believed that the recognition of monocular clues in the stereo pair were necessary for depth perception. Julesz's remarkable experiment discovery showed that human beings could invoke low-level processing, without recognition, and perceive depth. Later Marr and Poggio developed a computational theory (implemented by Grimson) that provided an explanation of matching filtered stereo pairs at different scales and gave even greater support for this view. Recently, however, there has been a shift away from this approach which is best exemplified by the following quote from Tanaka and Kak concerning depth from stereo:

During the last few years it has been recognised that while the Marr-Poggio paradigm may be an elegant model of the low level mechanisms for generating depth information, not to be ignored are the higher level cognitive phenomena that are also capable of producing the same type of information. In a majority of these higher level phenomena, there is first an explicit recognition of monocular cues in each image; depth perception is then generated either directly from the monocular clues, or through their fusion in a stereo pair.

At the outset we can make a distinction between **passive sensing** and **active sensing**. In passive analysis we attempt to analyze the scene from a reflected light detector such as a single frame from a TV camera. With active analysis we 'interfere' with the scene by introducing 'special' lighting conditions. We may, for example, illuminate the scene with grid-encoded light to considerably simplify subsequent analysis. Alternatively we may introduce radiation into the scene from, say, a laser ranger. Using a dense range image, of course, would seem to obviate the need for 'shape from' methods that try to extract depth, but even having access to a range image still leaves a large problem for computer vision. The active versus passive sensing debate was taken up in the previous chapter; for the moment we note that two-dimensional projections from passive sensors that measure reflected light intensity are easily and cheaply available (and are, of course, similar to our human low-level vision).

Purists tend to exclude active sensing from computer vision but the distinction seems somewhat harsh. If, for example, we look at Horn's shape from shading method we find that it needs to be loaded with mathematical constraints to enable a solution; so that the practical effect is no different in a sense to introducing constrained lighting. It makes no difference in the end if the scene is constrained from the mathematics – thus causing physical constraints to exist – or whether these constraints are part of the technology to begin with; both are less than ideal solutions.

In this chapter and Chapter 18 we will only look at shape from shading, stereo and motion. More 'shape from' methods exist, such as shape from texture, but these three are probably the most explored. Of the three, shape from shading is the least successful. Shape from motion algorithms, used in motion analysis problems, find many applications outside computer vision, for example in image compression as discussed in Chapter 26 and in photo-modelling (Chapter 21).

16.1 Shape from shading

This topic is concerned with extracting knowledge on the shape of an object solely from the intensity variation in the image plane. It was one of the first areas of study in computer vision and the initial work was carried out by Horn in 1977. Despite the time that has elapsed since, work in this area still remains mainly experimental.

A simple way to look at the problem is to consider it as the inverse of shading, using a local reflection model in computer graphics (Chapters 3 and 5). Here we make certain assumptions concerning the scene which enable us to shade an object quickly using 'easy' geometric properties, such as the orientation of the surface normal at each point on the surface with respect to the light source. Given a projection that exhibits shading variations, and the assumption of a light reflection model that produced these variations, we can work out the geometry of the object. The problem here is that real projections do not correspond to their 'pure' computer graphics counterparts and the simple light reflection models used in computer graphics only approximately simulate real light behaviour. The subsequent differences exhibited by real projections, compared to the expected differences predicted by an assumed light refection model, together with the normal noise variations that always occur in a real image, underpin the difficulties that this method possesses.

Thus computer graphics models are not 'real' enough for computer vision. But this is something that we should expect. The manifestation of using less than real models in computer graphics is the production of images that do not look completely real – they are recognizably computer graphics images. Idealized light reflection models produce perfect images in computer graphics and it follows that we cannot use them inversely in the analysis of real projections. Alternatively if we do use them we have to make certain assumptions concerning the nature of the light/object interaction in the scene.

In the quantitative recovery of shape from shading we can, as a first approximation, make virtually the same assumptions as are made in computer graphics. These are:

- We consider the light source that illuminated the object to be a point source at infinity.

- We ignore any illumination incident on the surface of interest that is due to global illumination. (In local reflection models in computer graphics we do not implement this component.)

- We assume that no shadows are cast on the object. (Consider the computer graphics case. We recall that we do not implement shadows in a local reflection model but require a separate 'add on' algorithm.)

Using these assumptions, and assuming that the image was formed from an orthographic projection, it is possible to recover shape from shading. Additionally we need knowledge concerning the reflectance properties of the surface that we are trying to describe. Again, if we consider the computer graphics local reflection model, we recollect that we were able, with a single object such as a sphere, to produce a wide variety of different images; that is, images that are different in the appearance of their overall shading. These differences were achieved by altering the parameters in the Phong reflection model – the ratio of the diffuse to the specular reflection coefficient. Thus the method must have knowledge of the reflectance properties of the surface. In other words, the shading of a surface depends on both how it is illuminated and its reflectance properties. We approached the problem in computer graphics by 'ignoring' all aspects of illumination, except direction, and by having knowledge of surface reflectance. This approach in computer vision uses the same constraints on light/object interaction.

Horn's method relies on a two-dimensional representation called **gradient** space. It uses this space to represent both the orientation of a surface and its reflectance properties. We will now describe gradient space and the reflectance map which uses this space.

16.1.1 Gradient space

Gradient space is a two-space representation of the orientation of every point on a surface. We consider that the surface that we are viewing has been projected into a two-space or image plane representation. Further, we take the projection direction along the $-z$ axis and consider only orthographic projections. Our surface is:

$$z = f(x,y)$$

and every visible point on the surface is projected into the image plane. Each of these points has a world space surface normal and we can represent the orientation of the surface normal of each by a single point in two space. This space is called the gradient space. An example of the relationship between gradient space and a surface normal is shown in Figure 16.1. This shows a surface normal N at a point on a surface. All visible points on this surface – the points that are visible in the image plane – will have surface normals with negative z components. To represent such normals in two space we first extend the vector back to the (x,y,z) origin and assign coordinates (a,b,c) to it (Figure 16.1(b)). If we consider a plane normal to the z axis positioned at $z = -1$ then the vector intersects this plane at coordinates (p,q), where:

$$p = -a/c$$
$$q = -b/c$$

This is shown in Figure 16.1(c) and the plane is known as gradient space. Now the direction of the normal to a surface $z = f(x,y)$ is:

$$(\partial f/\partial x, \partial f/\partial y, -1)$$

and thus we have:

$$p = \partial f/\partial x$$
$$q = \partial f/\partial y$$

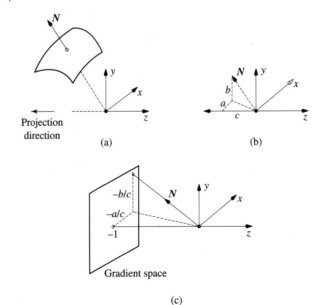

Figure 16.1
Gradient representation of the orientation of a surface normal. (a) The surface normal of a visible point; (b) moved to the (x,y,z) origin; (c) extended to intersect the plane $z = -1$.

hence the name gradient space. We can note that a surface point with a positive *z* component is invisible and the boundary between visibility and invisibility are points with normals of zero *z* component. Consider, for example, a cylinder with its long axis parallel to the *z* axis. This would project, or be viewed, as a circle in the image plane and would appear as a single point (0,0) in gradient space – there is only a single normal for the (visible) flat surface of the cylinder. Normals on the curved surface of the cylinder are points at infinity in every direction in gradient space. Alternatively a sphere would appear as an infinity of points everywhere in gradient space. As we move from the pole (the point (0,0) in gradient space) to the equator along a line of longitude, surface normals would have every orientation in gradient space and we would move from point (0,0) along a straight line towards infinity where the normal vector on the line of longitude intersects the equator. The further any point (vector) in gradient space is from the origin the steeper is its surface.

The reflectance map

The reflectance map is an encoding of the reflecting properties of the surface in gradient space for a particular direction of incident illumination. Such a map, together with the gradient space representation of the surface orientation, is used as input to the algorithm that attempts to solve the shape from shading problem. The reflectance map encodes only the reflectance properties of the surface and the direction of illumination. Thus we have, for a simple scene consisting of a single object, surface orientation encoded in gradient space and the surface reflectance properties and illumination direction encoded in the same space.

To see how a reflectance map works we start with the simplest type of reflection – Lambertian. You will recall that a Lambertian surface is a perfect matte surface that looks the same from all directions. (That is, a point on the surface is equally bright from all viewing directions.) In our Phong reflection model we called this the diffuse component and we recollect that the intensity of the reflected light depended only on the cosine of the angle between the light direction vector and the surface normal at the point of interest. Figure 16.2 shows two reflectance maps for such a surface differing only in the direction of incident illumination. The map is represented by iso-brightness contours or contours of constant $N \cdot L$. That is, the reflectance map is plotted from:

$$N \cdot L = k$$

where *k* is a constant between 0 and 1.

Staying with our computer graphics local reflection model we now consider a reflectance map for a surface that is both a specular and a diffuse reflector. First, consider a perfect specularly reflecting surface. As we know, this reflects light from a point source only along a particular direction – which in the computer graphics section we called the 'mirror' direction. Such a surface would have a reflectance map that is a single point – a single surface orientation reflecting

Figure 16.2
A diffuse sphere illuminated
from two different
directions, (a) and (c),
with the corresponding
reflectance maps, (b) and
(d).

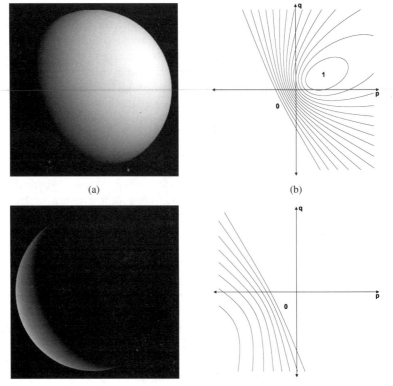

light. In computer graphics we considered specularly imperfect surfaces and introduced a model where the outgoing or reflected light was spread about the mirror direction. This resulted in a 'lobe' which was linearly combined with the hemispherical distribution of the diffuse reflection to give a characteristic of the type shown in Figure 16.3. Such a characteristic is a function of incident illumination direction and specular/diffuse reflectance properties.

A reflectance map representation of such behaviour will contain a set of small concentric circles (centred on the point that specifies the orientation that surface points must have to reflect specularly). These will give way to the diffuse behaviour of Figure 16.2 as the reflected intensity decreases. Thus we can interpret such a map as being a combination of the diffuse map and a set of concentric circles specifying, for a particular orientation, the dominance of the specular component. (Note that the figure contains no information concerning the colour change that would occur, for a coloured object, as we move from an area exhibiting a specular reflection or highlight into an area that only exhibited diffuse reflection.)

It is useful to consider the difference between the two forms (the computer graphics representation shown, for example, in Figure 3.14 and the reflectance map) of representing the reflectance behaviour of a surface. Both are characteristics from a particular illumination direction. In the computer graphics charac-

Figure 16.3
As Figure 16.2(a), with a
specular component added.

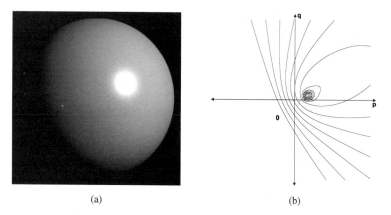

(a)   (b)

teristic the behaviour of a single point on the surface is represented as a function
of viewing direction. The different reflected intensities encountered as the
viewing direction is changed are shown. With the reflectance map the reflected
intensities for every point on the surface are represented for a single viewing
direction.

Solving the problem

We can state the problem as follows. We have an intensity function $I(x,y)$, the
image or projection of the scene, and a reflectance function $R(p,q)$. For the
constraints already stated, the reflectance function relates reflected light intensity to surface orientation and is a function only of light direction. If we can find
a correspondence between $I(x,y)$ and $R(p,q)$ and then for every point (x,y) we
have a surface orientation. We can then integrate to find the variation (but not
the absolute value of) z or $f(x,y)$.

Consider

$$I(x,y) = R(p,q)$$

This is one equation in two unknowns; all we know is that the surface orientation that has produced $I(x,y)$ must lie somewhere on a contour of R. An infinity
of surface orientations lies on a single contour. Thus we need constraints.

The constraint employed is that we consider surfaces to be smooth over any
small region. Horn's method of solving the problem relies on 'growing' a
solution by starting at a single point in the image plane $I(x_0,y_0)$ where the surface
orientation is known. This gives us a corresponding unique point $R(p_0,q_0)$ in
gradient space. The method then 'grows' a solution by moving a small amount
in the image plane in a special direction. This direction tells us what the equivalent direction is in gradient space, and the solution proceeds by moving incre-
mentally in image space and at the same time moving in gradient space. The
curve traced out in image space is then supplied with the surface orientation
along its length from which, by integration, we can find z.

First we note that:

$$dp = \partial p/\partial x \, dx + \partial p/\partial y \, dy$$
$$dq = \partial q/\partial x \, dx + \partial q/\partial y \, dy$$

From the definitions for p and q we have:

$$\partial p/\partial y = \partial^2 f/\partial y \partial x = \partial^2 f/\partial x \partial y = \partial q/\partial x$$

and we can write:

$$dp = \partial p/\partial x \, dx + \partial q/\partial x \, dy$$
$$dq = \partial p/\partial y \, dx + \partial q/\partial y \, dy$$

Now consider that from our start point $I(x_0,y_0)$ and $R(p_0,q_0)$ we take small steps, ds, in the image plane in a special direction. We choose, for a reason that will become obvious soon, this special direction to be the direction of steepest descent in gradient space. That is, our increment in $I(x,y)$ is

$$dx = \partial R/\partial p \, ds$$
$$dy = \partial R/\partial q \, ds$$

This gives us a new point in image space $(x_0 + dx, y_0 + dy)$ and we have to find the orientation of this point from $R(p_0 + dp, q_0 + dq)$. Substituting our values for

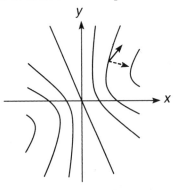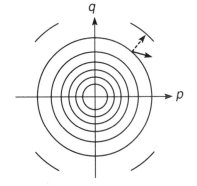

(a)

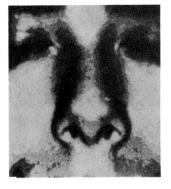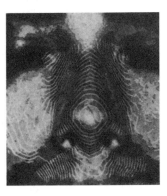

(b)

Figure 16.4
Horn's characteristic strip method of shape from shading. (Courtesy of B.K.P. Horn.)

dx and *dy* in the initial equations for *dp* and *dq* yields:

$$dp = (\partial p/\partial x \; \partial R/\partial p + \partial q/\partial x \; \partial R/\partial q) \; ds$$
$$= \partial I/\partial x \; ds$$

similarly:

$$dq = \partial I/\partial y \; ds$$

That is, we need to move in gradient space in the direction of the gradient of *I*. For a general point in the process, $I(x,y)$, $R(p,q)$, we:

(1) Move to a new point $(x + dx, y + dy)$ by moving in the direction of the gradient of $R(p,q)$.

(2) At the new point we move in a direction in *R* space given by the gradient of *I*.

This is demonstrated in Figure 16.4. In this way a set of surface normals are associated with a curve in image space and from this information the variation of depth along the curve can be obtained to within a constant spatial displacement along the direction of the projection.

16.1.4   Problems with Horn's method

The method is an elegant approach that relies on having a characteristic reflectance function for a surface. We developed much of the argument as an inverse computer graphics problem. However, this would only be the case if we were indeed analyzing synthetic images that had been produced by a computer graphics renderer. In practical images we are likely to be dealing with noisy projections of real objects which do not exhibit idealized reflectance functions.

In a multi-object scene we may have a number of different objects that not only possess different reflectance functions but, worse, may also exhibit different reflectance functions over their surface extent. Thus we are faced with the problem that we may have to recognize the object to know what reflectance function to use. Otherwise we need prior knowledge of the scene. Thus we conclude that the method could only function in practice as a single component of a vision system. We could not base a computer vision system on this technique alone.

Other constraints come from within the mathematical solution for the method. The method relies on $I(x,y)$ being smooth or continuous. This is turn implies that the surface contains no discontinuities. Other problems are that we need a start point to grow a solution and because the equations that are solved are not overconstrained the method is extremely susceptible to noise in the image. These comments explain the remark that we made at the beginning of this chapter: the method which strives for generality ends up being loaded with so many constraints that it becomes almost akin to practical constraint systems such as active vision.

16.2 Shape from stereo

Human beings possess stereo vision. That we appear to perceive depth from the disparity of images received in each retina has been known for a long time. This facility is sometimes called **geometric stereo**. (It does not appear, however, that we only utilize geometric stereo in depth perception. It is apparent that we can function, certainly in familiar surroundings, with one eye closed.)

Most 'shape from stereo' approaches in computer vision work by trying to extract shape information by decoding the disparity information in two or more projections taken from different viewpoints and reconstructing, from this information, the depth of points in the scene. This is mostly done by establishing correspondence between the stereo images. This means first recognizing which structures in each image correspond to each other – a task that, as we shall see, is not as easy as it sounds. If this can be successfully performed we can extract disparity and establish depth information which gives us shape.

In Chapter 20 we discuss the remarkable ability of the human visual system to perceive depth in images that are apparently structureless – the famous Julesz random dot stereograms. We remark that there is no obvious use of this attribute, but never the less it appears to exist in most people. Also, it is not clear how much of our depth perception depends on structure recognition. Do we as human beings recognize large-scale structure in the images and then use the disparity between such structures to sort out the depth of the objects, or is depth perception independent of structure recognition? An obvious conclusion that we could draw is that depth perception from stereo exists as a continuum. If large-scale structure is present then we use its geometry to aid our depth perception; if it is not, we can still perceive depth by analyzing structure at a smaller scale, and indeed even at the scale of a single pixel (as the random dot stereograms demonstrate). It is perhaps significant that with the random dot stereograms there is a delay before we can actually perceive the structure that is hidden in the image. (As I write this my visual field is filled partly with the foliage of a large tree and partly with a house. How much easier it is to estimate scale and depth in the house than to determine the spatial relationships between clusters of leaves and branches.)

There is also the obvious fact that if there is clear geometric structure in an image, representing familiar types of objects such as, say, buildings, we do not need stereo pairs – we can interpret depth because of our skill at interpreting perspective projections. Also, we should bear in mind that in human history geometric structure with straight lines belongs to a very recent age. Structure in natural scenes does not tend to contain straight lines.

In computer vision the existing methods reflect exactly this structure/no structure duality. Some methods try to match structure such as lines or edges; others try to match intensity in corresponding areas in the images. The first approach, of course, requires images that exhibit structure and that this organization can be abstracted from the image.

The fundamental problem in geometric stereo, which we will now discuss, is to find pairs of corresponding points – one from each of the stereo images. By corresponding we mean that pair of points that is produced in each image by a particular point in the scene. If for a single point in one image we can locate the corresponding point in the other image, then establishing the distance of the object point is simple trigonometric calculation (see Chapter 24).

Correspondence establishment

Having disposed of the straightforward geometrical problem, we now come to consider the fundamental problem of shape from stereo – establishing correspondence between points in each image.

First consider the ambiguity implicit in the problem. If we are recovering depth using the simple geometry outlined in Chapter 24, then we deduce that the object point of interest is located at the intersection of two rays – each drawn through the image points and the centres of projection. Figure 16.5 shows four adjacent points in each image. If the exact correspondence between points is not known then there are 16 possible interpretations in object space, 12 of which are so-called false targets. Note here that the problem, as framed in this way, is exactly equivalent to the image reconstruction from projections by back projection problem in medical imagery (Chapter 22). The difference with image projections is, of course, that there is no correspondence problem because the correspondence is implicit in the projection system and we know exactly which rays correspond in each image. Thus the problem in medical imagery is merely the reconstruction.

Establishing correspondence is complicated by many fairly obvious factors. Refer to Figure 16.6 and suppose that we are trying to match the indicated area in the left-hand image by searching along the same scan line in the right-hand image. First, points in one image may simply be missing from the other. In a scene that contains many objects, certain points in one image may be occluded by other objects in the other image. Occlusion areas are like shadows in computer graphics whose shape depends on the shape of the object causing the shadow and the position of the light source. They are geometrically the same as

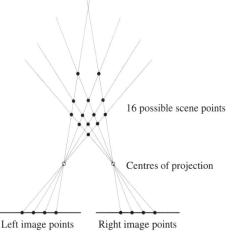

Figure 16.5
Four points whose exact correspondence is not known could have been produced from 16 possible scene points.

16 possible scene points

Centres of projection

Left image points   Right image points

Figure 16.6
A representation of
the common problems
in establishing
correspondence.

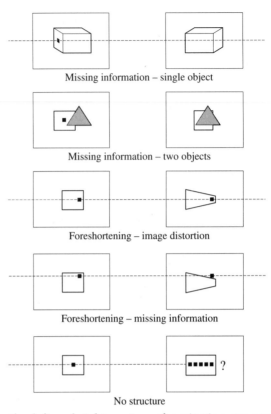

Missing information – single object

Missing information – two objects

Foreshortening – image distortion

Foreshortening – missing information

No structure

shadows where the left and right centres of projection are considered as light sources and the object casting the shadow is that causing the occlusion. Foreshortening can cause geometric distortion which makes the equivalent areas that we are trying to match dissimilar in the sense that one image is warped with respect to the other or completely different. Finally it may be impossible to find a correct match because the corresponding areas exhibit little difference – there is a lack of intensity variation or texture across the face of an object.

16.2.2

Constraints used in establishing correspondence

Most stereo matching algorithms use constraints to help with the search for correspondence. The constraints limit the scope of the search and enable confidence measures to be established for possible matches. The most obvious constraint is called the **uniqueness constraint** which means that a point in one image should have, at most, a single match in the other. Another is to place an upper bound on the disparity in the stereo projections by calculating a disparity gradient, which measures the rate of change of disparity of two points on the surface of an object with respect to the change in distance of the projection of the two points in a central (cyclopean) projection plane located centrally between the two stereo image planes. However, the most useful constraint is the so-called epipolar constraint, and this is now described.

Epipolarity is a powerful constraint that emerges from the geometry of simple stereo systems. If we consider a point in the source image and construct a ray from the centre of projection through that point, then we know that the object or scene point that produced the image point must lie somewhere on this line. The infinity of possible object points along this ray produce lines through the centre of projection of the right image that sweep out a plane containing the ray and the centre of projection of the right image (Figure 16.7). The inter-section of this plane with the right image plane is a so-called epipolar line. Thus if a point in the left image has a corresponding point in the right image, then this point must lie on the epipolar line formed by the projection of the left point's ray in the right image. So to search for a corresponding point in the right image, we know to constrain our search along the epipolar line. In general we have the concept of conjugate epipolar lines – a point in the left image has a conjugate epipolar line in the right image and vice versa. Conjugate lines have the property that the corresponding point on one epipolar line is restricted to lie on the conjugate epipolar line. It is easily seen that epipolar lines for one object or scene point come from the intersection of the epipolar plane for that point constructed by passing a plane through the scene point and the two centres of projection. For the simple geometry that we have used in the illustrations (projection planes coplanar and parallel to the line through their centres of projections), all epipolar lines are parallel to the x axis. A constraint that is required by simple correspondence matching algorithms – such as the intensity matching procedure described in the next section – is that the order of corresponding points along an epipolar line should not change. This is known as the monoticity constraint and it is violated, as Figure 16.8 shows, whenever a point can be imaged from either side of another point. The corresponding points then reverse their direction along an epipolar line.

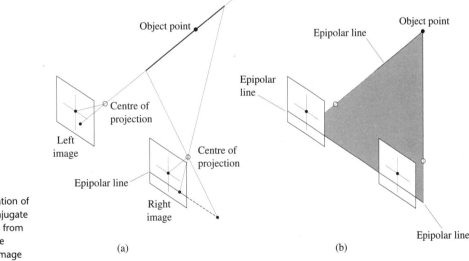

Figure 16.7
Epipolarity. (a) Formation of epipolar line. (b) Conjugate epipolar lines formed from the intersection of the epipolar plane with image planes.

Figure 16.8
Violation of monoticity
constraint.

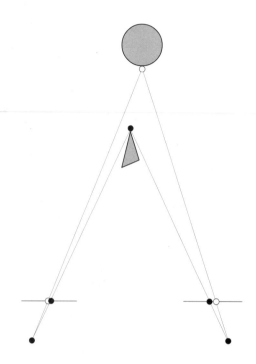

16.2.3 Establishing correspondence – intensity matching

So how do we establish correspondence? The simplest approach, which we will
now describe, is to ignore or not use structures in the scene and try to find a match
based solely on intensity. (Of course, structure is intensity variation; and intensity
matching means a simple pixel by pixel comparison that does not take into
account the fact that locally the pixels are forming a coherent structure such as a
straight line.) The idea is to consider a single point in one image, the left image
say, extract a region around this point giving a small sub-image, and then cross-
correlate (see Chapter 24) this sub-image with the right image. We then hope that
the maximum of the cross-correlation will be the corresponding point in the right
image. This idea is shown in Figure 16.9. Since we are utilizing the epipolar constraint we can restrict the cross-correlation to the epipolar line and the resulting
function is univariate as shown in the figure. More usually we would cross-correlate over a two-dimensional window as we describe in the case study below.

A number of important points now emerge. The first is that we should be
aware of the assumptions implicit in this approach. If we are going to match
intensities between two stereo images, taken by cameras from two different
directions, then we are assuming that the reflected intensity seen from the same
object point by each camera is the same. That is, reflected intensity is independent of viewing direction – something that is only true for perfect Lambertian
surfaces. Possibly an even more restrictive assumption is that the disparity is
constant across the extent of the window.

Figure 16.9
Correspondence establishment by intensity matching by cross-correlation.

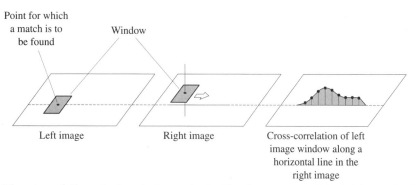

Point for which a match is to be found

Window

Left image

Right image

Cross-correlation of left image window along a horizontal line in the right image

The size of the window is important. Clearly we cannot just take a single point and attempt to match it with single points in the other image. But what size should the window region be? Too small a window may result in false matches which would inevitably occur as we reduced the size to approach a single point. A small window is also sensitive to image noise. Too large a window may result in no match at all because of the difference in the stereo pair that we have already discussed. As we increase the size of the window, the constraints that we assume become less and less likely to hold.

The simplest and easiest approach to implement, suggested by Levine et al. in 1973, is to have a window whose size varies adaptively according to the nature of the information that it encloses. We could, for example, increase the size of the window just until the variance of the enclosed intensity information reached a certain minimum.

Test images

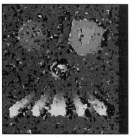

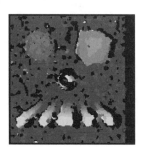

Figure 16.10
A simple intensity matching algorithm for a 3×3, 5×5 and 7×7 window.

3×3

5×5

7×7

Black pixels indicate no match found

The contradictions implicit in either increasing the window size or decreasing it point to the ideal solution being the capture of some distinctive structure in the source image to find a successful match from the cross-correlation.

Figure 16.10 shows an example of an intensity matching algorithm. Shown is a test image together with the results of using a 3×3, 5×5 and 7×7 window. Black pixels indicate that no match was found. One of the major problems, apart from matching, is the precision of the extracted depth. In this example the search is from a disparity of 10 pixels to 30 pixels giving only 20 levels in the depth map. The same algorithm operating on an image of a real scene is shown in Figure 16.11 (Colour Plate). The original image is shown as the left component and a composite of the left and right hand image indicates the disparity.

16.2.4   Establishing correspondence – structure matching

Establishing correspondence by intensity matching is computationally simple, but as we have seen certain tricky adjustments are required concerning the size of the window used in the cross-correlation. Essentially we are trying to capture, with a window, some reasonably unique structure that we can match in the conjugate image. The obvious question is: why do we not match structure directly? We can apply explicit edge detection and then try to match between the left and right images. Just as we had to assume a major illumination constraint in intensity matching – namely that the reflected intensity is independent of viewpoint, now we have to assume that edges are viewpoint independent. A simple example (Figure 16.12) demonstrates the concept of viewpoint dependence and independence in the context of edges. An object such as a rectangular solid exhibits a discontinuity in its surface normal as we move from one face to another. This discontinuity produces a viewpoint-independent edge in the stereo projections. Contrast this with an object, say, for example, a cylinder, whose surface normal is continuous (at least over a path traced out around its curved surface). In this case the position of the edge that is projected into each stereo image is different. Each projection sees a different pair of edges.

Edge detection is powerful in noisy images, as we have seen in Chapter 10, and can operate as a pre-process that is independent of the problem of matching. Coherence in an edge can be combined with the epipolarity to provide a powerful overall constraint. This means that if a match can be found for an edge at the intersection of a conjugate epipolar line, then all other points on the edge must match at conjugate epipolar line intersections.

Matching can be 'tightened' by using geometric constraints supplemental to the epipolarity. We can, for example, compute the following differences between the lines and ensure that each of these is less than a predefined maximum:

- the disparity between the lines measured, say, at the point of intersection between the line segments and the epipolar line;
- the length of each line;
- the orientation of each line.

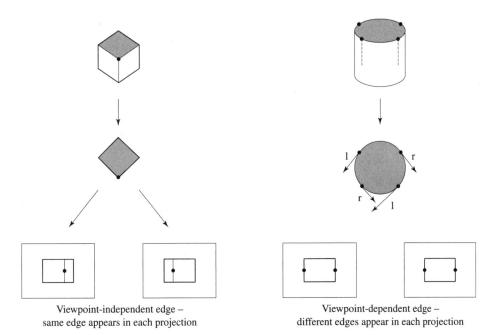

Viewpoint-independent edge –
same edge appears in each projection

Viewpoint-dependent edge –
different edges appear in each projection

Figure 16.12
Viewpoint independent and
dependent edges.

In addition there is the uniqueness constraint – a line segment in one image can have at the most one corresponding segment in the other.

One obvious problem that occurs is that we cannot deal with horizontal or nearly horizontal lines because they are parallel to the epipolar line. Using the epipolar constraint with straight lines means that we must have a well-defined intersection between the line segment and the epipolar line. As the line segments become horizontal we cannot define a unique intersection point.

Note that the categorization between intensity and structure matching is not as clear-cut as we have implied. With intensity matching we assume that the intensity of a single pixel is sufficiently unique to be the basis of a matching scheme, so we arrange for a match search to be based on windows that surround the pixels in each projection. We are using the structure in the windows and are thus implicitly using structure. The accepted categorization intensity and structure matching is somewhat misleading. With intensity matching we are using any structure present in the window. With structure matching, using, say, line segments, we are explicitly using a particular structure, extracting this first from each projection, then searching for a match. In this respect a better distinction may be between **implicit structure matching** using any coherent spatial configuration, and **explicit structure matching** using a particular structural configuration such as line segments.

16.2.5

More elaborate approaches – the MPG algorithm

Because of the discussed shortcomings of the above simple approaches, much research has centred around the development of relaxation or iterative algorithms.

One of the most well-known approaches in this category was originally developed by Marr and Poggio. This is an edge matching algorithm which uses coarse-to-fine edge resolution in the matching using the Marr–Hildreth edge operator (described in Chapter 10). This means that match estimates at coarse resolution are used to control those at finer resolution. The Marr–Poggio paradigm in its original form was presented as a computational theory which was implemented in 1981 by Grimson. It supplied a successful explanation of the random dot stereograms and, as we discussed in the introduction, provided support for the principle of the analysis of scenes by starting with low-level information extraction and working upwards to a high-level description without benefit of prior high-level knowledge or constraints.

Figure 16.13 shows the overall structure of the algorithm. The algorithm also incorporates matching at different degrees of resolution – structures that exhibit large scale variations are matched at a coarse resolution and those that exhibit small variations, such as, say, texture across the face of an object, at fine resolution. The matching is performed on the zero-crossings output of the filter where each output is produced from filter widths (see Chapter 10) of 64, 32, 16 and 8. The order of the matching is from coarse to fine and as each match is performed a 'vergence' control sets up the stereo pair for the next fine match in the sequence. This means that the disparity values for the previous (coarser) step are used to shift pixels in the current (finer) zero-crossing stereo pair. The matching itself is performed by using the epipolarity constraint and employing windows to constrain the search space. The filtering and matching stages are then followed by a disambiguation step which selects a particular match if there is more

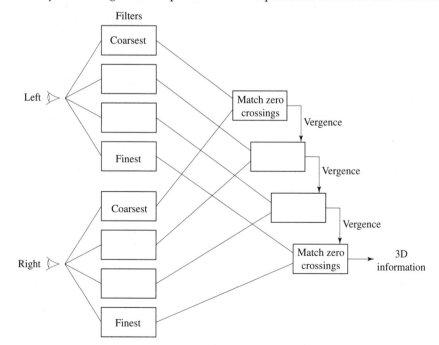

Figure 16.13
The structure of the Marr–Poggio–Grimson algorithm. Each filter consists of a Laplacian of a Gaussian followed by zero crossing detection at the appropriate resolution.

than one candidate. This is based on a notion that Marr and Poggio called the 'pulling effect'. This means simply that disparity variations in any neighbourhood of the image cannot be chaotic. Although there will be discontinuities in the disparity values, over any small neighbourhood the values should not change much. A candidate should be chosen whose disparity is consistent with the disparity values in a small neighbourhood (in the same resolution channel).

Depth recovery – the general problem

In recovering depth from a real scene, using either an intensity or edge-based scheme, we are faced with the problem that we will only have knowledge of depth at certain irregularly spaced points in the image. If we are matching using intensity then we will obtain no matches and have no information over surfaces that exhibit insufficient detail to obtain a match (textureless plane surfaces, for example). Using an edge-based scheme means that we only have information at detectable edges. And for most scenes an edge image is fairly sparse. The density of the depth image that we recover from the scene using the above methods will depend on the particular technique used and the nature of the scene.

Thus depth information at points in the scene that cannot be matched needs to be recovered by interpolation from known points. Intuitively this is only possible if heavy constraints are assumed concerning the nature of the scene, for example planar faces between edges. An alternative approach is to give the scene texture by illuminating it with a light source that casts random dots over the scene but this implies interference with the scene.

And what about the situation shown in Figure 16.6 where correct matching is impossible because each image contains information missing from the other? Both these problems point to a solution that involves high-level knowledge or experience of the nature of the objects in the scene.

Further reading

Grimson W.E.L. (1981). A computer implementation of a theory of human stereo vision. *Phil. Trans. of the Royal Society, Series B*, **292**, 217–53

Horn B.K.P. (1975). Obtaining shape from shading information. In *The Psychology of Computer Vision* (Winston P.H., ed.). New York: McGraw-Hill

Julesz B. (1960). Binocular depth perception of computer-generated patterns. *The Bell System Technical Journal*, **39**(5), 1125–61

Levine M.D., O'Handley D.A. and Yagi G.M. (1973). Computer determination of depth maps. *Computer Graphics and Image Processing*, **2**, 131–50

Marr D. and Poggio T. (1976). Cooperative computation of stereo disparity. *Science*, **194**, 283–7

Tanaka S.T. and Kak A.C. (1990). A rule based approach to binocular stereopsis. In *Analysis and Interpretation of Range Images* (Jain R.C. and Jain A.K., eds). New York: Springer-Verlag

17   The moving computer image

17.1 The moving image in entertainment – computer animation and morphing: introduction

17.2 A categorization and description of computer animation techniques

17.3 Motion control and the animator

17.4 Animation, modelling and physically based simulation

17.5 Image metamorphosis – morphing

17.6 The moving image in science

The manipulation of moving images is a relative newcomer to computer imagery and until very recently both the synthesis and the analysis of moving images generally took place offline. We are entering an era where there is a demand for the manipulation of moving images in real time and hardware resources to cope with this, and this fact has led to many new application areas. In this chapter we examine the techniques that have been used in the past together with current and emerging techniques. The chapter is structured by application because the techniques that have emerged are diverse and have mostly been developed out of the applications.

The particular moving image techniques that are relevant to virtual reality – quality image synthesis from very large scene descriptions and the use of computer vision techniques in interfacing – are dealt with in Chapter 20.

17.1   The moving image in entertainment – computer animation and morphing: introduction

Leaving aside some toys of the nineteenth century, it is interesting to consider that we have only had the ability to create and disseminate moving imagery for a very short period – since the advent of film. In this time it seems that animation has not developed as a mainstream art form. Outside the world of Disney and his imitators there is little film animation that reaches the eyes of the common man. It is curious that we do not seem to be interested in art that represents movement and mostly consign animation to the world of children's entertainment. Perhaps we can thank Disney for raising film animation to an art form and at the same time condemning it to a strange world of cute animals which are imbued with a set of human emotions.

With the advent of computer animation, will this situation change? Certainly it is too early to say. Computer animation has for many years been locked into its own 'artistic' domain and its most common manifestations are for TV title sequences and TV commercials. These productions, known derisively as 'flying logos', move rigid bodies around in three-dimensional space and have been the mainstream form of computer animation for around two decades. Their novelty having palled a long time ago, the productions exhibit a strange ambivalence: the characters have to retain their traditional function and at the same time have an 'animation personality'.

At first there was much optimism for computer animation. In the 1971 edition of the classic *The Techniques of Film Animation* (Hallas and Manvell, 1971), the author, commenting on early scientific computer animation, states:

The position at present is that the scientist and the animator can now create drawings that move in three or four dimensions, drawings that can rotate in space, and drawings involving great mathematical precision representing a complex mathematical factor or scientific principle. The process takes a fraction of the time for a production of a conventional cartoon, a condition every animator has wished for ever since the invention of cinematography. What may now be needed is an artist of Klee's talent who could invent a new convention for creating shapes and forms. The tools are there and the next ten years will surely lead to the development of exciting visual discoveries.

In fact the next 20 years saw little development of computer animation beyond its utilitarian aspects, but perhaps in the 1990s we are beginning to see evidence of this early prediction.

Computer animation is becoming increasingly used in the cinema, not, however, as a medium in its own right, but as a special effects tool. (And indeed one of the most ubiquitous tools used by recent productions – morphing – is strictly not computer animation at all, but the two-dimensional pixel by pixel post-processing of filmed imagery.)

What can computer animation offer to an animation artist? Two major tools certainly. First, the substantial shortening of routine workload over conventional cel animation. Second, the ability to make three-dimensional animation which means that we can 'film' the movement and interaction of three-dimensional objects. Film animation has been firmly locked into two-dimensional space with most effort being spent on movement and characterization with only a nod here and there to three-dimensional considerations such as shading and shadows. With the exception of *Toy Story*, the first full-length computer graphics animation film, it would seem that animators still need to use manual techniques in the main.

Here there is a parallel with paint packages and the lack of development of their use by painters – an issue taken up in Chapter 23. Despite the availability of elaborate computer metaphors for brushes and the like, such static graphic art facilities tend to be locked into the production of commercial art work. There is little use of such packages by established artists – art for art's sake. There are few exhibitions of computer art and few published books of work.

Leaving aside the issue of art, the main practical problem that is central to all computer animation is motion specification or control. Beyond the obvious problems of the static modelling of objects or characters that are going to make up a computer animation (which are the same problems faced by static rendering), there is the scripting or control of realistic movement – which is after all the basis of the art of animation. This becomes more and more difficult as models become more and more complex. Animating a single rigid body that possesses a single reference point is reasonably straightforward; animating a complex object such as an animal which may have many parts moving, albeit in a constrained manner, relative to each other is extremely difficult. Certainly at the moment the most complex computer animations are being produced in Hollywood and to highlight the difficult problem of movement control we will start the chapter by examining a contemporary example.

In film production more and more traditionally crafted special effects facilities that use modelmakers, matte painters and stop motion animators are being taken over by the computer. Digital manipulation techniques such as compositing, where images can be manipulated at the pixel level, are replacing time-honoured optical methods, giving the benefits of cost reduction and an increase in quality. Matte painting on glass – a technique that Hollywood has raised to an art form – looks like becoming obsolescent as digital techniques can be used to manipulate photographs to produce mattes. However, the innovative uses of computer image techniques have taken special effects into a realm that simply could not be achieved by manual techniques – an early example of this is the use of morph sequences in the mid-1980s.

Steven Spielberg's film *Jurassic Park* is reckoned to be the most lifelike computer animation accomplished to date. It has an interesting history, and recognizing that it is a pinnacle of achievement in realistic animation we will look briefly at the techniques that were used to produce it. The role of computer animation in this case was to bring to life creatures that could not be filmed and the goal was 'realism'. This, however, is not the only way in which computer animation is being used in films. In a recent Disney production, *The Lion King* (1994), computer animation is used to imitate Disney-type animation – to give the same look and feel as the traditional animation so that it can mix seamlessly with traditional cel animation. In this production a stampede sequence was produced by computer animation techniques. The sequence was perhaps more complex, in terms of the number of animal characters used and their interaction, than could have been produced manually; and this was the motivation for using computer techniques.

For *Jurassic Park* Spielberg originally hired a stop-motion (puppet or model) animation expert to bring the creatures to life using this highly developed art form. The only computer involvement was to be the post-processing of the stop-motion animation (with motion blur) to make the sequences smoother and more realistic. This task was to be undertaken by Industrial Light and Magic – a company already very experienced both in the use of 'traditional' special effects and the use of digital techniques such as morphing. However, at the same time ILM developed a Tyrannosaurus Rex test sequence using just computer animation techniques and when Spielberg was shown this sequence, so the story goes, he immediately decided that all the animation should be produced by ILM's computers. *Jurassic Park* is viewed as a turning point in the film industry and many people see this film as finally establishing computer graphics as the preferred tool in the special effects industry and as a technique, given the commercial success of *Jurassic Park*, that Hollywood will make much of in the years to come.

The advance in realism that emerged from this animation was the convincing movements of the characters. Although great attention was paid to modelling and detail such as the skin texture, it is in the end the motion that impresses. The realism of the motion was almost certainly due to the unique system for scripting the movements of the model (described in some detail in Section 17.2.2). Although the computer techniques gave much freedom over stop-motion puppet animation, where the global movements of the model are restricted by the mechanical fact that it is attached to a support rig, it is the marriage of effective scripting with the visual realism of the model that produced a film that will, perhaps, be perceived in the future as *King Kong* is now.

17.2 A categorization and description of computer animation techniques

Computer animation techniques can be categorized by a somewhat unhappy mix of the type and nature of the objects that are going to be animated and the programming technique used to achieve the animation. We have chosen to describe the following established types of computer animation:

- rigid body animation
- articulated structure animation
- particle animation
- behavioural animation
- procedural animation.

(The potentially important case of facial animation is dealt with in the final section – The Moving Image in Science.)

These categories are not meant to be a complete set of computer animation techniques; for example, we have excluded the much studied area of soft body or deformable object animation. Techniques that have been used are as wide and varied as the animation productions – we have chosen these particular five because they seem to have become reasonably well established over the relatively short history of computer animation. Some animation may, of course, be produced using a mixture of the above techniques.

Rigid body animation is self-explanatory and is the easiest and most ubiquitous form. In its simplest form it simply means using a standard renderer and moving objects and/or the viewpoint around.

Articulated structures are computer graphics models that simulate quadrupeds and bipeds. Such models can range from simple stick figures up to attempts that simulate animals and human beings complete with a skin and/or clothes surface representation. The difficulty of scripting the motion of articulated structures is a function of the complexity of the object and the complexity of the required movements. Usually we are interested in very complex articulated structures – humans or animals – and this implies, as we shall see, that motion control is difficult.

Particle animation means individually animating large populations of particles to simulate some phenomenon viewed as the overall movement of the particle 'cloud' such as a fireworks display. Particles, as the name implies, are small bodies each of which normally has its own animation script.

Behavioural animation means modelling the behaviour of objects. What we mean by 'behaviour' is something more complex than basic movement, and may depend on certain behavioural rules which are a function of object attributes and the evolving spatial relationship of an object to neighbouring objects. Behavioural animation is like particle animation with the important extension that particle scripts are not independent. A collection of entities in behavioural animation evolve according to the behaviour of neighbours in the population. The stampeding animals in *The Lion King*, for example, moved individually and also according to their position in the stampeding herd. Another example is the way in which birds move in a flock and fish move in a shoal. Each individual entity in such situations has both autocratic movement and also movement influenced by its continually changing spatial relationship with other entities in the scene. The goal of the behavioural rules in this context is to have a convincing depiction of the herd as an entity.

Finally, procedural animation is where we simulate the behaviour of an entity by writing a procedure that, most commonly, implements a mathematical model controlling movement.

17.2.1 Rigid body animation

Rigid body animation is the oldest and most familiar form of computer animation. Its most common manifestation is the ubiquitous 'flying logo' on our TV screens and it appears to have established itself as a mandatory technique for titles at the beginning of TV programmes. Dispensing with centuries of graphics design, we are invited to be impressed with block characters gracefully tumbling in space before freezing into their final position. Whatever charm these things held for us when they first appeared is debatable, but they have long since been artistically moribund. Their inertia is a tribute to the perceived power of the computer image. News programmes, for example, seem to use them very much; maybe to give a veracity to their reporting that the producers presume derives from the impressiveness of the characters' gymnastics. The message appears to be: we gather and interpret news for you, using the power and immediacy of modern electronic communication techniques. Our titles, together with some excruciating but dramatic musical motif, reinforces this message.

Rigid body animation could be described as the fundamental animation requirement and is likely to be used in some form by all of the other categories. It is the simplest form of computer animation to implement and is the most widely used. It is mainly used by people who do not have a formal computer or programming background; consequently the interface issue is critically important, and we will structure our treatment of it around this. This type of animation was an obvious extension of programs that could render three-dimensional scenes. We could produce animated sequences by rendering a scene with an object in different positions, or by moving the viewpoint (the virtual camera) around, recording the resulting single frames on video tape or film.

The problem is: how do we specify and control the movement of objects in a scene? Either the objects can move, or the virtual camera can move, or we could make both move at the same time. We will describe how to move a single object but the technique extends in an obvious way to the other cases.

The most obvious requirement is that an interface should enable motion specification in some kind of high-level manner, equivalent, say, to the implementation of the statement 'move object A from its current position to position X'. An early idea was to imitate the process of 'in-betweening', established by Disney in the 1930s, to enable the production of his feature film length animations. In this process the top animators produced difficult sections of animation – particularly complex movements or facial animation – by drawing key frames. These frames established the nature of the movement and were frames that represented some samples in the sequence at intervals greater than the inter-frame interval of the final production sequence. 'In-between' artists, lower down in the Disney hierarchy, and consequently paid less, would be presented with these key frames and would produce the in-between frames. Early computer animation investigators realized that they could repeat this process. A computer animator could place an object at appropriate positions in the scene and the computer could produce the key frames by interpolation. Thus the well-established idea of mathematical interpolation between two points was an obvious mechanism to imitate Disney in-betweening.

This idea, although perfectly adequate in simple cases, suffers from certain disadvantages. First, there is no explicit script which means that the animators cannot record and reuse their actions, a necessary tool if they are going to be able to evolve animations from previous experience. Second, the nature of the motion that emerges from the interpolation process is a function of the interval between key frames and the type of interpolation used, and the motion produced may not be exactly what the animator requires. If this happens it may not be apparent to the animator exactly where and when to place more key frames to achieve the desired result. So the approach does not offer good interaction facilities and the movement used for a sequence cannot be easily reused or imitated in other sequences. Interpolation can in the end only be a crude approximation to manual in-betweening. An in-betweener is an intelligent artist who is directed by key frames. An interpolation procedure fits a curve through points in three-dimensional space. The two techniques are poles apart.

So we are led towards the idea of an explicit script in computer animation and some kind of interface that enables a person to write the script. The best approach is to use a graphical interface. This will suffer from the usual problem of trying to perceive the three-dimensionality of a scene or scene representation from a two-dimensional projection, but if we can produce the sequences, or a wireframe version of the finished sequence, in real time then this difficulty is ameliorated. (As we discuss in Chapter 20, moving an object in real time is one way in which we can enhance perception of the three-dimensional scene that has been compressed into two dimensions.)

An obvious idea is to use cubic parametric curves as a script form (Chapter 7). Such a curve can be used as a path over which the reference point or origin of the object is to move. These can be easily edited and stored for possible future use. The best approach, called the double interpolant method, is to use two curves, one for the path of the object through space and one for its motion characteristic along the path. Then a developer can alter one characteristic independently of the other.

An interface possibility is shown in Figure 17.1. The path characteristic is visualized and altered in three windows that are the projections of the curve in the xy, yz and xz planes. The path itself can be shown embedded in the scene

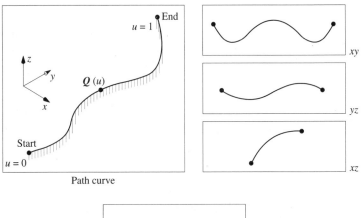

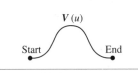

Figure 17.1

Motion specification for rigid body animation – an interface specification.

Path curve

Motion curve

with three-dimensional interpretative clues coming from the position of other objects in the scene and vertical lines drawn from the curve to the xy plane. The animator sets up the path curve $Q(u)$, applies a velocity curve $V(u)$ and views the resulting animation, editing either or both characteristics if necessary.

Generating the animation from these characteristics means deriving the position of the object at equal intervals in time along the path characteristic. This is shown in principle in Figure 17.2. The steps are:

(1) For a frame at time t find the distance s corresponding to the frame time t from $V(u)$.

(2) Measure s units along the path characteristic $Q(u)$ to find the corresponding value for u.

(3) Substitute this value of u into the equations for $Q(u)$ to find the position of the object (x,y,z).

(4) Render the object in this position.

This simple process hides a subsidiary problem called reparametrization. V is parametrized in terms of u, that is:

$$V(u) = (t,s)$$

$$t = T(u) \text{ and } s = S(u)$$

Given the frame time t_f we have to find the value of u such that $t_f = T(u)$. We then substitute this value of u into $s = S(u)$ and 'plot' this distance on the path characteristic $Q(u)$. Here we have exactly the same problem. The path characteristic is parametrized in terms of u, not s. The general problem of reparametrization in both cases involves inverting the two equations:

$$u = T^{-1}(t) \text{ and } u = Q^{-1}(s)$$

An approximate method that given t or s finds a close value of u is accumulated chord length. Shown in principle in Figure 17.3 the algorithm is:

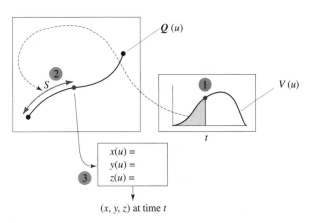

Figure 17.2
Finding the object position (x,y,z) at time t.

Figure 17.3
Accumulated chord-length
approximation.

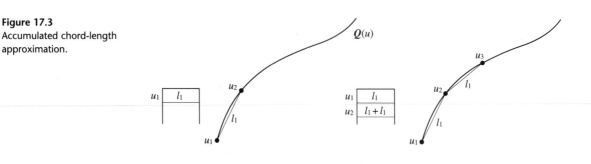

(1) Construct a table of accumulated chord lengths by taking some small interval in u and calculating the distances l_1, l_2, l_3, ... and inserting in the table l_1, (l_1+l_2), $(l_1+l_2+l_3)$, ... the accumulated lengths.

(2) To find the value of u corresponding to s, say, to within the accuracy of this method, we take the nearest entry in the table to s.

This simple approach does not address many of the requirements of a practical system, but it is a good basic method from which context-dependent enhancements can be grown. In particular it can form the basis for both a scripting system and an interactive interface. We briefly describe some of more important omissions.

The first is that if we freely change $V(u)$, then the total time taken for the object to travel along the curve will in general change. We may, for example, make the object accelerate more quickly from rest, shortening the time taken to travel along the path. Many animations, however, have to fit into an exact time slot and a more normal situation would involve changing $V(u)$ under the constraint that the travel time remains fixed.

Another more obvious problem is: what attitude does the object takes as it moves along a path? The method as it stands is only suitable for single particles or, equivalently, a single reference point in an object which would just translate 'upright' along the path. Usually we want the object to rotate as it translates. Simplistically we can introduce another three script curves to represent the attitude of the object as it moved along the path. The easiest way to do this is to parametrize the rotation by using three angles specifying the rotation about each of three coordinate axes rigidly attached to the object. These are know as Euler angles and are called roll, pitch and yaw. There are certain well-known problems with this parametrization. These are discussed at length in the book by Watt and Watt.

If we are producing an animation with many objects moving in the scene and if these objects are animated, one at a time, independently then what do we do about collisions? If we use a standard rendering pipeline (with a Z-buffer) then colliding objects will simply move through each other, unless we explicitly detect this event and signal it through the design interface. Collision detection is a distinctly non-trivial problem. Objects that we normally want to deal with in computer animation can be extremely complex – their spatial extent specified by a geometric description that in most cases will not be amenable to collision detection. Consider two polygon mesh objects that each contain a large number of polygons. It is not obvious how to detect the situation that a vertex from one object has moved inside the space of another. A straightforward approach would involve a comparison between each vertex in one object and every polygon in the other – an extremely time-consuming problem. And the detection of a collision is only part of the problem; how do we model the reaction of objects, their deformation and movement after a collision?

(17.2.2)
Articulated structure animation

Scripting of the movement of quadruped or biped models in computer animation has, for some time, been an energetically pursued research topic. The computer models are known as articulated structures and most approaches for movement control in animation have attempted to extend techniques developed in the industrial robotics field. Just as interpolation was the first idea to be applied to rigid body animation, parametrizing the movement of links or limbs in an articulated structure using robotic methodology seemed the way to proceed. Although this is perhaps an obvious approach it has not proved very fruitful. One problem is that robot control is itself a research area – by no means have all the problems been solved in that field. Probably a more important reason is that the techniques required to control the precise mechanical movements of an industrial robot do not make a comfortable and creative environment in which an animator can script the freer, more complex and subtler movements of a human or an animal. (This is a general problem in computer graphics that we have discussed elsewhere. Despite the exotic claims of the software developers, artists tend to be constrained by the nature of the interface tools supplied. Rather than have their creative abilities expanded by the medium, they are usually shrunk.) Yet another reason is that animal structures are not rigid and the links themselves deform as illustrated in Figure 17.4. In fact the most successful articulated structure animation to date – *Jurassic Park* – used an ad hoc technique to represent or to derive the motion. Let us look briefly at these techniques. This will give an appreciation of the difficulty of the problem faced by the animators in *Jurassic Park* and the efficacy of their solution.

First, what is an articulated structure? It is simply a set of rigid objects, or links, connected to each other by joints which enable the various parts of the structure to move, in some way, with respect to each other. Consider a simple example – a single human leg. We might model this as represented in Figure 17.5(a) using two links connecting three joints – the hip joint, the knee joint and the ankle joint. Simplistically we could constrain movement to the plane containing the joints and allow the link between the hip and the knee to rotate, between certain limits, about the hip joint and allow the link between the ankle and the knee to rotate about the knee joint (and, of course, we know that this link can only rotate in one direction). The rotation of the foot about the ankle

Figure 17.4
Spine flexion in a horse and
a cheetah (after Gray
(1968)).

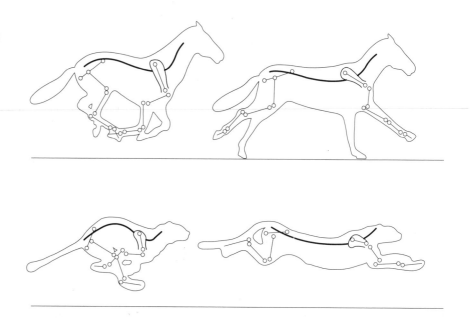

joint is more complicated since the foot itself is an articulated structure. Given such a structure, how do we begin to specify a script for, say, the way the leg structure is to behave to execute a walk action? There are two major approaches to this problem, both of which come out of robotics – **forward kinematics** and **inverse kinematics**.

Forward kinematics is a somewhat tedious low-level approach where the animator has to explicitly specify all the motions of every part of the articulated structure. Like any low-level approach the amount of work that has to be done by the animator is a function of the complexity of the structure. The articulated structure is considered as a hierarchy of nodes (Figure 17.5(b)) with an associated transformation which moves the link connected to the node in some way. We could animate such a structure by using curves to specify the transformation

Figure 17.5
A simple articulated
structure and its hierarchical
representation.

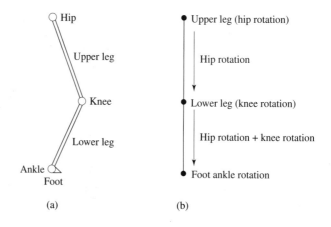

values as a function of time. Instead of having just a single path characteristic which moves a reference point for a rigid body, we may now have many characteristics each moving one part of the structure. An important point is that each node in the hierarchy inherits the movement of all the nodes above it. The hip rotation in the example causes the lower leg as well as the upper leg to rotate. The following considerations are apparent:

> Hip joint: this is the 'top' joint in the structure and needs to be given global movement. In our simple walk this is just translation.

> Hip–knee link rotation about the hip joint: we can specify the rotation as an angular function of time. If we leave everything below this link fixed then we have a stiff-legged walk (politely known as a compass gait but possibly more familiar as the 'goose step').

> Knee–ankle link rotation about the knee joint: to relax the goose step into a natural walk we specify rotation about the knee joint.

And so on. To achieve the desired movement the animator starts at the top of the hierarchy and works downwards, explicitly applying a script at every point. The evolution of a script is shown in Figure 17.6. Applying the top script would result in a goose step. The second script – knee rotation – allows the lower leg to bend. Applying both these scripts would result in a walk where the foot was always at right angles to the lower leg. This leads us into the ankle script.

Even in this simple example problems begin to accrue. It is not too difficult to see that when we come to script the foot, we cannot tolerate the hip joint moving in a straight line parallel to the floor. This would cause the foot to penetrate the floor. We have to apply some vertical displacement to the hip as a function of time and so on. And we are considering a very simple example – a walk action. How do we extend this technique for a complex articulated structure that has to execute a fight sequence rather than make a repetitive walk cycle? Figure 17.7 shows a simple character executing a somewhat flamboyant gait that was animated using forward kinematics.

Inverse kinematics, on the other hand, is a more high-level approach. Here an animator might specify something like: walk slowly from point A to point B. And the inverse kinematics technique works out a precise script for all the parts of the structure so that the whole body will perform the desired action. More precisely, inverse kinematics means that only the required position of the end (or ends) of the structure are specified. The animator does not indicate how each separate part of the articulated structure is to move, only that the ends of it move in the desired way. The idea comes from robotics where we mostly want the end effector of a robot arm to take up precise positions and perform certain actions. The inverse kinematics then works out the attitude that all the other joints in the structure have to take up so that the end effector is positioned as required. However, herein lurks the problem. As the articulated structure becomes more and more complex, the inverse kinematics solution becomes more and more difficult to work out. Also inverse kinematics does not, generally, leave much

Figure 17.6
Evolution of a script for a leg.

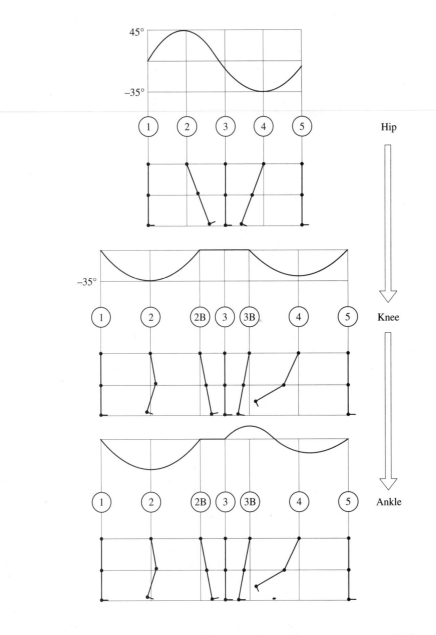

scope for the animator to inject 'character' into the movements, which is after all the art of animation. The inverse kinematics functions as a black box into which is input the desired movement of the ends of the structure, and the detailed movement of the entire structure is controlled by the inverse kinematics method. An animator makes character with movement. Forward kinematics is more flexible in this respect, but if we are dealing with a complex model there is much expense.

Figure 17.7
Simple characterization using an articulated structure – the flamboyant gait was animated using forward kinematics.

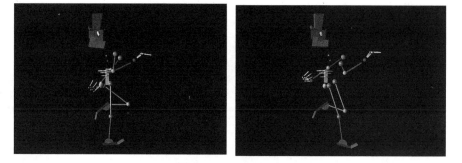

Thus we have two 'formal' approaches to scripting an articulated structure. Inverse kinematics enables us to specify a script by listing the consecutive positions of the end points of the hierarchy – the position of the hands or feet as a function of time. But the way in which the complete structure behaves is a function of the method used to solve the inverse kinematic equations and the animator has no control over the 'global' behaviour of the structure beyond the movement constraints built into the model. Alternatively if the structure is complex it may be impossible to implement an inverse kinematics solution anyway. On the other hand forwards kinematics enables the complete structure to be explicitly scripted but at the expense of inordinate labour, except for very simple structures. Any refinements have to be made by starting at the top of the hierarchy again and working downwards.

An illustrative example from the world of dance nicely illustrates this gulf. Figure 17.8 shows an allegory of a forwards kinematics script – in this case for a dance movement. Different notations are used to try to describe the movements of the human body, considering it as an articulated structure, that are required to execute a certain movement in dance. In each illustration an attempt is made to describe the individual movements of each part of the human body that is involved in the expression of the dance movement.

The second example, Figure 17.9, simply gives a script for emplacement of the feet as a function of time. The footprints occur at equal time subdivisions of the

Figure 17.8
An allegory of a forward kinematics script – four examples of dance notations. *Source*: Tufte, E.R. (1994) *Envisioning Information*, Cheshire, Conn.: Graphics Press.

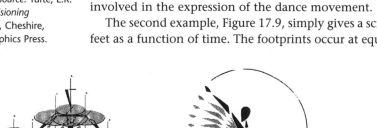

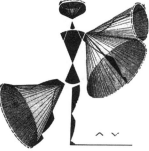

Figure 17.9
An allegory of an inverse kinematics script.
Source: Tufte, E.R. (1994) *Envisioning Information*, Cheshire, Conn.: Graphics Press.

music. This is an analogy of an inverse kinematics script. Only the positions of the end points of the hierarchy are specified. The reader of the script can move his body in a large number of different ways, all of which fit the footprint script. This is in fact one of the difficulties encountered in implementing an inverse kinematics solution for a structure – there are a large number of possible solutions. Note also that this script specifies part of a complete dance sequence whereas the previous illustration only specifies a single gesture, nicely illustrating the fact that we end up with a low-level script in forward kinematics and a high-level script in inverse kinematics.

In the high-level script the gestural movements of all parts of the body except the feet are left up to the interpretation of the dancer. Again this highlights the difference in artistic flexibility between the two approaches where computer animation is concerned. With forward kinematics the animator has complete freedom over the movement of any part of the structure – the problem is how the movement required by the animator is going to be imposed on the model. What is going to be the nature of the interface that facilitates the ideas of the artist? Using inverse kinematics the animator specifies 'footprints' but unfortunately the model being driven by this script does not possess the interpretation of a human being and the overall movement of the structure depends on the inverse kinematics solution. The same footprints produce the same body movements.

We now illustrate the distinction between forward and inverse kinematics more formally using as an example the simplest articulated structure possible – a two-link machine where one link is fixed and each link moves in the plane of the paper (Figure 17.10). In forward kinematics we explicitly specify the motion of all the joints. All the joints are linked and the motion of the end effector (hands or feet in the case of an animal figure) is determined by the accumulation of all transformations that lead to the end effector. We say that:

$$X = f(\Theta)$$

where X is the motion of the end effector and Θ is a state vector specifying the position, orientation and rotation of all joints in the system. In the case of the simple two-link mechanism we have:

$$X = (l_1 \cos \theta_1 + l_2 \cos (\theta_1 + \theta_2), l_1 \sin \theta_1 + l_2 \sin (\theta_1 + \theta_2))$$

but this expression is irrelevant in the sense that to control or animate such an arm using forward kinematics we would simply specify:

$$\Theta = (\theta_1 , \theta_2)$$

and the model would have applied to it the two angles which would result in the movement X.

In inverse kinematics we specify the position of the end effector and the algorithm has to evaluate the required Θ given X. We have:

$$\Theta = f^{-1}(X)$$

and in our simple example we can obtain from simple trigonometry:

$$\theta_2 = \frac{\cos^{-1}(x^2 + y^2 - l_1^2 - l_2^2)}{2l_1l_2}$$

$$\theta_1 = \frac{-(l_2 \sin\theta_2)x + (l_1 + l_2 \cos \theta_2)y}{(l_2 \sin \theta_2)y + (l_1 + l_2 \cos \theta_2)x}$$

Now as the complexity of the structure increases the inverse kinematics solution becomes more and more difficult. Quickly the situation develops where many

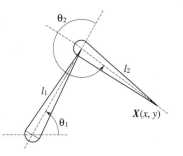

Figure 17.10
A two-link structure.

configurations satisfy the required end effector movement. In the simple two-link mechanism, for example, it is easy to see that there are two link configurations possible for each position X, one with the inter-link joint above the end effector, the other with it below. The attitude or state of this mechanism is specified by two angles (degrees of freedom) and we can easily foresee that as a structure becomes more complex it becomes increasingly difficult to derive an expression of the form $\Theta = f^{-1}(X)$. Thus with forward kinematics the animator has to handle more and more transformations while in inverse kinematics a solution may not be possible except for reasonably simple mechanisms. A human body possesses more than 200 degrees of freedom. An inverse kinematics solution for this is practically impossible and a forward kinematics script is inordinately complicated. A way forward is to invest such models with prewritten forward kinematic scripts for common gestures such as walking, running, grasping and so on. An animator then creates a script by putting together a sequence from prewritten parts.

In animating the dinosaurs in *Jurassic Park*, ILM used neither of these approaches, and in the time-honoured tradition of efficacious innovations, came up with a much simpler solution than those offered by the literature of articulated computer graphics animation. Their approach was to drive the models with a low-level forwards kinematics script but they bypassed the script complexity problem by creating a script semi-automatically. They effectively enabled stop-motion animators to input their expertise directly into the computer. The stop-motion animators moved their models in the normal way and the computer sampled the motion, producing a script for the computer models. ILM describe their technique in the following way:

The system is precise, fast, compact, and easy to use. It lets traditional stop-motion animators produce animation on a computer without requiring them to learn complex software. The working environment is very similar to the traditional environment but without the nuisances of lights, a camera and delicate foam-latex skin. The resulting animation lacks the artefacts of stop-motion animation, the stops and jerkiness, and yet retains the intentional subtleties and hard stops that computer animation often lacks.

The general idea is not original. For many years it has been possible to train industrial robots by having a human operator hold the robot's hand, taking it through the actions that the robot is eventually going to perform in the stead of the human operator. Spot welding and paint spraying in the car industry are good examples of the application of this technique. Movements of all the joints in the robot's articulated structure are then read from sensors and from these a script to control the robot is produced. Future invocations of the motion sequence involved in a task can then be endlessly and perfectly repeated – indeed the robot will go on reproducing the sequence perfectly even if something else has gone wrong and the car is not in position ....

In the *Jurassic Park* film robots were already available because the stop-motion animators had already built 'animatronic' models in anticipation of the film being produced by stop-motion techniques. These were then used, in reverse as it were, by the stop-motion animators, to produce a script for the computer models. Figure 17.11 shows a stop-motion animator working out the movements for the dinosaur wrestling with the car scene. The models now, instead of being clothed and filmed one frame at a time, are turned into an input device from which a script is derived.

A similar approach to what is coming to be known as 'motion capture' is to use human actors from whom to derive a motion script for a computer model. This involves fixing motion tracking devices to the appropriate positions of the actor's body and deriving a kinematic script in this way from the real movements of the actor. This approach is particularly popular in the video games industry which in recent years has made a transition from two-dimensional to three-dimensional animation. The requirements of the animation in games is somewhat less demanding in the sense that all that is required is certain sequences in response to user interaction events. It is natural and economic to use motion capture in this context to record the original motion scripts for the computer models.

Thus we see from these examples that we are only at the beginning of this difficult problem of specifying motion for complex articulated structures and that many solutions to the problem have involved going outside the computer and deriving a script from the real world. (Reminiscent somewhat of early photographs of Disney animators who were to be seen building up facial animations by using their own image in a mirror as a guide.)

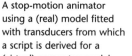

Figure 17.11
A stop-motion animator using a (real) model fitted with transducers from which a script is derived for a (virtual) computer model.
Source: Halas (1971)
The Techniques of Film Animation, Oxford: Butterworth Heinemann

Procedural animation

This form of animation is the most varied of our categorization and means using a mathematical model, encapsulated in a procedure, to simulate some physical behaviour. In other words, the motion is generated procedurally rather than being explicitly scripted through an interface by an animator. The motion control emerges from the procedure. Although an animator may use procedural animation as part of a production and be able to alter parameters of the controlling procedure, the idea is that explicit scripting is replaced by some procedural simulation.

Procedural animation may consist solely of physical simulation and the behaviour of objects modelled according to their interaction with, say, gravitational or magnetic fields. It may involve modelling the behaviour of colliding objects. Usually we would consider this kind of animation to be categorized as part of visualization and this begs the question: what do we mean by procedural animation and can it be considered as part of a separate category? The answer lies in the end in the nature of the simulation and the application. If we are investigating, say, some fluid dynamics problem and using animation techniques to visualize the output from a Navier–Stokes model, then the resulting animation is best considered as visualization. It is a direct reflection of the underlying mathematics and its purpose may be to assist pure research into a particular scientific or engineering problem.

On the other hand, if we are using a mathematical model to simulate the shape and motion of an object to produce, say, a TV commercial then we could say that we were using procedural animation. The crucial difference is that we are not interested in the veracity of the mathematical model as a description of the physical behaviour, merely in its ability to produce a visual sequence that looks like the real phenomenon. Examples of applications that have been investigated are animating cloth, animating water waves and snake locomotion. In each case the simulation is primarily visual. For example, in the case of water waves, Fourier synthesis can be used to simulate wave shape. It may well be that a physical model of wind-driven waves would not produce perfect sinusoidally shaped waves, but that is normally of no concern to us.

Procedural animation is characterized by its diversity – unique procedures are written to visually simulate particular phenomena. We will approach the topic by looking at two examples that illustrate the idea. The first – particle animation – has a certain generality in that variations of the basic technique will enable simulation of a number of different phenomena.

Procedural animation – case study: particle animation

Particle animation is a classic technique that was invented more than a decade ago. It has found wide acceptance and is still a popular tool. The basic idea is that certain (natural) phenomena can be simulated by scripting the movement of and rendering a large population of individual particles. A particle is usually a primitive whose geometrical extent is small or zero – that is, many particles can project into a single pixel extent – but which possesses certain fixed attributes such as colour. Each particle is scripted and the idea is that rendering a population of particles from frame to frame produces a sort of cloud object that can grow, shrink, move, change shape, and so on. An animation may involve literally tens or hundreds of thousands of particles and supplying an individual script for each one is out of the question. Rather a general script is provided for each particle with in-built random behaviour which produces the requisite differences for each particle as the position, say, of the particle evolves over time. Different phenomena are modelled by using general particle scripts and varying the attributes of the particle such as colour. For example, in simulating a firework the basic particle script may be a parabola. Parameters that would be varied for each particle may include the start point of the parabola, its shape parameters, the colour of the particle as a function of its position along its parabolic path and its lifetime (extinction) along the path.

Thus the dynamic behaviour of the particles and their appearance, as a function of time, can be merged into the same script. Stochastic processes can be used to control both these aspects of particle behaviour. The overall result is an animated object such as a cloud which changes shape as the scripts for the thousands of particles that make up its overall shape are obeyed. The pioneer in this field is Reeves, who published a paper in 1983 that used particle sets to model 'fuzzy' objects such as fire and clouds. Other people have used his idea to model, for example, the behaviour of water in fountains, in waterfalls and in the spray of breaking waves.

Reeves describes the generation of a frame in an animation sequence as a process of five steps:

(1) New particles are generated and injected into the current system.

(2) Each new particle is assigned its individual attributes.

(3) Any particles that have exceeded their lifetime are extinguished.

(4) The current particles are moved according to their scripts.

(5) The current particles are rendered.

The instantaneous population of a particle cloud is controlled or scripted by an application-dependent stochastic process. For example, the number of particles generated at a particular time t can be derived from:

$$N(t) = M(t) + \text{rand}(r)V(t)$$

where $M(t)$ is the mean number of particles perturbed by a random variable of variance V. The time dependency of this equation can be used to control the overall growth (or contraction) in cloud size. Reeves used a linear time dependency with constant variance in the examples given, but he points out that the control can incorporate quadratic, cubic or even stochastic variations. The number of particles can also be related to the screen size of the object – a mechanism that allows the amount of computation undertaken to relate to the final size of the object.

Although this mechanism will clearly contribute something to shape evolution of the cloud, this is also determined by individual particle scripts. The combination of these two scripting mechanisms was used to animate phenomena such as an expanding wall of fire used in the motion picture *Star Trek II: The Wrath of Khan*, and has been used to simulate multicoloured fireworks. Individual particle scripting is based on the following attributes:

- initial position
- initial velocity and direction
- initial size
- initial transparency
- shape
- lifetime.

Velocity and lifetime scripts can be based on dynamic constraints. An explosion, for example, may cause a particle to be ejected upwards and then be pulled down under the influence of gravity. Associated with both the attribute script and the population script is a 'generation shape' – a geometric region about the origin of the particle cloud into which 'newly born' particles are placed. For example, an exploding firework might have a spherical generation shape. Figure 17.12 is an example of part of an animation sequence produced using these techniques.

Although the applications Reeves described are generally growing phenomena, where the population of the particle cloud tends to increase, the method is general enough to model phenomena where, say, the population remains

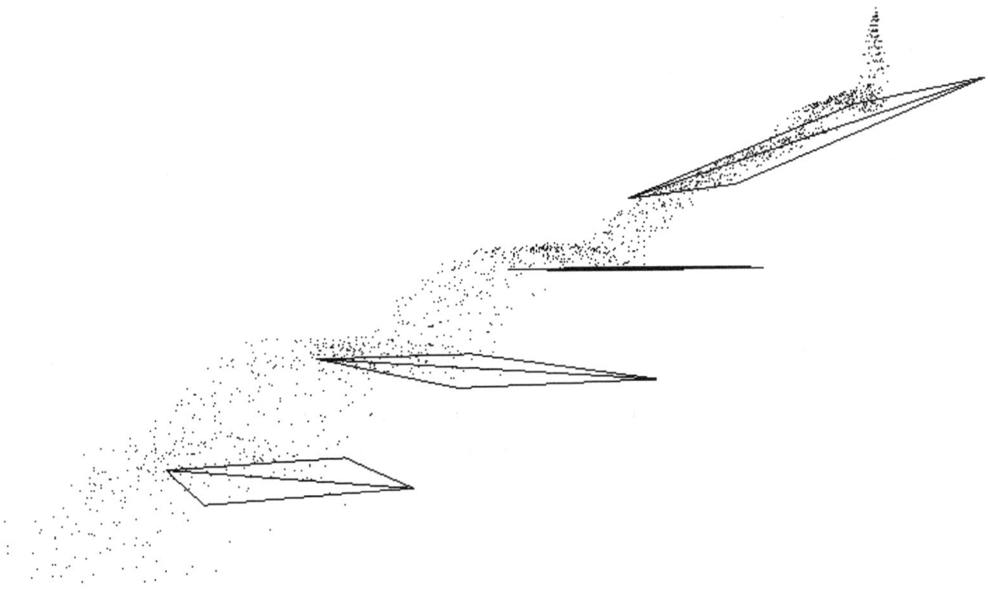

Figure 17.12
An example of physically-based particle animation. A stream of particles is released at the top of the space and falls under gravity, bouncing off each step.

constant, while the shape of the cloud perturbs or where the population decreases or implodes. As we have already pointed out, the final object appearance is determined from the net effect of individually rendering all the particles. Rendering is carried out by simply treating each particle as a single light source and using the final value of the appearance parameters.

In a later paper Reeves and Blau further develop particle systems. Moving away from using particles to model amorphous and continually changing shapes, they use them as 'volume filling' primitives to generate solid shapes whose form then remains generally constant, but which have the ability to change shape in such situations as blades of grass moving in the wind. These techniques were used in the film *The Adventures of Andre and Wally B* to generate the three-dimensional background images of a forest and grass.

The primary significance of particle systems in this context is not their ability to model shape-changing objects, but rather the property of 'database amplification' – the ability of a simple database to describe the general characteristics of an object that can then be modelled to the required level of detail. Objects are modelled with a resulting complexity that is far higher than that obtainable by conventional techniques. For example, in a forest scene, Reeves states that typically well over a million particles will be generated from basic tree descriptions.

Procedural animation – case study: light/water interaction

Figure 6.19 (Colour Plate) shows a frame from an animation that uses a procedure to generate the movement. In this case a procedure is used to control the geometry of the model that is being animated – a water surface. The animation is a simulation of light/water interaction and imitates the strange undulating patterns of light that are most commonly seen on the underwater surfaces of a swimming pool. These dancing ellipsoidal figures are produced by rays of sunlight striking the perturbed water surface. Wind makes the water surface non-planar and the parallel rays striking the surface are refracted and travel under water with bundles of rays diverging and converging. The converging rays deposit a high light intensity on the pool walls and bottom, and the nature of the refraction and the geometry of the perturbed surface form these bright depositions into closed loops. The patterns are known as 'caustics'.

In this animation each frame was rendered using a ray tracing model and a simple procedure modelled the wind-perturbed water surface. The procedure used modelled both the shape and the motion of the water surface. We now describe how to simulate wind-perturbed water waves.

Water waves can be modelled to within a good degree of geometric realism by using 'long crested travelling waves'. Fourier synthesis, or modelling the geometry of certain natural phenomena, by using a sum of sinusoidal functions has a long history in computer graphics and was first used in the early 1980s to provide texture patterns of landscapes for flight simulators. A long crested cosinusoidal surface $z(x,y)$ is shown in Figure 17.13. It is given by:

Figure 17.13
A long crested cosinusoidal
wave.

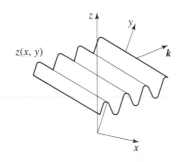

$$z(x,y) = A \cos (\boldsymbol{k} \cdot \boldsymbol{x})$$

where

> $\boldsymbol{k}$ is the wave vector $(u,v,0)$ specifying a wavelength of $(u^2 + v^2)^{-1/2}$
> $\boldsymbol{x}$ is the vector $(x,y,0)$
> A is the wave amplitude

This is the equation for a static wave whose peaks and troughs align in the direction:

$$\boldsymbol{k} \cdot \boldsymbol{x} = \text{constant}$$

and this equation can be used as a height field to modulate the vertices of a polygon mesh initially lying in the (x,y) plane. The equation for a travelling wave is given by

$$z(x,y,t) = A \cos (\boldsymbol{k} \cdot (\boldsymbol{x} - \boldsymbol{c}t))$$

where

> $\boldsymbol{c}$ is the velocity vector (in the $\boldsymbol{x}$ direction)

This generates a perfect cosinusoidal surface like the one shown in the figure and in practice we use:

$$z(x,y,t) = \sum_i A_i \cos (\boldsymbol{k}_i \cdot (\boldsymbol{x} - \boldsymbol{c}_i t))$$

For water waves it is best to select a bundle or sum of waves that consists of a group of high frequency and a group of low frequency waves together with a perturbation about the wave direction. These variations are easily incorporated in a procedure. For each frame the animation is generated by using the ray tracing model in conjunction with the current surface $z(x,y,t)$.

Radial waves can be simulated using:

$$z(x,t) = A \cos (\boldsymbol{k}(|\boldsymbol{r}| - \boldsymbol{c}t)$$

where each wave is radial with a centre $\boldsymbol{C}$ and where $\boldsymbol{r} = \boldsymbol{x} - \boldsymbol{C}$.

This model is used extensively to imitate raindrops hitting a water surface and other such effects.

Behavioural animation

Behavioural animation is, in many of its manifestations, an elaboration of particle animation. Usually we set up a kind of rudimentary 'sociological' model involving the behaviour of a population of entities (or a single entity). The significant difference between behavioural and particle animation is that in behavioural animation each entity is allocated a set of rules that govern its behaviour as a function of its relationship (usually spatial) to neighbouring entities.

An early and influential example of a behavioural model was developed by Reynolds in 1987 to simulate the flocking phenomena in birds and fish. Here each bird or fish possessed a set of rules that governed its behaviour with respect to neighbouring members of the group which was controlled by supplying global direction vectors. This basic idea was used to great effect in the Disney production *The Lion King* (1994) where a stampede sequence was controlled in this way.

Reynolds points out that flocking behaviour consists of two opposing factors – a desire to stay close to the flock and a desire to avoid collision within the flock. He simulated this behaviour as three rules which in order of decreasing precedence are:

(1) Collision avoidance: avoid collisions with nearby flock mates.

(2) Velocity matching: attempt to match the velocity of nearby flock mates.

(3) Flock centring: attempt to stay close to nearby flock mates.

The behaviour of the model is summarized by Reynolds as follows:

The flocking model described gives birds an eagerness to participate in an acceptable approximation of flock-like motion. Birds released near one another begin to flock together, cavorting and jostling for position. The birds stay near one another (flock centring) but always maintain prudent separation from their neighbours (collision avoidance), and the flock becomes quickly 'polarized' – its members heading in approximately the same direction at approximately the same speed (velocity matching); when they change direction they do it in synchronization. Solitary birds and smaller flocks join to become larger flocks, and in the presence of external obstacles, larger flocks can be split into smaller flocks.

From the pioneering work of Reynolds we now look at a recent ambitious system of behavioural animation. This work by Tu and Terzopoulos, simulating the behaviour of fish, is a self-animating system where the models are equipped with rudimentary vision, a physics-based locomotion capacity that reacts with hydrodynamic forces to simulate swimming behaviour and a set of behavioural rules. This appears to be the first attempt in computer animation to integrate all these aspects into one system.

The autonomous model that makes up each fish is made up of different levels of abstraction. Internal to the fish body is an 'animate spring-mass system'. This is a set of 23 nodes interconnected by 91 springs, some of the springs also serving as contractile muscles. The position of the nodes controls the shape of the fish. The fish swims like a real fish by contracting its muscles – decreasing the rest length of a muscle spring. The characteristic swinging of the tail, for example, is set up by contracting muscles on one side of the body while simultaneously relaxing muscles on the other side. An equation is set up for each node relating the mass and acceleration of the node together with the forces exerted, through the springs, from all other nodes to the external hydrodynamic force. These equations are solved at each time step to give the overall movement of the nodes. Thus the basis of this part of the model is a cloud of nodal points moving forward through the water and at the same time moving with respect to each other. Motion is initiated by motion controllers which translate a desired action such as swimming ahead or turning into detailed muscle actions.

To these nodes is coupled the control points of a parametric surface which models the skin of the fish. This results in a deformable body whose deformation is controlled by the underlying physical model. Additionally controlling the orientation of fins gives pitch, yaw and roll control to the basic motion. To this model, which successfully imitates fish locomotion to a high level of fidelity, is added a behaviour system to which is input information from a rudimentary visual perception and a temperature sensor. The visual sensor extracts such information as the colour, size, distance and identity of objects that enter its field of view.

The behavioural aspect is implemented as a set of routines that generate the appropriate actions to control the muscles. These are selected by an intention generator which selects a behaviour based on the sensory information, the fish's current mental state and its habits. Habits are represented as parameters and the mental state by variables. A state such as hunger is incremented by time and decremented when a fish eats a food particle. The behavioural routines simulate such activities as avoid-static-obstacle, avoid-fish, eat-food, mate, escape, school, and so on. A representation of information flow in a fish model is shown in Figure 17.14.

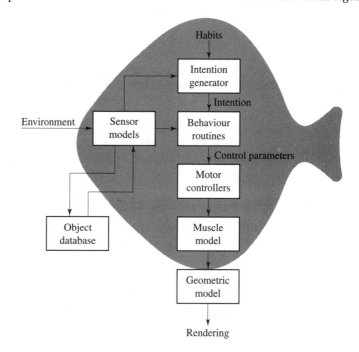

Figure 17.14
Information flow in the artificial fish (after Tu and Terzopoulos).

The developers claim that their system yields 'some astonishing behaviours' and indeed their production 'Go Fish' is extremely impressive. The visual success of their animations, however, begs some questions. Again we see problems with artistic freedom. If all the animation is to emerge from the model, how can animators use the tool? What are the potential applications of complete self-animation? As an experimental test bed on which behavioural scientists can test or simulate their theories? As a virtual environment? The authors make this exotic claim: 'We may be within reach of computational models that imitate the spawning behaviour of the female and the male, hence the evolution of new varieties of artificial fishes through simulated sexual reproduction.'

17.3   Motion control and the animator

We now discuss the crucial issue of high-level versus low-level motion control in computer animation. It is a crucial issue because for animation to pass from the hands of programmers into the artistic community requires the development of high-level scripting tools. There is an analogy here with the development of high-level languages and APIs (application programming interfaces). Originally using a computer was exclusively in the hands of machine-code programs. Development of high-level program languages enabled a vast expansion of computer usage. Nowadays the almost universal use of computers is by running programs through APIs. It could be said that at the moment the ease of using computer animation is roughly equivalent to the relative ease with which people could program in the late 1960s and early 1970s with the emergence of high-level languages.

How do the terms high level and low level relate to computer animation? Consider rigid body animation by explicit scripting. In this method the animator has total control over the motion at every point in the animation sequence. This is low-level motion specification. As far as the animator is concerned there is complete artistic control over the motion – the animator has complete freedom to choose whatever motion is appropriate for the application. The price paid for this freedom is the labour involved in the specification albeit that the use of curves as a scripting form cuts the workload down to an acceptable level.

In the case of articulated structures there is a choice – at least in theory. If a forward kinematics system is used then this is a low-level motion specification – every joint has to be separately scripted. The workload depends on the complexity of the system but again the animator has complete freedom. However, even using a curve script for each link, the workload is prodigious. Generally articulated structures are ordered into a hierarchy. For example, with a leg, the structure can be represented as a tree with the hip joint as the topmost node, the knee joint as the next node down, the ankle the node below the knee, and so on. An animator will script such a model by starting at the top node and working downwards. Every node 'inherits' the transformation of the node above it and a problem occurs if the movement of the end effector is wrong. The animator has to start again at the topmost node and work downwards .... The alternative is to use an inverse kinematics system – a high-level system. Here the animator may simply specify that a character is to walk from point A to point B. There is no control over the nature of the walk – this is evaluated by the inverse kinematics algorithm. The work is less but there is no detailed artistic control possible.

Procedural animation is, in most of its manifestations, a high-level specification. Some control may be invested in the variation of the parameters that have been built into the model, but usually you simply set the procedure going and the animation is calculated without any further intervention. The efficacy of the animation depends on how the movement is simulated by the procedure(s).

Behavioural animation, as we have seen, can be totally autonomous. The system is self-animating after it is set up. All the design freedom is incorporated in designing the system. If no alterations are made to the design of the system then it only has the ability in the end to produce a very large but finite number of animations. The artistic freedom is invested in the design of the society and the members. Although an animator could have access to the system through an interface and alter, for example, the behavioural routines, the system that we discussed is impressive in the motion realism that it produces, but the technique suffers from the disadvantage that it involves highly detailed modelling strategies that are in the end restricted to one species – in this case, fish. This problem of specificity occurs often in image synthesis. It means that we design a modelling strategy which, although it suits a particular physical reality well, does not have general application. Classic examples here are the use of fractal strategies to model mountainous terrain and the use of L systems in the modelling of plants.

So we can conclude that, in general, the current techniques in computer animation carry a trade-off which results in a contradiction. Low-level motion specification can be inordinately tedious, especially if the animated object has many degrees of freedom, but it leaves an opportunity for animators to invent their own motion at the cost of much work. High-level specification is easier for an artist to use but generally results in less artistic freedom. Perhaps it is the existence of this contradiction that has prevented the dissemination of computer animation, with its attendant advantages, into the artistic community, and the continuance of animation as a manual art form.

17.4 Animation, modelling and physically based simulation

In this section we will explore the relationship between animation possibilities, modelling or representational techniques and the use of physically based animation vs. visual simulation techniques. The connection between animation and modelling is most obvious in soft/deformable body animation which is still an unsolved problem. In this field the model must have a form that accepts an animation script that causes it to deform or change shape in some desired manner. The demands that virtual reality will make on computer animation will emphasize this relationship more.

Computer animation has long found most applications in the bland world of TV commercials and in the exotic creations of Hollywood, with most of the drive for new techniques coming from the latter. Both media have utilized techniques where frame generation times have been a secondary consideration. Productions have a long development time, sometimes involving the invention of new techniques, and the final sequence is rendered at high (film) resolution offline, perhaps taking tens of minutes for each frame.

With the arrival of virtual reality new demands are likely to be made on computer animation techniques. Although most early virtual reality applications involve a virtual viewer moving through a static environment, we are likely to see this extended to include environments with moving objects. Virtual environments may contain virtual humans and making these models move convincingly and realistically is likely to become a major area of investigation in virtual reality. Consider, for example, a historic site that is to be populated with ghosts – virtual human beings – the Madame Tussauds of the twenty-first century.... Here animation sequences have to be generated in real time and also as the virtual viewer usually moves, for a continuously changing viewpoint.

In the immediate future we are more likely to see the demands from such areas as medical training, surgical simulation and the simulation of human beings in industrial design applications. A virtual body, to be effective, would have to display most of the physical characteristics of a real body, reacting in a realistic manner to virtual dissection and surgery. Such a requirement would require a physically based deformation model of high complexity. The advantages, however, would be enormous and such a facility would be as valuable in medicine as flight simulation is in the aircraft industry. Pathologies could be produced on demand, for example.

In industrial design, virtual bodies are being applied to areas such as the interior design of a car. A virtual body can be immersed in a particular design, made to perform driving actions, and the possible arrangements of the seat, steering wheel and pedals tested, without having to resort to prototype building.

These applications all require a connected modelling and animation strategy far beyond current capabilities and the successful development of such techniques will be as necessary for the emergence of virtual reality technology as the much discussed hardware and display problems. Just how far away we are can be divined from the simple metric of frame generation time. Virtual reality requires a frame update time of, say, less than 20 ms which is between three and four orders of magnitude away from frame times used in complex (offline) animation productions.

We now consider the important relationship between modelling techniques and animation. That they are connected results from a general need in animation to control the motion and dynamic shape changes of objects other than rigid bodies. This comes about partly from the new demands of virtual reality, where in many applications it may be desirable to create an environment that contains, for example, virtual human beings moving around, fully clothed. In Section 17.2.2 we looked at the motion control of articulated structures but such techniques only attend to one aspect of animating a human body – the movement of the limbs. The appearance of the skin and the way it moves and wrinkles when limbs move and the complex nature of the movement of the clothes that we wear are as important to the final appearance of the animation as accurate motion control of the underlying articulated structure.

The new demands made of computer animation are resulting in a research movement that rivals the major efforts that were made in rendering techniques in the 1980s. We may require not only to animate a human being as a complex articulated structure, but to control the complex movement of clothing as part of the animation. General modelling techniques, from static computer graphics, are not sufficient. Although a polygon mesh structure is capable of representing an object at whatever level of detail is required, it is useless for objects that exhibit complex shape changes. Thus modelling techniques are being developed that attend to both the detailed shape of an object and its dynamic shape change. Animation and modelling are merging in these new areas.

Like the area of modelling static natural phenomena, such as plants and terrain, the current state of the art is exemplified by a plethora of models that are application dependent and this is one of the current outstanding problems of computer graphics. The nature and diversity of complex objects does not admit a universal modelling approach – different categories of objects spawn different solutions. It remains to be seen if a good general modelling approach will emerge from these efforts.

To illuminate this discussion we will consider two examples that are being energetically pursued and relate to the simulation of human beings – facial and body animation and the simulation of fabric movement. Although the methods vary enormously in detail there are possibly just two underlying categories. Either the model is physically based and relates to the underlying forces that produce the dynamic shape changes – the use of elastic forces in fabric simulation, for example – or it is a pure visual simulation. By a visual simulation we mean a model that enables control of the shape of the object but which does not do this by attempting to simulate the natural forces that underpin the dynamic shape change. Both approaches tend to work through a hierarchy. One layer of the model will accept the shape change control and this level of the model will be connected, perhaps through other layers, to the detailed geometry. The bicubic parametric patch is a perfect example of this paradigm. A few control points can be scripted which control the overall geometry of a patch which is everywhere defined in three-dimensional space. However, as we saw in Chapter 7, bicubic parametric patches are not extendible outside a few well-defined areas such as engineering CAD. Bicubic parametric patch modelling suffers from the lack of a high-level modelling abstraction for shape control. Low-level control implies controlling the position of 16 control points in three-dimensional space to effect a shape change of a single surface modelling element and this factor has meant that the much-vaunted free-form sculpting metaphor is currently unrealized.

A good example of a pure visual simulation for control of shape of fabric is shown in Figure 17.15 (Colour Plate). Here a square cloth has been embedded in an FFD lattice – a volumetric version of a parametric patch which is a function of three rather than two parameters. The idea here is identical to surface patches except that now the patch is a volume. The object – a square cloth – is embedded in this volume and the volume is deformed by moving its lattice of control points. The embedded object is dragged around by the volume deformation. Here we are deforming or warping the space that the object is locked into. It is a pure visual simulation – there is no attempt to deform the cloth by considering its physical construction and the shape it will take under the influence of gravity due to being draped across a circular table top.

We can easily consider the disadvantage of a visual simulation in this context and the reason why most fabric models are physically based. Although the model can produce complex shapes such as the folds, every change of shape has to be explicitly modelled albeit at a higher level than controlling the underlying polygon mesh of the cloth. Simulating the draping of a cloth over a circular table means setting up a circular control volume with a sufficient number of points to produce the desired number of folds. A completely different structure would be required if we were going to simulate the wrinkling of the fabric of a garment as an elbow bends. The model offers a higher level of abstraction than pure surface elements, such as polygons, but one that is not general enough.

The seduction of physically based modelling now becomes apparent. One of its most important aims is to avoid explicit modelling of every shape change by imitating the underlying physical interaction that leads to geometric changes in the render surface of the object. Instead we simulate the underlying physical interaction and allow this to produce the shape change. It is another way of looking at procedural animation in the particular case of dynamic simulation using known physical laws. This is not to dismiss visual simulations – it is too early to say. The history of computer graphics to the present time has certainly favoured visual simulations or empirical models in rendering (static) objects.

The physically based approach is easily exemplified by a quote from recent work by Lie Ling et al. on fabric movement. They state

...clearly show that this approximate physics based model, incorporating (a) elements of low speed incompressible, inviscid and irrotational aerodynamic flows to construct an unsteady distributed force model and (b) the cloth deformation model based on classical rigid body dynamics and elastic theory, has been able to give very realistic animations of cloth motion in air flow.

Although this work is restricted to such objects as flags blowing in the wind, the implication is that a physically based model can produce a wide variation of shapes under control of the setting of the environmental conditions. The flow and wrinkling of the cloth in the wind emerges from the model.

Figure 17.16 (Colour Plate) is an example of using physically based principles to control the deformation of an object. Like the FFD method, the object is immersed in a field that is used to deform the object globally. The animator specifies the properties of the field and the deformation of the object is then automatic. Unlike the FFD method, where the animator has to explicitly script the movement of the control points of the volumetric patch, the assignment of elastic properties to the field is all that is required.

In this example the object is a dress, attached to an (invisible) body that has associated motion capture data controlling its movement. As the body moves around, the dress follows the body but, at the same time, is controlled by its status as a deformable object in an 'elastic field'. It is as if the object was made up of elastic material with its own properties. The designers term the object material 'hypermatter'.

Work on the shape animation of human bodies also exhibits the two approaches of modelling through visual simulation and physically based modelling. An early example of a rendered image was produced by Don Herbison-Evans in 1978. It was constructed from overlapping ellipsoids, which serve as both a geometric element for rendering and a link in an articulated structure for motion control or scripting. (A not to be ignored advantage of using implicitly linked ellipsoids is that by overlapping them at the joins, a primitive form of surface blending is achieved which prevents discontinuities in the surface.)

From this there evolved models with underlying (stick-figure) skeletons, which accepted the articulated structure motion control, surrounded by a render surface – the skin – which deformed as a function of the joint movement. These models effectively separate the animation into a two-level hierarchy: the motion control is applied to the skeleton and the skin deformation is calculated as a function of the type of joint, its angle and the position of the point on the skin relative to the joint. An example in this category is the 'Joint-dependent Local Deformation' or JLD operators of Thalman and Thalman.

Recently models of joints have began to appear which are physically based and which produce shape changes at the render surface as a function of the internal structure and biomechanics of the limb. These models usually consider the limb to be a hierarchy with the render surface – the skin – enclosing a bulk of interacting flesh, muscle and bone. Flesh is attached to muscle which is attached to bone. In the work of Chen et al. the muscle occupies the position at the top of the hierarchy. Using finite elements and physiological data a muscle is itself modelled as a rendered entity whose shape changes according to contractile force. In the illustration shown in Figure 17.17 the muscle activation causes the biceps to shorten and the forearm (or the forearm skeleton) flexes inverse kinematically to track the end of the muscle.

This kind of work is the beginning of a tendency that is taking human body animation away from kinematic modelling of a skeleton, together with some attached empirical shape model, into physically based modelling where the shape changes due to the physical properties of limbs. The implications for this kind of model go beyond just visual simulations. Consider again the interaction of a person with car controls or any such application where a human is interacting with a machine. We could begin to simulate the complex spatial totality

Figure 17.17
A physically based shape model for a limb (after Chen and Zeltzer (1992)).

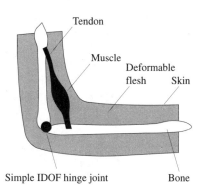

Tendon

Muscle

Deformable flesh   Skin

Simple IDOF hinge joint   Bone

of all the forces that need to be applied by a person to operate the controls which in the end is as important to simulate as the positional constraints.

Facial animation issues are dealt with in some length in Chapter 19. Here we will consider those factors that relate to modelling. The hierarchy is similar to those suggested for modelling of limbs, except that the shape changes that we are interested in are facial expressions, rather than simply bulk changes in a mass of flesh. Although in the end there is no physical difference – expressions are just very detailed changes in the shape of a skin surface – their subtlety demands very careful modelling.

The most well-known work in this area is due to Terzopoulos and Waters who have developed a hierarchical model that facilitates high-level motion control that is separated from the geometrical detail. But the model does more than just achieve this necessary separation. They describe it as a model which decomposes into levels of abstraction, such a decomposition facilitating the injection of specialized knowledge into each aspect of the model. They describe the levels as follows:

(1) **Expression**: At the highest level of abstraction, the face model executes expression (or phoneme) commands. For instance, it can synthesize any of the six primary expressions within a specified time interval and with a specified degree of emphasis.

(2) **Control**: A muscle control process translates expression (or phoneme) instructions into a coordinated activation of actuator groups in the facial model.

(3) **Muscles**: As in real faces, muscles comprise the basic actuation mechanism of the model. Each muscle model consists of a bundle of muscle fibres. When fibres contract, they displace their points of attachment in the facial tissue of the jaw.

(4) **Geometry**: The geometric representation of the facial model is a non-uniform mesh of polyhedral elements .... Muscle-induced synthetic tissue deformations distort the neutral geometry into an expressive geometry. An example of the model up to this level of complexity is shown in Figure 17.18.

Figure 17.18
A classic image from facial animation research. The muscle model was originally produced by Keith Waters in 1988. The image on the left is the rest face. The image on the right was produced by controlling the muscle parameters for the eyebrows and the right side of the mouth. (Image generated using a program available on Waters's web site: www.research.digital.com/ crl/books/facebook/ appendix1/appendix1.html) Courtesy of Keith Waters

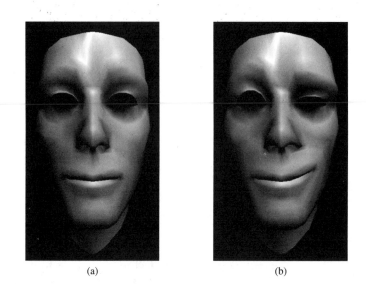

(a)   (b)

(5) **Physics**: Later versions of the face model incorporate a physical approximation to human facial tissue. The tissue model is a lattice of point masses connected by non-linear elastic springs. Large-scale synthetic tissue deformations, which are subject to volume constraints, are simulated numerically by continuously propagating, through the tissue lattice, the stresses activated by the muscle fibres.

Thus we can see that this model is a multi-level physically based modelling approach, where the final geometry, in the form of a polygon mesh, is pulled around by other abstractions above it in the hierarchy. Unlike the fabric in the wind example it is designed to respond to detailed high-level scripting that trickles down through a hierarchy, producing detailed shape changes at the render surface.

This model is one of the most layered approaches reported in computer graphics and it is not possible to estimate its future value. Certainly the price paid for this level of abstraction is the complexity of the model and subsequent processing requirements. Another of the apparent drawbacks of the model is the creation of the script. In the work reported, the authors obtain scripts by analyzing video sequences of actual human faces. Control parameters are extracted to resynthesize the expressions on the computer graphics model.

Further reading – computer animation

A good insight into the motivations for using computer graphics in *Jurassic Park* can be obtained from the issue of the magazine *American Cinematographer* (December 1993) which dealt in some depth with this film. Two articles are listed below.

The double interpolant method, which is a straightforward way to implement the scripting of rigid body animation, is described in the paper by Steketee and Badler.

The above treatment of parametric scripting curves completely avoided specifying any particular basis. Although the B-spline basis is commonly used, this basis was developed for specifying geometric shapes and has certain disadvantages when used in animation. There is a class of splines that has been specially developed to service the particular requirements of animation scripts. These are described in the paper by Kochanek.

The book by Badler et al. is a useful reference to the theoretical techniques that have been developed in computer animation to control movement in articulated structures.

Reeves's paper on particle animation is the classic in this field. Most work that has been done in this area is an application of the techniques described in it. The procedural animation example is described in more detail in the book by Watt and Watt. This text also contains a comprehensive treatment of the mathematics required for computer animation.

The paper by Tu and Terzopoulos contains much detail on behavioural strategies as well as information on the modelling techniques used. The acknowledged pioneer of behavioural animation is Reynolds, whose seminal paper on flocking behaviour was published in 1987.

The geometric shape control of fabric example is taken from Coquillart's work and this contrasts nicely with the somewhat daunting physically based model of Ling et al.

The Herbison-Evans, Thalmann and Thalmann, and Chen and Zeltzer papers give a good account of the evolution of different methods in the simulation of limbs, from an imitative visual simulation to a complex physically based model.

Badler N.I., Barsky B.A. and Zeltzer D. (1991). *Making them Move: Mechanics, Control and Animation of Articulated Figures*. San Mateo, CA: Morgan-Kaufmann Inc.

Chen D.T. and Zeltzer D. (1992). Pump it up: computer animation of a biomechanically based model of muscle using the finite element method. *Computer Graphics*, **26**(2), 89–98 (Proc. SIGGRAPH '92)

Coquillart S. (1990). Extended free form deformation. *Computer Graphics*, **24**(4), 23–7 (Proc. SIGGRAPH '90)

Gray, J. (1968). *Animal Location*. London: Weidenfeld & Nicholson

Hallas J. and Manvell R. (1971). *The Techniques of Film Animation* 3rd edn. London: Focal Press

Herbison-Evans D. (1989). Nudes 2: A numeric utility displaying ellipsoid solids. *Computer Graphics*, **12**(3), 354–6 (Proc. SIGGRAPH '89)

Kochanek D.H.U. (1984). Interpolating splines with local tension, continuity and bias control. *Computer Graphics*, **18**(3), 35–44 (Proc. SIGGRAPH '84)

Ling L., Damodaran M. and Gay R.K.L. (1995). Physical modelling for animating cloth motion. In *Computer Graphics: Developments in Virtual Environments* (R. Earnshaw and J. Vince, eds), New York: Academic Press

Magid, R. (1993). After *Jurassic Park*, traditional techniques may become fossils. *American Cinematographer*, December, 58–65

Magid R. (1993). ILM's digital dinosaurs tear up effects jungle. *American Cinematographer*, December, 46–57

Reeves W.T. (1983). Particle systems – a technique for modelling a class of fuzzy objects. *Computer Graphics*, **17**(3), 359–76

Reeves W.T. and Blau R. (1985). Approximate and probabilistic alogorithms for shading and rendering structured particle systems. *Computer Graphics*, **19**(3), 313–22

Reynolds C.W. (1987). Flocks, herds and schools: a distributed behavioural model. *Computer Graphics*, **21**(4), 25–34 (Proc. SIGGRAPH '87)

Steketee S.N. and Badler N.I. (1985). Parametric keyframe interpolation incorporating kinetic adjustment and phrasing control. *Computer Graphics*, **19**(3), 255–62 (Proc. SIG-GRAPH '85)

Thalmann N.M. and Thalmann D. (1990). *Computer Animation: Theory and Practice*. Berlin: Springer-Verlag

Tu S. and Terzopoulos D. (1994). Perceptual modelling for the behavioural animation of fishes. In *Proc. Second Pacific Conf. on Computer Graphics* (PG '94), Beijing, China

Watt A. and Watt M. (1992). *Advanced Animation and Rendering Techniques*. Wokingham: Addison-Wesley

17.5 Image metamorphosis – morphing

Morphing appeared to be an overnight discovery. It was found that by using a method that was locked into two-dimensional space, a remarkable illusion of three-dimensional shape change could be created. This meant that it could be used as a post production technique in films of reality and in this way it effectively bypassed the problems that would arise if three-dimensional graphics techniques were used in this context. It is in reality a two-dimensional image processing technique, but produces an effect that appears to have originated by filming an actual scene. (Although three-dimensional morphing techniques are used, where three-dimensional objects change into other objects, most morphing is a two-dimensional process.) We include morphing as a moving image technique because either it is used to produce a moving sequence from two static images or it is used to produce a new sequence from two sets of already moving sequences. Examples of morphing abound in TV commercials, music videos and films.

Outside the world of entertainment, morphing techniques are finding applications. It is the most commonly used technique in a set of emerging image-based or two-dimensional techniques that are being investigated as alternatives to the standard three-dimensional rendering pipeline which computes a new projection every time the viewpoint is changed by starting again at the detailed geometric description of the scene. In Chapter 21 we look at an application where morphing is used to quickly generate images in a virtual walkthrough, from pre-rendered images of the scene. The goal here is to perform the equivalent of three-dimensional key frame animation, but perform all the operations in two-dimensional or image space. Later in this chapter, we will look at an application in medical imagery which uses morphing in reverse, that is, it analyzes deformations in medical images considering that these could have been produced by a morphing transformation and then uses the information from this analysis to 'correct' the images.

An early illustration of the idea can be found in a classic book by D'arcy Thompson entitled *On Growth and Form* (Thompson, 1942). In this publication he made the observation that certain fish species could be mapped into others using a non-linear transformation that was based on the warping of a coordinate system. In fact, as the reproduction shows (Figure 17.19), he proposed a model that underlies most of the approaches that are in use today.

Morphing is a classic example of the replacement, by a computer implementation, of more rudimentary techniques employed by film makers for many years. The most common is the cross-dissolve, used, for example, to great effect in 1941 in *The Wolfman*. In a cross-dissolve one image sequence is faded out while another is simultaneously faded in. (In fact cross-dissolving is a component of most morphing techniques.) Another traditional technique used by film makers to accomplish a metamorphosis is stop-motion animation, in which the subject is progressively transformed (by make-up or whatever) and photographed one frame at a time. As can be imagined this device requires much skill and patience.

We can define morphing loosely to be the production of a set of frames that shows one object transforming into another. It has some overlap with the term in-betweening in animation, where a set of in-between frames are generated from two key frames. We define the term warping or self-morphing to mean that we warp between two frames of the same object in different attitudes. This has an important application in facial animation. Thus morphing means a transformation from one object to another, both objects usually being startlingly different. Warping means transformation between two attitudes of the same object. Alternatively we could simply take an object and warp it into some (grotesque) attitude that it could not possess in reality. This is often done in newspapers where a celebrity's or politician's face is twisted to better match the perception that the caricaturist has of him or her.

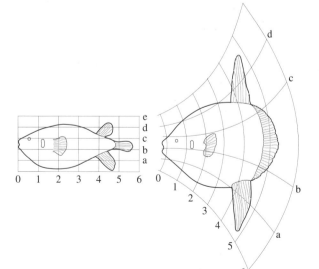

Figure 17.19
An illustration from D'arcy Thompson's *On Growth and Form*.

We will deal with the subject by considering the following aspects:

● morphing two-dimensional images – currently the most common application
● morphing in three-dimensional space – creating a set of images by changing the shape of a three-dimensional object
● morphing between animated sequences
● morphing as an image registration technique.

In morphing two-dimensional images we usually use film or video images of reality. The metamorphosis occurs in the two-dimensional domain. Although all of the operations are locked into two-dimensional space, the idea of two-dimensional morphing is to give the illusion of the source object changing into the target object as if the metamorphosis had actually been filmed. Currently most morphing is of this type.

This was employed to great effect by ILM (Industrial Light and Magic – the special effects division of Lucasfilms) in the 1988 film *Indiana Jones and the Last Crusade* to depict the untimely demise of the villain. Believing he has found the grail, he drinks, only to find that it is the wrong cup. He ages in seconds and dies shrivelling horribly in the process. Two-dimensional morphing was used in conjunction with three increasingly grotesque masks to produce this sequence.

Three-dimensional morphing is a technique that consists of utilizing three-dimensional graphics techniques to effect shape transformations in a three-dimensional graphics domain. By definition, in three-dimensional morphing we can only deal with computer graphics objects, that is, either abstract models or models of reality that have been converted into a computer graphics object. The problem with this type of morphing, used with a real object, is complexity. To retain the illusion of reality the real object, if it is, for example, an animal, must be represented by an extremely complex computer graphics object. This then raises the problem of choreographing the deformation of such an object.

Although both two-dimensional and three-dimensional morphing create an animated sequence – the transformation of one object into another – most morphing is carried out between two sequences of live action rather than between two still images. The source and target are moving sequences rather than still frames. A classic example of this is the Michael Jackson video *Black and White* (produced by Pacific Data Images) where dancers are morphed into each other and Jackson turns into and out of a black panther while moving. Also, in this sequence the morphs were staggered so that different parts of each dancer changed at different times.

17.5.1 Morphing two-dimensional images

Morphing between two-dimensional images of three-dimensional reality is the most common kind of shape metamorphosis. We effect a shape transformation from source image to target image producing a sequence of intermediate images. A much used example of a morph sequence is to use two facial images, say a man and a woman, or a baby and an old man. The early intermediate images will look like the source image and the later images will resemble the target image. The metric of the quality of the morph is that the intermediate images should look lifelike. In the case of facial images the intermediates should look like real people (Figure 17.20).

We can describe the complete process of two-dimensional morphing as the sequential application of two sub-processes – image warping followed by a colour transformation. Image warping is the process of mapping a pixel in the source image to a (generally different) pixel in the target image, without changing the value of the pixel:

$$S(x,y) \rightarrow T(x',y')$$

where

$$S = T \text{ and } (x',y') = warp(x,y)$$

warp is an image warping function that will be derived from an algorithm (rather than a mathematical function). Implied in this process is the ability to generate a sequence of intermediate images.

A colour transformation is where we change the colour of a pixel without changing its coordinates:

$$S(x,y) \rightarrow T(x,y)$$

For example, we can specify the traditional cross-dissolve by the following:

$$I(x,y,t) = F_1(x,y,t) S(x,y) + F_2(x,y,t) T(x,y)$$

where

for $t = 0$ (the first image in the sequence)

$$F_1(x,y,0) = 1, F_2(x,y,0) = 0$$

for $t = 1$ (the final image in the sequence)

$$F_1(x,y,1) = 0, F_2(x,y,1) = 1$$

Figure 17.20
An author ages during the production of his book.

for all t

$$F_1(x,y,t) + F_2(x,y,t) = 1$$

(a)   (b)   (c)   (d)   (e)

A linear cross-dissolve would be specified by

$$F_1(x,y,t) = 1 - t \text{ and } F_2(x,y,t) = t$$

The overall process can be accomplished by first applying an image warping followed by a colour transformation such as the above linear cross-dissolve. The warping is bi-directional, the source warping towards the target and vice versa. This produces two sets of images which are cross-dissolved into a single sequence. Figure 17.21 shows how a morph sequence is manufactured. We realize a single frame in a morph sequence by cross-dissolving between a pair of shape-warped images. For example, the first frame in a sequence showing a morph from source to target would consist of cross-dissolving between S_1 and T_n. For $n = 0 \ldots 10$ we have an 11-frame sequence and S_1 would consist of a 10% deformation of source towards target. T_9 would be a 90% deformation of target towards source.

We will now describe in detail the operation of the two classic image warping algorithms that have produced most of the warps seen in TV and film imagery. The simple process of cross-dissolve does not require further explanation. The algorithms are called two-spline mesh warping and feature-based warping.

Morphing algorithms usually have two components:

(1) They need a mechanism whereby a user can establish correspondenece between the two images. A common way to do this, for example, is to mark the sihouette edge of the object of interest in one image into the corresponding feature in the other. This specifies a sparse correspondence between the images.

(2) From this sparse correspondence the algorithm has to determine a dense (pixel) correspondence which is the warp transform.

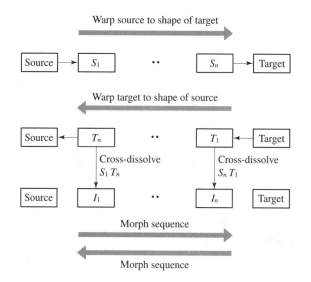

Figure 17.21
Forming a mesh sequence by shape warping followed by cross-dissolving.

Two-spline mesh warping

This classic algorithm was developed by Douglas Smythe at ILM. The algorithm was used to produce sequences in the films *Willow, Indiana Jones and The Last Crusade* and *The Abyss*.

The sparse correspondence is supplied by the user who specifies a grid of points in the source and target images. Splines are fitted through these points and the user has the visual concept of a spline mesh. Mesh elements are shaped by the user to specify the nature of the warp for each part of the image. Effectively the user selects a patch in the source image and sets a distortion for that patch in the destination image. A rectangular topology is imposed on the grid and the meshes must be topologically equivalent.

The meshes can be thought of as two coordinate systems and the morphing as a transformation from one coordinate system to the other. For a complete morph sequence we require a source mesh G_s, a destination mesh G_T and a set of *in-between* meshes – one for each frame in the morph sequence. Consider the in-between mesh G_{Ii}. The ith warp in a sequence is achieved by distorting the source image S using G_s and G_{Ii}, then G_T and G_{Ii}. The set of in-between grids is obtained by some kind of interpolation – for example, linear. Alternatively the interpolation can be positionally dependent making it possible to have some parts of the object change at different rates to other parts.

The algorithm utilises the two-pass transform technique described in Chapter 24. This makes for both efficiency and reduction in complexity. We will describe the implementation of the algorithm in terms of such a structure but the warp process does not, of course, depend on being implemented as a two-pass process.

At any point in the morph sequence we have to generate two frames and cross-dissolve. Thus the basic algorithm is a procedure that accepts as input one image and two grids. At this stage we can simplify the convention and consider two grids G_1 and G_2 (Figure 17.22(a)). In practice this procedure would be called twice for the ith frame with parameters:

$$(G_1,G_2) = (G_s,G_{Ii}) \text{ and } (G_1,G_2) = (G_T,G_{Ii})$$

Figure 17.22(a) shows two grids superimposed with the transform conceptualized as a migration of the points G_1 into the points G_2. Note that the points on the edge of each grid are constrained to remain at the edge. Because of the rectangular topology, correspondence can be established between the points.

The first, or horizontal, pass of the two-pass implementation provides an intermediate grid. This intermediate grid is used by the two-pass structure and it is that set of points having the y coordinate of G_1 and the x coordinate of G_2 (Figure 17.22(b)). We then fit a vertical spline through the column of points in the intermediate grid and G_1 (Chapter 7). Thus we have two sets of vertical splines, one set for G_1 and one set for G_{12}, the intermediate grid. These two sets are used to control the distortion in the first pass or the horizontal warp.

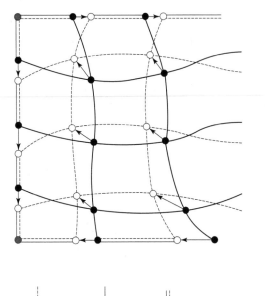

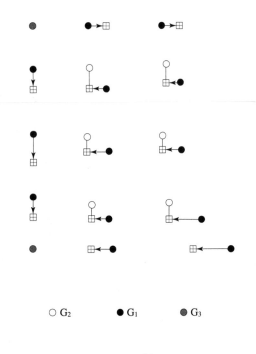

(a)

(b)

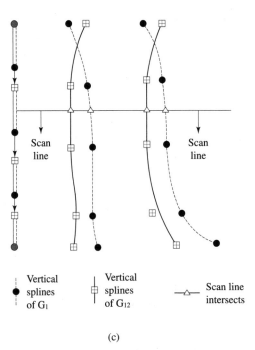

Figure 17.22
(a) Two grids G_1 and G_2.
(b) The formation of an 'intermediate' mesh G_{12}.
(c) Splines are fitted through columns of G_1 and G_{12} and finding the x intersects of each scan line with these two sets of vertical splines.

(c)

This is achieved by, for each scan line, finding the x intercepts with the vertical splines through G_1 and G_{12} (Figure 17.22(c)). From these intercepts a pixel mapping function for the current scan line is derived. Figure 17.23 shows the intercepts plotted on an x and y axis, producing a set of points through which a spline is fitted. This spline provides a row or scan line mapping function and a complete row of pixels is mapped from the source to an intermediate image that contains the result of the first pass. Note that there is a separate mapping function for each scan line. At this stage, in common with any other two-pass transform, all the x coordinates of the output image are now correct and this image is used as input to the second pass.

The second pass is completely analogous to the first pass and performs a vertical warp. This time we fit horizontal spines through G_{12} and G_2. These splines are now sampled vertically for each pixel boundary, creating two sets of y intercepts. A spline is fitted and a y mapping function is realized. This is used to perform the vertical warp which completes the entire transform.

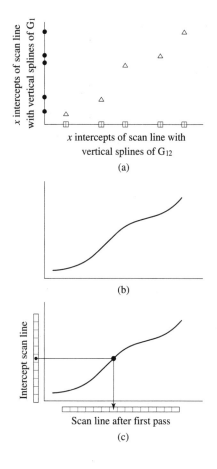

Figure 17.23
Building a mapping function. (a) Scan line intercepts; (b) a spline fitted to the points in (a); (c) (b) is used to map a row from the input image to the output image from the first pass.

The overall process can be summarized as

for the ith frame in the sequence

derive the in-between grid G_{1i} by interpolation from G_S and G_T

warp the source towards the target using G_S and G_{1i} producing G_1

warp the target towards the source using G_T and G_{1i} producing G_2

The warp process itself, between G_1 and G_2, can be summarized as

First pass (rows or horizontal warp)

create G_1 vertical splines and find x intercepts

create G_{12} vertical splines and find x intercepts
for each scan line find the x mapping function and warp in x

Second pass (columns or vertical warp)

create G_{12} horizontal splines and find y intercepts

create G_2 horizontal splines and find y intercepts

for each pixel boundary or column find the y mapping function and warp in y

Feature-based morphing

This algorithm was developed by Beier and Neely at Pacific Data Images. The rationale for the algorithm is greater artistic control over the morph sequence. In the mesh warping algorithm there is no way that certain areas can be assigned an importance greater than others. In practice a certain feature may require a high spatial density of points so that a more accurate or detailed deformation may be achieved in the area of interest. Because the mesh resolution is homogeneous, the entire mesh resolution must be increased. The practical effect of this is that the animator may find that he does not have sufficient control in one region and too much in another.

The basis of feature-based morphing is that important features that correspond in the source and target image are marked or selected by the animator. This is achieved by a remarkably simple device. A line is drawn over a feature of the source image and associated with a corresponding line in the target image. For a single line pair the algorithm effects a 'local' change. The idea is shown in Figure 17.24.

The dense correspondence is derived as a simple mapping function. Consider first a single line pair (Figure 17.24). The problem is, given a pixel X in the target image, what pixel X' in the source image does that correspond to (inverse mapping or reverse mapping is used in this algorithm). The mapping is defined by the line pair. Each line defines a uv coordinate system. A point X has uv coordinates found as follows: u is the proportional distance along the line (from its start) and v is the distance (in pixel units) along the perpendicular from the point to the line. The point X' in the source image is found by applying u and v

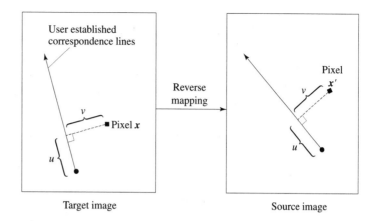

Figure 17.24
The line correspondence reverse mapping morphing technique of Beier and Neely.

to the corresponding coordinate system or line in the source image. Beier and Neely state:

Because the u co-ordinate is normalised by the length of the line, and the v co-ordinate is not (it is always distance in pixels), the image is scaled along the direction of the lines by the ratio of the lengths of the lines. The scale is only along the direction of the line. We have tried scaling the v co-ordinate by the length of the line, so that the scaling is always uniform, but found that the given formulation is more useful.

Now the use of more than one pair of line segments produces a set of coordinate system transformations that must be blended in some way. Beier and Neely proposed using weights for each coordinate pair system such that the weight is strongest if the point lies on the line and decreases the further the points are from it. In particular they suggest:

$$\text{weight} = \left(\frac{\text{length}^p}{a + \text{dist}} \right)^b$$

where

'length' is the length of the line

'dist' is the shortest distance from the pixel to the line

'a' is a strength coefficient that specifies the influence of the line. As 'a' approaches zero the strength of the line increases. For $a = 0$ and dist $= 0$, strength = infinity.

'b' determines how the relative strength of different lines decreases with distance. If $b = 0$ then each pixel will be affected by all lines equally.

'p' relates the length of the line to weight . If $p = 0$ then all lines have the same 'weight'. For $p = 1$ longer lines have a higher relative weighting.

Now for a destination pixel X we will have i source pixels X_i (where i is the number of line pairs). 'Weight' is used to find an average displacement from the set:

$$D_i = X_i' - X$$

The authors point out that with two or more line pairs the transformation effected is not simple and is non-affine. However, they claim that it is fairly obvious to the user what happens when lines are moved and added.

A complete morph sequence is achieved by drawing line pairs on the source and target image. The program finds an intermediate line map for each frame in the morph sequence by interpolation and the system calculates a complete sequence, as in the case of mesh warping, by warping both the source and target image using the source and target line maps. Beier and Neely used two different ways of interpolating the line maps – interpolating the end points of each line or interpolating the centre point and orientation. Figure 17.20 was produced using this method.

Morphing in three-dimensional space

As we defined earlier, morphing in three-dimensional space means effecting a morph sequence between two objects in three-dimensional space. Necessarily this means that the objects are computer graphic representations, most commonly polygon objects. This section is about the potential difficulties of morphing in three-dimensional space rather than any effective solution.

For example, in the film *The Abyss*, a computer graphics object – the pseudopod – was animated as a three-dimensional object and matted with live action sequences. This was made convincing by using environment mapping to cause scene features to be reflected in the object (which was incidentally made to look as if it was water). The face of the pseudopod was, however, scanned from several facial expressions of a real person. This resulted in a complex three-dimensional computer graphics object made up of a high resolution array of range data. To provide the in-between frames for the face, the two-dimensional array was manipulated using the two-pass mesh warping algorithm. These warped frames were then converted back into three-dimensional data and rendered using standard three-dimensional rendering techniques as the face of the pseudopod. Thus the pseudopod is a pure three-dimensional graphics object with the geometrical changes in the face produced by a two-dimensional morphing process.

Most of the difficulties with potential three-dimensional morphing are difficulties of complexity rather than of theoretical principles. In theory we can scan an object with a polygonal representation, then control its deformation in any desired manner by moving the vertices around. But this results in vast practical problems. And it is a fact that most of these difficulties are resolved by the simple expedient of resorting to two-dimensional morphing, to give the illusion of the three-dimensional process.

The complexity issue arises because the major demand for morphing is currently from the world of film special effects. If objects are scanned into a three-dimensional computer graphics object, then to achieve the necessary realism, hundreds of thousands of polygons are likely to result. This is not even taking into account other important aspects of real objects such as the hair and fur in animals. Given such a complex polygon object the question is how to control the deformation. We have problems with large numbers of polygon vertices. How do we script their movement in the morph? Whenever polygon vertices are moved with respect to one another, the original polygonal resolution changes, leading to potential artefacts or geometric aliasing. For example, if we change the aspect ratio of a four-sided polygon, making two opposite sides much longer than the other pair, this polygon may cause aliasing in the final image but exhibit no aliasing artefact in the source image. What if the topology of the source and target object is different (as in a sphere and toroid, for example)? It is not clear how this problem can be easily handled.

Morphing between animated sequences

All of the preceding discussion has been about morphing between two static images. Most morphing productions, however, take place between animated sequences and here the illusion of an actual change in three-dimenaional space is most effective. It is difficult to believe, looking at such sequences, that this is not actually happening.

When morphing between animated sequences, the source and the target image are both frames in an animated sequence. Figure 17.25 shows a possible morph sequence that can be calculated from two animated sequences.

In animation, certain possibilities and difficulties arise that are not present in morphing between static images. A possibility used to great effect is to control the morph such that different areas of the object change at different rates. This process is extremely effective in an animated sequence. A difficulty that arises with animation is when two different objects are moving against the same background. It is clearly undesirable for the background detail to become involved in the morph.

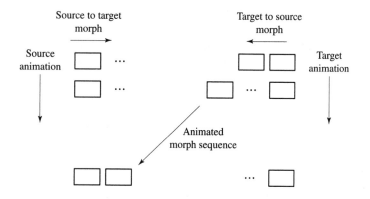

Figure 17.25
Generating a morph between the animated sequences.

17.5.4   Morphing and image registration

In standard applications of morphing an object in one image is morphed into an object in another image and along the way produces a sequence of intermediate images. The pixels migrate in the image plane according to a morphing script and this is derived from an underlying model and some user association of features in the source and target image. In the application we now describe, we are presented with a series of medical images, taken from different people, and we make the assumption that the differences between the images can be described by a morphing model. That is, we assume that if we applied a morphing model to one image we could produce all the others by using the model to warp the image. The important practical application of this philosophy is that the information obtained by using such an approach to analyze the differences in the images can be used to produce a 'standard' image. This technique helps in the production of biomedical atlases and in understanding the nature of the variability between images. Atlases are more appropriately constructed from such 'corrected' images than from images of any single form, however typical.

This is a particular example of a problem known as image registration which generally means pulling images around in their own image plane to satisfy some registration criterion. One of the most common requirements for registration comes again from medical imagery where there may be differences between images of the same part of the same patient due to the use of different imaging modalities, patient movement, and so on. The morphing model is used to analyze and quantify the differences between images and this information can then be used to register the images.

To return to the specific example: the study reported by Bookstein uses a set of images which are mid-sagittal MRI images taken from different patients. In each of the images a set of 13 'landmarks' are identified. These are unique points that can be identified manually, or perhaps by pattern recognition techniques, and are used to control the reverse morphing which morphs each sample image into the standard image. Bookstein's algorithm can be summarized as follows:

For each image, identify the landmarks

Evaluate a standard set of landmarks by spatially averaging the landmark samples from each image

For each image evaluate a morphing function – Bookstein uses thin plate splines. Thus a rectangular grid system is warped into a non-linear grid. The warped grid is just iso-parametric contours on the spline plate and the plate interpolates by minimizing a bending energy as if the landmark displacements had been normal to the image plane instead of being contained within it.

Use the morphing function to reverse morph or unwarp each image into its standard form.

Evaluate a standard image by pixel averaging the set of unwarped images. Such images, Bookstein says, all have the same 'biological coordinate system' after being unwarped.

Further reading – morphing

The most comprehensive treatment of image morphing, using splines, is given in an excellent text by George Wolberg. The book also includes colour pictures of the spline morphing algorithm being applied in various films.

The details of the feature-based image morphing technique, developed by Pacific Data images, is given in a paper by Beier and Neely. This paper contains a discussion on the problems that can arise with the technique. It also exhibits frames from the Michael Jackson video showing the line correspondences set up by the animators.

Beier T. and Neely S. (1992). Feature based image metamorphosis. *Proc. SIGGRAPH '92*, 35–42

Bookstein F.L. (1991). *Thin Plate Splines and the Atlas Problem for Biomedical Images*. Lecture Notes in Computer Science 511 (Colchester and Hawkes, eds), pp. 326–42. Berlin: Springer-Verlag

Smith A.R. (1987). 2-pass texture mapping and warping. *Proc. SIGGRAPH '87*, 263–72

Thompson D. (1942) *On Growth and Form*, 2nd edn. Cambridge: Cambridge University Press

Wolberg G. (1990). *Digital Image Warping*. Los Alamitos, CA: IEEE Computer Society Press

17.6 The moving image in science

The real world lives – it moves, objects in it move and grow and many phenomena of interest to scientists are dynamic. Growth in plants, flow in liquids and gases, catastrophes in the weather, and earthquakes are just a few examples of fields in which models are set up to simulate dynamic behaviour. It is natural that scientists should want to visualize this behaviour using animation techniques, just as they visualize the behaviour of mathematical models using static devices such as graphs of functions.

The use of animation techniques in science is not, of course, new. One of the most familiar devices is to animate images whose changes take place in, say, a day-to-day time mode – time lapse photography. Studying a film of growth and enfloration of plants is one of the most impressive uses of this much used technique. Information denied to us by studying static frames is suddenly revealed when the individual pictures, taken at, say, intervals of 24 hours, are used as frames in a 25 frames per second film. The dynamic nature of changes that are so slow that they are invisible from second to second or even day to day are suddenly perceivable and reveal behaviour invisible by observing individual photographs.

The use of computer animation has a long history and like the moving image in entertainment most scientific computer animation is just a convenient way of producing films that previously had been created manually. However, the inflexibility of film animation and the labour required in the productions tended to restrict scientific animation to education. With the advent of computer animation scientists are beginning to use the tool as a research technique.

We will now look at two historical examples which were produced before the advent of rendering engines. In these examples the emphasis is very clearly on visualizing the underlying motion. The addition of rendering techniques adds little to this type of animation. Three examples spanning 60 years illustrate the common representations and techniques that have been used. All examples use stylizations or abstractions in the form of line drawings; all that changes in the examples is the production technology. The emphasis is on making the drawing move accurately and the producers simply took the well-developed imagery of static scientific illustration and made it move. They reproduced the dynamics of the driving equations to highlight non-linearities or whatever in the dynamic behaviour.

A remarkable example of this technique appeared in 1935. This was a scientific 'flick' book authored by the famous physicist Max Born. (Born was a collaborator in quantum theory with Heisenberg, Shrödinger and Oppenheimer and won the Nobel prize for physics in 1954.) The book, published two years after Born fled Nazi Germany, was printed with wide page margins on which Born's 'films' were drawn. The films supported Born's explanation of the difficult concept of the wave particle duality in atomic theory. Figure 17.26 shows two pages with frames from four films, from top to bottom:

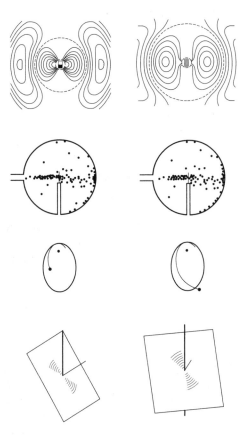

Figure 17.26
Two pages from Max Born's *The Restless Universe*, published in 1935. *Source*: Born, M. (1935) *The Restless Universe*, London: Blackie & Sons.

Hertzian oscillator

Scattering of α particles

Motion of the electron in the hydrogen atom

Rotation of the orbital plane in which the electrons motion is embedded

These beautiful demonstrations run to 118 frames (pages) and deal with most of the problems that have to be addressed in scientific animation. The moving entities or elements that are incorporated in the film are commonly in use today. The top film shows the evolution of iso-contours as a time varying function of three spatial variables shown as field lines in a single cross-sectional plane. The second film, which demonstrates Rutherford's law of scattering, is perhaps the first implementation of particle animation, rediscovered by computer graphics in the 1980s. (It is not clear from Born's text if the illustration tracks the particle paths accurately or if the particles are drawn intuitively.) In the bottom two films Born tries to introduce the effective visualization of three-dimensional space. The upper film shows the path an electron follows while rotating in its orbital plane (which also rotates). The path of the electron and its evolution over time is visualized by a trailing line and the plane in which the electron is embedded is reinforced by causing an image of the plane to rotate (the lower film). Unfortunately the efficacy of these carefully drawn animations (Born does not explain how the drawings were produced – that is, to what degree of accuracy) in the end depends on your ability to operate a flick book with the appropriate degree of expertise.

Beginning in the 1930s, scientific animation was refined and developed using film. For example, in a film *The Gas Turbine* produced by the Shell Film Unit in 1954, real turbine parts are used as a background with animated particles and flow lines, presumably drawn on cels, superimposed.

The 1960s saw the birth of computer animation which offered a virtually labour-free and automatic conversion of equations governing dynamic behaviour. Thus the tedious manual reproduction of hundreds of accurate line drawings could be replaced by sampling the equations at equal intervals in time and drawing the model or stylization on a graphics device that produced individual frames for the film. Displays at the time were 'calligraphic', either incremental pen plotters or cathode ray tubes. (They were called calligraphic because the program controlled the device as if it was a pen on paper – which was exactly what the flat bed plotter was. They were 'incremental' because both devices drew straight lines between two points supplied by the program. The minimum distance between the points, however, could be extremely small and curves, which appeared to be visually perfect, could be drawn as a set of increments. Because of their accuracy such devices produced better line drawings than today's pixel-based raster devices.) The CRT device simply used an electron beam instead of a pen, which produced a bright line on the screen – not unlike a modern laser device that can be controlled to 'paint' an outline image on a surface.

In 1966, Dr Zajac of Bell Telephone Laboratories published a paper in the *New Scientist*, describing such a facility that he had developed and used to produce 1000-frame (42s) films. He says:

To those who have tried to make an animated scientific film by conventional means, this account may sound Utopian .... Yet at Bell Telephone Laboratories, I can today write the program I have shown and obtain 16 mm film, ready for viewing, within three or four hours. At present there is only a handful of installations in the world where this procedure is possible. But within a few years, I suspect it will be available at most major universities and industrial laboratories in the USA and Western Europe.

Very soon the calligraphic CRT or plotter would be overtaken by the raster device and the expense of film replaced by video tape or the production of sequences in real time.

Zajac wrote his programs in Fortran. Figure 17.27 shows an example from his work, which he describes in the following terms:

At first I had the computer print out the numbers giving the satellite at successive instants of time. The problem of visualizing the satellite motion from the printed numbers was formidable, so I wrote a sub-program which took the numbers that would normally be printed out and used them to compute a perspective drawing of a box representing a satellite ... shows the superposition of every fifth frame of the movie for the first satellite orbit (in the movie itself the Earth turns). An orbital clock in the upper right-hand corner counts off the orbits.

Although it reads somewhat naively now, we have to bear in mind that this was a pioneering effort.

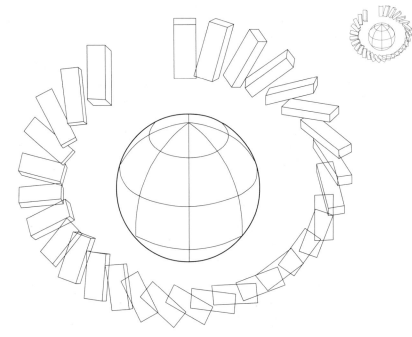

Figure 17.27
A frame from one of Zajac's animations. Redrawn after Zajac's animations.

Further reading

Halas and Manvell's text on film animation, first published in 1959, gives an excellent comparative treatment of the subject. It also contains a reprint of Zajac's early work on scientific computer animation.

Born, M. (1935). *The Restless Universe*. Glasgow: Blackie & Son, Ltd

Halas J. and Manvell R. (1971). *The Techniques of Film Animation* (3rd edn). New York: Focal Press

The moving image in computer vision

18.1 Introduction

18.2 Motion fields – global interpretation

18.3 A historical digression, a discussion, the difficulties

18.4 Motion field estimation

18.5 Principles of structure from motion

18.1 Introduction

Analysis of moving images has long been a research area in computer vision. Originally the motivation was the extraction of three-dimensional scene geometry and camera motion for robot navigation but now there are many and diverse applications. Motion analysis techniques are merging with image synthesis. We deal with a relatively new one in Section 19.5 – the analysis of facial expressions, where we attempt to measure or track the shape changes in a human face from frame to frame. Other examples are given in Chapter 20 where a motion field is used to control image warping for frame generation in virtual reality and recovery of camera motion is used to derive a computer graphics object from a set of photographs. Another area of the computer image which deals with motion is the compression of moving imagery in communications contexts. This is dealt with in detail in Chapter 19.

Motion analysis is one of the most difficult problems in computer vision. The reasons for this are fairly obvious. We need to be able to extract information on three-dimensional motion through space when we only have available the projection of this motion in the pixel plane – in other words, two-dimensional motion. Not only this but the two-dimensional motion in the image plane, for reasons that will shortly become apparent, is difficult to extract from an image sequence.

Motion analysis is highly context dependent and might be one or any combination of the following:

- Tracking a rigid body moving through space with a static camera. This immediately raises the problem that the projected shape of the object will in general change as it moves across the image plane.

- Tracking the changing shape of an object as a function of time with a static camera. In applications, such as the tracking of lip movements, we may only be interested in the two-dimensional or projected motion in the image plane

- Tracking an object is related to the segmentation issue (Chapter 12). Isolating a moving object from its background involves segmenting the information according to what is moving and what is not. This implies that motion analysis techniques can be used as segmentation tools.

- We may have a camera moving through a static or moving scene. The most oft-quoted application here is robot motion where we continually need to extract information concerning the position of the robot with respect to objects around which it has to navigate. This is often called ego motion. In this context we may have access to a single image at each time instant, or we may have a stereo pair available. Here the complexity of the motion problem is reduced if we assume that depth is available from the stereo information (although as we see from Chapter 16 the stereo problem itself is not solved).

- Shape from motion or the extraction of three-dimensional object properties from time-dependent projections is a much studied area. When the object motion is highly constrained and known, shape extraction is straightforward, and, for example, we can extract the shape of a rotating object from a time-varying sequence. One of the potentially important areas of shape from motion is in modelling for virtual reality (as we discuss in Chapter 21). If the quality and complexity of virtual environments is going to increase in the way its adherents claim, then there is a need to automate the modelling process and capture, say, a city centre environment using a video camera rather than attempting to build the scene manually.

Motion analysis techniques are sometimes seen as a subset of the image registration problem. This may be required in medical imagery where data in the form of transverse scans has been collected from some part of the patient using two different devices or modalities – X-ray and NMR, for example. Here, because of patient movement or some other alignment problem, we need to register the two images such that they can be superimposed. The connection between this and motion is that we can approach the registration problem by using the same techniques – we assume that local pixel motion has occurred.

To perform motion analysis we need to characterize or extract motion from the image plane. This is known as motion estimation. Relative motion between a scene and an observer is characterized in two main ways. First, we can observe the changing position of points, or groups of points, that make up a distinctive feature as they move across the image plane in consecutive frames. Clearly this representation of motion implies feature detection and includes such difficulties as the fact that features may disappear due to occlusion. Second, we can try to associate a motion vector with each pixel in the image plane that specifies how a projected point moves in the image plane between two consecutive frames. This is called an optical flow field.

There are differences between these two characterizations which impact on the nature of the algorithms which produce and analyze the motion information. The derivation of an optical flow field depends on continuity constraints and small interframe distances to make the mathematics valid. Point correspondence on the other hand may deal with large inter-frame distances. The image plane information in an optical flow field can be dense – we try to associate a motion vector with each and every pixel. Derivation of the optical flow field is the ideal, but it may not be necessary to have dense motion information for every application. There is no difference in principle between deriving motion information by point correspondence and from an optical flow field – after all, if we have correspondence for every pixel in two projections then we have an optical flow field – it is simply the case that optical flow field methods attempt to derive the field using low-level context-independent operations on the entire image whereas point correspondence explicitly searches for structural matches – a high-level context-dependent operation.

An appreciation of the difficulties of motion estimation can be gleaned by considering the simple case of a difference image formed by the subtrahend between two consecutive frames in a motion sequence. Image subtraction is a simple low-level operation that is often used in medical imagery to highlight moving information. (For example, if it is desired to enhance the detail from blood vessels – which contain moving texture – this can be done by taking X-rays of a patient who has been injected with X-ray opaque dye and then forming difference images in which the static information – anything that does not have blood flowing through it – disappears.) This is a pixel-by-pixel operation where pixels are operated on without considering their local context. Consider two images I_1 and I_2 and their difference image $(I_1 - I_2)$. Non-zero pixels (x,y) in the difference image can then be due to a variety of different events:

- $I_1(x,y)$ is a projection of part of a moving object and $I_2(x,y)$ is from a stationary object. (See front and rear of buses in Figure 9.8 for example.)

- $I_1(x,y)$ is a part of a moving object and $I_2(x,y)$ is from a different part of the same object. (See centre section of buses in Figure 9.8 for example.)

- $I_1(x,y)$ is a projection of part of a moving object and $I_2(x,y)$ is from another moving object.

- The difference has resulted from noise.

This simple example is intended to illustrate the difficulty of motion analysis using context-independent pixel operations and it would seem that a higher-level operation involving feature recognition and tracking is the way forward.

Despite this, most effort has been expended on fairly low-level mathematical analysis that attempts to recover a dense motion field.

Many of the problems in motion analysis stem from noise, but this is no different from any other branch of computer vision. The extracted motion is likely to be noisy. However, the interpretation of such information requires high precision and the interpretation itself is thus extremely susceptible to noise. Another notorious problem is that the extraction of an optical flow field depends, as we shall see, on an assumption that is rarely justified. In fact there is a school of thought which says that the information in an optical flow field is so noisy and unreliable that we should only make qualitative deductions from it.

If we consider the information presented to an observer who is moving through a scene then it is immediately apparent that consecutive images contain information concerning the nature of the motion through the environment. What is less apparent is that such information can also be used to deduce shape or depth information on the scene. Say that we have available images sampled at equal intervals in time by a camera moving at uniform speed through an environment. If we have complete knowledge concerning the correspondence of points in each frame in the time sequence, then comparing consecutive frames will give an optical field – a two-dimensional array of vectors where a single vector defines the motion of a scene point in the image plane. If we are using point correspondence, then because in any image we are only likely to be able to locate a few distinctive points, then this method only gives a sparse motion information. It may be used, for example, in an object tracking application where the motion of certain points on the objects (edges or corners, say) will suffice to track the object. If we need to extract dense information, concerning the shape of objects, for example, then we need dense motion information. We can attempt to deduce an optical flow field without recourse to point correspondence using differential methods to observe time-varying changes in image intensity.

Deriving three-dimensional information from a set of projections that exhibit relative movement between a camera and the scene – structure or shape from motion – is similar in principle to shape from stereo (Chapter 16) and the material that follows should be read in conjunction with Chapter 16. The difference is in the constraints that are usually invoked concerning the camera. Shape from stereo is the name used for a context where two (or more) projections from cameras of known relative position and orientation are considered. Successful solution of the correspondence problem then gives depth. Note that the similarity with the stereo problem decreases somewhat if we consider the case of scene objects moving relative to each other. We may not be looking at two different projections of the same scene, but two different scenes due to object motion. Structure or shape from motion is the term used when we have no information concerning the camera position that has produced each projection. The camera's motion is unknown. Determining both the structure in the image and the camera's motion is a much more complex problem unless heavy constraints are employed. For example, if we obtain correspondence between pairs of points in two projections, where camera motion has occurred, then the rigid displacement motion of the camera can be recovered and scene information can be determined to within a scale factor. In fact we need a minimum of five correspondences or five pairs of points to recover the rigid motion of the camera between the two viewpoints, consisting of three rotational parameters and two translational. But we are now up against the problem that we cannot, without camera knowledge, employ the epipolar constraint to assist in the correspondence search.

Another somewhat confusing point is: what do we mean by recovering camera motion? This is usually better interpreted in an equivalent way by saying that we wish to recover the camera position from which each projection was taken. For example, in Chapter 24 we describe a technique whose goal is to obtain a geometric model, to be used in a computer graphics context, from a set of photographs, of say a building, where the camera viewpoints are unknown. It is the discrete positions of the camera that we require. Camera motion tends to imply that we are interested in intermediate camera positions which in this context we are not.

At this stage we should clear up some potential confusion in terminology between the terms optical flow field, motion field and velocity field. A velocity field is generally used to describe the real motion of scene points in three-dimensional space and would thus consist of three-dimensional vectors. A motion field is the projection of this real motion onto the image plane and thus consists of an array of two-dimensional vectors – one for each visible point projected onto the image plane. An optical flow field is the field extracted by an algorithm from the consecutive frames with the goal that it should exactly correspond to the motion field. The reason this distinction is made is, of course, that in most cases an optical flow field does not correspond to a motion field. There is not only the problem with noise but the fact that different velocity fields can produce the same optical flow field. In particular, two objects can produce an optical flow field that is compatible with the motion of a single object.

Thus we can see that the general problem of motion analysis splits into two sub-problems – determination of the motion field and its subsequent analysis where the techniques involved in both cases will be context dependent. We may require simply knowledge of the motion or we may need to reconstruct the shape of the scene from the motion information.

Many of the problems that we encountered in shape from stereo reappear in shape from motion and there are many parallels with the stereo reconstruction problem. In particular, we can note that the same dichotomy exists in approaches to the problem. We can base an analysis on an approach akin to intensity matching in that we can attempt to analyze changes in the intensity of, say, two frames in a sequence to derive a motion field, or we can extract structure from the time varying images and try to track this in some way to gain the same information.

Like many aspects of computer vision, the motion problem is still an open research area and at the moment many constraints are invoked to narrow the problem. For example, in optical flow field determination we may assume that the relative motion between the scene and the observer or camera is constant and that frames are available at equal intervals in time. In addition, frames are

Figure 18.1
Examples of
spatio-temporal
sequences.

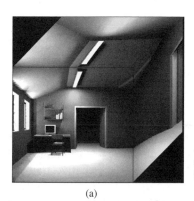

A visualization of a dense spatio-temporal
sequence. The camera is tracking towards
the desk and the door.

(a)

The first and last
frames in the sequence.

(b)

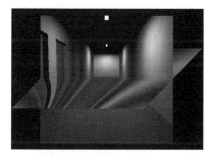

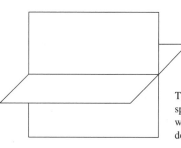

The cross-sections of a
spatio-temporal sequence
where a camera is tracking
down a corridor.

(c)

The first and last
frames in the sequence.

(d)

collected at appropriately small intervals in time – the motion is sampled at a high enough rate to facilitate an estimation of the motion field. We may also assume that objects are stationary (or do not move relative to each other) and are rigid or do not deform (although analyzing facial expressions is an important exception to the rigidity assumption).

We conclude this section with an image demonstration that illustrates the nature of the information in a motion sequence. Figure 18.1(a) shows a dense spatio-temporal sequence generated by translating a camera. The images represent equal samples in time as the camera moves. Figure 18.1(b) shows the first and last frame taken from this sequence. Consecutive frames may be used in motion estimation to derive a dense optical flow from the flow of intensity in the images. Associated with each pixel in the image is a motion vector. A practical application of the use of such information is in view interpolation, detailed in Chapter 21. The third illustration (Figure 18.1(c)) shows a slice of the three-dimensional data in the (x,t) plane. Here we see the coherence exhibited over the entire sequence. It is this information that we exploit in image compression techniques. It may also serve in structure from motion applications where we have no information concerning the nature of the camera motion. Clearly the coherence is a function of both the scene geometry and the relative motion between the scene and the camera. We see in this image yet another difficulty, which is that although the image depicts quite clearly the shift in grey-level structure over time, to make use of this in structure from motion we need to identify those surface elements that are responsible for the coherences. The final illustration, Figure 18.1(d), shows the first and last frame. An example where such frames, taken from far apart viewpoints, are used is in photomodelling, described in detail in Chapter 21. Here we are interested in recovering both the scene structure and the camera viewpoint. In the method described in Chapter 21, correspondence between such images is established by a mix of user intervention and prior knowledge of the nature of the scene (geometric constraints exhibited by the architecture). This problem is also categorized as structure from motion, even although in practice the camera motion consists of the photographer picking up the camera and locating it to a new viewpoint.

18.2 Motion fields – global interpretation

The first thing to do is to get an intuitive idea of what motion fields are. In other words, to see how the qualitative properties of a motion field relate to the motion that produced it. We will then see to what extent such information is amenable to analysis.

A motion field is a formalization or generalization of an observation originally made by Euclid in 300 BC: 'when objects move at equal speed, those more remote seem to move more slowly'. When we move quickly through an environment, say in a fast-moving train or aircraft, objects near to us move so quickly that they may appear blurred, whereas very distant objects appear stationary.

If we take two consecutive frames in a time sequence, then simply by comparing corresponding points we can derive a two-dimensional vector that represents the motion of a point in the two-dimensional image space as it moves its position in this space between frames. If we do this for every point in the image space we obtain a motion field. A (partial or sparse) motion field for a fictional train driver is shown in Figure 18.2, together with the scene that produced it. This simple example demonstrates a number of important points. First, note that the

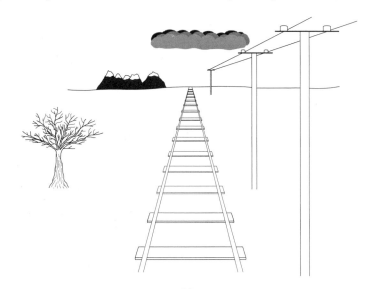

(a)

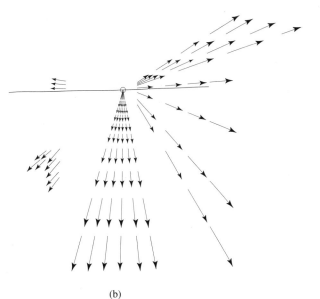

(b)

Figure 18.2
Illustrating the concept of a motion field. (a) The view of a train driver. (b) The motion field for the scene in (a).

field can be sparse or dense not only as a function of the method used to derive the field, but also of the nature of the surfaces in the field. An object whose surfaces are completely smooth will exhibit no detectable motion except at its edges.

Second, note that the vectors all diverge from a single point (on the horizon) known as the **focus of expansion**. At this point the magnitude of the motion vectors goes to zero. Sometimes it is described as being the point at which the **optic flow** is zero. For a set-up with a single translating camera there will be exactly one focus of expansion. Conversely, if we consider the case of an observer moving in the opposite direction in our simple example, then the singular point now becomes a **focus of contraction** because the situation is exactly the same, except that now the direction of the vectors is reversed.

Third, it is intuitively apparent that the motion field contains information concerning the motion of the camera. In our illustration we easily deduce that the camera is currently moving in a straight line towards the focus of expansion.

Let us now see how the optical flow is related to the velocity field. Consider a camera with a coordinate system (X,Y,Z) fixed at the centre of projection and an image plane with coordinate system (x,y) (Figure 18.3). If we assume a perspective projection then we have (Chapter 24):

$$x = X/Z \quad y = Y/Z$$

Now consider a point P at position (X,Y,Z) in the scene projecting onto point P' at position (x,y) in the image plane that possesses an instantaneous translational velocity T relative to the camera. It is easily shown that the motion vector at point (x,y) has components:

$$u = (T_x - T_z\, x)/Z \quad v = (T_y - T_z\, y)/Z$$

Figure 18.3
Projecting the velocity of
point **p** into the image
plane.

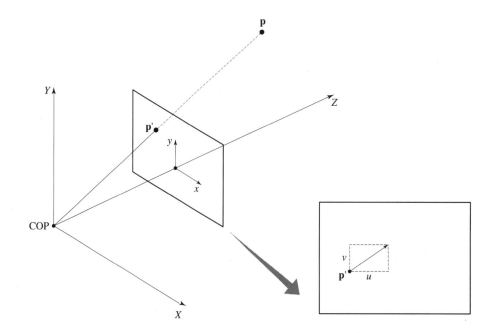

We can see from this that a knowledge of $\boldsymbol{T}$ and an algorithm that extracts u and v enables us to calculate the relative depth $Z(x,y)/r$ corresponding to a pixel, where r is the magnitude of $\boldsymbol{T}$. If $\boldsymbol{T}$ is unknown then the problem is still solvable if certain constraints are satisfied, as we have indicated.

Performing this analysis for the more general case where the relative velocity possesses a rotational component leads to formulae for the case known as **rigid flow**. This is where a camera with a general motion (translation plus rotation) moves through a static scene, or where an object moves with a similar general motion with respect to a camera.

Some simple motion fields can be represented by a single global description. This may be possible, for example, when the distance between the camera and the scene is large so that distances within the scene are negligible by comparison. In global flow each motion vector is a function only of global motion parameters and (x,y) its position in the image plane.

Most fields of practical interest are local and we usually attempt to assign a motion vector to each pixel or to a rectangular block of pixels. In the case of rigid flow, for example, each motion vector is a function of the motion parameters and (x,y) plus the z depth of the point that projected onto (x,y).

Now that we have established the idea of a motion field for a simple intuitive example of a general scene, let us now look at a few simple particular cases and consider the motion field from total knowledge of the geometry and relative motion. Figure 18.4(a) to (g) shows a set of such fields constructed for a variety of simple single objects. The purpose of the figure is to illustrate the qualitative relationship between different kinds of motion fields and the relative motion between the camera and the objects that produced them. In each case we have contrived a single motion 'type' concerning different relative motion between a planar object and a camera.

The images in Figure 18.4 were produced using computer graphics images and a fairly coarse intensity matching procedure (see the following section). The demonstrations attempt to show the nature of motion fields, as a function of object and motion type and, at the same time, the immediate difficulties that arise because of the assumption that the light reflected from the scene does not change due to relative motion between the camera and the scene. This assumption is discussed further in the next section.

The demonstrations are also important in the context of Chapter 26 which includes a discussion on the compression of image sequences. Here, intensity matching of areas of images is the main technique employed; the critical difference is that the motion vectors and difference information (which is zero if a perfect match is found) is encoded. In other words it is used as an encoding symbol, not to extract information concerning the motion in the scene.

Now consider Figure 18.4

(a) **Translation in depth – camera moves towards a sphere**   The focus of expansion is at the centre of the object – where the view vector intersects the object. The distribution of vector angles should be equiprobable and all velocities should occur.

Figure 18.4
Examples of motion fields.
(a) Translation in depth –
camera moves towards a
sphere; (b) translation in
depth – camera moves
towards a cylinder;
(c) translation in depth –
camera moves towards
both objects; (d) translation
in depth – camera
moves down a corridor;
(e) translation at constant
depth – camera moves from
left to right; (f) rotation in
depth; (g) rotation in depth.

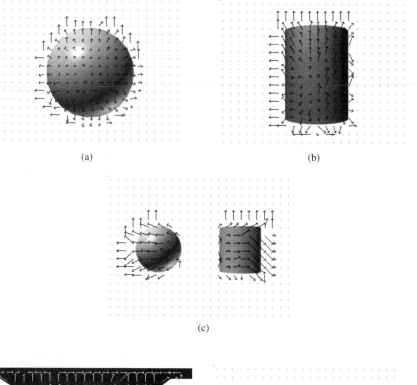

(a)

(b)

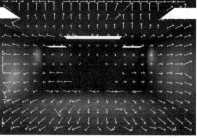

(c)

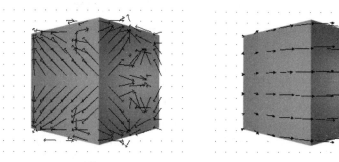

(d)

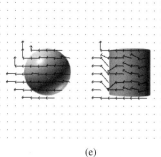

(e)

(f)

(g)

(b) **Translation in depth – camera moves towards a cylinder**   The field is now different from (a) as a function of the difference in shape of the objects. There are also more errors. This is because the cylinder was only illuminated with a single light (the sphere is lit by two lights) and the right-hand side is more or less constant dark.

(c) **Translation in depth – camera moves towards both objects**   The camera is moving towards a point that is situated between the two objects. The resulting field is noisy, exhibiting large inaccuracies.

(d) **Translation at depth – camera moves down a corridor**   Here, a simple program has no difficulty in deriving the motion field because the images are constructed using a radiosity renderer. The radiosity solution is independent of the camera position and, providing the effect of the perspective projection in the two frames does not cause too much inter-frame difference, the simple program can easily match pixel blocks.

(e) **Translation at constant depth – camera moves from left to right**   This motion occurs, for example, when a camera moves parallel to its own image plane. There is no focus of expansion or contraction and the motion vectors should be everywhere parallel. We can consider a pan which is caused by a camera rotation about an axis parallel to the image plane to be translation at constant depth for small angles of rotation.

(f) **Rotation in depth**   The cube is rotating about an axis that is parallel to the image plane. We should see a focus of both expansion and contraction – the object is moving both towards and away from the camera. In this case the result is hopeless because of the high rate of change of reflected light from the cube face between frames.

(g) **Rotation in depth**   This image is the field that should have been produced in image (f). This was generated by explicitly tracking the position of a regular texture mapped onto the surface of the object.

The two images shown in Figure 18.5 were produced by introducing relative motion between the objects and the camera.

(a) **Objects in relative motion – camera stationary**   Here we see two spheres in relative motion, the nature of which should be apparent from the fields.

(b) **Objects in relative motion – camera moving towards the scene**   The same object motion as in Figure 18.4(a) with the camera also moving towards the objects.

Perhaps we can conclude from these studies that it is difficult or impossible, except in very simple cases, to make global interpretations from the motion field. This is to be expected from a two-dimensional domain where the structure of the motion field depends on both the geometry of the scene and the relative motion of objects. Global interpretation of a motion field inevitably reduces to local interpretation; here we may be able to categorize groups of motion vectors according to the following:

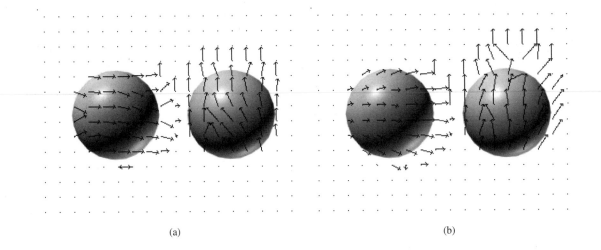

(a)   (b)

Figure 18.5
Further examples of motion fields. (a) Objects in relative motion, camera stationary; (b) objects in relative motion, camera moving towards the scene.

- Groups of parallel vectors have originated from translation at constant depth – panning.

- Groups exhibiting a focus of expansion have originated from motion along the z axis – zoom. More than one focus of expansion implies that there are several objects each with their own motion with respect to the camera.

- Groups of concentric vectors have originated from rotation at constant distance.

18.3   A historical digression, a discussion, the difficulties

Shape from motion using motion fields is another example of an area that has a long history of speculation concerning human vision which has influenced possible approaches to machine vision. It is not clear how important motion fields are to human beings. The first work on the importance of motion fields as a perceptual mechanism was carried out by J.J. Gibson and reported in a book published in 1950. In it he argues:

the fundamental visual perception is that of approach to a surface. This precept always has a subjective component as well as an objective component, that is, it specifies the observer's positional movement and direction, as much as it specifies the location, slant and shape of the surface.

A classic series of experiments initiated by Johansson in 1973 is as influential in the field of shape from motion as Julesz's stereograms are in shape from stereo. Just as Julesz demonstrated that shape could be perceived in stereograms from which all monocular clues had been removed, Johansson highlighted our ability to perceive shape from motion sequences, where each frame in the sequence contained no apparent structural clues. In this experiment viewers see a few lights attached to various parts of the body of a person moving in the dark. Individual frames prove meaningless but in a moving sequence, a viewer is able to provide such complex information as, for example, the nature of the gaits (in walking or running) and even gender and the recognition of familiar individuals from just the moving dots of light. These experiments have come to be known as moving light displays or MLDs.

This idea is strongly related to a technique currently being used to create scripts for computer animated sequences (Chapter 17). Here we circumvent the difficulty of obtaining a motion script for a complex articulated structure model, such as a computer graphics model of a human being, by deriving a script from a set of position detectors attached to a performing human being. The emplacement of these detectors on the body of the performer corresponding to the links in the articulated structure that we need to control. So if we can convincingly animate an articulated structure using as a script the motion of certain points attached to a real person, then perhaps it is no surprise that it is possible for observers to extract information from a moving light display.

A perhaps less impressive demonstration is based again on structure hidden by random dots. Frames for an animated sequence are generated by considering the scene to be made up of a random dot background and a small planar object – such as a square – also made up of random dots that forms the foreground. The sequence consists of the square object translating parallel to the background object. Just as in the random dot stereo demonstration (Chapter 20) examination of single frames reveals no apparent structure – only a pattern of random dots are seen. When the animation is viewed the viewer easily perceives the moving square. This demonstration vividly shows the importance of movement clues in our visual perception.

Nelson and Polana (1992) argue that to human beings familiar moving patterns have significance that their stationary counterparts do not. We can do no better than quote from their poetic introduction:

Who has not watched the ripples spread across a pool and known water nearby? Or seen leaves shimmer their silver backs in a summer breeze and known a tree? Who has not known the butterfly by her fluttering? Or seen a distant figure walking and known there goes a man?

They claim that such a global interpretation of the self-similarity of motion fields may be an important component of the human visual system. They suggest that such patterns as they describe could exhibit features that are invariant. We recognize the motion field of shimmering leaves independent of the tree type and all other detailed variables as we see in such a pattern as different from that produced by, say, the ripples on a pond.

Marr (1982) on the other hand states:

It is doubtful whether these facts are used much by our visual systems. So Gibson's hypothesis, that the centre of optical expansion plays a major role in the control of locomotion, is probably false for humans, although it may be more relevant to birds.

This would appear to be a reasonable assumption. After all, leaving aside twentieth-century modes of transport, we can only travel at a very small velocity relative to our environment. It is certainly the case that we are never explicitly aware of the presence of a motion field unless we are travelling in a fast-moving method of transport. We have plenty of time to analyze individual images of a scene through which we are moving in exactly the same way that we analyze the scene when we are stationary. We could make an analogy with sampling images in time (like a film camera). Our sampling rate is so high, relative to our velocity through the scene, that the perceptual mechanisms that we employ may be no different to those that we use when we are stationary. We probably have no perceptual mechanisms that rely on the relative velocity between the scene and the moving observer. Possibly it is more accurate to say that out interpretation of a scene is not disturbed in any way by relative motion.

We now know enough about shape from motion to be able to appreciate the underlying problems. We can only derive comprehensive knowledge of the scene if we can recover accurate knowledge of the motion field. We will now address this problem.

18.4 Motion field estimation

We can attempt to determine the motion field from **intensity flow** information or from **edge flow information**. Intensity flow implies that we will extract a dense motion field – a motion vector – for each pixel and this in turn means that we must have a high temporal sampling rate. Using edges or other image features usually implies a sparse motion field band establishing correspondence between features in separate frames.

In the first approach we track the flow of iso-brightness contours in the image. This, of course, assumes that the reflected intensity from an object does not change as the object moves and/or the camera moves. This is not strictly true even for Lambertian surfaces under invariant illumination unless the surface is only translating. It also assumes that the optical flow is smooth – adjacent points in the image plane move in a similar manner – something that does not occur at object edges.

An extreme example of the restrictiveness of this condition is provided by Horn who asks you to consider a sphere rotating under constant illumination. For an untextured surface this will appear as a stationary sphere. The motion field is non-stationary. Conversely consider a stationary sphere and a rotating light source. Here the motion field is stationary but a motion sequence will appear as if it is the sphere that is rotating. So in the first case we have a stationary motion – zero motion field – where we should have movement and in the second case we have motion where there is none.

Motion field estimation from the flow of intensity – differential methods

If we have a number of frames sampled at short intervals in time then we have a function of three variables $I(x,y,t)$. We assume that I is everywhere continuous and we can differentiate to give:

$$\frac{dI}{dt} = \frac{\partial I}{\partial x}\frac{dx}{dt} + \frac{\partial I}{\partial y}\frac{dy}{dt} + \frac{\partial I}{\partial t}$$

Now as we described in the previous section, we assume that the intensity of a point in the scene never changes in the motion sequence and so we can write

$$dI/dt = 0$$

and we have

$$\frac{\partial I}{\partial x}\frac{dx}{dt} + \frac{\partial I}{\partial y}\frac{dy}{dt} + \frac{\partial I}{\partial t} = 0$$

where

$$\left(\frac{dx}{dt}, \frac{dy}{dt}\right)^T = \frac{d\boldsymbol{x}}{dt} = \boldsymbol{v}$$

is the instantaneous velocity of the point $\boldsymbol{x}$ in the image plane at time t. The equation relates grey-level structure in the image to this velocity.

This is known as the optical flow constraint or more particularly the intensity flow constraint. As it stands it is a single equation in two unknowns – the two components of the motion vector, and requires additional constraints/ assumptions to be solved. We note that it is the dot product of the image gradient or iso-brightness contours with the image velocity and it can be written more succinctly as

$$\nabla I \cdot \boldsymbol{v} = -\partial I/\partial t$$

or

$$\boldsymbol{v} = (-\partial I/\partial t)/\nabla I \tag{18.1}$$

where we assume that $\partial I/\partial t$ is available from two consecutive images in a temporal sampling sequence.

This gives us an optical flow field specifying that component of image velocity in the direction of image gradient. This means that we only have knowledge of the velocity of the intensity in a direction normal to the iso-brightness contour at a point – we have no knowledge of any component tangential to the contour. This is a consequence of solving with a constraint that is local and it is known as the aperture problem. We are merely observing, locally, positional shifts in the grey-level structure of the image.

Figure 18.6
A contrived example that illustrates the aperture problem. Using methods that analyze local intensity flow we can only derive information concerning motion that is normal to the iso-brightness contour. (a) True motion field; (b) derived motion field.

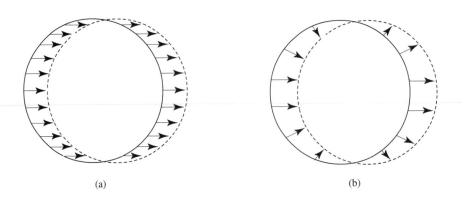

(a)   (b)

This problem is illustrated in Figure 18.6 for a simple and somewhat contrived case. Say we have two consecutive images in a time-varying sequence that exhibit a circular iso-brightness contour which has translated parallel to the image plane between the frames. The true motion field is shown in Figure 18.6(a) and the field derived by Equation (18.1) is shown in Figure 18.6(b). Thus we see that the derived field – the optical flow – is in general different from the true motion field.

A practical algorithm would operate in two phases – an application of Equation (18.1) followed by a procedure that operates on the derived field to produce a result that is closer to the true motion field. This can be done by using a procedure that minimizes the variation of the motion vectors over the iso-brightness contours computing the field of least variation. Such an approach is fully described in the text by Hildreth.

We have introduced the mathematical concept of the motion field constraint but we see that there are many problems in trying to extract a motion field from this information alone. A significant problem is that the method is local and in any real context the extension to a global solution is not easy.

18.4.2 Intensity-based correlation

This approach is identical to correlation techniques in stereo correspondence. It involves finding correspondence between adjacent frames in a sequenceand as with the stereo problem this implies that the image must exhibit features for this correspondence to be established. (Note that this contrasts with the previous method where no correspondence was required – we simply evaluate the first derivative of the image intensity.) Again we try to find correspondence by considering small areas in the image and we assume that the structure that produced these areas in the image plane is displaced rigidly by a displacement (u,v).

The problem is easily stated. Consider two consecutive frames $I(x,y,t_{n-1})$ and $I(x,y,t_n)$ in a time sequence. We assume that small areas in one image can be correlated with small areas in the other thus

$$I(x+u,y+v,t_n) = I(x,y,t_{n-1})$$

where (u,v) are the components of the displacement vector which is the same as the motion vector for constant velocity. Given a small area centred on (x,y) of $w \times w$ pixels we minimize:

$$E_{ij}(u,v) = \sum_{i-w}^{i+w} \sum_{j-w}^{j+w} (I(x+u,y+v,t_n) - I(x,y,t_{n-1}))^2$$

This approach is now used routinely in the compression of image sequences as we describe in Chapter 26. However, here the problem is somewhat easier in this sense. The accuracy of the motion estimation is not critically important; we are not subsequently going to require the motion field for further analysis. Instead we are simply trying to reduce the total amount of information required to specify a spatio-temporal sequence.

Multiframe motion analysis

Up to now we have talked about tracking points or features over time or extracting optical flow from image brightness information. We will now look at a method that exploits the fact that many frames may be available for analysis and it should be possible to exploit this and extract information from the frame to frame coherence.

This simple and elegant approach was reported by Bolles et al. in 1987 and is based upon analyzing a three-dimensional 'stack' of images that have been collected by sampling in time as a camera moves with respect to a scene (see Figure 18.1).

Consider the stack of data formed by consecutive camera images to be u,v,t space, where $v = z$ if the camera is moving parallel to the x,z plane of object space. If we consider a scene containing just a single point, then if we induce relative motion between the camera and the scene, the point will describe a three-dimensional space curve in u,v,t space. Similarly an edge will sweep out a surface. This concept is illustrated in Figure 18.7 (compare with Figure 18.1c) which shows a stack of images that have been sliced with a plane parallel to the u,t plane. These are called epipolar planes. Edge detail in the scene sweeps out 'streaks' in this cross-section. Bolles et al. utilized this fact in an approach that estimates motion field directly from such information. In a sense, the edges 'detect themselves'. There is an obvious coherence in the streaks. Also, we are directly tracking scene points and thus eliminate one of the main problems with the previous method – which was that we had to invoke a major constraint to be able to guarantee that movement of image intensity was equivalent to the movement of a scene point.

The significant difference between this technique and the intensity flow method is really embedded in the coherence of the streak method. Here we are considering information over a large number of temporal samples or frames. In the intensity flow method we are restricting ourselves to two consecutive frames and trying to lift out information concerning motion that is corrupted by noise

Figure 18.7
(a) Scene/camera geometry.
Camera moves in *zx* plane
in direction parallel to *x* axis.
(b) Data geometry.
(c) One epipolar plane.

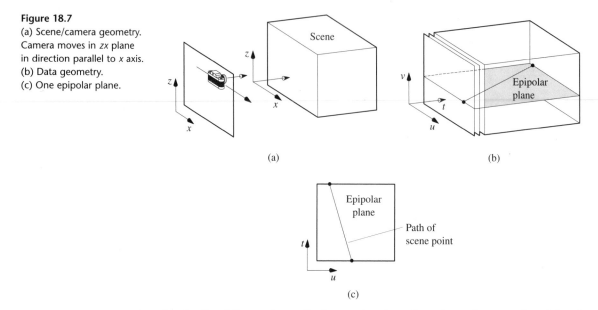

(a)

(b)

(c)

due to the failure of practical cases to obey the constraints employed by the method. It is rather like trying to fit a straight line through two noisy points.

It is easily seen that some streaks are linear and other are curves. For example, if the camera is translating in a direction that is parallel to its image plane and it sees an object with a view-independent edge then this will produce a linear streak in $I(x,y,t)$. If the camera moves in a direction not parallel to its image plane, then the streak traced out by the view-independent edge will be a curve. Straightforward analysis of $I(x,y,t)$ is enabled by introducing the following constraints:

- The camera is tracking parallel to its image plane. We assume that the camera moves with uniform velocity which is known.

- The scene only contains view-independent edges, so the streaks that are produced by the edges in the scene will be straight lines.

- The sampling rate is high so that the resolution in the (u,t) plane is sufficient to enable easy detection of the streaks.

Bolles et al. point out that although the general ambition in computer vision has been to estimate both the camera motion and the scene structure, assuming precise knowledge of camera motion is not unreasonable and could be obtained from, for example, an inertial guidance system.

Figure 18.7 shows the geometry of the system. The camera is moving in a straight line parallel to the *x* axis and is embedded in the *zx* plane. Consecutive images are placed on top of each other and we build up a stack of data in coordinate system *u,v,t*, where *u* is the horizontal image coordinate. Any plane parallel to the *ut* plane is an epipolar plane and will exhibit streaks which will have a negative slope for a camera that is moving towards increasing *x*. Any scene point remains at a constant distance in the *y* direction from the camera. If we start the camera at time $t = 0$ and move it along the x axis it is easily shown that the equation of a streak in an epipolar plane is given by:

$$t = -\left(\frac{y_o}{af}\right)u + \frac{x_o}{a}$$

where a is the velocity of the camera

f is the distance from the camera reference point to the centre of projection

x_o, y_o is the coordinate of the scene point that produced the streak line

The slope of a streak and x_o are known and we can thus determine the corresponding depth y_o. So in this way scene points in the image plane that are part of a feature such as an edge produce streaks in $I(x,y,t)$ from which their depth can be determined.

18.5 Principles of structure from motion

We will now consider the general principle of structure from motion. As we have already discussed, this is an unsolved problem in computer vision and the many and varied techniques are somewhat outside the scope of this text.

We start by recalling from Section 17.2.1 that for a rigid body constraint any relative motion between the object and the camera can be decomposed into two components – translation and rotation about a line through the centre of projection. This means that any motion field can be expressed as the sum of two components – the motion field for the translational component and the field for the rotational component. We further note that the translational motional field depends on the camera motion and the geometry of the scene, but the rotational component depends only on the camera rotation. This suggests that one way to tackle the motion analysis is to try to separate the estimated motion field into a translational and rotational component.

First consider the relationship between the three-dimensional motion and structure and the corresponding motion field in the image plane. Consider a scene point $\boldsymbol{p}$ at position (x_p, y_p, z_p). We represent the velocity of $\boldsymbol{p}$ with respect to

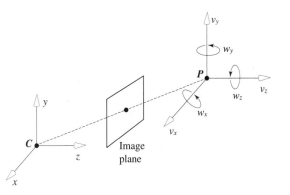

Figure 18.8
Motion geometry.

the coordinate system of the camera (Figure 18.8). That is, three translational components v_x, v_y and v_z and three rotational components ω_x, ω_y and ω_z. The velocity of the scene point is:

$$-(\boldsymbol{v} + \omega \times \boldsymbol{p})$$

which can be written as:

$$\frac{dx_p}{dt} = -v_x - \omega_y z_p + \omega_z y_p$$

$$\frac{dy_p}{dt} = -v_y - \omega_z x_p + \omega_x z_p$$

$$\frac{dz_p}{dt} = -v_z - \omega_x y_p + \omega_y x_p$$

Letting the distance to the image plane be 1, we have the coordinates of the point in the image plane:

$$x_s = \frac{x_p}{z_p} \text{ and } y_s = \frac{y_p}{z_p}$$

Substituting and differentiating then gives:

$$\frac{dx_s}{dt} = T_x + R_x \text{ and } \frac{dy_s}{dt} = T_y + R_y$$

where

$$T_x = \frac{-v_x + v_z x_s}{z_p} \quad T_y = \frac{-v_y + v_z y_s}{z_p}$$

$$R_x = \omega_x x_s y_s - \omega_y (1 + x_s^2) + \omega_z y_s$$

$$R_y = -\omega_y x_s y_s + \omega_x (1 + y_s^2) - \omega_z x_s$$

Further reading – motion analysis

Most of the approaches to motion analysis relate to intensity flow between two consecutive frames in a sequence. A good introduction to this is given in the book by Hildreth. In contrast the paper by Bolles et al. is a straightforward exploitation of the coherence that emerges over many frames.

Bolles R.C., Baker H.H. and Marimont D.H. (1987). Epipolar-plane image analysis: An approach to determining structure from motion. *Int. J. Computer Vision*, **1**, 7–55

Gibson J.J. (1950). *The Perception of the Visual World*. Boston, MA: Houghton Mifflin Co.

Hildreth E.C. (1983). *The Measurement of Visual Motion*. Cambridge MA: MIT Press

Johansson G. (1964). Perception of motion and changing form. *Scandinavian J. Psychology*, **5**, 181–208

Julesz B. (1971). *Foundations of Cyclopian Perception*. Chicago, IL: Univ. of Chicago Press

Marr D. (1982). *Vision – A Computational Investigation into the Human Representation and Processing of Visual Information*. San Francisco, CA: W.H. Freeman and Co.

Nelson R.C. and Polana R. (1992). Quantitative recognition of motion using temporal texture. *CVGIP: Image Understanding*, **56**, 78–89

The moving image in communications – facial animation

19.1 Introduction

19.2 Cut and paste – lips and eyes

19.3 Speech-driven synthetic heads – two-space techniques

19.4 Analysis–description–synthesis approaches

19.5 Facial expressions in facial animation: modelling issues

19.6 Summary

19.1 Introduction

The two great revolutions in communications technology in the twentieth century were the development of radio, or wireless, and television. John Logie Baird's machine was heralded by an advertisement in *The Times* dated 27 June 1923 which read:

Seeing by Wireless. Inventor of apparatus wishes to hear from someone who will assist (not financially) in making the working model.

Incredible as it may seem now, Baird's apparatus was wholly electromechanical and incorporated a scanning device – the Nipkow disc patented in 1884. Ignoring developments in the cathode ray tube, Baird stubbornly persisted with his cumbersome system, with scanning discs made from old tea chests, and on 30 September 1929, he transmitted his first broadcast via a BBC channel. Eight years later the BBC bowed to the inevitable and dropped the Baird system in favour of the all-electronic Marconi-EMI equipment. Apart from the increase in quality that resulted from the improvements in resolution and the introduction of colour, the basic principles of television transmission and its utilization remain the same today.

It seems that the computer image is about to change the basic image communication mode of TV systems which is to transmit 25 or 30 (potentially independent) images a second without the intervention of any processing operation that attends to image content. TV images are only subject to such processes as are concerned with retaining image quality and other routine operations such as modulation. The interest now is in having a computer intervene in the TV transmission process and using computer image techniques to facilitate, for example, image compression. Although facial animation obviously has conventional applications in computer animation, it is its use in communication that is becoming important as it offers a solution to human 'face to face' communication and human communication with a computer.

A television channel has the ability to transmit a very large amount of information every second. Although there is normally little change in image content from frame to frame, a television channel has the capacity to transmit consecutive frames that are completely different from each other – as in the case of a chequerboard where each square is a pixel and the black–white pattern alternates between white–black and black–white once per frame. This requires a high bandwidth channel to carry the information (approximately 6 MHz for standard systems) and leaving aside whatever developments will come out of fibre optics, bandwidth is the predominant cost factor in any communications channel.

Individuals do not have access to TV channels, but they do to low bandwidth links such as telephone lines and lately to computer networks. A goal that has long been sought by developers is to use computer image techniques to enable live video to be squeezed down such channels – video telephony. We are, of course, talking about image compression, but the compression ratios that we require are far in excess of conventional image compression techniques and in this section we will look at novel approaches to this problem, most of which are associated in some way with facial animation. It remains to be seen if such approaches to information reduction will be developed to any significant extent. With the advent of fibre optics it may be that bandwidth cost reduction will obviate the need for such techniques and individuals will have access to links of sufficient bandwidth to handle images.

There is also an emerging application of facial animation in GUIs and virtual reality where instead of being interested in face-to-face communication we are interested in using a human-like or 'personable' talking head as an interface. Given a speech synthesizer and a speech recognizer, vocal communication with a computer could be enhanced in the sense that the normal disembodied nature of synthetic speech would be avoided.

Consider conventional image compression techniques which we deal with in Chapter 26. Generally conventional image compression techniques are context independent. They do the same thing to each pixel without considering the image context that the pixel is part of. (Although we could argue that a common compression technique – run length encoding – is context dependent, pixels that are identical along a scan line are grouped together.) The compression issue we discuss in this section is intelligent image compression. We wish to extract and transmit the information that is required by the context. Such compression techniques essentially rank image information. Important information is maintained at the expense of less important. In Section 19.2 we give a simplistic example of this where the lips of a talking head are 'cut' out and transmitted as they move, then superimposed on a background of a static head transmitted once only, or less frequently than the mouth. A crude approach but it illustrates the point.

Such techniques are best considered, not as compression schemes at all, but as analysis–synthesis systems. The image is analyzed at the transmitter and synthesized at the receiver. It is sometimes called model-based image coding but because of the diversity of the techniques this term is sometimes inappropriate. A moving image is analyzed and a description of the movement or script is transmitted over the channel to a receiver which interprets the movement script and attempts to construct an imitation of the source image from which the script was derived. This is a completely different approach to classical image compression where image information is simply 'repacked' efficiently using its statistical properties tolerating, or not, some reduction in the quality of the reconstructed image.

Because this area of the computer image is very new it makes sense to base the discussion on a particular example and the example we choose is the main application – the videophone, the science fiction dream of the 1950s that we alluded to in the introduction. This means transmitting a coded sequence of moving images representing the face and, say, shoulders of a person – a so-called talking head. A simple hierarchy of approaches arranged in order of bandwidth and image quality/fidelity is shown in Figure 19.1 which aims to be self-explanatory.

The methods we describe in this section are aimed at reducing the channel capacity from thousands of bits per second, which we would require for, say, a DCT compressed system, to something in the order of hundreds of bits per second. Clearly we do this by trading the channel capacity requirement against the processing costs involved in the analysis and synthesis stages.

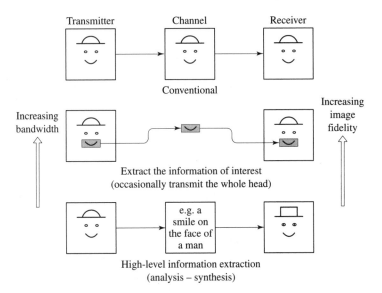

Figure 19.1
A simple hierarchy of the possibilities for a talking head.

We should start the discussion by talking about quality or the difference between the original image and the reconstructed image. This is the key to videophone transmission – too low a quality and the system will be unacceptable to the users; too high a quality demand will make the analysis–synthesis unattainable in real time. But how do we specify quality? Certainly the quantitative measures that we specified to compare classical image compression techniques would be completely inappropriate in this context. A 'traditional' method of setting an acceptable quality level that is used in public telephone systems may be appropriate here. This approach is simply to reduce the bandwidth of a channel as much as possible while retaining the vocal signatures of the users. That is, if it is your mother speaking, the received speech, although low pass filtered and thus degraded, still sounds like your mother. Originally the telephone bandwidths were set to about 3 kHz. It was decided that although human speech occupies a much wider bandwidth (up to around 10 kHz), the distortion produced by a 3 kHz bandwidth would be acceptable and indeed we can manage without the frequency components in the human voice above 3 kHz without too much trouble. The equivalent operation in the transmission of a talking head might be to retain sufficient bandwidth so that visual identity of the speaker persists. But, of course, things are far more subtle with face-to-face communication. Many facial expressions that signal a wide variety of emotions may need to be communicated in an application. How do we avoid destroying these sometimes imperceptible signals? For example, consider the fine difference between a genuine and a forced smile. Most people would find it difficult to give any image-based description of this difference, so how do we get a computer to extract it?

In a moving image of a talking head, and leaving aside the qualifications of the previous paragraph, the main components that we are concerned with are the expressions that derive from lip position and movement, the expressions that come from eye movement and movements of the hands and arms. We can say straight away, for example, that lip motion must be accurately encoded to a degree that can accomplish synchronization with the speech. We find unsynchronized lip movements very disturbing as happens, for example, in a dubbed film. However, the encoding of arm and hand movement is not so critical. Although most people use arm and hand movements for emphasis, the precise nature or timing of the motion is not so critical as is the motion of the lips.

There are useful analogies here with computer animation. In the simplest case the animation script may specify the movement of a model or object from one attitude to another. We have a single instance of the model plus a script that moves it. In model-based image coding, if we are trying to transmit an image of a moving body, then we need only transmit once the model of the body and then subsequently transmit the movement script. The receiver, with knowledge of the model, repeats the animation at the transmitter by synthesizing (or duplicating) the animation from the transmitted script. The example is somewhat obvious but the important point is that the animated image at the receiver may be highly or arbitrarily detailed and involve the movement of a complex polygonal object. However, the frame to frame information required to drive the receiver synthesizer may only require a few hundreds of bits per second.

This analogy falls down in two respects which are instructive to consider. First, we are not concerned in the videophone application with three-dimensional rigid body animation but with shape change that occurs in a face due to changing expressions. Second, we are in effect 'locked' into two space. We have to derive a specification of the change in shape of a two-dimensional projection of a three-dimensional object. This is not unlike the morphing techniques which also were locked into two space, but convincingly gave the visual effect of a three-dimensional object appearing to change shape in reality (that is, in three space). In a videophone context we can say that we need to invert the morphing process – we need to derive the morphing script that caused the changing expression in the source images. We can then transmit this script only down the channel and use it to warp a rest face at the receiver. Thus in Figure 19.1 the high-level information that we extracted would be a script for some morphing method.

Facial expressions are concerned with movements that may be evident to a greater or lesser extent over the whole of the face. How do we analyze such expressions? Many current approaches effect some kind of local selectivity and do not attempt to analyze facial movements as being a function of the whole head. This is because of the inherent difficulty of such an approach. The work that has been carried out in this area in the past few years is conceptually and practically quite simple, reflecting the need for quick analysis and synthesis processing. We will develop a description that starts with a simple and obvious approach and then develop refinements on this.

Most of the work in this area is speculative. No standard techniques have yet emerged. We will concentrate therefore on a few of the representative examples rather than attempt any kind of structural review. The work chosen is mainly by Waters, Terzopoulos and Waters and Kaneko et al.

19.2 Cut and paste – lips and eyes

The first method is in principle extremely simple and involves transmitting only those parts of the image or face that move. The image is edited in two-dimensional space by cutting out windows of pixels around the eyes and lips and sending these across the transmission channel. Although not strictly an analysis–synthesis based approach this simple technique gives the flavour of the analysis–synthesis methods and illuminates, through its drawbacks, the problems that we need to address in the development of a 'full' model-based scheme.

If we assume that facial expressions are effectively embodied in eye and lip movements, then we can simply **cut** an area enclosing the eyes and lips and restrict the information transmitted to a representation of these windows. If we make the further assumption that eye and lip movements are constrained to a small set then we can build a LUT of typical movements for a particular person.

Thus for any frame we simply transmit the LUT entry number. If we decide that 64 eye movements and 64 lip movements are sufficient we only require 12 bits per frame or 300 bits per second for a 25 frames per second system. This can generate a total of 64×64 different combinations or expressions made up of eye/lip shapes.

This crude but simple approach has the following requirements. First, we need a pre-processing phase where the catalogue of expressions is derived for a particular person or transmitter. (This is not unlike the training phase used by speech recognizers or handprinted character recognition devices.) In the operating phase the eye and lip windows are then extracted and compared with the LUT entries for the closest match to obtain the code for transmission.

We can easily build a LUT if we consider that the head is static. We construct, say interactively, an eye and lip window and run a video sequence. We add the windows from the first frame to the LUT and for any current frame we add the windows if they differ from all previous stored windows by some threshold. (We would use, say, cross-correlation for matching – Chapter 24.) The threshold controls how large the LUT grows. In this way we build an expression catalogue for a particular person.

Before an operating phase can begin this catalogue, together with a rest head, must be transmitted to the receiver. (But only once for any person and people that communicated regularly would build up a library of catalogues.) Once the operating phase begins, a face is synthesized by reproducing in every frame the full face from the first frame overwritten with the current expression windows from the receiver's catalogue indexed by the transmitted LUT entries.

The efficiency of the scheme depends on the length of the LUT – the shorter the LUT the less channel capacity is required. However, the accuracy decreases as the LUT is shortened. Too few entries means that we will see a time quantization effect because a single entry will become established for a few frames followed by a sudden jump to another entry.

And what about head movement? Here there are a number of problems. The idea is that the receiver displays a static head from the first frame with moving eyes and lips. This is extremely artificial and machine-like and perhaps its dehumanizing quality is unacceptable. But even accepting this quality drawback there is a problem with movement at the transmitting end. Unless we impose the somewhat unrealistic constraint that the transmitting subject does not move, then we have to track or move the eye and lip windows along with the head. This is only straightforward when the head moves in a motion parallel to the image plane where we can 'lock' the windows to reference points on (say) the head outline. Rotation about any axis is going to require a more elaborate tracking scheme.

Another problem is that we not only have to consider global head movement but important local movement that should not be ignored – up/down jaw displacement as the mouth opens and closes. So although this is a very simple and fast scheme with extremely low channel capacity requirement, its disadvantages are somewhat significant and this leads us on to the greater complexity of more elaborate schemes.

19.3 Speech-driven synthetic heads – two-space techniques

An obvious approach, which is similar in effect to the previous method but differs in the means used, is to use speech to drive mouth or lip movements. We do this, like the previous method, by assuming that any head is only going to execute a fixed vocabulary of lip movements, storing these, and deriving a animation by indexing into this set of movements using the speech uttered by the transmitter. This enables us to transmit speech only down the channel and lip-synchronize (lip-sync) this to a synthetic head. The head can be that of a real person which moves using a warping method to provide the appropriate face movements. In terms of our morphing script analogy, we set up a fixed vocabulary of warps in advance and use the speech to index into our list of warp scripts.

Face-to-face communication could be implemented with the availability of speech recognition. The graphical face used for the synthesis would be transmitted once only. The transmitter's speech would then be recognized, that is, mapped from a continuous time-varying signal into a sequence of discrete phonemes. This sequence would be used to drive the lips of the synthetic graphical head at the receiver. Thus to within the visual limitations of the system, apparent video communication would take place using only a voice channel. (Speech recognition by programs trained to recognize one particular speaker at a time is currently possible in a noise-free environment, at least for non-continuous speech or speech with gaps inserted between words.)

This approach has a number of potential applications and could function both as a communication system and as a 'human' GUI. It may be that this latter application will become the more important as the cost of bandwidth for communication drops significantly with the spread of fibre optics cables.

Speech synthesizers are now well developed and cheap. We could have such a device driving a graphical head. In this case the source data would be text with obvious uses in GUIs. A user can interact with what appears to be a real person rather than with graphical icons. The addition of a speech recognition facility would take us into a new era of interface modes and would perhaps alleviate the difficulties that non-expert computer users still have with interfacing. There is also a major application in implementing interfaces into databases or indeed as a front-end into any electronic service. An oft-suggested application is a synthetic head in a public telephone kiosk, where an enquirer of some service, such as a directory enquiry, would have the ability to hear the speech and see the lip movements which would enhance intelligibility in a noisy environment. Two possible scenarios are represented in Figure 19.2.

An intriguing application of such a facility would be dubbing in film productions. The current manual method – laborious, crude and visually defective – could be automated; the language into which the film is to be dubbed would drive a warping method which would accurately lip-sync deformations and speech. Deviations from the actual facial expressions that would be made by the actors if they were really speaking the foreign language would be preferable,

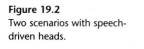

Figure 19.2

Two scenarios with speech-driven heads.

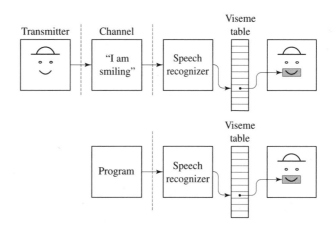

perhaps, to the current crude system which only achieves synchronization at the start and stop of a phrase; the visual expression changes between pauses are still synchronized with the original soundtrack.

As the previous paragraphs have implied, the method is locked into two space. Although we refer to a synthetic or graphical head the method for deforming the head is a warping technique and relies for its efficacy on the 'morphing illusion': that changes effected entirely in two space result in an image sequence that appears to be a projection of three space events. We are locked into a two-space method because we only have access at the transmitter to a two-dimensional image. We cannot easily obtain depth information at the source and this leads us naturally into considering a warping method at the receiver.

There are three problems to be overcome in this method. We need to be able to set up a convincing synthetic head and derive and represent a fixed set of lip shapes that correspond to phonemes. We need to be able to generate an animation from these patterns of pixels which are the shapes that the mouth takes between these patterns. In this respect, can we simply use standard in-betweening or do we need something more elaborate? Finally we need to be able to generate the appropriate shade or texture values in the in-between frames.

Let us deal with the simplest problem first – the texture map or synthetic head. The source image for the texture map is a silent or rest face. We overlay this with a two-dimensional polygon mesh with high polygonal resolution in the areas of interest – the lips and eyes (including eyebrows). The polygon mesh nodes can then be used to parametrize movement of the lips and eyes.

The polygons expand and dilate as the areas of interest move and the nodes cause texture pixels to migrate. Thus we can consider the technique as a warping method or just plain texture mapping that changes from frame to frame. Figure 19.3 shows an example of a single polygon from the face texture map. When this polygon changes shape to form part of a lip movement, we simply map the contents of the texture map enclosed by the 'rest' polygon into the new polygon. This is easily done using Gouraud interpolation and we do not

Figure 19.3
Warping or texture mapping polygons for lip movements.

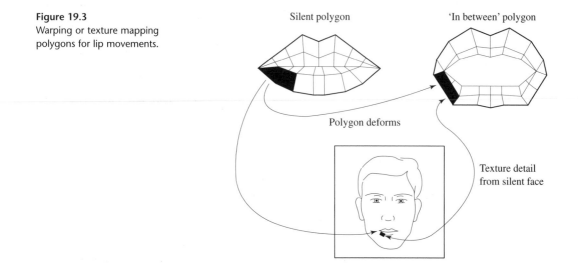

encounter any of the difficulties of texture mapping in three-dimensional computer graphics because it is a two space to two space mapping.

This is obviously not correct but it gives a good visual impression, given our constraint of two-dimensionality. It implies that as the face changes shape we can derive the new shade for a pixel for a polygon in the synthesized model by simply dilating or shrinking the shade values in the original model. But as we know, when a polygon mesh model changes shape in three space its new shade values come from the fact that the three-dimensional orientation of the polygon has changed with respect to the light source. However, this discrepancy does not seem to worry us and the warping illusion persists.

Lip shapes that correspond to phonemes are called visemes and an example is shown in Figure 19.4 which was derived from a real face. Armed with such a table, which can be derived for any face according to application, we need a method of generating in-between shapes and a method of synchronizing the synthetic speech to the resulting animation. The in-betweens together with the polygon-based warping method can then be applied to the head to animate it.

Waters and Levergood use a physically based empirical method to interpolate the in-between frames because, as they point out, the mouth shapes rarely converge to discrete viseme target shapes during continuous speech and the problem is to determine suitable in-between shapes by considering co-articulated

Figure 19.4
Four examples from a table of 55 mouth shapes based on an observation of real lips (after an illustration in Waters and Levergood, 1993).

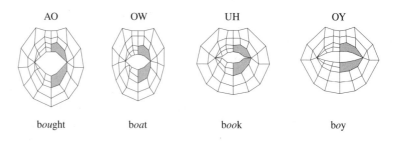

visemes rather than separate ones. In practice this means that the target nodes in the visemes, which function as key frames, are never reached. This is done by assigning a mass m_i to a polygon mesh node x_i. A force f_i is then associated with the node. f_i is made proportional to the vector formed from the current position of the node and its final position. The following equations of motion are then numerically integrated:

$$v_i = v_i' + (f_i/m_i)\,\Delta t$$

$$x_i = x_i' + v_i\,\Delta t$$

where v_i, x_i are the new velocity and position of the node along its trajectory

v_i', x_i' are the previous velocity and position

f_i is an elastic force that is made proportional to the vector joining the nodes

Waters states that this approach has the attribute that it does not peak at the discrete viseme mouth shapes and also that the system is able to adapt to different rates of speech.

19.4 Analysis–description–synthesis approaches

Finally we arrive at the most general of the methods which is to analyze the source image, extract a suitable animation script or description, transmit this over the channel and use it to synthesize an animation at the receiver. It differs from the previous methods in that we extract a moving description that is continually updated on a frame by frame basis. In the previous approach we only need prior knowledge of a two-dimensional silent face and a library of visemes. Figure 19.5 gives an overview of the approach. It shows that both the analyzer and the synthesizer have access to, or knowledge of, a common model which could be a polygon mesh model of the head. The other major difference is that we now consider a three-dimensional model to enable us to include small head movements. However, as we have already remarked, the analysis phase is always going to be locked into the source image plane and as we shall see, this results in somewhat unsatisfactory hybrid methods that use both two-dimensional and three-dimensional techniques.

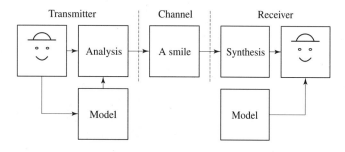

Figure 19.5
A schematic representation of an analysis–synthesis approach.

This kind of approach can also potentially cope with those subtle facial expressions, apart from lip movements, that must be included in any system that can claim to capture the 'essence' of facial movements important in the communication of emotions. Here we can make an analogy with loss-free compression in classic image compression techniques. A perfect analysis–synthesis scheme would be indistinguishable from a TV transmission. No information that is important to the communication of all the subtle clues that convince the receiver that the animation is as good as TV should be lost. Although we cannot reconstruct an image that is identical to the source image on a pixel by pixel basis – the case with loss-free classical image compression – we could say that we aim to reconstruct a received image that is 'emotionally identical' to the source image. (We discuss this aspect of facial expressions and the computer graphic approaches that attempt to simulate these as a separate issue in the next section.)

Despite years of research into this kind of approach, many problems are not resolved and relatively complex analysis–synthesis methods result in high overall processing requirements which have to be met in a frame interval. Usually as a description is made more and more succinct, the more 'artificial' the synthesized image becomes. (Of course this kind of analysis in image processing is not a well worked out problem; neither is shape animation in computer graphics.) Consider an obvious comparison. A high-level description of an expression might just be a symbol for 'a smile'. A less succinct description may be a list of key points representing the position of the lips that form into a smile. Clearly synthesizing an image from the latter will produce a visual effect closer to the original than could be achieved by using the former description. But do we measure quality in the synthesized image by whether the smile is convincing, in that the computer graphics head is actually smiling in a reasonably human-like manner, or do we take as our metric the nearness of the synthesized image to the source image? Surely we use the latter criterion. It would seem pointless to design a system in which the 'humanity' or individuality of the source's appearance and particular way of smiling had been replaced by an automaton that bore a resemblance to the source but which had its own computer expressions – in a way reducing the person to an animated caricature of himself. Thus there is a limit to how far we can 'reduce' the description and it is not clear from examining current research if this method is going to be in the end superior to conventional or classical compression approaches to videophony.

What follows is based on the work by Terzopoulos and Waters and Kaneko et al. These approaches exhibit similarities and are a good example of analysis–synthesis approaches. Kaneko et al. use a standard three-dimensional polygon mesh model that is the same model for all source heads. This has a polygonal resolution that increases in the critical areas such as the mouth and eyes. The standard model is fitted to a particular head. This can be done by setting, say interactively, a set of key points, such as the centre of the nose, in the source image. The standard model, with the same set of keys, is overlaid onto the source and 'pulled' or deformed until it fits the source image. (Eventually in a practical system this stage would be automated.) This is done with a frontal view and no depth information is used. (Here again is the two/three-dimensional hybridity that we described earlier.) Thus we get a polygon mesh that fits the source in the xy plane and it is assumed that the errors in the z coordinates of the polygon mesh (in general every z coordinate will be erroneous) will not be noticeable for small rotations of the head. (A similar modelling scheme was used in an intriguing animation application in 1985 by Bergeron (1986). This was a production called 'Tony de Peltrie' – a cartoon piano player character. Human expressions were taken photogrammetrically and mapped onto the polygon mesh model of the cartoon character.)

Terzopoulos and Waters report a more accurate approach in this phase where two maps, range and texture or colour, are obtained using a three-dimensional colour digitizer. Both the range and colour are mapped onto a three-dimensional polygon mesh which Waters calls the epidermal mesh. This process is carried out semi-interactively. Effectively the polygon mesh nodes sample the depth and colour. Terzopoulos and Waters claim that the head rendered from this model is comparable in visual quality to a display of the original three-dimensional data (the range and colour maps) that the mesh has sampled.

However the model is obtained it needs to be transmitted to the receiver and becomes the common knowledge used by both the transmitter and the receiver in the working or analysis–synthesis phase of the method. In the operating phase we need to extract a movement or animation script, based on the model, and transmit this to the receiver. The receiver gets this script and uses it on a frame by frame basis to make corresponding changes in the model which is then rendered to produce the final result. The rendering is straight forward and changing the texture map can be effected in the same way as we described in the previous section – we can use the x,y coordinates of the nodes in, say, a bi-linear (Gouraud) interpolation which warps the texture as the node positions move around.

A more difficult problem is how to extract the animation script from the frame sequence at the transmitter. Both authors come back to the expediency of selecting particular features to track using two-dimensional methods because, although in both approaches a three-dimensional model is set up, we only have access in the working phase to two-dimensional or image plane information. Herein lies the basic difficulty. Although we can set up a three-dimensional model, the script for this model has to be obtained from two-dimensional image plane information. Also, as we will see in the next section, with fairly elaborate face models, where hierarchical parametric control enables facial expressions to be produced (rather than local eye or lip movements), it is not clear how the information to control such models can be extracted from a two-dimensional sequence.

It is instructive to compare this approach with the previous method. In the previous method we obtained an animation script by in-betweening from a dictionary of predetermined facial expressions. This implies that we are always going to obtain exactly the same script for a given sentence or phrase – a situation that can hardly simulate a fairly common reality: a person might utter an identical sentence using a variety of vocal and facial expressions depending on the context. In the analysis–synthesis approach no such constraint is imposed and we attempt to continuously extract a script from the source images without recourse to a dictionary.

Kaneko et al. use a simple analysis or script extraction that concentrates on the eyes and mouth scheme. Consider the outline of the mouth. They process the image (by thresholding) so that they can track the movement of four key points; then these points are used to deform the polygon mesh of the common model. Essentially they are superimposing a very rudimentary 'sketch' or 'caricature' on the thresholded image and distorting the sketch to track the changes in the actual two-dimensional image.

They take the same approach for the eyes and then transmit only 12 coordinates (eight for the eyes plus four for the mouth) resulting in a channel requirement of

$$8 \text{ bits/coordinate} \times 2 \times 12 \text{ coordinates} \times 25 \text{ frames/second} = 4.8 \text{ kbits/sec}$$

Compared with the cut and paste (with dictionary) method we have increased the data rate by one order of magnitude and at the same time increased the processing requirements in the analysis and synthesis phases. So what have we gained with this more elaborate method? Possibly not much in the way of quality of expression, and the advantage at this stage of the research has to be the potential of the method to achieve something that can appear more realistic than that obtainable with crude cut and paste.

There are, however, a number of hidden problems that can only be dealt with in an ad hoc manner. The tracking can be misled by shadows. For example, the shadow cast by the lower lip may be interpreted as part of the lip itself. Another tricky problem is that it is not possible to use pixel values from just a single frame in the common model. To take an obvious example: if there are no teeth in the common model pixels then there is no way that they can be produced for an open mouth expression. Another example is the synthesis of a closed eye. If the common model contains pixels taken from an open eye only, the closed eye pixels will be taken from a dilation of the eyebrow shadow pixels, giving a dark appearance.

Terzopoulos and Waters tackle the analysis phase by using deformable contours, or snakes, to track the movement of facial features. These are contours which can be set up to lock on to moving image features. They are given certain pseudo-physical attributes that enable them to interact with images as if they were force fields (see Chapter 14 for a fuller description). Snakes are set up to track prominent facial features such as lip outlines and eyebrows and the method in effect reduces the face to a caricature and the snakes track the caricature movements. This process is represented in Figure 19.6. (Waters neatly side-steps some practical problems in the determination of the caricature he requires to set the snakes onto, by having his source head wear heavy make-up.)

The unique aspect of his approach is that he does not then use the 'snake script' in the synthesis phase as a reflection of the analysis phase. In other words,

Figure 19.6
A classic image from analysis/synthesis research in facial animation by Terzopoulos and Waters. The left column shows a face exhibiting different expressions, the middle column shows snakes tracking the features enhanced in the first column and the final column shows Waters's muscle model being controlled by the extracted information to synthesize the expressions shown in the first column. (Courtesy of Demetri Terzopoulos.)

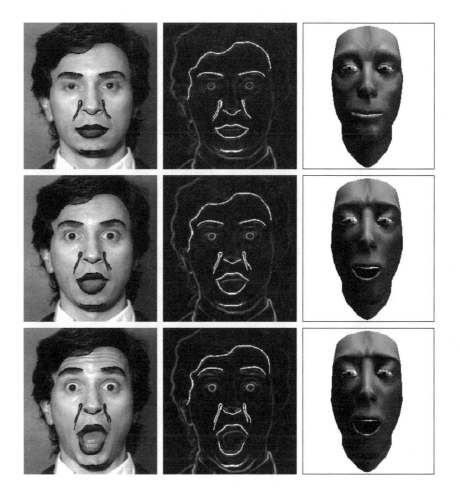

this is not a warp approach where the snake script is simply used to pull pixels around in the receiver image plane. The scripts are use to control parameters in a hierarchical model of the face. This is described in some more detail in the next section.

Finally, an important advantage of setting up a three-dimensional model is its potential ability to deal with global head movement such as some rotation. This eliminates the major defect of the cut and paste method – its machine-like rendition of a completely static head. Here we have exactly the same problem described in Chapter 18 which is estimation of the three-dimensional motion of an object from a set of two-dimensional projections. Kaneko et al. describe a specific technique that involves dividing the image into 13×13 blocks and using a gradient method to derive a motion vector for each block. Assuming that head movement between frames is small, these motion vectors can then be used to estimate translation and rotation. These values are then applied to the three-dimensional polygon mesh to synthesize global movement.

(19.5) Facial expressions in facial animation: modelling issues

As we have discussed, it is an open question at the moment if we can achieve a sufficiently high human-like quality at low bit rates or whether the distinctly dehumanizing effect of the techniques will obviate such methods so that we would rather pay the high rate penalty of conventional compression techniques.

How do we get away from this emphasis on certain features or local operations and consider the face as a whole model and try to emulate the totality of facial expressions? The few researchers that have dealt with this subject have from the outset emphasized model hierarchy with parametric control. Of course the geometric or low-level model (the model injected into the rendering pipeline) has to be highly detailed, but how do we set up the motion control for the deformation of such a model that is going to result in realistic-looking expressions?

Some early pioneering work (1987) by Waters using three-dimensional polygon mesh models addressed the problem of producing expressions and tackled the motion specification problem by introducing an underlying muscle model. The polygon mesh nodes were distorted to produce expressions using the muscle model which was itself parametrically controlled. The overall model then became hierarchical with a few parametric muscle models controlling many polygon mesh nodes in their zone of influence.

Waters produced recognizable expressions of happiness, fear, anger, disgust and surprise. But the video sequences that he produced had the appearance of animated caricatures. The source sequences that he used were of famous people (famous actors and so on) and the distinct visual signature of his method originates no doubt partly from the coarseness of the polygon mesh and partly from the fact that he presented us with known or familiar faces all animated by exactly the same model.

Pixar attempted to solve the problem with high model complexity, setting up a model of a baby's face using thousands of small parametric patches whose control points were scripted by a muscle model of 40 muscles. The animation, called 'Tin Toy', was released in 1989 and won an animation Oscar – the first computer graphics animation to do so. Despite the accolade, viewing the animation will confirm that this attempt was unsuccessful – the baby's expressions are somewhat bizarre and a little sinister. The animation is a good example of the failure of increased model complexity. Adding more and more detail, by increasing the element resolution of the three-dimensional geometry, fails to solve the problem in that, despite the extremely detailed structure, it could not be deformed or animated in a convincing manner.

The facial animation model of Waters consists of a parametric muscle model that controlled the deformation of a polygon mesh representation of a human face using 'muscle vectors'. The model is based on a notation system called FACS (Facial Action Coding System) and features muscle processes controllable by a limited number of parameters and is non-specific to a particular polygon mesh.

Thus his parametrization deals with the 'motivators of the facial action' and can be applied to a representation of any face.

The motivations for such an approach are twofold. It is a hierarchical model enabling a reduction in the complexity of a script required to control a geometrically complex model. The required expression maps into parameters which control the muscle model and not the polygon mesh. It is a physical or biomechanical model which itself controls the geometry of the polygon mesh. This must be the best interface for an expression script – providing that it a good model of the real process. Particular parameter values are assigned to muscle models which are consistent between faces. The parameters are abstractions and do not attempt to model underlying physical or neuro-physiological mechanisms. The polygon mesh vertices of different faces are controlled by the parametric muscle models attached to the vertices. Thus individual facial topology is maintained in the model of the object, while dynamic movement of the object to form different expressions is controlled by the muscle model.

Three types of muscles are active in controlling facial movements – linear, sphincter and sheet. Linear muscles are responsible for such movements as raising the corner of the mouth and are sets of muscle fibres that have a common emergence point in bone. Sheet muscles are flat sheets of fibres with no focus point and perform functions like raising the eyebrows. Sphincter muscles are loops around holes and control, for example, pouting expressions in the lips. There are around 200 facial muscles and they act by pulling facial tissue to which they are attached in a way that depends on the degree of motivation and their type.

Waters's muscles models are parametrized with vectors. They are embedded in the model as such from a point of attachment in the underlying bone with a direction that is towards their point of attachment in the skin. The muscle vector has a surrounding region or zone of influence defined so that skin in this region is subject to a displacement when the muscle operates. This is a function of the muscle type and the position of the skin point with respect to the muscle vector. Indeed this technique, when considered in two space, bears a similarity to feature-based morphing or warping (Chapter 17). So again we get back to the morphing or warping metaphor, this time somewhat indirectly. Figure 17.18 is an example of Waters's original parametrized muscle model controlling the mesh.

The synthesis from the snake analysis is facilitated by the vector parametrization. Node points on the snakes are tracked from frame to frame and the muscle contractions estimated from this operation. The snake reference points give us a motion field and this is mapped directly onto the muscle vectors. Although the muscle models are three-dimensional, this operation, like the analysis–synthesis of Kaneko et al., operates in two space.

Waters's original work (1987) consisted of a muscle model that directly controlled polygon mesh nodes. Recently he has added another biomechanical layer simulating the skin and works now with a muscle model – skin model – polygon mesh model hierarchy. It is not clear what visual advantages accrue from this increase in complexity.

19.6 Summary

A brief comparison of the above methods is now given. In each case we consider the information that is going to exist on the channel. A channel could be a normal communications channel or simply an interface to an applications program or a database.

Method	Information on channel	Other requirements
Cut and paste	Pixels – selected subsets of the image	
Cut and paste with predetermined dictionary	Dictionary codes	Offline construction of LUT representing lip and eye movements of a particular person.
Lip-synching with speech synthesizer	Text	Offline extraction of visemes of head to be used.
Lip-synching with transmitted speech	Speech	Offline extraction of visemes. For a particular speaker needs speech recognition.
Analysis–description–synthesis	Extracted description+speech	Offline determination of the common model. Tracking global movement.

Further reading

Model-based image coding is a relatively new idea and like any new field the approaches are diverse. We have chosen three methods that are representative of current research. The cut and paste method is fully described in the book by Pearson. This book also deals, in some detail, with real-time or communication technology aspects considering, for example, the use of a channel whose capacity varies in time (packet video).

The report by Waters et al. deals in detail with lip-synching synthetic speech to a synthetic head and also addresses the problem of how to interpolate between viseme shapes. The paper by Kaneko et al. contains many useful illustrations showing the strengths and weaknesses of their approach. Also, they implement a texture mapping method that is more elaborate than Gouraud interpolation. Waters's analysis–synthesis approach is described in some detail in Terzopoulos and Waters. The report gives an account of how all the elements in the muscle model–skin model–geometric model hierarchy relate together with details on the control of the snakes used in the analysis–synthesis.

Waters's original work on facial animation contains examples that show its 'caricature' aspect and the FACS system is described in the paper by Ekman and Friesman. This system is often used/referenced by researchers and is used in an approach described in the Pearson book.

Bergeron P. (1986). Techniques for animating characters. *SIGGRAPH Course Notes*, **22**, 240–65

Ekman P. and Friesman W. (1977). Manual for the Facial Action Coding System. *Consulting Psychologist*, Palo Alto, CA

Kaneko M., Koike A. and Hatori Y. (1991). Coding of facial image sequence based on a 3D model of the head and motion detection. *J. Visual Comm. and Image Repres.*, 2(1), 39–54

Pearson D., ed. (1991). *Image Processing*. London: McGraw-Hill

Terzopoulos D. and Waters K. (1993). Analysis and synthesis of facial image sequences using physical and anatomical models. *IEEE Trans. on Pattern Analysis and Machine Intelligence*, **15**, 569–79

Waters K. (1987). A muscle model for animating 3D facial expressions. *Computer Graphics*, **21**(4), 17–24 (Proc. SIGGRAPH '87)

Waters K. and Levergood T.M. (1993). DECface: An Automatic Lip-Synchronization Algorithm for Synthetic Faces. Digital Equipment Corporation Research Lab., CRL 93/4

The computer image and the third dimension

20.1 Introduction

20.2 The three-dimensional computer image

20.3 Interacting with two-dimensional projections of a three-dimensional scene – direct manipulation

20.4 The computer image and stereo

20.5 Virtual reality

20.6 Immersive virtual reality elements

20.1 Introduction

In this chapter we will look at how the computer image attempts to go beyond the normal display mode of projecting a three-dimensional scene onto a two-dimensional image plane. Now that we are leaving behind the yoke of tens of minutes of rendering time for a single frame, and are approaching being able to render scenes of some complexity at, say, 30 frames per second, the new ways that we can interact with three-dimensional information has provoked much interest and a new set of techniques and interface modalities have emerged – the most ambitious collection of techniques being called virtual reality. As well as looking at this important area (mostly the computer imagery aspects), we will examine some relevant aspects of human depth perception and look at how to inject more 'three-dimensionality' into two-dimensional imagery. Enhancing two-dimensional projections to improve their interpretation as representations of three-dimensionality and facilitate interaction is currently an under-explored area; this may be due to the assumption that three-dimensional display devices will eventually predominate.

As an antidote to the exaggerated claims that surround virtual reality we will, in the next chapter, look at how image synthesis and modelling techniques need to evolve to satisfy the short frame generation times and high scene complexity required by most applications. Currently this is a much under-studied aspect of virtual reality – the stock solution being that hardware advances will take care of such demands.

20.2 The three-dimensional computer image

Although by no means a new idea, it is only recently that enabling technology has made it possible to create three-dimensional images from stereo pairs displayed on small monitors inside a helmet in which the user sticks his head. The most talked about application of the three-dimensional computer image goes under the oxy moron of virtual reality. Like many innovations in computer technology, virtual reality was developed because it was possible – not out of a perceived need However, the concept of virtual environments has intrigued many and an industry has developed, virtually overnight, offering a plethora of low quality product Despite the exotic claims from the optimistic futurologists, we are a long way from reasonably priced high quality systems and the current technology is bedevilled with problems other than the high processing requirements – notably cumbersome viewing and interactive devices and low quality image synthesis. The limitations of the current technology leave us well short of the much-quoted goal of immersive virtual reality systems – that the user should be 'immersed' in a virtual environment that goes some way towards convincing him that he is actually in the virtual space.

In this chapter we will examine this technology and its possible applications. Before this we will look at the 'connections' between the computer image and human depth perception – in particular, the important issue of aiding depth perception in a two-dimensional image – since it is likely that two-dimensional display devices are going to be with us for the foreseeable future.

Of course the efficacy of a virtual environment also depends on other forms of feedback such as directional sound, tactile and kinaesethic feedback, but the imagery, rightly or wrongly, has been considered the most important, and most virtual reality systems concentrate, at the moment, on this aspect.

Although the specific requirements of a virtual reality system are, to some extent, application dependent, we can state that most will require:

- High quality imagery generated in real time; high quality in this context means being able to render a scene of a sufficiently high complexity appropriate to the application.

- High resolution display devices that facilitate a reasonably convincing immersion experience by presenting the immersee with a wide angle stereo display (the most common manifestation being the stereo head-mounted display or HMD).

- 'Natural' interface devices that enable a user to move through a virtual environment and interact with it. The basic requirement for an HMD system is a head tracking device that enables the system to track the viewer's (virtual) position and viewing direction coupling the image generator to the user.

The apparent feasibility of these requirements – all are currently available to a greater or lesser extent – and the promise of quick improvements in their quality has led to an avalanche of proposed uses.

Much of the current work in virtual reality is applications oriented and the particular facilities that are employed are highly application dependent. For example, in the now well-established area of flight simulation, there is no head tracking or stereo display. The virtual exterior is presented to the pilot via monitors, which replace the aircraft's windows, and the display responds to the pilot's use of the controls. Despite this, there is emerging the concept of a general purpose virtual reality platform that will run any application, in the same sense that modern workstations are general purpose running a wide variety of applications programs all with their own unique GUI.

As well as looking at the software and hardware techniques used, we will devote some effort to examining intriguing psychophysical demonstrations that tell us something about the fallibility of human depth interpretation of pictures and three-dimensional reality. In most virtual reality applications there is little in the way of novel computer image techniques – they simply have to work in real time. The major research in virtual reality is directed towards developing the above requirements and inventing new uses for this intriguing new manifestation of the computer image. We will look at the special demands that virtual reality makes on computer imagery, and try to examine the possible and probable uses of this much-vaunted topic and the sci-fi atmosphere that it has cloaked itself in.

20.2.1 Human beings and pictures

While it seems not a little pompous to discuss the relevance of computer imagery in contemporary culture, in some ways we are entering into a new era of imagery. Man-made images have gone through a number of significant evolutions. The most important early innovation for our purposes was the discovery (or rediscovery) of perspective by Italian artists in the fifteenth century, enabling viewers to perceive, for the first time, representations of reality that looked three-dimensional. In the nineteenth century the invention of photography made it possible, for the first time, to record and reproduce recorded images of reality. The twentieth century saw the development of the moving picture first with film and then with TV imagery. With these latter inventions man-made imagery left the isolated and rarefied world of art and became part of the everyday life of the common man. Our remarkable skill at the interpretation of depth in complex two-dimensional images is an extremely recent facility. For photographic images it is not much more than 100 years. It cannot be that we have structures in our brain that are specialized for this task; certainly we do not need such a facility to survive or even to build complex civilizations.

With the advent of computer imagery at the end of this century we are entering a further evolutionary stage of imagery. Currently we need to accurately perceive depth relationships in a projection so that we can interact with two-dimensional images that represent a three-dimensional domain of interest. Images now become something that we actively participate with rather than passive entities to be interpreted. Virtual reality takes this one step further. We now want to 'go inside' the image – interacting with three-dimensional scenes or immersing ourselves in a virtual environment. It could be argued that the problem is solved by immersion in a virtual environment. Here stereo images mounted in a helmet that isolates the user from the real environment give the impression that the user is actually part of the artificial environment. However, virtual reality is still at an early stage of development and is expensive. Certainly in the immediate future, most computer graphics imagery is going to be produced on mono-displays. Other than the use of perspective projections, the work that has been carried out in computer graphics concerning enhancing their interpretation is somewhat fragmented.

The design of interactive devices, both hardware devices and interpretative aids that are added to the two-dimensional image to enhance its interpretation as three-dimensional reality, is a very recent development. It seems a good idea, before we examine the design of such elements, to look at some existing knowledge on how we as human beings perceive depth in pictures. Such is our familiarity with the interpretation of photographs and suchlike that we hardly give it a second thought. And yet it is remarkably fragile in the sense that it is very easily tricked or confused.

Also, our ability to interpret depth in two-dimensional images is often dependent on the nature of the image. The famous Necker cube illusion is well known and is shown in Figure 20.1(a). A wireframe cube without perspective, the figure persistently offers two interpretations, our brain switching from one to the other. Even adding perspective often does not help as Figure 20.1(b) shows – the illusion persists with two cubic interpretations. Also, we may convince ourselves that the object in Figure 20.1(b) is a truncated pyramid; but we prefer the more familiar interpretation. In the third example we have a very familiar object – the branch of a tree – in which depth perception is totally impossible. This is because such objects exist in reality in an infinite number of shape guises and we cannot have any stored knowledge concerning them to aid our perception.

Although wireframe objects are not encountered very much in reality we use them in computer graphics, and in particular they are used as 'containers'

Figure 20.1
Some problems of depth perception in pictures. (a) Ambiguous depth perception – the Necker cube. (b) Adding perspective – the illusion persists. (c) A familiar but 'structureless' object in which depth perception is impossible. We cannot even tell which branch is in front of the others. (After an illustration by R. L. Gregory.)

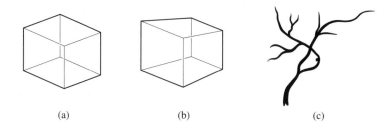

(a)   (b)   (c)

to enhance three-dimensional interpretation, as we discuss below. It may be thought that the problem stems solely from the fact that we are viewing two-dimensional projections but it seems that this is not the whole story. A surprising demonstration of the persistence of the Necker cube is due to R.L. Gregory and is described in his classic text *The Intelligent Eye* in which he studies the problem of perception of pictures compared with the perception of reality. He showed that even touch information cannot dispel the ambiguity. Figure 20.2 shows a hand-held skeleton cube. When this is coated with luminous paint and held in the dark, even the holding of the object cannot prevent the illusion. This demonstration may have implications in modelling and display for virtual environments.

These examples demonstrate simply ambiguity. There exist startling examples where our perception of reality is completely fooled or breaks down. The examples are important, not because of their surprise and novelty, but because they contain clues concerning the way in which we interpret depth. Figure 20.3 shows a classic example known as the Ames room. In this bizarre and unforgettable illusion we assume (wrongly) that the room has a normal rectangular shape. In fact, the far wall recedes more to one side and at the same time the height of the room increases. The projection of the structure of the room is the same as it would be if the room was actually rectangular. Because of our perceptual misassumption we see the women as being of somewhat different size, although they are both the same size. Despite the existence of other clues – such as the fact that the women look the same age and we 'know' that they are probably the same size – the illusion cannot be expelled. This illusion is perceived in reality, not just as a photograph. It is reported that the illusion can only be dispelled by letting the observer explore the real dimensions of the room with a long stick. Perhaps this is one of the best demonstrations of our reliance on pre-knowledge in interpreting a scene; albeit in this case wrongly. It also demonstrates our heavy reliance on supporting clues to enable us to correctly perceive depth – in this case the straight lines from the room structure.

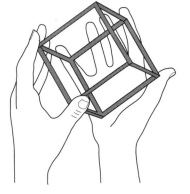

Figure 20.2
The Necker cube illusion persists even with touch information. A luminous wireframe cube is held in the dark. Does this raise problems for VR? (R. L. Gregory)

Figure 20.3
The Ames distorting room.

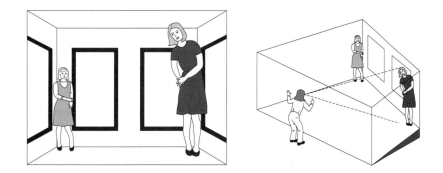

An equally remarkable illusion was discovered by Gregory (Figure 20.4). This concerns a real object – an image which is a photograph of the **inside** of the mould that made the statue. It is impossible to see, in the photograph, that it is a concave image of a face. Gregory postulates that this is due to high-level perceptual processes and is simply explained by the sheer improbability of a 'negative' face. Such objects rarely occur in reality and so we do not correctly interpret the photograph. Even when the concave face is viewed in stereo the illusion stubbornly persists.

Gregory comments on our interpretation of two-dimensional images as follows:

Pictures are unique among objects; for they are seen both as themselves and as some other thing, entirely different from the paper or canvas of the picture. Pictures are paradoxes .... Pictures are flat projections of three-dimensional objects. But it is strictly impossible to compress into two dimensions without loss of information. So pictures are always ambiguous in depth. The remarkable thing is that we are able to make sense of them, for any projection is infinitely ambiguous: it could represent an infinity of different objects, but generally we see but one.

Figure 20.4
The mask illusion of preconceived notions. The image is the familiar visage of Vladimir Ilyich Lenin and is a photograph of the inside of a mask made by taking a mould of a bust. It is impossible to perceive the mask, we can only see a 'convex' face. The illusion appears to have been discovered by R.L. Gregory and it persists even when the mould is viewed. The effect is quite startling – the face appearing to jump out of the mould.

So of what relevance is this to computer imagery? Just this. It seems that if we are going to persist with interaction with a two-dimensional projection we need to know much more about how human beings interpret depth in two-dimensional images. The three-dimensional Necker cube illusion (Figure 20.1) raises possible problems in virtual reality where interaction with three-dimensional virtual objects is a feature of many proposed and existing systems.

Before the era of rendering, wireframe displays were the norm in three-dimensional computer graphics. These were generally presented without depth cues (such as depth fading) and anyone who has used such systems for any length of time will have experienced variations of the above illusions. Shaded images (of single objects) have certainly removed much of the perceptual uncertainties; but there is now a need for direct manipulation of three-dimensional objects and as we shall see in Section 20.3 one approach to this is to use subsidiary objects as guides or 'widgets'.

It seems that our perception is only reliable with images of familiar scenes. This is indeed a problem in many computer graphics applications where we may be viewing and trying to interact with an object that we have never seen before – a possible scenario in many visualization applications.

With virtual reality we try to immerse a person in a virtual environment by relying on presenting an immersee with a pair of stereo images. The major efforts in the development of this field are all directed towards the improvement of quality of these images in terms of spatial resolution, field of view and so on. This philosophy embraces the popular view of human visual perception that it is a low-level information processing activity that can operate in isolation and takes low-level information through a succession of stages that enable us to extract the scene knowledge that we require. Virtual reality assumes that we can trick this visual perception by using stereo images whose generation is coupled to head movement. However, the three-dimensional illusions tend to demonstrate that high-level processing may be significant. Prior knowledge or experience of our environment may be very significant. It would seem that it is not just hardware limitations that are going to bedevil our attempts to create high quality virtual environments, particularly if we are going to create environments that are completely unfamiliar to the immersee. Perhaps the development of computer imagery for virtual reality can only proceed as our knowledge of human depth perception advances and currently this is not particularly advanced.

Further reading – human beings, pictures and depth

There is no better introduction to this fascinating topic than Gregory's book. It contains a wealth of information of interest to computer graphicists.

Gregory R.L. (1970). *The Intelligent Eye*, London: Weidenfeld and Nicolson

⟨20.3⟩ Interacting with two-dimensional projections of a three-dimensional scene – direct manipulation

Most applications of three-dimensional computer graphics involve a user interacting in some way with a two-dimensional representation of three-dimensional object space. Yet attention to this important aspect of computer graphics has been low. Direct manipulation of the object from an interactive device has generally been ignored and indirect manipulation, using interaction techniques originally developed for two-dimensional graphic applications, have instead been employed. Control panels, using say, sliders, are what the user interacts with directly. For example, three sliders representing the three components of a vector may be manipulated by a user to effect, say, some three-dimensional transformation of an object on the screen. The disadvantage of this kind of interactive mode is obvious – it is difficult for the user to relate the control of the sliders to the consequent movement of the projection of the object on the screen. What is required is direct manipulation of the object, retaining the user's perception of the object as a particular three-dimensional entity, and trying, at the same time, to assist the user's extraction of a three-dimensional perception from a two-dimensional projection.

A number of ad hoc solutions have emerged. The traditional way to do this, and a method adopted by many CAD programs, is to have alternative projections simultaneously displayed on the screen: say, for example, orthographic projections onto the three coordinate planes. However, moving points around in the space using a two-dimensional locator device is not easy and the relationship between movements in the standard projections, movement of the mouse and movement of the point in three-dimensional space is torturous to say the least. Also, the relationship between the projections and the three-dimensional shape is not always easy to interpret and depends strongly on object familiarity. With the possible exception of engineering draughtsmen, we are unskilled at the interpretation of multiple projections. Figure 20.5 demonstrates this point.

We can enhance the ease of interaction with a two-dimensional projection of an object in a number of ways. For example:

● Movement – the structure of an object can be enhanced by, for example, simple rotation about a vertical axis. An attempt to demonstrate this 'statically' is given in Figure 20.6. Here two space curves are drawn with dots. The curves are embedded in vertical planes at different orientations and any

Figure 20.5
Our ability to interpret and thus interact with orthographic projections depends on our familiarity or a priori knowledge of the object. (a) One view of a complex but familiar object. (b) Three orthographic projections of a simple but unfamiliar object.

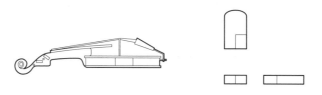

(a)   (b)

Figure 20.6
A demonstration of how structure and depth are revealed by rotation.

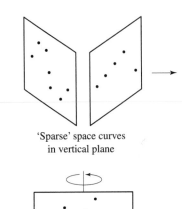
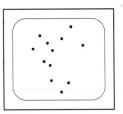

'Sparse' space curves in vertical plane

When projected into 2D screen space no structure or depth is perceived

Rotating about y axis ...

... enables the viewer to perceive the structure of the curves and their depth relationship

static screen space projection is difficult if not impossible to interpret. As the implementation of this demonstration will confirm, rotating the screen plane about the vertical axis reveals the structure of the separate curves and their depth relationship.

Movement can occur in three-dimensional interaction 'incidentally' as a consequence of user interaction. In other words, the fact that a desired rotation or scale change produces movement in the projection enhances the overall interpretation of the object or scene. Also it can be made to occur as a deliberate action, when the user simply moves the viewpoint of the object to aid interpretation, and no alteration is made to the geometry or position of the object.

These somewhat simplistic mechanisms involve changing the nature of a two-dimensional projection in the image plane by changing, in some way, the position of the viewpoint. They are imitative of the process in human visual perception known as motion parallax where an observer moves his head around – changing his viewpoint – so as to enhance depth perception.

● Enclosing an object in a stylized or 'surrogate' container such as a cube or sphere. The interface facilities then operate on the container and the object that is contained is subject to the identical space transformations that the interface subjects the container to.

● Additional stylized objects or handles can be added to the object to be manipulated. The user interacts directly with these objects – curiously known as three-dimensional widgets – to facilitate manipulation of the object itself. This device enables shape changing operations to be specified.

The first of these aids simply enables a better perception of depth but the second and third enable us to operate on and manipulate objects in the two-dimensional screen space. (Implementations of the container technique on a workstation, powerful enough to facilitate real-time interaction, include the first. As the container is manipulated the movement occurs.) The need for such devices depends on how secure our prior knowledge or internal concept is of the object or scene that is being manipulated. This may be very strong as in the case of CAD in industrial design, where we may be making variations on the shape of a familiar object. It may be much less secure in the case of an unfamiliar object – say, for example, a complicated surface that has emerged from a mathematical simulation of some physical behaviour.

The use of a container is an obvious extension or exploitation of our apparent use, as human beings, of structural information to perceive depth in pictures. We seem to rely on recognizing structural clues as well as using our a priori knowledge that we are viewing a perspective projection. Say that, for example, we are looking at a scene in a room. We sense depth because of the receding lines of the room structure.

We can compare the three-dimensional interaction problem with the equivalent and familiar two-dimensional interactive method. In two-dimensional graphics the operation of selecting an object with a mouse, and moving or altering it in some way, is well established and forms the basis of two-dimensional CAD and graphic design software. In three-dimensional interaction we have the equivalent operations of selecting an object or object part and dragging it. Consider selecting an object. This can be done either as a pure software operation or with hardware assistance. Given the coordinates of the pixel currently being pointed to, we can generate an object hit by ray tracing in world space. An initial ray is generated from the pixel into the scene, an intersection test is invoked, and the nearest object found. Clearly this has all the speed problems of ray tracing, where as you may recall, most of the cost is in intersection testing. Alternatively, if available, an item buffer can be used. This is an auxiliary frame buffer. Accessing this buffer with the coordinates of the pixel being pointed to by the interactive device gives a pointer to the object that is currently covering that pixel.

(20.3.1)

Direct manipulation of objects – linear transformations

Having selected an object we can enclose it in a wireframe container – the object whose familiarity is so strong that we can interpret its depth relationships from a two-dimensional projection. Two commonly used containers are the wireframe bounding box and the wireframe sphere. The wireframe bounding box can be used to perform translation, rotation and scaling. In this way the difficult visual feedback link that must somehow indicate movement in three-dimensional space is made easier. Two-dimensional mouse movement can be made to produce understood, but constrained, movement in three-dimensional space using the perceptual understanding emerging from our a priori familiarity with the wireframe container. Click–drag–release mouse events are applied to the container through the interface and, of course, movements and alterations applied to the container affect the contained object. We will now look at some specific examples.

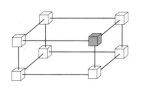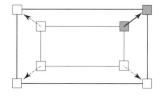

(a)

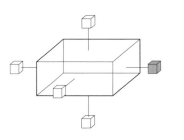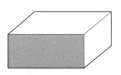

(b)

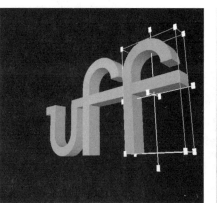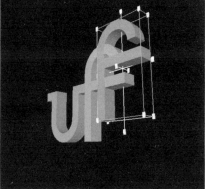

Figure 20.7
The Open Inventor manipulator 'Handle box'. (a) Eight vertex draggers implement uniform scaling. (b) Three axis draggers implement scaling in *x*, *y* or *z*. (c) Selecting a visible plane effects translation of the whole manipulator in that plane.

(c)

It appears that the first company to use such devices was Silicon Graphics and we will use simple examples based on the containers that they have developed. These devices, which they term 'interactive manipulators', are available to C and C++ programs through a toolkit called Open Inventor. The name manipulator is given to the geometry of the container which is further embellished with 'draggers' which are small rendered boxes (or other shapes) attached to the vertices and axes of the manipulator. The edges of the manipulator provide visual geometric feedback and the draggers react to click–drag–release mouse events. (The Silicon Graphics distinction between manipulators and draggers is somewhat confusing as it seems possible to interact with parts of the manipulator that are not draggers.) Enclosure of the object in the bounding box also defines an origin – the centre of the manipulator.

An example of a manipulator based on a bounding box is called 'Handle box'. This is a wireframe box which enables uniform and non-uniform scaling and translation. Figure (20.7) shows uniform scaling effected by a click–drag–release using any of the eight vertex draggers. Three-dimensional movement of the draggers is along a line from the dragger to the manipulator centre. To effect scaling in the direction of one of the manipulator axes, one of the three axis draggers is selected. Translation is achieved by moving parallel to one of the

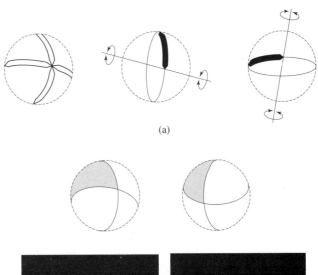

(a)

(b)

Figure 20.8
The Open Inventor manipulator 'Trackball'. (a) Selecting a strip facilitates rotation about the perpendicular axis. (b) Selecting an octant enables 'trackball' rotation.

manipulator faces. A visible face is selected and the complete manipulator is dragged in a movement that is locked into the selected plane.

The 'Trackball' manipulator enables two modes of rotation. First, rotation constrained about one of the three mutually perpendicular axes. The manipulator appears as a wireframe sphere represented by the three grand circles that divide the sphere into octants. Each circle is drawn as strips or ribbons and selection of a strip facilitates rotation about an axis perpendicular to the plane of the circle (strip) selected (Figure 20.8). Selecting any point on the (virtual) surface of the sphere that is outside a strip facilitates 'trackball' movement. Here mouse movement is like placing a finger on a trackball device (a sphere placed in a hemispherical cradle which can move in any direction within the cradle). Rotation now occurs about any axis through the centre of the manipulator.

20.3.2 Direct manipulation of objects – non-linear transformations

The manipulators of the previous section exploit our familiarity with the stylized containers in which the object is placed. Another idea, which was suggested initially by Snibbe et al. in 1992, is to attach handles, or 'racks', to objects that have some associated function with respect to the object in which they are embedded. These handles, equipped with limited degrees of freedom, can be used to facilitate shape changing operations such as twisting, tapering and bending. Figure 20.9 shows the idea. A twist handle is rotated in an indicated plane, producing a twist in the object normal to that plane. A taper handle is shortened to taper the object and a bend handle bends the object. The metaphor is that of real tools which are in some way stuck into the real object and levered or pushed or what-

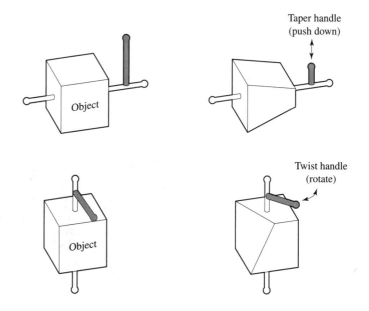

Figure 20.9
Using handles, or racks, to effect shape changing transformations (after Snibbe et al. (1992)).

ever to produce the desired effect. The user can select tools with different functions and place them on different parts of the object to be manipulated. The handles themselves are rendered (stylized) objects and can be designed to reflect their function, by using either different colours or different shapes. These example shape changing operations are more complicated than the linear transformations of the previous section and it is apparent that effecting such operations through a two-dimensional interface would be difficult.

These are early suggestions in an area which is largely unexplored. What we can say for certain is that they enable us to effect direct manipulation of the object rather than through the indirect medium of a two-dimensional interface.

20.3.3 Direct manipulation of objects – high-level shape manipulation

Recent work at Brown University concentrates on direct manipulation interfaces for the control of parametric surfaces. One of the motivations of the work is to enable the union of engineering constraints with aesthetic considerations. That is, to make it possible for an industrial designer to operate directly on objects and have the system take care of the engineering constraints. Although surface blending has long been incorporated into CAD packages, the researchers at Brown point out that little effort has been expended on helping the designer figure out exactly how to specify blending operations.

Figure 20.10 is an example showing two tubes to be joined. The second illustration (Figure 20.10(b)) shows the control points of the horizontal tube being moved

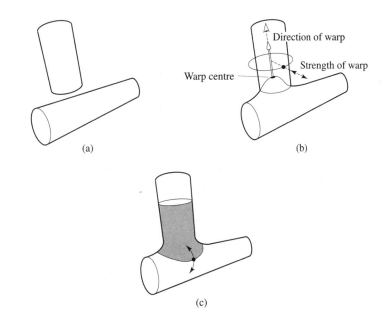

Figure 20.10
Direct manipulation in surface blending (based on illustrations at www.cs.brown.edu).
(a) Tubes to be joined;
(b) warping the horizontal tube into the vertical;
(c) editing a blend surface.

to effect a 'warp' operation that pulls the surface of the horizontal tube up into the vertical tube. The warp is directly manipulated using the arrow that specifies the direction of the warp and whose tail is embedded in its centre. The 'strength' of the warp is controlled by directly manipulating the sphere, or handle, on the circle enclosing the vertical tube to increase or reduce the radius of the circle.

Figure 20.10(c) shows a scheme for the direct manipulation of a blend surface. The curves are the boundaries of the blend surface and are embedded in the respective surfaces of each tube. Direct manipulation of the blend surface is effected by operating on the two spheres that lie in each boundary curve. A sphere can be moved along the curve and then pushed or pulled to move the curve around according to the wishes of the designer.

(20.3.4) ## Direct manipulation of objects – free-form sculpting

Free-form sculpting, or the unconstrained manipulation of parametrically defined surfaces, has long been a suggested application in computer graphics (see Chapter 7). However, because of the difficulties involved, this idea has not been realized to any great extent. The problems are well known and are tied up in controlling the movement of control points in three-dimensional space in order to effect a desired deformation or shape change.

There are two problems to be addressed. The first emerges from the control point representation. The simplest surface element – a Bézier patch – possesses 16 control points. Complex objects may possess hundreds or even thousands of control points. Allowing a user to move individual control points around is hopeless. Free-form sculpting implies that the sculptor can make shape changes just as if the object was a piece of modelling clay – the metaphor most often employed. The nature of the shape changes will depend on a multiplicity of factors concerning control point movement: which control points are moved, how are they moved and how many of them are moved. And in the end the exact nature of the movement depends on the mathematics of the representation. A depression, say, of a large extent of an area of a surface will require simultaneous movement of many points. A protrusion of small extent may require only a few or even just one point to be moved.

The second problem is that effective and creative free-form sculpting implies that the user can experience a strong perceptual connection between the tool used to effect the deformation and the resulting shape change. This is a more challenging problem than constrained industrial design where the designer has some familiarity with the three-dimensional nature of the object being created. Virtual reality can address this problem by giving a sculptor a three-dimensional visualization of the object that he is shaping, and virtual reality platforms or possibly augmented reality techniques will surely fuel further interest in the free-form sculpting metaphor.

So to return to the first problem, what interactive devices can we employ that will enable us to directly manipulate a three-dimensional object as if it was a piece of soft clay? This aspect is considered independent of whether we implement such a tool as part of a virtual reality system or as part of a conventional computer graphics set-up.

An obvious idea for sculpting is to have metaphors of real sculpting tools. Alternatively, for simple clay-like deformations we could have a 'repelling' tool to produce depressions in the object and an 'attracting' tool for protrusions. Such an approach was suggested by Hsu et al. who used a tricubic hyperpatch representation – known in the computer graphics community as an FFD representation – in which to implement this metaphor. Here the object is embedded in the space of a tricubic B-spline hyperpatch and deformation of the control points of the patch – a three-dimensional lattice – causes a shape change in the object.

The FFD representation has the singular advantage that the representation of the space – the tricubic patch – and the representation of the object are separate entities. The object could, for example, be a polygon mesh representation. The best metaphor of an FFD space is an extremely viscous fluid initially in the form of a rectangular or cubic solid. The vertices of the object representation are immersed with their initial configuration into this fluid. The FFD representation – the fluid – is then formed into the desired shape by, say, bending, causing the embedded object to deform in a similar manner because it is dragged along in the fluid. Control points will generally be far fewer in number than the vertices of the object.

In Hsu's algorithm the direct manipulation tools operate on the object itself rather than the control points of the FFD lattice. Consider just a single point on the surface. The user specifies the new position of the point. Transparent to the user, the algorithm works out the new position of control points that accommodate this change. That is, the program finds the movement necessary in the FFD lattice to fit the movement in the change of the surface point. This new lattice then deforms the complete object and the user sees a smooth deformation resulting from changing a single surface point. Note that this is the reverse of normal FFD deformation operations. Normally the FFD lattice is deformed by the user who drags the object into its new shape. Here we deform the object directly to facilitate a 'graceful' deformation. The algorithm finds the FFD defor-

Figure 20.11
Free-form sculpting and direct manipulation with tool metaphors. *Source*: Hse, Hughes and Kaufman (1992) 'Direct Manipulation of Free-Form Deformations' in Siggraph Proceedings *Computer Graphics* **26** (2), July.

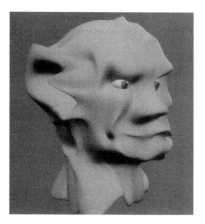

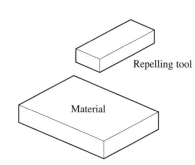

Material

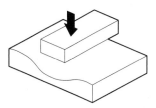

Repelling tool

mation that fits the new object position. Thus the user directly manipulates the object but sees a nice deformation resulting from the interaction. Figure 20.11 shows the idea working with a repelling tool.

In all of these systems, however, the use of the term 'direct manipulation' is somewhat oxymoronic. The interaction is indirect in the sense that we have to operate the handles or whatever through a conventional interface. An object may possess a handle that enables it to be tapered, but the handle needs to be pushed down using a mouse. For 'true' direct manipulation of a virtual object we would have to use a virtual reality system of some kind and in this respect Hsu et al. comment:

We envision an environment where users will be able to sculpt objects using a DataGlove-like input device, The finger tips, digits and palm of the hand will be tracked to offset selected points in a malleable object, with smooth valleys and hills attained by the FFD operation. Different elasticities can be assigned to the object by varying the resolution of the control point lattice. Perhaps a metaphor of molten metal or glass may be appropriate, where a blow torch and cold air are used to heat and cool the object to give it different moulding properties. By making modelling as natural as possible, or by imitating the ways in which it is done in the real world, a greater number of users can be reached and an increase in expressiveness in modelling attained.

Halfway between an immersive virtual reality system and direct manipulation through a two-dimensional interface is the work of Galyean and Hughes. They use conventional image synthesis techniques in conjunction with a three-dimensional input device. The input device is a hybrid of a three-dimensional pen pointer (which returns a stream of x,y,z samples of the pen position) embedded in a force feedback device. They describe their manipulation tools as follows:

Routing or Subtractive Tool: The tool acts like a milling head or router.

Additive Tool or Toothpaste Tube. This tool leaves a trail of material wherever it moves, much like a tube of toothpaste that is squeezed as it is moved.

Heat Gun. This tool 'melts away' material much as a heat gun melts Styrofoam. If held in one place for a while, it removes all the material, like the routing tool; if moved quickly past a region, it melts the material there slightly.

Sandpaper. This 'smoothing' tool alters the object by wearing away the ridges and filling the valleys.

Unlike the other systems where the object representation was a bicubic or tricubic parametric patch, Galyean and Hughes use a voxel representation for the object. The tools then add or subtract voxels from the current structure which is then rendered using a contextually optimized version of the marching cubes algorithm.

Let us now summarize from these efforts. There are many issues involved in the ways in which we interact with three-dimensional virtual objects. The major ones are:

- The choice of an appropriate three-dimensional metaphor for a tool – the handle or widget. How this is to be connected or associated with the object. How the spatial relationship between the tool and the object is best visualized – subsidiary graphical devices, such as axes, for example, may be employed.

- How are the degrees of freedom of the tool to be constrained to the tool to assist in its 'indirect' manipulation? How is the potential movement of the tool to be signalled to the user? Here the most common device is an arrow. But there are many more possibilities.

- How the functionality of the tool is to be reflected in its appearance. It must be identifiably a tool that is distinct from the object. Shape and colour are the candidates here. A twisting tool, for example, could itself be in the form of a twisted object.

- How is the tool to be moved? 'Directly' using a three-dimensional interface device or a virtual reality system, or 'indirectly' using a mouse and a conventional interface?

Further reading – direct manipulation of objects

This is an emerging area which should develop rapidly. The published work is currently somewhat sparse. The container philosophy is to be found in the paper by Strauss and Carey. The paper by Snibbe et al. is extremely short and does not contain much more information than that given in this text.

Hsu W.H. (1992). Direct manipulation of free-form deformations. *Computer Graphics*, **26**(2), 177–84 (Proc. SIGGRAPH '92)

Snibbe S.S., Herndon K.P., Robbins, D.C., Conner D.B., and v. Dam, A. (1992). Using deformations to explore three-dimensional widget design. *Computer Graphics*, **26**(2), 351–2 (Proc. SIGGRAPH '92)

Strauss P.S. and Carey R. (1992). An object-oriented three-dimensional graphics toolkit. *Computer Graphics*, **26**(2), 341–9 (Proc. SIGGRAPH '92)

20.4 The computer image and stereo

The generation of stereo pairs to drive an HMD is currently the most popular virtual reality display mode. In this section we will look at the history of stereo in computer imagery and how it relates to current developments.

Since the discovery in the nineteenth century that human beings could merge stereoscopic images into a single image in which depth is apparently perceived, stereoscopic entertainment devices have appeared and become popular many times. Its fascination is bound up in stereo pairs enhanced by interaction and immersion. There have been many 'stereo cycles'. Each time it seems that the lifetime of the craze has got shorter and shorter. Recently computer imagery has entered into the arena with virtual reality. Here an animated stereo pair is presented to a viewer through a pair of small monitors contained in a helmet, which also serves to isolate the user from the real environment. In this way, so we are assured, he experiences 'immersion' in a virtual three-dimensional reality – that presented by the monitors. It remains to be seen if virtual reality will develop for public use and last longer than, say, three-dimensional cinema did in the 1950s, or whether it will become locked into specialized areas like training and scientific visualization.

Computers have come lately into stereo originally with the fascinating discovery of Bela Julesz in the 1960s (see next section) and the advent of virtual reality in the 1990s, but the field of stereoscopy has a long and fascinating history. Shortly after the invention of photography, photographers turned to stereoscopy, producing millions of stereo pairs, mounted on card, which were viewed using a simple stereoscope. Figure 20.12(a) shows a wooden Victorian stereoscope designed to view snapshots taken by a stereo camera.

Stereography spawned a vast industry and by the end of the nineteenth century, such viewers could be found in most middle class homes in Europe and

(a)

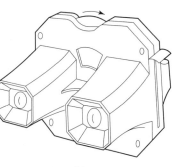

(b)

(c)

Figure 20.12
The persistence of the stereoscope.
(a) 1890
(b) 1950
(c) 1990

America. Stereoscopic photography was the progenitor of the newsreel. Natural disasters and wars (in particular the American Civil War and the First World War) were photographed in stereo. Even hard-core pornography was produced in stereo. However, the interest of the public in this form of photography disappeared very quickly with the rise of cinema in the 1920s. Although there have been many attempts in the twentieth century to revive the public's interest in stereo photography – principally the mass production of stereo cameras – these have generally failed. The wooden stereo viewer of the nineteenth century survives today in the form of a long-running toy – the ViewMaster (Figure 20.12(b)). In this device stereo pairs are mounted in a card disk (at opposite ends of a diameter). A child can view a sequence of images by rotating the disk in the viewer. A stereo fad, notable for its short life, occurred between 1950 and 1953. This was stereo cinema which used the anaglyph method. (Hitchcock's *Dial M for Murder* was made on stereo, although it was never released in that format.) Here one image of a stereo pair was superimposed on the other, with each component image coded respectively in red and green. Each image was 'steered' into the appropriate eye by special spectacles which contained for one eye a red filter and for the other a green one. The anaglyph technique was also used in comic books at about the same time.

20.4.1   The stereograms of Bela Julesz

All the devices discussed in the previous section rely on our ability to perceive depth from stereo pairs, but it is not clear how much of our depth perception depends on 'pure' geometric disparity and how much is due to our familiarity with an environment filled with objects that are long known to us.

That we can operate with only geometric disparity was shown in a remarkable and highly influential series of demonstrations developed by Bela Julesz in the 1960s. These are stereo pairs from which all monocular or structural clues are removed and each image consists of a random dot pattern. The simplest of these was generated from two initially identical random dot arrays. A central square in each image is then shifted horizontally by a small amount. The two monocular images still look identical – they are still patterns of random dots. When, however, the images are viewed stereoscopically, a square appears, vividly floating in front of a background and at a distance from it. Such a stereo pair is shown in Figure 20.13. (With some practice these stereo pairs can be fused 'manually' – that is, without using any devices. Place a small piece of card between the two images to restrict each image to one eye and then stare at the centre of one image until the two images merge. When the images merge the coherent structure will emerge vividly from the background.)

Fusion of random dot stereograms by human beings is a remarkable demonstration. But it is not clear what it means. Certainly it demonstrates that we can perceive depth in binocular images from which all structure has been removed. A number of questions remain. Why should we possess this ability? Are we

Figure 20.13
The generation and
structure of a random
dot stereogram.

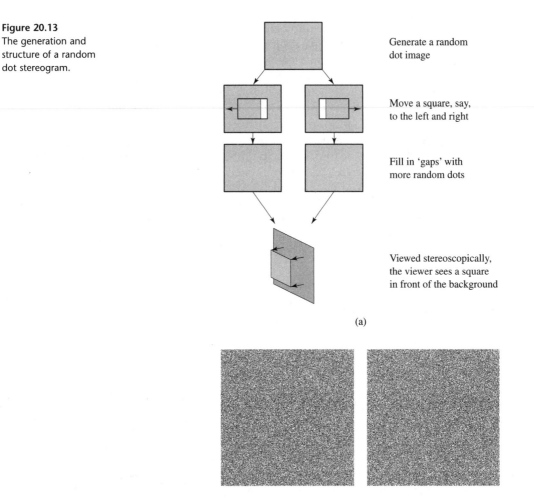

Generate a random
dot image

Move a square, say,
to the left and right

Fill in 'gaps' with
more random dots

Viewed stereoscopically,
the viewer sees a square
in front of the background

(a)

(b)

analyzing these images by establishing the correct correspondence between each pair of points in the left and right image? This seems like a monumental processing task even for the human visual system, but it is difficult to see what else could be happening. However, the demonstration was influential in stimulating much research based on the assumption that human stereopsis operated in low-level processes rather than high-level cognitive processes. In fact Marr and Poggio (see Marr's book, *Vision* (1982)) developed a theory based on Marr's famous zero crossings technique (Chapter 16) that 'explained' the Julesz experiments. Explanation in this case does not, of course, mean that they explained how the human visual system performed this feat, but that when they applied the theory to the random dot stereograms it extracts the hidden structure. This point is further taken up in Chapter 16 where we discuss using stereo information to extract shape from two-dimensional projections.

Bela Julesz's stereograms remained locked into the world of psychophysical experiments and research into perception until 1990 when a sudden new craze, using a technique developed from his work, propagated around the world.

Autostereograms

In the early 1990s a remarkable fad, reminiscent of the earlier brief cycles of popularity of stereoscopy, took off. These were single image random dot stereograms or autostereograms, where the random dot pairs of Bela Julesz had somehow been merged into a single image. This craze, still going strong at the time of writing, manifested itself in the form of books of images and posters. It is probably the case that together with 'Mandelbrot set imagery' (see Chapter 1) these images are the only two productions of computer graphics purchased on a wide scale by members of the public (leaving aside the successful computer graphics film productions of the 1990s). Intended to be viewed without any device, just as Julesz's original random dot pairs can be viewed without a fusing device, a three-dimensional structure suddenly jumps out of the apparently random image.

Apparently a colleague of Bela Julesz, Christopher Tyler, produced the first image in 1983, but the technique remained unpopularized until 1990 when Don Dyckman published one in the May/June 1990 issue of *Stereo World*, a little-known magazine produced by The National Stereoscopic Association in the USA. It appeared to be this single event that started the craze.

Like Julesz's stereo pairs they demonstrate some remarkable properties of human stereo vision, and like the random dot pairs we can describe the functioning of an algorithm that will produce them, but we can only guess at what mechanism the human visual system uses to decode them and indeed its purpose.

So what is their relevance to computer imagery beyond their apparent ability to generate profit and their fascination? Perhaps none, but any technique that enables depth to be encoded in a single image for human consumption is worthy of more than passing consideration. It may be relevant in the development of stereo viewing devices. Certainly the effect is startling – because it is unexpected – and remarkably clear.

Let us now look at how an autostereogram can be produced. It is simplest to consider an autostereogram made up of repetition of a motif or small sub-image rather than random patterns. Also, it is easiest to consider the production of a special case. First of all you need to be able to view a finished product (Figure 20.14 (Colour Plate)). To view this the best way is to hold the image vertically in front of your nose and gradually remove it further and further from your face until it is about 8 inches distant. At the same time you need to relax and try to 'look through the page'.

Figure 20.15
Overall disparity plan of
encoded image.

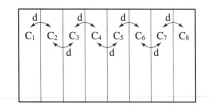

Now consider Figure 20.15 which shows the overall 'disparity plan'. In the autostereogram, the encoding pattern, in our case the motif, is organized into repeating columns with depth disparity, d, between pairs of columns. Remarkably the human visual system organizes the columns into pairs – (C1,C2), (C2,C3) and so on – and decodes depth information from the horizontal disparity between these groupings. The left eye looks at a particular column and the right eye looks at the next column on the right. We use the repeating motif to encode the depth of an object or scene. Consider Figure 20.16(a). This shows a 64×64 motif and the depth map of an object that is to be encoded into the autostereogram. The depth map has dimensions which are multiples of 64. In this case the object is, say, a folded card and the depth map values are constant along any horizontal line. Figure 20.16(b) shows what is happening for the first two lines. For the first line the object depth is 1 and we tile the encoded image, the autostereogram, with the first line from the motif image. Each pair of

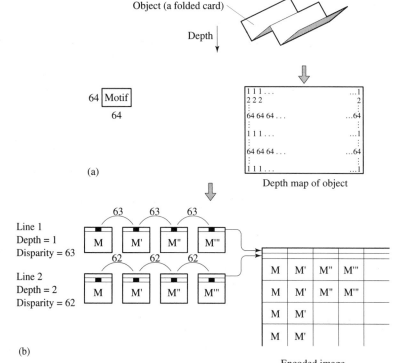

Figure 20.16
Showing how an
autostereogram is built up.

corresponding pixels in the repeated sub-images must exhibit a constant disparity of 63 and this means that each motif line segment M, M', M'', M''' must be stretched or scaled by 64/64, 64/63, 64/62, 64/61 and so on. For the second line the encoded depth must be 2 and the constant disparity between columns 62. So the scaling factors for this line are 64/64, 64/62, 64/60, 64/58 and so on. This process is easily seen in the encoded image where the motifs are subject to this line by line stretching.

Further reading – stereo

Marr D. (1982). *Vision – A Computational Investigation into the Human Representation and Processing of Visual Information*. San Francisco, CA: W.H. Freeman and Co.

20.5 Virtual reality

20.5.1 The strange invention of Mort Heilig

One view of virtual reality is that it is a promise bolstered in the main by exotic words and predictions rather than by technological reality. This is because the current enabling technology is a very long way from that required by most predicted applications. Although computer imagery is the foundation of virtual environments, it is a fact that few innovative computer imagery techniques are used in virtual reality and in this section and the next chapter we will try to answer these questions:

- What is virtual reality now?
- What might it become or what do the pundits think it might become?
- What are the outstanding image generation problems that need to be solved?

We will answer the first question by looking at some current applications. The second question we will deal with by delving into some of the predictions. *Caveat emptor*: they may strike you as irrelevant, exciting, nonsensical or even profound, depending on your viewpoint.

Where do we begin? It is a technology that was predicted 35 years ago in almost every important functional detail and it has already been in use for many years in areas like flight simulation. Now, according to the predictions of some researchers and entrepreneurs, it will invoke a revolution in the life of human beings.

Although there are many possible 'serious' uses of virtual reality, most of the technology and most of the exotic language is directed towards the personal or entertainment uses of virtual reality. A technology dealing in the science of illusions, it may be that the predicted impact of the technology on ordinary lives will be the biggest illusion of all. Like many new technologies its social effect will probably be marginal. The great technological revolutions have changed societies, have touched and altered human lives: the industrial revolution in Britain, the invention of the motor car, the impact of TV – all have affected the lives, to some extent, of most who live on the planet. Computer technology, in contrast, has affected little. Despite the hyperbole there is little that can be performed by a computer that was not previously accomplished by human beings. And, certainly, there is much done by human beings that could never be carried out by machines.

To begin at what appears to be the beginning: in 1960 Morton Heilig filed a patent in the US Patent Office (Figure 20.17 shows an excerpt from this). The invention was called 'Stereoscopic TV Apparatus for Individual Use' in which he claimed:

My invention is directed to improvements in stereoscopic television apparatus for individual use.

My invention generally speaking comprises the following elements: a hollow casing, a pair of optical units, a pair of television tube units, a pair of earphones and a pair of air discharge nozzles, all coacting to cause the user to comfortably see the images, hear the sound effects and to be sensitive to the air discharge of the said nozzles.

In most respects this patent predicted what we understand today by virtual reality. A user dons a head-mounted display (HMD) which presents him with a pair

Figure 20.17
An extract plan from Mort Heilig's patent.
Source: Morton, L. and M. Heilig October 4, 1960 Stereoscopic-television extract plan from Mort Heilig's patent 'Virtuality Reality Apparatus for Individual Use'.

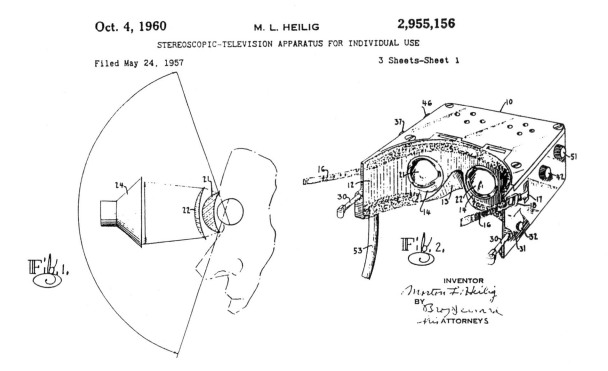

Oct. 4, 1960   M. L. HEILIG   2,955,156
STEREOSCOPIC-TELEVISION APPARATUS FOR INDIVIDUAL USE

Filed May 24, 1957   3 Sheets-Sheet 1

INVENTOR
Morton F. Heilig
BY
ATTORNEYS

of stereo images and at the same time visually isolates him from the real world. He is 'immersed' visually in a virtual reality. Other inputs, such as sound (and in Morton's invention even evocative odours), engender a more complete illusion of immersion.

But Morton's patent would nowadays be classified as 'passive' and 'non-immersive'. It does not allow the immersee to interact with the environment. It contains no head tracking device that alters the imagery according to the immersee's direction of gaze. It contains no device that enables the user to touch or grasp a virtual object.

One of the best analogies of an immersive virtual environment is that it is like, or should be like, allowing a user to wander through the environment and look around, but only through a set of wide angle binoculars. In a sense the computer image becomes transparent to the viewer. The user does not, or should not, explicitly perceive a computer image; although it is the power of the imagery that can make this illusion 'real'.

At the time of writing, most financial investment is being directed towards passive virtual reality – vast sums being invested in **ride simulations**. Using the technology of flight simulators the audience sits on a motion platform – the most elaborate of these has 6 degrees of freedom. Either the motion platform is in the form of a capsule with a screen inside, where both the screen and the audience move with the action, or an open platform moves in front of a static screen. Synchronized with the video is software that controls the platform movements to give the sensation that the audience is actually taking the place of the camera that produced the video that they are enjoying.

Ride simulators are interesting applications of computer imagery because they try to create a real three-dimensional experience but do not use stereo imagery or indeed any kind of interaction. Interaction is generally considered impossible because operators require a throughput of between 2000 and 3000 customers per hour. Interactive simulations are by definition very low capacity. For the same reasons operators do not want to supply the accoutrements necessary for three-dimensional vision. In these toys reality is imitated by using oversize film formats and relying on the sensations created by synchronizing the film action with the motion platform. Although the film action was originally made from live action, the difficulty of choreographing real cameras, in such a way that the resulting images could be convincingly synchronized with the motion platform, has meant that computer graphics imagery is now used extensively.

Interactive or immersive virtual reality, on the other hand, is possible but to within current limitations of the technology. A virtual grasp device, coupled to a real glove that the user wears, can be used to grab selected virtual objects; a user can walk around and a positional body sensor can use his real movements in real three-dimensional space to appropriately control his position and direction of gaze in virtual three-dimensional space.

Perhaps we should ask why anyone would want to do it anyway. There seems to be something profoundly depressing about the idea of putting on an HMD and a suit of body sensors and strolling around in a computer-created environment. Sure it's an interesting experience, but in the end ephemeral. Like your first trip in a hall of mirrors. And perhaps this is, in the end, the real future of virtual reality – these modern manifestations of our childhood fairgrounds, the giant theme parks.

At the moment the virtual reality presents us with a number of faces. They are

● Non-immersive (and usually special purpose) systems of which flight and ride simulators are a good example. The categorization emphasizes that the user looks into the virtual environment, or observes it, rather than being immersed in it.

● Immersive systems, that most commonly employ an HMD and a DataGlove, and which claim some generality. Unlike non-immersive systems whose form tends to depend on the application, immersive systems are much less application dependent and we can consider this form to be supported by a general purpose platform. Different virtual reality applications can be implemented on such a platform, analogous to different application programs mounted on a general purpose processor.

● Hybrid or augmented reality systems that use aspects of both. Here the idea is to 'mix' computer generated imagery with the user's real-world view. The real environment is augmented with a virtual environment.

● And lastly the irresistible rise of the prophets.

20.5.2 Non-immersive vs immersive virtual reality

Established (non-immersive) simulators using motion platforms have, of course, been around for many years in the form of flight simulators. They are important to consider because they exist and have well-developed technology and also because they operate outside the immersive virtual reality paradigm. They highlight the dichotomy between non-immersive special purpose applications – where the interactive modes and devices are determined by the application – and the idea of an immersive general purpose virtual reality platform that can accept any application.

A modern flight simulator could be considered non-immersive because the pilot sits in a mock-up cockpit – a real environment – and views virtual space on a 200-degree panoramic mirror onto which the computer imagery is projected. His interaction with the replica controls determines what computer images are presented and motion feedback is provided by computer controlled hydraulic rams that move the platform. Originally flight simulators consisted of a video camera, with position and attitude controlled by the pilot from the simulator controls, moving over a model landscape. With the advent of fast image generators in the early 1980s this cumbersome system died naturally. Virtual environments, although not exactly cheap to construct, are cheaper, more flexible and more realistic than models.

Many of the benefits of using computer generated imagery in flight simulators can be seen as advantages of virtual reality systems in general. Hazardous and emergency conditions can be presented to the pilot without danger. Training operators inexpensively and safely in hazardous tasks may become one of the major applications of virtual reality. In flight simulators it is not just the simulation of general hazards that is created. Databases exist of every international airport in the world, enabling pilots to become familiar with new airports before actually flying to them. Different weather conditions can be simulated using the same databases.

Current implementations of the immersive model are mainly locked into research labs and mount applications on systems that are put together from high performance graphics workstations, head-mounted or boom-mounted displays and DataGloves. These efforts usually investigate the efficacy of immersion and interactive modes and struggle against the limitations of the display and the interactive devices.

Such efforts form a continuum of experience that goes from applications that to some extent can be serviced by the technology, to applications that will require a revolution in the technology to be achieved. A good example of the former is the NASA Ames Virtual Wind Tunnel. This uses a boom-mounted display to immerse a scientist in the three-dimensional data fields that emerge from complex fluid dynamics simulations enabling better interpretation and exploration than would be possible with a two-dimensional display. This is an application where such limitations as the DataGlove inaccuracy and resolution limitations seem curable by extrapolation from current technology.

At the opposite end of the achievability spectrum, we could put product visualization. The hope here is that rather than just being able to visualize a product, such as a car, by using conventional CAD, we want to immerse a person in a virtual car. The person would be able to fully experience the car interior – the feel of the seats, the comfort of operating the controls, and so on. Such applications need a quantum leap in the development of devices that make a person feel physically immersed in an environment. Although we can achieve high quality visual feedback, the whole question of tactile and force feedback is mainly unexplored. Force feedback, in particular, is fraught with overwhelming problems. It would seem that almost by definition this can only be achieved by inserting the operator in some kind of exoskeleton. It remains to be seen if such application demands will attract the vast research and development costs.

20.5.3 Augmented reality

Hybrid systems, sometimes called augmented reality, use aspects of both the immersive and the non-immersive model. In their simplest form they consist of a general virtual reality system employing a see-through HMD so that the user views the real world in conjunction with computer generated imagery.

Curiously, although it is likely that augmented reality systems will find more applications than (immersive) virtual reality systems, augmented reality is more or less free from the mystique surrounding virtual reality.

The best (non-military) example of this is in medicine where a clinician may view, say, internal ultrasound data, superimposed on the body of the patient from whom it was collected. Using a 'see-through' HMD, the clinician is presented with ultrasound imagery superimposed on his view of the patient's body. The positional trackers on both the clinician and the hand-held scanner enable, as it were, the user to see – at least ultrasonically – inside the patient. The clinician has the ultrasound data presented in its 'correct' position in three-dimensional space. It is just as if the hand-held scanner has made the patient's flesh transparent.

Augmented reality systems may in the end turn out to be the more useful virtual reality mode for serious applications. Most applications are going to be concerned with real objects in real environments rather than virtual objects in virtual environments. One way of looking at augmented reality is to consider that real-world objects can gain or be assigned computer facilities without losing their real-world appearance. The functionality of the computer is superimposed on the object. The allegory is that we bring the facilities of the computer out of the monitor screen, where they are normally visualized, and make them part of the object.

Augmented reality implies that demands, additional to those of a virtual reality system, will be made of any implementation. First they bring another potentially expensive overhead into the frame generation cycle, namely the costs associated with registering the computer generated image with the real image. In medical applications such techniques will be useless without accurate and reliable registration. In most virtual environment applications some tracking inaccuracy is tolerable. The user is seeing virtual objects in a virtual environment. Small errors are tolerable. In augmented reality the user is extremely sensitive to misalignment of the virtual and real image. Connected with this is the requirement that there be no noticeable lag or delay between head movement and image update. Again in a virtual reality system some lag may be tolerable before it becomes noticeable or bothersome to the user. In augmented reality, where the user is looking at a static real environment, the effect of lag is to cause the synthetic image to 'swim' around the real image – a disturbing effect when both images must align and contain common structural details. Another potentially expensive demand comes from interaction. Interaction with real objects implies that the processor can sense some attribute of the object. So, for example, some computer vision facility may be included in an interaction loop.

The display requirement of augmented reality is a device that enables image superposition of the real and virtual world. This can be a see-through HMD where the user sees a view of a normal real world augmented with a computer image. Alternatively it can be a device that projects a computer image onto an object.

Augmented reality can be either passive or interactive. The medical application described above is non-interactive in the sense that the user does not engage in any explicit interaction – although passive interaction takes place through tracking. Here the clinician is equipped with a see-through HMD and is continually changing his direction of gaze. As in a normal virtual reality system gaze direction is tracked as the clinician looks at different parts of the body area under examination. At the same time a hand-held scanner, also with its own position and orientation in three-dimensional space, is sending ultrasonic information into the system. Information collected by the scanner is restricted to a two-dimensional plane or cross-section. The position of the HMD and that of the ultrasonic scanner are used to generate a correctly oriented plane of ultrasonic data which is overlaid on the view of the patient. In this way the clinician sees a composite image of the ultrasonic data registered in its true three-dimensional location.

Other obvious possibilities suggest themselves for augmented reality applications. One often suggested is the 'burning building scenario'. Fire fighters could be equipped with a see-through HMD to help them navigate through a smoke-filled building. The requirements would be identical to those of a normal architectural walk-through except that the fireman would be in a real environment, viewing it through an augmented display. Again in this application there is an obvious and critical requirement for accurate registration information.

In neither of these applications is explicit or deliberate user interaction involved. Explicit user interaction potentially offers intriguing possibilities. An interesting interactive augmented reality application is currently being studied at Cambridge University (UK). Its potential importance derives, not perhaps from the immediate application – the office desk – but as a demonstration of the interactive possibilities in augmented reality implementations.

People like paper, or so it seems. Despite the coining of the phrase 'desktop metaphor' and the subsequent predictions of a paperless office, we still want to keep paper. It seems that paper possesses properties that we do not want to give up and in fact use of paper has increased in the face of the computerized office. What has happened is that people have accepted the advantages of electronic documents alongside those of paper and this has resulted in two desktops – the computer screen and the real one. Pierre Wellner suggests a solution that he calls the 'DigitalDesk'. He states

'... but imagine if we did not have to choose and had a space where documents could be both paper and electronic at the same time. Instead of putting the user in the virtual world of the computer, we could do the opposite: add the computer to the real world of the user and create a Computer Augmented environment for paper. Instead of replacing paper with computers, we could enhance paper with computation.'

Figure 20.18(a) is a schematic illustration of the DigitalDesk. A computer image can be superimposed on the desk via a projector and an image can be analyzed via a television camera. (This idea is also described in Krueger's influential book, but without the projection facility, where it is called 'VideoDesk'.) A but-

Figure 20.18
The 'DigitalDesk'.

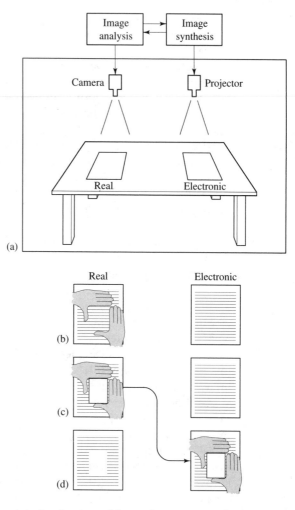

ton click event is implemented by a finger tap picked up by a microphone. Shown on the desk is a real document and a computer image of a document. One of the many interaction possibilities is merging operations between the two documents. Consider cutting from the real document and pasting into the electronic document – eliminating the need for scissors and glue. A user selects the area to be cut with his hands (Figure 20.18(b)). The computer in this mode projects a grey transparent overlay rectangle onto the document to enable precise positioning. The final area is then grabbed, projected onto the electronic document and finally positioned (Figures 20.18(c) and (d)). Implied in this facility is the ability of the computer vision program to recognize the forefinger–thumb image which delineates the rectangle. The selected image can be grabbed as a bit map or as text using an OCR facility.

Alternatively the real document and the electronic document can be merged on a single piece of paper. This opens up the possibility of an artist sketching using a real pencil and then making such operations as scaling or rotating the drawing or producing operated versions on different parts of the paper. Clip art can be placed and rotated into position and made permanent in the document. The tedious and limiting operations available in graphic design packages – freehand sketching with a mouse, pulling sub-images around on the screen with a mouse, and so on – are dispensed with. The advantages of the paper and pencil medium are retained and the computer facilities are added to the paper without the overwhelming restrictions of mouse/screen interaction.

These are only two possibilities out of many that can be suggested for this augmented reality system and they give some idea of the under-explored potential of this approach. The author states:

'The goal is not to enhance computers by giving them better access to paper; it is to enhance paper by giving it better access to computers. There is a difference between integrating the world into computers and integrating computers into the world ... Do we think of ourselves as working primarily in the computer but with access to physical world functionality, or do we think of ourselves as working primarily in the physical world but with access to computer functionality? Much of the research in human–computer interaction seems to emphasize the former ...'.

An alternative assessment of such a system could be that it is a reflection of our current uncertainty with regard to a hundred per cent paperless office. Perhaps we wish to retain paper along with computer facilities because we need its indisputable permanence as a record. We still cannot trust computer systems to retain important documents in perpetuity. Despite precautions we still fear the loss of computer files.

20.5.4 The prophets

A loud and sometimes absurd aspect of virtual reality is the prediction business which explores the possible applications and benefits that will come from having a general purpose immersive platform. Many suggestions make an analogy with the programmable computer and see a general purpose programmable virtual reality platform whose applications can be changed by simply swapping the software. For example, the successful DataGlove is often seen as a progenitor of a body suit that will enable complete immersion. Problems tend to be treated by the familiar 'vision extrapolation philosophy' which says that anything is achievable as an extrapolation from basic current technology through the appropriate effort and investment. This atmosphere has been responsible for much of the dynamics of early commercial developments of virtual reality and has led to the market release of decidedly immature systems. They have spurred a haphazard development of devices, in particular the manufacture of research devices, still at an early stage of development, and the manufacture of devices without any kind of specification and agreement on standardization.

It is the immersion aspect of virtual reality that gives it its science-fiction appeal and which seems to cause many people to see it as something that will significantly affect our lives. We are clearly a long way from convincing immersion where a user may be persuaded to forget about the fact that he is connected to a computer – the virtual environment becoming the reality. And anyway this is an unrealistic goal. Suspension of belief could only ever occur in a weak-minded person. We should not want to see virtual reality as a kind of electronic hypnotist. The realistic goal is to provide a virtual environment together with sufficient interaction so that a user would be as happy with a visit to a virtual museum as he would by a walk around the real thing.

Will it be what the harbingers of a new order predict or will it be like three-dimensional cinema and simply end up as a tool in certain specialized areas – just as flight simulation has been for two decades or so? In this respect we can do no better than present a few statements for you to judge. These were taken, it should be pointed out, not from the popular press, but from the pages of one of the most respected computer graphics journals. Here are three examples:

Virtual reality as a cure for social disintegration: 'Our urban society has fallen from an exciting metropolitan culture filled with amusement parks, picture palaces, dance crazes and other vital public group spaces and activities, into a sterile suburban landscape. The older urban entertainments nurtured a sense of community (however fleeting). Ethnic and regional differences dissolved as diverse groups discovered a common identity as a "republic of pleasure seekers". This middle class melding survived the Great Depression and World War Two, but not white flight and the spread of commercial TV. The mass audience was carved up into innumerable market segments based on age, sex and income. People no longer had a coherent culture or a sense of belonging to a unified "public". Now the opportunity exists to develop a new unification based on collaboration-focused activities supported by advanced technology ...'

(M. Harriss, AT&T Human Interface Technology Center)

Virtual reality to influence our evolution: 'If virtual realities actually attained immersion, we could feel and sense them – indistinguishable from real life. Recreating real life, however, is only one type of experience .... We can use virtual reality to experience things not possible in the real world ... It is this promise and prediction that the world-wide virtual reality network can fulfil. It could, in fact, function as the major stimulus to our evolutionary development'

(Written, apparently without any sense of the absurd, by J.F. Morie)

Virtual reality as a hallucinogenic drug: 'Virtopia is a step towards ultimate involvement. What we are testing is what it takes to provide an emotional experience/evoke an emotional response from a person in a virtual environment. Experiences range from the psycho-physical to the extremely cerebral. The interface for Virtopia is a vast barren desert. Scattered across the desert are various oases. Each oasis has a pool that provides a threshold into a rich experimental world. For example, you might find yourself in the spider world, where against a blood red sky a 30 foot high spider looms over you ...'

Frightening or absurd? It is indeed strange that our high tech societies energetically persecute and outlaw persons who try to change their consciousness and perception by taking chemicals. And yet we wholeheartedly embrace the concept that people may indulge in an experience where digital technology will interfere with our perception of reality. Because this is what in the end these prophets are saying. They are predicting that if we simply overcome the nagging technological inadequacies we can indulge in experiences that according to their descriptions sound not unlike a trip into the strange world induced by taking LSD.

20.6 Immersive virtual reality elements

The extent to which immersive virtual reality systems are convincing will determine their ultimate utility. This in turn will depend on the functionality and quality of the enabling devices that are used. It is not only the quality of the devices that is important, for example the quality and complexity of the computer imagery, but how well they 'fix' a user in a virtual environment. Can the user touch, hear and maybe smell the virtual objects? In most applications the goal is to present the user with a realistic experience of being part of a virtual environment. The point of the experience may be entertainment or training or scientific research but in any case accuracy or veracity is an important general goal. The most basic requirements of such systems then are a vision facility together with a touching or grasping device. A vision facility means that the user can look around the virtual environment which implies a display for the computer generated imagery and a tracking device that senses the user's position and direction of view. Most current manifestations of virtual reality have the following implementations of these facilities:

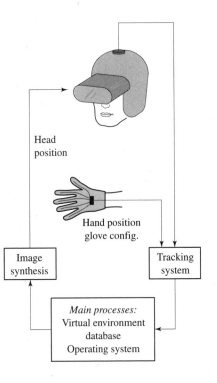

Figure 20.19
Components in a mainstream VR system.

- A stereo display device, usually miniature display monitors inside a head-mounted display.

- A computer graphics generator to provide the images and handle the interaction.

- A sensor that provides the current position of the viewer and his current viewing direction. This is usually a sensor mounted on the helmet.

- A device that enables such interaction as grasping a virtual object. The most popular device currently is a 'DataGlove'.

In passive systems a user is simply a viewer and the first two elements are required. In interactive systems some manifestation of the third and fourth elements is necessary. The way in which these elements are organized is shown in Figure 20.19.

20.6.1 Head-mounted display

A head-mounted display device presents a user with a stereo display and at the same time isolates him from the real environment. Like the DataGlove there is much debate on the utility of HMDs and their future as a vision facility in virtual reality systems is by no means certain. The first use of stereo computer graphics imagery was by the graphics pioneer Ivan Sutherland in 1965, who only two years earlier had published his seminal work on 'Sketchpad' which laid the foundation of two-dimensional interactive graphics. Sutherland provided images of wireframe objects that could be mixed in with the viewer's normal vision in a system called 'Ultimate Display'. This development is usually considered the progenitor of today's stereo-based virtual reality systems.

Along with a viewing facility a helmet also includes a head position sensor so that as the viewer changes his head position and/or direction of view in the virtual environment, so does the display change appropriately. New frames are generated from the changed viewpoint. Thus the helmet position sensor is used to control computer graphics imagery although there are applications where source images may come from TV cameras. Also, as we have seen, some applications mix real and computer graphics imagery into the same display.

Having imagery that is controlled by the viewer's position and gaze directions is called visual coupling and the idea goes back a surprisingly long time. In 1961 the Philco Corporation developed a device called 'Headsight' which consisted of a head-mounted monocular TV display. The helmet positional sensor was used to control the attitude of a remote TV camera and the idea was to invoke 'telepresence' or to give the user the impression that he was in the remote environment of the TV camera. The system was designed to be part of a remote control set-up for hazardous environments such as ocean or space exploration or radioactive areas. Indeed such applications are still suggested as one of the eventual major applications of virtual reality.

The debate about HMDs centres around their obvious inconvenience – they are bulky and heavy and current models need to be physically connected to a computer with cables. They suffer from a quality/weight convenience trade-off. To convince the user that he is in the virtual environment the resolution of the display must be high and the field of view afforded by the monitors should approach the human vision system's field of view. Both these factors are not realized to a sufficiently high quality within the size and weight constraints of a head-mounted display. The most expensive devices achieve a horizontal field of view of up to 140 degrees (against the human vision system's 200 degrees) by using complex anamorphic lenses which necessitate a pre-distorted image. Current spatial resolutions of the small eye monitors are a long way from the limiting resolution of the eye and those achieved by high quality conventional monitors.

We can note that for many applications a head-mounted display may not be necessary and some systems have the display mounted on a counter-balanced arm. The overall system is then a stereoscopic viewer that reacts to the movement of the arm. Positional sensing is far simpler in such devices and the display quality/weight trade-off is not so severe.

Finally, although the HMD is currently the preferred display system for virtual reality it is not the only possible candidate system for immersive displays. The CAVE system, first reported in 1992, is a major research effort that offers the same 'degree of immersion' while losing one of the major disadvantages of the HMD. Using an HMD makes enormous demands on an image generator. To prevent head latency, the lag between head movement and the supply of an updated image to the display, image generators must function at 30 frames per second, 60 being ideal. Using a standard rendering pipeline for this immediately places an upper limit on scene complexity. The CAVE system enables a user to look around at images because the images are projected onto an encapsulated environment that physically surrounds the immersee, rather than being fixed in front of his eyes. In other words, the image plane does not rotate as the user moves his head around.

CAVE works by projecting the synthesized images onto a display surface that physically encapsulates the immersee. For simplicity the geometry of the encapsulation is chosen to be a cube and images are projected onto the walls and floor. As a user moves around a room his position is tracked and the appropriate wall projections of the virtual environment are calculated. The immersee wears synchronized shutter glasses and sequential stereo projections are merged from each eye to give stereo views of the environment. A significant practical advantage here is that using such glasses means that the immersee is relatively unencumbered compared to wearing a large HMD.

(20.6.2) ## Graphics generators

No new techniques are demanded of a graphics generator in a virtual reality system beyond the ability to generate stereo pairs in the time interval demanded by the interaction. The system must present new displays as soon as an interactive event has been invoked, such as hand or head movement.

The requirements of the image generator are prodigious. To maintain a reasonable immersion illusion, the projected image has to change very quickly as an immersee moves his head. Any delay between head movement and updated image, called latency, results in a disturbing effect for the immersee. The lag perceived by the user is the difference between the stereo images presented by the graphics generator and the correct images, given the current position of the user's head or the current state of any interactive device being used. The visual manifestation of lag is that objects appear to jump – there is no illusion of scene constancy as the user moves his head. Thus we can identify two related performance factors: lag or latency and the frame update time. Lag depends on the processing necessary to sample the current state of the interactive device and supply updated information to the graphics generator. Frame update depends on the power of the graphics generator and the graphics complexity of the environment. In general we have to consider not only head movement but also movement of objects in the environment. Objects may move independently of the user or they may move because the user is interacting with them – virtual objects may be grasped, for example, by the user. A general rule of thumb is that the frame update time must always be greater than $0.1 \, s$ and twice the highest frequency of motion of objects in the scene with an ideal that is much higher – say $1/60 \, s$. The end to end delay in response to user interaction should also always be greater than $0.1 \, s$. To achieve a reasonable frame update time the compromise that is made on medium workstations is, of course, image quality, with the image being degraded or simplified, sometimes to an extent that obviates the point of the system, to maintain the frame rate.

A more considered solution to the lag problem is to accept a constant delay in the image update time and diminish the effects of lag by employing a predictive approach. Instead of sensing the head position at time t and generating the image for this position at time $t+\triangle t$, where t is the frame update time, the likely position of the head is predicted at time $t+\triangle t$ and the image for this position is rendered. However, this in itself can introduce problems. If linear extrapolation is used and if the prediction interval is too long then overshoot will result during, for example, deceleration of a movement, producing an effect that is as disturbing as the lag that it is intended to cure.

An obvious image generation problem arises out of the more extravagant predicted applications – such as wandering around a virtual city. This is the initial production of the database. To build even part of a real city using computer graphics imagery that would be of sufficient quality to satisfy users and impart any degree of immersion is a task that is extraordinarily expensive using current modelling tools. Existing models of such environments are inadequate. The databases are generated by duplication of standardized buildings resulting in uniformity. Unique complex buildings have to be constructed without the detail that contributes to their uniqueness and so on. The creation of such environments seems a bigger problem than that of display quality and processing capability and in the end will probably be the limiting factor in the early development of such applications. Here there is a parallel with the display limitation – the graphics generator can display images of high quality and detail but a very large virtual environment cannot be built at that level of fineness. The issue of hardware advances versus new or altered image synthesis techniques as a way out of this problem is further discussed in the next chapter.

20.6.3 Interaction and virtual hand controllers

Interaction with objects or entities in the image is becoming a more and more important aspect of computer imagery. Virtual reality systems require some kind of interaction unless they are restricted to passive viewing. We may have virtual three-dimensional objects that a user wants to grasp, rearrange or change in some way. In the case of selecting and moving objects it is a simple matter of extending the two-dimensional interaction model and this is easily implementable using a device equivalent to a three-dimensional version of the ubiquitous mouse. The mode of interaction, where a two-dimensional icon is moved under mouse control, is easily extended into three-dimensional space if the user is stationary. Another type of interaction is called immersee navigation where the user travels through the virtual environment.

Usually an immersee is physically constrained to moving within some restricted zone in reality (usually by cables that connect him to the computer) and some indirect interactive mode is required to enable the user to navigate freely in the virtual environment. This is normally accomplished by the user specifying a direction of travel and 'flying' in this direction using a start/stop control. Alternatively an immersee can specify a destination and be 'teleported' to it – the system updating the display with a view from the new location. Neither of those two interactions is satisfactory – flying is tedious and tends to induce motion sickness, teleporting suffers from the disadvantage of difficult specification of the destination which may require the introduction of a secondary display, such as a plan, to enable this. Both navigation and object interaction can be implemented using a glove device.

In 1987 *Scientific American* published an article featuring the VPL DataGlove and it seems to have been this event more than any other which sparked off media and public interest in virtual reality. The DataGlove (Figure 20.20) is the most popular interactive device at the moment and satisfies some of the (realistic) demands of a general purpose virtual reality platform; that is, one on which different applications can be loaded. Generically known as a virtual hand controller, such a device provides a number of functions. First, a position and orientation sensor enables a computer graphics hand to appear in the virtual environment, moving around (albeit disembodied) just as a user would see his own hand moving around in the equivalent real environment. Second, it acts as a select or grasp device enabling the system to determine when a virtual object has been touched.

Figure 20.20
The VPL DataGlove.

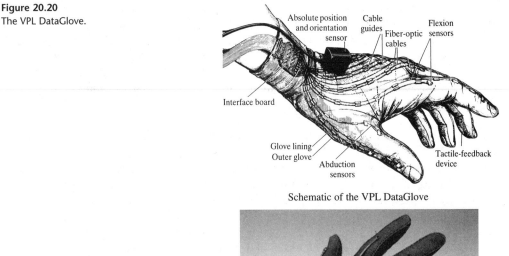

Schematic of the VPL DataGlove

VPL DataGlove

Simply being able to touch and cause an object to move only requires detection of a hit or selection. The object can then be 'glued' to the hand and moved around just like a click–drag–release with a mouse. However, most hand controllers are much more than the equivalent of a three-dimensional joystick and buttons, although in practice, because of current accuracy problems, in many applications they are reduced to being just that. For example, the VPL DataGlove uses fibre optics to sense the angles between finger joints. The device is controlled by its own computer which abstracts the device to a higher level. For example, an LUT containing min/max values that define a range of finger sensor values for certain finger postures enables gesture events to be generated.

The use of more elaborate gestures as a step forward in increasing the richness of user interaction is an obvious suggestion but it is not clear at the moment whether a DataGlove is the best way to implement such a tool. Given the complexity, cost and fragility of devices that sense the detailed attitude of a human hand, it may be that the way forward is to use computer vision techniques to recognize hand attitude, rather than using a glove.

Gloves are being extended with tactile and force feedback. The idea is that such feedback means the user is able to feel surface texture, the hardness/softness of the object and make him feel that he has picked up and is moving a real object. Tactile feedback can be simulated by inflatable air sacs in the finger tips and palms and force feedback by inserting the hand in an exoskeleton.

Leaving aside the substantial problems of tactile and force feedback there are many difficulties with the required visual feedback between a glove and a three-dimensional image. If accurate applications are to be developed, such as the oft-suggested surgical training, then the interaction has to support accurate movement of the real hand and produce an accurate visual simulation of this. How is this to be achieved? We might take the gross position of the fingers and hand from the hand controller, but leave the final accurate intersection calculations in virtual space. That is, we would calculate the intersection between the virtual object and the computer graphics model of the hand. This will give accurate visual feedback and would prevent the occurrence of a user being able to grasp a virtual object that his virtual hand is (visually) not in contact with; or seeing the virtual hand enter the space of the object. The big disadvantage of this approach is the processing cost. Human beings use different grasp motions depending on the nature of the object and the task. It is not just a matter of determining when a fingertip comes into contact with the object. For example, if a palmar grasp is employed then a large area of the hand comes into contact with the object.

Further reading – virtual reality

Most current books on virtual reality seem to split into two categories. Either they are collections of papers detailing diverse applications that use the mainstream HMD plus stereo display, or they herald the beginnings of a new phase in the history of humanity and all that jazz. Most of those in the latter category are not worth reading. The books listed below are exceptions. In particular, Krueger's well-considered work is probably the best book on the wider issues (both technological and cultural) of virtual reality.

The DigitalDesk is described in a special issue of *CACM* devoted to augmented reality; Krueger's Videodesk is described in his book.

Mort Heilig's patent for Stereoscopic-Television Apparatus for Individual Use is reproduced in full in a recent issue of *Computer Graphics*.

Bajura M., Fuchs H. and Ohbuchi R. (1992). Merging virtual objects with the real world: seeing ultrasound imagery with the patient. *Computer Graphics*, **26**, 203–10 (Proc. SIGGRAPH '92)

Galyean T.A. and Hughes J.F. (1991). Sculpting: an interactive volumetric modeling technique. *Computer Graphics*, **25**, 267–74 (Proc. SIGGRAPH '91)

Heilig M. (1994). Stereoscopic-Television Apparatus for Individual Use. US Patent no. 2,955,156, reproduced in *Computer Graphics*, **28**(2), May, 131–4

Kalawsky R.S. (1993). *The Science of Virtual Reality and Virtual Environments*. Wokingham, UK: Addison-Wesley

Krueger M.W. (1991). *Artificial Reality II*. Reading, MA: Addison-Wesley

Rheingold H. (1991). *Virtual Reality*. London: Secker and Warburg

Wellner P. (1993). Interacting with paper on the DigitalDesk. *Comms. ACM*, **36**(7), July, 86–95

Virtual reality and efficiency in image synthesis

21.1 Complexity, modelling and rendering

21.2 Image-based rendering

21.3 Image-based rendering using view interpolation – introduction

21.4 Photo-modelling for image-based rendering

21.5 The complexity problem – organizing scene data – hidden surface removal

In Chapter 20 we made the point that many current applications in virtual reality fall somewhat short of acceptable quality in the sense that the systems cannot cope with a degree of image complexity sufficient to convincingly imitate the reality. Also, much of virtual reality research is concerned with demanding novel applications and this proceeds on the assumption that the image synthesis difficulties will eventually be solved by hardware advances. In this chapter we will look at the costs that hold up real-time quality image generation of complex scenes and discuss potential algorithmic solutions that are independent of hardware improvements. Before we do that perhaps it is in order to examine the reasons that these problems have not been vigorously addressed in the past. There is a legacy of unsolved problems in computer graphics which now beset virtual reality developers.

Problems with virtual reality implementations flow from the wide acceptance of the standard approach to rendering which consists of building an accurate geometric model, setting a viewpoint and then evaluating a projection using shading and hidden surface removal. The inertia of this approach is partially due to the fact that it is now embedded – as fixed program hardware – in many graphics workstations. The approach is potentially wasteful for virtual reality image generation applications where a new view of a complex scene, which may be only marginally different to the previously generated view, is required in, say, one-sixtieth of a second. This is beginning to be recognized and it is possible that the demands of image generation in virtual reality will be responsible for a new generation of computer graphics algorithms.

The development of graphics workstations in the 1980s tended to stabilize, as far as three-dimensional graphics is concerned, around the fast rendering of polygon mesh objects using the Z-buffer algorithm for hidden surface removal, an approach consolidated by the development of special hardware. This rendering approach became written in stone as manufacturers have chased higher and higher polygon throughput rate. Academic researchers perceived this kind of basic image generation as being solved as far as the theory went and moved on to more and more complex light transport models – a process that began in the early 1980s with the appearance of ray tracing followed a few years later by the radiosity method. The failure of the CG community to address the problems of short image generation time has resulted in their resurfacing in the plethora of low quality virtual reality platforms. If anything, the photo-realism goal tended to increase image generation times as more complex rendering methods and more complex scenes moved ahead of mainstream hardware advances. With poor image quality making the exotic language that surrounds the immersion goal of virtual reality manifestly nonsensical, we are now seeing the start of explorations into alternative approaches to basic image generation. This area is called image-based rendering to signify that the algorithms operate (mostly) in two-dimensional image space.

It is not only the rendering cost that has important implications for the development of virtual reality but the associated modelling cost. Even although modelling has the benefit of being performed offline, the use of low-level representations, such as the polygon mesh, implies high manual costs for applications like cityscapes. Image-based rendering techniques offer a potential solution to both the rendering and the modelling cost by employing methods based on photographic imagery.

Image generation time problems have long been recognized by one image synthesis industry. Flight simulator manufacturers have been grappling for many years with these issues and have used, for example, special hidden surface removal algorithms, where much processing is accomplished offline, and objects are rendered at different levels of detail depending on their projected screen area. However, such techniques have tended to be locked into this specialized field which has developed historically without the same hardware cost constraints of a mass market application such as virtual reality. A new generation of developers is now tackling the same problem in the video games market, where animation of some complexity needs to be generated in real time on a PC.

At the time of writing, the problems have been addressed by a few people, but their work has not yet resulted in general acceptance. There has been no emergence of an agreed approach to coping with complexity in a virtual environment and certainly much of the difficulty is rooted in the wide diversity of virtual reality applications. It is interesting to consider that the current state of the research into rendering methods for virtual reality is not unlike the situation in the early 1970s where, because of contemporary memory constraints, the Z-buffer algorithm had not emerged as a de facto standard and there was an energetic search, motivated by efficiency requirements, amongst many diverse hidden surface removal algorithms.

We will discuss the following problems in virtual reality relating to scene complexity:

● Modelling approaches: The cost of traditional methods in computer graphics, where all of the geometry of a scene is defined by some three-dimensional point sampling method, such as the polygon mesh representation, become wholly inappropriate for very complex scenes.

● Connected with modelling is the potential of new approaches to rendering. Apart from its inertia there is no good reason for staying with the standard rendering approach. What are the alternatives to injecting a complex low-level description of a scene into the input of complete rendering pipeline for every frame?

Apart from novel approaches in image synthesis for virtual reality, we will also look at how we can adapt existing rendering approaches to deal better with scene complexity. The areas of interest here are:

● The organization of scene data: with a large complex scene we are only interested in rendering part of the scene in any frame. We need to couple the virtual reality positional interaction to the scene database in some way that enables us to get access only to the information we currently require.

● The ubiquitous scale problem: at any render instant we need access to object representations that are appropriate to their image plane projections. The lack of object descriptions that are accessible at any level of detail implies that we must always render the entire detail in a scene which then causes high costs in shading and hidden surface removal.

● Hidden surface removal: for very complex scenes the convenience/efficiency trade-off of the Z-buffer tips into inefficiency. It is likely that virtual reality demands will bring about a renewal of interest in hidden surface removal research.

21.1 Complexity, modelling and rendering

Traditional modelling techniques in computer graphics, described in Chapter 2, were in the main evolved for single objects, and quickly become unworkable when we wish to build a very complex scene that may contain thousands of objects – cityscapes, for example. Although in virtual reality the cost of rendering complex scenes is often dismissed as being solvable in the future with hardware advances, there is also a large (albeit once-only) cost associated with building complex scenes if manual or semi-manual methods are used. One possibility is to use photography as an alternative source of models and imagery. In this context photography can help in two ways. We can attempt to build conventional computer graphics models by extracting three-dimensional information from photographs. Another possibility, and one that is now being pursued, is to use panoramic photographs as the basic input to a virtual reality system. This eliminates both modelling and rendering and replaces it with an image-based or two-dimensional process that reconstructs the desired view from the panorama or environment map to use a traditional computer graphics term. The time taken to produce the image is now decoupled from the scene complexity and, just as important, real world detail, whose richness and complexity elude even the most elaborate photo-realistic renderers, is easily captured.

Photographs have always been used in texture mapping and this classical tool is still finding new applications in areas which demand an impression of realism that would be unobtainable from conventional modelling techniques, except at great expense. A good example is facial animation (Chapter 19) where a photograph of a face is wrapped onto a computer graphics model or structure. The photo-map provides the fine level of detail necessary for convincing and realistic expressions, and the underlying model is used as a basis for controlling the animation.

In building geometric representations from photographs, many of the problems that are encountered are traditionally part of the computer vision area but the goals are different. Geometric information recovered from a scene in a computer vision context usually has some single goal, such as collision avoidance in robot navigation or object recognition, and we are usually concerned in some way with reducing the information that impinges on the low-level sensor. We are generally interested in recovering the shape of an object without regard to such irrelevant information as texture; although we may use such information as a device for extracting the required geometry, we are not interested in it *per se*. In modelling a scene in detail, it is precisely the details such as texture that we are interested in as well as the pure geometry.

Consider first the device of using photography to assist in modelling. Currently available commercial photo-modelling software concentrates on extracting pure geometry using a high degree of manual intervention. They use a pre-calibrated camera, knowledge of the position of the camera for each shot and a sufficient number of shots to capture the structure of the building, say, that is being modelled. Extracting the edges from the shots of the building enables a wireframe model to be constructed. This is usually done semi-automatically with an operator corresponding edges in the different projections. It is exactly equivalent to the shape from stereo problem using feature correspondence except that now we use a human being instead of a correspondence-establishing algorithm. We may end up performing a large amount of manual work on the projections, as much work as that would be entailed in using a conventional CAD package to construct the building. The obvious potential advantage is that photo-modelling offers the possibility of automatically extracting the rich visual detail of the scene as well as the geometry.

It is interesting to note that in modelling from photographs approaches, the computer graphics community has side-stepped the most difficult problems that are researched in computer vision by embracing some degree of manual intervention. For example, the classical problem of correspondence between images projected from different viewpoints is solved by having an operator manually establish a degree of correspondence between frames which can enable the success of algorithms that establish detailed pixel by pixel correspondence. In computer vision such approaches do not seem to be considered. Perhaps this is due to well-established traditional attitudes in computer vision, which has tended to see the imitation of human capabilities as an ultimate goal, as well as constraints from applications.

Using photo-modelling to capture detail has some problems. One is that the information we obtain may contain light source and view-dependent phenomena such as shadows and specular reflections. These would have to be removed before the imagery could be used to generate the simulated environment from any viewpoint. Another problem of significance is that we may need to warp detail in a photograph to fit the geometric model. This may involve expanding a very small area of an image. Consider, for example, a photograph – taken from the ground – of a high building with a detailed facade. Important detail information near the top of the building may be mapped into a small area due to the projective distortion. In fact this problem is identical to view interpolation which we discuss later.

Let us now consider the use of photo-modelling without attempting to extract the geometry. We simply keep the collected images as two-dimensional projections and use these to calculate new two-dimensional projections. We never attempt to recover three-dimensional geometry of the scene (although it is necessary to consider the three-dimensional information concerning the projections). This is a form of image-based rendering and it has something of a history.

Consider a virtual walk through an art gallery or museum. The quality requirements are obvious. The user needs to experience the subtle lighting conditions designed to best view the exhibits. These must be reproduced and sufficient detail must be visible in the paintings. A standard computer graphics approach may result in using a (view-independent) radiosity solution for the rendering together with (photographic) texture maps for the paintings. The radiosity approach, where the expensive rendering calculations are performed once only to give a view-independent solution, may suffice in many contexts in virtual reality, but it is not a general solution for scenes that contain complex geometrical detail. As we know, a radiosity rendered scene has to be divided up into as large elements as possible to facilitate a solution and there is always a high cost for detailed scene geometry.

This kind of application – virtual tours around buildings and the like – has already emerged with the bulk storage freedom offered by videodisc and CD-ROM. The inherent disadvantage of most approaches is that they do not offer continuous movement or walk-through but discrete views selected by a user's position as he (interactively) navigates around the building. They are akin to an interactive catalogue and require the user to navigate in discrete steps from one position to the other as determined by the points from which the photographic images were taken. The user 'hops' from viewpoint to viewpoint.

An early example of a videodisc implementation is the 'Movie Map' developed in 1980. In this early example the streets of Aspen were filmed at 10-foot intervals. To invoke a walk-through, a viewer retrieved selected views from two videodisc players. To record the environment, four cameras were used at every viewpoint – thus enabling the viewer to pan to the left and right. The example demonstrates the trade-off implicit in this approach: because all reconstructed views are pre-stored the recording is limited to discrete viewpoints.

An obvious computer graphics approach is to use environment maps, originally developed in rendering to enable a surrounding environment to be reflected in a shiny object (see Chapter 4). In image-based rendering we simply replace the shiny object with a virtual viewer. Consider a user positioned at a point from which a six-view (cubic) environment map has been constructed (either photographically or synthetically). If we make the approximation that the user's eyes are always positioned exactly at the environment map's viewpoint then we can compose any view direction-dependent projection demanded by the user changing his direction of gaze by sampling the appropriate environment maps. This idea is shown schematically in Figure 21.1. Thus we have, for a stationary viewer, coincidentally positioned at the environment map viewpoint, achieved our goal of a view-independent solution. We have decoupled the viewing direction from the rendering pipeline. Composing a new view now consists of sampling environment maps and the scene complexity problem has been bound by the resolution of the pre-computed or photographed maps.

The highest demand on an image generator used in immersive virtual reality comes from head movements (we need to compute at 60 frames per second to avoid the head latency effect) and if we can devise a method where the rendering cost is almost independent of head movement this would be a great step forward. However, the environment map suggestion only works for a stationary

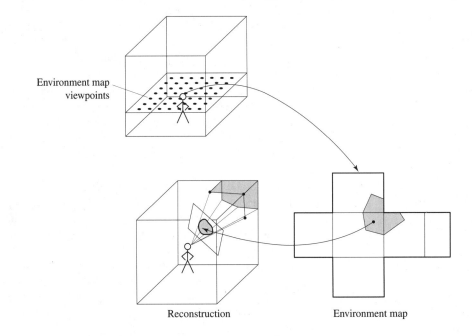

Figure 21.1
Compositing a user projection from an environment map.

Environment map viewpoints

Reconstruction   Environment map

viewer. We would need a set of maps for each position that the viewer could be in. Can we extend the environment map approach to cope with complete walk-throughs? Using the constraint that in a walk-through the eyes of the user are always at a constant height, we could construct a number of environment maps whose viewpoints were situated at the lattice points of a coarse grid in a plane, parallel to the ground plane and positioned at eye height. For any user position could we compose, to some degree of accuracy, a user projection by using information from the environment maps at the four adjacent lattice points? The quality of the final projections are going to depend on the resolution of the maps and the number of maps taken in a room – the resolution of the eye plane lattice. The map resolution will determine the detailed quality of the projection and the number of maps its geometric accuracy.

To be able to emulate the flexibility of using a traditional graphics pipeline approach, by using photographs (or pre-rendered environment maps), we either have to use a brute force approach and collect sufficient views compatible with the required 'resolution' of our walk-through, or we have to try to obtain new views from the existing ones. This is known as view interpolation. View interpolation is based on the idea that if a new viewpoint is close to one for which a view has been photographed or pre-rendered, then it should be possible to construct the new view from the existing one.

Currently, viewing from cylindrical panoramas is being established as a popular facility on PC-based equipment (see Section 21.2.1). This involves collecting the component images by moving a camera in a semi-constrained manner – rotating it in a horizontal plane. The computer is used merely to 'stitch' the component images into a continuous panorama; no attempt is made to recover depth information.

This system can be seen as the beginning of a development that may eventually result in being able to capture all the information in a scene by walking around with a video camera, resulting in a three-dimensional photograph of the scene. We could see such a development as merging the separate stages of modelling and rendering; there is now no distinction between them. The virtual viewer can then be immersed in a photographic quality environment and have the freedom to move around in it without having his movement restricted to the excursions of the camera. It may be that this demand from the virtual reality community will bring computer vision research out of the research laboratories, where it has remained for over two decades, and away from its long assumed applications – robot vision and object recognition – and give a much needed impetus to this weighty problem.

21.2 Image-based rendering

In this section we will discuss image-based rendering which means using algorithms in two-dimensional image space to construct new views from photographs or pre-rendered imagery. We begin by giving some definitions relating to how a user, or virtual camera, may want to move in a virtual environment. These are based on categories suggested by Chen in his report on QuickTime VR (described shortly) and concern the requirements of systems that recompose planar projections from photographic panoramas or environment maps. Chen defines three types of virtual camera movement:

- **Camera rotation**: this refers to a camera fixed at a particular viewpoint which has three rotational degrees of freedom (DOF): pitch (rotation about a horizontal axis), yaw (pivoting about a vertical axis) and roll (rotating normal to the view plane). Reprojection from an environment map can simulate the first two DOFs for a virtual viewer positioned at the camera or viewpoint from which the environment map was constructed. The third can be accomplished by image rotation. Thus a virtual viewer can position himself at the viewpoint and look around in any direction. This is the basic facility implemented in QuickTime VR. In an HMD-based virtual reality system this means that as long as a viewer stands still he can look around in any direction.

- **Object rotation**: refers to orbiting a camera around an object which is oriented such that it is always pointing to the centre of the object. That is, the motion is equivalent to rotating an object about its centre. Although the camera viewpoint is now moving, the movement is restricted, in particular the depth from the viewpoint to the centre of the object is fixed. This means that the virtual viewer who wants to travel around the object in any orbit can be serviced by recording frames which correspond to all allowable orientations of the object. Chen calls this a 'navigable movie' method and suggests storing 504 frames (at 10 degree increments) for an object with 360 degrees rotation in one direction and 140 in the other. The user then composes a movie of choice.

- **Camera movement**: this is the general case of the camera viewpoint changing – the requirement of a walk-through. This can be implemented approximately by storing a set of environment maps synthesized or photographed from a set of discrete viewpoints and hopping from viewpoint to viewpoint when travel is required. The viewer can look around from each viewpoint but a discontinuity is experienced when moving between viewpoints. This can be alleviated by increasing the number of environment maps stored or by interpolating in-between views from adjacent environment maps. Thus the choice is between high storage and data collection costs and the additional complexity of view interpolation. However, in this connection Chen quotes a CD-ROM as being capable of storing 1000 cylindrical panoramas (at a 10:1 compression ratio), so in practice the limitation may turn out to be the manual work of photographing the environment, rather than storage limitations.

We can summarize the above categories in terms of viewpoint and viewing direction movement as:

- **Camera rotation**: Viewpoint fixed
  Viewing direction (theoretically) unconstrained

- **Object rotation**: Viewpoint constrained (moves over the surface of an enclosing sphere)

  Viewing direction constrained (to point to the centre of the sphere)

- **Camera movement**: Viewpoint unconstrained

  Viewing direction unconstrained

Image-based rendering is new and it is difficult to predict the extent to which it will replace or supplement the conventional computer graphics rendering pipeline. What we can do is identify and describe the various approaches that are currently under development and investigation. It is difficult at this stage in the development of the field to define a detailed taxonomy and we resort to listing the main approaches that have so far emerged:

- **Viewing of photographic panoramas** The best current example of this is Apple Computer's QuickTime VR which uses a cylindrical environment map or photographic panorama. QuickTime VR operates with panoramas collected from fixed viewpoints enabling the user to look around 360 degrees and up and down. Walk-throughs need to be implemented by hopping and their accuracy depends on the number of panoramas collected to represent an environment. Thus QuickTime VR implements (limited) camera rotation. A warping operation is necessary in the process whose purpose is to derive a planar projection from (part of) the panorama.

- **Viewing synthetic panoramas or environment maps** This is identical to the first category except that we are now dealing with computer graphics or synthetic imagery. Instead of using photographs the environment maps are rendered offline. This means that there is a potential to update the imagery and combine the advantages of generating imagery offline with on-the-fly alterations. We can also represent environments that do not exist or which cannot be photographed. Also, there is no reason why synthetic and photographic imagery cannot be combined in a single application. Again this method implements camera rotation.

- **View interpolation of synthetic imagery and panoramas** This means using something akin to an image warping or morphing approach to interpolate new views from panoramas taken from discrete or fixed recording viewpoints. This time, image warping or morphing is used to construct an interpolated image from, say two, reference images. In principle it is no different to the morphing or warping techniques discussed in Chapter 17. However, there we were usually considering a morph sequence between two views of different objects. In view interpolation we are concerned with generating a view of the same scene from a viewpoint that is different to the viewpoints from which the reference images were taken. Another important difference is that in conventional morphing programs the user sets up sparse correspondence between the two images, whereas in view interpolation we require dense correspondence information between the reference views.

To do this we require the external camera parameters associated with the reference views.

View interpolation is an interesting and challenging problem because it throws up the obvious demand that we have, in general, to deal with information in an interpolated view that may be missing from the stored views that it is interpolated from. Also, as will become apparent, we need to store additional information such as depth and camera information for this approach. View interpolation can operate with one or (usually) more images taken from predetermined viewpoints and can potentially implement camera movement.

● **View interpolation of photographic imagery and panoramas**
This is the same in effect as the previous category except that now we have to establish camera information and depth values using computer vision approaches. Although there is no theoretical difference between this method and the previous category, the need to resort to computer vision techniques makes the approach a separate category in practice.

(21.2.1)

Image-based rendering using photographic panoramas

Developed in 1994, Apple Computer's QuickTime VR is a classic example of using a photographic panorama as a pre-stored virtual environment. A cylindrical panorama is chosen for this system because it does not require any special equipment beyond a standard camera and a tripod with some accessories. As for reprojection, a cylindrical map has the advantage that it only curves in one direction, thus making the necessary warping to produce the desired planar projection fast. The basic disadvantage of the cylindrical map – the restricted vertical field of view – can be overcome by using an alternative cubic or spherical map but both of these involve a more difficult photographic collection process and the sphere is more difficult to warp. The inherent viewing disadvantage of the cylinder depends on the application. For example, in architectural visualization it may be a serious drawback.

Figure 21.2 (see colour plate section) is an illustration of the system. A user takes a series of normal photographs, using a camera rotating on a tripod, which are then 'stitched' together to form a cylindrical panoramic image. A viewer positions himself at the viewpoint and looks at a portion of the cylindrical surface. The reprojection of selected parts of the cylinder onto a (planar) view surface involves a simple image warping operation which, in conjunction with other speed-up strategies, operates in real time on a standard PC. A viewer can continuously pan in the horizontal direction and the vertical direction to within the vertical field of view limit.

Currently restricted to monocular imagery, it is interesting to note that one of the most lauded aspects of virtual reality – three-dimensionality and immersion – has been for the moment ignored. It may be that in the immediate future monocular non-immersive imagery, which does not require expensive stereo viewing facilities and which concentrate on reproducing a visually complex environment, will predominate in the popularization of virtual reality facilities.

(21.2.2)

Image-based rendering using synthetic panoramas

The advantage of the technique described in the previous section is that it makes photographic quality (real-time) virtual reality possible on mainstream computers. Its disadvantage is that it is limited in two ways. Reconstructions can only take place from fixed viewpoints and the complete environment is fixed at the time the photographs are created. Visual interaction potential is limited to whatever facilities have been predicted by the designer. This drawback is eliminated by applying the same technique to synthetic imagery. Standard computer graphics techniques are used to render environment maps offline which are then viewed in the same way as for the photographic panorama, but without losing the ability to update parts of a scene according to user interaction. The fact that the bulk of the rendering can be done offline eliminates the time penalty of scene complexity but we are still left with the modelling cost – so easily sidestepped by photographs.

An interesting study of this approach was undertaken in 1994 by Regan and Pose who called it priority rendering because it combined the environment map approach with updating the scene at different rates. They used a six-view cubic environment map as the basic pre-computed solution. In addition a multiple display memory was used for image composition and on-the-fly alterations to the scene were combined with pre-rendered imagery.

The method is a hybrid of a conventional graphics pipeline approach with an image-based approach. It depends on dividing the scene into a priority hierarchy. Objects are allocated a priority depending on their closeness to the current position of the viewer and their allocation of rendering resources and update time are determined accordingly. The scene is rendered as environment maps and, as before, if the viewer remains stationary no changes are made to the environment map. As the viewer changes position the new environment map from the new viewpoint is rendered according to the priority scheme.

Regan and Pose utilized multiple display memories to implement priority rendering where each display memory is updated at a different rate according to the information it contains. If a memory contains part of the scene that is being approached by a user then it has to be updated, whereas a memory that contains information far away from the current user position can remain as it is. Thus overall different parts of the scene are updated at different rates – hence priority rendering. Regan and Pose used memories operating at 60, 30, 15, 7.5 and 3.75 frames per second. Rendering power is directed to those parts of the scene that need it most. At any instant the objects in a scene would be organized into display memories according to their current distance from the user. Simplistically the occupancy of the memories might be arranged as concentric circles emanating from the current position of the user. Dynamically assigning each object to an appropriate display memory involves a calculation which is carried out with respect to a bounding sphere. In the end this factor must impose an upper bound on scene complexity and Regan and Pose reported experiments with a test scene of only 1000 objects. Alternatively objects have to be grouped into a hierarchy and dealt with through a secondary data structure as is done in some speed-up approaches to conventional ray tracing.

(21.2.3) ## Compositing panoramas

Compositing environment maps with synthetic imagery is straightforward. For example, to construct a cylindrical panorama we map viewspace coordinates (x,y,z) onto a cylindrical viewing surface (θ,h) as:

$$\theta = \tan^{-1}(x/z) \qquad h = y/(x^2 + z^2)^{1/2}$$

Constructing a cylindrical panorama from photographs involves a number of practical points. Instead of having three-dimensional coordinates we now have photographs. The above equations can still be used, substituting the focal length of the lens for z and calculating x and y from the coordinates in the photograph plane and the lens parameters. This is equivalent to considering the scene as a picture of itself – all objects in the scene are considered to be at the same depth.

Another inherent advantage of a cylindrical panorama is that after the overlapping planar photographs are mapped into cylindrical coordinates (just as if we had a cylindrical film plane in the camera), the construction of the complete panorama can be achieved by translation only – implying that it is straightforward to automate the process. The separate images are moved over one another until a match is achieved – a process sometimes called 'stitching'. As well as translating the component images, the photographs may have to be processed to correct for exposure differences that would otherwise leave a visible vertical boundary in the panorama.

The overall process can now be seen as a warping of the scene onto a cylindrical viewing surface followed by the inverse warping to re-obtain a planar projection from the panorama. From the user's point of view the cylinder enables both an easy image collection model and a natural model for viewing in the sense that we normally view an environment from a fixed height – eye level – looking around and up and down.

(21.3) ## Image-based rendering using view interpolation – introduction

View interpolation means that, given certain reference projections taken from certain viewpoints, we attempt to construct a set of in-between projections, employing some kind of interpolation procedure that eliminates the normal procedure of re-rendering the scene from the in-between viewpoints. Such a procedure thus has the potential to eliminate the viewing constraint of pre-stored or photographed imagery which is that we cannot move continuously between (reference) viewpoints, we have to jump from one to the other. Providing we can supply a sufficient number of reference images taken from discrete viewpoints, we can interpolate the required views for a continuous walk by a viewer between the viewpoints. In terms of our camera definitions we are implementing camera movement rather than just camera rotation.

A brute force way of doing this is reprojection. We simply consider the pixels in an environment map, together with their associated depth values, to be (two-dimensional) objects in a scene. In other words, we remove each pixel from the image plane and position it at a point determined by its depth value, and then consider this collection of objects as a scene which we project from our new or required viewpoint. Although this gives us a method of calculating a new view, without re-injecting the scene through an entire graphics pipeline, it is still lengthy in that we now have a number of polygons equal to the pixel resolution of the image plane. It does, however, result in a process that is independent of scene complexity.

View interpolation can be looked upon as an image warping procedure. Two images from different but adjacent viewpoints have been constructed using a (non-linear) perspective projection; they can be seen as relating to each other in image space by some warping transformation. With synthetic imagery we can establish complete correspondence between pixels and, leaving aside some geometric problems (discussed in the next section), we can set up a dense warp script between two reference views. Figure 21.3 shows the idea for a single pair of corresponding pixels in two reference images. The correspondence tells us how a pixel in the first reference image moves towards a pixel in the second reference image. View interpolation can then be quickly carried out for any in-between image by moving pixels in either (or both) reference images along their warp path. This is precisely the approach taken by Chen et al. in their Virtual Museum work undertaken in 1993. Note at this point that we are assuming a

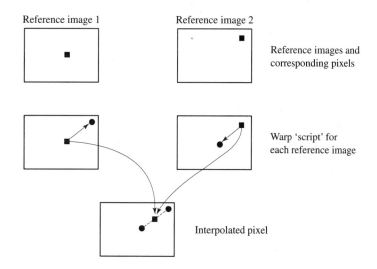

Figure 21.3

Simple view interpolation: a single pair of corresponding pixels define a path in image space from which an interpolated view can be constructed.

Reference image 1

Reference image 2

Reference images and corresponding pixels

Warp 'script' for each reference image

Interpolated pixel

linear path in image space between corresponding pixels. This assumption imposes certain constraints on camera movement between the two reference viewpoints and we deal with this shortly.

It is possible to implement view interpolation using one of a number of strategies. The main differences between these relate to the way in which visibility problems are resolved which in turn depends on whether we are dealing with photographic or synthetic imagery. Visibility problems will always occur and the severity of these, and whether they can be ignored or not, relates to how far the interpolated viewpoint is from the reference viewpoints.

The important implication here is that we require correspondence at the outset. Pixel correspondence can be established if we have knowledge of the external camera parameters; this is no problem with synthetic imagery but with photographic imagery we are up against the classic problems that occur in computer vision and, as we have already hinted, these tend to be dealt with in part by manual intervention or the injection of some constraint into the system that facilitates its establishment.

With this process two categories of visibility problems occur. Areas in a reference view may become obscured in an interpolated view – this is variously called image folding or overlaps. This is easily shown for a single point in the scene (Figure 21.4(a)). P_1 and P_2 project onto different pixels in the reference view but onto a single pixel in the interpolated view. Equivalently many pixels in the reference image may map into a single pixel in the interpolated image. We can resolve this problem by using depth information.

Conversely areas hidden in the reference image may need to become visible in the interpolated view (Figure 21.4(b)). This is known variously as holes or

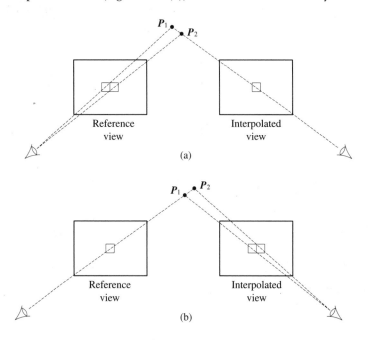

Figure 21.4
Image folding and stretching in view interpolation. (a) Image overlaps or image folding (two pixels map into one in the interpolated view). (b) Image holes or image stretching (one pixel maps into two in the interpolated view).

image stretching (because it can also occur because of zooming) where a single pixel in the reference image may map into many in the interpolated image. Theoretically there is nothing to be done about image holes – we cannot recover information that was not there (in the reference image) in the first place but we can adopt strategies to alleviate the problem. In particular, as we increase the number of reference images that represent a scene, less and less information will be occluded and fewer holes will occur in any interpolated image provided we use information from all the images.

Thus despite their geometric symmetry we note that the image overlap problem can be routinely solved but the hole problem requires some kind of heuristic or approximate solution – it has no exact solution. With both overlaps and holes we can detect where they occur in the interpolated image. Overlaps occur when we attempt to assign a value to a pixel that already has a value and holes occur where no value has been assigned. This enables us to adopt strategies that are local to the problem pixel to resolve the problem.

Another potential problem is that view-dependent illumination differences can occur. For example, we know that specular reflection is not independent of viewpoint and this means that the same point in a scene may have a different colour in different views. A basic strategy to deal with some of these problems is to use the cross-dissolve operation of conventional image morphing. This will simply blur areas in the image with contributions, in the appropriate proportion from the reference images.

We now look in more detail at view interpolation – in particular the details of algorithms that have been used.

(21.3.1) View interpolation – geometry

We first look at a constrained problem that demonstrates, without the visibility complications, the overall principles and geometric considerations. Let us consider two reference images where every point in one image is visible in the other. If we can establish pixel by pixel correspondence then we have a motion or flow field between pairs of pixels in the two reference images and we can move pixels in either image along paths determined by the motion field into their new positions in the interpolated image.

This approach is taken in recent work by Seitz and Dyer who show that if certain constraints are satisfied then interpolating in two-dimensional space between two projections – image interpolation – gives valid in-between views. The key word here is 'valid'. View interpolation by warping a reference image into an interpolated image proceeds in two-dimensional image plane space. A warping operation is just that – it changes the shape of the two-dimensional projection of objects. Clearly the interpolation should proceed so that the projected shape of the objects in the interpolated projection is consistent with their real three-dimensional shape. In other words, the interpolated view must be equivalent to a view that would be generated in the normal way (using either a camera or a conventional graphics pipeline) by changing the viewpoint from the reference viewpoint to that of the interpolated view. A 'non-valid' view means that the interpolated view does not preserve the object shape. If this condition does not hold then the interpolated views will correspond to an object whose shape is distorting in real three-dimensional space. This is exactly what happens in conventional image morphing between two shapes. 'Impossible', non-existent or arbitrary shapes occur as in-between images because the motivation here is to appear to change one object into an entirely different one. The distinction between valid and invalid view interpolation is shown in Figure 21.5.

An example where linear interpolation of images produces valid interpolated views is the case where the image planes remain parallel (Figure 21.6). Physically this situation would occur if a camera was allowed to move parallel to its image plane (and optionally zoom in and out). If we let the combined viewing and perspective transformations (Chapter 24) be V_0 and V_1 for the two reference

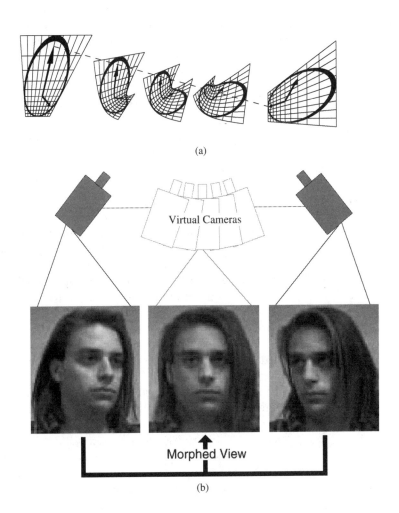

(a)

(b)

Figure 21.5
Distinguishing between valid and invalid view interpolation. In (a), using a standard (morphing) approach of linear interpolation produces gross shape deformation (this does not matter if we are morphing between two different objects – it becomes part of the effect). (b) The interpolated (or morphed view) is consistent with object shape (Courtesy of Steve Seitz.)

Figure 21.6
Moving the camera from C_0 to C_1 (and zooming) means that the image planes remain parallel and P_i can be linearly interpolated from P_0 and P_1 (after Seitz and Dyer).

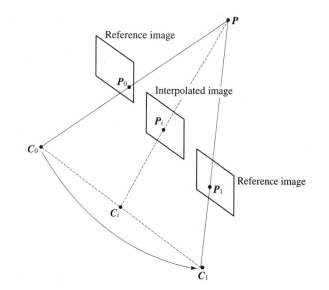

images then the transformation for an in-between image can be obtained by linear interpolation:

$$V_i = (1-s)\ V_0 + sV_1$$

If we consider a pair of corresponding points in the reference images p_0 and p_1 which are projections of world space point P, then it is easily shown (see Seitz and Dyer) that the projection of point P from the intermediate (interpolated) viewpoint is given by linear interpolation:

$$p_i = p_0(1-s) + p_1 s$$
$$= V_i P$$

In other words, linear interpolation of pixels along a path determined by pixel correspondence in two reference images is exactly equivalent to projecting the scene point that resulted in these pixels through a viewing and projective transformation given by an intermediate camera position providing parallel views are maintained; in other words, using the transformation V_i which would be obtained if V_0 and V_1 were linearly interpolated. Note also that we are interpolating views that would correspond to those obtained if we had moved the camera in a straight line from C_0 to C_1. In other words, the interpolated view corresponds to the camera position:

$$C_i = (sC_x, C_y, 0)$$

If we have reference views that are not related in this way then the interpolation has to be preceded (and followed) by an extra transformation. This is the general situation where the image planes of the reference views and the image plane of the required or interpolated view have no parallel relationship. The first transformation, which Seitz and Dyer call a 'prewarp', warps the reference images so that they appear to have been taken by a camera moving in a plane parallel to its image plane. The pixel interpolation, or morphing, can then be performed as in the previous paragraph and the result of this is postwarped to form the final interpolated view, which is the view required from the virtual camera position. A simple geometric illustration of the process is shown in Figure 21.7. Here R_0 and R_1 are the reference images. Prewarping these to R_0' and R_1' respectively means that we can now linearly interpolate these rectified images to produce R_i'. This is then postwarped to produce the required R_i. An important consequence of this method is that although the warp operation is image based we require knowledge of the viewpoints involved to effect the pre- and postwarp transformations. Again this has ramifications for the context in which the method is used, implying that in the case of photographic imagery we have to record or recover the camera viewpoints.

The prewarping and postwarping transformations are derived as follows. First, we have shown in Chapter 24 that any two perspective views that share the same centre of projection are related by a planar projective transformation – a 3×3 matrix obtained from the combined viewing perspective transformation V. Thus R_0 and R_1 are related to R_0' and R_1' by two such matrices T_0 and T_1. The procedure is thus as follows:

(1)   Prewarp R_0 and R_1 using T_0^{-1} and T_1^{-1} to produce R_0' and R_1'

(2)   Interpolate to calculate R_i', C_i and T_i.

(3)   Apply T_i to R_i' to give image R_i.

We will now look at a set of recent examples of the techniques that we have outlined for image-based rendering.

Figure 21.7
Prewarping reference images, interpolating and postwarping in view interpolation (after Seitz and Dyer).

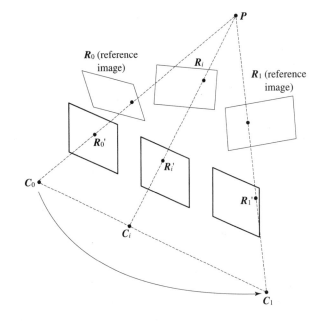

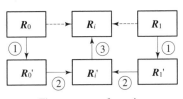

Three-step transformation sequence

View interpolation case studies

View interpolation of synthetic imagery

In a report that preceded his paper on QuickTime by two years, Chen et al. describe a view interpolation method that, with some constraints, allows the reconstruction of a projection from an arbitrary viewpoint from two reference images. For a pair of adjacent images, pixel by pixel correspondence is known from the depth information and the virtual camera parameters and thus an image flow field can be established. Each pixel in one reference image is related to a pixel in the other by a vector from the image flow field. To generate an in-between image, such a vector is linearly interpolated and a pixel is moved from one of the source images to a destination in the interpolated image specified by the interpolated image flow vector. (In fact Chen pre-computes the transformations from the camera movement and reduces them to three-dimensional (screen space) offset vectors for each pixel. Pre-computation of the offset vectors between reference or source images is facilitated by making constraints on the nature of the virtual camera between reference viewpoints.)

The first visibility problem – image folding or image overlap – is handled by a Z-buffer algorithm, the depths of each pixel having been retained in the reference images. Image stretching (or holes) are handled by literally stretching the image. Any missing pixels are filled with a colour interpolated from its neighbours. Holes are identified by using a reserved background colour to initialize the interpolated image. Any pixel that has this colour after the transformation is then subject to an adjacent pixel colour interpolation. Although this simple method cannot recover information hidden in both source images, Chen et al. point out that this can be recovered by ray casting to render the missing pixels.

Figure 21.8 (Colour Plate) shows the algorithm in operation. Figure 21.8(a) shows the pixels from the first key or source moved into their new position when the camera is moved to the right. Note that many holes result. The result of the operation after both sources have been composited is shown in Figure 21.8(b). (The mapping can be bi-directional and both pixels from both source images can be mapped into the destination image.) This results in a reduction of the holes leaving scene features not visible in either image. Figure 21.8(c) shows that the number of such holes depends on the spacing between the two source images and Figure 21.8(d) shows the final result after the holes have been filled.

View interpolation of photographic panoramas

The main practical difference between interpolating photographic and synthetic imagery is that we need to establish correspondence between two reference images before we can proceed with the interpolation. If we have total correspondence then the problem reduces to that of view interpolation of synthetic imagery. Thus we have to resort to computer vision techniques to find correspondence. However, the requirements are not so severe. In applications such as shape from stereo we need to find pixel by pixel correspondence to find pixel by pixel depth variation. Generally we do this by searching for correspondence along epipolar lines. One of the problems is that the pixel intensity within a line segment may exhibit insufficient variance to enable correspondence to be established. In the case of view interpolation we can work with line segments rather than individual pixels. Seitz and Dyer point out that correspondence or shape information within uniform regions is not necessary to predict in-between views. In other words, the correspondence problem is not so severe. We may also have to estimate camera position from the reference views although in most applications this will be known. Camera positions can be found – but only to within a scale factor – from pairs of corresponding points called tie points.

In recently reported work, McMillan and Bishop deal with the view interpolation of cylindrical panoramas. This approach potentially solves the main disadvantage of QuickTime VR which is that the user can only hop from viewpoint to viewpoint. Thus the method retains the advantage of reprojecting from panoramas – the ability to generate planar views from a fixed viewpoint but in any gaze direction – while being potentially able to generate any view in between two or more reference cylinders.

McMillan and Bishop first find correspondence between a pair of cylinders using the epipolar geometry for a pair of cylinders. The epipolar geometry of cylinders is such that to find the point on cylinder B corresponding to a point on cylinder A we search along a sinusoid on the surface of B.

Next the angular part of the disparity between the reference cylinders and a new cylinder is established using a simple geometric relationship. Finally the angular part of the disparity is substituted into the epipolar constraint equation and the height part found. This enables a forward mapping from one of the reference cylinders onto the new or interpolated cylinder. The process is shown for one pixel in Figure 21.9. Given that the relationships between reference cylinders can be calculated offline, McMillan and Bishop describe their system as an image-based renderer which takes as input the reference cylinders and automatically generates arbitrary cylindrical panoramas from which the desired planar views are then obtained.

The authors formalise the problem of image based rendering by introducing the term 'plenoptic function' and defining this in computer graphics terms as the set of all possible environment maps for a given scene. For example, Figure 21.1 shows a set of environment maps for a scene constrained to an eye-level plane. Such a function is in effect a scene representation and to generate a view of the scene we 'plug-in' the viewpoint coordinates into the representation – the plenoptic function – and generate a projection (as shown in Figure 21.1). The authors state:

Within this framework we can state the following problem definition for image based rendering. Given a set of discrete samples (complete or incomplete) from the plenoptic function, the goal of image based rendering is to generate a continuous representation of that function. This problem statement provides for many avenues of exploration, such as how to optimally select sample points and how to best reconstruct a continuous function from these samples.

Figure 21.9
(a) Establishing correspondence using epipolar constraint searching along the quadratic in B.
(b) Corresponding points on A and B enable the angular part of the disparity β to be found. (c) Substituting into the epipolar constraint equation enables the height part of the disparity *v* to be found.

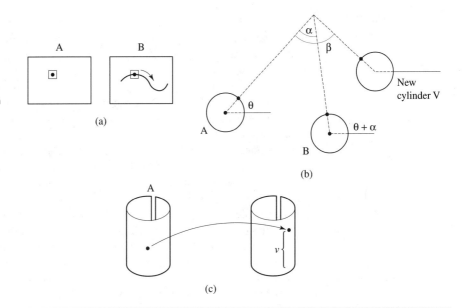

21.4 Photo-modelling for image-based rendering

In one of the first comprehensive studies of photo-modelling for image-based rendering, Debevec et al. describe an approach with a number of interesting and potentially important features. Their basic approach is to derive sufficient information from sparse views of a scene to facilitate image-based rendering (although the derived model can also be used in a conventional rendering system). The emphasis of their work is architectural scenes and is based on three innovations:

(1) **photogrammetric modelling** in which they recover a three-dimensional geometric model of a building based on simple volumetric primitives together with the camera viewpoints from a set of sparse views;

(2) **view-dependent texture mapping** which is used to render the recovered model;

(3) **model-based stereo** which is used to solve the correspondence problem (and thus enable view interpolation) and the recovery of detail not modelled in (1).

Debevec et al. state that their approach is successful because:

it splits the task of modelling from images into tasks that are easily accomplished by a person (but not by a computer algorithm), and tasks which are easily performed by a computer algorithm (but not by a person).

The photogrammetric modelling process involves the user viewing a set of photographs of a building and associating a set of volumetric primitives with the photographic views to define an approximate geometric model. This is done by invoking a component of the model, such as a rectangular solid, and interactively associating edges in the model with edges in the scene. In this way a box, say, can be fitted semi-automatically to a view or views that contain a box as a structural element. This manual intervention enables a complete geometric model to be derived from the photographs even although only parts of the model may be visible in the scene. The accuracy of the geometric model – that is, the difference between the model and the reality – depends on how much detail the user invokes, the nature of the volumetric primitives and the nature of the scene. The idea is to obtain a geometric model that reflects the structure of the building and which can be used in subsequent processing to derive camera positions and facilitate a correspondence algorithm. Thus a modern tower block may be represented by a single box and depth variations, which occur over a face due to the windows that are contained in a plane parallel to the wall plane, are at this stage of the process ignored.

The process is identical in principle to CAD-based vision (Chapter 15). Here pre-stored volumetric models are tested against projection of scenes that contain objects constrained to be made up of elements contained in a pre-stored vocabulary of primitives. The main difference is manual intervention – a user invokes the appropriate volumetric primitives and their spatial juxtaposition. Also, the user has to correspond the model with the projection. In CAD-based vision the idea is that these two functions are performed completely automatically.

Once a complete geometric model has been defined, a reconstruction algorithm is invoked, for each photographic view. The purpose of this process is to recover the camera viewpoints which, you will recall, are necessary for view interpolation, together with the world coordinates of the model, which are necessary if the model is going to be used in a conventional rendering system. This is done by projecting the geometric model, using a hypothesized viewpoint, onto the photographic views and comparing the position of the image edges with the position of the projected model edges. The algorithm works by minimizing an objective function which operates on the error between observed image edges and the projected model edge. Correspondence between model edges and image edges having already been established, the algorithm has to proceed towards the solution without getting stuck at a local minimum. An illustration of the concept of the process is shown in Figure 21.10 (Colour Plate).

These two processes – photogrammetric modelling and reconstruction – extract sufficient information to enable a conventional rendering process that Debevec calls 'view-dependent texture mapping'. Here a new view of a building is generated by projecting the geometric model from the required viewpoint, treating the reference views as texture maps and reprojecting these from the new viewpoint onto the geometric model. The implication here is that the building is 'over sampled' and any one point will appear in two or more photographic views. Thus when a new or virtual view is generated there will, for each pixel in the new view, be a choice of texture maps with (perhaps) different values for the same point on the building due to specularities and unmodelled geometric detail. This problem is approached by mixing the contributions in inverse proportion to the angles that the new view makes with the reference view directions

Figure 21.11
The pixel that corresponds
to point **P** in the virtual view
receives a weighted average
of the corresponding pixels
in the reference images.
The weights are inversely
proportional to θ_1 and θ_2.

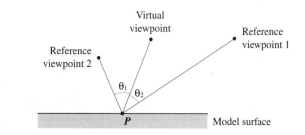

Figure 21.11
The pixel that corresponds
to point **P** in the virtual view
receives a weighted average
of the corresponding pixels
in the reference images.
The weights are inversely
proportional to θ_1 and θ_2.

as shown in Figure 21.11. Hence the term view-dependent texture mapping: the contributions are selected and mixed according to the position of the virtual viewpoint with respect to the reference views.

The accuracy of this rendering is limited to the detail captured by the geometric model and there is a difference between the real geometry and that of the model. The extent of this difference depends on the labour that the user has put into the interactive modelling phase and the assumption is that the geometric model will be missing such detail as window recesses and so on. For example, a facade modelled as a plane may receive a texture that contains such depth information as shading differences and this can lead to images that do not look correct. The extent of this depends on the difference between the required viewing angle and the angle of the view from which the texture map was selected. Debevec et al. go on to extend their method by using the geometric model to facilitate a correspondence algorithm that enables a depth map to be calculated and the geometric detail missing from the original model to be extracted. Establishing correspondence also enables view interpolation.

This process is called 'model-based' stereo and it uses the geometric model as a priori information which enables the algorithm to cope with views that have been taken from relatively far apart – one of the practical motivations of the work is that it operates with a sparse set of views. (Chapter 16 contains a discussion on traditional stereo correspondence algorithms that try to operate without prior knowledge of scene structure. Here the extent of the correspondence problem predominantly depends on how close the two views are to each other.)

Consider two photographic views that Debevec et al. refer to as the key and offset view (Figure 21.12 – Colour Plate). A third view is generated which is obtained by projecting the offset image onto the geometric model and reprojecting the model onto the image plane of the key camera; an operation made possible by the fact that an approximate geometric model has been established. This is known as the warped offset view and correspondence is established between the key view and the warped offset view (rather than the key and offset views). This has a number of implications.

- The warping of the offset view removes foreshortening and enables a correspondence algorithm to proceed using simple correlation techniques (along epipolar lines). As we discuss in Chapter 16, the warping or geometric distortion between structure in stereo pairs is possibly the biggest bar to correspondence establishment using a simple correlation-based approach.

Figure 21.13
Recovering detailed
geometry from disparity
between the key image and
the warped offset image.

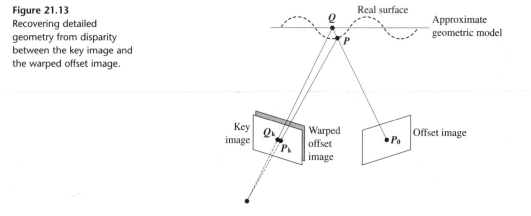

● Epipolar lines in the key image correspond to epipolar lines in the warped offset image.

● The difference between the (approximate) geometric model set up by the user and the reality can be established by looking at the disparity between the key and warped offset image. Alternatively we can say that any real point that coincides with the approximate geometric model will have zero disparity between the key and warped offset images.

Consider the third implication with respect to Figure 21.13. This shows a simple example of a point P that is located on a real structure that does not correspond to the geometric structure. Such a point is imaged as P_0 in the offset image and as P_k in the key image. This enables a third image to be formed – the warped offset image – by projecting P_0 onto the model and viewing the result from the key viewpoint. This projects as point Q_k in the warped offset image. Establishing correspondence between P_k and Q_k reveals a disparity that corresponds to the distance between P and Q or the distance between the real surface and the model surface. Calculating the corresponding depth enables the model to be refined to include the detail missing from it when the user set up the geometric model. If there is no disparity between the key image and the warped offset image then the model and the real surface coincide.

21.5 The complexity problem – organizing scene data

Having looked at image-based techniques as a way to cope with real-time generation of complex scenes we will now look at variations that can be made to standard rendering. The first problem is fairly obvious and will generally be context dependent. An issue raised by extremely high scene complexity is memory cost – to render a scene quickly we need to have all of it in memory – and we need to devote much more effort to data structure organization than is normal in computer graphics. For example, in a very complex scene such as the interior of an office block we would need to have something equivalent to a secondary data structure that broke the scene down into manageable portions. The user's position would be coupled to the secondary data structure which would point to the appropriate section of data needed to render the current environment that the user occupies. This is straightforward for an interior scene and more problematic for an exterior scene such as a cityscape.

For a building interior, the normal computer graphics hierarchical organization can be used. A building consists of corridors and rooms. A room has contents, which may be common to more than one room and so on. If, simplistically, when we are in a room we cannot see into another room then we only need to consider, for rendering, the representation of the room we are currently in. The coupling between the data structure and the viewpoint interaction can easily be implemented by a two-dimensional map for each floor of the building (given that the viewpoint is locked into a plane parallel to the ground plane). As the viewpoint moves, its position is plotted on the map. Each element on the map contains a pointer to that part of the data structure currently required to render the part of the scene that the user is in. Simplistically all the elements in the two-dimensional map of the room would contain pointers to the room data. Bi-directional 'sensors' can be positioned at each entrance so that when a user enters a room this action causes the new data to be accessed. The two-dimensional map can also be used for viewpoint constraint to prevent a user walking through walls. Thus in this case the secondary data structure is a two-dimensional map with a pointer out of each region in the map that represents a visually bounded part of the scene. Such a device can also be used to predict the next part of the scene that has to be accessed by the renderer.

(21.5.1) The complexity problem – object representation

As early as 1976, one of the pioneers of three-dimensional computer graphics, James H. Clark, wrote:

> It makes no sense to use 500 polygons in describing an object if it covers only 20 raster units of the display ... For example, when we view the human body from a very large distance, we might need to present only specks for the eyes, or perhaps just a block for the head, totally eliminating the eyes from consideration ... these issues have not been addressed in a unified way.

Did Clark at that time realize that not many years after he had written the paper, 500 000 polygon objects would become fairly commonplace and that complex scenes might contain millions of polygons?

Existing systems tend to address this problem in a somewhat ad hoc manner. For example, many cheap virtual reality systems adopt a two-level representation switching in surface detail, such as the numbers on the buttons of a telephone as the viewer moves closer to it. This produces an annoying visual disturbance as the detail blinks on and off. More considered approaches are now being developed and lately there has been a substantial increase in the number of papers published in this area.

What would we like to do? When we render an object we would like to use the viewing distance and the object size to index into a data structure at an appropriate level of detail. As we moved towards or away from the object, the geometric detail that we fetched from the database would be correspondingly larger or smaller. Why is this difficult? Because the de facto representation is polygon mesh and the commonest data generation methods produce some kind of single polygon mesh. We can easily generate very large numbers of polygons from an object using any of the modelling methods described in Chapter 2, but given such a structure how do we then produce a hierarchy of representations with fewer and fewer polygons? And in such an approach we need to ensure that we can traverse the levels without producing blinks on the screen.

Such considerations seem necessary and cannot be dismissed by relying on increased polygon throughput of the workstations of the future. The position we are in at the moment is that mainstream virtual reality platforms produce a visually inadequate result even from fairly simple scenes. We have to look forward not only to dealing with the defects in the image synthesis of such scenes, but to being able to handle scenes of real-world complexity implying many millions of polygons. The much vaunted 'immersive' applications of virtual reality will never become acceptable unless we can cope with scenes of such complexity. Current hardware is very far away from being to deal with a complex scene in real time to the level of quality attainable for single object scenes.

An obvious solution to the problem is to generate a polygon mesh at the finest level of detail and then use this representation to spawn a set of coarser descriptions. As the scene is rendered an appropriate level of detail is selected. Certain algorithms that use this principle have emerged from time to time in computer graphics. An example of a method that facilitates a polygon mesh at any level of detail is bicubic parametric patches (Chapter 7). Here we take a patch description and turn it into a polygon description. At the same time we can easily control the number of polygons that are generated for each patch and relate this to local surface curvature. This is exactly what is done in patch rendering where a geometric criterion is used to control the extent of the subdivision and produce an image free of geometric aliasing (visible polygon edges in silhouette). The price we pay for this approach is the expense and difficulty of getting the patch description in the first place. But in any case we could build the original patch representation and construct a pyramid of polygon mesh representations offline.

The idea of storing a 'detail pyramid' and accessing an appropriate level is established for two-dimensional imagery as image pyramids (Chapter 11). In the case of mip-mapping, for example, texture maps are stored in a detail hierarchy and a fine detail map selected when the projection of the map on the screen is large. In the event that the map projects onto just one pixel, a single pixel texture map – the average of the most detailed map – is selected. Also, in this method the problem of avoiding a jump when going from one level to another is carefully addressed and an approximation to a continuous level of detail is obtained by interpolation between two maps.

The problem of simplifying a polygon mesh that is too detailed is referred to as 'mesh optimization'. Usually this means taking a single object, represented by a very large set of polygons extracted from some data collection scheme (like the output from a marching cubes algorithm applied to X-ray CT data), and reducing it to a simpler form without the loss of any geometry. This means that areas where the surface exhibits a low curvature are simplified most.

The diversity of current approaches underlines the relative newness of the field. Currently techniques are being developed for medical images, which generate very large numbers of polygons from the marching cube algorithm (Chapter 22). Typically the marching cubes algorithm, which you will recall can output up to five triangles per voxel, can easily produce two million triangles from a medium resolution voxel set. A direct and simple approach for triangular meshes derived from voxel sets was reported by Schroeder et al. in 1992. Here the algorithm considers each vertex on a surface. By looking at the triangles that contribute to or share the vertex, a number of criteria can be enumerated and used to determine whether these triangles can be merged into a single one exclusive of the vertex under consideration. For example, we can invoke the 'reduce the number of triangles where the surface curvature is low' argument by measuring the variance in the surface normals of the triangles that share the vertex. Alternatively we could consider the distance from the vertex to an (average) plane through all the other vertices of the sharing triangles (Figure 21.14). This is a local approach that considers vertices in the geometry of their immediate surroundings.

A non-local approach can be seen in the work of G. Turk in 1991 and 1992. Although the original motivation for this work was to produce a single simplified mesh, with around a few hundred vertices, from a surface that contained many thousands of vertices, his method can be used to produce a hierarchy of models.

The algorithm can be described as follows:

(1) A set of points is placed on the polygons of the original surface which will eventually form the vertices of the new polygonal mesh. This is accomplished by first distributing a set of points randomly over the surface, then using 'point-repulsion' within the framework of a relaxation method to

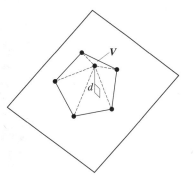

Figure 21.14
A simple vertex deletion criterion. Delete **V**? Measure d, the distance from **V** to the (average) plane through the triangles that share **V**.

ensure that the points are evenly distributed. The motivation is that such a set of points will be amenable to the construction of a new polygon mesh which will best retain the location, curvature and geometry of the original surface. (Note that this is a completely different approach to the previous one in that new vertices are created. The previous method functioned by deleting vertices that were deemed to be unnecessary, retaining a subset of the original vertices.) To do this, each point P is visited and its nearby points ascertained. The repulsive forces that the nearby points exert on P are calculated and stored. When this process is complete the algorithm revisits each point and repositions it according to its repulsive force vectors. The overall process iterates and the random distribution has turned into an even distribution of points over the surface. This may seem a complex process but we have to remember that a surface can be of any arbitrary shape. The creation of evenly distributed new vertices is that part of the process that makes it possible to create a hierarchy of representations.

(2) The second step is to connect the new vertices together to form a triangular mesh. This has to be done in a way that retains the connectedness of the original surface. The new points cannot simply be joined on a distance basis and carry in themselves no connectivity information – this has to be regained from the original representation. An intermediate polygonal surface is set up which Turk calls a 'mutual tessellation'. This mesh uses as vertices both the original vertices and the new vertices that the previous step has dispersed evenly over the surface represented by the original mesh. Then the old vertices are removed one at a time. It is at this stage that topological consistency checks are made. Figure 21.15 shows an illustration of the different stages in the algorithm.

Figure 21.15
Re-tiling of a radiation iso-dose surface. Upper left: Original surface. Upper right: Candidate vertices after point-repulsion. Lower left: Mutual tessellation. Lower right: Final tessellation. (Courtesy G. Turk). *Source*: Turk, G. (1992) 'Re-Tiling Polygonal Surfaces' in Siggraph Proceedings *Computer Graphics* **26** (2), July.

Despite its power, a drawback of the method is its inability to deal with the surface curvature problem – areas of high surface curvature should be tiled with more polygons than areas of low surface curvature. The algorithm results in a mesh in which the polygons are all approximately the same size. Turk deals with this problem by setting up a procedure that measures the surface curvature over the original surface and then concentrating the position of the new points in areas of high surface curvature.

Turk also addresses the problem of interpolation. If we are going to have a pyramid of models then the levels of detail in the hierarchy will be separated by discrete jumps. We would like to index into such a representation, using a continuous indexing parameter, which then causes a 'detail interpolation' between the two neighbouring levels (just as we did with mip-mapping in Chapter 4). Turk does this by 'flattening' some of the vertices and polygons of a higher-detailed model onto the polygons of the model with less detail. Turk refers to this process as 'inflating' the low detail model towards the higher detail one.

Being able to represent objects in the scene at many levels of detail, however, is only part of the story. What criteria do we use to select a particular level of detail? We have mentioned the obvious criteria of viewing distance and projected area in pixels but these are somewhat crude in the following sense. In the context of a walk through a very complex environment we need to maintain constant (interactive) frame generation times. If frame rate drops much below this then the quality of the interaction starts to diminish and the user experiences jerkiness. If we independently select a level of detail for each object in the scene, rather than considering the scene as a whole, then the overall frame generation time will be determined by the number of objects in the viewing frustum and their complexity. Individual selection of an appropriate level of detail for each object does not necessarily guarantee that the frame time will be less than a chosen limit. Funkhauser and Sequin point out that what is required is an image synthesis approach that bounds the frame generation time to some specified limit. In other words, a rendering strategy is selected that ensures the frame generation time falls within this limit. The limit can be fixed or itself react to the current interaction. When a user slows down or comes to a halt it can increase thereby allowing more detail onto the screen.

They suggest a level of detail selection algorithm that adapts to overall scene complexity. This they suggest should be predictive, rather than reactive (based on the time taken to render previous frames), as sudden changes in scene complexity often occur in walkthroughs. (Reactive schemes are commonly used in flight simulators where level of detail selection is based on the render time of previous frames.)

They do this by evaluating a *benefit* heuristic that is maximized subject to a *cost* heuristic that must be less than the required frame generation time. The cost heuristic is simply the overall rendering cost per object through the rendering pipeline. The benefit heuristic depends primarily on the projected size of the object in the image plane – larger object contribute more to the final image – and the level of detail or accuracy of the representation. Other factors can be built into the benefit heuristic – some objects may be more important than others in a particular context, objects in the periphery of the viewer's vision may be considered less important, and so on.

The scene complexity problem – hidden surface removal

Research into hidden surface removal tended to predominate in computer graphics in the 1970s but then with the industry acceptance of the Z-buffer algorithm, hidden surface removal was regarded as solved and the main research effort in rendering moved towards light transport models in the 1980s (although research continued into methods of improving the Z-buffer algorithm – dealing with aliasing and image composition methods). The Z-buffer algorithm suffers from well-known efficiency problems and perhaps the demands of virtual reality image generation will re-emphasize the importance of efficient hidden surface removal.

The disadvantage of the Z-buffer is that it causes unseen polygons to be rendered. If we wish to retain the advantages of the traditional Z-buffer approach then this is a major cost factor that we must avoid. The main advantage of the Z-buffer, apart from its simplicity, is that the computing cost per polygon is low. It exploits image space coherence and adjacent pixels in a polygon projection are handled by a simple incremental calculation. However, this advantage rapidly diminishes as the scene to be rendered becomes more and more complex and the polygons smaller and smaller. The set-up computations at the polygon vertices predominate over the pixel by pixel calculations.

Depth complexity of a scene is a function of the number of objects in a scene just as much as object complexity, and scenes that we wish to render in virtual reality applications will tend to possess both depth and object complexity.

An approach reported by Greene et al. in 1993 takes the basic Z-buffer algorithm and develops it into a method that is suitable for complex scenes. Compared with a standard Z-buffer, Greene reports a reduction in rendering time from over an hour to 6.45 seconds on a complex scene containing 53 million polygons (although an important practical factor that enables this reduction is the fact that the large scene is constructed by replicating a smaller scene of 15 000 polygons). It does this by exploiting object space, image space and temporal coherence whereas the Z-buffer, as we know, only employs image space coherence. Another important attribute of the algorithm is that it can be implemented on existing hardware designs with only minor design changes.

The reason for the inefficiency of the Z-buffer algorithm is that it is an image space algorithm. It exploits image space coherence but not object space coherence. An algorithm that does exploit object space coherence is a ray tracing algorithm that uses a spatial subdivision scheme (an octree, for example) for ray tracking. For each ray cast, the first surface that the ray hits is the visible surface and no surfaces behind are considered by the algorithm. (A ray tracing algorithm, on the other hand, does not exploit image space coherence and each pixel calculation is independent of every other.) Greene's development recognizes this and employs spatial subdivision to incorporate object space coherence in the traditional Z-buffer. It also uses a so-called 'Z-pyramid' to further accelerate the traditional Z-buffer image space coherence.

The object space coherence is set up by constructing a conventional octree for the scene and using this to guide the rendering strategy. A node of an octree is hidden if all the faces of the cube associated with that node are hidden with respect to the Z-buffer. If such is the case then, of course, all the polygons or complete objects that the cube contains are hidden. This fact leads to the obvious rendering strategy of starting at the root of the tree and 'rendering' octree cubes, by rendering each face of the cube, to determine whether the whole cube is hidden or not. If it is not hidden we proceed with the geometry inside the cube. Thus a large number of hidden polygons are culled at the cost of rendering cube faces. So we are imposing a rendering order on the normally arbitrary polygon ordering in the Z-buffer. Greene points out that this in itself can be expensive – if the cube being rendered projects onto a large number of pixels – and this consideration leads to further exploiting the normal Z-buffer advantage of image space coherence.

The Z-pyramid is a strategy that attempts to determine complete polygon visibility without pixel by pixel elaboration. A Z-pyramid is a detail hierarchy with the original Z-buffer at the lowest level. At each level there is a half resolution Z-buffer, where the z value for a cell is obtained from the largest of the z values of the four cells in the next level down (you might say a depth mip-map). Maintaining the Z-pyramid involves tracking down the hierarchy in the direction of finer resolution until we encounter a depth that is already as far away as the current depth value. Using the Z-pyramid to test the visibility of a cube face involves finding the finest detail level whose corresponding projection in screen space just covers the projection of the face. Then it is simply a matter of comparing the nearest vertex depth of the face against the value in the Z-pyramid. Using the Z-pyramid to test a complete polygon for visibility is the same except that the screen space bounding box of the polygon is used.

In this way the technique tries to make the best of both object and image space coherence. Using spatial subdivision to accelerate hidden surface removal is a old idea and seems to have been first mooted by Schumaker et al. in 1969. Here the application was flight simulation where the real-time constraint was, in 1969, a formidable problem.

Temporal coherence is exploited by retaining the visible cubes from the previous frame. For the current frame the polygons within these cubes are rendered first and the cubes marked as such. The algorithm then proceeds as normal. This strategy plays on the usual event that most of the cubes from the previous frame will still be visible – a few will become invisible in the current frame and a few cubes, invisible in the previous frame, will become visible.

Further reading

Clark's discussion of the problems of object representation are to be found in the paper published in 1976. The work of G. Turk was originally motivated by texture generation and appears in the two papers given below, together with some excellent explanatory images. Mesh generation occurs in finite element techniques where the need is to generate a mesh by subdividing a surface so that the elements of the mesh can be used to model some physical phenomenon such as heat dissipation or stress and strain. A review of work in this area is given in the paper by Ho-Lee.

Chen S.E. (1995). Quicktime VR – An image based approach to virtual environment navigation. *Proc. SIGGRAPH 1995*, 29–38

Clark J.H. (1976). Hierarchical geometric models for visible surface algorithms. *CACM*, **19**(10), 547–54

Debevec P.E., Taylor C.J. and Malik J. (1996). Modelling and rendering architecture from photographs: A hybrid geometry and image based approach. *Proc. SIGGRAPH 1996*, 11–20

Funkhauser T.A. and Sequin C.H. (1993). Adaptive display algorithm for interactive frame rates during visualization of complex virtual environments. *Proc. SIGGRAPH 1993*, 247–54

Greene N., Kass M. and Miller G. (1993). Hierarchical Z-buffer visibility. *Proc. SIGGRAPH 1993*, 231–8

Ho-Lee K. (1988). Finite element mesh generation methods: A review and classification. *Computer Aided Design*, **20**(1), 27–38

Lippman A. (1980). Movie maps: An application of the optical videodisc to computer graphics. *Proc. SIGGRAPH 1980*, 32–43

McMillan L. and Bishop G. (1995). Plenotopic modelling: An image based rendering system. *Proc. SIGGRAPH 1995*, 39–46

Regan M. and Pose R. (1994). Priority rendering with a virtual reality address re-calculation engine. *Proc. SIGGRAPH 1994*, 155–62

Schroeder W.J., Zarge J.A. and Lorenson W.E. (1992). Decimation of triangular meshes. *Proc. SIGGRAPH 1992*, 65–70

Schumaker R.A., Brand B., Guilliland M. and Sharp W. (1969). Applying Computer Generated Images to Visual Simulation. *Technical Report AFHRL-Tr-69*, US Airforce Human Resources Lab.

Seitz S.M. and Dyer C.R. (1996). View morphing. *Proc. SIGGRAPH 1996*, 21–30

Sutherland I.E., Sproull R. and Schumaker R.A. (1974, 1982). A characterization of ten hidden surface removal algorithms. *ACM Computing Surveys* 1974, and *Computer Graphics Tutorial* (ed. Beatty and Booth), IEEE Computer Society, MD, 1982

Turk G. (1991). Generating textures on arbitrary surfaces. *Computer Graphics*, **20**(4), 289–98 (Proc. SIGGRAPH '91)

Turk G. (1992). Re-tiling polygonal surfaces. *Computer Graphics*, **26**(2), 55–64 (Proc. SIGGRAPH '92)

Williams L. and Chen S.E. (1993). View interpolation for image synthesis. *Proc. SIGGRAPH 1993*, 279–88

Seeing the unseen – the computer image in medicine

In 1979 the Nobel prize in medicine was awarded to G.N. Hounsfield and A.M. Cormack for their respective contributions to the development of X-ray computer tomography. This was probably the most significant development in diagnostic medicine since the invention of the X-ray machine. The development was a classic wedding of new technology – in this case the advent of the minicomputer – to an established body of knowledge – the reconstruction of an image from a set of projections.

At a stroke the new machines revolutionized X-ray imagery while retaining the same basic X-ray technology. For the first time clinicians were able to view an X-ray in which information was confined to a single cross-sectional slice through some part of the body. This contrasts with traditional X-ray images where information is superimposed. In a chest X-ray, for example, we see the spine, the back ribs, and the front ribs as 'shadows' and organs such as the lungs are all superimposed in the X-ray. Much information is projected onto a single plane, forming the familiar image of superimposed shadows. To interpret these conventional X-ray images is a skilled and demanding perceptual task.

A tomographic X-ray on the other hand is a single cross-section that is a rectangular array of X-ray absorption coefficients. Such cross-sections, known as tomograms, are usually in a plane normal to the spine – called transaxial slices. A clinician can examine the information in a single cross-section without having to mentally separate other information from other planes. Figure 22.1 shows schematically how the system works. A source emanates a fan of X-rays in the plane of interest which are detected on the other side of the patient by an array of detectors. The source detector system rotates in this plane and a number of one-dimensional projections are built up. The value of each detected X-ray is a function of the sum of the absorption of the tissue it meets along its path. When sufficient projections are collected, an algorithm reconstructs a two-dimensional array of absorption coefficients. One of the most important facts concerning such a system may be intuitively apparent at this stage – the quality or resolution of the reconstruction depends on the amount of information or the number of projections collected, which in turn determines the X-ray dosage

Figure 22.1

A schematic illustration of X-ray transmission computer tomography (CT).

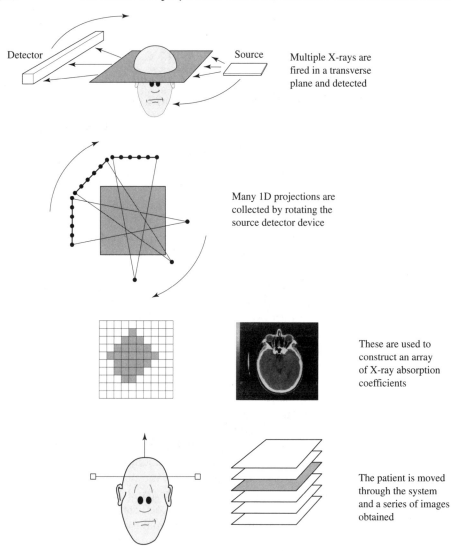

Multiple X-rays are fired in a transverse plane and detected

Many 1D projections are collected by rotating the source detector device

These are used to construct an array of X-ray absorption coefficients

The patient is moved through the system and a series of images obtained suffered by the patient. This fact has led to the development of different data collection technologies, or modalities as they are known. The basic idea of image reconstruction from projections remains unchanged, but the rays are changed. Other modalities are MRI (magnetic resonance imaging), PET (positron emission tomography) and ultrasonography. As well as their assumed harmlessness, alternative modalities produce different images inasmuch as the interaction of tissue with these different rays is different to X-ray interaction.

After data has been collected for a slice, the patient is moved a distance through the system and a new slice is constructed. Thus a stack of cross-sectional data is built up. The full name for the technology is X-ray transmission computed tomography – usually abbreviated to CT.

Normally these slices are examined by the clinician side by side. The images are known as tomograms. Recently computer graphics visualization techniques have entered the field and volume rendering has been used to reconstruct a three-dimensional object from the stack of slice data (Figure 22.2). Images are produced which attempt to represent the actual three-dimensional appearance of the structure being examined. This has the singular advantage that when a clinician needs to perceive the three-dimensional shape of an object, such as, say, a tumour that appears in a number of consecutive tomograms, he does not have to do this by imagination using cross-sectional information. It also brings the advantage of interactivity – the data volume can be rotated and viewed from different viewpoints, and cross-sections can be produced at any orientation in the three-dimensional space of the data.

The initial applications of this three-dimensional extension to conventional viewing techniques have tended to be in X-ray CT scans for planning orthopaedic surgery. Such problems as the positioning of plates and screws to strengthen a limb are more easily planned if the surgeon can interpret a three-dimensional view rather than consecutive slices.

When constructing a three-dimensional visualization one of the problems is that the data is usually non-isotropic. The resolution in a single plane may be 256×256 or 512×512 which in reality will represent a fraction of a square centimetre. However, the distance between planes can approach, or be more than, one centimetre and this discrepancy means that approximations are necessarily involved in computer graphics reconstructions.

Figure 22.2
CT and computer graphics visualization.

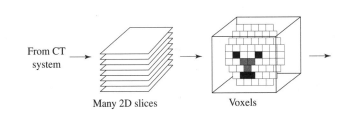

From CT system →

Many 2D slices   Voxels

Computer graphics visualization

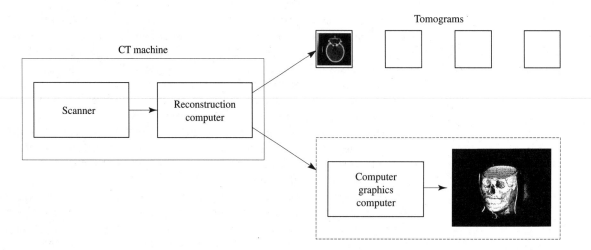

Figure 22.3
The current equipment set-up in medical imaging and visualization.

The overall nature of a complete system is shown in Figure 22.3. At the moment the scanner and reconstruction computer are part of a system that has been commercially available since the mid 1970s. The computer graphics visualization is not yet used routinely by clinicians and the separating dotted line indicates that this part of the system is carried out on separate computers in research institutes. It is likely that these two parts will merge and a single dedicated machine will perform both reconstruction and visualization.

In this chapter we will examine the theory of image reconstruction from projections and the subsequent visualization. Although medicine is by no means the only application of image reconstruction from projections it is now by far the most important and the most common. Also, visualization of tomographic data is one of the commonest applications of volume rendering and we will thus use medicine as an example throughout this chapter. We will of course not be concerned with the actual technology of the data collection system which is a subject in its own right.

22.1   The reconstruction problem

Consider first a single X-ray beam. An X-ray is attenuated as it passes through tissue according to

$$N = N_0 \exp(-\mu x)$$

where

N_0 is the number of incident photons

N is the number of photons travelling through the material without being scattered

μ is a linear absorption or attenuation coefficient that is a function of tissue density

x is the thickness of the material

If we have a composite material whose attenuation varies as a function of x then:

$$N = N_0 \exp(-\int \mu(x) \, dx)$$

or

$$\log N/N_0 = \int \mu(x) \, dx$$

In a CT system the factor on the LHS of this equation is measured by the system for as many beams as are required and these measurements, or projections, are used to reconstruct an image in the form of a two-dimensional array of absorption coefficients over the plane of the data collection. In Hounsfield's original system 28 000 measurements were taken to determine an array of 80×80 absorption coefficients.

Now consider the two-dimensional problem in more detail. We consider a thin slab of tissue in the x,y plane and assume that the tissue absorbs X-rays as some function of its density $\mu(x,y,z)$ at any point. If we shoot a set of rays parallel to the x axis (Figure 22.4(a)) then at each point along the y axis we can determine a ray sum and we have:

$$p(y) = k \int_L \mu(x,y) \, dx$$

where k is some factor and L is the path length. We call the function $p(y)$ a 'projection' and note that it is constructed from 'samples' which are obtained in this case by integrating $\mu(x,y)$ along a set of paths parallel to the x axis. Now the integrations are carried out by the source detector system which rotates and we collect a set of projections $p(t,\phi)$ at different values of ϕ (Figure 22.4(b)). $p(t,\phi)$ for a particular value of t is given by integrating along the line:

$$x \sin\phi - y \cos\phi = t$$

and we can define $p(t,\phi)$ as the projection function

$$p(t,\phi) = k \int \int \mu(x,y) \, \delta(x \sin\phi - y \cos\phi - t) \, dxdy$$

where $\delta()$ is the delta function – zero everywhere except when its argument is zero, when it takes the value unity. This is just a notational way of including the equation for the projection path in the integral definition of a general projection

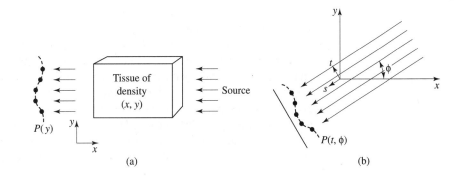

Figure 22.4
Projection notation. (a) A projection function $P(y)$ formed by projecting along paths parallel to the x axis. (b) A projection function $P(t,\phi)$.

(a)

(b)

function. The equation is a transform that takes us from the spatial domain into the projection domain. Each point in (t,ϕ) space corresponds to a line in the spatial domain.

The reconstruction problem is to take our set of projections $p(t,\phi)$ and reconstruct the density function $\mu(x,y)$. To do this certain assumptions are made which are:

● Slices are infinitely thin.
● For a source/detector path we assume that the transmitted X-ray travels in a straight line to the corresponding detector. Specifically the area is divided into small squares and an X-ray absorption coefficient – a CT number – is calculated for each square. We will describe three methods of reconstruction: a simple intuitive method called back projection, the Fourier transform method which has certain practical difficulties and the algebraic reconstruction technique (ART) – versions of which are used in commercial machines.

Although the above analysis is for parallel beams, in practice projection data is collected using fan beams as we implied in Figure 22.1. The practical advantage of fan beams which diverge from a single source is that they facilitate more rapid data collection.

22.1.1

Reconstruction by back projection

An extremely simple but approximate method of reconstruction is to consider each pixel in the reconstruction and give it a value which is the **sum** of the intensities of all the projection rays that pass through it. This is known as back projection. That is, for a single cell in the reconstructed image we assign the intensity

$$(1/N)\ p(t,\phi)$$

for all the projection rays that pass through the cell and where N is the number of cells that each projection ray has encountered. That is, the magnitude of p is distributed equally amongst the cells through which it has passed.

A simple example using this technique is generated in Figure 22.5 which shows an original image whose projections were calculated. We can see the efficacy of the reconstruction method by comparing the original with the image reconstructed from the simulated projections. You can see that the reconstruction is of poor quality – most noticeably it appears blurred. This effect is easily explained by considering an image that consists of just a single point. Consider that n projected rays pass through the point. The reconstruction of such an image from its projections would result in a reconstruction of a high value at the point together with n 'spokes' radiating outwards from the point. The energy at the point is 'spread' into the spokes. In general, every point in a reconstructed image is spread in this way, causing a degradation whose nature and severity is characteristic of the reconstruction method. Observe the important point

Figure 22.5
Back projection of a simple image.

Original image

Reconstruction from one projection

From two projections

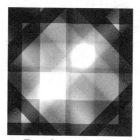

From four projections

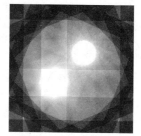

From eight projections

From 32 projections

that the ratio of the reconstructed intensity at the point to the intensity in the spokes is a function of the number of projections. The higher the number of projections, the greater the intensity of the point to the background noise in the spokes.

Back projection reconstruction methods are characterized by the filtering technique that they employ to reduce the visibility of the noise introduced by the process and the order in which they perform the filtering.

22.1.2 Algebraic reconstruction

The algebraic reconstruction or ART algorithm is a simple iterative approach that calculates a more accurate reconstruction than that obtained from the previous method. We start with initial (arbitrary) values in the two-dimensional array of absorption coefficients. At any point in the iteration we have a certain reconstruction (not yet the correct one). We consider this reconstruction and examine one projection path and calculate the path sum. This will be, in general, different to the actual data value for that path. The difference between the current value and the actual value is then divided amongst the pixels along the path and the two path sums now match. Now, although the sums match, the image pixels along the path are not necessarily correct. Also, distributing the difference along the path has now altered all the other path sums that every pixel in current path contribute to. Nevertheless it can be shown that repeating this iterative process a sufficient number of times will lead to convergence.

Figure 22.6
Fourier transform
reconstruction method.

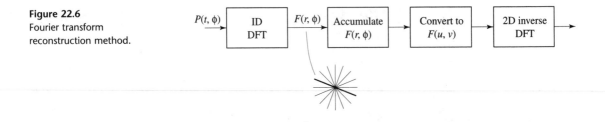

22.1.3

Reconstruction using the Fourier transform method

This is a simple method that follows from the fact that the Fourier transform (Chapter 11) of a single projection $p(t,\phi)$ is a radial slice through the two-dimensional Fourier transform of $\mu(x,y)$. If we define the two-dimensional transform of $\mu(x,y)$ to be $F(u,v)$, and $F(r,\phi)$ to be a radial slice of $F(u,v)$, then we have:

$$\Im(p(t,\phi)) = F(r,\phi)$$

This leads to the reconstruction process shown schematically in Figure 22.6. The method breaks down into three stages:

(1) Transform each of the $p(t,\phi)$ into $F(r,\phi)$ and build up $F(u,v)$ in polar coordinates from $F(r,\phi)$.

(2) Estimate $F(u,v)$ in rectangular coordinates from the information in the first stage using, say, bi-linear interpolation.

(3) Calculate $\mu(x,y)$ from $F(u,v)$ using a reverse FFT transform.

If we remember (Chapter 11) that the loci of spatial frequencies of the same value are concentric circles centred on the origin, then we see that higher and higher spatial frequencies are less and less well defined and the reconstruction of $\mu(x,y)$, compared to the original, will be consequently blurred to an extent that depends on the number of projections $p(t,\phi_i)$.

22.2 Volume rendering and the visualization of volume data

We will now extend the X-ray CT example and consider techniques for visualizing the stack of CT slices as a three-dimensional volume of data. All of the techniques described in this part of the chapter apply to most volume data. They are more or less completely general. It is simply easier to consider the different possibilities in the context of a particular application area.

As we mentioned previously, our reconstructed CT data consists of a number of infinitely thin slices or two-dimensional arrays, where the interslice distance is in practice greater than a pixel dimension within the slice. To turn this stack into a regular three-dimensional array of cubic voxels we have to invoke some form of interpolation. We can then consider the various possibilities, or modes, of displaying this volume data.

Figure 22.7
(a) Volume rendering by
casting parallel rays from
each pixel (after Levoy
(1990)). (b) Using planes
parallel to the view plane to
construct a view volume of
the dataset.

For any application, because we are dealing with volume data, the options available are much greater than with rendering the surface of an object; and the particular mode of display will depend on the applications. The nature of these requirements and also the nature of the data determines the algorithm that is used. One of the easiest ways to visualize the possibilities is to consider an algorithm which is conceptually the simplest method of converting the contents of a volume data set into a two-dimensional image – ray casting. The idea is shown in Figure 22.7 which shows a volume data set, represented as a cube, rotated into a desired viewing orientation and intersected by a bundle of parallel rays – one for each pixel. We will now discuss the following general options and considerations:

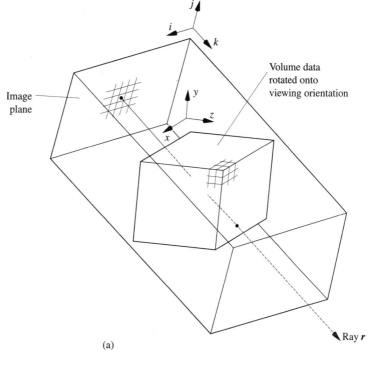

(a)

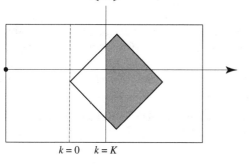
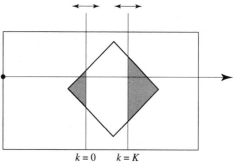

(b)

- **What properties of the data do we want to see in the image plane?** We may want to see the external boundary surface as a shaded object. In medical imagery this could be the skin surface and this implies that we have to 'find' this surface and shade it. In the ray casting case this would simply involve terminating the ray when it strikes the first non-zero voxel, evaluating a surface normal for the voxel and applying a local shading model. Alternatively we may want to visualize an internal object and shade it. In medical imagery we might want to see bone structure underneath the skin/ flesh layer. This implies that we have to extract such a surface for the data set, before we can render it as a computer graphics object. We may want to move a cross-sectional cutting plane through the data as shown in Figure 22.7(b) and view the contents of the intersection of the cutting plane with the data as it moves. We may want to see both bones, such as the rib cage, and the organs contained within. This could be accomplished either by rendering the bones as opaque so that the viewer sees the organs through the gaps in the bones, or by rendering the bones as partially transparent. Other possibilities are easily imagined from the figure. We could compose a projection that, for each pixel, was the maximum data value encountered along the ray. A less obvious mode is to display the sum along each ray path. This will then give an image analogous to a conventional X-ray, giving us the facility of being able to generate a (virtual) X-ray type image from viewing angles that would be impossible with conventional equipment.

- **What is the physical nature of the reality?** If we are sampling a morphous substances such as smoke or clouds, then this will determine the mode of display required; here we would not wish to use conventional computer graphics surface rendering techniques.

- **What is the relationship between the reality and the data?** Our volume data set will consist, in general, of a three-dimensional array of points, representing a three-dimensional sampling of the reality. This may be a very large data set; say 512^3. We associate the single sample with the entire voxel volume, just as a sample in two-dimensional image processing is associated with a square pixel extent. But what does that single sample represent? Here the simpler case to consider is binary occupancy. We assume that the voxel resolution is fine enough so that any voxel only contains a single material, or it contains nothing. Alternatively we could consider that a voxel contained a mix of materials. In medical imagery it may be that the physical extent of a voxel corresponds to a region which straddles both bone and tissue. Another consideration that arises is: do we consider the value of a voxel to be constant throughout its extent, or do we consider that the value varies throughout? If the latter, what model do we use to interpolate the variation between neighbouring voxels?

- **What are the implications of voxel size?** Unlike conventional surface rendering, where we have a definition associated with an object for each pixel, it is likely that the projection of a voxel extent onto the image plane will occupy many pixels.

We will now look at these considerations in greater detail and then examine the implications of using algorithmic structures other than ray casting from the image plane.

22.2.1 'Semi-transparent gel' option

The most general viewing option is to somehow give a viewer the facility to see all the data. No voxel is considered completely opaque and all the data is therefore seen. The physical analogue is an object that made of different coloured transparent gels. Each voxel is assigned a colour C and a transparency α. The colour associated with the material type can be chosen 'aesthetically'. In the CT example white could be chosen for bone and the transparency would be made proportional to density so that bone could be made almost completely opaque.

We then cast a ray from each pixel into the data volume which has been rotated into the desired viewing orientation and perform an operation called compositing. This accumulates a resultant colour and opacity for that pixel. The process is like considering the volume to be made up of a semi-transparent gel of different colours and opacities. It is as if behind the volume we had diffuse white light and we are looking into it from the front side. The process is analogous to taking a conventional X-ray of the volume in the viewing direction; but now we are transmitting parallel beams of light through a volume whose opacity relates to tissue density and displaying the result. However, unlike an X-ray we can compose a projection from any viewing angle we desire.

In clinical application at the John Hopkins Medical Institution, Ney et al. state:

The images generated using this unshaded rendering process are reminiscent of a conventional radiographic image. These images are particularly useful for examining bony abnormalities. The bones are semi-transparent and therefore internal detail is visible as well as surface detail. Unfortunately the unshaded technique does not work well for imaging soft tissue. The high variability of bone density causes the unshaded algorithm to produce the perceived detail. Soft tissue attenuation values are confined to a far narrower spectrum, making it more difficult to separate, for example, a vessel or node from adjacent muscle.

Thus we see that this visualization involves a number of steps:

(1) Classify each voxel in the original data with colour and opacity values.

(2) Transform the (now classified) volume data into the viewing direction.

(3) For each pixel cast a ray and find, by compositing along the ray, a colour for that pixel.

We now describe each of these steps separately.

22.2.2 Voxel classification

Considering the more general case of a voxel containing more than one tissue type, a typical classification scheme was introduced by Drebin et al. (for the particular

Figure 22.8
Material classification in
CT data (due to Drebin et
al. (1988)). (a) Trapezoid
classification function
for one material.
(b) Classification functions.

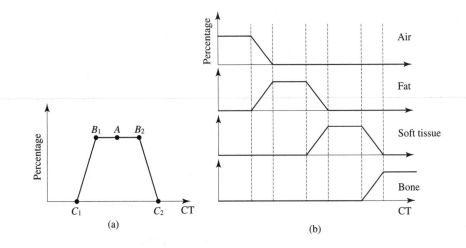

case of X-ray CT data). In this scheme voxels are classified into four types according to the value of the X-ray absorption coefficient. The types are: air, fat, soft tissue and bone. The method is termed 'probabilistic classification' and it assumes that two, but not more than two, materials can exist in a voxel. Thus voxels can consist of seven types: air, air and fat, fat, fat and soft tissue, soft tissue, soft tissue and bone, and bone. Mixtures are only possible between neighbouring materials in the absorption coefficient scale – air, for example, is never adjacent to bone.

The classification scheme uses a piecewise linear 'probability' function (Figure 22.8). Consider a specific material assigned such a function. There will exist a particular CT number that is most likely to represent this material (point A in Figure 22.8(a)). Points B_1 and B_2 represent the maximum deviation in CT number from point A that is still considered this material. Any CT number less than B_1 or greater than B_2 and contained within the limits defined by C_1 and C_2 is classified as a mixture of 'neighbouring' materials. A complete scheme is shown in Figure 22.8(b). Voxels are assigned (R,G,B,α) values according to some scheme and if a mixture of two materials are present in a voxel the two colours are mixed in the same proportion as the materials.

22.2.3   Transforming into the viewing direction

Theoretically a simple process, this step produces difficulties. A simple illustration of the viewing process is shown in Figure 22.9. In general the data volume can be rotated into any desired orientation and when pixel rays are cast into the rotated volume this involves a resampling operation and aliasing has to be considered (discussed in Section 22.4). One of the main options in the overall construction of a volume rendering algorithm is the way in which this transformation is performed and its position in the order of the three stages described in Section 22.1.3.

Figure 22.9
Ray casting implies
resampling the data.
A ray will not, in general,
intercept voxel centres.

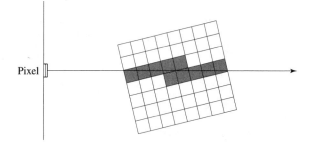

In the CT example it is only useful to rotate about the z axis (spinal rotation) and about the x axis (somersault rotation). This means that the rotation of the volume can be performed by rotating two-dimensional planes perpendicular to these axes.

22.2.4 Compositing pixels along a ray

The simplest compositing operation (Figure 22.10) is the recursive application of the formula:

$$\boldsymbol{C}_{\text{out}} = \boldsymbol{C}_{\text{in}} (1 - \alpha) + \boldsymbol{C}\, \alpha$$

where:

$\boldsymbol{C}_{\text{out}}$ is the accumulated colour emerging from a voxel
$\boldsymbol{C}_{\text{in}}$ is the accumulated colour into that voxel
α is the opacity of the current voxel
$\boldsymbol{C}$ is the colour of the current voxel

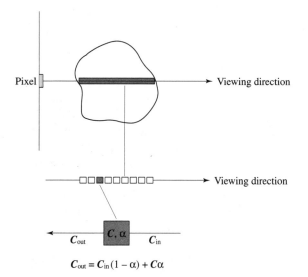

Figure 22.10
The ray compositing
operation.

It does not matter in this model where the light comes from. We simply note that any light exiting from the voxel of interest along the viewing direction has the colour of that voxel plus the product of the incoming light and $(1 - \alpha)$. There are elaborations that can be made on this simple model. For example, α should in reality be a vector quantity since it will differ according to the R, G or B component of the colour of the voxel.

22.3 Semi-transparent gel plus surfaces

If we assume that opaque surfaces are present in the data volume then we supplement the previous scheme with a shading scheme, and present the surfaces as part of the display according to the various options that we described in Section 22.4. Assuming that a voxel can contain part of a surface we can evaluate a normal and a shading component is calculated as a function of this normal and the direction of the illuminating source. This shading component can then replace C in the compositing operation.

The shape of surfaces is now perceived in the normal way as the lighting model enhances the details in the surface. Various options now emerge. We can display just those voxels that contain, say, bone together with its surface shape detail, visible through a fuzzy cloud of soft tissue. Bone can then be made completely opaque or still be given an opacity so that detail behind the bone is still visible.

A surface is detected by evaluating a normal using the volume gradient. The components of this normal are:

$$\mathbf{N}_x = R(x+1,y,z) - R(x-1,y,z)$$
$$\mathbf{N}_y = R(x,y+1,z) - R(x,y-1,z)$$
$$\mathbf{N}_z = R(x,y,z+1) - R(x,y,z-1)$$

where for each voxel, R is evaluated by summing the products of the percentage of each material in the voxel times its assigned density. If a material is homogeneous these differences evaluate to zero and the voxel under consideration is deemed not to contain a surface segment. This scheme is illustrated diagramatically in Figure 22.11.

The presence of a surface is quantified by the magnitude of the surface normal – the larger this magnitude the more likely it is that a surface exists. The magnitude or 'strength' of the surface ($|\mathbf{N}|$) can be used to weight the contribution of the shaded component. No binary decision is taken on the presence or absence of a surface. A normalized version of the surface normal is calculated and can then be used in a shading equation such as the Phong reflection model. We should bear in mind that this technique is purely for the purposes of visualization. It has absolutely no relation to physical reality. We assume that each voxel has an uninterrupted view of the light source even though it may be buried in the middle of a volume.

The localness of this operation means that it is sensitive to noise. This can be diminished by reducing the localness. In the above formula the gradient is eval-

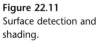
Figure 22.11
Surface detection and
shading.

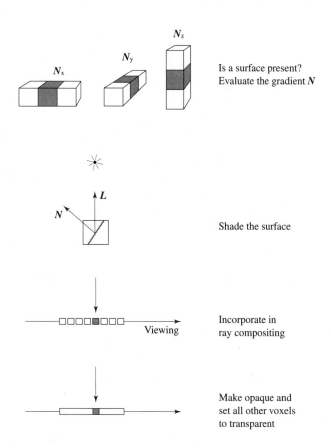

Is a surface present?
Evaluate the gradient N

Shade the surface

Incorporate in
ray compositing

Make opaque and
set all other voxels
to transparent

uated by considering six neighbouring voxels. We can extend this to 18 or even 24 voxels.

We have shaded surfaces by calculating the interaction of a normal of the voxel containing the surface with a light source. Then the surface shape detail becomes visible. We can either incorporate the shaded surface in the semi-transparent gel model or we can make the surface opaque and remove all voxels that do not contain a surface. This makes the first surface the ray hits the surface that is seen by the viewer. These options are indicated schematically by Figure 22.11.

It is important to realize that the surface detection is local and is evaluated for single voxels. No decision has to be taken about the existence or otherwise of a surface if the shading component is included in the semi-transparent gel model. This is important in medical applications where clinicians are (rightly) suspicious of methods where binary decisions on the existence of a surface are made. There are, however, applications where such an approach – explicit extraction of an (assumed) continuous surface – is desirable as we describe in the next section.

Explicit extraction of iso-surfaces

If the volume data is such that it is known to contain continuous iso-surfaces, then they can be explicitly extracted and converted into polygon mesh structures and rendered in the normal way. Such an approach finds one or more appropriate polygons for each voxel and produces a continuous set of such polygons from the set of voxels comprising the surface.

So why go to the trouble of finding a polygon mesh surface when we can find and shade surfaces in the volume by using the density gradient? One of the motivations is that conventional rendering techniques can be used if the surface is represented with conventional graphics primitives, and volume rendering then reduces to a pre-processing operation of surface extraction.

The technique used is known as the marching cubes algorithm, reported by Lorenson and Cline in 1987. An actual surface is built up by fitting a polygon or

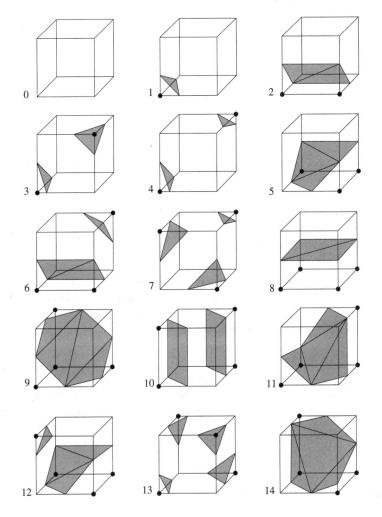

Figure 22.12
The 15 possibilities in the marching cubes algorithm. Dot (•) used in figure represents a vertex that is inside a surface.

polygons through each voxel that is deemed to contain a surface. A voxel possesses eight vertices and if we assume at the outset that a voxel can sit astride a surface, then we can assign a polygon to the voxel in a way that depends on the configuration of the values at the vertices. By this is meant the distribution of those vertices that are inside and outside the surface over the eight vertices of the cube. If certain assumptions are made then there happen to be 256 possibilities. From considerations of symmetry these cases can be reduced to 15 and these are shown in Figure 22.12. The final position and orientation of each polygon within each voxel type is determined by the strength of the field values at the vertices. A surface is built up that consists of a normal polygon mesh and the difference in quality between rendering such a surface and effecting surface extraction by appropriate zero–one opacity assignment in volume rendering is due to what is effectively an inferior resolution in the volume rendering method. In the volume rendering method a surface may exist somewhere within the voxel. If the opacity of such a voxel is set to 1 the information on the position and orientation of the surface fragment is lost. In the marching cubes algorithm the surface fragment is positioned and oriented accurately within the voxel – at least within the limitations of the interpolation method used. However, explicit surface extraction methods sometimes make errors by making the assumption that a surface exists across neighbouring voxels. They can fit a surface over what in reality are neighbouring surface fragments. In other words, they make a binary decision that may be erroneous. Another problem with the marching cubes algorithm is the sheer volume of primitives that can be generated. This can run into millions where many primitives project onto the same pixel.

22.4 Structural considerations in volume rendering algorithms

There are many options in setting up a volume rendering algorithm. As we have seen, the process of viewing a volume data is conceptually simple, involving as it does the rotation of the volume into the viewing orientation, then ray casting (or an equivalent operation) into the volume to discover a suitable value for each pixel. The main research thrust in volume rendering arises out of the importance of efficient hardware implementation. Interactivity and animation are important in most application areas because of their contribution to the interpretation of the data. Because we are generally dealing with very large datasets – routinely in the order of 512^3 – the relationship between the algorithm design and available hardware (such as parallel processors) becomes of critical importance if interactivity/animation demands are to be met.

The terminology used to describe algorithmic options in volume rendering is somewhat confusing. The confusion seems to arise out of what names to give to the main categories. There are two main categories:

● Ray casting methods (with two variants). Also called image or pixel space traversal or back projection.

● Voxel projection methods (with two variants). Also called object or voxel space traversal or forward projection.

These options are illustrated diagramatically in Figure 22.13. In ray casting we can either transform and resample the volume data so that it is oriented with a coordinate axis parallel to the image plane, or we can leave it untransformed. If the data is transformed prior to ray casting then we generate a set of rays parallel to rows (or columns) of the transformed data. For untransformed data the ray set is subject to the inverse viewing transform. Ray casting methods are also categorized as image space methods in that the outermost loop of the algorithm traverses image space.

Although at first sight, it would seem that ray casting methods can be implemented in parallel, memory bottleneck problems arise. If arbitrary viewing directions are allowed there is no way to distribute voxels in memory to ensure that no contentions occur.

A potential problem with forward projection is that holes may arise in the image plane. For voxel projection methods we have to bear in mind that in most applications a single voxel will form a projection in the image plane that spreads over many pixels. (This has been called a footprint.) If we ignore perspective projections then this footprint is the same for all voxels – for a given view – and such coherence can be used to advantage for fast implementation and efficient anti-aliasing. We will now consider these options in greater detail. The important

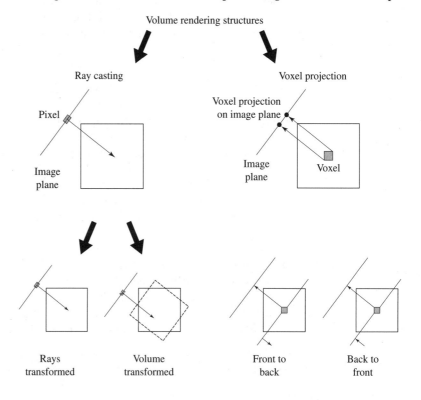

Figure 22.13
A taxonomy of volume rendering structures.

differences between the methods are manifest in the suitability for parallel implementation and how resampling is accomplished.

Ray casting (untransformed data)

In ray casting we traverse image space and cast a ray from each pixel to find a single colour for that pixel by the compositing operation previously described. (The method bears little or no relationship to **ray tracing** which traces a pixel ray in any direction through the scene depending on the geometry and nature of the objects that are hit. In volume rendering we cast a set of parallel pixel rays which all remain travelling in the same direction.) To do this two non-trivial tasks have to be performed. First, we have to find these voxels through which the ray passes; second, we have to find a value for each of the voxels from the classified dataset.

Consider the first problem. This in itself breaks down into two parts. Finding the voxels through which a pixel ray passes is a well worked out problem – we simply use a 3DDA (three-dimensional differential analyzer), an extension into three-dimensional space of knowledge worked out over the years to deal with the two-dimensional line/pixel problem. However, once we find these voxels how do we deal with their values? How do we obtain values to insert into our compositing scheme? Using the basic values of each encountered voxel is wrong. One reason is obvious. The path lengths through each voxel will vary from a very small distance, for a ray that just cuts the corner of a voxel, to a large distance for a ray that is close to the diagonal across opposite corners. We are effectively viewing along a ray and a long journey through a voxel should produce a higher contribution to the compositing than a short one. This is, of course, one of the consequences of sampling a practical volume dataset with an infinitely thin ray – or more precisely, resampling. It is a three-dimensional problem of the equivalent resampling process in image processing. We start with sampled data, rotate it into a new orientation, and resample it. We have to filter when we are resampling to avoid aliasing. The complication in volume rendering is that the data is three-dimensional and the resampling is in three-dimensional space. An appropriate way to proceed, therefore, is to measure equal points along the ray and find a resampled value at these points by filtering over a three-dimensional region, using the equally spaced ray sample points as a centre for the three-dimensional filter kernel.

The algorithm is sometimes described as an image space traversal algorithm and the outermost loop is usually defined as 'cast a ray for each pixel'. However, we need to recognize that we can do no better than cast a parallel set of rays into the volume that pass through every voxel in the data. A simple scheme to achieve this is shown in cross-section in Figure 22.14. The ray set is constructed by passing each ray through the centre point of each voxel in the front face of the dataset.

The same concept is used by Yagel and Kaufman (1992) who use the idea of a ray 'template'. The ray template method adopts the simple approach of mov-

Figure 22.14
An appropriate set of rays in a ray casting algorithm.

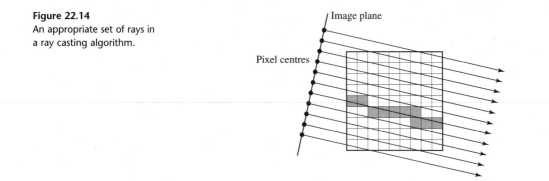

ing the ray one voxel at a time along a line called the base plane. Thus the ray, or ray template, is computed once only and stored in a data structure. All rays are then followed by obtaining the appropriate displacements from this information. The shaded voxels in Figure 22.14 form a ray template. In effect this approach is exploiting the coherency between rays.

We now consider the question of resampling. If the volume is left undisturbed, then the rendering (or compositing) process and resampling process are merged into one operation. We step along the ray at equal sample points and evaluate, for each sample point, a C to be used in the compositing. We could simply use a value for C that was the value of the voxel that contained the sample point. But normally the more accurate process of tri-linear interpolation is used. This is shown in cross-section in Figure 22.15 where it becomes in two dimensions bi-linear interpolation. To evaluate C_S we interpolate from the surrounding grid points, evaluating first the horizontal and vertical intersects of the ray with the voxel grid lines. We can then find the value of C_S. The process is a simplified version of bi-linear interpolation used in polygon shading (Chapter 24) where the polygon is a square.

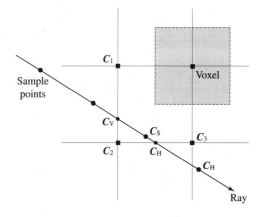

Figure 22.15
C_S, the value at a sample point on the ray, is evaluated by bi-linear interpolation. C_V is evaluated from C_1 and C_2. C_H is evaluated from C_2 and C_3. C_S is evaluated from C_V and C_H.

Figure 22.16
Resampling is performed during *each* shear.

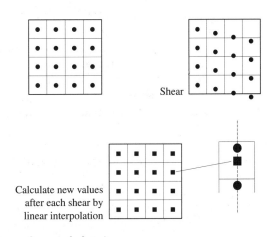

Shear

Calculate new values after each shear by linear interpolation

Ray casting (transformed data)

The second variant of ray casting involves pre-transforming the data into the desired orientation. The geometry of the actual ray casting is then trivial (or eliminated) in that we simply composite along rows or columns of the transformed data.

To transform the data the three-pass (all shear) decomposition described in Chapter 9 can be used. A viewing transformation then becomes a sequence of pure shears – three for each axis. So a general transformation is a set of nine shears. The importance of a shear-only process lies in its implementation in special purpose hardware. In particular, it possesses the property that every voxel in a single shear is moved through a constant amount.

The significant difference in the two ray casting variants is involved in the resampling. Now resampling must be performed during each shear and the process of resampling is performed **before** the compositing. Resampling during a shear involves simple linear interpolation (Figure 22.16).

In ray casting methods an important efficiency enhancement is ignoring empty space in the data volume. A cast ray advances through empty space until it encounters an object. It penetrates the object until sufficient opacity has accumulated, and for high opacity this may be a short distance compared with the traversal through empty space. The empty space does not contribute to the final image and because of the large number of voxels, it is important to implement some space skipping procedure. This can be based on a bounding volume, just as in speed-up schemes in conventional ray tracing, the traversal of the data set starting from the surface of the bounding volume.

Voxel projection method

This variant of volume rendering possibilities involves traversing the dataset and projecting each voxel onto the image plane, as we indicated in Figure 22.13. If we move a plane through the data as shown in this figure, then the frame buffer is used as an accumulator and all pixels are updated simultaneously until all the data is completely traversed and the pixels have their final values.

We can traverse the data either from front to back or from back to front. The significant difference between these two variants is that with back to front traversal we only need to accumulate colour, while with front to back traversal we need to accumulate both colour and transparency. (This is exactly equivalent to saying that with front to back traversal we require a Z-buffer.)

Voxel projection algorithms are important because they are easier to parallelize. At each point in the process, that is, at each voxel, we only need knowledge about a small surrounding neighbourhood. This contrasts with ray casting into untransformed data where we generally require the entire dataset when we cast a single ray.

Possibly the most well-known voxel projection algorithm is due to Westover and is termed 'splatting'. This strange word is used to describe the effect that one pixel has in the image plane. The algorithm depends on two important facts:

- In many applications, and certainly in the case of CT data, one voxel projects onto many pixels.

- In the case of parallel projection, for a particular view, all voxels produce the same projection in the image plane – called a footprint (Figure 22.17).

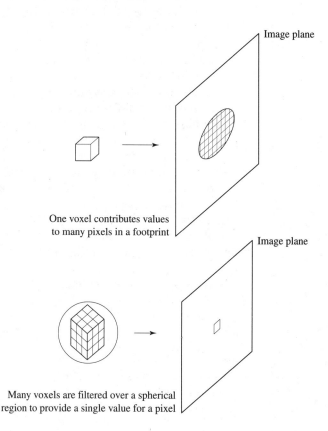

Figure 22.17
Filtering schemes in resampling a volume.

Effectively the algorithm considers the contribution of many points in the data volume, spreading these in the image plane according to the footprint. The process considers each point separately, spreading its contributions to the output samples.

22.5 Perspective projection in volume rendering

So far we have not mentioned the issue of perspective projection. In the case of medical imaging it is not clear that a perspective projection is useful. The volume data in medical applications usually has limited spatial extent of some centimetres and we would not expect to perceive significant perspective clues over this distance. Also, it is not usually the shape of the overall structure that is important to the viewer, but some detail such as a fracture or a tumour and its relationship to surrounding structures. Some specific applications in medicine do require a perspective projection. An example is the construction of a 'beam's eye view' in radiation therapy planning. Here the clinician requires a view of the volume looking down a treatment beam. Treatment beams diverge and so a perspective projection is required.

A number of obvious difficulties occur in constructing a perspective projection in a volume renderer. The most serious results from the divergence of rays from the centre of projection (Figure 22.18). If the ray density is such that the nearest plane in the volume data is sampled with one ray per voxel, then in the example shown, this will quickly drop to one ray per two voxels and small details can be missed. Another problem is anti-aliasing during re-sampling. If we consider travelling along the four rays that pass through each of the four corners of a pixel and the centre of projection, the geometry of the volume at the centre of the neighbourhood over which we must filter is no longer a cubic voxel but a truncated pyramid.

One of the easiest ways of implementing perspective projection is to augment the voxel projection or footprint algorithm. Full details of this are given by Westover.

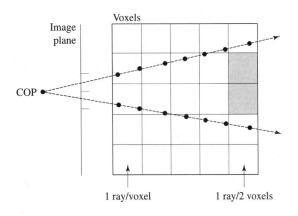

Figure 22.18
Ray density and perspective projection (after Novins, Sillion and Greenberg (1990)). One ray/pixel results in decreasing sampling rate.

Case study – an example of CT data

A series of images that were produced using a selection of volume rendering, image processing and computer graphics techniques are shown in Figures 22.19 to 22.24 (Colour Plate). The original data is 23 planes of X-ray CT data with a 512×512 resolution in each plane. Figure 22.19 shows a skull rendered using the marching cubes algorithms. The second illustration (Figure 22.20) uses exactly the same data but this time it is rendered using a volume rendering algorithm with the bone opacity set to unity. Although it may not be apparent in the reproductions, the marching cube version appears to be of higher quality or resolution – this is an illusory consequence of the algorithm; it is accessing the same data but creating an explicit computer graphics model. The volume rendering algorithm is simply assigning normals to each voxel based on local information. Figures 22.21 and 22.22 show the same data but this time with superimposed computer graphics structures. The first image shows spheres enclosing the eyeball rendered in the normal way and merged into a volume rendered image with bone opacity set to unity. The next illustration is the same as the previous one but now the bone is made transparent. This shows another computer graphics structure enclosing the spinal column and a (highlighted) brain tumour.

The computer graphics structures are a potential aid to radiotherapy planning and provide a means of reassuring the oncologist that the critical structures are not touched by an oblique treatment beam. (Treatment beams are produced by a radioactive source and oriented such that they concide at the cancer site.) The computer graphics objects (spheres for the eyeball and generalized cylinders for the spinal column) are bounding volumes – they fully enclose the critical structures. In effect they are stylizations of the anatomical structure. The process to produce these bounding volumes is classical image segmentation. Image processing operations are performed on the original data in the two-dimensional data plane and 'move through' the three-dimensional dataset by assuming the existence of (a variation of) the two-dimensional structure in adjacent planes. For example, the eyeball sphere is derived by fitting a circle of varying radius to the two-dimensional data using the a priori knowledge that the circles should grow into a sphere.

The final two illustrations (Figures 22.23 and 22.24 (Colour Plate)) show other possibilities. The first shows a visualization of treatment beams together with the areas that they 'shadow' on the skin surface and the second shows a 'beam's eye view' showing that it coincides with a critical structure.

Further reading

For image reconstruction from projections the classic text is by one of the pioneers in the field – Gabor T. Herman. This gives the underlying theory of all reconstruction methods and describes many interesting applications (apart from X-ray CT). It is, however, somewhat demanding mathematically and could only be used superficially by anyone without a strong mathematical background. A more accessible 'popular' article by Gordon, Herman and Johnson appeared in *Scientific American* in 1975. This article contains interesting historical background and also describes a quantitative study of a beating dog's heart.

The classic paper by the inventor of the first machine – Hounsfield – was published in 1973 and this gives a clear description of how the first scanner worked. Present-day scanners differ considerably in the arrangement of X-ray beams and the way in which data is collected.

Like ray tracing was in the early 1980s, volume rendering is an energetic research area in computer graphics which has spawned much investigation. Much of this is concerned with efficiency and the problems that stem from dealing with very large datasets. Volume rendering is conceptually straightforward and the general reader is best referred to application-oriented papers in which its possibilities are described. A good paper on X-ray CT visualization is by Ney et al. Full details of the footprint method are given in Westover's paper.

At the time of writing a good and easily digested introduction to the relationship between parallel hardware and volume rendering algorithms is given in a special issue of *The Visual Computer*.

Papers

Drebin R.A., Carpenter L. and Hanrahan P. (1988). Volume rendering. *Computer Graphics*, **13**(2), 270–5

Gordon R., Herman G.T. and Johnson S.A. (1975). Image reconstruction from projections. *Scientific American*, **233**, 37–46

Hounsfield G.N. (1973). Computerized transverse axial scanning (tomography): Pt 1. Description of the system. *British Journal of Radiology*, **46**, 1016–22

Levoy M. (1990). Efficient ray tracing of volume data. *ACM Trans. on Graphics*, **9**(3), 245–61

Lorenson W.E. and Cline H.E. (1987). Marching cubes: A high resolution 3D surface reconstruction algorithm. *Proc. SIGGRAPH 1987*, 163–170

Ney D.N., Fishman E.K., Magid D. and Drebin R.A. (1995). Volumetric rendering of computed tomography data: principles and techniques. *IEEE Computer Graphics and Applications*, **10**(2), 33–40

Novins K.L., Sillion F.X. and Greenberg D.P. (1990). An efficient method for volume rendering using perspective projection. *Computer Graphics*, **24**(5), 95–102

Various authors (1993). *The Visual Computer* (Special Issue on Interactive Visualization), **9**(3)

Westover L. (1990). Footprint evaluation for volume rendering. *Computer Graphics*, **24**(4), 367–76 (Proc. SIGGRAPH '90)

Yagel R., Cohen D. and Kaufman A. (1992). Discrete Ray Tracing. *IEEE Computer Graphics & Applications*, **12**(5), 19–28

Books

Herman G.T. (1980). *Image Reconstruction from Projections – The Fundamentals of Computed Tomography*. New York: Academic Press

The computer image and art

23.1 Introduction

In Chapter 1 we briefly discussed the use of computer imagery in 'serious' art, that is, art where the end result does not have a commercial motivation (other than selling the work, perhaps). There we made the point that there is very little takeup of computer tools by artists and we can say that, with some notable exceptions, serious art produced by using computer tools does not exist. There are few or no exhibitions of computer art in major galleries, there are no computer artists well known to the public and you cannot buy books of reproductions (leaving aside the now tedious exception of Mandelbrot sets). Why this is so is something of a mystery. Perhaps it is that the artistic community perceive computers as being associated with a world that is somewhat at odds with their domain – computers are part of commerce, they are mechanistic, and so on. They carry with them an aura of absolute predictability that may be considered the antithesis of creativity. Perhaps the computing community do not produce tools of sufficient 'artistic power'. It is certainly the case, for example, that supplying an artist with a freehand sketching facility controlled by a mouse is a worthless exercise. What we do not appear to have developed is a creative tool equivalent to a paintbrush and palette where artists can bring to life creations of their imagination.

It is not immediately obvious why this should be. For example, computers can offer extremely accurate and thus subtle control over colour, much finer control than can be exercised by mixing paint on an artist's palette. They can offer endless fast experimentation with shape and form. One can think of many well-known artists whose work could have been produced on a workstation. Two that come to mind are the paintings of Piet Mondrian and Bridget Riley.

Perhaps something more fundamental than inappropriate interface metaphors for paint brushes is involved. It may be that the direct manipulation of tools – the dragging of paint over a canvas, for example – is an irreplaceable part of the artistic process. Perhaps such devices will never be replaced by computer metaphors, however exotic the facilities offered. Consider in support of this point the haunting collage *El Pensador* (The Thinker) by a little-known Spanish artist (Figure 23.1, Colour Plate). This image, curiously reminiscent of the work of Francis Bacon, was made by tearing pieces out of magazines. The point here is that although the computer is supreme at cut and paste operations, or manipulating small two-dimensional blocks of colour on the viewing surface, somehow it is difficult to conceive of the artist producing works like this using computer facilities. In a sense the medium is the art as much as the art is of the medium.

This is not, however, the situation in the applied visual arts. Here there has been an explosion of usage of DTP programs incorporating typographical design facilities and image processing. The publishing industry and the graphic design industry are now heavily computerized. Pictorial layout for magazines, advertising copy and the like are now handled by DTP programs which incorporate image processing and typographical facilities that are flexible enough not to impede in any way the aspirations of graphical designers.

At one level this is due to the mechanization of 'cut and paste' and the ability to freely mix text and imagery. Complex layouts can be set up and experimented with on a computer screen. A creative process that was before in the mind of the designer and which previously could only be made real through making some physical copy of the desired layout can be visualized and changed at will.

The exploitation and development of image processing techniques by graphics designers has popularized this area and disseminated knowledge of operations that were previous confined to research laboratories. Illustrations in magazines, advertisements and the like are full of images that have been passed through an edge detection filter, sheared and subject to bizarre colour transformations. Even the domain of the caricaturist has been invaded by warping programs that bizarrely distort images of well-known personages.

Adobe's Photoshop is currently the most popular example. Although, as the name suggests, the original motivation for such facilities was to enable basic image processing operations to be performed on scanned or photographed imagery, it was soon realized that simple combinations of common image processing operations could themselves be used as artistic tools. The popularity of these tools has been no doubt in part due to the invention of non-technical names for most of the operations. Although the term 'filter' is retained, operations like edge enhancement or high pass filtering become 'embossing filters'. Thus operations that were previously the domain of the image processing scientist have become the property of the computer-based graphic designer. In some ways categorizing such tools as 'image processing' is somewhat misleading in that many operations, although composed of known techniques, apply a degree of innovation in the way in which the techniques are used. Figure 23.2 (Colour Plate) is a good example of this.

It is indeed the case that currently the ubiquitous manipulation of existing imagery is the only popular manifestation of what could be called 'using the computer as an artistic tool'. But is it art? Certainly it requires little skill other than the knowledge required to operate the program interface. In image processing packages the originality or artistic input is in the ability to combine and manipulate supplied effects.

The influence of the computer image in applied art is probably greatest in typography. Overtaking phototypesetting, which enjoyed only a brief life, in the 1990s personal computers offer a user the freedom of hundreds of typefaces and quality laser printed documents. Sumner Stone commented in 1991:

Before personal computers came into general use in businesses, schools and homes, a vast technological chasm separated the machines used for producing informal personal documents, namely typewriters, and the machines used by the printing and publishing industry for setting type for formal purposes. Graphic designers have never considered the distinctive monospaced typewriter letter forms to be a 'real' type. A typewritten manuscript became a true typographic document only by the transforming agency of the typesetting house. Now these two historically separate worlds of typography have merged. The same personal computers are used for creating both informal and formal written communications; a letter and a book can be produced on the same machine. The same typefaces work on all of the machines, from computer screens with very low resolution to colour thermographic printers and sophisticated laser typesetters. We have only recently begun to realize the far-reaching implications of this technological change.

In this chapter we will look at tools which offer some kind of 'artistic input'. These are many and varied; some have existed for many years and others, particularly those that offer interaction with three-dimensional rendering engines, are still in the research stage. It is an area that, aside from simple paint packages and image processing facilities, has seen little innovation. Indeed it is difficult to say whether the lack of innovation has led to poor take-up by the artistic community or whether the potential artistic market is perceived as being too small and is insufficient to motivate research and development. Because of this a taxonomy is impossible. The major division is between facilities for two-dimensional imagery and facilities that operate with three-dimensional objects or scenes.

Usually known by the generic term 'painting packages', two-dimensional programs operate on individual pixels using some kind of brush metaphor. Brush styles and various compositing operations are usually included in such programs.

Various approaches are now emerging that use three-dimensional scene information either interactively or as part of the rendering system to produce painterly effects. This is surely one of the potentially important features of the computer image in art. A major branch of this area goes under the somewhat negative title of non-photo-realistic rendering (NPR) which, as the name implies, means producing a projection of a scene, described geometrically in one of the standard ways, in such a way that the image emulates what might have been produced by an artist sketching or painting the scene.

In what follows we will look only at techniques that are to all intents and purposes inherent computer techniques, rather than imitations of existing artistic tools. If there is any future for the development of computer facilities as mainstream artistic tools then it is surely in the exploitation of such developments. We will begin by looking at innovative developments for creating and manipulating two-dimensional imagery and then explore the intriguing potential of techniques where an artist can work in three-dimensional space.

23.2 User-originated imagery – painting

Painting in the context of the computer image is a generic term that is used to describe some operation on an image surface that is controlled by moving a virtual stylus over the view surface from which flows a trail of 'paint'. At its most basic level painting is a fairly dire imitation of the artistic act, but the novelty of this computer painting is invested in the exotic brush styles or paint that can be implemented and the possibility of interaction of the paint with any existing imagery.

For reasons that we have already speculated about, computer graphics facilities have not been taken up by the serious artistic community. This is particularly true of paint programs and we should begin by looking at the differences between using such a program and natural painting media. They are in the end a combination of clear disadvantages and potentials. Despite this, they have certainly been popularized by the DTP industry even if they have not been explored by serious artists.

The biggest drawback with computer painting is the virtual brush or pen. Most ideally this is a stylus/tablet device but more usually it is just the ubiquitous mouse. Either way the physical act of placing marks is indirect – the physical movement of the device is separated from the movement of the paint and the artist has to focus on the screen, which is normally perpendicular to the interface surface. The concept of a stroke with beginning and end has to be implemented in some way and this is achieved most conveniently by maintaining and releasing stylus pressure.

Paint programs began making an appearance in the early 1970s but were restricted to research institutes because of the high cost of 24-bit framestores and workstations. Alvy Ray Smith of Lucasfilm (now Pixar) described in 1979 such a program operating at NYIT. This work contains most of the facilities implemented in current paint programs. Elaborations in modern programs are mostly a matter of detail.

Facilities that were implemented in this seminal system included allowing the artist to define brush shape – the particular area of pixels that are coloured as the stylus, whose position maps into a single pixel, moves. The brush definition includes both shape and the colour of pixels within the shape. Interaction with existing imagery included 'single attribute' colour application where, for example, the value of a colour is selected and changes only the value of the pixels under the brush, leaving their hue and saturation unchanged. Another interaction with existing imagery or colour was 'wet paint' where the brush colour (A) and the existing colour (B) were mixed according to:

$$wA + (1-w)B$$

Using a brush shape as a random distribution over a circular radius, clustering towards the centre with higher weights simulated air brushing. Other novel facilities implemented included priority or Z-painting where each applied colour has an associated priority enabling the brush to go 'over' certain colours and 'under' others. This could be used in conjunction with the brush definition to produce interesting effects. For example, if a brush is defined as the image of a smooth-shaded sphere then as the spheres appear along the brush stroke they intersect with one another.

Paint programs have continued to evolve by exploring more interaction possibilities between the brush and existing imagery and more exotic simulation of brushes (although it is the case that there has been little work in the area that might result in more take-up by the artistic community – the development of an input device that is as expressive as a real brush). For example, Strassman reported work in 1986 that he entitled 'hairy brushes'. Perhaps the most complex brush simulation to date, the brush was emulated by a set of bristles where each bristle could have its own colour and this colour could evolve as a function of time into the stroke to simulate such effects as the volume of paint reducing as it is transferred from brush to paper and brush pressure. Brush strokes had B-splines fitted through them to refine their trajectory. Even the interaction of bristles was considered to simulate the transfer of paint from bristle to bristle.

In this context painting can be regarded in general as a compositing operation. It is an action which is applied to a foreground layer which is subsequently composited with a background layer. Compositing has important ramifications for both two-dimensional and three-dimensional imagery and we will now deal with some of its important points.

23.3 Compositing images

Compositing finds diverse uses in many applications. It can be used together with Z-buffer information to combine images produced by different renderers or rendering algorithms or alternatively to combine computer generated imagery with photographic background imagery (see Chapter 26 for more discussion on an application of this facility).

Composites can be specified by a binary operator that combines two sub-images:

C = A **op** B

where the images A, B and C are three-channel RGB images.

Consider the operator $\mathbf{Z_{min}}$. We may have two sub-images, say of single objects, that have been separately produced and their Z-buffer information retained. Compositing the images into a scene means creating a projection of both of them by combining them using the depth information, and the effect of

A $\mathbf{Z_{min}}$ B

is

C = (**if** $Z_A < Z_B$ **then** A **else** B)

$Z_C = \mathbf{min}(Z_A, Z_B)$

Unfortunately this simple approach carries over and may make worse aliasing artefacts in the component images. In particular, component images that have been anti-aliased may have their quality diminished in compositing. In recognizing this Porter and Duff in 1984 (at Lucasfilm Ltd – now Pixar) suggested that for quality composition an image needs to have four channels – RGBα. The extra α channel is a matte or coverage channel. If the α value is one for a pixel, then an object covers a pixel at that point – if it is zero it does not. In painting programs the matte channel can be used in combination with the component images to invoke painting modes. In the context of composition its primary use is to ensure quality (although the same combination modes can be invoked within a pixel). Here the α channel is used to retain fractional pixel coverage information at the silhouette edges which emanate from the anti-aliasing method in the renderer that produced the component image and it is used to 'carry' anti-aliasing into the composite image. Straightforward compositing, where one image is placed on top of another, is then defined as:

C = A **over** B

where the operator **over** is defined as:

C = A + $(1 - \alpha_A)$B

and

$\alpha_C = \alpha_A + (1 - \alpha_A)\alpha_B$

Compositing using Z information is then enhanced by examining the Z depth at the four corner points of a pixel. Z_A is compared with Z_B at each pixel corner and if the comparison is not the same at all corners then the pixel is said to be confused. There are 16 possible outcomes of this comparison and subtracting the two cases when there is no confusion – Z_A is less than Z_B or vice versa – this leaves 14 cases. Identification of the particular case and linear interpolation of the Z values enable the calculation of a factor β – the fraction of the pixel for which A is in front of B. An operator **comp** can then be defined which combines $\mathbf{Z_{min}}$ and **over**:

$$C = \beta(A \text{ \textbf{over} } B) + (1 - \beta)(B \text{ \textbf{over} } A)$$

23.4 Manipulation of two-dimensional imagery – multi-resolution painting

Multi-resolution painting means being able to manipulate an image at any scale. It is a facility that has no manual analogue. Its simplest application is the ability to make sweeping changes to the image by working at a coarse resolution and fine changes by operating with a high resolution. In other words, the artist can apply minute changes at the limiting resolution, or zoom out and make changes across a large area with the same 'brush stroke'.

A multi-resolution image is represented as an image pyramid and all three representations (described in more detail in Chapter 11) – low pass pyramids, bandpass pyramids and wavelet representations – have been used to implement multi-resolution paint systems.

An important aspect of multi-resolution paint systems is how the image representation is updated when a user makes a change to one of its constituent levels. Most systems operate by postponing changes and as a user works with an image at a current level of detail, only the changes at that level are recorded. Perlin and Velho, in their report 'Live Paint', categorize two strategies for updating the structure: re-execution and lazy evaluation. In the re-execution strategy changes are stored as prescriptions for redrawing. When a user moves to another level in the detail pyramid the stored operations are re-executed at the new level. Re-execution is used with lowpass pyramids. The other strategy, lazy evaluation, propagates the changes from the operated level when the user moves to a new level. This strategy is used with bandpass pyramids.

One of the advantages of bandpass or wavelet representation is that they make lazy evaluation straightforward. All that has to be done when a user travels towards a higher resolution level after applying paint at a current level is to propagate the paint mask. The detail or bandpass coefficients at higher levels of detail depend only on the product of the opacities of the paint applied at lower levels. The changes need only be propagated when the user moves and only as far in the hierarchy as the user moves. Some marker needs to be left at the highest level of detail that the user has currently visited so that in the event of a future descent in the hierarchy beyond this level the system knows to reinitiate a propagation of previous changes. Perlin and Velho use the metaphor of 'ink' that flows 'downhill' and 'pools' that form at the current highest level visited. As it propagates to a higher level it is erased from the lower one. They also use 'ink' to invoke procedural texture, which when travelling down to a higher level of detail from the one at which it added into the image needs to be refined. As the ink flows downhill it causes the procedural texture definition to be activated and generate more detail.

23.5 Manipulation of two-dimensional imagery – using image processing techniques

It is curious to consider that the use of image processing operations, confined until fairly recently to research institutes that processed scientific imagery like satellite or medical images, are routinely used as 'effects' by the DTP people who presumably have little interest and no knowledge of the mathematics and algorithms that implement the facilities. Software like Adobe's Photoshop offer straightforward image processing operations like contrast enhancement and colour manipulation as well as a variety of more exotic techniques. This may, for example, involve some interaction between two images, one of which is a source, such as a photograph, and the other a 'manipulator' image such as stylized water vortex. The result is the source image distorted in some way by the manipulator image. Image processing operations tend to be used to idealize images and to remove unwanted parts of images and the artistic effects are used to, for example, make a photograph look as if it was an oil painting.

It is easy to see the reasons for the success of such programs. Photo-processing or retouching, an expensive, time-consuming and skilled operation, has been replaced by a computer program. Anyone can retouch a photograph of a holiday destination, removing the clouds and changing the greyness in the sky to a deep tropical blue. It is a strange development in our visual culture. Most of the applications are in advertising in magazines and the like which seem to want to retain the 'underlying truth' of a photographic image but to idealize it by removing any aspects that the creator feels would detract from its attractiveness to a potential customer. Such idealization of the photographic image – some might call it falsification – is now universal and goes way beyond the possibilities of traditional retouching techniques.

23.6 Manipulation of three-dimensional imagery – non-photo-realistic rendering

'Non-photo-realistic rendering' (which we will subsequently refer to as NPR) is a new approach to image synthesis that gives an image-maker the ability to use 'painterly' effects while still retaining the advantages of a conventional rendering system. It has come into being because of a certain dissatisfaction with photo-realistic renderers. Photo-realism has long been a goal of image synthesis. Great advances have been made since the Gouraud shaded images of single objects emerged in the early 1970s. The motivation behind almost all the research into advances in image synthesis has always been attempts to imitate reality more and more accurately. This tendency is exemplified in the development of physically based local reflection models and global illumination models. Recent years, however, have seen the emergence of NPR where the apparent perfection of photo-realistic imagery is perceived as being less than ideal in many application areas – particularly in areas, such as architecture, where a designer has to present his creation to a client. Of course, this may have as much to do with the designer's desire to sell an illusion as anything else – designers' presentations are often idealized and omit any negative aspects of reality. The designer can emphasize the idealism of his creation and give its ordinariness or defects less visual prominence.

Consider the two architectural illustrations shown Figure 23.3 (Colour Plate). One is a computer graphics view of a proposed development. Its attributes, common to most computer images of this type, are a mixture of the good and the bad. The light intensity throughout the image has been calculated extremely accurately – at least to within the limits of the local reflection model that has been used. (It is noticeable, however, that the shadows are too dark and incur a visual prominence in the image that is out of proportion to their function.) The image projection is exactly correct and the only geometric defects that we may notice will be due to inaccuracies in the scene database. But in the end it is somehow sterile – devoid, we might say, of a human touch. It is no better than a cardboard model and could not be improved to any great extent by adopting better (more photo-realistic) rendering strategies. Now consider the other illustration which is a seventeenth century engraving. Somehow it is preferable and more evocative of Paris in the seventeenth century than a computer graphics image would be.

In many areas the message to be communicated by the image is more functional. Educational medical illustrations, for example, are generally stylized to a certain extent and hand drawn. In such pictures the medical artist will emphasize the important features and de-emphasize information irrelevant to the function of the illustration. Maintenance manuals for complex machines employ sketches (and non-realistic renditions such as exploded views) rather than photographs. For example, Winkenbach states:

at Boeing, even when CAD databases of aeroplane parts exist, all high quality manuals are still illustrated by hand in order to provide more effective diagrams than cannot be achieved with either photo-realistic rendering or simple hidden line drawings

Landsdown and Schofield make the point that in our pursuit of photo-realism we simulate effects that are considered defects in photography and state:

Other techniques such as simulated depth of field, lens flare and motion blurring can also be applied to the image. Intriguingly, these effects are sometimes unwanted artefacts of conventional photography, yet they are deliberately introduced into computer graphic scenes to convince us of their 'photographic' veracity.

They assess photo-realism in image synthesis as follows:

When viewed from a broader cultural perspective, photo-realism is only one pictorial style among many. The use of alternative and more radical forms of representation is particularly strong in art and design, where photo-realism can sometimes be less than desirable.

We will now attempt a definition of NPR by saying that it facilitates additions to the normal rendering pipeline in such a way that the final rendered image is more akin to what an artist or designer may produce manually than a photograph. NPR is concerned with making changes to the final image by adding or taking away information that would appear in an image rendered in the normal way. This may be achieved by modifications of rendering parameters prior to the generation of the image in the framestore or it may involve altering the framestore in conjunction with Z-buffer information. (Of course, many effects can be obtained by operating on the final rendered image using conventional image processing utilities; we do not consider these to be NPR techniques although they may produce similar effects. Image processing utilities only use two-dimensional or pixel information.)

Finally we should address the question 'why do it anyway?'. If the final effect is to be artistic and it is so difficult to wrest artistic imagery out of systems designed for photo-realism, then why not use conventional artistic tools? The answer is that NPR should be able to exploit the advantages of both approaches and there is the labour-saving advantage of using a renderer to provide the staring point for a scene representation. The artist has the potential freedom of a painting tool together with access to the model that has created the light/object interaction.

There are many potential applications where the accuracy (both the geometric accuracy and the accuracy of the lighting calculation) and ability to accurately display complex shapes and detail need to be combined with stylized or artistic effects. Complex technical illustrations require stylization to aid their interpretation; architectural representations need to retain accuracy but also have some illusion of free artistic effects to enhance their presentation. (It is interesting to note that photographs were rarely used in either of these applications as a representation prior to computer graphics and CAD.)

It is certainly the case that NPR is in a somewhat immature state and much development with collaborative input from artists is required. Of course the full potential of such ideas can only be realized by artists and designers using them creatively – that is, after all, their function.

The remainder of this chapter is a description of the possibilities of NPR based on developments already reported. We begin by looking at a few examples, then see what conclusions can be drawn from this study.

23.7 NPR imitating natural media – pen and ink illustration

It is often argued that imitating natural media – like having a virtual paintbrush under interactive control produce oil or water colour brush strokes – is futile. What artist would prefer these to the real thing? On the other hand, it can be argued that there is a demand in DTP systems for quality illustration techniques that go some way to approaching those that might be produced by an illustrator.

Pen and ink illustrations, where shading is accomplished by hatching or cross-hatching, is a well-established traditional technique in book illustration and the like. It has the obvious advantage – its *raison d'être* in fact – that it can be used on the printed page, using the same ink and paper. A three-dimensional rendering facility that produced convincing pen and ink illustrations would be invaluable in DTP. A good example of computer-produced pen and ink illustration is the work of Winkenbach and Salesin reported in 1994. (It is curious that, given the decades of research that has gone into producing grey scale images by dithering, it is only in 1994 that we saw the emergence of this alternative.)

The input is a three-dimensional scene description and the output is a convincing pen and ink illustration version of the scene. The motivation of the system is to enable a non-artist (DTP user, say) to produce artist quality illustrations. Although the work described is non-interactive the techniques used do not in themselves preclude interaction.

The basis of pen and ink illustration is the use of a texture – pen strokes that conform to some pattern like nearly parallel lines – to indicate both texture and tone or reflected light intensity. Textural patterns representing stone will be different to those representing wood. The tone of a texture is the amount of blackness per unit area – complete absence of texture indicates very bright light and as the reflected light intensity decreases the density of the strokes increases towards complete blackness. These two properties are not always independent – the texture pattern itself can be changed to indicate more blackness. Instead of increasing the number of parallel strokes to get increasing blackness we can add strokes at right angles, say. These concepts are illustrated in Figure 23.4. Note that this figure suggests the normal convention in pen and ink illustration which is very few quantization levels from white to black.

To create pen and ink illustrations Winkenbach and Salesin use all the three-dimensional information that is routinely processed in a normal renderer. Textures are associated with an object in the normal way and so change their orientation and scale just as the face orientation and scale of the object change. Reflected light intensity – calculated in the normal manner from a local reflection model – is used to select an appropriate texture tone. (Note that this is different to the normal texture model in computer graphics where texture controls the surface colour of an object, usually by modulating the diffuse reflection coefficients, but the texture pattern remains unchanged.) Although the basis of their system is simple, its visual success is no doubt due to careful attention to subtle changes in strokes that an artist would incorporate automatically. These are:

- Strokes should occasionally stray outside their face boundaries; clipping a texture pattern exactly to face boundaries produces an unnatural effect.

- Creating the same texture and tone at very different scales can require modification of the pattern. Simplistically we have to alter the pattern to maintain the same overall density of blackness over the face.

Figure 23.4
Examples of the use of
pen and ink techniques to
indicate different texture
values.

Density of a pen stroke texture represents different tonal values

Adding strokes at different orientations to darken a texture

- The texture may have to change according to view direction, particularly along silhouette edges.

- The boundary between two faces needs to be outlined in a way that varies as, for example, the contrast between faces.

- The textures themselves should only be suggested. This means that a face should not be completely filled with the selected texture, but partially filled – a process known as indication. Winkenbach and Salesin point out that this is a difficult process to automate and introduce an interactive element, allowing the user to specify where the texture detail is to appear.

To implement the above features requires a rendering system that departs from the (easy) scan conversion of individual polygons using a Z-buffer. The final operation in screen space proceeds by drawing one pen stroke at a time. These emerge out of a stroke generator whose parameters are set up using three-dimensional information – the original texture style, the tone or stroke density and the scale. Each stroke has to be clipped to a polygon or face boundary and in a multi-object scene, for the strokes to cover the entire surface, the strategy has to take into account the fact that faces will be fragmented with holes due to other partially obscuring faces. In other words, a stroke has to stop and restart according to the visible projection of the face in screen space. This implies using a partitioning of screen space. The algorithm initially computes face visibility using a three-dimensional BSP tree. This is used to compute an auxiliary data structure – a two-dimensional BSP tree of projected faces in screen space. Each leaf is the group of pixels onto which visible portions of the face project and a pointer to the corresponding face in the three-dimensional structure. The two-dimensional BSP tree is used to effect efficient clipping of the pen strokes. The

Figure 23.5
An example of Winkenbach and Salesin's work. In this example, the ideas discussed in the text are extended to parametric surfaces. (Traditional texture mapping was used for the pattern on the bowl; bump mapping was used to modulate the surface of the jug.) (Courtesy of Georges Winkenbach and David H. Salesin.)

path of a stroke is pushed down the tree until it reaches one, or, in general, more than one leaf nodes. This operation enables the determination of the portions of the path that belong to the face currently being rendered. (Presumably Winkenbach and Salesin adopt this screen space clipping to avoid the inefficiencies inherent in the simpler strategy of rendering each face in reverse depth order – the Painter's algorithm.)

An example of the work produced by them is given in Figure 23.5.

23.7.1 Interaction and NPR

Crucial to any form of creative NPR is the ability to interact with the renderer that produces the artistic or stylistic effects. Non-interactive techniques, like those described in the previous section, have by definition limited utility.

What parameters of a rendering engine should we offer to an artist and what functions will be desirable? Most recent approaches try to combine the metaphors (such as brushes and brush styles) of a two-dimensional painting program with access to some aspect of the scene information and offer what is sometimes called three-dimensional painting. NPR methods are usually distinguished by interactive painting of effects together with new modes of operation facilitated by access to three-dimensionality. The distinction between two-dimensional image space and world or scene space in respect of the effect being applied is quite subtle. For example, if cross-hatching is automatically applied to create a sketch-type stylization, the three-dimensional information may be used to associate a particular line density with reflected light intensity. But the cross-hatching itself is a screen space effect which can be under control of the artist and is part of the image rather than a projection of part of the object.

Any interaction with the screen space image using a conventional brush metaphor exhibits immediate differences from conventional painting programs. As the brush moves in two space the colour that it imparts to the image changes according to light/object interaction. Painting an object, the artist would see colour changing from dark to bright to white in areas of highlight. There is also the consideration that once a user starts painting an object it does not make sense to allow the brush to wander outside the object projection. Another consideration is that the brush metaphor can now possess a three-dimensional orientation with respect to the object surface.

The first discussion of three-dimensional painting appeared in a paper published in 1990 entitled 'Direct WYSIWYG painting and texturing on 3D shapes' (Hanrahan and Haeberli) and the implication of the title is that the artist paints in two-dimensional space but sees the correct interaction of the new paint with a local reflection model as he paints. The paint, in effect, becomes the co-efficients of a local reflection model and is loaded onto a brush using a materials interface that would normally be used to set up a batch renderer with sliders controlling the relative contribution of ambient, diffuse and specular light. In this work the brush position in screen space is mapped back into object space via texture maps. A screen space identity buffer stores the object identity and the texture coordinates associated with a pixel. In effect the interface for the rendering engine is the rendered image itself. Although the paper discusses many possible modes of operation for three-dimensional painting, the authors' examples are finally conventional photo-realistic images albeit produced in this novel way. The key point in this method is that the user is interacting with the renderer's parameters via the two-dimensional image that the renderer is currently producing.

(It is interesting to note that techniques that enable interactive operations with a renderer have been around for a long time. As early as 1981 Bass suggested a method that uses a colour lookup table indexed by a quantized surface normal. This has come to be known as a reflectance map and each vector orientation has an associated RGB colour. To effect a change in the rendering of the object specific to the lookup table, the new colours are calculated. Recalculating the entries in the lookup table requires little work compared with recalculating the pixels' shades in the conventional way. Despite this early interest, interactive rendering has not seen much development beyond standard interface devices such as material editors that allow parameter selection and show the effect on a single 'standard' object like a sphere. Perhaps this is due to the tendency of photo-realistic models to soak up hardware advances. Hardware benefits have been used to service more elaborate and more complex rendering devices rather than interactivity.)

Consider now some of the interaction possibilities available with a rendering system as shown in Figure 23.6. Type 1 restricts interaction to post-processing the rendered image in a way that uses three-dimensional information such as the Z-buffer. We might, for example, edge enhance the Z-buffer or depth map and use this as a stylized overlay for the original image. This technique was used

Figure 23.6
Interacting with a rendering engine for NPR.

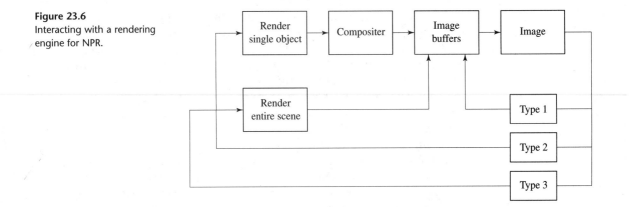

by Saito and Takahashi in 1990. The other possibility (Type 2) is to restrict changes to a single object in the scene, using a compositor to merge the operated object back into the scene. The advantage of this type of interaction over the previous is that the changes can be recorded in the object database and any subsequent scene creation, say from a different viewpoint, will include these changes. A restriction of both of these interaction modes is that we can only conveniently effect changes to scenes rendered using local reflection models. In type 2 interaction if we change the colour, say, of an object, then we cannot by definition transmit the effect of this change to other interacting objects in the scene. Changing the position or orientation of a single object would only be possible if we recalculated any areas in the image that were previously behind the object being operated on. This can be done by ray tracing from the revealed pixels. Previously visible pixels that are obscured by the new object position can be handled by the compositor. Conventional re-rendering of the entire scene (Type 3) is necessary if changes are made to the viewpoint or light sources.

An interesting Type 1 example called PIRANESI was reported by Schofield in 1996. This is a post-processor that operates on RGB files, a Z-buffer file and a 'material' file and enables the facilities of three-dimensional painting by recalculating certain three-dimensional information from the Z-buffer or depth image. The material buffer contains a pointer to the shading equation coefficients of the object that projects onto the pixel. If the viewpoint does not change, and this can be finalized in producing the basic RGB image, then a material pixel together with an associated surface normal is all that is required to recalculate shading.

This information is used in the implementation of various painterly effects that are invoked interactively in the normal way. The obvious advantage of this approach is that it gives most of the benefits of using a renderer in a three-dimensional painting mode, but it is independent of any specific rendererer – it works with the files produced by the renderer. An advantage of pixel resolution information is that there is no dependence on object complexity – all the geometry is recalculated from Z-buffer pixels.

PIRANESI works with the following geometric and image information extracted from the Z-buffer:

$P = (x_e, y_e, z_e)$, the coordinate in eye space corresponding to a pixel (x, y, z_e) in three-dimensional screen space, is given by:

$$P = T^{-1}(x, y, z_e)$$

where T is the perspective transformation.

N, the normal and hence the plane equation containing P, is given by:

$$N = (P_2 - P_1) \times (P_3 - P_1)$$

where $\quad P_1 = T^{-1}(x, y, z_e)$
$\qquad P_2 = T^{-1}(x+1, y, z_e)$
$\qquad P_3 = T^{-1}(x, y+1, z_e)$

An edge image is calculated, together with the screen space gradient, using a Sobel edge detector (see Chapter 10) operating on the Z-buffer as a depth image.

As we have discussed earlier, there has been very little work done on this potentially important topic. What can we conclude from the above approaches? Consider the limitations of PIRANESI. This is a system that is essentially a post-processor. A conventional rendering cycle is invoked to produce a basic RGB image which the artist then develops interactively. The further development is essentially image based but it uses painting effects which are influenced or modulated by three-dimensional information retrieved from the Z-buffer. The key point is that no alterations are made to the object database or scene description and no alteration to the viewpoint can be made after this phase of the interaction is entered. It would seem self-defeating to exclude viewpoint changes from an artistic process, but one of the advantages of the system is that it can work with files produced by any renderer.

We conclude with a simple comparative case study that demonstrates some of the techniques that we have discussed. These are simple variations in rendering of a machine part and are all produced without interaction – they are post-processes, some of which use depth information. Figure 23.7(a) (Colour Plate) is a conventional rendered representation, using stylized colours and shadows. Figure 23.7(b) is an image of the Z-buffer of the object. A so-called depth map, it can be retained then used to apply NPR techniques as we have discussed. The third image (Figure 23.7(c)) is an edge-enhanced version of the depth map. This could be used as an illustration in its own right, in, say, a maintenance manual or in a spare parts publication. A subtle problem here is the choice of a suitable threshold for the edge-enhanced image. We must remember that the image has been derived from a polygon mesh model and the edge-enhancing operation will detect polygon edge discontinuities in either the rendered image or the depth map. Ideally we would like to be able to automatically select a threshold that does not make visible the polygon edges. Figure 23.7(d) is a simple allusion to cross-hatching. The intensity of the final rendered image is coarsely quantized and used to modulate the horizontal lines. The limitations of this technique compared with Winkenbach and Salesin's cross-hatching are obvious. The 'chalk sketch' shown in Figure 23.7(e) was produced by point sampling the rendered image and jittering the samples. Finally the 'brush stroke' image in Figure 23.7(f) was produced by point sampling the rendered image to obtain basic brush stroke attributes. These are then sorted in depth using the Z-buffer information at each sample point before being drawn.

Further reading

Bass D.H. (1981). Using video lookup tables for reflectivity calculations. *Computer Graphics and Image Processing*, **17**, 249–61

Hanrahan P. and Haeberli P. (1990). Direct WYSIWYG painting and texturing on 3D shapes. *Proc. SIGGRAPH 1990*, 215–23

Landsdown J. and Schofield S. (1995). Expressive rendering: A review of nonphotorealistic techniques. *IEEE Computer Graphics and Applications*, May

Perlin K. and Velho L. (1995). Live paint: painting with procedural multi-scale textures. *Proc. SIGGRAPH 1995*, 153–60

Porter T. and Duff T. (1984). Compositing digital images. *Proc. SIGGRAPH 1984*, 253–9

Saito T. and Takahashi T. (1990). Comprehensible rendering of three-dimensional shapes. *Proc. SIGGRAPH 1990*

Schofield S. (1996). PIRANESI: A three-dimensional paint system. *Eurographics UK 96 Conf. Proc.*

Smith A.R. (1982). *Paint*. Tutorial: Computer Graphics (ed. Beatty J.C., Booth K.S.). Silver Spring, MD: IEEE Computer Society Press

Stone S. (1991). *On Stone: The Art and Use of Typography on the Personal Computer*. San Francisco, CA: Bedford Arts Pub.

Strassman S. (1986). Hairy brushes. *Proc. SIGGRAPH 1986*

Winkenbach G. and Salesin D.H. (1994). Computer generated pen-and-ink illustration. *Proc. SIGGRAPH 1994*

Fundamentals of the computer image

The idea of this chapter is to isolate fundamental information that is used throughout the text. It can be read in sequence or skipped and referred to when necessary when reading the other chapters. There is mathematical detail dispersed throughout the text and the information given in this chapter is that which is common to more than one chapter or field.

24.1 Representation – sampling and quantization

As we discussed in Chapter 1 the fundamental information unit of the computer image is a pixel. A rectangular array of pixels makes up a digital or computer image. A pixel encapsulates two separate pieces of information – it has a size which relates to the size of the reality that it represents and this is most easily imagined in the context of image processing where we can relate the size of a pixel to the physical area on, say, a source image such as a photograph. Here it may, for example, be equivalent to a square millimetre on the photograph. The second piece of information is its value or colour. Most commonly we represent the colour of an area to which a pixel corresponds in a photograph as an RGB triple of, say, 8 bits per component, making the value of a pixel a 24-bit integer number.

In image processing we transform an image of reality – a TV image or a photograph – into a digital image. We have the concept of a pixel enclosing a small square extent on a very high, but finite, resolution photograph. We assign a single value to a pixel despite the fact that in general there will be variation of detail within the pixel extent on the image. This is called sampling and quantization. Sampling is digitization of the spatial dimension and quantization is digitization of the intensity or colour dimension. We wish to sample and quantize an image at the highest possible resolution to retain the quality of the original reality. The cost of this in image processing is the time it takes to process the image and its cost of storage or equivalently its transmission cost over a communications channel.

The trade-off between the amount of digital information that we use to represent an image and its quality is best illustrated by varying the sampling and quantization resolution independently of each other. Figure 24.1 shows a digital image subject to decreasing spatial resolution or increasing pixel size. Figure 24.2 shows the same image with the pixel size maintained at its smallest size and reducing the quantization resolution. The relationship between the quantity of information used to represent an image and its quality is discussed in more detail in Chapters 8 and 26. In particular a fundamental theorem – the sampling theorem – is introduced. This gives a precise relationship between the spatial or

Figure 24.1
Coarsening the resolution of an image – the familiar pixelization effect.

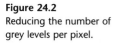

Figure 24.2
Reducing the number of
grey levels per pixel.

sampling resolution of an image and information loss. It gives us the minimum sampling resolution that we have to apply if all the information in the image being sampled is to be retained in the digital image.

Images are almost always represented in this uniform way. Non-uniform representations, where a large pixel size may be used in areas of little detail and vice versa, are clearly a more economical way of representing an image. This concept is extremely important in image compression which has gained a new importance as the image communication becomes more and more ubiquitous. Non-uniform representations are not used much outside of this specialized area for fairly obvious reasons – image capturing hardware deals with uniform areas and it is easier to write algorithms that can make the assumption that all pixels are of the same size. The concept of a uniform pixel is used by most image synthesis approaches and there are only a few algorithms whose rendering 'granularity' depends on the local detail of the image in the image plane. The main reason for this is the inertia accumulated by uniform pixel algorithms due to the development of special hardware for the mainstream rendering method described in Chapter 3.

In computer graphics, the issues of sampling and quantization, although still important, are not so easily related to the source information, in this case a three-dimensional model or geometric description of an object. Also, they are only a single factor – and usually not a predominant factor – in the quality of the final image. In computer graphics we are synthesizing an image, calculating individual values for pixels in the frame memory. The quality of the image is usually deemed to be the extent of the photo-realism of the final image and this depends on the accuracy of the original scene representation and the rendering method used, rather than the number of pixels in the frame memory. However, the number of pixels determines the rendering time and this is of prime import in interactive work and virtual reality, and image quality in terms of pixel resolution is traded off against rendering time.

A central problem in computer graphics is the resolution of the representation of the three-dimensional geometry of the scene or object. Most objects are stored as a single representation, that is, a single geometric description at the greatest level of detail available. When the relative positions of the viewer and the object are such that the object projects only onto a few pixels on the screen then it is an extremely wasteful strategy to render a complex object as if it was going to project onto thousands of pixels. In other words, the resolution of the source information – the geometric description of the object – is often too high. Representational issues in computer graphics are discussed at length in Chapters 2 and 21.

Thus computer vision and computer graphics both operate at their lowest level with a uniform pixel. In computer vision we first try to extract or determine structural relationships between pixels and then eventually determine relationships between three-dimensional entities that produced these structures in the projection or image plane. In computer graphics we have a three-dimensional structure or model and the aim is to break this down, determining the interaction of the structures with light in the environment and eventually produce a set of pixels in the image plane.

24.2 Transformations and the computer image

Transformations that operate on three-dimensional points are used extensively in the computer image. In computer graphics we may use transformations to move and orient objects to construct a scene, or we may apply transformations in the form of an animation script to move objects and/or a virtual camera to produce an animation sequence. In any object description the lowest level of representation consists of single points in three-dimensional space and it is on these points that transformations are usually applied.

In computer vision we may wish to infer transformations or object movement from detail in one or more two-dimensional images that have been formed by pointing a camera at a scene.

24.2.1 Three-dimensional linear transformations

A set of vertices or three-dimensional points belonging to an object can be transformed into another set of points by a linear transformation. Both sets of points remain in the same coordinate system. Matrix notation is used in computer graphics to describe the transformations and the de facto convention in computer graphics is to have the point or vector as a column matrix, preceded by the transformation matrix T.

Using matrix notation, a point V is transformed under translation, scaling and rotation as:

$$V' = V + D$$
$$V' = S\ V$$
$$V' = R\ V$$

where D is a translation vector and S and R are scaling and rotation matrices.

These three operations are the most commonly used transformations in computer graphics and to enable them to be treated in the same way and combined, we use homogeneous coordinates which increase the dimensionality of the space. The practical reason for this in computer graphics is to enable us to include translation as matrix multiplication and thus have a unified scheme for linear transformations. In a homogeneous system a vertex

$$V(x,y,z)$$

is represented as

$$V(w{\cdot}X, w{\cdot}Y, w{\cdot}Z, w)$$

for any scale factor $w \neq 0$. The three-dimensional Cartesian coordinate representation is then:

$$x = X/w$$
$$y = Y/w$$
$$z = Z/w$$

If we consider w to have the value 1 then the matrix representation of a point is

$$\begin{bmatrix} x \\ y \\ z \\ 1 \end{bmatrix}$$

Translation can now be treated as matrix multiplication, like the other two transformations, and becomes

$$V' = T\ V$$

$$\begin{bmatrix} x' \\ y' \\ z' \\ 1 \end{bmatrix} = \begin{bmatrix} 1 & 0 & 0 & T_x \\ 0 & 1 & 0 & T_y \\ 0 & 0 & 1 & T_z \\ 0 & 0 & 0 & 1 \end{bmatrix} \begin{bmatrix} x \\ y \\ z \\ 1 \end{bmatrix}$$

This specification implies that the object is translated in three dimensions by applying a displacement T_x, T_y and T_z to each vertex that defines the object. The matrix notation is a convenient and elegant way of writing the transformation as a set of three equations:

$$x' = x + Tx$$
$$y' = y + Ty$$
$$z' = z + Tz$$

The set of transformations is completed by scaling and rotation. First scaling:

$$V' = S \ V$$

$$S = \begin{bmatrix} S_x & 0 & 0 & 0 \\ 0 & S_y & 0 & 0 \\ 0 & 0 & S_z & 0 \\ 0 & 0 & 0 & 1 \end{bmatrix}$$

Here S_x, S_y and S_z are scaling factors. For uniform scaling $S_x = S_y = S_z$, otherwise scaling occurs along these axes for which the scaling factor is non-unity. Again the process can be expressed less succinctly by a set of three equations:

$$x' = x \cdot S_x$$
$$y' = y \cdot S_y$$
$$z' = z \cdot S_z$$

applied to every vertex in the object.

To rotate an object in three-dimensional space we need to specify an axis of rotation. This can have any spatial orientation in three-dimensional space, but it is easiest to consider rotations that are parallel to one of the coordinate axes. The transformation matrices for anti-clockwise (looking along each axis towards the origin) rotation about the X, Y and Z axes respectively are:

$$R_x = \begin{bmatrix} 1 & 0 & 0 & 0 \\ 0 & \cos\theta & -\sin\theta & 0 \\ 0 & \sin\theta & \cos\theta & 0 \\ 0 & 0 & 0 & 1 \end{bmatrix}$$

$$R_y = \begin{bmatrix} \cos\theta & 0 & \sin\theta & 0 \\ 0 & 1 & 0 & 0 \\ -\sin\theta & 0 & \cos\theta & 0 \\ 0 & 0 & 0 & 1 \end{bmatrix}$$

$$R_z = \begin{bmatrix} \cos\theta & -\sin\theta & 0 & 0 \\ \sin\theta & \cos\theta & 0 & 0 \\ 0 & 0 & 1 & 0 \\ 0 & 0 & 0 & 1 \end{bmatrix}$$

The Z axis matrix specification is equivalent to the following set of three equations :

$$x' = x \cos\theta - y \sin\theta$$

$$y' = x \sin\theta + y \cos\theta$$

$$z' = z$$

Figure 24.3 shows examples of these transformations operating on a cube with one of its vertices at the origin.

The inverse of these transformations is often required. T^{-1} is obtained by negating T_x, T_y and T_z. Replacing S_x, S_y and S_z by their reciprocals gives S^{-1} and negating the angle of rotation gives R^{-1}.

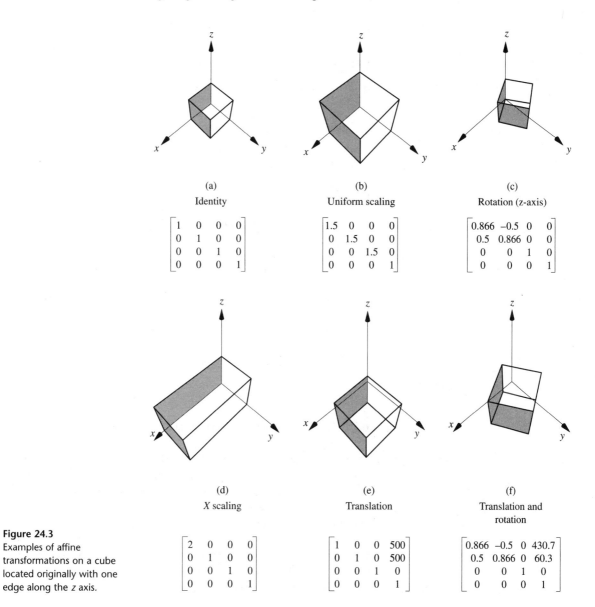

Figure 24.3
Examples of affine transformations on a cube located originally with one edge along the *z* axis.

Any set of rotations, scalings and translations can be multiplied or concatenated together to give a net transformation matrix. For example if:

$$\begin{bmatrix} x' \\ y' \\ z' \\ 1 \end{bmatrix} = \textbf{\textit{M1}} \begin{bmatrix} x \\ y \\ z \\ 1 \end{bmatrix}$$

and

$$\begin{bmatrix} x'' \\ y'' \\ z'' \\ 1 \end{bmatrix} = \textbf{\textit{M2}} \begin{bmatrix} x' \\ y' \\ z' \\ 1 \end{bmatrix}$$

then the transformation matrices can be concatenated:

$$\textbf{\textit{M3}} = \textbf{\textit{M2}}\ \textbf{\textit{M1}}$$

and

$$\begin{bmatrix} x'' \\ y'' \\ z'' \\ 1 \end{bmatrix} = \textbf{\textit{M3}} \begin{bmatrix} x \\ y \\ z \\ 1 \end{bmatrix}$$

Although translations are commutative, rotations are not and

$$\textbf{\textit{R1 R2}} \neq \textbf{\textit{R2 R1}}$$

A general transformation matrix will be of the form:

$$\begin{bmatrix} a_{11} & a_{12} & a_{13} & T_x \\ a_{21} & a_{22} & a_{23} & T_y \\ a_{31} & a_{32} & a_{33} & T_z \\ 0 & 0 & 0 & 1 \end{bmatrix}$$

The 3×3 upper left sub-matrix $\textbf{\textit{A}}$ is the net rotation and scaling while $\textbf{\textit{T}}$ gives the net translation.

(24.2.2) Transformations for changing coordinate systems

Up to now we have discussed transformations that operate on points all of which are expressed relative to one particular coordinate system. In many contexts in computer graphics we need to derive transformations that take points from one coordinate system into another.

Consider two coordinate systems with axes parallel, that is, the systems which only differ by a translation. If we wish to transform points currently expressed in system 1 into system 2 then we use the inverse of the transformation that takes the origin of system 1 to that of system 2. That is, a point $(x,y,z,1)$ in system 1 transforms to a point $(x',y',z',1)$ by:

$$\begin{bmatrix} x' \\ y' \\ z' \\ 1 \end{bmatrix} = \begin{bmatrix} 1 & 0 & 0 & -T_x \\ 0 & 1 & 0 & -T_y \\ 0 & 0 & 1 & -T_z \\ 0 & 0 & 0 & 1 \end{bmatrix} \begin{bmatrix} x \\ y \\ z \\ 1 \end{bmatrix}$$

$$= \boldsymbol{T}_{12} = (\boldsymbol{T}_{21})^{-1}$$

which is the transformation that translates the origin of system 1 to that of system 2 (where the point is still expressed relative to system 1). Another way of putting it is to say that the transformation generally required is the inverse of the transformation that takes the old axes to the new axes within the current coordinate system.

This is an important result because we generally find transformations between coordinate systems by considering transformations that operate on origins and axes. In the case of viewing systems a change in coordinate systems involves both translation and rotation and we find the required transformation in this way by considering a combination of rotations and translations.

24.3 Vectors and the computer image

Vectors are used in a variety of contexts in computer graphics. A vector is an entity that possesses magnitude and direction. A three-dimensional vector is a triple:

$$\boldsymbol{V} = (v_1, v_2, v_3)$$

where each component v_i is a scalar.

24.3.1 Addition of vectors

Addition of two vectors $\boldsymbol{V}$ and $\boldsymbol{W}$, for example, is defined as:

$$\boldsymbol{X} = \boldsymbol{V} + \boldsymbol{W}$$
$$= (x_1, x_2, x_3)$$
$$= (v_1 + w_1, v_2 + w_2, v_3 + w_3)$$

Geometrically this is interpreted as follows. The 'tail' of $\boldsymbol{W}$ is placed at the 'head' of $\boldsymbol{V}$ and $\boldsymbol{X}$ is the vector formed by joining the tail of $\boldsymbol{V}$ to the head of $\boldsymbol{W}$. This is shown in Figure 24.4 for a pair of two-dimensional vectors together with an alternative, but equivalent, interpretation.

Figure 24.4
Two geometric interpretations on the sum of two vectors.

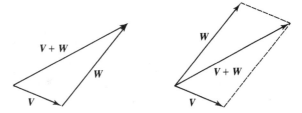

Length of vectors

The magnitude or length of a vector is defined to be

$$|\mathbf{V}| = (v_1^2 + v_2^2 + v_3^2)^{1/2}$$

and we interpret this geometrically as the distance from its tail to its head.

We normalize a vector to produce a unit vector which is a vector of length equal to one. The normalized version of $\mathbf{V}$ is:

$$\mathbf{U} = \mathbf{V}/|\mathbf{V}|$$

which is a vector of unit length having the same direction as $\mathbf{U}$. We can now refer to $\mathbf{U}$ as a direction. Note that we can write:

$$\mathbf{V} = |\mathbf{V}|\mathbf{U}$$

which is saying that any vector is given by its magnitude times its direction. Normalization is used frequently in computer graphics because we are interested in calculating and representing the orientation of entities and comparative orientation requires normalized vectors.

Normal vectors and cross products

In computer graphics considerable processing is carried out using vectors that are normal to a surface. For example, in a polygon mesh model (Chapter 2) a normal vector is used to represent the orientation of a surface when comparing this with the direction of the light. Such a comparison is used in reflection models to compute the intensity of the light reflected from the surface. The smaller the angle between the light vector and the vector that is normal to the surface, the higher is the intensity of the light reflected from the surface (Chapters 3 and 5).

A normal vector to a polygon is calculated from three (non-collinear) vertices of the polygon. Three vertices define two vectors $\mathbf{V}_1$ and $\mathbf{V}_2$ (Figure 24.5) and the normal to the polygon is found by taking the cross product of these:

$$\mathbf{N}_p = \mathbf{V}_1 \times \mathbf{V}_2$$

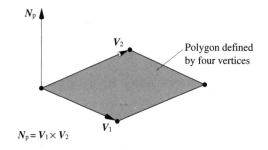

Figure 24.5
Calculating the normal vector to a polygon.

The cross product of two vectors V and W is defined as:

$$X = V \times W$$
$$= (v_2 w_3 - v_3 w_2)\mathbf{i} + (v_3 w_1 - v_1 w_3)\mathbf{j} + (v_1 w_2 - v_2 w_1)\mathbf{k}$$

where $\mathbf{i}$, $\mathbf{j}$ and $\mathbf{k}$ are the standard unit vectors:

$$\mathbf{i} = (1,0,0)$$
$$\mathbf{j} = (0,1,0)$$
$$\mathbf{k} = (0,0,1)$$

that is, vectors oriented along the coordinate axes that define the space in which the vectors are embedded.

Geometrically a cross product, as we have implied, is a vector whose orientation is normal to the plane containing the two vectors forming the cross product. When determining the surface normal of a polygon, the cross product must point outwards with respect to the object. In a right-handed coordinate system the sense of the cross product vector is given by the right-hand rule. If the first two fingers of your right-hand point in the direction of V and W then the direction of X is given by your thumb.

If the surface is a bicubic parametric surface (Chapter 7), then the orientation of the normal vector varies continuously over the surface. We compute the normal at any point (u,v) on the surface again by using a cross product. This is done by first calculating tangent vectors in the two parametric directions. (We outline the procedure here for the sake of completeness and give full details in Chapter 7.) For a surface defined as $Q(u,v)$ we find:

$$\frac{\partial}{\partial u} Q(u,v) \text{ and } \frac{\partial}{\partial v} Q(u,v)$$

We then define:

$$N = \frac{\partial Q}{\partial u} \times \frac{\partial Q}{\partial v}$$

This is shown schematically in Figure 24.6.

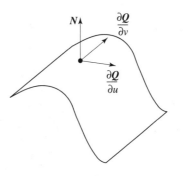

Figure 24.6
Normal N to a point on a parametric surface $Q(u,v)$.

In computer vision we often try to determine, from an image plane projection, the orientation of the surface normal of the surface element that produced the projection. Here the only information we have is intensity variations in the local area of the pixel for which we are trying to determine the surface normal. In other words, the problem is the opposite to that of computer graphics – we have to determine the surface normal from the image whereas in computer graphics we use the surface normal to produce the image. The surface normal orientation thus has to be determined from derivative information calculated from local intensity variations. It is immediately obvious that this will be sensitive to noise variations because the neighbourhood over which derivatives are calculated is necessarily small. Surface normals and computer vision is a topic we return to in Chapter 15.

24.3.4 Normal vectors and dot products

The most common use of a dot product in computer graphics is to provide a measure of the angle between two vectors, where one of the vectors is a normal vector to a surface or group of surfaces. Common applications are shading (the angle between a light direction vector and a surface normal) and visibility testing (the angle between viewing vector and a surface normal).

The dot product of vectors V and W is defined as:

$$X = V \cdot W$$
$$= v_1 w_1 + v_2 w_2 + v_3 w_3$$

Figure 24.7(a) shows two vectors. Using the cosine rule we have:

$$|V - W|^2 = |V|^2 + |W|^2 - 2|V||W| \cos\theta$$

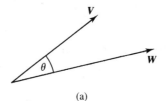

(a)

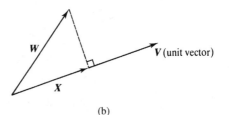

(b)

Figure 24.7
(a) The dot product of the two vectors is related to the cosine of the angle between them:

$$\cos\theta = \frac{V \cdot W}{|V||W|}$$

(b) $|X| = V \cdot W$ is the length of the projection of W onto V.

where θ is the angle between the vectors. Also it can be shown that:

$$|V - W|^2 = |V|^2 - 2VW + |W|^2$$

thus

$$V{\cdot}W = |V||W| \cos\theta$$

giving

$$\cos\theta = V{\cdot}W/|V||W|$$

or the angle between two vectors is the dot product of their normalized versions.

We can use the dot product to project a vector onto another vector. Consider a unit vector V. If we project any vector W onto V (Figure 24.7(b)) and call the result X, then we have:

$$|X| = |W| \cos\theta$$
$$= \frac{|W|\ V{\cdot}W}{|V||W|} \tag{24.1}$$
$$= V{\cdot}W$$

because V is a unit vector. Thus the dot product of V and W is the length of the projection of W onto V.

A property of the dot product used in computer graphics is its sign. Because of its relationship to $\cos\theta$ the dot product of V and W (where V and W are of any length) has sign:

$$V{\cdot}W > 0 \text{ if } \theta < 90 \text{ degrees}$$
$$V{\cdot}W = 0 \text{ if } \theta = 90 \text{ degrees}$$
$$V{\cdot}W < 0 \text{ if } \theta > 90 \text{ degrees}$$

(24.3.5)

Vectors associated with the normal vector

There are three important vectors that are associated with the surface normal. They are the light direction vector L, the reflecting vector or mirror vector R and the viewing vector V. The light direction vector L is a vector whose direction is given by the line from the tail of the surface normal to the light source, which in simple shading contexts is defined as a the point on the surface that we are currently considering. This vector is shown in Figure 24.8(a). The reflection vector R is given by the direction of the light reflected from the surface due to light incoming along direction L. Sometimes called the mirror direction, geometric optics tells us that the outgoing angle equals the incoming angle as shown in Figure 24.8(b).

To find R in terms of N and L consider the construction shown in Figure 24.9. This shows:

$$R = R_1 + R_2$$
$$R_1 = -L + R_2$$

Figure 24.8
Vectors associated with the normal vector. (a) **L**, the light direction vector. (b) **R**, the reflection vector. (c) **V**, the view vector, is a vector of any orientation.

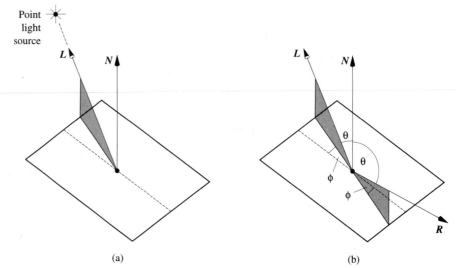

(a)   (b)

(c)

Figure 24.9
Construction of the reflection vector **R**.

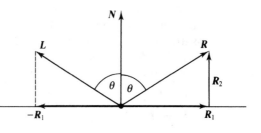

Thus

$$R = 2R_2 - L$$

from Equation (24.1)

$$R_2 = (N \cdot L)N$$

and

$$R = 2(N \cdot L)N - L$$

Finally, Figure 24.8(c) shows a view vector V. Note that this vector has any arbitrary orientation and we are normally interested in that component of light incoming in direction L that is reflected along V. This will depend in general on both the angles ϕ_v and θ_v. We also note that the intensity of outgoing light depends on the incoming angles ϕ_i and θ_i, and this is usually described as a bidirectional dependence because two angles, ϕ_v, θ_v and ϕ_i, θ_i in three-dimensional space are involved.

24.4 Rays and the computer image

In computer graphics we are interested in an entity called a ray (mathematically known as a directed line segment) that possesses position, magnitude and direction. We use this mostly to simulate light as an infinitesimally thin beam – a ray. If we imagine a ray to be a physical line in three space, then its position is the position of the tail of the line, its magnitude the length of the line between its head and tail and its direction the direction of the line. A ray can be specified by two points or by a single point, and a vector. If the end points of the ray are (x_1, y_1, z_1) and (x_2, y_2, z_2) respectively then the vector is given by:

$$V = (x_2 - x_1, \ y_2 - y_1, \ z_2 - z_1)$$

Rays are not only used in ray tracing, but they find uses in volume rendering, rendering CSG volumes and in calculating form factors in radiosity. We will now look at some of the more important calculations associated with rays.

24.4.1 Ray geometry – intersections

The most common calculation associated with rays is intersection testing. Here we test a ray against all objects in the scene for an intersection. This is potentially a very expensive calculation and the most common technique used to make this more efficient is to enclose objects in the scene in bounding volumes – the most convenient being a sphere – and test first for a ray/sphere intersection. The sphere encloses the object and if the ray does not intersect the sphere it cannot intersect the object.

Intersections – ray/sphere

The intersection between a ray and a sphere is easily calculated. If the end points of the ray are (x_1, y_1, z_1) and (x_2, y_2, z_2) then the first step is to parametrize the ray (Figure 24.10):

$$x = x_1 + (x_2 - x_1)t = x_1 + it$$
$$y = y_1 + (y_2 - y_1)t = y_1 + jt \qquad (24.2)$$
$$z = z_1 + (z_2 - z_1)t = z_1 + kt$$

A sphere at centre (l, m, n) of radius r is given by:

$$(x - l)^2 + (y - m)^2 + (z - n)^2 = r^2$$

Substituting for x, y and z gives a quadratic equation in t of the form:

$$at^2 + bt + c = 0$$

where:

$$a = i^2 + j^2 + k^2$$
$$b = 2i(x_1 - l) + 2j(y_1 - m) + 2k(z_1 - n)$$
$$c = l^2 + m^2 + n^2 + x_1^2 + y_1^2 + z_1^2 + 2(-lx_1 - my_1 - nz_1) - r^2$$

If the determinant of this quadratic is < 0 then the line does not intersect the sphere. If the determinant equals 0 then the line grazes or is tangential to the sphere. The real roots of the quadratic give the front and back intersections. Substituting the values for t into the original parametric equations yields these points. Figure 24.10 shows that the value of t also gives the position of the points of intersection relative to (x_1, y_1, z_1) and (x_2, y_2, z_2). Only positive values of t are relevant and the smallest value of t corresponds to the intersection nearest to the start of the ray.

Other information that is usually required from an intersection is the surface normal (so that the reflected and refracted rays may be calculated) although, if the sphere is being used as a bounding volume, only the fact that an intersection has occurred, or not, is required.

If the intersection point is (x_i, y_i, z_i) and the centre of the sphere is (l, m, n) then the normal at the intersection point is:

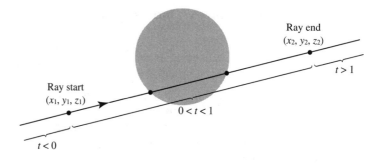

Figure 24.10
Values of parameter t along a ray.

$$N = \left(\frac{x_i - l}{r}, \frac{y_i - m}{r}, \frac{z_i - n}{r} \right)$$

24.4.3 | Intersections – ray/convex polygon

If an object is represented by a set of polygons and is convex then the straight-forward approach is to test the ray individually against each polygon. We do this as follows:

(1) Obtain an equation for the plane containing the polygon.

(2) Check for an intersection between this plane and the ray.

(3) Check that this intersection is contained by the polygon.

For example, if the plane containing the polygon is:

$$ax + by + cz + d = 0$$

and the line is defined parametrically as before, then the intersection is given by:

$$t = -(ax_1 + by_1 + cz_1 + d)/(ai + bj + ck)$$

Figure 24.11
(a) A ray in the half space that does not contain the object ($t < 0$). (b) A possible exit condition. The ray is parallel to the plane containing the polygon currently being tested. It is either inside or outside the object.

We can exit the test if $t < 0$. This means that the ray is in the half space, defined by the plane that does not contain the polygon (Figure 24.11(a)). We may also be able to exit if the denominator is equal to zero which means that the line and plane are parallel. In this case the ray origin is either inside or outside the polyhedron. We can check this by examining the sign of the numerator. If the numerator is positive then the ray is in that half space, defined by the plane that is outside the object, and no further testing is necessary (Figure 24.11(b)).

The straightforward method that tests a point for containment by a polygon is simple but expensive. The sum of the angles between lines drawn from the

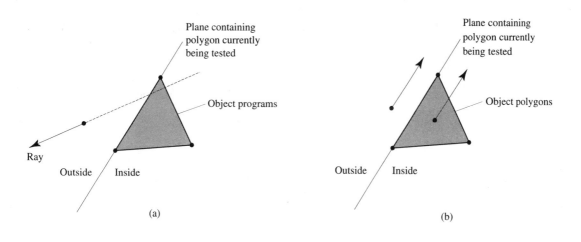

(a)

(b)

point to each vertex is 360 degrees, if the point is inside the polygon, but not if the point lies outside.

There are three disadvantages or inadequacies in this direct approach. We cannot stop when the first intersection emerges from the test unless we also evaluate whether the polygon is front- or back-facing with respect to the ray direction. The containment test is particularly expensive. It is also possible for errors to occur when a ray and a polygon edge coincide.

Intersections – ray/box

Ray/box intersections are important because boxes may be more useful bounding volumes than spheres, particularly in hierarchical schemes. Also, generalized boxes can be used as an efficient bounding volume.

Generalized boxes are formed from pairs of parallel planes, but the pairs of planes can be at any angle with respect to each other. In this section we consider the special case of boxes forming rectangular solids, with the normals to each pair of planes aligned in the same direction as the ray tracing axes or the object space axes.

To check if a ray intersects such a box is straightforward. We treat each pair of parallel planes in turn, calculating the distance along the ray to the first plane (t_{near}) and the distance to the second plane (t_{far}). The larger value of t_{near} and the smaller value of t_{far} is retained between comparisons. If the larger value of t_{near} is greater than the smaller value of t_{far}, the ray cannot intersect the box. This is shown, for an example in the xy plane, in Figure 24.12. If a hit occurs then the intersection is given by t_{near}.

A more succinct statement of the algorithm comes from considering the distance between the intersection points of a pair of parallel planes as intervals. Then if the intervals intersect, the ray hits the volume. If they do not intersect the ray misses.

Again, because our convex polygon is reduced to a rectangular solid, we can define the required distances in terms of the box extent. Distances along the ray are given for the X plane pairs as follows: if the box extent is (x_{b1}, y_{b1}, z_{b1}) and (x_{b2}, y_{b2}, z_{b2}) then:

$$t_{1x} = \frac{x_{b1} - x_1}{x_2 - x_1}$$

is the distance along the ray from its origin to the intersection with the first plane, and:

$$t_{2x} = \frac{x_{b2} - x_1}{x_2 - x_1}$$

The calculations for t_{1y}, t_{2y} and t_{1z}, t_{2z} are similar. The largest value out of the t_1 set gives the required t_{near} and the smallest value of the t_2 set gives the required t_{far}. The algorithm can exit at the y plane calculations.

Figure 24.12
Ray–box intersection.

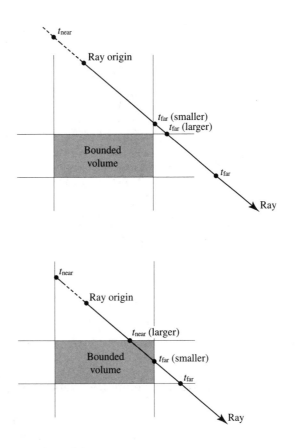

Intersections – ray/quadric

The sphere example given in Section 24.4.2 is a special case of rays intersecting with a general quadric. Ray/quadric intersections can either be dealt with by considering the general case, or 'special' objects, such as cylinders, can be treated individually for reasons of efficiency.

The general implicit equation for a quadric is:

$$Ax^2 + Ey^2 + Hz^2 + 2Bxy + 2Fyz + 2Cxz + 2Dx + 2Gy + 2Iz + J = 0$$

Following the same approach as we adopted for the case of the sphere, we substitute Equations (24.2) into the above equation and obtain the coefficients a, b and c for the resulting quadratic as follows:

$$a = Ax_d^2 + Ey_d^2 + Hz_d^2 + 2Bx_dy_d + 2Cx_dz_d + 2Fy_dz_d$$

$$\begin{aligned}b = 2(&Ax_1x_d + B(x_1y_d + x_dy_1) + C(x_1z_d + x_dz_1) + \\ &Dx_d + Ey_1y_d + F(y_1z_d + y_dz_1) + Gy_d + Hz_1z_d + Iz_d)\end{aligned}$$

$$c = Ax_1^2 + Ey_1^2 + Hz_1^2 + 2Bx_1y_1 + 2Cx_1z_1 + 2Dx_1 + 2Fy_1z_1 + 2Gy_1 + 2Iz_1 + J$$

where $x_d, y_d, z_d = i, j, k$ of Equation (24.2).

The equations for the quadrics are:

- Sphere

  $(x - l)^2 + (y - m)^2 + (z - n)^2 = r^2$

  where (l,m,n) is, as before, the centre of the sphere

- Infinite cylinder

  $(x - l)^2 + (y - m)^2 = r^2$

- Ellipsoid

  $$\frac{(x - l)^2}{\alpha^2} + \frac{(y - m)^2}{\beta^2} + \frac{(z - n)^2}{\gamma^2} - 1 = 0$$

  where α, β and γ are the semi-axes

- Paraboloid

  $$\frac{(x - l)^2}{\alpha^2} + \frac{(y - m)^2}{\beta^2} - z + n = 0$$

- Hyperboloid

  $$\frac{(x - l)^2}{\alpha^2} + \frac{(y - m)^2}{\beta^2} - \frac{(z - n)^2}{\gamma^2} - 1 = 0$$

(24.4.6)

Ray tracing geometry – reflection and refraction

The formulae presented in this section are standard formulae in a form that is suitable for incorporation into a simple ray tracer.

Each time a ray intersects a surface it produces, in general, a reflected and refracted ray. The reflection direction, a unit vector, is given (as we saw in Section 24.3.5) by:

$$\boldsymbol{R} = 2\boldsymbol{N}\cos\theta - \boldsymbol{L}$$
$$= 2(\boldsymbol{N}\cdot\boldsymbol{L})\boldsymbol{N} - \boldsymbol{L}$$

where $\boldsymbol{L}$ and $\boldsymbol{N}$ are unit vectors representing the incident ray direction, which is equal but opposite to the light vector, and the surface normal respectively. $\boldsymbol{L}$, $\boldsymbol{R}$ and $\boldsymbol{N}$ are co-planar. These vectors are shown in Figure 24.13.

A ray striking a partially or wholly transparent object is refracted due to the change in the velocity of light in different media. The angles of incidence and refraction are related by Snell's law:

$$\frac{\sin\theta_1}{\sin\theta_2} = \frac{\mu_2}{\mu_1}$$

where the incident and transmitted rays are co-planar with $\boldsymbol{N}$. The transmitted ray is represented by $\boldsymbol{T}$ and this is given by

$$\boldsymbol{T} = \mu\,\boldsymbol{I} - (\cos\theta_2 + \mu\cos\theta_1)\,\boldsymbol{N}$$

Figure 24.13
Reflection and refraction
geometry.

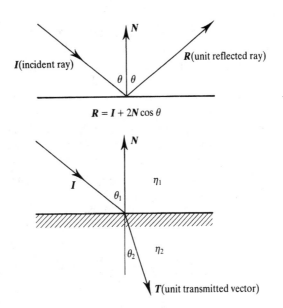

$$R = I + 2N \cos \theta$$

$$T = \mu I - (\cos \theta_2 - \mu \cos \theta_1)N$$

$$\mu = \mu_1/\mu_2$$

$$\cos \theta_2 = (1 - \mu^2(1 - \cos^2 \theta_1))^{\frac{1}{2}}$$

as shown in Figure 24.13.

If a ray is travelling from a more to a less dense medium then it is possible for the refracted ray to be parallel to the surface (Figure 24.14). θ_c is known as the critical angle. If θ is increased then total internal reflection occurs.

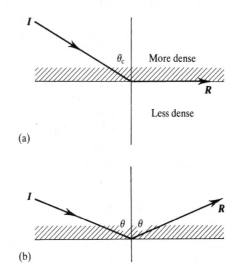

Figure 24.14
Internal reflection in an
object. (a) θ_c = critical
angle, (b) $\theta > \theta_c$.

24.5 Cameras and virtual cameras

In computer vision a scene is input into a program via some kind of camera or similar device. To derive or infer information from the two-dimensional projection of the scene we need to know and be able to parametrize the characteristics of the camera. In computer graphics we construct a view of a scene or an object by positioning a virtual camera at a point in the three-dimensional space that contains the scene or object. In other words we consider the act of setting up a viewpoint and producing a projection of the scene from that viewpoint as equivalent to positioning a camera at the viewpoint and taking a snapshot.

Cameras often move or equivalently there is relative motion between the scene and the camera. Extracting information from moving scenes is a major research area in computer vision. The most common applications of cameras in motion in computer graphics is in animation sequences where the virtual camera is choreographed and in virtual reality where the virtual viewer is the camera and can walk about and change his gaze direction.

In what follows we will, for simplicity, consider only the geometric properties of a perfect pinhole camera and ignore the non-linear effects of lens distortion. Although lens distortion necessarily has to be taken into account in a computer vision system, in computer graphics lens effects are not usually simulated. The common exception to this is distributed ray tracing where blurring due to depth of field can be incorporated.

24.5.1 Camera image formation – perspective projection

The most common projection used in real and virtual cameras is the perspective projection. It is important because it approximates the projection formed by the real world on our retinas and exhibits our expectation of foreshortening. In a perspective projection a distant line is displayed smaller than a nearer line of the same length. Although the perspective projection was only incorporated into art and stylized representations of our environment in the sixteenth century, we have become remarkably adept at perceiving depth relationships in paintings and photographs.

A perspective projection is characterized by a point known as the centre of projection, or COP, and the projection of a three-dimensional point onto the image plane is just the intersection of a line, from the point to the COP, with the image plane (Figure 24.15).

In a (lenless) computer graphics system we usually for convenience consider the COP to be behind the image plane and consider the transformation or projection of points in three-dimensional (world space) onto the image plane.

Consideration of similar triangles easily gives the coordinates (x_s, y_s) in the image plane of a point (x_v, y_v, z_v) as (Figure 24.15):

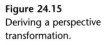

Figure 24.15
Deriving a perspective
transformation.

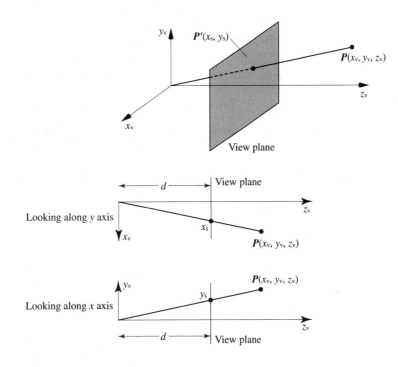

$$x_s = \frac{x_v}{z_v/d}$$

$$y_s = \frac{y_v}{z_v/d}$$

If we use homogeneous coordinates with w set to a non-unity value then we can write the above transformation as:

$$\begin{bmatrix} x_h \\ y_h \\ z_h \\ w \end{bmatrix} = \begin{bmatrix} 1 & 0 & 0 & 0 \\ 0 & 1 & 0 & 0 \\ 0 & 0 & 1 & 0 \\ 0 & 0 & \frac{1}{d} & 1 \end{bmatrix} \begin{bmatrix} x_v \\ y_v \\ z_v \\ 1_v \end{bmatrix} = T_{pers}P$$

$$w = \frac{z}{d}$$

Note that this specification also includes a value for z. In other words, we can consider the projection of a point in three-dimensional space onto an image plane as a three-dimensional to three-dimensional transformation. In computer graphics the target space is known colloquially as three-dimensional screen space and the value of z as the screen space depth. This is used in screen space hidden surface removal algorithms, such as the Z-buffer algorithm (Chapter 3). In computer vision systems we often want to try to find the value of z given that we only have (x_h, y_h), the goal of 'Shape from X' algorithms described in Chapter 16.

In imaging systems or real cameras the image is normally inverted and the projection lines, or projectors, pass from a point in three-dimensional world space through a point in front of the image or film plane which is the lens centre. This is positioned at a distance from the image plane which is known as the focal length. The transformation for this system is given as:

$$\begin{bmatrix} x_h \\ y_h \\ z_h \\ w \end{bmatrix} = \begin{bmatrix} 1 & 0 & 0 & 0 \\ 0 & 1 & 0 & 0 \\ 0 & 0 & 1 & 0 \\ 0 & 0 & -\frac{1}{f} & 1 \end{bmatrix} \begin{bmatrix} x \\ y \\ z \\ 1 \end{bmatrix} = T_{pers}P$$

$$w = 1 - \frac{z}{f}$$

There are other practical differences in image formation between a computer graphics camera and a real camera. If we define a line from the COP to the centre of the image plane to be the viewing direction, we note that in the computer graphics system we can orient the image plane at any angle with respect to this direction. This has applications in certain contexts, for example inflight simulation systems where the view surface or screen (the cockpit windows) may not be normal to the viewer. With real cameras normally the film plane is perpendicular to the lens axis (although specialist cameras exist where the film plane can be slanted). A more important difference is that in computer graphics we can have a view volume which is defined by dropping a near and far clipping plane into the view frustum formed by the four lines from the COP through the view plane (window) corners (Figure 24.16). Points or parts of objects that lie outside this volume are discarded and do not appear in the projected image. This facility is mandatory when the virtual camera finds

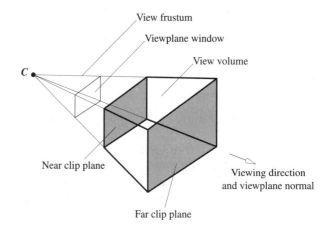

Figure 24.16
Computer graphics viewing system allows a subset of the view frustum – a view volume to be defined with near and far clip planes.

itself inside a scene with objects both behind and in front of it. In this case we cannot simply pass every point in the scene through an image plane projection. Although at first sight it seems like a powerful facility, apart from its necessity for points that cannot be seen, it does not find much application – perhaps because there is no real-world equivalent: imaging devices which capture only a slice of the scene positioned in front of it, discarding objects near to it and objects that lie far away.

24.5.2

Camera geometry

By camera geometry we mean the parameters that encapsulate the position and orientation of the camera in three-dimensional space. In computer graphics this is called the viewing system and the geometric parameters set up by the user include not only the attitude of the camera but also parameters associated with the view volume and orientation of the image plane. The minimum practical requirements in a computer graphics viewing system are the ability to position the camera anywhere in the scene and to specify from this selected position a pan, a tilt and a roll (or rotation of the camera about its view direction). Equivalently from a camera point we could define a viewing direction and a rotation of the camera about this viewing direction.

The easiest convention for a computer graphics viewing system just consists of two vectors and a point. These define a space, known as the viewing space, which can be considered an intermediate space between world space and screen space. To set up this space we define (Figure 24.17):

- A camera position **C**. This is the origin of the view space which, for simplicity, we also make equal to the COP.

- A viewing direction vector **N** which forms the positive z axis of view space. This vector is normal to the view plane.

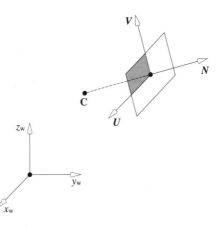

Figure 24.17
UVN coordinate system plus a camera point **C** defines a viewing coordinate system.

- An up vector V that orients the camera about the view direction and which can be considered as the y axis of the view coordinate system.

- (An optional vector U to denote the direction of increasing x in the view coordinate system. This establishes a right- or left-handed coordinate system UVN.)

To transform points from world space into view space we have:

$$T_{\text{view}} = \begin{bmatrix} U_x & U_y & U_z & -C_x \\ V_x & V_y & V_z & -C_y \\ N_x & N_y & N_z & -C_z \\ 0 & 0 & 0 & 1 \end{bmatrix}$$

This can be viewed as a change of the origin to C (the translation component) and a change of basis, or composite rotation component, which rotates the world coordinate axes into alignment with the view UVN axes.

We are now in a position to list all the coordinate spaces that are used in computer graphics and consider the formation of an image as a series of transformations through these spaces. The spaces and transformations are as follows:

- Objects are normally defined in some convenient coordinate system that is established with respect to the object itself. For example, we may position the origin of the local coordinate system to be coincident with the centre of the object. To make up a multi-object scene we would transform the geometry of the object from the local coordinate system to world coordinate space – a space that is common to all objects in the scene. The transformation that does this is know as the modelling transformation.

- The user defines camera geometry through a suitable interface and points which define objects in world coordinate space are transformed into view coordinate space using T_{view}.

- Points in view coordinate space are transformed into three-dimensional screen space using T_{pers}. In the absence of complications arising from the clip to view volume procedure these two transformations can be concatenated and a single transformation takes us from world coordinate space to screen space.

Examples of viewing a simple object using this system are shown in Figure 24.18.

In computer vision imaging systems the question of camera geometry depends on the context or application. Either we have explicit knowledge of the camera or we have to recover the camera geometry using the camera itself as a measuring device and a set of image points whose world coordinates are known. Alternatively we may try to extract the camera position(s) from a set of views – the so-called 'structure from motion problem'.

If we consider the concatenation of the transformations which we described for the computer graphics camera then we have an overall transformation that takes us from world space into the image plane:

Figure 24.18
Altering parameters in the viewing system. (a) Reference view; (b) as (a) but **C** is moved further away from world origin; (c) **V** is given a non-zero *y* component; (d) **N** is rotated about the z_w axis; (e) **C** is moved towards the world origin and *d* is reduced at the same time.

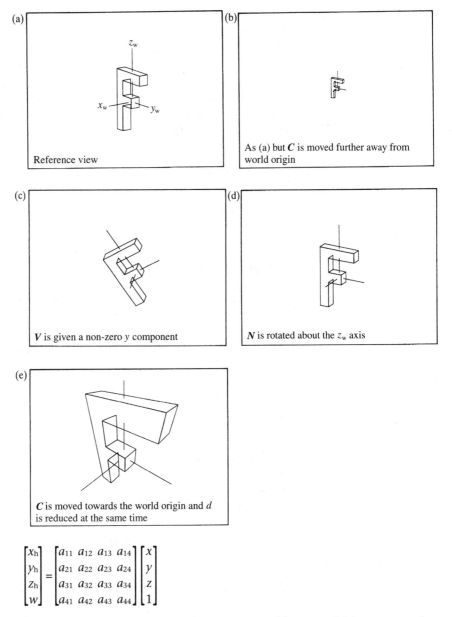

(a) Reference view

(b) As (a) but **C** is moved further away from world origin

(c) **V** is given a non-zero *y* component

(d) **N** is rotated about the z_w axis

(e) **C** is moved towards the world origin and *d* is reduced at the same time

$$\begin{bmatrix} x_h \\ y_h \\ z_h \\ w \end{bmatrix} = \begin{bmatrix} a_{11} & a_{12} & a_{13} & a_{14} \\ a_{21} & a_{22} & a_{23} & a_{24} \\ a_{31} & a_{32} & a_{33} & a_{34} \\ a_{41} & a_{42} & a_{43} & a_{44} \end{bmatrix} \begin{bmatrix} x \\ y \\ z \\ 1 \end{bmatrix}$$

If the world coordinates (x,y,z) of points in world space which correspond to known points in the image plane are known, then the problem can be stated as finding the unknown parameters associated with the camera. Substituting

$$x_h = x_s w \qquad y_h = y_s w$$

in the previous equation, where (x_s, y_s) are the Cartesian image plane coordinates, gives:

$$x_s w = a_{11}x + a_{12}y + a_{13}z + a_{14}$$
$$y_s w = a_{21}x + a_{22}y + a_{23}z + a_{24}$$
$$w = a_{41}x + a_{42}y + a_{43}z + a_{44}$$

Substituting for w yields two equations with 12 unknown coefficients requiring at least six points whose world coordinates are known.

An important relationship bridges image collection and image synthesis. This is that any two (planar) projections of a scene that are taken from a common camera position are related by:

$$\begin{bmatrix} u \\ v \\ w \end{bmatrix} = \begin{bmatrix} a_{11} & a_{12} & a_{13} \\ a_{21} & a_{22} & a_{23} \\ a_{31} & a_{32} & a_{33} \end{bmatrix} \begin{bmatrix} x_{s1} \\ y_{s1} \\ 1 \end{bmatrix}$$

$$x_{s2} = \frac{u}{w} \qquad y_{s2} = \frac{v}{w}$$

where (x_{s1}, y_{s1}) and (x_{s2}, y_{s2}) are the image plane coordinates of the same point in world space in two different projections taken from the same camera position. In other words the camera has imaged the point and then been subject to some combination of pan, tilt and roll. It tells us how a point moves in the projection plane when the camera changes its orientation. (It relates projections in a zoom sequence.) This important result is used, for example, in creating computer graphics imagery from panoramas (photographic or rendered). A panorama is constructed from photographs or pre-rendered imagery and then used in, say, a virtual reality system, where a virtual camera or viewer can pan or tilt around the panorama (see Chapter 21 for a detailed description of this image synthesis technique).

24.5.3 Stereo camera geometry

Generating a stereo pair for a head- or boom-mounted display is at the moment the standard display method in virtual reality systems. Although three-dimensional display devices exist, the mainstream method in virtual reality presents a stereo pair to a viewer usually on two small monitors in a head-mounted display or HMD. In computer vision, imaging a scene with a pair of cameras – a stereo camera – has long been the standard approach in contexts where the goal is to recover dense depth information from a scene. As we discuss in Chapter 16, this has proved to be an extremely difficult problem because to extract the depth from a pair of stereo images requires knowledge of the correspondence between individual points in each projection and it is solving the correspondence problem that has proved remarkably difficult.

If for a single point in one image we can locate the corresponding point in the other image, then establishing the distance of the object point is geometrically simple. Figure 24.19 shows a simple example. Consider two cameras, rigidly attached and pointing in the same direction parallel to the z axis. Further assume

Figure 24.19
Simple stereo geometry.

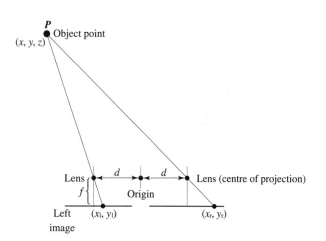

that the image planes of the cameras are co-planar and that no distortion is produced by the lenses. Consider a coordinate system, with an origin on the line joining the lens centres, which are separated by a distance $2d$, imaging an object or scene point P with coordinates (x,y,z). Then similar triangles give:

$$x_l/f = (x + d)/z \qquad x_r/f = (x - d)/z$$

and

$$z = 2fd/(x_l - x_r)$$

$|x_l - x_r|$ is known as disparity and we see that z, the depth of the imaged point, is inversely proportional to this quantity.

A practical set-up will not normally correspond to the simple situation depicted in Figure 24.19, but using the calibration measurements the incoming images can be transformed so that they appear to come from such a set-up. This process is known as rectification and it has the distinct advantage of considerably simplifying the epipolar constraint geometry described in Chapter 16.

24.6 Differentiating and averaging images

Up to now we have been concerned with mathematics involved in the representation and synthesis of digital imagery from geometric models. We will now look at two common operations carried out on existing imagery and used widely in image processing and computer vision. These operations are averaging – whose function is usually to eliminate or reduce noise – and differentiation, whose function is usually to 'sharpen' an image by emphasizing detail.

The most widely used differential operator in digital imagery is the gradient operator ∇. In practice we use the magnitude of this operator:

$$|\nabla I(x,y)| = ((\partial I/\partial x)^2 + (\partial I/\partial y)^2)^{1/2}$$

Digital approximations to the derivatives can be specified as **mask** operations. Here a small mask is placed over the pixel of interest and a sum of the products of the mask weights and the corresponding image pixel values is computed. This sum replaces the current value of the pixel. The operation is just digital cross-correlation between the image $I(x,y)$ and the mask.

The smallest mask dimension is usually taken to be 3×3. To avoid proliferating subscripts we can represent the product of a mask element and the corresponding image pixel by a single letter as:

$a \ b \ c$
$d \ o \ e$
$f \ g \ h$

and the operation is then specified by:

for all x,y
$|\nabla I(x,y)| = f(a,b,c,d,e,f,g,h,o)$

where

a means the product of the weight of the mask element a with image element $I(x{-}1,y{-}1)$
b means the product of the weight of the mask element b with image element $I(x,y{-}1)$, and so on
and f specifies the digital function of these products that approximates the gradient at $I(x,y)$

We can then write an approximation to $\partial I/\partial x$ and $\partial I/\partial y$ as:

$\partial I/\partial x = (c+e+h) - (a+d+f)$ and $\partial I/\partial y = (f+g+h) - (a+b+c)$

Sometimes this operation is specified by writing down the mask weights as:

$$\begin{bmatrix} -1 & 0 & 1 \\ -1 & 0 & 1 \\ -1 & 0 & 1 \end{bmatrix} \text{ and } \begin{bmatrix} -1 & -1 & -1 \\ 0 & 0 & 0 \\ 1 & 1 & 1 \end{bmatrix}$$

A gradient approximation can be written as:

$$|\nabla I(x,y)| = |(c + e + h) - (a + d + f)| + |(f + g + h) - (a + b + c)|$$

where the gradient expression is approximated for computation by replacing the square root of each of the partials squared by absolute values. The first term or mask is an approximation to the derivative in the x direction and the second an approximation to the derivative in the y direction.

A second-order spatial derivative that finds applications in the computer image is the Laplacian:

$$\nabla^2 I(x,y) = \partial^2 I/\partial x^2 + \partial^2 I/\partial y^2$$

The easiest way to implement this is:

$$\nabla^2 I(x,y) = 4o - (b + d + g + e)$$

Averaging or smoothing an image is accomplished most simply by replacing a pixel with the average of its neighbours. Thus:

$$o := (a + b + c + d + o + e + f + g + h)/9$$

or specified as mask weights:

$$\frac{1}{9} \begin{bmatrix} 1 & 1 & 1 \\ 1 & 1 & 1 \\ 1 & 1 & 1 \end{bmatrix}$$

Simple neighbourhood matching smoothes the image by getting rid of isolated noise spots – sudden perturbations in the value of a pixel that we suppose should not be there. However, it also has the consequence of blurring the image. We can see this by considering that overall the operation is just equivalent to taking the image and eight copies displaced in the horizontal, vertical and diagonal directions. These displaced copies go with the original to form the sum. There are many ways in which the blurring effect of a smoothing operation can be reduced or eliminated. These usually involve examining each neighbourhood and invoking a strategy that depends on some function of these values. The commonest operation in this class is simply to replace the pixel with the median of the brightness values in its neighbourhood.

24.7 Interpolating properties in the image plane

In mainstream rendering techniques – that is, rendering polygons – various properties required for interior pixels are interpolated from the values of these properties at the vertices of the polygon (that is, the pixels onto which the vertices project). Such interpolation is known as bi-linear interpolation and it is the foundation of the efficiency of this kind of shading.

Referring to Figure 24.20, the interpolation proceeds by moving a scan line down through the pixel set representing the polygon and obtaining start and end values for a scan line by interpolating between the appropriate pair of vertex properties. Interpolation along a scan line then yields a value for the property at each pixel. The interpolation equations are (for the particular edge pair shown in the illustration):

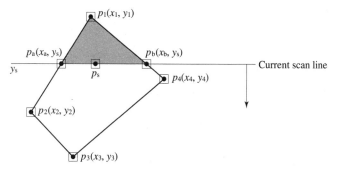

Figure 24.20
Interpolating a property at a pixel from values at the vertex pixels.

$$p_a = \frac{1}{y_1 - y_2} \left[p_1(y_s - y_2) + p_2 (y_1 - y_s) \right]$$

$$p_b = \frac{1}{y_1 - y_4} \left[p_1(y_s - y_4) + p_4 (y_1 - y_s) \right]$$

$$p_s = \frac{1}{x_b - x_a} \left[p_a(x_b - x_s) + p_b (x_s - x_a) \right]$$

These would normally be implemented using an incremental form, the final equation, for example, becoming:

$$p_s := p_s + \Delta p$$

with the constant value Δp calculated once per scan line.

Colour and the computer image

25.1 The sensation of colour

Most computer images are coloured. Colour is a subjective perceptual experience. In computer imagery we are mostly concerned with trying to imitate this real experience by reproducing colours on a display monitor. Sometimes we are interested in coding an image with colour to transmit to the viewer an impression of the variation of numerical information in the image; for example, in pseudo-colour displays of medical imagery or in displaying the output from a simulation. We will find in the course of this chapter that there are many limitations in display technology that prevent us from imitating the reality of colour and this forms one of the main topics of study together with methods of quantifying colour. In image analysis we are concerned at recovering information from a two-dimensional projection of a scene. In this respect certain aspects of the higher-level processing in the human visual system may be of some significance.

Human beings react to colour stimuli in a number of ways. There is the mysterious psychophysical reaction, of which little is known, that enables us to perceive light as a colour sensation. Except for people who suffer from colour blindness this reaction is the same for everyone. There are loose physiological reactions to colour – most people deem reds and purples to be warm and blues to be cold. There are cultural and religious associations pertaining to colour – particularly when the colour is combined with symbols. In the creation of that icon of the corporate state – the company logo – colour is usually an integral part of the design. Technological societies make heavy use of colour in all applications of graphic design and education. Complex natural phenomena and man-made systems are often explained in textbooks and other educational media by using stylized coloured diagrams. Colour is used in such contexts to enhance certain areas, to distinguish certain areas from their neighbours and to aid the perception of connectivity. The London Underground (metro) map is an old example (the original version was produced in 1933) of the effective and elegant use of colour for connectivity and identification of different lines (and incidentally stylization – geographical accuracy was sacrificed to enable horizontal, vertical and diagonal lines only and to have equal distances between stations on the map).

In computer imagery a large number of colours are normally available to the programmer or designer. Graphics terminals have usually a minimum of 256 colours (that is, any 256 selected from a palette of 16 million) and increasingly direct access to 16 million. To be able to use these colours effectively and to produce a colour display that is optimal for a particular application, a reasonable understanding of the way in which colours can be designated and specified is required.

Because colour sensation is a phenomenon that is dependent on higher-level processes in the human brain, we need a specification for the parametrization of colour that is related to human perceptual experience. This is the reason for the study of the CIE standard. This leads us to two ways of specifying colour. We can use a spectrophotometer which measures the power at each wavelength and gives us a function known as a spectral power distribution or SPD. This is a physical measurement that characterizes the relative power at each wavelength. Alternatively we can use a colorimeter to measure the colours in the CIE system. This instrument 'sees' the reflected light like a human being. The CIE system allocates a label in the form of a triple to the light. The three numbers are based on colour matching data collected from human observers and the measurements are thus related to the colour perception, defined in terms of colour matching, of human observers.

Colour vision is a field that is a scientific orthodoxy. There are accepted theories that have high inertia but no objective proof. It seems that the best we can say is that first-level processes are wavelength dependent and occur in the retina. Higher-level processing occurs in the brain. Much objective work has been carried out on the first-level processes but little is known about the working of the high-level processes. As we shall see, the way in which we 'name' colours is not necessarily directly related to the SPD of the light that we are observing.

In the retina there are three types of receptors, called cones, which operate in daylight. They have spectral sensitivities, shown in Figure 25.8(a), and each curve peaks at different points in the visible spectrum of 400 nm to 700 nm with considerable overlap occurring between the curves. This low-level processing is the fundamental reason for the specification of colour as three components (even though it was known since Newton's time that colour could be labelled in this way).

As far as the higher-level processes are concerned, little is known, but what is certain is that the perception of colour is only partially a wavelength-dependent purely local phenomenon. In a series of classic experiments Harold Land, the inventor of the Polaroid process, has shown that the perception of colour is dependent on the spatial content of scenes. It is as if somehow colour was an attribute of an object like shape, that does not change under different lighting conditions. These facts must have implications in computer imagery that have not yet been explored. They have implications in computer vision where we are trying to recover intensity information from the scene without knowledge about the lighting conditions or under varying lighting conditions. Physics tells us that this is impossible but Land's experiments show us that this task is routinely carried out by the human visual system.

25.2 Colour and the computer image

How is colour used in computer imagery? In image synthesis, at the present time, colour is mainly arbitrary or decorative. By this we mean that a designer simply selects arbitrary colours perhaps on some coarse aesthetic basis because the final image is as much an abstraction as it is an image of reality. These colours are then used in shading equations and because this is a process that operates with just three samples in wavelength space, colour aliasing is produced. Colour aliasing means that the colour produced from light with a certain SPD reflecting from a real object will not in general be the same colour produced in a computer graphics simulation of this light/object interaction.

However, it is curious that an industry which has devoted major research effort to photo-realism has all but ignored a rigorous approach to colour. After all, framestores whose pixels are capable of displaying any of 16 million colours have been commonplace for many years. We suspect three reasons for this:

- the dominance of the RGB or three-equation approach in rendering methods such as Phong shading, ray tracing and radiosity, and the high cost of evaluating these models at more than three wavelengths,

- the rendering models themselves have obvious shortcomings that are visually far more serious than the unsubtle treatment of colour (for example, spatial domain aliasing is visible, colour domain aliasing is generally invisible), and

- the current lack of demand from applications that require an accurate treatment of colour.

With some exceptions, Hall's work for example, little research into rendering with accurate treatment of colour has been carried out. There are, however, a growing number of applications that would benefit from accurate colour simulation, and a rendering method exists (the radiosity method) that is subtle enough in its treatment of light/object interaction to benefit from such an approach. Undoubtedly this will be one of the major developments in CAAD (Computer Aided Architectural Design) in the future. A computer graphics visualization of an architectural design, either interior or exterior, is usually recognizable as such. We know that the image is not a photograph. This appears to be due predominantly to the lack of fine geometric detail. Modelling costs are high and approximations are made. (In the radiosity method a coarse detail model is mandatory.) So we first notice the inadequate geometry. However, 'second order' effects are no doubt just as important and such aspects as unrealistic shadows and light that 'doesn't look quite right' contribute to the immediate visible signature of a computer graphics image.

In both image processing and computer graphics colour coding is used to highlight variations in both visual data, such as satellite imagery, and non-visual data such as mathematical models. Many important application areas involve the display of non-visual data or invisible reality as we called it in Chapter 1. This may be superimposed on, or combined with, visual structure. Colour may combined with shape to display the data in physical conjunction with the object to which the data relates. This is one of the most powerful application areas in computer graphics, giving us in effect visualizations of invisible reality as in the case of medical imagery. Here X-ray tomography or ultrasonic scanning will produce a two-dimensional array or cross-section of intensity values. A stack of these can be displayed as a three-dimensional volume (volume rendering) and colour and transparency allotted to intensity values in the original image which is related to tissue density. An example in image processing is in earth resources studies and visualizations. Colours are used to represent reflectance from the visual and non-visual part of the spectrum and such data can be combined with non-geographical data (economic data, for example), again using colour, to provide thematic maps. Stress data in structures can be collected from transducers and these values superimposed on the outline of a structure. This may be a two-dimensional section or a three-dimensional model. In all of these cases, appropriate choice of a colour mapping is important.

In computer vision or image synthesis there is currently not as much attention to colour as in the other two fields. One intriguing problem in computer vision is the recovery of shape information from image brightness. This is discussed in detail in Chapter 16. The thrust of this research is to interpret changes of intensity in grey scale images. This is difficult for the following reasons:

● The image brightness varies according to surface orientation with respect to the scene illumination. In general recognition tasks we may have no knowledge of the surface orientation. (The inverse situation in computer graphics, where we shade a surface according to its attitude with respect to the scene illumination, is of course straightforward because we do know the relationship between the surface and the light source.)

- The image brightness varies according to scene illumination – the amount of light falling on the object. This in turn depends on the nature of the light sources and the relationship of the object to other objects in the scene – whether, for example, the object is in shadow.

Both these reasons are simply statements that the light incident on a surface depends usually on unknown conditions. The incident light and surface reflectance determine image brightness; so how do we extract surface reflectance information from image brightness? If we now add the complication that the reflected light from an object surface depends on the colour of the incident light – its SPD and the reflectivity of the object as a function of wavelength – then using colour (as opposed to just intensity) is going to be difficult without knowledge of the SPD of the incident light. Intriguingly both these problems seem to be dealt with automatically by the human visual system.

Consider a famous demonstration/experiment carried out by Harold Land. Believing, as he put it, that 'the study of colour in fully coloured images is best begun by examining images that are completely devoid of and completely uncomplicated by the experience of colour', Land evolved an experiment that showed conclusively that human beings accurately perceive surface reflectance in an image, completely independent of the energy radiated from the surface.

Sheets of grey paper were positioned around a room that was subject to varying illumination. The reflectance of the paper was chosen to be inversely proportional to the illumination of the position of the room in which it was placed. Dark sheets were placed in brightly lit areas, light sheets in dimly lit areas. A photometer was used and the set-up adjusted to ensure that the light received by a viewer, from each sheet, was exactly the same. Despite this, viewers could accurately determine the reflectance of the sheets of paper.

Higher-level processes also ensure that, except under degraded conditions, we perceive colour as an attribute of an object that is independent of the wavelength of the incident light. We perceive the colour of an orange as orange under a wide variety of lighting conditions. Our colour vision system does not rely solely on wavelength and we do not function in this respect as a wavelength-dependent filter. If we did then the colour of the orange would alter according to the colour of the illuminant. This phenomenon is called colour constancy and is another area investigated by Land.

Extending the idea of the previous experiment into the colour domain, Land provided what is probably his most convincing demonstration that colour vision can be completely independent of the information reaching the eye in the form of the product of surface reflectance times incident illumination on a wavelength by wavelength basis.

The idea of the experiment is conveyed by Figure 25.1. A pattern called a 'Mondrian' (after the Dutch painter who produced works that the experimental patterns are similar to) is made up of a pattern of coloured matte paper. Each

Figure 25.1
Land's famous 'Mondrian' experiment. Illumination is set up so that the triplet of energies reaching the eye of a viewer is the same for a different coloured path for each Mondrian.

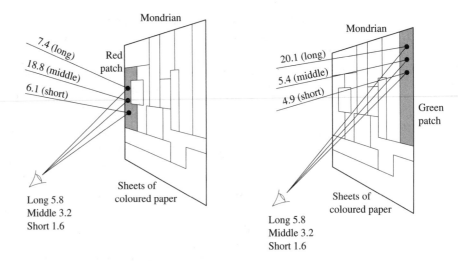

patch is surrounded by at least five or six others of different colours. Two identical Mondrians are used in the experiment. The first (left) is illuminated by three projectors operating in wavelengths determined by sharp bandpass filters. These partitions are the long, medium and short wave regions of the visual spectrum. The illumination (relative strength of each projector) is chosen so that overall the colours look 'deep' and a white patch looks white. Then using a photometer, the reflected energy reaching the eye from one patch – say a red patch – is measured in each wavelength band. Moving to the right Mondrian the illuminating projectors are now adjusted so that the reflected energy from a patch of different colour – say green – is exactly the same as for the red patch in the left Mondrian in each waveband.

When the two Mondrians are viewed simultaneously the patch in the left Mondrian looks red and the patch in the right Mondrian looks green, despite the fact that the triplet of energies reaching the eye from each patch is exactly the same.

Oliver Sacks elegantly sums up this phenomenon as follows:

These demonstrations, overwhelming in their simplicity and impact, were colour 'illusions' in the Goethe sense, but illusions that demonstrated a neurological truth – that colours are not 'out there' in the world, nor (as classical theory held) an automatic correlate of wavelength, but, rather, are *constructed by the brain*.

This concept of colour as a phenomenon internal to higher perceptual processes of humans, rather than something unambiguously associated with the wavelength of reflected light, is not well understood or accepted.

Now the purpose of these excursions is to emphasize that colour is a topic that exists at two levels. One is the subject of this chapter – how do we make calculations with colour in computer graphics and the like? The other is that colour is constructed in the brain – a process of which we know little. Many questions concerning colour and computer imagery are in the air because of this. For example, consider the phenomenon of colour constancy. Does it operate for a monitor screen view of a real scene in the same way when the viewer looks directly at the real scene? If not then this has implications in rendering for global models which transport colour from surface to surface (see Chapter 6). In this respect consider Figure 8.22 (Colour Plate) which shows colour bleeding in a photograph of a real scene. The camera system sees this effect and records it on the film. However, does the photographer see it? We record the image in this way because we can do no other with a camera/film system. But should we be doing this in trying to imitate reality in a computer graphics system? As far as colour is concerned, should a rendering system imitate a camera? Consider a simple ray tracer. Here shiny coloured objects operate as coloured mirrors. The specular–specular colour transport in a ray tracing program simply mixes the colour of the reflected object with the colour of the object that it is reflected in. This does not seem to be correct and is one of the reasons that ray traced imagery carries a heavy computer signature (although the effect is further compounded by colour shifts if a three-sampling or RGB colour model is used). If you look at the reflection of one coloured object in the other – a good example is to look into a car body surface – you are faced with an enigma. Both the reflected object and the reflecting object seem to retain their colour identity. Our eyes refuse to see a mix of colours in the reflection. The way in which we combine colours in global rendering destroys the effect. The message is that computer graphics has proceeded with rendering models by ignoring these aspects of human visual perception.

25.3 Colour sets in computer imagery

To deal with colour in the computer image we need to quantify it in some way and this gives us the notion of a colour space or domain. This is a three-dimensional space in which reside all the colours that we have an interest in. First of all, we need to define the hierarchy of colour sets that we will be referring to. These are:

(1) The set of all colours perceivable by human beings with normal colour vision.

(2) The set of colours that can be displayed by a monitor screen or captured by an input device. This is a subset of (1) for reasons that will become clear in the course of this chapter.

(3) The set of colours that can be calculated by a program and stored in a frame memory. This is generally a subset of (2). In the case of an 8-bit framestore, then only 256 colours can be specified by a synthesis program and the subset is very small indeed. However, we should make the qualification that it is a numerical subset, not a subset in colour space, as Figure 25.2 demonstrates. Even with 256 colours we can still generate colours that are outside the range or gamut of the monitor.

Figure 25.2
The hierarchy of colour sets relevant to computer imagery. A colour is a two-dimensional point in this space.

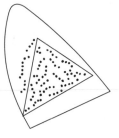

All perceivable colours
(the human visual system)

Colours reproducible
on a monitor

Colours calculated by a program
(normally we would require these
to fall within the monitor gamut)

The hierarchy is illustrated (Figure 25.2) in a cross-section of a three-dimensional colour space that will be explained later. For the moment it suffices as a base for comparing the different sets. The 8-bit colour set is represented as discrete dots (in reality there would be 256) on the diagram. These can be anywhere in the range or gamut of perceivable colours but normally we would want them to fall within the monitor gamut (undisplayable colours can be inadvertently generated by a rendering program, unless it makes checks on this eventuality).

Eight-bit colour still persists as the most commonly available option (although 24-bit colour as the default option cannot be far away) and many algorithms have been developed to 'squeeze' 24-bit images into 8-bit images by calculating, for each image, the best 8-bit set (see Section 25.8). This approach has been remarkably successful and may in itself account for the lack of dissemination of 24-bit colour into the mass market.

25.4 Colour and three-dimensional space

Why is colour a three-component vector? Again we have to bear in mind that colour is a human sensation. Traditionally we describe colours in words, usually by allusion to common objects: 'apple green', 'blood red' and so on. More precisely, colour is communicated in the painting and dyeing industry by the production of charts of sample colours. The numerical specification of colour has a long history that began with Isaac Newton, but it was only in the twentieth century that numerical systems became important industrially.

The answer to the question why colour is specified by three numerical labels is that we have three different types of cones in our retinas which have different sensitivities to different wavelengths (Figure 25.8(a)). Light can be specified physically as an SPD and we should be able to categorize the effect of any SPD on a human observer by three weights – the relative response of the three different types of cones. And so it happens that we can visually match a sample colour by additively mixing three coloured lights. We can, for example, match a sample or target colour by controlling the three intensities of a red, a green and a blue light. However, note the important point that in using matching with primary colours red, green and blue we are not basing the labelling of an SPD on the cone spectral sensitivity curves, but are using the human vision system to match colours with a mix of primaries. To do this for all colours on a wavelength by wavelength basis leads to spectral sensitivity curves that our retinas would have if the cones responded maximally to these colours. The reason for this somewhat convoluted approach is that we can derive these functions easily from colour matching experiments; precise knowledge of the actual spectral sensitivity curves of the retina is harder to come by.

Thus numerical specification of colour is by a triple of primary colours. Most, but not all, perceivable colours can be produced by additively mixing appropriate amounts of three primary colours (red, green and blue, for example). If we denote a colour by $\mathbf{C}$, we have:

$$\mathbf{C} = r\mathbf{R} + g\mathbf{G} + b\mathbf{B}$$

where r, g and b are the relative weights of each primary required to match the colour to be specified. The important point here is that this system is not specifying information related directly to the SPD of the colour. It is saying that a colour X can be specified by a numerical triple because if a matching experiment was performed an observer would choose the components r,g,b to match or simulate the colour X.

In a computer graphics monitor a colour is produced by exciting triples of adjacent dots made of red, green and blue phosphors. The dots are small and the eye perceives the triples as a single dot of colour. Thus we specify or label colours in reality using three primaries and the production of colours on a monitor is also specified in a similar way. However, note the important distinction that colour on a monitor is not produced by mixing the radiation from three light sources but by placing the light sources in close proximity to each other.

Unfortunately in computer graphics this three-component specification of colour together with the need to produce a three-component RGB signal for a monitor has led to a widely held assumption that light/object interaction need only be evaluated at three points in the spectrum. This is the 'standard' RGB paradigm that tends to be used in Phong shading, ray tracing and radiosity. If it is intended to simulate accurately the interaction of light with objects in a scene, then it is necessary to evaluate this interaction at more than three wavelengths; otherwise aliasing will result in the colour domain because of undersampling of the light distribution and object reflectivity functions. Of course, aliasing in the colour domain simply consists of a shift in colour away from a desired effect and in this sense it is invisible. (This is in direct contrast to spatial domain aliasing which produces annoying and disturbing visual artefacts.) Colours in most computer graphics applications are to a great extent arbitrary and shifts due to inaccurate simulation in the colour domain are generally not important. It is only in applications where colour is a subtle part of the simulation, say, for example, in interior design, that these effects have to be taken into account.

In image processing, we may be dealing in coarsely sampled spectral space. A satellite image, for example, may comprise four or eight component images sampled at different wavelengths. Colour is used with such imagery to produce the beautiful colour composites that form the new cartography of the late twentieth century. Colours are assigned to different parts of the spectrum and combined to produce the composites – a powerful, precise and immediately interpretable image that can show, for example, urban usage highlighted against agricultural usage, temperature of water – indeed, whatever property of reflected radiation that can be resolved by the scanner. Such images are exact and powerful imitations of the traditional cartography technique of colouring a map according to height with blue for sea, green for low-level land, brown for higher land and eventually white for snow-capped mountains.

Given that we can represent or describe the sensation of colour, as far as colour matching experiments are concerned, with numeric labels we now face the question: which numbers shall we use? This heralds the concept of different colour spaces or domains.

It may be, as we suggest in the previous section, that a calculation or rendering domain is a wavelength or spectral space. Eventually, however, we need to produce an image in RGB monitor space to drive a particular monitor. What about the storage and communication of images? Here we need a universal standard. RGB monitor spaces, as we shall see, are particular to devices. These devices have different gamuts or colour ranges all of which are subsets of the set of perceivable colours. A universal space will be device independent and will embrace all perceivable colours. Such a space exists and is known as the CIE XYZ standard. A CIE triple is a unique numeric label associated with any perceivable colour.

Another requirement in computer graphics is a facility that allows a user to manipulate and design using colour. It is generally thought that an interface that allows a user to mix primary colours is anti-intuitive and spaces that are inclined to perceptual sensations such as hue, saturation and lightness are preferred in this context.

We now list the main colour spaces used in the computer image.

- CIE XYZ space: the dominant international standard for colour specification. A colour is specified as a set of three tri-stimulus values or artificial primaries XYZ.

- Variations or transformations of CIE XYZ space (such as CIE xyY space) that have evolved over the years for different contexts. These are transforms of CIE XYZ that better reflect some detail in the perception of colour, for example linearity.

These first two spaces relate to all colours perceivable by human beings. The following relate to the colours used in computer imagery and TV.

● Spectral space: In image synthesis light sources are defined in this space as n wavelength samples of an intensity distribution. Object reflectivity is similarly defined. A colour specified on a wavelength by wavelength basis is how we measure colour with a device such as a spectrophotometer. As we have pointed out, this does not necessarily relate to our perception of an SPD as one colour or another. We synthesize an image at n wavelengths and then need to 'reduce' this to three components for display.

● RGB space: the 'standard' computer graphics paradigm for Phong shading. This is just a three-sample version of spectral space. Light sources and object reflectivity are specified as three wavelengths Red, Green and Blue. We understand the primaries R, G and B to be pure or saturated colours.

● RGB$_{monitor}$ space: A triple in this space produces a particular colour on a particular display. In other words, it is the space of a display. The same triple may not necessarily produce the same colour sensation on different monitors because monitors are not calibrated to a single standard. Monitor RGBs are not pure or saturated primaries because the emission of light from an excited phosphor exhibits a spectral power distribution over a band of frequencies. If the usual three-sample approach is used in rendering then usually whatever values are calculated in RGB space are assumed to be weights in RGB$_{monitor}$ space. If an n-sample calculation has been performed then a device-dependent transformation is used to produce a point in RGB$_{monitor}$ space.

● HSV space: a non-linear transformation of RGB space enabling colour to be specified as Hue, Saturation and Value.

● YIQ space: a non-linear transformation of RGB space, variations of which are used in analogue TV.

We will now deal with the computer image issues surrounding these colour spaces. We will start with RGB space because it is the most familiar and easiest to use. We will then look at certain problems that lead us on to consideration of CIE space.

25.4.1 RGB space

Given the subtle distinction between the fourth and fifth points above we now describe RGB space as a general concept. This model is the traditional form of colour specification in computer imagery. It enables, for example, diffuse reflection coefficients in shading equations to be given a value as a triple (R,G,B). In this system (0,0,0) is black and (1,1,1) is white. Colour is labelled as relative weights of three primary colours in an additive system using the primaries Red, Green and Blue. The space of all colours available in this system is represented by the RGB cube (Figures 25.3 and 25.4 – Colour Plate). Important points concerning RGB space are:

Figure 25.3
The RGB colour solid. See also Figure 25.4 (Colour Plate).

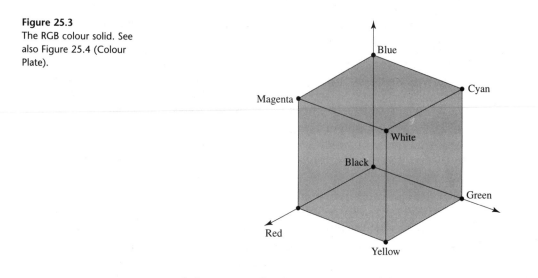

- It is perceptually non-linear. Equal distances in the space do not in general correspond to perceptually equal sensations. A step between two points in one region of the space may produce no perceivable difference; the same increment in another region may result in a noticeable colour change. In other words, the same colour sensation may result from a multiplicity of RGB triples. For example, if each of RGB can vary between 0 and 255, then over 16 million unique RGB codes are available.

- Because of the non-linear relationship between RGB values and the intensity produced at each phosphor dot (see Section 25.7), low RGB values produce small changes in response on the screen. As many as 20 steps may be necessary to produce a 'just noticeable difference' at low intensities, whereas a single step may produce a perceivable difference at high intensities.

- The set of all colours produced on a computer graphics monitor, the RGB space, is always a subset of the colours that can be perceived by humans. This is not peculiar to RGB space. Any set of three visible primaries can only produce through additive mixing a subset of the perceivable colour set.

- It is not a good colour description system. Without considerable experience, users find it difficult to give RGB values to colours known by label. What is the RGB value of 'medium brown'? Once a colour has been chosen it may not be obvious how to make subtle changes to the nature of the colour. For example, changing the 'vividness' of a chosen colour will require unequal changes in the RGB components.

25.4.2

The HSV single hexcone model

The H(ue) S(aturation) V(alue) or single hexcone model was proposed by A.R. Smith in 1978. Its purpose is to facilitate a more intuitive interface for colour than the selection of three primary colours. The colour space has the shape of a hexagonal cone or hexcone. The HSV cone is a non-linear transformation of the RGB cube and although it tends to be referred to as a perceptual model, it is still just a way of labelling colours in the monitor gamut space. Perceptual in this context means the attributes that are used to represent the colour are more akin to the way in which we think of colour; it does not means that the space is perceptually linear. The perceptual non-linearity of RGB space is carried over into HSV space; in particular, perceptual changes in Hue are distinctly non-linear in angle.

It can be employed in any context where a user requires control or selection of a colour or colours on an aesthetic or similar basis. It enables control over the range or gamut of an RGB monitor using the perceptually based variables Hue, Saturation and Value. This means that a user interface can be constructed where the effect of varying one of the three qualities is easily predictable. A task such as make colour X brighter, paler or more yellow is far easier when these perceptual variables are employed, than having to decide on what combinations of RGB changes are required.

The HSV model is based on polar coordinates rather than Cartesian and H is specified in degrees in the range 0 to 360. One of the first colour systems based on polar coordinates and perceptual parameters was that due to Munsell. His colour notation system was first published in 1905 and is still in use today. Munsell called his perceptual variables Hue, Chroma and Value and we can do no better than reproduce his definition for these. Chroma is related to saturation – the term that appears to be preferred in computer graphics.

Munsell's definitions are:

- Hue: 'It is that quality by which we distinguish one colour family from another, as red from yellow, or green from blue or purple.'

- Chroma: 'It is that quality of colour by which we distinguish a strong colour from a weak one; the degree of departure of a colour sensation from that of a white or grey; the intensity of a distinctive hue; colour intensity.'

- Value: 'It is that quality by which we distinguish a light colour from a dark one.'

The Munsell system is used by referring to a set of samples – the Munsell Book of Colour. These samples are in 'just discriminable' steps in the colour space.

The HSV model relates to the way in which artists mix colours. Referring to the difficulty of mentally imagining the relative amounts of R, G and B required to produce a single colour, Smith (1978) says:

Try this mixing technique by mentally varying RGB to obtain pink or brown. It is not unusual to have difficulty. ... the following (HSV) model mimics the way an artist mixes paint on his palette: he chooses a pure hue, or pigment and lightens it to a tint of that hue by adding white, or darkens it to a shade of that hue by adding black, or in general obtains a tone of that hue by adding some mixture of white and black or grey.

In the HSV model, varying H corresponds to selecting a colour. Decreasing S (desaturating the colour) corresponds to adding white. Decreasing V (devaluating the colour) corresponds to adding black. The derivation of the transform between RGB and HSV space is easily understood by considering a geometric interpretation of the hexcone. If the RGB cube is projected along its main diagonal onto a plane normal to that diagonal, then a hexagonal disc results.

The following correspondence is then established between the six RGB vertices and the six points of the hexcone in the HSV model.

RGB		HSV
(100)	red	(0,1,1)
(110)	yellow	(60,1,1)
(010)	green	(120,1,1)
(011)	cyan	(180,1,1)
(001)	blue	(240,1,1)
(101)	magenta	(300,1,1)

where H is measured in degrees. This hexagonal disc is the plane containing V = 1 in the hexcone model. For each value along the main diagonal in the RGB cube (increasing blackness) a contained sub-cube is defined. Each sub-cube defines a hexagonal disc. The stack of all hexagonal discs makes up the HSV colour solid.

Figure 25.5 shows the HSV single hexcone colour solid and Figure 25.6 (Colour Plate) is a further aid to its interpretation showing slices through the achromatic axis. The right-hand half of each slice is the plane of constant H and the left-hand half that of H + 180.

Apart from perceptual non-linearity, another subtle problem implicit in the HSV system is that the attributes are not themselves perceptually independent. This means that it is possible to detect an apparent change in Hue, for example, when it is the parameter Value that is actually being changed.

Finally, perhaps the most serious departure from perceptual reality resides in the geometry of the model. The colour space labels all those colours reproducible on a computer graphics monitor and implies that all colours on planes of con-

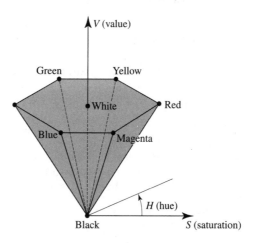

Figure 25.5
HSV single hexcone colours solid. See also Figure 25.6 (Colour Plate).

stant V are of equal brightness. Such is not the case. For example, maximum intensity blue has a lower perceived brightness than maximum intensity yellow. We conclude from this that because of the problems of perceptual non-linearity and the fact that different hues at maximum V exhibit different perceptual values, representing a monitor gamut with any 'regular' geometric solid such as a cube or a half-cone is only an approximation to the sensation of colour and this fact means that we have to consider perceptually based colour spaces. A simpler way of expressing this fact is to reiterate that colour is a perceptual sensation and cannot be accurately labelled by dividing up the RGB voltage levels of a monitor and using this scale as a colour label. This is essentially what we are doing with both the RGB and the HSV model and the association of the word 'perceptual' with the HSV model is unfortunate and confusing.

(25.4.3) YIQ space

YIQ space is a linear transformation of RGB space that is the basis for analogue TV. Its purpose is efficiency in terms of bandwidth usage (compared to the RGB form) and to maintain compatibility for black and white TV (all the information required for black and white reception is contained in the Y component).

$$\begin{bmatrix} Y \\ I \\ Q \end{bmatrix} = \begin{bmatrix} 0.299 & 0.587 & 0.144 \\ 0.596 & -0.275 & -0.321 \\ 0.212 & -0.523 & 0.311 \end{bmatrix} \begin{bmatrix} R \\ G \\ B \end{bmatrix}$$

Note that the constant matrix coefficients means that the transformation assumes that the RGB components are themselves defined with respect to a standard (in this case an NTSC definition). The Y component is the same as the CIE Y primary (see Section 25.5) and is called luminance. Colour information is 'isolated' in the I and Q components (equal RGB components will result in zero I and Q values). The bandwidth optimization comes about because human beings are more sensitive to changes in luminance than to changes in colour in this sense. We can discriminate spatial detail more finely in grey scale changes than in colour changes. Thus a lower bandwidth can be tolerated for the I and Q components, resulting in a bandwidth saving over using RGB components.

Colour representations where the colour and luminance information are separated are important in image processing where we may want to operate on image structure without affecting the colour of the image.

(25.5) Colour, information and perceptual spaces

We now come to consider the use of perceptual spaces in computer imagery. In particular, we shall look at the CIE XYZ space – an international numerically based colour labelling system first introduced in 1931 and derived from colour matching experiments.

To deal with colour reality we need to manipulate colours in a space that bears some relationship to perceptual experience. We have already alluded to applications where such considerations may be important. For example, in CAAD for interiors, the design of fabrics or the finish on such expensive consumer durables as cars, it will be necessary for computer graphics to move out of the arbitrary RGB domain into a space where colour is accurately simulated. Of course, in attempting to transmit an illusion of reality in a computer graphics simulation there are many other factors involved – surface texture, the macroscopic nature of the colour (metallic paint or ordinary gloss paint, for example) and geometrical accuracy, but at the moment in computer graphics it is the case that the RGB triple is the de facto standard for rendering.

The use of colour to communicate numerical information has a long history. Possibly the most familiar manifestation is a coloured terrain map. Here colours are chosen to represent height. Traditionally colours are chosen with green representing low heights. Heights from 0–100 m may be represented by lightening shades of green through to yellow. Darkening shades of brown may represent the range 1000–3000 m. Above 3000 m there are usually two shades of purple, and white is reserved for 6000 m and above.

This technique has been used in image processing and computer graphics where it is called pseudo-colour enhancement. It is used most commonly to display a function of two variables, $f(x,y)$, in two space where before such a function would have been displayed using 'iso-f' contours. In pseudo-colour enhancement a deliberately restricted colour list (of, say, 10 colours) is chosen and the value of f is mapped into the nearest colour. The function appears like a terrain map with islands of one colour against a background of another. (See Figure 9.4 (Colour Plate) for an example of this technique.)

In computer graphics and image processing the most popular mapping of $f(x,y)$ into colour has been some variation of the rainbow colours with red used to represent high or hot and blue used for low intensity or cold – in other words, a path around the outer edge of HSV space. One of the problems with this mapping is that depending on the number of colour steps used, transitions between different colours appear as false contours. Violent colour discontinuities appear in the image where the function f is continuous. There is a contradiction here: we need these apparent discontinuities to highlight the shape of the function but they can easily be interpreted as transitions in the function where no transition exists. This is particularly true in non-mathematical images which are not everywhere continuous to start with. Natural discontinuities may exist in the function anyway – say in a medical image made up of the response of a device to different tissue. The appearance of false contours in such an image may be undesirable.

Thus, whether the contours add to or subtract from the perception of the nature and shape of f depends in the end on the image context. The effect of false contours is easily diminished by adding more colours to the mapping but this may have the effect of making the function more difficult to interpret.

The use of perceptual colour spaces in the context of numerical information is extremely important. If an accurate association between colours and numeric information is required, then a perceptually linear colour scale should be used (perceptual colour spaces are dealt with in the next section). We discussed in Section 25.5 the perceptual non-linearity of RGB space and it is apparent that unless this factor is dealt with, it will interfere with the association of a colour with a numeric value. There is no good reason, apart from cultural associations like the example of the terrain map coding in cartography, why a hue circle should be used as a pseudo-colour scale.

The use of pseudo-colour in two space to display functions of two spatial variables has been around for many years. The past 10 years have seen an increasing application of three-dimensional computer graphics techniques in the visualization of scientific results and simulations (an area that has been awarded the acronym ViSC). The graphics techniques used are mainly animation, volume rendering (both dealt with elsewhere in this text) and the use of pseudo-colour in three space, which we will now examine.

Figure 25.7 (Colour Plate) illustrates an application. It shows an iso-surface extracted from a Navier–Stokes simulation of a reverse flow pipe combustor. In this simulation the primary gas flow is from left to right. Air is forced into the chamber under compression at the left, and dispersed by two fans. Eight fuel jets, situated radially approximately halfway along the combustor, are directed in such a way as to send the fuel mixture in a spiralling path towards the front of the chamber. Combustible mixing takes place in the central region and thrust is created at the exhaust outlet on the right. The iso-surfaces shown connect all points where the net flow along the long axis is zero – a zero velocity surface.

Such an iso-surface can be displayed by using conventional three-dimensional rendering techniques as the illustration demonstrates. In the second illustration we have sought to superimpose a pseudo-colour that represents temperature. A spectral colour path, from blue to magenta, around the circumference of the HSV cone is used.

Thus in the same three-dimensional image we are trying to represent two functions simultaneously: first, the shape of an iso-surface, and second, the temperature at every point on the iso-surface. Perceptual problems arise in this case because we are using colour to represent both shape and temperature, whereas normally the colour is experienced as an association with a single phenomenon. For example, it tends to be difficult, in such representations, to interpret the shape of the iso-surface in regions of rapidly varying hue or temperature. Nevertheless representational schemes like this are becoming commonplace in visualization techniques. They represent a kind of summary of complex data that, prior to the use of three-dimensional computer graphics, could only be examined one part at a time. For example, the simulation in the illustration may have been investigated by using a rotating cross-section. This leaves the difficult task of building up a three-dimensional picture of the data to the brain of the viewer.

25.5.1 CIE XYZ space

We have seen in the previous section that we need spectral space to try to simulate reality. This implies that we need a way of 'reducing 'or converting spectral space calculations for a monitor display. Also, we saw that we need perceptual colour spaces for choosing mappings for pseudo-colour enhancement. Another *raison d'être* for perceptual colour spaces in computer graphics is for the storage and the communication of files within the computer graphics community and for communication between computer graphicists and industries that use colour.

In image processing our ability to work in spectral space is entirely limited by the nature of the image collection device. In the case of a TV camera we are back to RGB space. With satellite imagery the number of bands depends on the technology. Eight is common. The use of perceptual spaces in image processing is not at the moment therefore very great.

The CIE standard allows a colour to be specified as a numeric triple (X,Y,Z). CIE XYZ space embraces all colours perceivable by human beings and it is based on experimentally determined colour matching functions. Thus, unlike the three previous colour spaces, it is not a monitor gamut space.

The basis of the standard, adopted in 1931, are colour matching experiments where a user controls or weights three primary light sources to match a target monochromatic light source. The primary sources used were almost monochromatic and were $\mathbf{R}$ = 700 nm, $\mathbf{G}$ = 546.1 nm and $\mathbf{B}$ = 435.8 nm. In other words, the weights in:

$$\mathbf{C} = r\mathbf{R} + g\mathbf{G} + b\mathbf{B}$$

are determined experimentally.

The result of such experiments can be summarized by colour matching functions. These are shown in Figure 25.8(b) and show the amounts of red, green and blue light which when additively mixed will produce in a standard observer a monochromatic colour whose wavelength is given by λ. That is:

$$C_\lambda = r(\lambda) + g(\lambda) + b(\lambda)$$

For any colour sensation C exhibits an SPD $P(\lambda)$, r, g and b are given by:

$$r = k\int_\lambda P(\lambda)r(\lambda)d(\lambda)$$

$$g = k\int_\lambda P(\lambda)g(\lambda)d(\lambda)$$

$$b = k\int_\lambda P(\lambda)b(\lambda)d(\lambda)$$

Thus we see that colour matching functions reduce a colour C with any shape of spectral energy distribution to a triple rgb. At this stage we should make the extremely important point that the triple rgb bears no relationship whatever to a triple RGB specified in the aforementioned (computer graphics) system. As we

Figure 25.8
The 'evolution' of the CIE
colour matching functions.

Spectral sensitivity curves
of the ρ, δ and β cones in the
retina and their relationship
to the monochromatic colours:
red = 700 nm
green = 546.1 nm
blue = 435.8 nm

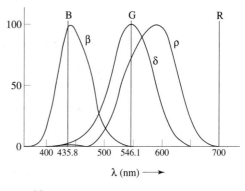

(a)

RGB colour matching
functions for the CIE 1931
Standard Colourimetric
Observer

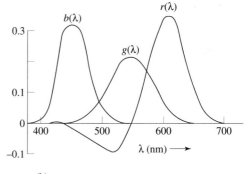

(b)

CIE matching functions
for the CIE 1931 Standard
Colourimetric Observer

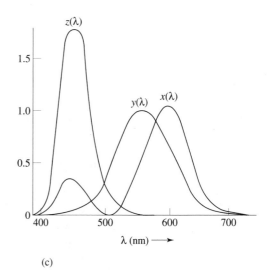

(c)

discussed in Section 25.6, computer graphicists understand the triple RGB to be three samples of the SPD of an illuminant or three samples of the reflectivity function of the object which are linearly combined in rendering models to produce a calculated RGB for reflected light. In other words, we can render by working with three samples or we can extend our approach to working with *n* samples. In contrast the triple rgb is **not** three samples of an SPD but the values obtained by integrating the product of the SPD and each matching function. It is a specification of the SPD as humans see it (in terms of colour matching) rather than as a spectrophotometer would see it.

There is, however, a problem in representing colours with an additive primary system, which is that with positive weights, only a subset of perceivable colours can be described by the weights (r,g,b). The problem arises out of the fact that when two colours are mixed the result is a less saturated colour. It is impossible to form a highly saturated colour by superimposing colours. Any set of three primaries form a bounded space outside of which certain perceivable highly saturated colours exist. In such colours a negative weight is required.

To avoid negative weights the CIE devised a standard of three supersaturated (or non-realizable) primaries X, Y and Z, which when additively mixed will produce all perceivable colours using positive weights. The three corresponding matching functions $x(\lambda)$, $y(\lambda)$ and $z(\lambda)$ shown in Figure 25.8(c) are always positive. Thus we have:

$$X = k\int_{\lambda} P(\lambda)x(\lambda)d(\lambda)$$

$$Y = k\int_{\lambda} P(\lambda)y(\lambda)d(\lambda)$$

$$Z = k\int_{\lambda} P(\lambda)z(\lambda)d(\lambda)$$

where:

$k = 680$ for self-luminous objects

The space formed by the XYZ values for all perceivable colours is CIE XYZ space. The matching functions are transformations of the experimental results. In addition the $y(\lambda)$ matching function was defined to have a colour matching function that corresponded to the luminous efficiency characteristic of the human eye, a function that peaks at 550 nm (yellow-green).

The shape of the CIE XYZ colour solid is basically conical with the apex of the cone at the origin (Figure 25.9). Also shown in this space is a monitor gamut which appears as a parallelepiped. If we compare this space to HSV space we can view the solid as distorted HSV space. The black point is at the origins and the HSV space is deformed to embrace all colours and to encompass the fact that the space is based on perceptual measurements. If we consider, for example, the outer surface of the deformed cone, this is made of rays that emanate from the origin terminating on the edge of the cone. Along any ray is the set of colours of identical chromaticity (see the next section). If a ray is moved in towards the

Figure 25.9
(a) CIE XYZ solid. (b) A typical monitor gamut in CIE XYZ space.

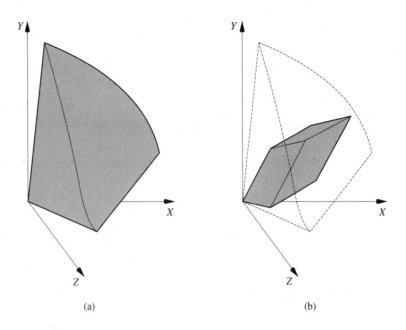

(a)   (b)

white point, situated on the base of the deformed cone, then we desaturate the set of colours specified by the ray. Within this space, the monitor gamut is a deformed (sheared and scaled) cube, forming a subset of the volume of perceivable colours.

(25.5.2)

CIE xyY space

An alternative way of specifying the (X,Y,Z) triple is (x,y,Y) where (x,y) are known as chromaticity coordinates:

$$x = \frac{X}{X + Y + Z}$$

$$y = \frac{Y}{X + Y + Z}$$

Plotting x against y for all visible colours yields a two-dimensional (x,y) space known as the CIE chromaticity diagram.

The wing-shaped CIE chromaticity diagram (Figure 25.10) is extensively used in colour science. It encompasses all the perceivable colours in two-dimensional space by ignoring the luminance Y. The locus of the pure saturated or spectral colours is formed by the curved line from blue (400 nm) to red (700 nm). The straight line between the end points is known as the purple or magenta line. Along this line are located the purples or magentas. These are colours whose perceivable sensation cannot be produced by any single monochromatic stimulus, and which cannot be isolated from daylight.

Figure 25.10
CIE chromaticity diagram showing typical gamuts for colour film, colour monitor and printing inks.

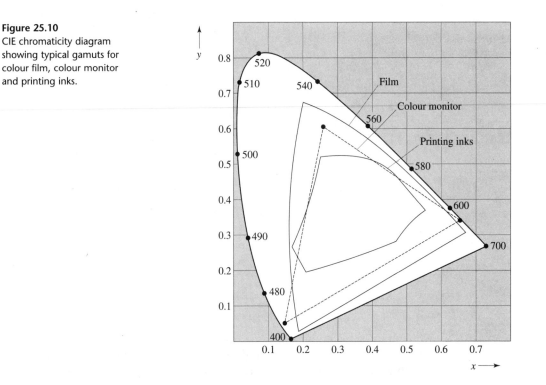

Also shown in Figure 25.10 is the gamut of colours reproducible on a computer graphics monitor from three phosphors. The monitor gamut is a triangle formed by drawing straight lines between three RGB points. The RGB points are contained within the outermost curve of monochromatic or saturated colours. Examination of the emission characteristics of the phosphors will reveal a spread about the dominant wavelength which means that the colour contains white light and is not saturated. When, say, the blue and green phosphors are fully excited their emission characteristics add together into a broader band, meaning that the resultant colour will be less saturated than blue or green.

The triangular monitor gamut in CIE xy space is to be found in most texts dealing with colour science in computer graphics, but it is somewhat misleading. The triangle is actually the projection out of CIE xyY space of the monitor gamut, with the vertices formed from phosphor vertices that each have a different luminance. Figure 25.11 shows the general shape of monitor gamut in CIE xyY space and Figure 25.12 (Colour Plate) shows three slices through the space. The geometric or shape transformation from the scaled and sheared cube in XYZ space to the curvilinear solid (with six faces) in xyY space is difficult to interpret. For example, one edge of the cube maps to a single point.

There are a number of important uses of the CIE chromaticity diagram. We give one important example. It can be used to compare the gamut of various display devices. This is important in computer graphics when an image is eventually to be reproduced on a number of different devices. Figure 25.10 shows a CIE

Figure 25.11
Monitor gamut in CIE $_{xy}$Y space (see also Figure 25.12 (Colour Plate)).

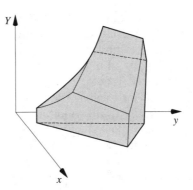

chromaticity diagram with the gamut of a typical computer graphics monitor together with the gamut for modern printing inks. The printing ink gamut is enclosed within the monitor gamut, which is itself enclosed by the gamut for colour film. This means that some colours attainable on film are not reproducible on a computer graphics monitor, and certain colours on a monitor cannot be reproduced by printing. The gamut of display devices and reproduction techniques is always contained by the gamut of perceivable colours – the saturated or spectral colours being the most difficult to reproduce. However, this is not generally a problem because spectral and near-spectral colours do not tend to occur naturally. It is the relative spread of device gamuts that is important rather than the size of any gamut with respect to the visual gamut. The general problem of transforming a gamut so that it fits within the range of a practical device is discussed in Section 25.7.

25.6 Rendering and colour spaces

We have discussed reasons for the lack of accurate colours in computer graphics and now look at one of these reasons in more detail – colour aliasing is invisible.

Physics tells us that the light reflected from a surface, as a function of wavelength, is the product of the wavelength-dependent surface reflectance function times the spectral energy distribution function of the light source. If we simply evaluate this product at three wavelengths (the RGB Phong shading model discussed in Chapter 3) then clearly, because of the gross undersampling, we will not produce a result that simulates the real characteristic. What happens is that the three-sample approach will produce a colour shift away from the real colour. However, this shift is in most contexts completely invisible because we have no expectations of what particular colour should emerge from a computer graphics model anyway. A wrong colour does not necessarily look wrong.

To try to simulate real colour interaction numerically we can simply expand our three-sample rendering approach to n samples and work in spectral space, sampling the light source distribution function and the reflectivity of the object at appropriate wavelength intervals.

We look at three approaches which are summarized in Figure 25.13. The first – the de facto standard approach to rendering – takes no account of colour except in the most approximate way. The illuminant SPD is sampled at three wavelengths, or more usually arbitrarily specified as 1,1,1 for white light. Similarly the reflectivity of the object is specified at each of the R, G and B wavelengths. Three rendering equations/models are applied and the calculated RGB intensities are fed directly to the monitor without further alteration. This method produces works with input values that are arbitrary in the sense that a user may want to render a dark red object, but may not be concerned with specifying the colour of the object and illuminant to any degree of accuracy. Only three rendering equations are used.

The second approach applies the rendering equations in spectral space for a set of wavelengths ($n = 9$ appears to be a good compromise). Here the rendering cost is at least a factor of three greater than the 'arbitrary' colour method. The output from the renderer is a sampled intensity function and this must be transformed into (three sample) $RGB_{monitor}$ space for display. The implication here is that if we have gone to the trouble to render at n wavelengths then we wish to display the result as accurately as possible and we need certain monitor parameters to be able to derive the spectral to $RGB_{monitor}$ transformation (see Section 25.7).

In the final approach we render in CIE space. This means specifying the SPD illuminant as CIE XYZ values using the matching functions. However, we have the problem of the surface reflectivity. What values do we use for this? This is a subtle point and the reader is referred to the paper by Borges which addresses exactly this issue. Here we can note that we can simply express the reflectivity function also as a CIE XYZ triple and use this in a three-equation rendering approach. The output from the renderer is a CIE XYZ triple and we then require a CIE to $RGB_{monitor}$ transform to display the result.

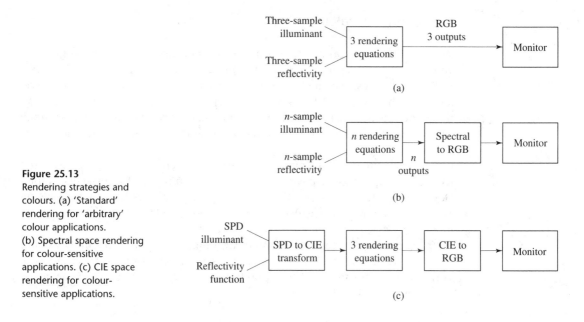

Figure 25.13
Rendering strategies and colours. (a) 'Standard' rendering for 'arbitrary' colour applications.
(b) Spectral space rendering for colour-sensitive applications. (c) CIE space rendering for colour-sensitive applications.

The difference between an image produced by 'spectral rendering' and 'RGB rendering' is shown (to within the limits of the reproduction process) in Figure 25.14 (Colour Plate) for a ray tracer.

We must remember that we are only attending to a single aspect in the simulation of reality – which is the prevention of erroneous colour shifts due to undersampling in spectral space. Colour is also determined by the local reflection model itself. Defects in the accuracy with which the reflection model simulates reality still exist. We cannot overcome these simply by extending the number of samples in spectral space.

25.7 Monitor considerations

25.7.1 $RGB_{monitor}$ space and other monitor considerations

Serious use of colour in computer imagery needs careful attention to certain aspects of the display monitor. Computer graphics monitors are not standardized and the application of the same RGB triple to different monitors will produce different colours on the screen. The most important factors are:

- Colour on a monitor is not produced by the superposition mixing of three lights, but relies on the eye to spatially mix the tiny light sources produced by three phosphor dots. There is nothing that we can do about this. One of the consequences is that saturated colours are not displayed at their full brightness – an area of pure red is only one-third red and two-thirds black. This means that, for example, even though we as human beings seem to compensate for this effect, taking photographs directly from the screen produces poor results.

- Different monitors are manufactured with phosphors that have different spectral energy distributions. For example, different phosphors are used to achieve different persistences (the length of time a phosphor glows for after being activated). This can be corrected by a linear transformation as we demonstrate in the next section.

- The relationship between the RGB values applied to the monitor and the intensity of light produced on the screen is non-linear. The cure for this, gamma correction – a non-linear transformation – is described in the next section.

- In image synthesis, shading equations can produce colours that are outside the gamut of the monitor – undisplayable colours. We have somehow to clip these colours or bring them back into the monitor gamut. This is also a non-linear operation.

25.7.2 Monitor considerations – different monitors and the same colour

Contexts in which real colours are produced in computer imagery are, for example, rendering in spectral space and using perceptual space mapping. With spectral space we can produce a CIE XYZ triple from our final set of results. CIE XYZ space is used as a final standard and we need a device-specific transformation to go from CIE XYZ space to the particular RGB$_{\text{monitor}}$ space.

We can write:

$$\begin{bmatrix} X \\ Y \\ Z \end{bmatrix} = \begin{bmatrix} X_r & X_g & X_b \\ Y_r & Y_g & Y_b \\ Z_r & Z_g & Z_b \end{bmatrix} \begin{bmatrix} R_m \\ G_m \\ B_m \end{bmatrix}$$

$$= T \begin{bmatrix} R_m \\ G_m \\ B_m \end{bmatrix}$$

where T is particular to a monitor and a linear relationship is assumed between the outputs from the phosphors and the RGB values. (X_r, X_g, X_b) are the tri-stimulus values required to produce a unit amount of the R primary on the monitor, (Y_r, Y_g, Y_b) are the tri-stimulus values to produce a unit amount of the G primary, and so on. T can be calculated in the following way. We define:

$$D_r = X_r + Y_r + Z_r$$
$$D_g = X_g + Y_g + Z_g$$
$$D_b = X_b + Y_b + Z_b$$

giving:

$$\begin{bmatrix} X \\ Y \\ Z \end{bmatrix} = \begin{bmatrix} D_r x_r & D_g x_g & D_b x_b \\ D_r y_r & D_g y_g & D_g y_b \\ D_r z_r & D_g z_g & D_b z_b \end{bmatrix} \begin{bmatrix} R_m \\ G_m \\ B_m \end{bmatrix}$$

where:

$$x_r = X_r/D_r \qquad y_r = Y_r/D_r \qquad z_r = Z_r/D_r$$

Writing the coefficients as a product of two matrices we have:

$$\begin{bmatrix} X \\ Y \\ Z \end{bmatrix} = \begin{bmatrix} x_r & x_g & x_b \\ y_r & y_g & y_b \\ z_r & z_g & z_b \end{bmatrix} \begin{bmatrix} D_r & 0 & 0 \\ 0 & D_g & 0 \\ 0 & 0 & D_b \end{bmatrix} \begin{bmatrix} R_m \\ G_m \\ B_m \end{bmatrix}$$

where the first matrix is the chromaticity coordinates of the monitor phosphor. We now specify that equal RGB voltages of $(1,1,1)$ should produce the alignment white:

$$\begin{bmatrix} X_w \\ Y_w \\ Z_w \end{bmatrix} = \begin{bmatrix} x_r & x_g & x_b \\ y_r & y_g & y_b \\ z_r & z_g & z_b \end{bmatrix} \begin{bmatrix} D_r \\ D_g \\ D_b \end{bmatrix}$$

For example, with standard white D$_{65}$ we have:

$$x_w = .313 \qquad y_w = .329 \qquad z_w = .358$$

and scaling the white point to give unity luminance yields

$$X_w = .951 \quad Y_w = 1.0 \quad Z_w = 1.089$$

Example chromaticity coordinates for an interlaced monitor (long persistence phosphors) are:

	x	y
red	0.620	0.330
green	0.210	0.685
blue	0.150	0.063

Using these we have:

$$\begin{bmatrix} X \\ Y \\ Z \end{bmatrix} = \begin{bmatrix} .584 & .188 & .179 \\ .311 & .614 & .075 \\ .047 & .103 & .939 \end{bmatrix} \begin{bmatrix} R_m \\ G_m \\ B_m \end{bmatrix}$$

Inverting the coefficient matrix gives:

$$\begin{bmatrix} R_m \\ G_m \\ B_m \end{bmatrix} = \begin{bmatrix} 2.043 & -0.568 & -0.344 \\ -1.036 & 1.939 & 0.043 \\ 0.011 & -0.184 & 1.078 \end{bmatrix} \begin{bmatrix} X \\ Y \\ Z \end{bmatrix}$$

The significance of the negative components is that RGB space is a subset of XYZ space and XYZ colours that lie outside the monitor gamut will produce negative RGB values.

(25.7.3) Monitor considerations – colour gamut mapping

Monitor gamuts generally overlap and colours that are available on one monitor may not be reproducible on another. This is manifested by RGB values that are less than zero, or greater than one, after the transformation *T* has been applied. This problem may also arise in rendering. In accurate colour simulation, using real colour values, it is likely that colour triples produced by the calculation may lie outside the monitor gamut. In other words, the image gamut may be in general greater than the monitor gamut. This problem is even greater in the case of hard copy devices such as printers which have smaller gamuts than monitors. The problem should not arise in image processing with pseudo-colour mapping.

The goal of the process is to compress the image gamut until it just fits in the device gamut in such a way that the image quality is maintained. This will generally depend on the content of the image and the whole subject area is still a research topic. There are, however, a number of simple strategies that we can adopt. The process of producing a displayable colour from one that is outside the gamut of the monitor is called 'colour clipping'.

Clearly we could adopt a simple clamping approach and limit out of range values not 0 or 1. Better strategies are suggested by Hall in his book (see Further reading). Undisplayable colours fall into one of two categories:

- Colours that have chromaticities outside the monitor gamut (negative RGB values).

- Colours that have displayable chromaticities, but intensities outside the monitor gamut (RGB values greater than one).

Any correction results in a shift or change from the calculated colour and we can select a method depending on whether we wish to tolerate a shift in hue, saturation and/or value.

For the first category the best approach is to add white to the colour or to desaturate it until it is displayable. This maintains the hue or dominant wavelength and lightness at the cost of saturation. In the second case there are a number of possibilities. The entire image can be scaled until the highest intensity is in range; this has an effect similar to reducing the aperture in a camera. Alternatively the chromaticity can be maintained and the intensity scaled. Finally the dominant hue and intensity can be maintained and the colour desaturated by adding white.

25.7.4 Monitor considerations – gamma correction

All of the foregoing discussion has implicitly assumed that there is a linear relationship between the actual RGB values input to a monitor and the intensity produced on the screen. This is not the case. That we need to maintain linearity comes from the fact that as far as possible we require a person viewing, say, a TV image of a scene on a monitor to see the colour relationships as he perceives them from the scene. This implies that the end-to-end response of the TV system should be linear (Figure 25.15(a)). In a TV system gamma correction is applied at the camera (for reasons that also have to do with coding the signal optimally for noise) to pre-compensate for the monitor linearity. This is shown in Figure 25.15(b) which shows gamma correction introduced in the camera compensating for the non-linear relationship at the monitor. A computer graphics system (Figure 25.15(c)) is analogous to a TV camera with a linear intensity characteristic because the rendering calculations are linear. Because of this, gamma correction is required after the calculation and this is usually implemented in the form of an LUT.

Now consider the details. The red intensity, for example, produced on a monitor screen by an input value of R_i' is:

$$R_m = K(R_i')^{\gamma_r}$$

where γ_r is normally in the range 2.3 to 2.8. The goal of the process is to linearize the relationship between the RGB values produced by the program and if γ_r, γ_g and γ_b are known then so-called gamma correction can be applied to convert the

Figure 25.15
Gamma correction. (a) A viewer should ideally see the same colours on a TV monitor as if he was viewing the scene. (b) Gamma correction is applied in a TV camera. (c) Computer graphics system.

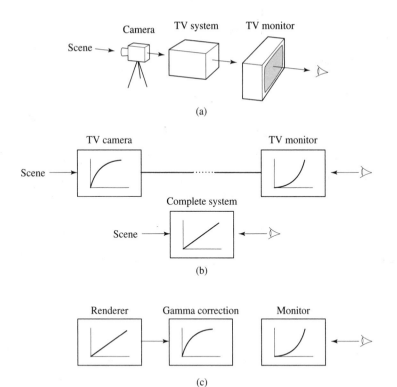

program value R_i to the value that when plugged into the above equation will result in a linear relationship. That is:

$$R_i' = k(R_i)^{1/\gamma_r}$$

An inexpensive method for determining γ is given in a paper by Cowan. The two relationships are shown in Figure 25.16. The second graph is easily incorporated in a video lookup table. Note that the price paid for gamma correction is a reduction in the dynamic range. For example, if k is chosen such that 0 maps to 0 and 255 to 255 then 256 intensity levels are reduced to 167. This can cause banding and it is better to perform the correction in floating point and then to round.

Using a monitor with uncorrected gamma results in both intensity and chromaticity shifts away from the colour calculated by the program. Consider, for example, the triple (0,255,127). If this is not gamma corrected the display will decrease the blue component, leaving the red and green components unchanged.

Gamma correction leaves zero and maximum intensities unchanged and alters the intensity in mid-range. A 'wrong' gamma that occurs either because gamma correction has not been applied or because an inaccurate value of gamma has been used in the correction will always result in a wrong image with respect to the calculated colour.

Figure 25.16
Gamma correction.
(a) Intensity as a function
of applied voltage values.
(b) Corrected values as a
function of applied values.

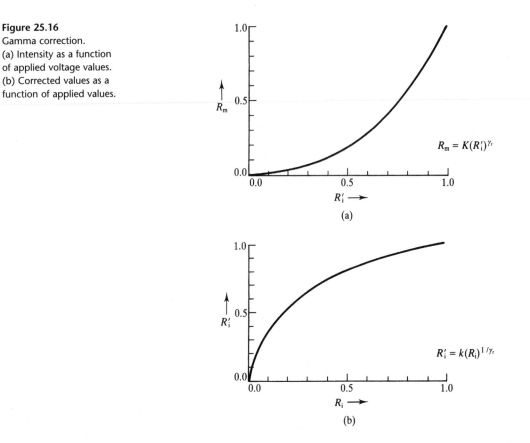

(a)

$$R_m = K(R'_i)^{\gamma_r}$$

(b)

$$R'_i = k(R_i)^{1/\gamma_r}$$

25.8 Colour quantization

Colour quantization (or more accurately colour re-quantization) is responsible for the high visual quality of 24-bit images that are displayed on 8-bit systems. As we have discussed, the need for such an approach may not be around for too long in the future; but it is a common colour processing technique at the moment and very many powerful algorithms have been designed.

It is a form of image compression but is not usually regarded as such which is why we describe it here rather than in Chapter 26. Image compression techniques are usually global in the sense that a selected technique is applied to an image regardless of content (although, of course the selection of the particular technique may depend on the nature of the image as does the amount of compression achieved). With colour quantization a strategy is determined from an analysis of the colours in the image. It is a two-pass approach: analysis of the image colours followed by a selection of the best (reduced) set of colours to represent it.

We may evaluate an image at 24 bits (8 bits for each of the RGB components) and have to re-quantize to 8 bits for the display. In image processing we would usually be working with raw image data that is 24 bits and again we may have to re-quantize. If we are taking images from a scanning device then there is another quantization process but generally the colour resolution of such input devices is at least as great as, and usually greater than, the colour resolution of the output process.

This cut-down, which we will assume in the worst case is from 24 bits to 8 bits, is not as drastic as it may at first sight seem. There are two simple reasons for this. First, the gamut of an image may be predominantly restricted to a subset of RGB space. Consider, for example, the image of a human face with blonde hair against a black background. Second, we can resort to 'dither' or 'jitter' to mollify the effects of false contours that begin to appear whenever we coarsen the quantization.

In our worst-case example, the overall process is to find somehow the best 256 colours to use in the colour map that converts the 8-bit framestore value into a display colour. Equivalently we can say that we need to divide up the RGB space into 256 regions, where each region is represented in the framestore by a single 8-bit colour. (There is a subsidiary question here which is: what colour space should we use for the subdivision? We know that the RGB space is perceptually non-uniform. Ought we to use this fact to influence the subdivision? The answer is, of course, yes; but in going from 24 to 8 bits the size of the range reduction masks this consideration.)

The task is broken down into three steps. First, we need to select the colours that we will use to represent the image. Two approaches are possible. We can either analyze the statistics of the colours in the image or we can define a new colour space – that of the image gamut – and divide this up.

The second phase of the process involves the problem of taking each of the image values or colours and finding what region in the subdivided space they occupy so that the mapped value or label can be applied to the lookup table to get the display colour.

The final process is adding dither to reduce the effects of false contouring. This is more or less mandatory with a 24 to 8 bit reduction.

Choosing colours to represent the image

For the sake of simplicity and because this will be the experience of most readers, we will consider the colour range reduction to be from 24 bits to 8 bits. The first step is to analyze or parametrize the image gamut. There are at least two ways in which we could do this. We could use statistics and compile a histogram of image colours and select the set of the 256 most frequently occurring. This is called a popularity approach and it has the effect of excluding infrequently occurring colours from an accurate representation. The popularity algorithm generally functions well unless the image contains a wide range of colours, when its performance degrades markedly. It relies on image colours clustering.

A better approach appears to have been first introduced by Heckbert in 1982. Called the 'median cut algorithm', this method relies upon directly subdividing the colour space of the image gamut into 256 sub-spaces. In the median cut algorithm this is achieved by originally enclosing the image gamut in a rectangular box, in, say, RGB space. The box is a 'minimax' box defined by finding the two points with the minimum and maximum RGB coordinates. The longest dimension of the box is found and this box is then subdivided by finding the median plane or that plane, normal to the axis of the longest dimension, that divides the box occupancy into two equal populations. This process continues until the image gamut has been divided into 256 boxes. The process is represented in Figure 25.17.

The two approaches can be combined and a weighted subdivision algorithm used, where the position of the subdividing plane is influenced by the weight (frequency of occurrence) of each of the image colours.

In each approach the 256 colours that are going to be used to represent the image are loaded into the colour map or LUT. In the histogram approach, these colours are already determined. In the median cut algorithm we have to find a colour that is representative of each subdivision box – say, for example, the centroid.

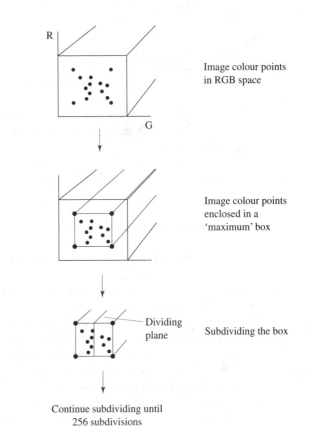

Image colour points in RGB space

Image colour points enclosed in a 'maximum' box

Dividing plane — Subdividing the box

Continue subdividing until 256 subdivisions

Figure 25.17
A conceptual view of the subdivision method of requantizing the image gamut.

(25.8.2)

Colour mapping – second pass

After the first phase, which determines the colours that are going to be used to represent the image, we rescan the image to find an LUT index and map the image colours from their source colour through the LUT into their screen colour. With the histogram approach we need to change unrepresented colours to the nearest represented colours in the histogram. This is most simply carried out by, for each colour, finding the nearest representative colour. A brute force approach would then involve calculating the distance in RGB space from an unrepresented colour to each represented colour and selecting the colour that has the smallest distance. With the median cut algorithm we have to find, for an image colour, the colour label of the space that the colour occupies. Here the straightforward approach is to build up a tree representing the subdivision history of the space, then descend the tree in the colour allocation phase (See Chapter 2).

(25.8.3)

Adding jitter

When the number of available colours is only 256 the phenomenon of 'false contouring' invariably occurs. It is particularly prevalent in image synthesis where a smooth change in the calculated intensity over a surface maps into a series of steps – the false contours. For example, consider a sphere illuminated by a single light source (Figure 25.18(a)). False contours appear as concentric rings which tend to interfere with and destroy the desired effect of smooth shading. The visual predominance of false contours can be diminished by adding noise – usually called jitter or dither (Figure 25.18(b)) – which breaks them up.

(a) Original image showing banding

(b) Adding random noise

Figure 25.18
Options with 8 bit images. (a) An 8 bit image showing false contours. (b) Adding noise. (c) Dithering. The final image (d) is a popular and enduring technique that used only 1 bit per pixel.

(c) Error diffusion

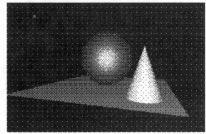

(d) 1 bit version using different symbols

A classic dithering technique, due to Floyd and Steinberg, is called 'error diffusion'. Here we consider the quantization error at each pixel – the difference between the actual image colour and the nearest displayable colour (calculated as described in the previous section) – and propagate fractions of this to neighbouring pixels. In other words, the error is spread or diffused. The algorithm can be implemented as a single pass through the image if the error is propagated only to the right of and below the current pixel. A view of the process is shown in Figure 25.19. The image is scanned from left to right and from top to bottom. For each pixel, the error between the nearest displayable colour and the actual colour is calculated and used to increment the three neighbouring pixels.

Although the principle of the error diffusion algorithm is extremely simple there are practical complications when using it in conjunction with the median cut algorithm. This is because propagating the error term may result in the production of a colour that falls into a space that is not represented by any colour.

Consider Figure 25.20. This shows a colour plane subset at the nth subdivision. This subdivision produces two clusters which are themselves tightly

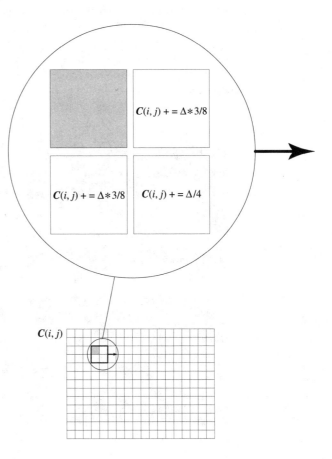

Figure 25.19
One-pass error diffusion.

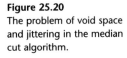

Figure 25.20
The problem of void space and jittering in the median cut algorithm.

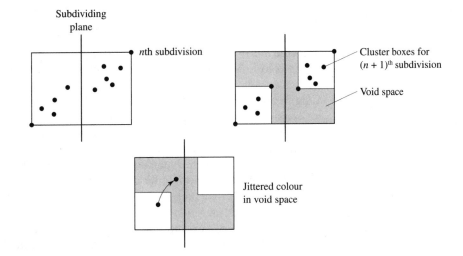

enclosed in boxes in preparation for the (n+1)th subdivision. At this stage a void space or a 'no colour'space is created (shaded). When we come to add jitter it may be that a colour is displaced outside of a cluster into a void space. This state has to be detected and the appropriate action taken. Thus at the nth subdivision the void space must be 'remembered' – that is the coordinates of the two subdivision products at this level need to be maintained along with the coordinates of the two new cluster boxes.

The question then arises: what to do with a jittered colour that falls into void space? We can map it back into the cluster box from which it was displaced. This sometimes gives poor results if the jittered colour C_j (as in Figure 25.21) happens to be nearer to a colour C_x, from another cluster box, than it does to the representative colour C_r. This suggests another strategy which is to search for the nearest colour.

Figure 25.22 (Colour Plate) shows a 24-bit image and two 8-bit equivalents using the median cut and popularity algorithm that we have described.

Figure 25.21
C_j, the jittered colour, may be much closer to a colour C_x than the representative colour, C_r, of the category from which it was displaced.

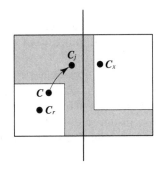

25.9 Colour and computer vision

It is true to say that to date there has not been much research in computer vision using colour. Most investigation has been carried out with grey scale imagery. This is a somewhat strange state of affairs given that many computer vision paradigms are based on assumptions concerning the human visual system and that colour appears to be extremely important to us.

Colour is used in computer vision mainly to perform segmentation or as an aid in this classic image analysis problem. This is particularly true in contexts where the reflected colour of an object relates to a physical property that is to form the basis for the segmentation. For example, in the classification of areas in satellite imagery (Chapter 14), colour as a multi-wavelength property of a pixel in a multi-band image is routinely used to categorize different types of vegetation. Different crops exhibit different spectra and such data varies not only with the vegetation type but also as a function of the health of the crop, the stage in the growth cycle and the time of the day.

To start with, we can make the obvious statement that the colour of light reflected from a point in a scene will depend on many factors, some of which may be relevant to the problem in hand, and others that may be considered as noise which we have to eliminate from consideration. The main factors are:

- the intrinsic colour of the object and how homogeneous this is over the object surface;
- variations such as specular reflection which depend on the geometry of the object with respect to the light source and the viewpoint;
- the colour of the illuminant or illuminants;
- the interaction of the object with other objects in the scene – the global illumination problem in computer graphics – which means that the reflected colour of an object may be indirect light from another object in the scene.

In other words, the same factors that are recognized in computer graphics and that are simulated to a greater or lesser extent by a variety of algorithms, occur in computer vision when we try to extract information from the scene by examining the colour of the reflected light.

It is certainly the case that colour is not much used in computer vision and that most established approaches to scene analysis spend most effort in attempting to extract geometry or structure from the scene. Colour may be used as a part of the overall process but we do not, for example, attempt to extract, say, depth from colour.

Also, it is not altogether clear what the importance of colour is to us as human beings. We could certainly survive in a black and white world although we find such an experience somewhat dull. Why then is such a large part of our visual system devoted to processing colour? In part it may be that our relative ignorance concerning the role of colour in our lives reflects its lack of use as a tool in computer vision.

Consider again the above list of variables. The effect of these is manifest in the fact that in scenes of interest, variations occur in both the intensity of reflected light and its spectral make-up across a scene.

Normally in computer vision we are interested at first in detecting object boundaries or edges and in this regard spectral changes in colour are probably more important than intensity changes. De Valois et al. put it this way:

Although in principle neither the intensity nor the spectral distribution of the light reflected from various parts of a complex scene should be perfectly correlated with the presence of object boundaries, the differences in spectral distribution that do not directly signal borders are effectively minimal, while the differences in intensity are large and obvious. ... Regions of the same colour are more likely to belong to the same object, while regions of different colour are more likely to belong to different objects.

Further reading

The classic text on colour science is Wyzecki and Stiles. More easily comprehensible to computer graphicists are the books by Hall and Poynton. The best introduction to the work of Harold Land is his article in *Scientific American*.

Papers

Borges C.F. (1991). Trichromatic approximation for computer graphics illumination models. *Computer Graphics*, **25**(4), 101–4 *(Proc. SIGGRAPH 1991)*

Cowan W. (1983). An inexpensive scheme for the calibration of a color monitor in terms of CIE standard coordinates. *Proc. SIGGRAPH 1983*, 315–21

Floyd R. and Steinberg L. (1975). An adaptive algorithm for spatial gray scales. Society for Information Display 1975 Symposium Digest of Technical Papers

Heckbert P. (1982). Color image quantization for frame buffer display. *Proc. SIGGRAPH 1982*, 297–307

Land H. (1977). The retinex theory of colour vision. *Scientific American*, **237**(6), 108–28

Smith A.R. (1978). Color gamut transform pairs. *Proc. SIGGRAPH 1978*, 12–19

Books

Hall R. (1989). *Illumination and Color in Computer Generated Imagery*. New York: Springer-Verlag

Munsell Color Company (1976). *Book of Color*. Baltimore, MD: Munsell Color Company

Poynton C. (1996). *A Technical Introduction to Digital Video*. Chichester: Wiley

Wyszecki G. and Stiles W.S. (1982) *Color Science: Concepts and Methods, Quantitative Data and Formulae*. 2nd edn, New York: Wiley

Reducing the information: compressing images – a new frontier

In our twentieth century desire to shrink the world, transmitting images electronically has been perhaps the most important factor. Towards the end of the twentieth century, the word communications has become ubiquitous. We have phrases like 'breakdown of communications' or 'lack of communication'. We have communication industries, communication media and nowadays there is a strong association of that word with electronic imagery. Because of the global ubiquity of TV imagery, the common man of today has much more visual knowledge of the world than his great-grandfather did. For technological reasons, computer imagery has been late to enter the communication field and until now communication associated with computers has been concerned with numerical data and words. This appears to be about to change with digital TV, the transmission of image traffic on the Internet and our curious desire to fulfil that sci-fi dream of the 1950s – the 'videophone'.

Electronic image transmission began with the grandfather of the fax, when in the 1930s newspapers began using electromechanical drum scanners to encode photographs into a signal that could be transmitted over a standard telephone line. With the advent of TV it was thought that videophones were just around the corner but of course this has not proved to be the case. The transmission of static pictures over a telephone link and that of TV images over a UHF channel illustrate a fundamental point concerning image transmission. The predominant cost of any communications channel is related to its bandwidth or its capacity to transmit information per unit of time. The early news photograph systems took, say, one hour to transmit an image over a telephone line that has sufficient bandwidth to cope only with human speech. A modern TV channel has the capacity to transmit 30 completely independent high resolution colour images every second. Low bandwidth telephone lines are more or less available to everyone whereas a nation will only possess a few TV channels. The dream of the videophone is to make it as ubiquitous as the telephone and to do this it has to use a channel with a comparable capacity. Numerically this means reducing the information in the image so that it 'fits' into the telephone bandwidth or else giving everyone access to high bandwidth lines. The digital bandwidth that is equivalent to an analogue telephone line is around 64 kbits/sec. This contrasts with the capacity of a TV channel, which digitally is about 19 Mbits/sec.

In this chapter we will examine what is usually known as classical image compression. This operates by considering statistical and other properties of the image and uses this information to reduce spatial and/or temporal redundancy. These techniques operate without using any high-level or structural knowledge of the content of the image and have been used traditionally to solve image storage problems. The reduction achievable by such means is generally not great enough for videophone-type applications and the approach taken for this application is variously called **model-based** or **intelligent** image coding. Here some kind of **description** of the image is transmitted and at the receiver end an image is reconstructed from that description. The idea is that such techniques can exploit image redundancy to a much higher degree, particularly for moving images. This, of course, is at a cost of higher complexity or encoding/decoding penalty. Although the ultimate utility of a videophone may bemuse you it is a fascinating problem and one that we address separately in Chapter 19.

Consider again that apparently vital part of our day-to-day life in the late twentieth century – the fax machine. This device is functionally identical to the devices of the 1920s in that it scans a document a line at a time using a mixture of electromechanical and electronic technology. (Strangely a fax machine, although predominantly concerned with the transmission of words, albeit in the form of documents, deals with the image of words.) The addition is that a small processing facility enables a simple image compression and decompression so that a document image can be sent in an economical few seconds.

Perhaps almost as important as economical transmission of images is their efficient archiving. An 'old' example is satellite imagery. A Landsat satellite transmits 85×10^6 bits of data every second, resulting in a vast amount of information to be archived and examined at a later point in time. A contemporary example is storing imagery on CD-ROM. For example, Microsoft use fractal compression technology to store 10 000 images in their multimedia CD-ROM encyclopaedia, 'Encarta'.

Recently there has been much interest in the compression of moving images or image sequences. Apart from the special case of the videophone, the advent of HDTV has meant that there is a need to transmit far more information, in the form of moving sequences over existing TV channels. For example, a format of 1280×720 pixels at 24 bits per pixel at 60 frames/s gives a rate of 1.32 Gbits/s. This needs to be compressed by a factor of 70 to be transmitted on existing TV channels. Moving image sequences are compressed by considering not only compression within a frame but inter-frame compression and generally the compression achieved over a number of frames is much higher than the compression that can be achieved by considering single frames independently.

A good way of looking at the compression of moving sequences is from the point of view of the data rate as a function of the 'action' in the movie or animation sequence. Since frames are regular samples of data in time, as the action in a movie becomes more vigorous then there is less opportunity for inter-frame compression and the data rate increases. Thus the data flow increases and decreases following the amount of movement in the sequence to optimize the image quality with respect to the desired overall compression goal. The importance of moving image compression is further highlighted by the publication of recent standards – MPEG-1 and MPEG-2.

The idea of image compression, then, is to process images in such a way that the information required to transmit (or store) an image is reduced either with no loss in quality (lossless compression) or with some (tolerable) reduction in image quality. The cost of image compression is the encoding and decoding time and we trade bandwidth requirements against these penalties incurred at the transmitter and receiver.

Image compression techniques operate on one or a number of aspects of image representation. We can try to reduce the number of pixels in an image. The classic technique of run length encoding encodes 'runs' of identical pixels so that areas where there is no variation in the image have fewer information units allocated to them. We can try to reduce the number of bits per pixel. This is a classic technique in analogue TV where the colour specification comprising a luminance channel and two chrominance channels is allocated bandwidths in the ratio 2:1:1 because the eye is more sensitive to changes in the brightness (luminance) than it is to changes in hue (chrominance). The most common implementation of this technique in digital imagery is transform encoding where an image is mapped into the Fourier domain and different frequency components are allocated a different number of bits. This is one of the mechanisms used in the JPEG standard.

At the time of writing (1995) the use of the Internet for still image communication is rapidly expanding. However, the transmission time for imagery between, say, Europe and the USA is so long at peak periods as to render the facility unusable except by the most patient. (It is indeed a measure of the scale of the illusions fostered by commercial interests that this situation persists and even worsens in a year in which the Internet is being 'sold' to the general public.) Whether the effective bandwidth available to a user is going to expand in the future to alleviate this problem is uncertain. At the moment demand is increasing faster than bandwidth. Thus image compression, and in particular a progressive mode of operation, where an image is sent in an approximate form followed by a progressive refinement of quality, has become extremely important. This aspect of image compression is also addressed by the JPEG standard.

Because of the factors described above which have led to an expansion of demand for image communication between computers, image compression has now become an urgent problem. Two major recent advances, one a careful optimization of classical techniques (JPEG) and the other a completely new approach (fractal image compression), have made significant advances and a science (or technology) that was, a few years ago, virtually unheard of in mainstream applications is used routinely by anyone who stores or communicates digital imagery.

Finally we list a number of aspects of image compression that will continually crop up in this chapter:

● **Compression ratio or bit rate**   The data volume required to transmit or store a compressed image can be expressed either as the before: after compression ratio, or as the (average) number of bits/pixel that the compressed image uses.

● **Lossy vs. lossless compression**   Lossy compression, where some loss in the quality of the image is tolerated, is now more common than lossless because of the demand for high compression ratios. Lossy compression implementations normally allow the user to select the degree of quality loss.

Different lossy compression schemes cause visually different degradations in the image. When we say that two images subject to different lossy compression schemes produce decoded images of equal quality, this is a subjective estimation which does not mean that the images are equivalent on a pixel by pixel basis. The nature of the degradation is a function of the type of lossy compression employed. DCT-based schemes, such as JPEG, produce blurring; fractal compression produces an effect where the image seems to be just as sharp but individual pixels appear to be slightly displaced, causing jagged edges. Toleration of lossy schemes obviously depends on application. In scientific studies such as satellite imagery or medical imagery, for example, no loss in quality may be tolerable.

● **Symmetric vs. asymmetric compression**   An important compression technique – fractal based – is highly asymmetric: the encoding time is much longer than the decoding time. The same is true for most methods that deal with moving imagery. The importance of this depends on the application in which the technique is being used. For example, it is not important in entertainment video where we may compress a film (once only) that is to be stored on a server and accessed on demand by viewers.

● **Symmetric vs. asymmetric applications**   Symmetric applications are where there is equal use of the encoding and decoding process, for example video telephony and video conferencing. Asymmetric applications are those in which there is no inconvenience incurred in using an asymmetric compression technique, for example electronic publishing on CD-ROM or entertainment videos.

Classical image compression techniques

Classical image compression is a loose term that applies to (old) methods that are not model based, are not optimized to exploit characteristics of the human visual system, do not employ fractal block encoding, and so on. This category of image compression techniques divides naturally into two categories: **loss-free** or information preserving and **lossy compression**.

In the first category redundancy in the data is exploited without any loss of image information. Here we invent an encoding of pictorial information that is more economical than uniform sampling and quantization. There are numerous examples of computer imagery where we require compression without any loss of information. In medical imaging, for example, it is undesirable that less information be presented to a clinician for diagnosis than was collected by the primary imaging system. The vast expense of satellite images and the demanding and detailed research to which these images are subjected makes it undesirable that there is the slightest reduction in quality. Indeed any images from 'other worlds' – medical images, images from space or images from an electron microscope – should not be compressed in case unwittingly the compression process deletes detailed but important information. With lossy compression we aim for higher compression at the expense of losing some image information. We try to invent methods where this loss is more or less insignificant to the human viewer.

The scale of the reduction available from these two approaches is, of course, a function of the content of the image to which they are applied, but we can say that for full colour images as a general rule, with error-free compression we should achieve a compression ratio of 2:1 and for lossy compression 20:1. The amount of compression achieved by any image compression scheme can be expressed as either a ratio (of the original source image to the compressed image) or the average number of compressed bits per pixel. The latter tends to be preferred since it relates directly to the cost of storage or transmission of the image.

26.1.1

Loss-free compression – coding redundancy

Loss-free image compression exploits coding redundancy or inter-pixel redundancy. Coding redundancy simply refers to the fact that if we represent the value of a pixel with a natural binary code (the de facto standard being 8 bits per pixel per RGB component image) then for almost any image the total number of bits used to represent the image will be greater than if we used a **variable length** code rather than a fixed length code. This follows simply from the nature of images that are of interest to us. Images contain objects. Objects of interest are almost always much bigger than one pixel. Objects tend to occupy a small range of pixel values. All of these facts mean that an image histogram, as we saw in Chapter 9, is never equiprobable – some values are more probable than others.

This leads us naturally to the simple concept of variable length coding, also known as entropy encoding. We design a code where the bit length varies and we assign few bits to those values that occur most frequently and longer bit lengths to infrequently occurring values. In this way we achieve a measure of loss-free image compression.

An approach to this type of image compression is to first construct a code based on the image histogram. This can then be loaded into an LUT. Note that since we no longer have fixed length words we need the coded image to be **uniquely decodable** – we must be able to unravel the coded image in only one way. For ease of implementation we would also like the process to be **instantaneous**. This means that we can decode one word at a time by working from left to right – we have no need of knowledge of any other code word.

The commonest form of coding redundancy reduction is **Huffman** coding. This is most easily explained by using a simple illustrative example (Figure 26.1(a) and (b)). In this example we consider that a pixel, $I(x,y)$, can take one of eight values. These are listed as I_1 to I_8 together with their probabilities in the figure. A tree is constructed by operating on this row of probabilities as follows:

while number of uncombined probabilities ≥ 2
      find the two lowest and add these together

From this tree a code is assigned to each pixel value. This is done by traversing the tree from the root and assigning a 1 to the left branch and a 0 to the right branch. As the tree is descended we build up codes by appending, to the end of the current code at a node, a 1 for the left branch and a 0 for the right branch. Eventually, as Figure 26.1(b) demonstrates, the following codes are assigned to each value that $I(x,y)$ can take.

Pixel value	Probability	Assigned code
I_1	0.4	1
I_4	0.25	01
I_5	0.10	0010
I_2	0.09	0011
I_3	0.08	0001
I_6	0.07	00001
I_7	0.01	000001
I_8	0.00	000000

This reduces the number of bits per pixel from 3 to:

$$(0.4{\times}1) + (0.25{\times}2) + (0.10{\times}4) + (0.09{\times}4) + (0.08{\times}4) + (0.07{\times}5) + (0.01{\times}6) = 2.39$$

This kind of encoding need not be confined to the redundancy in pixel codes. It can be applied to any 'source symbol' such as, for example, some function of pixel values like the output from a run length encoder (described in the next section). In terms of the language of coding theory it generates the smallest number of code symbols per source symbol, given the constraint that the source symbols are encoded one at a time.

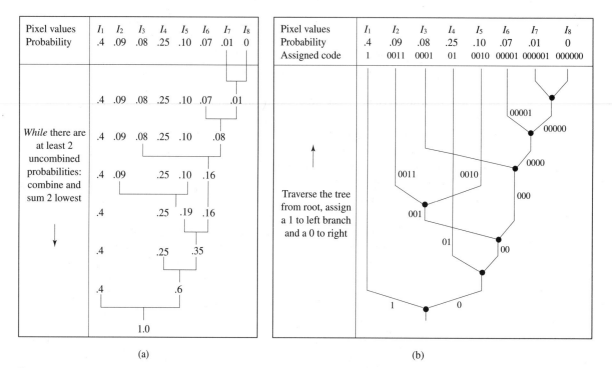

(a)   (b)

Figure 26.1
Huffman coding:
(a) constructing a tree;
(b) assigning a code.

The disadvantage of a Huffman code results from the computational cost of its construction. A unique code has to be constructed for each image and even for an 8-bit image this is non-trivial. Also, for infrequently used source symbols the code becomes very long, adding to the computational burden. Therefore some compromise is usually made between efficiency and compression. In practice it is better to implement such a compromise as a **truncated Huffman** code which is described in detail in Gonzalez and Woods.

26.1.2 Loss-free compression – inter-pixel redundancy

We noted in the previous section that structure in an image causes clustering in the occupancy of pixel values. For exactly the same reasons that pixels are not equiprobable, adjacent pixels normally correlate – they are not independent. The pixels that represent an object will tend to be the same or at least their values will change slowly except at the object edge. Thus some form of spatial encoding, where a group of adjacent pixels are considered and encoded, ought to be possible. Computationally, the easiest way to reduce inter-pixel redundancy is to operate on binary images and this means representing, say, an 8-bit image as eight binary images, where each component image is called a bit plane.

Note that before splitting an image into bit planes it is advantageous to represent pixel values using a **Gray code**. This code has the property that consecutive values differ in only one bit position. This simple transformation produces bit planes of larger (connected) black/white areas than those that occur when an image, where the pixels are represented with a natural binary code, is decomposed into bit planes. A little thought will show why this is so. It is the case with natural binary that a small change in image values between adjacent pixels, say from 127 to 128, or 01111111 to 10000000, will produce a 1/0 adjacency in every single bit plane. The change in neighbouring pixels is reflected in every bit plane. Using a Gray code, the transition is from 11000000 to 01000000 and a 1/0 adjacency will occur in only one bit plane in the decomposition. This is clearly advantageous to image compression. Another property of bit plane decomposition is that the higher bit planes tend to contain larger black/white areas than the lower ones.

Once an image has been decomposed into bit planes it can be subject to a variety of techniques that take advantage of the inter-pixel redundancy. The simplest is **run length encoding** where each row is represented by a series of numbers representing the length (in pixels) of successive runs of black and white.

Run length encoding can operate on an undecomposed image, for example an 8-bit image. Here the rows are encoded as duples – the values or amplitudes of the pixel followed by the run length. For efficiency, the coding scheme must be tailored to the image statistics. If a duple is used it must be decided how many bits are going to represent a run length and infrequently occurring long runs need to be broken up into 'pseudo' runs. In encoding a binary image or a bit plane a variable length encoding should be applied to the run lengths themselves.

Two-dimensional encoding techniques can be applied to bit plane images and run length encoding can be extended into a two-dimensional coding scheme. Alternatively **constant area coding** is an extremely simple scheme that we will now describe.

In constant area coding the bit plane is divided into rectangular blocks of some predetermined size. Each block can then be categorized according to whether it contains only white, black or mixed black/white. The most frequently occurring category is assigned the code 0 and the other two 2-bit codes 10 and 11. Clearly, if a block contains n pixels, all of which are either black or white, this number is reduced to one or two bits. If the block is mixed then the mixed code has to be followed by the bit pattern for the block.

(26.1.3) ## Predictive coding

Lossless predictive coding is another technique that exploits spatial redundancy or similarity between adjacent pixels. However, instead of sending information on runs of identical pixels, the encoder sends the difference between the current pixel and a predicted value. Runs of pixels identical to the predicted value will then cause the encoder to output a stream of zeros which can then be exploited by the entropy encoder. Its advantage over run length encoding is that the image

Figure 26.2
Lossless predictive coding.
(a) Encoder; (b) decoder.

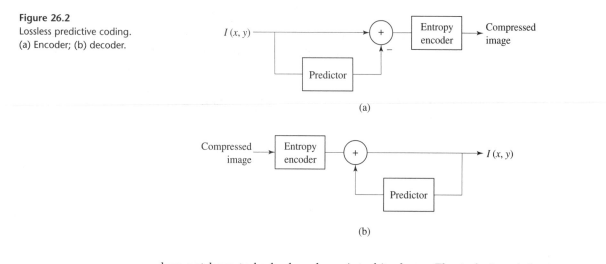

(a)

(b)

does not have to be broken down into bit planes. The technique is best represented as a block diagram (Figure 26.2) which shows an encoder and a decoder with identical predictors. The predictor calculates a value based on the immediate past history of pixel intensities. This can be just the value of the previous pixel or it can be some function of m previous pixels:

$$\text{current prediction} = \text{round} \left(\sum_{i=1}^{n} \alpha_i I_{n-i} \right)$$

where

Figure 26.3
One-dimensional predictive
coding.

I_{n-i} is the value of the ith previous pixel
$_i$ is a set of prediction coefficients

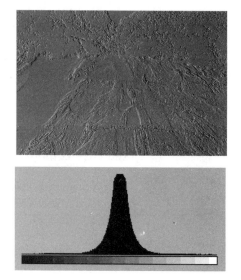

In one-dimensional predictive coding the previous pixels would just be those previously encountered along the current scan line. Alternatively, in two-dimensional predictive encoding 'previous' means that we index into some two-dimensional neighbourhood of the pixel for which we require a prediction value. In temporal or inter-frame encoding 'previous' means that we index the corresponding pixel(s) in previous frame(s). This scheme is shown in Figure 26.13(a) which should be compared with Figure 26.2. Figure 26.3 shows the efficacy of the scheme by comparing an image histogram with the histogram of the encoded pixels.

26.2 Lossy image compression

In the previous sections we used compression techniques that depended on neighbouring pixels correlating. This gave us a compression whose magnitude depended on the image statistics. This is sometimes inconvenient and the technique that we now discuss can be implemented to give a constant compression for each image. In one sense the approach is completely opposite in that we **de-correlate** the image. Most lossy image compression techniques are based on a re-encoding of the image, or more particularly an encoding of the transform of the image, where the nature of the transform is such as to de-correlate the image.

Let us now look at what we mean by de-correlation and how we can exploit it. The aim of the process is to find a set of parameters that represent the picture, and from which it can be reproduced. Each parameter is to be as independent of other parameters as possible – meaning that we should not be able to predict the value of a parameter from its neighbours. We would like each parameter to reflect or specify some property of the whole picture. We can do this by employing one of a family of linear reversible transforms, the Fourier transform being the most common example. This then opens up the possibility of **ranking** the de-correlated parameters according to their importance and deleting the least important of these.

As far as image coding transforms for compression are concerned, this is a subject in its own right and the study of these transforms is often the topic of a book. In this text we will try to give a feel for this technique and we will look in detail at the most commonly used transform: the discrete cosine transform or DCT.

In the Fourier transform one value represents the 'strength' of a single spatial frequency that exists everywhere in the image. The motivation for storing or transmitting the Fourier transform of an image, rather than the image, lies in the fact that we can make a measured decision on the importance of the spatial frequency components. We can then effect compression by quantizing less important components more coarsely, or not storing them at all. In other words, we are simply low pass filtering the image and deleting high frequency components according to how much compression we want to achieve. For most pictures of interest, most of the energy in the image is concentrated in the low frequency components. We can quantize these components accurately and coarsely quantize, or delete, the high frequency components with little reduction in image quality.

The point is demonstrated in Figure 11.6 which shows a plot of image energy against frequency. The energy value is obtained by summating elements within concentric circular regions centred on the origin of the Fourier domain. The efficacy of the point concerning the concentration of energy into low frequency components can now be qualified. We can also consider that when the image contains much coherent structure, there is more energy dumped in the high frequency components by the transform.

At this stage we should discuss the degree of compression that we can obtain. This depends on how much of a degradation the viewer of the reconstructed compressed image can tolerate. A commonly used **quantitative** measure is the RMS (root mean square) difference between the original image and the image that has been subject to lossy compression:

$$\text{error} = \left(\frac{1}{MN} \sum_{0}^{M-1} \sum_{0}^{N-1} (I'(x, y) - I(x,y))^2 \right)^{1/2}$$

where $M{\times}N$ is the image dimension
I' is the image that has been subject to compression
I is the original image

This is a quantitative measure of the average squared error per pixel and it has the advantage that it can be used to compare the efficiency of various lossy compression schemes against each other. It has the distinct disadvantage, however, that it is not a subjective measurement. It could be argued that a quantitative measure of image degradation is virtually useless since the only thing that matters is how the degradation appears to a human viewer. Also, the nature of the degradation depends on the type of compression technique that is being employed. In the case of a Fourier transform, using fewer bits to represent high frequency components will result in the entire image blurring. Gonzalez and Woods describe a simple subjective scale based on a 'side by side' comparison between the original and the reconstructed image.

The discrete cosine transform

The most popular lossy image compression technique is the discrete cosine transform, or DCT, and indeed the DCT forms part of the JPEG standard for image compression. The mathematics of the DCT are discussed in Chapter 11 and here we will restrict our discussion to a qualitative discourse on its suitability as a lossy compression transform compared with the Fourier transform or DFT.

First, we note that to perform a DCT, in practice, we divide the image into either 8×8 or 16×16 blocks and encode the DCT of each block. Of course, there is no mathematical justification for chopping an image into blocks without regard to its content. This is a simple practical decision. The computational complexity and cost is a function of block size and it is considerably more efficient to block divide the image rather than compute the DCT of the entire picture. It is the normal cost–benefit trade-off because the capacity for compression is a function of block size. An advantage of block encoding is that it is possible to vary the compression applied from block to block depending on the content of the DCT for each block. Thus we can effect a scheme that depends on actual image content (at least to within the limitations of the regular subdivision).

The reason for the choice of a DCT in image compression over, say, a DFT is that it has a superior information packing property. Informally this means that if we transform an image, compress it by some factor in the transform domain, transform the compressed transform back into the image domain and then measure the mean square difference between the compressed image and the original image, the DCT will be superior to the DFT. The DCT 'packs' more energy into fewer coefficients in the transform domain. A connected point is that the use of the DCT rather than the DFT diminishes the visibility of **blocking artefacts** that would otherwise occur because we divide the image up into rectangles. The visibility of blocking artefacts depends not only on the transform used but also on the compression factor. As information is reduced towards 1 bit per pixel, block boundaries become more and more visible in the reconstruction.

However, despite these points, the main justification for the use of the DCT is that it is better than almost all other transforms in its energy compaction properties. The DCT is the lossy part of the JPEG standard, an example of which is shown in Figure 26.4 (Colour Plate). Finally note that lossy image compression can be followed by loss-free compression to effect a higher compression factor.

26.2.2

The wavelet transform, compression and progressive transmission

Using a wavelet transform for image compression is a little more complicated than using a DCT in that we delete or requantize depending on the value of the coefficients for each image that we wish to compress rather than having a global scheme that we apply to every transformed image. First the coefficients are computed in a normalized two-dimensional Haar basis (Chapter 11). They are then sorted in order of decreasing magnitude and either a fixed proportion of the smallest coefficients is deleted or an amount is deleted that is consistent with an allowable error term. The former strategy results in a fixed compression independent of image content whereas the latter will result in a compression that depends on each image. The obvious cost involved here is the large processing overhead for sorting the coefficients and more efficient strategies are suggested by Stollnitz et al.

A comparision of compression by wavelets and by JPEG is shown in Figure 26.4 (Colour Plate). The original image is 64 kB and this is compressed using both techniques to 13 kB and 5 kB respectively. The superior quality of the JPEG compression is obvious, the main difference being the noticeable blocking artefacts in the wavelet compressed version. The advantage that wavelet compression exhibits is the simplicity of the transform and the fact that it is, for most

Figure 26.5
Image progression and
wavelets.

images, superior for progressive transmission. A simple comparison is shown in Figure 26.5 which shows three progressive sequences, a wavelet series, a sequence generated by resampling the image at progressively higher resolution and a JPEG series. The series is for a single, three and six updates containing 0.14%, 4.12% and 8.24% respectively. The algorithm used to generate the wavelet series is now described. The progressive mode of JPEG is described in Section 26.3.3.

Wavelet transform

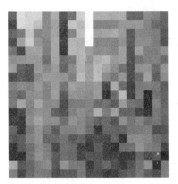

Image domain

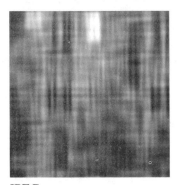

JPEG

First update
0.14%

Third update
4.12%

Sixth update
8.24%

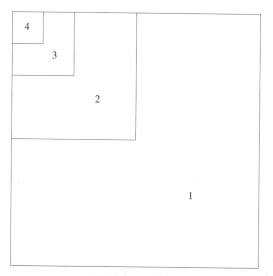

Weighting coefficients

Largest 5% of coefficients

Largest 5% of coefficients

Figure 26.6
Weighting wavelet
coefficients.

(1)   The wavelet transform is calculated and a weighting function applied to the coefficients. This applies a simple importance weighting to the coefficients as shown in Figure 26.6.

(2)   The weighted coefficients are sorted into order. This, of course, implies that their position must be remembered. This is done by resorting them back into scan line order, mapping their position into a binary bit map. This sparse array is then run length encoded and transmitted with the coefficients.

(3)   Establish a final image quality (data packet) for a given bandwidth (bytes/sec.) and speed of updates (updates/sec.)

$$\text{data packet} = \frac{\text{bandwidth}}{\text{speed of updates}}$$

(26.2.3)   ### Colour images and compression

For colour images we can transform from RGB to a video-based representation. This means using a colour representation where the three components are made up of two chrominance and one luminance channel like the CIE xyY encoding described in Chapter 25. Such a transformation means that overall the compression applied to the chrominance channels can be much greater than that applied to the luminance channel. This fact, that an acceptable image can be reproduced from chrominance channels that are spatially degraded more than the luminance, is the basis of colour TV broadcasting. The NTSC (USA) colour encoding scheme, which had to be compatible with existing black and white receivers, transmits a luminance component (for black and white and colour receivers) together with two chrominance channels of much lower bandwidth. Occupying a total of 5.8 MHz, the luminance channel takes up 4 MHz while both chrominance channels only occupy 1.8 MHz.

In Chapter 25 we deal with a technique that could be termed a special case of image compression – that of forcing a 24-bit colour image into 8 bits. In one sense this is image compression but for reasons that we now enumerate it usually called 'colour requantization' and considered part of computer graphics.

One of the simplest techniques that effected this data reduction is the popularity algorithm where we requantize the pixel values on the basis of an image histogram. However, the unrepresented 24-bit values appear as errors in the image which, depending on the nature of the image, may be highly visible. In classical lossy compression we are not requantizing but encoding in a way that diminishes the visibility of lost information. All pixels are encoded using, say, a DCT. There is no concept of unrepresented pixels that have to be 'moved' into the represented space. Also, in colour range compression we often positively interfere with the image by introducing noise or dither and so for these reasons colour range compression tends not to be treated as classical lossy image compression. However, the similarity between the approaches can be seen by looking at the way in which the image histogram is affected. Figure 26.7 (Colour Plate) shows an image lossily compressed using JPEG and the effect on its histogram together with the same image compressed using the median cut algorithm. Note that in both cases the compression technique has mapped the pixels into fewer colours – the smoothness of the original histogram is destroyed in both cases.

Practical classic image compression – JPEG

In the above sections we have looked at single classical techniques for image compression. We will now examine the current way in which most (still) image compression is accomplished, which is to use the ISO standard JPEG (Joint Photographic Experts Group). Work began on JPEG in the mid-1980s and it was finally adopted as ISO DIS 10918-1 in 1993.

The standard was developed to deal with still continuous-tone grey-scale or colour (photographic) images and the original aim was to achieve compression targets which were 0.25 bits per pixel for recognizable images, 1.0 bits per pixel for excellent quality images and four bits per pixel for images that are subjectively indistinguishable from the original. The feature of JPEG that distinguishes it from the routine application of a single classical data compression technique is that a number of facilities are selected from JPEG's capabilities. These include not only the option of lossy or lossless compression but the use of modes of operation that are appropriate to the user's application. These are sequential coding, progressive coding and hierarchical coding. An appropriate compatible set of functions can be selected according to the nature of the imagery, the way in which the images are to be used and the degree of compression that is required.

An overall block diagram of the encoding process is shown in Figure 26.8. The first operation is lossless – the decorrelation procedure in this case is a DCT transform. The second part is the variable quantization of the transform to which the remainder of this section is devoted and the third part is the redundancy remover, in this case a Huffman encoder.

Lossy image compression in JPEG is implemented by using a DCT. However, the way in which the coefficients are operated on to facilitate compression is based on a scheme that depends on the sensitivity of the human visual system to threshold intensity changes at different spatial frequencies. In other words, JPEG exploits the fact that the human eye does not perceive the intensity oscillations of different spatial frequencies equally to achieve the maximum possible compression of (DCT) information commensurate with the minimum loss of image quality. Thus JPEG is a system that achieves compression by exploiting both the image properties and statistics and the properties of the human visual system. Surprisingly, giving regard to information in an image according to its importance to the human visual system has been mostly ignored in classical image compression, although it has been long established in TV communications systems since the advent of colour TV where the bandwidth of the luminance channel is twice that of the chrominance channels.

In this brief treatment of JPEG we will mostly concentrate on lossy compression since this is the facility that is most used. (See Further reading for references that give a more comprehensive account of JPEG.)

The JPEG model for lossy image compression

As we implied earlier, when we are exploiting redundancy in symbols, these need not be the image pixels themselves but can be some other descriptors, symbols or representation of the image. This is precisely the approach in JPEG lossy encoding (Figure 26.8). As can be seen, the image is subjected to three processes. The first is a DCT that produces 64 coefficients from 8×8 blocks of the image. The coefficients comprise a single 'DC' coefficient which is the average intensity level of the 8×8 block and 63 'AC' coefficients. (The use of the terminology 'DC' and 'AC' in the JPEG standard seems somewhat absurd since they have no relevance whatever to imagery and spatial frequencies but relate to the field of signal processing. They stand for Direct Current and Alternating Current.)

The distinction between these coefficients is made because the DC coefficients are subject to a different (differential) coding scheme. Note at this stage that simply displaying the DC coefficients gives a blocky approximation to the image, where each 8×8 block is filled with a constant intensity. The 63 (variably) quantized AC coefficients are ordered into a zig-zag sequence which arranges them into a one-dimensional sequence in approximate order of increasing spatial frequency. For example, the zig-zag sequence through an 8×8 array visits the cells in the order shown in Figure 26.9. This ordering can be used in a progressive operational mode.

Figure 26.8
JPEG model for (lossy) image compression.

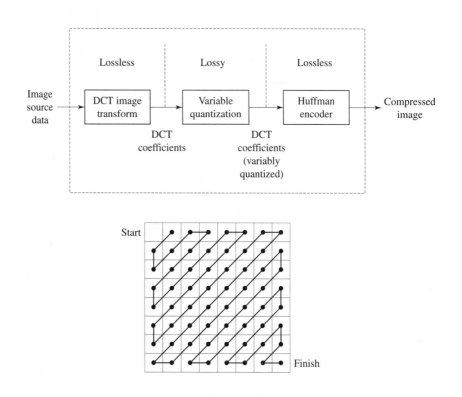

Figure 26.9
The zig-zag sequence for fetching elements in approximate order of increasing spatial frequency.

Each of the 63 AC coefficients is then subjected to a variable quantization scheme where the quantization accuracy used is in general different for each coefficient according to the relative importance of each as far as the human visual system is concerned (next section). This produces a set of source symbols for a Huffman encoder which produces the final compressed data. The first and final processes are lossless, the lossy information reduction occurring when variable quantization is applied to the DCT coefficients.

26.3.2 DCT coefficients and the human visual system

The lossy compression option of the JPEG standard accounts for its most popular usage. This is achieved by quantizing the coefficients unequally according to a table and is effected by dividing the DCT coefficients by a quantization value and truncating. Many of the high spatial frequency coefficients then become zero. The particular quantization values are set individually, based on the subjective measurements of the human visual system of the threshold of visibility of each spatial frequency. This aspect of JPEG underpins the lossy compression option and is responsible for the high quality of (lossy) compressed images.

The philosophy is summarized in Figure 26.10. Figure 26.10(a) shows the response of the human visual system to different spatial frequencies. Many different experiments have been carried out to measure the eye's response to sinusoidal gratings. All tend to show a peak in the response between 4 and 8

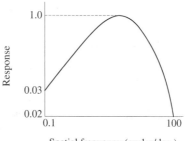

(a)

Figure 26.10
(a) Response of the human visual system to different spatial frequencies. (b) Luminance quantization table. (c) Chrominance quantization table.

16	11	10	16	24	40	51	61
12	12	14	19	26	58	60	55
14	13	16	24	40	57	69	56
14	17	22	29	51	87	80	62
18	22	37	56	68	109	103	77
24	35	55	64	81	104	113	92
49	64	78	87	103	121	120	101
72	92	95	98	112	100	103	99

(b)

17	18	24	47	99	99	99	99
18	21	26	66	99	99	99	99
24	26	56	99	99	99	99	99
47	66	99	99	99	99	99	99
99	99	99	99	99	99	99	99
99	99	99	99	99	99	99	99
99	99	99	99	99	99	99	99
99	99	99	99	99	99	99	99

(c)

cycles/degree and show a similar response for both horizontally and vertically oriented gratings which is different to diagonally oriented ones. This leads to the quantization value tables in the ISO which are shown in Figures 26.10(b) and (c).

Although this works, as evidenced by the efficacy and popularity of JPEG, there is a problem with the motivation. The subjective data is not being applied in the image domain – the domain of the experiments – but to individual DCT coefficients. These, as we know, do not relate directly to cosinusoidal corrugations in the image domain, but to the amount of that coefficient that is required to reconstruct the image from its value. The quantization value for a single coefficient affects the entire (8×8) image in a complex way and all that we can say is that it seems reasonable to use visibility data concerning the spatial frequencies as image domain patterns to rank their importance when they form a coefficient of an image in the transform domain.

26.3.3 JPEG operating modes

JPEG specifies four modes of operation:

- Sequential DCT based
- Progressive DCT based
- Lossless
- Hierarchical

Sequential DCT based

Sequential DCT based is the normal image communication mode where an image is transmitted at its final quality level one block at a time.

Progressive DCT based

As we pointed out in the introduction, progressive image communication modes are extremely important in such contexts as the Internet, where a user is tied to the lowest bandwidth link in the chain, and where at the moment, demand is increasing faster than bandwidth. Progressive image communication is analogous to progressive refinement in radiosity (Chapter 6) and it enables the viewer to see an entire image that progressively increases in quality, rather than waiting for an image to scan at its final level of quality (sequential mode). This gives the user the vital facility of being able to interrupt an image communication if necessary at an earlier stage than with a sequential mode of operation. The information in the image is sent as an initial approximation which, as more and more information is sent, 'gracefully' increases in quality towards the final version which contains all the information. ('Gracefully' just means smoothly or without noticeable visual jumps.) An example is shown in Figure 26.5.

Progressive modes are implemented at the expense of an image buffer, inserted between the quantizer and the entropy encoder. Multiple scans can then be made through the DCT coefficients and only part of the information sent for each scan.

The DCT offers a perfect vehicle for this mode of operation because it offers, through either selection of the coefficients (spectral selection) or through partially encoding each coefficient to less than its full quantized value (successive approximation), complete approximate images at each scan.

In spectral selection we can first send all the DC coefficients which gives an 8×8 blocky image, then send a specified band of coefficients from each block. (This is a trivial operation because, you will remember, the coefficients are ordered as a one-dimensional array – the zig-zag sequence.) In successive approximation a specified number of the most significant bits of each coefficient are encoded first, followed by the encoding of the remaining bits in subsequent scans. Thus a spectral selection proceeds from an 8×8 block to the final image by becoming progressively less and less blurred.

A successive approximation image exhibits visible blocking artefacts because of the approximate encoding of the coefficients. For a given number of bits/pixel the successive approximation image is thought to be of better quality. These two options can be used separately or their individual disadvantages can be diminished by using them in combination.

Note that although more processing has to be carried out in the encoder and the decoder for the progressive mode, the same amount of information is sent over the channel whether it is sequentially or progressively encoded. (More precisely, the same amount of information is input to the entropy encoder.) Finally, in progressive mode the image refines to its final quality which is still a lossy image – the mode simply reorders the way in which the information is sent.

Lossless mode

In its simplest form lossless coding operates as sequential DCT based with the DCT module removed. Each pixel in the image is differentially encoded and input directly to the entropy encoder.

Hierarchical mode

The hierarchical mode of operation is similar to the progressive DCT based mode but it is useful in environments that have multi-resolution requirements – i.e., an environment where different image destinations operate at different resolutions.

In the hierarchical mode of operation the image is ordered into a bandpass pyramid (see Chapter 11) and the difference images are encoded using either DCT-based or lossless options. The image sequence progresses, with increasing spatial resolution, towards the final resolution. This mode gives a higher quality image for low bits/pixel than progressive DCT-based modes, but the final bits/pixel is about 33% higher.

26.4 Fractal image compression

The most commonly used forms of image compression use combinations of classical techniques, like JPEG, discussed in the previous section, to effect a lossy compression that retains high image quality at a bit rate of around 1 bit/pixel. Fractal compression is a recently developed technique that can achieve lower bit rates – 0.5 bits per pixel and less – for the same high image quality at the expense of incurring a much higher encoding penalty. Fractal compression exploits self-similarity in images and finds a representation where blocks in an image can be represented as affine transforms of other blocks. This is sometimes called affine redundancy and it is this concept that is unique to fractal compression.

Elsewhere in the text we have become used to the idea of redundancy in images as areas over which there is little change. In a computer graphics image, a Gouraud shaded surface may change slowly over a large number of pixels, whereas a surface exhibiting a detailed texture may change at every pixel. As we have seen, these attributes are exploited in a straightforward way in classical image compression techniques.

Affine redundancy, or self-similarity, is a more powerful concept and carries the potential of greater compression. Simply stated, it says that all images are inherently self-similar and given any (smallish) image block, we can find another block in the image that it relates to through an affine transformation.

Fractal image compression depends on ideas formalized by M. Barnsley – the foremost pioneer in the practical application of fractal-based techniques and the author of the influential book *Fractals Everywhere*. The concepts used in fractal image compression are:

- The Collage Theorem
- The specification of a fractal as an IFS or Iterated Function System.

We can demonstrate these ideas using Barnsley's familiar fern leaf example (Figure 26.11). This image is a fractal – it is completely self-similar and infinitely scalable. It possesses (apparently) extremely high visual complexity with extremely low information content and this is the underlying concept that is applied to fractal image compression. The idea is that real images exhibit this tendency, if we can uncover it, to a greater or lesser extent. Fractal image compression thus involves modelling the image as a fractal object and the high redundancy inherent in such objects leads to the required compression potential.

Let us now return to the fern leaf image and examine these ideas in some more detail. The fern leaf can be totally specified by a set of four affine transformations whose coefficients are known as the code for the IFS. The IFS code for the fern is given in Figure 26.11 for the coefficients of the general affine transformation:

$$x' = ax + by + e$$
$$y' = cx + dy + f$$

The IFS code consists of the coefficients for four transformations and in the first iteration each transformation maps the main image into one of the smaller parallelograms p, q, r and s. Each of these recursively maps into four smaller ones and so on until eventually we get down to a parallelogram that just covers a pixel. This pixel is coloured black.

Figure 26.11

Ideal fractal image compression. The fern leaf is completely specified by 24 coefficients – the IFS code.

	a	b	c	d	e	f
p	0.85	0.04	–0.04	0.85	0.02	0.08
q	–0.13	0.24	0.22	0.20	0.12	–0.27
r	0.18	–0.24	0.21	0.20	–0.12	–0.30
s	0.0	0.0	0.0	0.16	0.0	–0.42

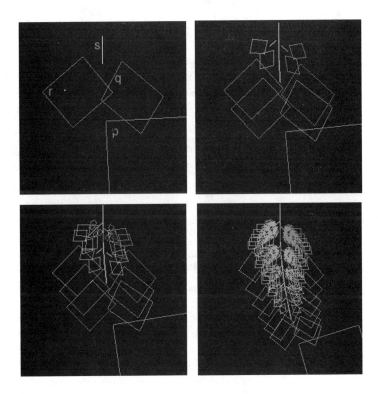

This simple demonstration is a graphics realization of the fact that the fern leaf image is constructed in its entirety from a 'collage' of transformed copies of itself. The implication for image compression is that the entire picture is represented by only 24 numbers. Note also that the representation can go on iterating irrespective of the final pixel size – it is infinitely zoomable. Of course, real images do not exhibit the 'perfection' of the fern leaf image and they have to be organized in such a way that we can consider the image as a potential fractal object and find its IFS code. This is the encoding part of the image compression procedure. Causing the IFS code to recurse, as we described above, produces the image and this is both the decoding and the rendering part of the process. The algorithm that decodes is the algorithm that renders. Options are available in both the encoding and decoding phases but encoding is a more expensive operation than decoding. Thus fractal compression is an asymmetric method in terms of our discussion in the introduction to this chapter.

Barnsley gives us the following informal description of his Collage Theory:

The theorem tells us that to find an IFS whose attractor is 'close to' or 'looks like' a given set, one must endeavour to find a set of transformations – contraction mappings on a suitable space within which the given set lies – such that the union, or collage, of the images of the given set under the transformation is near to the given set. Nearness is measured using the Hausdorff metric.

A contraction mapping means that points migrate under a transform in such a way that they become closer together. If we consider that an affine transform maps all the points in a parallelogram into all the points in another parallelogram, then this means that the destination parallelogram must be smaller. This constrains the coefficients:

$$\text{abs}(ad - bc) < 1$$

This constraint was implied by the rendering procedure we described above, which is known as the deterministic algorithm.

26.4.1 ### Encoding

In the previous section we demonstrated how a fractal object – the fern leaf image – could be specified and generated from an IFS code. The practical application of this concept to image compression means inverting this process – IFS code has to be found for a (real) image. This, when iterated in the decoder, then regenerates a copy of the image to within some error.

The processing penalty inherent in the encoding phase has meant that fractal compression is currently not generally accepted as a routine image compression method and it is this aspect that is being energetically researched.

The exception to this comment is Barnsley's own company Iterated Systems Ltd who produce a variety of products that with appropriate hardware will function in real time. Perhaps their most well-known user is Microsoft who use this fractal compression technology to store 10 000 images in their multimedia CD-ROM encyclopaedia 'Encarta'. This contrasts sharply with the observation Barnsley made in an article in *Byte* published in 1988: 'Complex colour images require about 100 hours each to encode and 30 minutes each to decode (on a Masscomp 5600 workstation).'

Most of what follows is based on the approach taken by Jacquin who comments: 'Our system is also plagued by high encoding times.'

The most popular approach to encoding is to divide the image into small blocks and find the IFS code that relates the block under consideration to some other (larger) block in the image. The smaller blocks of dimension $R{\times}R$ pixels, where R is typically 4, tile the image without overlapping and are called 'range' blocks. The larger blocks, domain blocks, cover the image as overlapping squares of $D{\times}D$ pixels (typically $D = 2R$) placed at intervals of S pixels horizontally and vertically, where S is typically R or $R/2$.

Encoding consists of initially setting up a pool of domain blocks where the aim is to make the size of the pool less than the maximum pool which would contain all the domain blocks in the image. Jacquin classifies the blocks in the (maximal) pool according to their perceptual geometric features, then trims and organizes the pool to reduce the search time for any range block. He defines three types of blocks: shade blocks, edge blocks and midrange blocks. A shade block contains only a smooth gradient, an edge block contains an edge and a midrange block has moderate gradient but no definite edge – a textured block.

The next stage in the process is for each range block to search for a matching (transformed) domain block after which each range block is specified as a domain block label together with a block transformation (the IFS code) that enables the range block to be regenerated in the decoder. Since it is this part of the process that incurs the time penalty, algorithms differ according to how they constrain and optimize the search. For example, one search strategy invoked is to restrict the domain blocks to be near to the range blocks. The compressed data consists of the IFS code for every range block. In other words, we have found a (set of) equation(s) for the image. This means that in a simple scheme the bit rate is going to be proportional to:

$$\frac{I}{R^2}$$

where I is the number of bits required to encode the information in the transformation.

Barnsley calls the overall process a Fractal Transform but as we have seen it is not an image transform in the sense of those described in Chapter 11 but an algorithmic process involving many design options and possibilities. (Also, the fact that the term is a trademark does not sit comfortably alongside the notion of an image transform.) The (non-trademarked) general term is fractal block coding.

Jacquin in addition adopts a two-level partitioning strategy for range blocks where a parent cell ($R{\times}R$) can be further split into up to four child cells. This enables the straightforward or classical exploitation of image redundancy where large blocks are used in smooth areas and smaller blocks in areas that contain pixel-level detail. The size of the range blocks is a determining factor in the encoding penalty – if the range block is small it can be encoded more quickly and more accurately than a large block. Jacquin also questions some of the apparently established notions of this type of compression, pointing out that image partitioning does not have to be square, and in addition he suggests that the whole notion of self-transformability needs further investigation, stating:

The notion of self-transformability should be investigated further. In particular it is not clear how localized a property this is for a given class of original images, i.e., how large the neighbourhood of a range block to encode should be, to permit efficient construction and search of the domain pool, thereby reducing encoding times.

We will now consider the extraction of the IFS code in more detail. The goal of the process is to derive an IFS code for each range block and an encoder can do this simply by comparing the image data in a range block with each of the transformed blocks formed by applying the affine transformations to each domain in the domain pool.

First consider that we are now dealing with real images which are functions of the two spatial variables and comparing this situation with the binary image of the fern leaf we can see that we now need a three-dimensional affine transform, where the Z direction is the pixel intensity.

$$x' = ax + by + e$$
$$y' = cx + dy + f$$
$$z' = gx + hy + i$$

Jacquin considers the overall transform as made up of two parts which he calls the geometric and massic parts. The geometric part is a contraction operator which in the simple case we have suggested ($D = 2R$), the pixel values in the range block are averaged from four pixels in the domain block.

The massic part, so-called because we can consider the range block to be a 4×4 stack of 'voxels' where each unit of height represents a step in the grey scale, can itself be split into two parts. The coefficients g, h and i represent operations on the grey scale values such as adding an offset (luminance shift), multiplying by a scaling factor less than one (contrast scaling) and subtracting the pixel value from its maximum value ('colour' reversal). The coefficients a, b, c, d, e and f represent the shuffling around of pixels in the range block, such as reflections about the horizontal, vertical and diagonal axes and rotation of 90 and 180 degrees about the centre of the block. Note that these operations are not contractive. Jacquin calls these operations isometries and defines eight to use in this context – a coding requirement of three bits for this part of the transformation.

(26.4.2) Decoding

Decoding is considerably easier and faster than encoding as we have already remarked. The block transformations are unpacked and two image buffers are set up. One of them is initialized with any arbitrary image – say, for example, a constant. This is the initial domain image. Then each range block in the other buffer is filled with the information obtained from the appropriate domain block (in the first buffer), using the block transformation and partitioning information associated with that range block. This completes the first iteration. This image is then made the new domain image and the process is repeated for the second iteration and continues until convergence – no further difference between images in the buffers.

Remarkably and somewhat anti-intuitively, it does not matter what the initial image is – it can be anything; after a few iterations (say, between four and eight) the decompressed image is complete, although, as you would expect, the number of iterations required depends on the similarity of the initial image to the final one. This fact can be exploited in schemes which actually transmit a low resolution copy of the image and in the compression of moving images where the previous frame can be used as the initial image when decoding the current frame. The difference between the lossy decoded image and the original unencoded image depends on the accuracy of the matching process in the encoding phase. Thus just as a single IFS code generates a fern leaf, a set of IFS codes or block transformations, derived by the encoder, regenerates any real image in the decoder.

Like JPEG, the basic technique can form the kernel of an overall scheme that includes other strategies. For example, consider transmitting (storing) extra information in the form of a low resolution image, or low pass – in particular, the average values of the pixels in each range block. This means that a low resolution image (identical to the first image in a progressive DCT-based sequence in JPEG) can immediately be constructed by the decoder. (Note that the penalty for transmitting (storing) this data is 1/16 of the image bit volume for $R = 4$.) It also means that convergence occurs after one iteration. If the low pass image is subtracted from the original, then we have a high pass image, and a high pass image is particularly suitable for a modified fractal encoding scheme because, as we know, it will contain many range blocks which have a constant intensity and much fewer which contain edge information. We can use this fact to implement a scheme where the information whether a range block is flat or edge type is transmitted (stored), and for the flat blocks we do not transmit the block transform. Thus the transmitted (stored) information consists of a low pass image plus a high pass image encoded using a modified fractal scheme. This scheme was reported by Beaumont in 1991.

26.5 Image compression in moving imagery

It is the case at the time of writing that most image compression is applied to still images. It is also certainly true that much effort will be applied in the immediate future to the compression of moving sequences. The demand for moving computer imagery comes from applications such as multimedia (moving images stored on CD-ROM) and communications applications such as digital TV (HDTV) and video telephony.

A number of important factors distinguish moving image compression from still image compression. One of the most important is that the achievement of good compression ratios almost always implies an asymmetric process – encoding is longer than decoding – which is inconvenient because the major applications of moving imagery are in real-time communication. The reason for this expense is that the encoding (motion estimation) usually involves an expensive search procedure (just like fractal block coding) whereas the decoding simply implies the application of the result of that process.

As we discussed in the introduction, in real-time communication the compression required by a particular application is dictated by the channel bandwidth. For using HDTV on existing TV channels the available bandwidth is 19 Mbit/s and for videotelephony it is 64 kbit/s. An intermediate requirement – addressed by MPEG 1 – is the encoding of entertainment video and moving imagery stored on CD-ROM. The available bandwidth here is 2 Mbit/s.

For real-time communication of images that are compressed, there are many subtle considerations that are outside the scope of this text and are more properly part of communications theory. For example, the rate at which the encoder outputs bits must be uniform to make full use of the channel bandwidth. (Note that this is not the same thing as the asymmetric encoding/decoding time.) Consider transmitting a run length encoded image as is done, for example, with a fax document. Because of the nature of run length encoding the symbols output by any encoder do not occur at equal intervals in time. Such a sequence will not achieve any bandwidth reduction and it is necessary to store the runs and input them into the transmission channel at a uniform rate, equal to their average rate of occurrence. Another problem with practical transmission channels is that they are subject to noise introduction to some degree. When an image is encoded for compression – say run length encoding plus variable length encoding of the runs – redundancy in the code representing the image is reduced. A one-bit error, due to noise, may have no visible effect in an uncompressed image because of the redundancy, but produce an error over some area of the picture in a compressed image. Thus a related consideration is to use a coding scheme that is also immune to errors. Generally this means that with any scheme the rate at which the coded image is sent **must** be less than the capacity of the channel. We must retain some redundancy so that error immunity can be built in.

Another distinguishing feat of moving imagery compression is that greater compression can be achieved per frame than with individual still images by exploiting inter-frame or temporal redundancy. In fact most popular motion compression schemes operate with inter-frame images as source images for compression rather than the original frames (usually in this context called intra-frames). Inter-frame redundancy can be further exploited by motion compensation. Movement between frames is caused either by movement of objects, movement of the camera or both, and the prediction of this motion and its use in image compression is called motion estimation, its use being called motion compensation.

In this section we will examine two approaches to moving image compression – MPEG (Moving Pictures Expert Group) which is, like its still image equivalent, a (proposed) standard that specifies a combination of schemes to achieve compression, and an extension of fractal-based compression to incorporate the time dimension.

Motion compensation in moving imagery

Motion analysis or estimation is dealt with in some detail in Chapters 18 and 19 and there we point out that it is a difficult and unsolved problem. Because of this and also the encoding time constraint, most motion analysis currently used in image compression takes the form of simple inter-frame block matching algorithms which can only approximately represent or model most motion. In the special case of translation of a single object in a plane parallel top the image plane then block matching will suffice. In any other motion, block matching will not work theoretically. That it does work is due to the fact that in practice motion is usually slow with respect to the frame rate or temporal sampling frequency. If we had detailed motion estimation, that is, if we had the motion associated with each pixel, we would only have to initialize a sequence with intensity values and then propagate pixels at the receiver along their motion trajectory in the image plane. We would only ever have to transmit the information required to specify the pixel trajectories. In practice the image is divided up into blocks (usually 16×16) pixels and the pixel motion is encoded using a motion vector for the entire block together with the difference between the blocks.

In moving image compression we can define two processes: motion estimation, or the motion analysis problem enumerated in Chapter 18, followed by the exploitation of this information in the encoding process. This is called motion compensation. It is fairly obvious that, for a given image resolution, the greater the degree of exploitation of motion estimation to enable higher compression, the more accuracy is required from the motion analysis. So the main trade-off in motion compensation is the degree of compression vs. the need for accurate motion estimation with its consequent difficulty and time penalty.

Once motion has been estimated it can be used in various ways. Compression can be achieved by skipping frames and using the motion information in the decoder to reconstruct the missing frames by interpolation along the motion trajectory. Alternatively the information in the current frame can be encoded by references to the previous frame.

The most common form of motion analysis used in image compression is simple block matching. In block matching algorithms, given a block in the frame currently being encoded, we need to find a block that matches it in a reference frame under a transformation. Using the same terms as in fractal encoding of images above, we need to find the domain block (in the reference frame) that under a transformation T matches a range block in the frame to be encoded. The idea of motion estimation and compensation in an image sequence is shown in Figure 26.12. An area in the current image – the range block – is constructed by referring to a matching area – the domain block – in

Figure 26.12

Motion compensation: a region in the current image is constructed from a (translated) region in the previous or reference image.

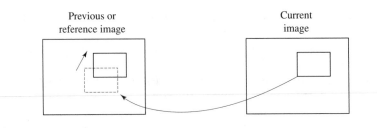

Previous or reference image

Current image

the previous or reference image. The information required to do this is the domain block label and its motion between frames.

The term 'motion vector' is often used to specify this transformation. This should not be confused with the same term that is used for the two-dimensional motion of individual pixels due to the projection of real motion into the image plane (see Chapter 18). In block matching algorithms we are saying that it is likely that we can find a match between a range block and a domain block under a transformation T due to object/camera motion. But, in general, it would have to be a transformation similar to that used in fractal encoding (in that it can be more than merely translation) and in this sense to call T a 'motion vector' is confusing. The term is only appropriate in the (assumed) simple case (which currently accounts for most algorithms) where the effect of the motion is pure translation in the image plane.

Thus for a given block, R, in the current image, we find a matching block D in the previous image. We can then use the transformation between R to align D; the motion of D between the previous and current frame is compensated for and this reduces the differences between the two frames. In practice we need not restrict ourselves to comparing a previous/current frame pair, but in general consider a reference frame and a number of frames to be encoded.

Just as in fractal block coding, we can have three components in the transformation: a geometric component and two massic components. The geometric component means that the shape of the domain and range blocks can be different and accounts for the fact that general motion produces a 'migration' of pixels in the image plane that can be modelled, for example, by an affine transformation. (See Chapter 21 for another development of the idea of image warping to model the changes in the image plane as a camera is moved relative to a scene.) In fractal block coding we used an affine transformation to match range blocks with domain blocks under the notion of self-transformability or affine redundancy – we were dealing with a single image. Here we are using the transformation to specify the changes between a pair of images due to motion that has occurred in the frame interval. Apart from this the general process is the same. An example of one of the main uses of the massic part of the transform in this context is the modelling of the change in reflected light intensity as an object moves with respect to a light source.

Most block matching algorithms currently in use do not attempt to determine the nine coefficients of the general three-dimensional affine transform but merely attempt to match rectangular range blocks with the same size rectangular domain blocks using a similarity criterion such as MAD (mean absolute difference) or MSE (mean squared error). Once a block is matched, a motion vector is defined for the block as the vector between the pixel in the range block and the corresponding pixel in the domain block. This, of course, assumes that all pixels in a block move by the same amount and the motion in the scene projected into the image plane results in pure translation of the block of pixels. Both of these assumptions are wrong in general and the inherent errors in this simple approach affect the quality of the reconstructed sequence to an extent that depends on the size of the blocks and the nature of the motion in the scene. In particular, blocking artefacts are noticeable. The errors in this method can be reduced by reducing the size of the block, but this mitigates against the potential compression because more motion vectors have to be sent.

Naive block matching algorithms differ in such aspects as the search strategy that is used to match blocks. The search can be constrained in various ways, for example, using the match from the previous (adjacent) match.

26.5.2 Strategies in the compression of moving imagery

As with the JPEG scheme described above, we can combine different compression schemes in moving imagery to achieve an optimal overall compression. The combination possibilities are greater with moving imagery because of the addition of the time dimension and motion compensation. We will consider the strategy adopted by MPEG-1 as an example. The best way to do this is with a hierarchy of block diagrams (Figure 26.13). We start with Figure 26.13(a) which shows simply temporal compression where the compressed image is formed by subtracting consecutive frames. We could also call this lossless inter-frame coding and it is identical to lossless predictive coding for still imagery (Section 26.1.3) except that we are now basing the prediction on corresponding pixels in different frames rather than neighbouring pixels in the same frame. Thus the structure is the same and if we are dealing with only pairs of frames the predictor is a frame delay or buffer. The next step is to make this lossy temporal coding and we do this by adding a JPEG strategy into the system (Figure 26.13(b)). This is called hybrid temporal/spatial compression and we can look at it as JPEG encoding applied to inter-frames. (There is a subtlety lurking behind the apparent simplicity of this diagram. Note that the difference image formed by the subtractor is the subtrahend formed by the current (lossless) image and the previous (lossy) image. We cannot simply delay/buffer the current image to form the previous component in the subtraction. This is because in the decoding process we can only ever reconstruct lossy images and so the difference image must be 'referred' to a lossy image.)

The final illustration (Figure 26.13(c)) shows the addition of motion compensation temporal/spatial compression and shows the motion estimation operating on two consecutive space domain images. Thus we apply motion compensation to blocks of the image so that when the subtrahend is formed the difference between

Figure 26.13
A hierarchy of motion compression schemes: (a) temporal compression (lossless interframe); (b) hybrid temporal/spatial compression; (c) motion compensated temporal/spatial compression.

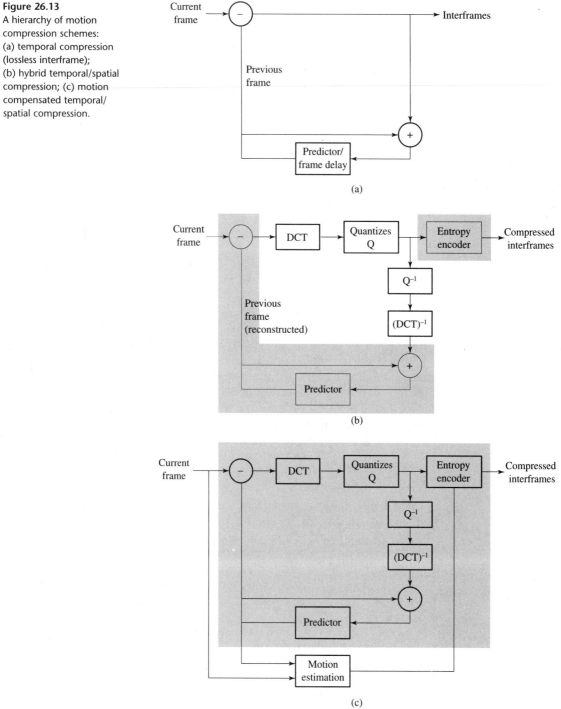

the blocks is much less than it would have been without motion compensation. Without motion compensation block pairs in consecutive image pairs are in identical positions in each frame. This is easily demonstrated for the simple example of a camera translating parallel to its own image plane with respect to a static scene. If we simply consider inter-frame images then the redundancy in these is a function of the speed of the motion with respect to the temporal sampling rate. If we motion compensate then, ignoring changes in field of view, the inter-frame will be made up of zeros.

This compression strategy represents a combination of four compression techniques:

- Exploiting temporal redundancy
- Lossy DCT encoding
- Entropy encoding
- Motion compensation.

The temporal redundancy is further exploited by motion compensation and spatial correlation is further reduced by lossy DCT encoding.

MPEG frame organization

The frame organization an encoding employs can vary in an MPEG sequence. The particular choice depends on application factors such as the degree of random access required and the coding delays that can be tolerated. MPEG uses 16×16 pixel blocks (called macroblocks) as the unit for motion estimation and as we implied in the previous section, an MPEG encoder works with a motion vector specifying the displacement between a current block and a block in some previous frame. Note that the motion vectors themselves are differentially encoded. Rather than having every frame (except the first) differentially encoded, MPEG uses three types of frames:

- **I frames (for Intra-coded)** As the name implies these frames are encoded without reference to any other frame. I frames are needed to start a sequence and are required for random access into a compressed sequence.
- **P frames (for Predicted)** These are frames produced by the encoder with a structure shown in Figure 26.13(c) and contain the motion vectors with respect to blocks in the previous P (or I) frame, together with the difference between the blocks in the two frames. Using I and P frames an encoded sequence can be of the form IPPP ... IPPP ... and so on.
- **B frames (for Bi-directional)** These are interpolated frames and have motion estimated from the nearest P (or I) frame in their past and future. The difference from the current block to the average of the nearest P (or I) block in the past and future is encoded. (Note that in an MPEG-1 application the entire sequence is available to the encoder and so future frames can

Figure 26.14
MPEG frame dependencies.

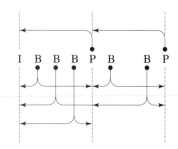

be exploited by the encoder.) One of the advantages of B frames is that they can deal with uncovered areas which are not predictable from past references alone. Another aspect of B frames is that they can be compressed more with coarser quantization.

Using all three types we can have sequences like, for example, IBBPBB ... IBBPBB ... and so on. The frame dependencies for a sequence are shown in Figure 26.14.

An example of applying wavelet compression to a moving image sequence is shown in Figure 26.15 (Colour Plate). The compression is first applied independently to frames (intra-frame compression) then applied to the inter-frames formed by subtraction in the image domain (inter-frame). The wavelet compression was made by applying a fixed threshold to the coefficients. The key observations to be made from the example are:

- The intra-frame compression reduces the image data from 192 kB to 6 kB/frame, but the inter-frame compression reduces it to 512 bytes/frame.

- The quality of the static information in the inter-frame compression is better, as we would expect. The moving cube object, which has large planar faces, does not break up whereas the sphere does quite noticeably.

26.5.4   FBC and moving images

Most of the interest in moving image compression is firmly in the communications field and because of the great asymmetry in fractal block encoding there has not been too much work reported on its application to real-time or communications applications. However, a recent report by Munro and Dudbridge details an approach that uses the Bath Fractal Transform (BFT) for encoding and the Accurate Fractal Rendering Algorithm (AFRA) for decoding/rendering. The authors state:

... analyses the differences between each successive frame and codes only a fraction of each frame, depending on the channel bit rate. The frame is divided into 99 blocks of 16×16 pixels. An activity value is calculated from the luminance of each block, and the most active blocks are coded in order of priority. Each block is coded into 8×8 fractal blocks, four luminance blocks and two chrominance blocks. Using this technique, it is possible to have bit rates as low as 40 kbit/s and still maintain lip-sync with a 25 frames/s source.

This contrasts with the following conclusion made by Lazar and Bruton in 1994:

However, the high computational cost of the encoding algorithm and the approximately fixed cost of decoding suggests that the proposed algorithm may be better suited to asymmetric applications such as multi-media.

Fractal block coding is easily extended, at least in theory, into three-dimensions (spatio-temporal compression) and three-dimensional range blocks are matched with three-dimensional domain blocks. In spatio-temporal compression no distinction is made between the time dimension and the spatial dimensions and the input to the compression process consists of three-dimensional blocks. The addition of a third dimension to the blocks means a consequent increase in search time for block matching and optimized search strategies become even more important than in the two-dimensional algorithm.

As in the previous section we are exploiting inter-frame redundancy and we would expect a greater compression per frame than would be possible by simply applying a two-dimensional fractal block coding scheme. Thus we expect that the information required to encode the three-dimensional block matching transformation is considerably less than the sum of each of the two-dimensional transformations that would result from applying a two-dimensional fractal block coding to each frame in the sequence.

Further reading

There is a whole family of image transforms that are used in encoding images. As well as the two aforementioned there are:

    Walsh transfom
    Hadamard transform
    Haar transform
    Slant transform
    Discrete sine transform
    Karhunen–Loéve transform

The topic of image compression is covered in most image processing texts and almost all texts compare in detail the properties of linear reversible image transforms. In particular, Gonzalez and Woods (Chapter 1) give a comprehensive coverage of this topic. A useful book that is devoted entirely to the transform coding of images is the text by Clarke.

Pennebaker and Mitchell's book on JPEG is an extremely comprehensive reference. However, much of the detail in the book is only of interest to implementors. It contains a copy of the (draft) ISO standard.

Beaumont J.M. (1991). Image compression using fractal techniques. *BT Technol. Jnl.*, **9**(4), October, 93–109

Clarke R.J. (1985). *Transform Coding of Images*. London: Academic Press

Jacquin A.E. (1992). Image coding based on a fractal theory of iterated contractive image transformations. *IEEE Trans. on Image Proc.*, **1**(1), January, 18–30

Lazar M.S. and Bruton L.T. (1994). Fractal block coding of digital video. *IEEE Trans Circuits Systems Video Technology*, **4**(3), 297–308

LeGall D. (1991). MPEG – a video compression standard for multimedia applications. *CACM*, **34**(4), April, 46–58

Mcfarlane M.D. (1972). Digital pictures 50 years ago. *Proc. IEEE*, **60**(7), 768–70

Munro D.M. and Dudbridge F. (1995). Rendering algorithms for deterministic fractals. *IEEE Computer Graphics and Apps.*, January, 32–41

Pennebaker W.B. and Mitchell J.L. (1993). *JPEG Still Image Data Compression Standard*. New York: Van Nostrand Reinhold

Stollnitz E.J., DeRose T.D. and Salesin D.H. (1995). Wavelets for computer graphics – Parts 1 and 2. *IEEE Computer Graphics and Apps.*, May, 76–84 and July, 75–84

Index